GENDER AND CLIMATE CHANGE FINANCING

This book discusses the state of global climate change policy and the financing of climate-resilient public infrastructure. It explains the sources of tensions and conflict between developing and developed countries with regard to global climate protection policies, and highlights the biases and asymmetries that may work against gender equality, women's empowerment and poverty eradication.

Gender and Climate Change Financing: Coming out of the margin provides an overview of the scientific, economic and political dynamics underlying global climate protection. It explores the controversial issues that have stalled global climate negotiations and offers a clear explanation of the link between adaptation and mitigation strategies and gender issues. It also maps the full range of public, private and market-based climate finance instruments and funds.

This book will be a useful tool for those engaged with climate change, poverty eradication, gender equality and women's empowerment.

Mariama Williams is Senior Programme Officer at the South Centre, Geneva, Switzerland.

ROUTLEDGE IAFFE ADVANCES IN FEMINIST ECONOMICS

IAFFE aims to increase the visibility and range of economic research on gender; facilitate communication among scholars, policymakers, and activists concerned with women's wellbeing and empowerment; promote discussions among policy makers about interventions that serve women's needs; educate economists, policymakers, and the general public about feminist perspectives on economic issues; foster feminist evaluations of economics as a discipline; expose the gender blindness characteristic of much social science and the ways in which this impoverishes all research, even research that does not explicitly concern women's issues; help expand opportunities for women, especially women from underrepresented groups, within economics; and, encourage the inclusion of feminist perspectives in the teaching of economics. The IAFFE book series pursues the aims of the organization by providing a forum in which scholars have space to develop their ideas at length and in detail. The series exemplifies the value of feminist research and the high standard of IAFFE sponsored scholarship.

1 **Living Wages, Equal Wages**
   Gender and labor market policies in the United States
   Deborah M. Figart, Ellen Mutari and Marilyn Power

2 **Family Time**
   The social organization of care
   Edited by Nancy Folbre and Michael Bittman

3 **Feminist Economics and the World Bank**
   History, theory and policy
   Edited by Edith Kuiper and Drucilla K. Barker

4 **Sexual Orientation Discrimination**
  An international perspective
  Edited by M. V. Lee Badgett and Jefferson Frank

5 **The Feminist Economics of Trade**
  Edited by Irene van Staveren, Diane Elson, Caren Grown and Nilufer Catagay

6 **Sex Markets**
  A denied industry
  Marina Della Giusta, Maria Di Tommaso and Steinar Strøm

7 **Gender and Chinese Development**
  Towards an equitable society
  Lanyan Chen

8 **Gender and the Contours of Precarious Employment**
  Leah Vosko, Martha MacDonald and Iain Campbell

9 **Questioning Financial Governance from a Feminist Perspective**
  Edited by Brigitte Young, Isabella Bakker and Diane Elson

10 **Challenging Knowledge, Sex and Power**
   Gender, work and engineering
   Julie E. Mills, Suzanne Franzway, Judith Gill and Rhonda Sharp

11 **Women and Austerity**
   The economic crisis and the future for gender equality
   Edited by Maria Karamessini and Jill Rubery

12 **New Frontiers in Feminist Political Economy**
   Edited by Shirin M. Rai and Georgina Waylen

13 **Gender and Climate Change Financing**
   Coming out of the margin
   Mariama Williams

GENDER AND CLIMATE CHANGE FINANCING

Coming out of the margin

Mariama Williams

LONDON AND NEW YORK

First published 2016
by Routledge
2 Park Square, Milton Park, Abingdon, Oxon OX14 4RN

and by Routledge
711 Third Avenue, New York, NY 10017

Routledge is an imprint of the Taylor & Francis Group, an informa business

© 2016 Mariama Williams

The right of Mariama Williams to be identified as author of this work has been asserted by her in accordance with sections 77 and 78 of the Copyright, Designs and Patent Act 1988.

All rights reserved. No part of this book may be reprinted or reproduced or utilized in any form or by any electronic, mechanical, or other means, now known or hereafter invented, including photocopying and recording, or in any information storage or retrieval system, without permission in writing from the publishers.

Trademark notice: Product or corporate names may be trademarks or registered trademarks, and are used only for identification and explanation without intent to infringe.

British Library Cataloguing in Publication Data
A catalogue record for this book is available from the British Library

Library of Congress Cataloging in Publication Data
Williams, Mariama.
  Gender and climate change financing : coming out of the margin/ Mariama Williams.
    pages cm. – (Routledge iaffe advances in feminist economics)
  Includes bibliographical references and index.
  1. Climatic changes – Economic aspects. 2. Environmental economics.
  3. Sustainable development. 4. Women in development. I. Title.
  QC903.W57 2015
  363.738′74561 – dc23
  2014047326

ISBN: 978-0-415-68853-6 (hbk)
ISBN: 978-0-415-68854-3 (pbk)
ISBN: 978-1-315-69476-4 (ebk)

Typeset in Bembo and Stone Sans
by Florence Production Ltd, Stoodleigh, Devon, UK

Printed and bound in Great Britain by
TJ International Ltd, Padstow, Cornwall

For Cynthia Gladys Blake Ebanks – your dedication and commitment to service and to your family continues to inspire us. Thank you.

CONTENTS

List of illustrations xi
Preface xv
Acknowledgements xviii
List of abbreviations xix

   Introduction 1

1 The global climate change policy environment 18

2 The ethical, equity and social development dimensions of global climate change policy 70

3 Climate change, gender equality and women's empowerment issues 117

4 The global climate change finance architecture 166

5 The state of play of bilateral and multilateral and market-based climate finance 237

6 Gender and the state of play in adaptation finance 261

7 Gender and the state of play in mitigation financing 289

8 Gender biases and asymmetries in global and climate change finance 339

x Contents

9 Private sector climate finance and gender equality   370

10 Towards an equitable and gender-sensitive post-2015 climate change financing regime   403

11 Summary and recommendations   427

Appendices   *431*
Bibliography   *484*
Index   *526*

ILLUSTRATIONS

Figures

1.1	Global land-ocean temperature index	23
2.1	Turning around the formula	91

Tables

1.1	Gender composition of constituted bodies established under the Convention and the Kyoto Protocol	37
1.2	Gender composition of party delegates to sessions under the Convention and the Kyoto Protocol	38
2.1	Carbon dioxide emissions per tonne per capita, 2009	82
2.2	Comparison of per capita principle, HR and SD approach to equity as aspects of equitable access to sustainable development	87
2.3	The WBGU budget approach option 1: historical responsibility, 1990–2050	92
2.4	The WBGU budget approach option 2: future responsibility, 2010–2050	93
2.5	Cross comparison emission only and double accumulations methods	95
2.6	Fair carbon shares and actual emissions of CO_2, 1850–2008	102
2.7	Cumulative emissions: fair shares, and carbon creditors and debts: selected countries, 1850–2008	103
2.8	Allocation for 2010–2050, global budget of 750 Gt CO_2	103
3.1	Key adaptation sectors	124
3.2	A typology of climate-proofing by selected sectors and activities	133
3.3	Distribution of authors by gender and developing countries for IPCC AR5 (2013)	155

3.4	A qualitative gender climate risk assessment for climate change financing	157
3.5	Climate change and gender operational domains plus finance-related issues	161
4.1	UNFCCC adaptation funds classification at a glance	207
4.2	Overview of the first generation climate funds under the UNFCCC's financial mechanism	215
5.1	Bilateral funding for climate change	247
6.1	Total adaptation costs (additional annual investment needed/financial flows) by sectors in US$ billion per year by 2030	271
6.2	Comparison of estimations of adaptation costs in developing countries, per annum (2010–2015 and 2030)	271
7.1	Global mitigation cost estimates	292
7.2	At-a-glance view of social and gendering potentials with the CIFs	304
7.3	Overview of opportunities, challenges and constraints of mitigation finance on gender equality and women's empowerment	308
9.1	Level of female entrepreneurship activity across countries	388

Boxes

1.1	The scope, nature and workings of the IPCC	25
1.2	The Bali Action Plan	29
1.3	Evolution of gender in the UNFCCC decision-making	35
1.4	Operational provisions of the Durban Gender Decision	36
1.5	What the science says	40
1.6	Climate change, its impacts and projection	42
1.7	Impact of climate change on Africa – agriculture	44
1.8	The Caribbean	45
1.9	When pledges are not pledges	46
1.10	Zambia and climate change	49
1.11	Jamaica and climate change	50
2.1	Climate change, poverty, vulnerability and food security	78
2.2	Climate change and human displacement	79
2.3	Gender and climate refugee	80
2.4	Poor and low-income blacks impacted the worst by Hurricane Katrina 2005	81
2.5	Historical accountability and historical responsibility and global climate policy	88
2.6	Developing countries mitigation update on NAMA efforts	101
3.1	The Global Burden of Disease Study 2010	122
3.2	Gender aspects of vulnerability and adaptive capacity	126
3.3	The gender equality domains	128

3.4	Targeted gender equality and non-targeted gender equality interventions	131
3.5	Snapshots of gender-related considerations from the NAPAs of the LDCs	137
3.6	Gender and the Cancún Adaptation Framework	138
3.7	Gender and NAPs	139
3.8	Gender equality, adaptation and the Durban outcomes	139
3.9	Small-scale agricultural activities and cost effective mitigation	146
3.10	Further identification of women-specific climate change vulnerabilities	153
4.1	Climate finance 'mantras'	173
4.2	Annex II financial commitments under the Convention	181
4.3	Evolution of climate finance under the UNFCCC	185
4.4	The nuts and bolts of climate change finance I: useful terms	189
4.5	Green bonds	190
4.6	The nuts and bolts of climate change finance II: carbon financing	193
4.7	National communications	204
4.8	GEF project cycle	206
4.9	The LDCF approval process for NAPA priority	209
4.10	Countries with completed NAPAs and approved NAPA implementation projects	210
4.11	The Adaptation Fund	213
5.1	Sustainable energy in the ADB framework	245
5.2	Market-based mechanisms under Kyoto	250
5.3	Steps to issuance of CERs	251
5.4	CDM at work	251
6.1	Basic elements of adaptation costing	267
6.2	Structural differences between adaptation and mitigation policy and financing regime	268
6.3	Strategic elements for gender mainstreaming for the enhancement of Cancún Adaptation Framework	276
6.4	Useful steps for integrating gender-related considerations into the medium- and long-term adaptation process	277
6.5	Elements of health adaptation costs	284
6.6	Some critical questions to be posed for engendering adaptation finance flows	285
7.1	Evolution of gender mainstreaming at the GEF	296
7.2	GEF-6: towards the gender plan of action and the future of gender mainstreaming at GEF	297
7.3	Small Grants Programme and gender	298
7.4	Gender empowerment and the SGP	298
7.5	The Climate Investment Funds since 2008	301
7.6	Gender sensitivity of the Asian Development Bank	313

7.7	Best practice tips for integrating gender into lending/investment programmes	313
7.8	The CDM	317
7.9	Brazil, the CDM and sustainable development criteria	328
8.1	Gender and discriminatory norms in financial markets	348
8.2	The AfDB Gender Policy Framework	355
8.3	Gender and Asian Development Bank	356
8.4	Implementing gender equality strategies in regional development bank portfolios – the case of the ADB	357
8.5	The IDB's Gender and Diversity Fund	358
8.6	The IDB's Gender Framework	358
9.1	Climate change financing and conventional finance instruments	377
9.2	Land grabbing	377
9.3	The private sector and adaptation in Africa	381
9.4	Women's SMEs world-wide growth and constraints	389
9.5	Women-owned businesses and the global financial market environment	390
9.6	Biogas recovery, heat and electricity generation from effluents ponds in Honduras	397
10.1	Further identification of women-specific climate change vulnerabilities	415
10.2	Gender equity language in finance and finance-related areas of the Durban outcome	425

PREFACE

Climate change impacts women and men differently. As a result of gender-based inequalities and discrimination, which tend to leave women as the poorest of the poor in many developing countries, women can least afford to respond effectively to the negative and destructive effects of climate change-induced extreme weather events. Women bear extraordinary losses in lives and livelihoods during and after such events. The same persistent unfavourable gender dynamics also limit the extent to which many poor women can take advantage of the opportunities presented by the responses to climate change in terms of securing and sourcing climate solutions such as clean energy or the building and construction of climate-proofing infrastructure. Unfortunately, the responses to climate change, in terms of the climate protection policies, may aggravate and further exacerbate underlying issues of inequities. These involve issues of the erosion of access to land (for example, initiatives aimed at managing emissions from forests and preventing land degradation may be unmindful of the exclusionary effects of land conversion on traditional users of the forests) and the negative impacts on food security for poor women and men (for example, as a result of land conversion for biofuels production and land grabbing).

The ever deepening and shockingly clear consensus of climate scientists is that the world must urgently end the utilization of fossil fuels. This transformation is requiring an unprecedented scale of financial and technology transfers between developed and developing countries – a scale of financial transfer that potentially, in a short time-frame, will exceed the last great transformation necessary as a result of man-made political, economic and social problems, the Marshall Plan, which transformed war-torn Europe into the developed economies that now exist today.

Climate finance therefore permeates every aspect of discussions about climate change. This is especially so in discussions of the developmental impacts of climate change that underlie and bedevil negotiations around global climate protection policy under the United Nations Framework Convention on Climate Change (UNFCCC), the current reigning and evolving global climate protection instrument. Climate finance is a central pillar of the UNFCCC. Poor and growing developing countries, which have historically contributed little to the current climate problem, and which need to mobilize resources for poverty eradication, decent job creation and social and economic development, are facing a quite stark choice: use scarce resources (and/or accumulate debt) for climate change adaptation and mitigation versus spending on poverty reduction and making both targeted and non-targeted gender equality interventions in the economic and social spheres of the economy.

In recognition of the serious nature of climate change and its negative impacts on the social and economic status and advancement of women in developing countries, a coalition of gender focal points of various United Nations (UN) agencies and women's non-governmental organizations came together in early 2005 to create the Global Gender and Climate Alliance (GGCA). The GGCA, which was formally launched in 2007, seeks to leverage the combined resources and efforts of agencies such as UNEP, IUCN, UNDP and the Women's Environment and Development Organization to engender climate change policy and practice so as to ensure that the gender-differentiated points of views, perspectives and concerns of women and men are mainstreamed into climate protection policy-making both at global and national level. Initial efforts galvanized around pinpointing how men and women were involved with and impacted by adaptation and mitigation strategies in developing countries. However, it soon became clear that, though the aggregate level and scale of climate financing going to developing countries was inadequate to their needs, there were also gender-based inequities in the distribution of this flow of financing. Not much of the financing seemed to go into projects and programmes that benefited women, as a group, relative to men.

In 2008, I was commissioned to undertake research on gender and climate change finance for the GGCA in collaboration with the United Nations Development Programme Gender Team. The research took place between 2008 and 2010 and the final product of that commissioned work, entitled *Ensuring gender equity in climate change financing*, was launched at the UNFCCC Seventeenth Meeting of the Conference of the Parties (COP), Durban, South Africa, 2011. Since 2010, further research and enhancement of my understanding of the milestones and pivots of climate change and climate change negotiations were made possible during my work for the South Centre, an inter-governmental think tank of developing countries, based in Geneva, Switzerland, which brought me into closer intimacy with the substance, processes and nuances of the negotiations taking place under the auspices of the UNFCCC.

This book builds on that work and benefited from my role also as trainer of trainers with the GGCA team (2008–2009), working with climate negotiators in the Caribbean and Africa. Since then I have researched, monitored and written on the state of play of the finance track in the UNFCCC process, both at the intersessional negotiations and the end of year meetings of the COP (in 2010, 2011 and 2012). I have also been privileged to participate, and give expert presentations for various topics on the negotiations agenda, at both the UNFCCC events as well as numerous expert, civil society and think-tank meetings and a brief spell as an expert reviewer for some of the chapters of the fifth Assessment Report of the Intergovernmental Panel on Climate Change.

Although emphasizing a gender perspective on climate change finance, this book is grounded in a developing countries and justice perspective on climate change. The book is focused on enhancing the understanding of a wider audience on the depth and severity of the climate change challenges facing the children, women and men in developing countries and the tremendous inequity that is being perpetuated on them as a result of the lack of timely, adequate and sustainable finance for undertaken adaptation and mitigation actions and for enhancing and building their capacity to respond to climate challenges effectively. This finance is also meant to support the transfer and development of technologies that will provide and promote real and effective responses in developing countries' economies.

The book offers insights into the debates about the architecture of global climate regulation, including the contestations around the role of equity in global climate protection and the debate over historical responsibility and accountability of developed countries for climate change and discusses how that aspect of the debate overshadows the issue of ensuring the appropriate scale and quantum of finance from primarily public (supported by appropriately managed and implemented innovating) sources. The private sector is expected to play its full and effective role in shifting from a business-as-usual trajectory towards a more climate-sensitive role, as well as complementing public finance for the transformation of low-carbon and climate-resilient development worldwide.

ACKNOWLEDGEMENTS

I am grateful to Martin Khor and Vice Yu of the South Centre and Matthew Stilwell of the Institute for Governance and Sustainable Development as well as the members of the Climate Justice Network (CJN) for helping to further deepen my understanding of the equity issues underlying the global climate change discussion and the central importance of the development dimensions of the global climate protection regime. Ms Bernaditas Mueller remains a constant source of admiration and inspiration for her knowledge and dedication to advocating and negotiating for the timely, adequate and sustainable flow of climate finance from developed to developing countries, as is required under the climate convention.

Specific inputs for this book on the equity and mitigation discussions are drawn from the work of the CJN, the South Centre and Sivan Kartha of the Stockholm Environment Institute. The consistent and highly valuable contributions of Liane Schalatek of the Heinrich Boll Foundation on gender and climate finance also provided an important benchmark for the evolution of this publication. Towards the end of writing the book, volume 61 (September 2012) of *Development Dialogue: What Next Volume III Climate, Development and Equity* and the book *Climate Protection and Development* by Frank Ackerman, Richard Kozul-Wright and Rob Vos were useful for rounding out the discussion on climate and development that permeates all chapters of this book.

Finally, without the persistence of the staff of Routledge and the encouragement of Robert Langham this work would not have been published. All errors and omissions remain mine.

ABBREVIATIONS

AAU	Assigned Amount Unit
ADB	Asian Development Bank
AfDB	African Development Bank
BAP	Bali Action Plan
CBD	Convention on Biological Diversity
CCS	Carbon Capture and Storage
CDM	Clean Development Mechanism
CEDAW	Convention for the Elimination of Discrimination Against Women
CEIF	Clean Energy Investment Framework
CER	Certified Emission Reduction
CIFs	Climate Investment Funds
CO_2	Carbon Dioxide
COP	Conference of Parties
CTF	Clean Technology Fund
EBRD	European Bank for Reconstruction and Development
ERU	Emissions Reduction Unit
EST	Environmentally Sound Technology
ETS	Emission Trading Scheme
FAO	Food and Agriculture Organization
GEF	Global Environment Facility
GEMCRA	Gender Empowerment Climate Risk Assessment
GGCA	Global Gender and Climate Alliance
GHG	Greenhouse gas
IFIs	International Financial Institutions
IPCC	Intergovernmental Panel on Climate Change
LDC	Least Developed Country

LDCF	Least Developed Country Fund
MATCH	Modelling and Assessment of Contributions to Climate Change
MDB	Multilateral Development Bank
MDG	Millennium Development Goal
NAMA	Nationally Appropriate Mitigation Action
NAPA	National Adaptation Programmes of Action
ODA	Official Development Assistance
OECD	Organisation for Economic Co-operation and Development
PPCR	Pilot Programme for Climate Resilience
PRSP	Poverty Reduction Strategy Paper
REDD	Reduced Emissions from Deforestation and Degradation
RMU	Removal Unit
SBSTA	Subsidiary Body for Scientific and Technological Advice
SFCCD	Strategic Framework for Climate Change and Development
SIDS	Small Island Developing States
SME	Small and Medium Enterprise
UNCTAD	United Nations Conference on Trade and Development
UNFCCC	United Nations Framework Convention on Climate Change
VAT	Value-Added Tax
WHO	World Health Organization

INTRODUCTION

> But today there is no 'normal' to return to. The earth's climate is now in a constant state of flux.
> Lester Brown, president of the Earth Policy Institute, August 2012

> Extreme heat and drought in the US and other major food-exporting countries had hit harvests badly and sent prices spiralling.
> *The Guardian*, 14 October 2012[1]

The long-term rise in the average temperature of the earth's surface is a serious dilemma confronting humanity. This shift in the state of the average weather over time (climate) and the resulting climate change and climate variability (for example, variations in precipitation and temperature) is dramatically contributing to rising sea level and frequent and extreme weather events such as droughts, cyclones, floods and hurricanes. The Intergovernmental Panel on Climate Change (IPCC) have stated that climate change is 'unequivocal'. The IPCC's 2012 Special Report, *Managing the Risks of Extreme Events and Disasters to Advance Climate Change Adaptation,* argues that 'climate change may increase the probability of some ordinary weather events reaching extreme levels or of some extreme events becoming more extreme'. The fifth Assessment Report (AR5) of the IPCC affirms these trends. It notes that 'warming of the climate system is unequivocal, and since the 1950s, many of the observed changes are unprecedented over decades to millennia' (IPCC 2013: 4). The report also highlights that the evidence for human influence has grown since AR4 and that 'it is *extremely likely* that human influence has been the dominant cause of the observed warming since the mid-twentieth century' (IPCC 2013: 17).

2 Introduction

It is crystal clear. Climate variability and change is not some far away possibility; climate variability and change is upon us. Human, anthropogenic sources of greenhouse gases (GHGs) arising from the way the world produces and consumes since at least the late 1750s is undeniably a significant causal factor behind our changing climate. According to the IPCC, '(t)here is evidence that anthropogenic influences, including increasing atmospheric greenhouse gas concentrations, have changed these extreme weather events' (IPCC 2013: 17).

The physical effects of climate change extreme events (fire) and extreme weather events (increased evaporation and increased fresh water) impact on the oceans (sea level rise and acidification) and the cryosphere (such as rapidly melting and thinning arctic sea ice), are occurring even quicker than scientists could ever imagine, much less predict. Rising sea levels that pose existential threats to the lives of women, children and men living in low-lying islands and on large swathes of coastlines from Africa, Asia, the Caribbean and the Pacific, with no potential for retreat and increased aridity, contribute to climate-related national disasters and impinge on the quality of natural resource balance. All of the events will have adverse impacts on both the quantity and quality of water resources, agriculture, food production and food security, and human health. Frequent droughts and floods result in the degradation of water supply and impact people's access to water for drinking and for household and agro-industrial production. Water degradation may also promote vulnerability to diaharroea and cholera as well as contribute to a rising incidence of waterborne diseases. Ultimately, these extreme events (floods, landslides and storms) are associated with direct injuries, morbidity and mortalities as well as indirect injuries and loss of lives due to increased conflicts over resources such as forests, land and water.

The Fourth Assessment Report (2007) of the IPCC highlights that floods and heat are linked to deaths, injuries, infectious diseases and the toxic contamination of water. Storm surges have severely injured or caused many people to drown. More severe and frequent droughts will cause water scarcity, and the destruction of agricultural lands and crop failures – contributing to nutritional deficiencies and food insecurity.

These consequences of global climate variability and extreme weather events are already affecting the lives of countless millions of women, men and children. The Global Humanitarian Forum (GHF) reports that every year, climate change and climate variability leave over 300,000 people dead, seriously affect[2] another 325 million people and create economic losses totalling $125 billion (GHF 2009). These stark realities point to the urgent need for countries and institutions to marshal the financial and human resources of the global community in order to address and arrest the causal factors behind climate change so as to protect lives of humans and the other species that inhabit the earth as well as ensure the sustainable livelihoods of men and women.

Climate science has shown that climate change and its impact are primarily a result of human interference with the climate system in terms of how mankind has produced and consumed goods and services. Science also shows that the accumulated stock of GHGs primarily from the burning of fossil fuels was central to the growth dynamics of the now developed countries of Europe and north America and that these economies include other developed countries such as Australia, New Zealand and Japan, which have benefited significantly from this growth. At the same time, the damaging effects of the climate are being experienced and will continue to be felt most severely in developing countries. Developing countries experience significant damages and losses from slow-onset events and extreme events. These include economic losses (infrastructure, livelihoods, crop loss) and non-economic losses: human life as well as cultural loss, displacement and loss of ecosystem and biodiversity. Ultimately, there are lost development opportunities which jeopardize the right to development.[3] This is especially so for particularly vulnerable countries such as Small Island Developing States (SIDS) some Asian states, such as the Philippines, and Least Developing Countries (LDCs). Some Pacific islands such as Kiribati, Maldives, Marshall Islands, Nauru and Tuvalu are facing loss of their geographic and political space and identities as nations and peoples as the IPCC projects that sea level will rise between 26 and 82 cm by 2100. The LDC, home to 12 per cent of the world population and with per capita GHG emission of 0.25, accounts for about 66 per cent of all deaths related to climate disasters in 1980–2011 (LDC Watch 2014). Furthermore, people living in LDCs are five times more likely to die from the climate catastrophe than those living in other parts of the world. According to the NGO group LDC Watch, the number of people living in LDCs affected by extreme weather events has almost doubled from 100 million in 1970–1979 to 193 million in 2000–2020.[4]

Hence, there are significant ethical and equity dimensions to climate change impacts and how the global community chooses to address the problem. Within the nation state there are also other equity dimensions such as the impacts of climate on portions of the population and groups who have been traditionally marginalized and with the least access to resources to enable themselves to respond to climate change. The two most dominant climate-related equity issues impacts are gender equality and the lives of indigenous people. (But there are also issue of the just transition of the workforce and the survival of some island nations as a consequence of sea-level rise.) This book, however, will focus on the gender dimensions of climate change and the global and national responses to it.

Climate change and equity – gender and social dimensions

Though climate variability and extreme weather events impact both men and women, their adverse effects and outcomes are likely to be more acute for women given men's and women's socially determined roles and responsibilities – gender (as distinct from men's and women's biological and reproductive characteristics) – sex roles in the economy and society. It is well known that gender roles and the way that women and men are treated in societies result in different types of gender inequalities through which men are systematically favoured relative to women in terms of access to social and economic resources. Differences in the social and economic treatment of women and gender discrimination give rise to continuing gender biases and gender gaps in access to information and economic and social resources. These gender biases and gaps work to heighten the vulnerability of women in times of extreme weather events and natural disasters.

In many developing countries, women and girls have primary responsibility for collecting water and firewood, cooking, washing and raising small livestock. Women are also dependent on natural streams and rainwater more than men, who tend to use irrigation schemes. Climate change events that lead to water degradation can increase the time that women and girls spend collecting water, increase their workload and, as in the case with natural disaster and conflict over resources, mean that they have to travel greater and greater distances in order to collect water. Women and girls are thus exposed to increased risk of sexual harassment, rape and loss of life. In some cases, climate variability and change may require new survival skill sets for women, such as tree climbing and swimming, which are not usual activities for some women based on cultural and religious prohibitions (Brody et al. 2008; Perlata 2008).

Hence, climate change is associated with a wide range of challenges for women and girls. For example, the IPCC's Fourth Assessment Report noted that 'climate change is likely to directly impact children and pregnant women because they are particularly susceptible to vector- and water-borne diseases, for example, malaria is currently responsible for a quarter of maternal mortality' (2007). Pregnant women are four times more likely to contract malaria than the general population (Bordallo 2008; WHO 2003).[5]

Gender biases and gender gaps in access to income and other economic and social resources may adversely impact women's ability to command resources or to secure durable and climate-resilient residences. In general women tend to dominate informal sector employment and self-employment activities.

The informal sector economy, which is 'the diversified set of economic activities, enterprises, and workers that are not regulated or protected by the state'[6] (WEIGO 2014), and the key occupational groups, which includes domestic workers, home-based workers, street vendors, waste pickers, construction workers, garment workers and small farmers, is most hurt by climate change and weather-related shocks. Women tend to make up the majority of the 'least visible of the informal workers ... [who] sell or produce goods from their homes: garment workers; embroiderers; incense-stick rollers; cigarette rollers; paper bag makers; kite makers; hair band makers; food processors; and others' (WEIGO 2014). Extreme weather events hence worsen the impact of women's lack of access to resources and lessen their capacity to cope. Because of low or irregular income, women may also lack savings to support post-disaster recovery efforts.

In some countries, women may face disproportionately more harm than men from weather events because of their reliance on rain-fed agriculture, food processing, cattle and chickens for their cash income (Khondker 1996). Pre-existing gender-related patterns of vulnerabilities such as lack of secure land rights (which is interrelated with access to credits and livelihood), gender gaps in the ownership of productive assets, higher illiteracy rates among women than men, unpredictable and less favourable access to employment and income, coupled with inequality in participation in decision-making, can block women's ability and capacity to effectively engage in eco-friendly technology, natural resource management and early warning systems.

Climate change also intensifies the effects of pre-existing gender gaps such as information asymmetry (in agricultural training, crop prices and technology diffusion) between men and women. While the older forms of gender asymmetries led to long-term chronic problems such as ill-health and endemic poverty, the 'newer' forms such as asymmetrical information sharing regarding early warning and disaster preparedness are a matter of life and death for some women. Research points out that women and children are fourteen times more likely to die from natural disaster than men. Evidence from the aftermath of extreme weather events analysed by Neumayer and Plümper (2007) show that 'natural disasters (and their subsequent impacts) on average kill more women than men or kill women at an earlier age than men'.

The gender-differentiated realities of climate change and extreme weather events point to the need to integrate and under-grid actions and solutions to resolve the climate change challenges within policy and programmatic frameworks that integrate gender equality and women's empowerment analysis and objectives. This includes ensuring that the means of implementation such as finance, technology development and transfer, and capacity building accompanying global and national climate protection policies flow in the required amounts and on a timely basis and are both gender-sensitive and poverty-eradication-friendly.

Dealing successfully with hazard management, disaster preparedness and climate change-induced weather challenges requires resources well beyond those that are available to meet the day-to-day needs faced by the average household in developing countries. Though this situation impacts both male and female-headed households, it is likely to be more acute for female-headed households due to gender gaps in income and social and economic resources. It may require resources to build permanent or stronger and more robust housing for families, better and strong water storage units and investment in energy-efficient household devices, such as solar-heated stoves. Women and men, therefore, not only will require access to income for day-to-day living but will also need additional financing for climate-proofing their residencies and making their businesses and farming activities climate resilient. This will require increased access to income, savings, grants, governmental transfers, low interest loans and other forms of finance. These financial resources must come from women's livelihood and labour market activities, or other forms of household income, or governmental transfers or earnings from assets in the financial markets. But climate change imposes an additional burden on development that can strain or distract from social development budgets. Therefore there is increasing need to ensure adequate flows of public-oriented climate finance for climate change needs.

Climate change equity development: potential and possibilities for securing women's and men's lives

The scientific community warns that, if humanity steadfastly maintains the present trajectory of fossil fuels-based production and high GHG emissions, the earth will reach a threshold beyond which there is no certainty of regeneration. Sustainability will require a path towards achieving and maintaining temperate well below 2 degrees Celsius and holding GHG emissions concentration levels in the atmosphere substantially below 450 ppm.[7] The global community in 2009 set the temperature target at 2 degrees Celsius but did not set a blueprint for how to maintain temperature changes well below this stabilization target. Conventionally, it is assumed that the proactive-reactive responses of human systems in the form of adaptation and mitigation will be the pathways for achieving this global temperature 'guardrail' (WBGU 2009). Implementation of both of these strategies entails serious economic and social costs as well as social and inter-generational equity issues.

The equity dimension with regards to the burden of obligations and responsibilities for climate change between developed and developing countries are addressed, though under serious threats in the current negotiations, as part of the discussions and normative framework of the United Nations Framework Convention on Climate Change (UNFCCC) (1992). This is best articulated by the principle of 'common but differentiated responsibilities and respective capabilities' (Article 3.1). This provision for equity enshrines the rights of developing countries to develop on a steady state path. It must continue to be the central core of climate protection policy. Subsequent Conference of the Parties (COP) decisions have consistently reaffirmed the idea of 'targeting to the most vulnerable'.[8] However, other equity and rights dimensions of climate change, such as ensuring and protecting the rights of indigenous peoples and gender equality and women's empowerment have not yet secured their rightful place in global climate change policy response framework.

Operationalization of equity and ethics in the governance of climate change

The current climate protection regime is premised on the twin strategies of adaptation and mitigation, facilitated by appropriate flows of finance and transfer of environmentally sound technology from developed countries to developing countries.

Adaptation strategies aim to reduce or avoid the harms caused by climate change (for example, building sea walls to protect communities from rising sea levels), whereas mitigation strategies aim to forestall or lessen the onset of climate change through reducing greenhouse gas concentrations (for example, switching from carbon-based fuel to renewable energy sources). While both adaptation and mitigation are critically important to economic growth, population growth and human development, they individually and jointly have serious gender, poverty and social equity dimensions.

Both adaptation and mitigation strategies are inextricably intertwined and must work synergistically to achieve the required alterations in human actions that will positively impact climate change. Successful adaptation to climate variability and change depends on the functioning (i.e., state of health/being), capabilities (education and acquisition of knowledge) and the empowerment (i.e., the ability to make choices) of men and women, especially those living in developing countries, to respond to the adverse consequences of climate variability and to manage climate change risks, including managing damages and losses arising from climate events. Under-girding this must be men's and women's equitable access to, the ownership of, and control over economic and social resources.

The financing of climate change adaptation and mitigation strategies in developing countries is one of the central issues at the heart of the political debate over the global climate protection policy architecture. Climate change finance is distinct from regular development finance as it arises from, and the architecture supervising it is grounded in, the UNFCCC (1992). At the heart of this Convention is the principle of equity and polluter pays. Climate financing, hence, is a legally binding obligation of developed countries whose development path has led to the existing overhang of GHGs in the atmosphere. Thus the planet is committed to a path of decades of warming trends despite whatever present actions might be taken. And, since according to the scientific literature, the impacts of this warming trend will be felt primarily and more acutely in developing countries, especially those most vulnerable to climate variability and change, adaptation actions and measures to cover the losses and damages incurred remain a global, regional, national and local imperative.

The historical responsibility of developed countries for climate change, in tandem with the polluter pay principle, and the recognition that developing countries still have significant challenges of poverty and lack of access to essential services such as proper sanitation, access to water and modern energy services, are factors behind the principle of common but differentiated responsibility, which has been an essential principle (Principle 7) in international environmental governance since the Rio Conference. However, this does not mean that developing countries have no responsibility to transform their economies to support the objectives of the convention. They do. And, developing countries have over the years been taking on increasingly more actions in their national economies to mitigate climate change. With each annual UNFCCC COP, especially since the post-2006 period, developing countries across all the global regions have also accepted more and more mitigation responsibilities beyond what they are obligated to undertake under the Convention. Furthermore, under so-called market mechanisms, such as the Clean Development Mechanism, many developing countries are also contributing to the mitigation actions of the developed countries.

Under the UNFCCC, developed countries committed to taking the lead on mitigation, to provide finance and technological development and transfer to developing countries in order to help these countries meet their obligations under the Convention and to support their mitigation and adaptation actions. The Kyoto Protocol further quantified the nature of the commitment of developed countries to take mitigations action to reduce the level of GHGs emitted into the atmosphere.

8 Introduction

However, there was no corresponding protocol or agreement quantifying the scale and scope of finance and technology transfers.

The UNFCCC has established the key pillars critical for the emerging system for mobilizing, managing and delivering financial resources and investments for adaptation and mitigation projects and programmes. The financial architecture that has evolved for climate change was established to ensure adequate flow of financing for adaptation, mitigation and technological transfer. Initially, the flow of finance has been implemented through the Global Environment Facility (GEF), which was contracted as an operating entity of the financial mechanism of the UNFCCC. Over time, an assortment of different funds have emerged both under the Convention (the Adaptation Fund, the Least Developed Country Fund, and the Special Climate Change Fund), and through the preference of developed contributing countries for bilateral and multilateral frameworks such as Japan's Cool Earth Partnership/Hatoyama Initiative, the Global Climate Change Alliance and the World Bank's Climate Investment Funds (CIFs). Existing Convention and related funding arrangements include a set of mechanisms based on voluntary contributions from developed countries as well as market-based instruments such as the Clean Development Mechanism, emissions trading, and Joint Implementation, which catalyse the carbon market.

Current dedicated climate resources under the UNFCCC framework have been estimated at about $10 billion per year (2005–2010 and during the fast start finance period 2010–2012) (IPCC 2013: chapter 16). This represents the combined total financing and investment flows available for financing adaptation and mitigation. However, there is widespread agreement that this is not sufficient to cover the scale and scope of required climate-related activities needed by developing countries in Africa, Asia, Latin America, the Caribbean and the Pacific (conservatively estimated at $171 billion per year by 2030 for adaptation and $210 billion per year for mitigation; UNFCCC 2008).

After many years of weak implementation of their finance commitment, in the 2009 annual climate meeting, held in Copenhagen, developed countries proposed fast start finance of about $30 billion for the period 2010–2013 and further committed to a goal of mobilizing $100 billion per year by 2020 from various sources, including public and private and innovative sources. A significant part of this amount plus any additional flow of funds generated through innovative financing mechanisms should flow through the Green Climate Fund (GCF) established by the Cancún 2010 agreement and whose governing instrument was endorsed by the Durban COP 17 in 2011. The rationalization of future climate finance under the UNFCCC is to be overseen by the now approved and implemented, as of 2012, Standing Committee on Finance, established by Cancún (2010) to oversee the coordination and coherence of climate finance.

Gender and climate finance

In terms of mitigation, successful long-term actions to promote clean energy and the transition to low carbon climate resilient development pathways will rely on the actions of men and women in their multiple roles as social and economic decision-makers in households, businesses and communities. As governments negotiate GHG emissions reduction targets – and establish innovative financial mechanisms and sustainable financing – it is important that they recognize and account for the gender and other equity dimensions of climate change policy. A salient approach to both adaptation and mitigation is the integration of a gender climate risk and vulnerability assessment framework that can help to clearly identify the risks that climate change poses for women's social and economic situation, and will provide the appropriate visibility so the risks can be fully addressed. Such a framework can be developed or grafted onto the numerous emerging climate risks and vulnerability approaches.

Careful reading and cross-referencing of the broad and growing literature on gender and the environment,[9] gender and energy,[10] gender and water,[11] gender and conflict,[12] gender and labour markets,[13] gender and the informal economy,[14] and gender and transport[15] will show that gender dimensions of climate change have profound implications for the success of climate change adaptation and mitigation strategies, and in turn that climate change poses significant challenges to the forward momentum of gender equality and women's economic empowerment objectives as highlighted in the Millennium Development Goals (MDGs) framework.

It is not clear how much of the total of $10 billion per year so far reported to have been spent on climate change actions in developing countries have supported women's empowerment and gender equality oriented projects and programmes. In the case of the approximately $30 plus billion of fast start finance reported to have been contributed by developed countries through various channels, there is widespread disagreement about the actual amount of fresh (new and additional) monies it earmarked or disbursed. A few contributing countries, mainly European countries, have specified a portion of their fast start financing for gender equity projects and programmes. But, apart from ensuring gender equity with regard to the governance structure of the GCF, there has been no commitment to fund gender equality interventions, either through a specific set of subfunds or under the funding of adaptation or mitigation.

At the national level, no government has yet broached the topic in their own national level planning around climate change, though gender has been identified in a number of National Adaptation Programmes of Action (NAPAs), the instrument through which least developing countries have pin-pointed their adaptation needs; nor is gender analysis incorporated into the emerging frameworks of the new National Adaptation Plans (NAPs) (applicable to all developing countries), the Cancún Adaptation Framework or to mitigation measures, such as the Nationally Appropriate Mitigation Actions (NAMAs) of developing countries.

The CIFs of the World Bank and the Adaptation Fund (under the UNFCCC) have both committed to integrate gender into their frameworks and this work is ongoing. It is, however, not clear how much of the funding stream is dedicated to women's projects as a distinct group of actors.

It is important that climate change policy and climate changing financing instruments, mechanisms and processes are made gender sensitive. At the present time, it is not clear to what extent climate change strategies and the financing of these impacts gender equality and women's empowerment, positively or negatively. This is a matter for empirical verification. The imperative for undertaking a thorough review of such impacts is now, given that the negotiations for bolstering and regirding the architecture of climate change finance is currently underway. An initial starting point in this direction is to demystify the subject-matter by carefully examining the scope, composition and direction of financial and investment flows. This must be complemented by a careful analysis and tracking of the specific dynamics and interrelationship between gender and climate change financing.

This book argues that the UNFCCC, as the normative framework for climate change finance, provides more than an adequate basis for integrating a gender social equity and women's empowerment approach into climate change policy and its related financing. Subsequent decisions of the COP (2001 and 2011) have contributed to enhancing the role and status of gender concerns into the Convention's governance framework. Yet more work needs to be done in integrating gender perspective into the various works of the substantive areas and bodies of the Conventions. At the same time, the overall climate change finance architecture and governance system has no systematic, consistent and coherent institutional framework for promoting gender equitable outcomes and the empowerment of women, to which most of the member states have made binding commitments under the Convention for the Elimination of Discrimination Against Women (CEDAW) and other human rights oriented instruments.

At best, climate change finance should strive to ensure that economic and financial resources for adaptation, mitigation and technology bolster and upgrade women's skills, knowledge, ownership and access to resources such as land, credit and technology. At worst, it should seek to 'do no harm', hence have no significantly negative impacts on women's access to and ownership of existing assets and resources. Therefore, it is imperative that social equity and gender equality are included as key cross-cutting principles in the normative and operational framework of global climate change as well as its financial architecture.

Unfortunately, the extent to which climate change financial and investment flows have contributed to improving peoples' capacities to withstand or rebound from climate change's adverse effects remains unclear. It is also difficult to track how much of these funds and investments have flowed to gender sensitive projects or programmes that promote gender equality outcomes. Social and gender impact assessments are critical to identifying improvements to adaptive capacity and resilience of vulnerable groups of men and women among and within countries. At present, however, these assessments are marginal to the distribution and utilization of flows of funds for climate change.

A key deliverable of the global climate change finance architecture is that it ensures adequate and balanced funding for both adaptation and mitigation, supports the transfer of technology and capacity building and promotes equity between regions and groups of developing countries. It should also seek to ensure that climate finance is gender equitable and gender sensitive in its distribution, supporting the efforts of poor women on the ground in developing countries and upscales their contributions to and benefits from mitigation programmes, projects and policies.

The final outcome of the climate negotiations in Durban (2011) maintained many of the Cancún, Mexico (December 2010), references to women and gender across several sections of agreement. The Doha 2012 negotiations for the most part maintained these advances and reaffirmed the gender decision of the Marrakesh negotiations of 2001, focusing on women's participation. This sets the stage for more focused discussions and actions around gender and climate change financing in the coming years. These advances were affirmed by the subsequent meetings of the parties, including Warsaw 2013 and Lima 2014.

With the full operationalization of both the GCF (2011–2015) and the Standing Committee on Finance (2012), which is dedicated to help the COP with the coherence and rationalization of climate finance under the UNFCCC, global attention will be focused on elaborating the financial framework for the post-2015 period, including issues of the financing gap between 2013 and 2020 and the long-term scale, sources and distribution of finance for climate change, starting with the Copenhagen promise of $100 billion per year by 2020.

This book therefore seeks to answer four interrelated questions. First, what is the nature, scope and extent of climate change finance and its implications for economic development and poverty eradication? Second, and the key concerns of this effort, what opportunities, challenges and risks do the current pattern of climate change finance pose for gender equality and women's economic empowerment processes now underway in developing countries? Or, alternatively, to what extent do climate change financial and investment flows enhance, bypass or marginalize women's concerns and priorities? Third, how are the challenges and risks to be mitigated or otherwise transformed into creative opportunities for financing the forward momentum of gender equality and women's economic empowerment? Fourth, what kinds of regulations, mechanisms, programmes and processes are required to achieve these goals within the context of the evolving global climate change financing architecture?

The analysis herein is based on the presumption that, at best, climate change finance should strive to ensure that economic and financial resources for adaptation, mitigation and technology bolster and upgrade women's and men's skills, knowledge, ownership and access to resources such as land, credit and technology. At worst, it should seek to 'do no harm', hence have no significantly negative impacts on women's access to and ownership of existing assets and resources. Therefore, it is imperative that social equity and gender equality are included as key cross-cutting principles in the normative and operational framework of global climate change as well as its financial architecture.

This book therefore synthesizes and analyses the information about the flow of finance in the global climate change finance architecture from a development, gender and social equity perspective. It analyses information on the trends in both public and private finance, and ascertains how these trends are impacting and will impact the lives of women and men in developing countries. The book thus seeks to provide a gender perspective of climate change finance, contributing to the debate about the efficacy of global climate finance for adaptation and climate resilient oriented poverty eradication.

The analysis in this book is driven by three underlying premises: (1) climate change is an issue of economic and social justice which cannot be effectively addressed without dealing with the underlying asymmetries and inequities between developed and developing countries; (2) climate change is an economic development issue which cannot be truly resolved without promoting sustainable economic development and upholding the right to development; (3) gender and other social equity issues must be factored into the global and national responses to climate change. Ultimately, the promotion of sustainable development and climate protection is, in all developing countries, tied into the promotion of the economic and social welfare of women and men by addressing their differentiated roles, contribution and responsibilities in the economy and society.

Climate change protection policy must invariably take into account the challenges and constraints of indigenous men and women's lives within the context of accounting for the historicity and continuity of their marginalization from natural and man-made resources. This has important implications for the present dilemma the world now faces and how the knowledge and practices of indigenous women and men can contribute meaningfully to help resolving some of these global challenges. Global and national approaches to climate protection must also pay attention to the other aspects of inequalities, including men and women with disabilities, young men and young women, the elderly and ethnic minorities in a framework that pays attention to the gender pathways of these inequalities and the challenges they pose for these groups' abilities and capacities to adapt to climate change and variability.

First, inequalities in the control and access to economic resources, including access to technology and scientific information as well as all types of infrastructural services, which are the results of historical forces, rooted in conquest, colonialism and imperialism, have led to the now developed countries controlling and utilizing a disproportionate share of the world's resources, including its atmospheric space. This inequitable sharing of the world's resources conditions the ability of different groups of countries, classes and groups of men and women to both undertake and maintain sustainable development and sustained poverty eradication. Though the development processes of the now rich countries of North America, Europe, Australia and New Zealand, in the period 1850–2002, have created about 76 per cent of the cumulative stock of carbon dioxide emissions (primarily from fossil fuel combustion)[16] fuelling the GHGs that now treacherously warm the planet, thus far they have been the least impacted by the consequences of this warming; it is the developing countries and the poorest men and women in these countries who are the primary victims of the impacts of the extreme weather events now unleashed by climate change. An added insult to this iniquitous situation is that there is very little atmospheric space left available for developing countries to grow and develop in a manner that could sustainably eradicate poverty and ensure access to a decent standard of living for the men and women in these countries. Yet in the face of rising extreme weather events linked to climate change and the continuing high per capita consumption and emissions patterns of the developed countries, it is the men, women and children of the developing countries who face increasing water shortages (between 3 billion and 7 billion people by 2075) and food shortages (one in six countries could likely face food shortages each year because of droughts), and untold millions face pending health crises.

Noting that 'the damage done to the environment by modern society is perhaps one of the most inequitable health risks of our time', *The Lancet* (May 2009) labelled climate change as the 'biggest global health threat of the twenty-first century'. It also argued that 'loss of healthy life years as a result of global environmental change – including climate change – is predicted to be 500 times greater in poor African populations than in European populations' (also cited in UNFPA 2009). Though the carbon footprint of the poorest 1 billion accounts for about 3 per cent of the world total footprint, the ultimate burden of climate change falls on the developing countries (Patz *et al*. 2005 cited in UNFPA 2009).

These and other types of inequality persist unabashedly in the climate debate. It is quite pronounced in debate over the nature of emissions reduction, especially in the push by the developed countries, as a group, to increasingly shift the burden of mitigation onto the developing countries, while they have not fully followed through on their own commitments, made under the Convention and the Kyoto Protocol, to reduce emissions. The cruellest of all ironies is that while these rich developed countries have had a difficult time making emissions cuts and transforming their economies towards a low carbon pathway, they nonetheless are insisting that developing countries, charged with being the future emitters and who have less resources and access to technology, shoulder the lion's share of the burden. This is evident in calls by the US, supported by other developing countries, for symmetry in rights and obligations and for ending the so-called 'firewall' between developed and developing countries in terms of mitigation obligations under the UNFCCC.

Unreservedly, developed countries, such as the US, are also putting greater emphasis on accounting for emissions of methane from agricultural fields, which from the point of view of developing countries are 'survival emissions' of short duration and should not be 'compared with the carbon dioxide emissions from fossil fuel burning and growing industrialization (Sethi 2012). The US, in particular, does this without, in parallel, placing emphasis on reducing and dramatically changing consumption patterns at home, specifically, and in the developed countries, broadly. As noted by Sethi, 'the focus on methane before the carbon dioxide emissions are addressed gives the rich countries a chance to get more headspace in the atmosphere to continue emitting "luxury emissions" for longer period of time' (Sethi 2012). It is indisputable that developing countries and the millions of women, men, boys and girls within their borders face the maximum risks to their lives and livelihoods from the chaos of climate change. This situation can only be lessened with appropriate attention and actions of the developed countries to reducing their own lifestyle-directed emissions and to providing the needed finance and technology that will enable developing countries to adapt to and transform their economies through the adoption of clean and renewable energy technologies. There will also be need for the financing of an international mechanism for loss and damage[17] in order to help the millions of women and men whose lives and livelihoods are imperiled. The economics of climate change is hence a serious concern.

Second, climate change is as much an economic issue as it is an ecological and environmental issue. It is definitively an economic development issue. Climate change arises from economic dynamics and is the result of acute market failure of not accounting for human production and consumption effects on the environment. That market-driven calculus is not the only thing that has driven the economy. The role of the household and women's role, activities and contribution to the economy are, likewise, under-recognized and neglected both in conceptual frameworks and in policy prescriptions, design and implementation. Climate change and the timely or lack of appropriate responses to mitigate its causal factors bode serious challenges for eradicating poverty and promoting economic growth and human development. This is because climate change has destructive impacts on critical sectors of agriculture and water resources as well as likely distributional impacts at all levels of the economy.

Yet many economists continue to underestimate both the urgency and the scale of mitigation and adaptation needed, while emphasizing mainly the impact on gross domestic production. Economic-based modelling also continues to put greater emphasis on mitigation, under-emphasizing adaptation and in some cases arguing that it can come later after mitigation. This is indeed a dangerous situation for developing countries and the lives of the millions of women, girls, boys and men in those countries, who face almost daily adaptation challenges now.

Since the first and second Earth Summits (1992, 2002), from the vantage point of economic analysis, there has been significant, though inadequate, attention paid to sustainability issues (mostly) at the micro and meso levels, to different degrees, in different economies. But these efforts have often been fragmented, weakly implemented and not integrated into the overall macroeconomic framework of countries. The global community is currently involved in a complex set of interrelated and somewhat intertwined processes: reviewing and making proposals for addressing the unfinished business of the MDGs; charting new terrain with the defining and elaboration of the content of yet another set of goals, the Sustainable Development Goals (SDGs)[18] and discussions of the framework for a new global agreement on climate change. This triplet of efforts (new development goals, sustainability goals, the new climate change agreement), which are currently on parallel tracks, are meant to set the roadmaps and rule books for tackling the most entrenched problems afflicting the modern political economy – endemic poverty and hunger, rising and persistent inequality (of all forms), financial instability, resource depletion, the state of ecology and climate change (the latter three being increasingly associated with the likely breach of the earth's planetary boundaries). All of these processes are set to conclude sometime in 2015.

Both the processes to design a new global sustainable development agenda (post-2015 and the SDGs) process are premised on sustainable development for all and thus are meant to set the world on a sustainable path. Thus both the post-2015, the SDG process and the new climate agreement meet at the crucial crossroads of sustainable development. The path towards sustainable development including addressing climate change and managing global commons, must be coherent in its content as well as coherent with the system of economic analysis, policy prescriptions and measurement utilized for both the national and the global economies.

Third, gender equality and women's empowerment issues, including the promotion of gender equity in climate finance, cannot be isolated from the broader discussions of climate change, its impacts and future dynamics, or the economic, political and scientific debates. All of these topics of debates set the broader envelope for the scale and intensity of adaptation and mitigation efforts to be undertaken by developing and developed countries, and give rise to the degree of sacrifice that is required at country and local levels. So gender equality concerns cannot be superficially or instrumentally used in a convenient manner. Gender inequality intervention for promoting and ensuring women's and men's lives in developing countries depends acutely on the outcomes and actions of historically based and just determination, and apportionment of climate protection polices and the appropriate and rapidly expedited flow of means of implementation of such policies: finance, technology and capacity building.

Ultimately, the over-riding framework of climate protection policy conditions and will significantly determine the life chances and opportunities for women and men in communities on the ground in developing countries. For example, though adaptation is a pressing concern in developing countries and of paramount importance for women's lives in those countries, the degree to which adaptation actions and the scale of funding that will be required for these, is inextricably linked to decisions and choices with regard to stabilising the climate system. This is occurring through ongoing negotiations about temperature targets (guard rail) and global goals and time frames for peaking and reducing GHG emissions. These so-called technical factors are not value-neutral decisions. They are informed by science but they are ultimately determined by economic and political considerations about tolerable risks and economic cost and benefit calculus. These decisions have implications for men's and women's daily lives now and in the future. Hence women's groups and gender advocates as much as farmers' groups and business organizations have vested interest in participating in this decision-making geared to specific outcomes and in ensuring that the policies and actions arrived at are driven by the concerns of those most vulnerable to the ill effects of climate change.

The fourth underlying premise of this book argues that solutions to the climate change challenges are intertwined with gender equality and the empowerment of women in developing countries. Sustainable achievements in gender equality and women's economic and social empowerment may entail positive effects on climate change solutions and vice versa. Meeting the climate change challenges and continuing to increase women's control and access to economic and social resources will require significant flows of financial resources geared to gender equality and women's empowerment outcomes within the framework of adaptation, mitigation and technology transfer and development. In this way, the implementing of sustainable gender equality interventions that enhance women's and men's empowerment and overall social equity can have large, sustainable economic development dividends, which can be immensely beneficial to the achievement of global climate change policy goals. *Gender equality and women's empowerment are complementary not antagonistic to the achievement of climate change goals. There is a gender equality dividend that will be beneficial to climate change goals and that can increase the efficacy and sustainability of climate finance.*

Notes

1 Failing harvests in the US, Ukraine and other countries this year have eroded reserves to their lowest level since 1974. UN warns of looming worldwide food crisis in 2013. www.guardian.co.uk/global-development/2012/oct/14/un-global-food.
2 According to the Global Humanitarian Forum, the term 'seriously affected' used in this context refers to those in 'need of immediate assistance either following a weather-related disaster, or because livelihoods have been severely compromised by climate change' (p. 3). In addition, natural disasters lead to both migration and internal displacement which puts women at great disadvantages and subject them to personal insecurity and vulnerability to sexual harassment, sexual assault and other forms of violence. In may also be associated with a rising prevalence of female households. The World Health Organization argues that since the 1970s there have been 150,000 excess deaths annually due to extreme heatwaves, storms or similar events due to climate change (WHO 2014). The Climate Vulnerability Monitor estimates that climate change causes 400,000 deaths on average each year today, mainly due to hunger and communicable diseases that affect above all children in developing countries (DARA 2012). DARA (ibid.) also reports that Climate change caused economic losses estimated close to 1 per cent of global GDP for the year 2010, or 700 billion dollars (2010 PPP).
3 The right to development is an inalienable human right by virtue of which every human person and all peoples are entitled to participate in, contribute to, and enjoy economic, social, cultural and political development, in which all human rights and fundamental freedoms can be fully realized, Article 2 (Declaration on the Right to Development).
4 Based on the IPCC's Fifth Assessment Report 'Climate Change 2014: Impacts, Adaptation, and Vulnerability'.
5 Climate change induced warming can lead to wider transmission of malaria; 'rising temperature extends the habitats of the mosquitoes that carry the malaria parasite, shifting the boundaries of latitude and altitude for malaria transmission – for example, many highland areas in Burundi, Kenya and Uganda that have historically been classed as malaria-free are now experiencing epidemics' (Sulaiman 2007). Floods and higher rainfalls are associated with new breeding grounds for mosquitoes in Mozambique and droughts in sub-Saharan Africa lead to declining water levels and rising stagnant pools of water.
6 Originally applied to self-employment in small unregistered enterprises, the concept of informality has been expanded to include wage employment in unprotected jobs. So defined, the informal economy comprises half to three quarters of the *non-agricultural* labour force in developing countries. When agriculture is included, the share of informal

employment in *total* employment is higher still: as high as 90 per cent in some countries in South Asia and sub-Saharan Africa (WEIGO 2014).
7 Pre-industrial levels of CO_2 concentrates in the atmosphere was about 280ppm, in 1998 377ppm. It is argued that CO_2 level beyond 450ppm is 'dangerous'.
8 In its fourth Assessment Report, the IPCC also flagged issues around equity. The IPCC made reference to three areas of equity: (1) Equity between developed and developing countries 'in the delineation of rights and responsibilities within any climate-change response framework'; (2) 'the need for equity across vulnerable groups that are disproportionately exposed to climate-change impacts; and (3) 'intergenerational ethics; i.e., the degree to which the interests of future generations are given relatively lower weighting in favour of short-term concerns' (IPCC 2007).
9 Agarwal (1995) Environment and Poverty Interlinks in Rural India: Regional Variation and Temporal Shifts, 1971–1991. United Nations Research Institute for Social Development (UNRSID).
10 Cecelski (2004) Re-thinking gender and energy: Old and new directions. ENERGIA/EASE Discussion Paper.
11 GWA/UNDP (2006). *Mainstreaming Gender in Water Management.*
12 Byrne (1996) *Gender, Conflict and Development: Volume I: Overview*. Bridge/IDS www.bridge.ids.ac.uk/Reports/re34c.pdf; Byrne, Marcus and Powers-Stevens (1995) *Gender, conflict and development Volume II: Case studies: Cambodia; Rwanda; Kosovo; Algeria; Somalia; Guatemala and Eritrea*. Bridge/IDS 1996 www.bridge.ids.ac.uk/Reports/re35c.pdf.
13 DAW (1999) *World Survey on the Role of Women in Development: Globalization, Gender and Work*. United Nations Division for the Advancement of Women.
14 ADB (2008) Asia's Urban Challenges. www.adb.org/documents/events/2008/adb-urban-day2008/presentation-Climate-Change.pdf; Chan and Pedwell (2008) Women, gender and the informal economy: An assessment of ILO research and suggested ways forward. ILO working paper series; and Chen and Carr (2002) *Globalization and the Informal Economy: How Global Trade and Investment Impact on the Working Poor*. Working Paper on the Informal Economy, No. 1. Geneva: ILO.
15 Gender and transport literature includes WIT 2014; ECE 2009; Riverson, Kunieda, Roberts, Lewis and Walker (2005), Peters 2002 and Fernando and Porter 2002.
16 This does not include emissions from land use change or recent deforestation – mainly emitted by developing countries (UNFPA 2009). Developing countries account for 24 per cent during the time period. However since 2005 their portion has increased to about 54 per cent of total emissions (IPCC 2007) and as a group developing countries will account for the majority of the growth in emissions of CO_2 2008–2030. (In 2007 China surpassed the US in total emission from fuel combustions. Nonetheless, as noted by UNFPA per capita emissions remains significantly higher in the developed countries Date on emissions distribution from WRI and cited in UNFPA 2009.
17 An international mechanism for loss and damage, which was formally mooted in the negotiation as of the Doha 2012 meeting of the Conference of the Parties, was agreed to in Warsaw (2013) as the Warsaw International Mechanism for Loss and Damage but the operational details have now to be worked on and there was no specific financing component agreed as part of the decision.
18 The path towards charting a set of sustainability goals is part of the implementation of the outcome from the United Nations Conference on Sustainable Development (UNCSD, Rio+ 20 2012 (*The Future We Want*). The SDGs, initially, were not on parallel track with the MDGs; it began in 2013. Its focus is to deal specifically with the interplay between economic, social and environmental parameters and the major challenges: poverty, environmental degradation and ecological limits.

1
THE GLOBAL CLIMATE CHANGE POLICY ENVIRONMENT

> The ultimate objective of this Convention and any related legal instruments that the Conference of the Parties may adopt is to achieve, in accordance with the relevant provisions of the Convention, stabilization of greenhouse gas concentrations in the atmosphere at a level that would prevent dangerous anthropogenic interference with the climate system. Such a level should be achieved within a time frame sufficient to allow ecosystems to adapt naturally to climate change, to ensure that food production is not threatened and to enable economic development to proceed in a sustainable manner.
>
> UNFCCC 1992: Article 2

This chapter presents an overview of the global climate change protection framework noting when and how gender considerations have entered. It also explores the scientific imperative behind the UNFCCC and discusses in brief the economic and political under-currents that have brought that process to a log-jam over the last 7 years.

It is undeniable. The evidence is unequivocal. At the planetary level, global temperature and the atmospheric concentration of GHGs is rising. This is causing specific kinds of impacts at global, regional, national and local levels posing wide ranging challenges for human beings, animals and plants.[1] These specific climate variability impacts include alterations in rainfall patterns and consequent storms, floods or droughts in different parts of the world. Adverse impacts on natural ecosystem, agriculture and food production, human health and limited access and availability to water are already being felt by millions of girls, boys, women and men in the developing countries of Africa, Asia, the Caribbean and the Pacific.

Climate change is driving the occurrence of more frequent storms such as super storm Sandy, typhoon Haiyan and rising sea levels. Super storm Sandy devastated the New York City area in 2012. Typhoon Bopha, also in 2012, killed more than 1,000 persons in the Philippines. It was followed the next year by Haiyan (Yolanda) which waged havoc in South East Asia and yet again 'devastated the Philippines'. According to *The Economist*, Haiyan, which was one of the worst storms ever recorded, created about $15 billion dollars' worth of damages (*The Economist* 2013). Rising sea levels, predicted to reach as much as 23 inches by 2100, will cause shore lines to move further inland posing danger to highly populated cities in a number of developing countries, such as Mexico, Venezuela, India, Bangladesh, the Philippines and Vietnam, as well as, play havoc on the lives of millions of women, men and children living in all small island states and the river delta regions of the world (World Bank 2012a).

The anthropogenic climate change (ACC) tenet outlined by the IPCC in its Fourth Assessment Report (2007) is well supported by the latest findings of the scientific community. Scientific research now more clearly show the link between extreme weather and man-made GHGs (IPCC 2012, 2013). Earth scientists, climate scientists, meteorologists and oceanographers all have expressed high levels of certainty about the basics of climate change and human activity as a primary driver.[2] While there remains uncertainty about how particular aspects of climate change (for example, changes in cloud cover, the timing or magnitude of droughts and floods) will unfold in the future,[3] by 2011 at least 34 national academies of science such as those in the major G8 countries, plus Brazil, China and India and Poland have made formal declarations or statements supporting the view that global warming is real and almost certainly caused by human activities. This consensus on global warming and its human causation has been long in the making. It is ultimately one of the key driving force behind the continuing, though political fraught and economically challenging, global effort to build a strong and effective global climate protection regime.

This chapter undertakes a forensic analysis of this global climate protection effort. The next section traces the evolution of the international environment and climate protection architecture which has been emerging in its contemporary form since the 1970s. The subsequent section presents an overview of the outcomes of climate negotiations, undertaken by a group of over 194 countries since 1992, under the umbrella of the United Nations Framework Convention on Climate Change (UNFCCC). The UNFCCC is currently the only legal framework responsible for the formation and implementation of climate protection policies on a global scale.

The chapter also explores how gender and other equity issues have been integrated into the policies, programmes, instruments and mechanisms of this global climate protection regime, focusing on the different turns and twists of the attempts by gender advocates to integrate gender equality concerns within the overarching structural framework of the UNFCCC. The remaining four sections of the chapter briefly discuss some of the key issues that challenge the global protection regime. These inextricably intertwined and challenging undertows that sometimes seems to cripple the global awareness and willingness to tackle the drivers of climate change are the economics of climate change and the tumultuous politics of climate change negotiations. The chapter also briefly explores the role of climate science in shaping the contours of the global climate protection. Chapter 2 will bring these strands together in a focused discussion of the fundamental debate about equity, fairness and climate justice in the global climate change regime. It will also highlight the debates on the critical gaps (development, emissions and fairness/equity, adaptation and finance) that are seemingly hamstringing the current negotiation process.

1.1 The evolution of the international environment and climate protection architecture

Since at least the 1970s, the global community has recognized the critical and far reaching dangerous interactions between human activities and the earth's atmosphere. Environmental activists, scientists and policymakers have since worked to raise global awareness of the environmental and ecological challenges posing danger for the earth's biological and physical systems that support life. The initial thrust of environmental activism on a global scale focused on air, water and marine pollution and the conservation and preservation of biological diversity and non renewable resources that enable ecological cycles and all human activities.

In the early 1970s a number of international conferences were convened on environmental issues geared towards developing a global consensus on the nature of the problems and to set up agreed frameworks for policy solutions (please see Appendix 1.1 for more details). Many of these early events were scientific and expert gatherings focused on examining the nature and processes of erratic weather patterns, the nature of environmental degradation and the consequent endangerment or near extinction of some species (such as amphibians, birds and tree snails)[4] and the using up of non-renewable resources (such as peat and minerals). Such meetings, which also attracted policy makers and environmental activists, highlighted the urgent need to deal with the effects of human activities on wetlands, marine eco-systems as well as climate factors impacting temperature, soil and humidity and desertification. These meetings helped to define and further clarify the elements that would be needed for ensuring sustainability and thus set the groundwork for high level political discussions that would culminate in the creation of a number of multilateral and plurilateral environmental agreements such as the Montreal Protocol, the Convention on Biodiversity and the UNFCCC. These agreements are now the bedrock of global environmental governance.

The first two major summit level international conferences on environment were the UN Conference on the Human Environment (Stockholm, 1972) and the United Nations Conference on Environment and Development (UNCED, the Earth Summit or the Rio Summit, 1992). The Stockholm Declaration on the human environment emphasized the shared responsibility for the quality of the environment, especially the oceans and the atmosphere. It made over 200 recommendations for international level actions on matters ranging from climate change, marine pollution and toxic waste focused on the management of the biosphere. Stockholm also set in motion processes that laid the foundation of modern environmental regulation, including the creation of a global environmental assessment programme (Earthwatch) and the United Nations Environment Programme (UNEP).

Twenty years later the more politically oriented 1992 UNCED, which focused on the theme of environment and sustainable development, culminated in three signature pieces of environmental landmarks: the Rio Declaration on Environment and Development, the Statement of Forest Principles and an ambitious action plan for catalysing and stimulating local, national, regional and international cooperation in addressing environmental degradation, Agenda 21. It also facilitated the signing of three multilateral environmental agreements that were negotiated on parallel tracks prior to and during the conference planning processes. These so-called Rio Conventions are the Convention on Biological Diversity, the Convention on Combatting and Controlling Desertification and the UNFCCC. Ten years after UNCED, the 2002 Johannesburg Conference sought to enhance and enlarge the operational domain of Agenda 21, the UN programme of actions from Rio, by proposing concrete steps and identifiable quantitative targets under the Johannesburg Plan of Implementation.

During the period of the 1970s to the 1990s a number of critically important international instruments and international and national institutions were set up to ground environmental protection policy globally and nationally. For example, in 1970, the US established the Environmental protection Agency and the European Union (formerly European Economic Community) also established an Environment and Consumer Protection Service (1973). Internationally, in 1972, the United Nations Environment Programme (UNEP)[5] was established to perform both the normative role of assessing global environmental state, facilitate international environmental policy development and formulate multilateral environmental agreement in the context of sustainable development as well as undertake operational functions such as supporting the implementation of environmental treaties and related action plans at local, national and regional levels.

In the developing countries, many governments also followed suit, establishing their own versions of national environment agencies. In Latin America, in 1973 Brazil established a Special Secretariat for the Environment later (by 1999) transformed into the Ministry of the Environment. In Africa, Tanzania, with long history of natural resource conservation, established a National Environment Management Council in 1983. In Asia, China established the National Environmental Protection Agency in 1984,[6] later upgraded to a State Environmental Agency (SEPA) in 1998, operating at ministerial level, and since 2008, it is the Ministry of Environmental Protection of the People's Republic of China (Wikipedia 2013).

In 1979 the Geneva Convention on Long Range Transboundary Air Pollution that regulated the emissions of noxious gases was adopted and concern with depletion of the ozone layer led to the Vienna Convention for the Protection of the Ozone Layer, 1985 and its Montreal Protocol on Substances that Deplete the Ozone layer.[7] The protocol facilitated the gradual withdrawal of the chlorofluoro-

22 The global climate change policy environment

carbons (CFCs) that destroy the ozone layer.[8] The capstone of this period was the World Commission on Environment and Development (the Brundtland Commission, 1983–1987), which issued the report *Our Common Future*[9] and placed emphasis on sustainable development (defined as: development that 'meets the needs of the present without compromising the ability of future generations to meet their own needs').

By the early 1980s, global attention was increasingly focused on the effects of the rising average temperature of the earth's atmosphere, identified as global warming, and its causes – GHGs, with carbon dioxide (CO_2) as a principal agent.[10]

The pattern of rising carbon dioxide CO_2 and the correlative warming links with atmospheric global temperature rise, through the so-called greenhouse effect, had been theorized since the nineteenth century by Jean Fourier (1820) and Svante Arrhenius (1896).[11] Anthropogenic (human caused) CO_2 as the key driver of global warming through the burning of fossil fuels was identified by Svante Arrhenius and Thomas Chamberlin (1896) and John Tyndall in the mid- to late nineteenth century. By the middle of the twentieth century, scientists such as Roger Revelle, Hans Seuss and Charles Keeling were able to empirically verify the threat of rising levels of overhang of CO_2 in the atmosphere.[12]

GHGs such as carbon dioxide, water vapour, nitrous oxide, methane, halo carbon and ozone prevent heat from escaping the earth's atmosphere much the same way as the locked windows of a car traps heat inside the car. This warming effect is raising the average temperature of the earth to current level of 0.8 degrees Celsius above pre-industrial level and could conservatively exceed 4 degrees Celsius by 2100 (Figure 1.1). There are noticeable, significant and growing interactions between carbon dioxide and climate parameters such as rainfall and temperature change as well as the adverse impact on sea level. These intertwined factors and their dire implications for food production, forest and ecosystem services and the availability of clean fresh water led to climate change becoming centre stage in the global environmental discussion.

Rising sea level puts at least 200 million people's lives at risk. Rising temperature is associated with natural migration of mosquitos and hence increased susceptibility to incidence of both vector borne diseases such as dengue (Eastern Caribbean) and malaria (Uganda and Rwanda),[13] and non-vector-borne infectious diseases such as cholera and salmonellosis. Floods and the salinity of water increase toxic intrusion into water catchment areas and pose severe consequences for human and health systems, biodiversity and the continuation of specific animal and plant species. Climate change, hence, is seen as a severe threat to human and ecological survival.

Though rising atmospheric carbon dioxide can occur due to naturally occurring warming processes such as the solar (sun) energy on the earth's orbital cycle and ocean circulation, empirical evidence show that anthropogenic GHG such as fossil fuels (coal, oil, natural gases) burning since the beginning of the industrial revolution (1700s) is the major cause of rising CO_2. Naturally generated carbon dioxide trend

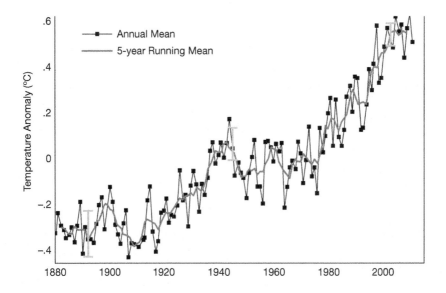

FIGURE 1.1 Global land–ocean temperature index

has not risen significantly and commensurately with the increasing warming of the earth's atmosphere to be the primary causal factor in global warming.

In the early 1980s, both the US National Academy of Science (NAS) and the Environmental Protection Agency issued studies that concluded that anthropogenic sources of CO_2 were likely responsible for the observed changes in the CO_2 levels. The NAS report argued that waiting to take action on climate change could result in permanent damage to the environment and potential disruption to the society. In addition, the Ad Hoc Working Group on carbon dioxide and climate change in 1978 argued that doubling of the level of carbon dioxide from pre-industrial time would eventual warm the earth by approximately 3 degrees Celsius.

Given that human causation has been identified as the key contributing factor to rising CO_2 level, global activities have centred on developing global understanding and a common consensus on how to deal with climate change. An intense process of diplomacy led to a global policy framework to examine and respond to the climate change challenge.

In 1979 and 1990, the first and second World Climate Conferences were convened to examine the issue of climate change. The First World Climate Conference 1979 was more of a scientific and experts meeting to improve the scientific understanding of atmospheric processes. It assessed the state of knowledge of climate and to consider the effects of climate variability and change on human society. The final declaration of the Conference 'identified the leading cause of global warming as increased atmospheric concentrations of carbon dioxide resulting from the burning of fossil fuels, deforestation, and changes in land use' (UNFCCC 2012).

One of the key outputs of the Conference was the creation of the World Climate Program and its associated research component the World Climate Research Programme. The World Climate Programme engendered the global collaboration of scientists and hence was a precursor to the creation of the Inter-governmental Panel on Climate.

After the first Climate Conference, there were a number of important meetings (Toronto 1988, the Hague 1989, Noordwijk 1989 and Bergen 1990) that mobilized political support around globally coordinate climate change responses at the highest political level.[14] For example, the Noordwijk Declaration in 1989 made the point that developed countries should stabilize CO_2 emission by 20 per cent with respect to 1990 level and that they should also provide assistance to developing countries. The Hague meeting called for a framework convention on climate change.

By the time of the second World Conference, which was a more political gathering than the first, there was general acceptance that it was indeed possible for developed countries to stabilize CO_2 emissions from the energy sector and reduced these by at least 20 per cent by the year 2005. Meeting participants also argued that developing countries should uses modern technologies (Gupta 2010). The second global climate meeting concluded with a Ministerial Declaration that helped to lay the framework for a global treaty on climate change. Two years later, under the auspices of the UNCED 1992, the UN Framework Convention on Climate Change was adopted. It came into force in 1994 with signatories of 155 countries.

A critical input into the formation of the current global climate policy was the establishment of the Inter-governmental Panel on Climate Change set up in 1988 under the auspices of the World Meteorological Organization and the United Nations Environment Programme, as an independent body of scientific advisers that 'reviews and assesses the most recent scientific, technical and socio-economic information produced worldwide relevant to the understanding of climate change' (IPCC 2009; see also Box 1.1).

The IPCC, which is an intergovernmental body currently comprised of scientific experts from the 194 member countries of the UN, presents its findings in a series of comprehensive assessment reports; since 1990 there have been five such reports: the first assessment report (FAR 1990), the second assessment report (SAR 1995), the third assessment report (TAR 2001), the fourth assessment report (AR4 2007) and the most recent (AR5 2013). These assessment reports provide the scientific basis for international climate change policy formulation.

The first report of the IPCC (FAR) provided the scientific basis for the international negotiations on climate change policy 1992. The second report, which discussed more strongly that human influences were impacting the climate system help to intensify efforts towards the Kyoto Protocol, while the third report, which offered stronger evidence of the warming trend helped the negotiations of the ninth meeting of the parties. AR4, while it did not specifically recommend a temperature target, its scientific analysis was the basis for the global consensus around the 2 degree C temperature guard rail. Likewise, AR5 will guide the negotiations

BOX 1.1 THE SCOPE, NATURE AND WORKINGS OF THE IPCC

The Intergovernmental Panel on Climate Change (IPCC) was established by the United Nations Environment Programme (UNEP) and the World Meteorological Organization (WMO) in 1988 'to provide the world with a clear scientific view on the current state of knowledge in climate change and its potential environmental and socio-economic impacts'.

The IPCC does not conduct any research nor does it monitor climate-related data or parameters. It reviews and assesses the most recent scientific, technical and socio-economic information produced worldwide relevant to the understanding of climate change. The IPCC relies primarily on peer reviewed literature complemented by non-peer reviewed publications from the private sector and governments including, industry journals, internal organisational publications, non-peer reviewed reports or working papers of research institutions, proceedings of workshops, etc. (so-called grey literature). Governments participate in the review process and the Plenary Sessions, where main decisions about the IPCC work programme are taken and reports are accepted, adopted and approved.

Thousands of scientists worldwide contribute on a voluntary basis to the work of the IPCC as authors, contributors and reviewers. This work is supported by a Secretariat based in Geneva and supported by voluntary and in kind contributions of its 195 Member governments, research institutions and researchers. Regular contributions and other forms of support are also provided through UNEP and WMO with contributions from the UNFCCC (as agreed by the Parties).

The IPCC is currently organized in three working groups and a task force on National Greenhouse Gas Inventories. *Working Group I* assesses the physical scientific aspects of the climate system and climate change, including changes in GHGs and aerosols in the atmosphere; observed changes in air, land and ocean temperatures, rainfall, glaciers and ice sheets, oceans and sea level; historical and paleoclimatic perspective on climate change; biogeochemistry, carbon cycle, gases and aerosols; satellite data and other data; climate models; climate projections, causes and attribution of climate change. *Working Group II* assesses the vulnerability of socio-economic and natural systems to climate change, negative and positive consequences of climate change, and options for adapting to it, taking into consideration the interrelationship between vulnerability, adaptation and sustainable development. *Working Group III* assesses options for mitigating climate change through limiting or preventing GHG emissions and enhancing activities that remove them from the atmosphere, taking into account the costs and benefits of the different approaches to mitigation, considering also the available instruments and policy measures, in a near-term and in a long-term perspective. The sectors

> include energy, transport, buildings, industry, agriculture, forestry and waste management.
>
> IPCC produces assessment reports (ARs)–five thus far, which include the Working Group contributions to the AR – a synthesis report, which synthesises and integrates materials contained in the Working Group reports, and special reports on specific issues (written in a non-technical style suitable for policymakers and which address a broad range of policy-relevant but policy-neutral questions), summaries for policymakers (which provide a policy-relevant but policy-neutral summary of that report) and methodology reports.
>
> Source: based on information from the IPCC website at www.ipcc.ch

around the new legally binding agreement now underway, under the framework of the Ad Hoc Working Group on the Durban Platform or the post-2015 agreement to be agreed in Paris at the twenty-first meeting of climate negotiations.

The initial climate change negotiations, which were undertaken by the Intergovernmental Negotiating Committee for a Framework Convention on Climate Change, culminated in the adoption of the UNFCCC in 1992. The Convention was agreed upon and adopted during its fifth session, second part, held at New York from 30 April to 9 May 1992. Currently, there are 195 parties (194 States and one regional economic integration organization). Negotiations also involve different group of countries and informal and recognized negotiation blocs such as the European Commission, the Group of 77 and China (see Appendix 1.2).

The UNFCCC (Article 1) defines climate change as 'a change of climate which is attributed directly or indirectly to human activity that alters the composition of the global atmosphere and which is in addition to natural climate variability observed over comparable time periods'.[15] Article 1 further defines emissions as 'the release of greenhouse gases and/or their precursors into the atmosphere over a specified area and period of time'. Given this framework, and consistent with the goal of the Convention (the '. . . stabilization of greenhouse gas concentrations in the atmosphere at a level that would prevent dangerous anthropogenic interference with the climate system), as articulated under Article 2, countries agreed to be guided by the principles adopted under the Convention and to take the actions necessary to meet the goals of the Convention, the gathering of countries made commitments to common but differentiated responsibility for achieving the objectives of the Convention (Article 4).

A group of countries made specific commitments to adopt national policies and take measures to mitigate climate change. These countries, referred to as Annex I countries, are 41 developed countries including 14 economies in transition to market economies and the European Economic Community. These are primarily the industrialized countries who have historically contributed the most to climate change.[16] They include both the relatively wealthy industrialized countries that were members of the Organisation for Economic Co-operation and

Development (OECD) in 1992, plus countries with economies in transition (the EITs), including the Russian Federation, the Baltic States, and several Central and Eastern European States (UNFCCC 2002). Annex I Parties are committed to adopting national policies and measures with the non-legally binding aim that they should return their greenhouse gas emissions to 1990 levels by the year 2000. According to the UNFCCC Secretariat, the Convention grants EITs 'a certain degree of flexibility', on account of the economic and political upheavals recently experienced in those countries.[17] Annex II Parties comprised the group of developed countries excluding countries in transition. They have commitment for financial resources and technology transfer to developing countries (Convention Article 4, in particular Paragraphs 2–5). The developing countries Parties, as a group, are generally referred to as non-Annex I parties (NAI).

In 1997, parties to the UNFCCC (at its third meeting, COP 3) adopted the Kyoto Protocol, a legally binding instrument requiring that Annex I signatories to reduce (individually or jointly) their aggregate greenhouse gas emissions to at least 5.2 per cent below 1990 levels between 2008 and 2012 (UNFCCC 1998: Decsion1/CP3).[18] Under the Protocol, which came into force in 2005, legally binding emissions reduction commitments of the Annex I countries (listed in Annex B of the Protocol) were to be implemented during the first commitment period, 2008–2012. Working with the principles of burden sharing and of 'respective capacities', developed countries could determine how to meet the goal of decreasing GHG emissions.[19] Countries had three ways of undertaking the emissions. They could do so by economy-wide efforts focused on integrating and increasing the use of fuel efficient and clean technology and promote greater energy efficiency in their domestic context; and/or promote emissions reduction projects in developing countries; or emissions trading. Developing countries were not required to adopt emissions reduction commitments; instead, it was agreed that these countries would undertake adaptation and (voluntary) mitigation efforts in line with their national development priorities and support with finance, including for technology development and transfer by developed countries Parties.

Under the Kyoto Protocol, the emissions reduction commitments of signatory members were limited to 5 years and thus the first commitment period of the protocol expired in 2012. After that, and with subsequent renewal of commitments for deeper emissions cuts there would be a progressive realization of the Convention's goal of stabilizing GHGs emissions. The Protocol has scope for a second (and subsequent commitment periods) beginning in 2013, and further reductions after that, unless the Protocol is explicitly ended (Khor 2008). Prior to the expiration of the first commitment period in 2012, the amendment of the Protocol was to be adopted in order to preclude a legal gap between the first and second commitment periods. It was anticipated that the second and subsequent commitment periods would progressively increase the emissions reduction commitments of Annex B Parties. As a result, there have been ongoing negotiations about the nature and scope of a second and subsequent periods under the Protocol.[20]

1.2 Overview of climate negotiations and the formation of the global climate protection regime

Since the inception of the UNFCCC, there has been a series of negotiating rounds under the auspice of what is called the Conferences of Parties (COP), the supreme body of the Convention: from its first session, COP 1 – Berlin 1995, to its twentieth session thus far, COP 20 – Lima 2014. With the coming into force of the Kyoto Protocol (in 2005), there have been combined meetings of the COP with the meetings under the Conference of the Parties serving as the meeting of the Parties to the Kyoto Protocol, the CMP, now in its tenth session (CMP 10 – Lima 2014).

In 2005, negotiations on furthering commitments under the Kyoto Protocol was instituted under the Ad Hoc Working Group on the Kyoto Protocol (AWG-KP) which explored the undertaking of 'future commitments for industrialized countries under the Kyoto Protocol' (UNFCCC 2009). The work of the AWG-KP aimed at setting further quantified emissions limitations or reductions by industrialized countries (Annex I) for the second commitment period 2013–2017 and beyond.

A comprehensive road map to achieving the ultimate goal of the Convention was launched in Bali (COP 13 2007) as the Bali Action Plan to be supported by the Bali Road Map – a two-year UNFCCC negotiating process (see Box 1.2). The Bali Road Map should have resulted in agreed outcomes on a science-based global goal for emissions reduction and a time frame for the peaking of GHGs emissions into the earth atmosphere so as to prevent dangerous climate change by 2009.

Under the Bali Action Plan (2007), countries agreed to take stronger (enhanced) actions on mitigation through a four pillar process: (1) Developed countries through quantified emissions reduction targets in a second (and subsequent) commitment period(s) under the Kyoto Protocol. (2) Comparability of efforts by the US and other non-Kyoto Protocol Parties (primarily the US) to the efforts of the other developed countries, who are taking mitigation commitment under the Protocol. (The US, though not party to the Protocol, nevertheless, has legal obligations under the Convention to 'adopt national policies and to take corresponding measures on the mitigation of climate change, by limiting its anthropogenic emissions of GHGs and protecting and enhancing its greenhouse gas sinks and reservoirs (Article 4 Paragraph 2a).) (3) Increased voluntary mitigations actions of developing countries through the creation of a new vehicle, the nationally appropriate mitigation actions (NAMAs), in the context of sustainable development. (4) The efforts of developing countries would be catalysed and sustained by scaled up finance, technological transfer and capacity building to be provided by developed countries, as agreed under the Convention. Bali also gave prominence to the adaptation to climate change.

Thus the Bali Road Map established another subsidiary body, the Ad Hoc Working Group on Long-term Cooperative Action (AWG-LCA), under the UNFCCC, to negotiate a shared vision for long-term cooperative action, including a long-term global goal for emissions reduction and comparability of efforts by

BOX 1.2 THE BALI ACTION PLAN

The Bali Action Plan in responding to the findings of the Fourth Assessment Report of the Intergovernmental Panel on Climate Change that warming of the climate system is unequivocal, and that delay in reducing emissions significantly constrains opportunities to achieve lower stabilization levels and increases the risk of more severe climate change impacts, decides to launch a comprehensive process to enable the full, effective and sustained implementation of the Convention through long-term cooperative action, now, up to and beyond 2012, in order to reach an agreed outcome and adopt a decision at its fifteenth session, by addressing, inter alia (Paragraph 1):

A shared vision for long-term cooperative action, including a long-term global goal for emission reductions, to achieve the ultimate objective of the Convention, in accordance with the provisions and principles of the Convention, in particular the principle of common but differentiated responsibilities and respective capabilities, and taking into account social and economic conditions and other relevant factors (Paragraph 1a);

(b) Enhanced national/international action on mitigation of climate change, including, inter alia, consideration of (Paragraph 1b):

(i) Measurable, reportable and verifiable nationally appropriate mitigation

Commitments or actions, including quantified emission limitation and reduction objectives, by all developed country Parties, while ensuring the comparability of efforts among them, taking into account differences in their national circumstances (Paragraph 1b1);

(ii) Nationally appropriate mitigation actions by developing country Parties in the context of sustainable development, supported and enabled by technology, financing and capacity-building, in a measurable, reportable and verifiable manner (Paragraph 1b2).

non-Kyoto Parties such as the US with the effort under taken by Kyoto Parties. This AWG worked in tandem with the already existing Ad Hoc Working Group on further commitments for Annex I parties to the Kyoto Protocol (AWG-KP). The AWG-LCA mandate was to undertake a 'comprehensive process to enable the full, effective and sustained implementation of the Convention through long-term cooperative action, now, up to and beyond 2012, in order to reach an agreed outcome and adopt a decision at its fifteenth session' (COP 15). The work of both working groups was on parallel tracks and was expected to be concluded at the Copenhagen Climate Conferences, COP 15, 2009.

However, by 2008, this Bali bargain was beginning to show signs of unravelling. Despite the developed countries achieving much of what they sought in Bali, such as a decision in which the developing countries agreed to undertake voluntary mitigation actions, that was ultimately to be measurable, verifiable and reportable (MRV), there was still dissatisfaction especially, with the need to provide enhance flows of financing, which was also to be MRV-ed. In the case of the US, though it had agreed to under-take comparable mitigation efforts to that of the other developed countries, who were Parties to the Kyoto Protocol, it was still not at ease. At the same time, developing countries were increasingly concerned that the finely achieved balance of rights and obligations achieved in the convention were being altered to their disadvantage: though in the Convention they had no explicit obligations for mitigation, under Bali, they had expressly committed to undertake mitigation actions (albeit, voluntarily). They also felt that developed countries were not taking the strong leadership in mitigating greenhouse gas that had been committed under the Convention, they also were slow in providing the means of implementation – finance, capacity building and technology transfer.

After a fractious negotiating process, the fifteenth meeting of the COP (Copenhagen 2009) partially collapsed due to a pushed by a US-led coalition of developed countries, including the UK, that focused on the twin strategies of over-throwing the current top-down (aggregate) legally binding emission reduction targets of the Kyoto system, which the US had walked away from, towards a voluntary bottom-up, 'pledge and review' system with low emissions reduction ambition, coupled with attempts to shift mitigations burden unto developing countries. The meeting ended with the infamous Copenhagen Accord that settled on an arbitrary temperature target of keeping global mean temperature well below 2 degrees Celsius. This was coupled with a proposed $30 billion 'fast start financing' (2010–2012) package and a commitment to a goal of mobilizing $100 billion per year, long-term (by 2020) finance for developing countries in the context of meaningful mitigation actions by developing countries.

Even though many developing countries left the Copenhagen meeting with grave, disquieting fearing that their voluntary mitigation actions was slowing becoming an albatross around their necks with the new proposal of international consultation analysis and other frameworks for MRV, while the obligations of the developed countries where at best left to 'best endeavour'. The diminished effect of sweetener of the $30 billion fast start finance and the vagueness of promise of $100 billion per year by 2020 began to settle in, hence by the 2010 Cancún meetings; many developing countries' were uneasy.

Nonetheless, the Cancún Agreements (COP 16, 2010) legitimated the Copenhagen Accord by incorporating most all of those provisions as part of its final outcome. Cancún, however, left the question of the extension of the Kyoto Protocol open. It did not set a global goal or peaking year or a means to ensure the achievement of the 2 degrees Celsius temperature goal. The Cancún Agreement did make some new ground. For example, it explicitly included references to the rights of indigenous people and gender and women in many provisions of the shared vision texts (for example the preamble of the Long-term Cooperative Action under the Convention (LCA) text and in some provisions on adaptation). It also had agreement on a framework for adaptation, the so-called, Cancún Adaptation Framework and established the world's first Green Climate Fund (GCF), a Standing Committee for Finance, a Technology Mechanism and associated components, the Technology Executive Committee and the Climate Technology Centre and Network. The first two set of institutions are meant to enhance and accelerate the flow of financial support to the developing countries, while the latter mechanisms would facilitate the transfer and development of environmentally sound technologies to those countries.

However, to date, there is still an ongoing struggle to operationalize these institutional frameworks to deliver significant and meaningful outcome to developing countries. This has raised a growing level of distrust between the Parties, which is further exacerbated by the push by developed countries to weaken the explicit differentiation between developed and developing countries in the Convention with regard to rights and responsibilities around addressing the climate challenge. Many observers as well as developing countries argue that this is the real motivation behind the call for a new legal instrument 'applicable to all' and an initial rejection of equity and common but differentiated responsibility principle. It is in fact perplexing what is meant by applicable to all as the Convention and its instrument are in fact applicable to all the parties; there are different levels of responsibilities and obligations having to do with the recognition of the historical nature of the problem of the accumulation of GHGs. Hence the issue it seems is more about developed countries now having second thoughts about the commitments they made in 1992. Hence, the US, among others, has been repeating the phrase 'the world has changed since 1992' as if it is a mantra.

Despite any misgivings about the intent behind the call for a new agreement both developed and developing countries agreed to the Durban Decision 2011 which launched 'a process to develop a protocol, another legal instrument or an agreed outcome with legal force under the Convention applicable to all Parties'. India was careful at the last minute to make it explicit that this new instrument would be grounded in the principles of the Convention, including equity and CBDR. Though both the EU and the US was dragged kicking and screaming into accepting this concession, realpolitik dictated that this was the only way to get an agreement in the early morning after a long night in Durban. The work toward the penultimate final outcome of the Durban agreement is to be undertaken by a new Ad Hoc Working Group on the Durban Platform for Enhanced Action, the ADP. Ultimately, the negotiation process, which is expected to conclude by 2015, aims at raising the level of ambition, and the adoption of a new protocol, legal instrument or legal outcome with force[21] to come into effect and be implemented from 2020 (Draft Decision-/CP.17 FCCC/CP/2011/L.10). However, the Indian concession on equity and CBDR has been the tail wagging the dog of the ADP, since at every turn the developed countries have been faced with the issue that the outcome of 2015 must be under the Convention, being the principles of the Convention including equity and CBDR.

The long anticipated amendment of the Kyoto Protocol, both to strengthen its emissions reduction potential and to ensure its continuation beyond the initial first commitment period, did not occur as anticipated in the last three remaining meetings of the COP, COP 15 (Copenhagen 2009), COP 16 (Cancún 2010) and COP 17 (Durban 2011) due to foot dragging and attempts to run down the clock by the major Parties to the Protocol. The Durban meeting (COP 17, 2011) decided that 'the second commitment period under the Kyoto Protocol shall begin on 1 January 2013 and end either on 31 December 2017 or 31 December 2020, to be decided at the eighteenth session' (COP 18 2012).[22] The eighteenth session of the COP and the eighth session of the CMP took place in Doha, Qatar, December 2012; it seemingly implemented the process for the ratification of a legal second commitment period for the Kyoto Protocol.

The Doha 2012 climate meeting agreed on the duration and ambition of the second commitment period of the Kyoto Protocol. It agreed to a much weakened, legally binding, 8 years (instead of 5 years), second commitment period. This agreement extended the Protocol until 2020. But with countries representing only 15 per cent of global emissions proposing to take on quantified emissions reduction target, the Kyoto Protocol is effectively on life-support. There are no provisions for subsequent periods beyond the second period. The second commitment period will be severely weakened by the withdrawal of Canada, which post-Durban announced its exit from the Protocol, and both Russia's and Japan's refusal to participate in a second commitment period. Australia and New Zealand have both only indicated conditional pledges, indicating less than enthusiastic support for the continuation of the Protocol. Australia, the EU and a few other European countries have offered to place their existing emissions targets under the legal framework of the Protocol: But the reality is that only a political commitment on the Protocol that was initially agreed in Durban (2011) even after the Doha meeting (2012) there is still much legal uncertainty about the Protocol. There is still uncertainty as to whether, despite the Doha Outcome, there is a second commitment period that is ratifiable and legally binding. A meaningful and legally effective second commitment period of the Protocol should come into effect on 1 January 2013 and provisionally applied so that there is immediate implementation. But Doha did not agree on a process or set terms for the ratification of the Protocol. Even with the EU, the mainstay of the Protocol, ratification is hardly likely to be a quick process given the resistance of Poland among others of the Eastern European countries. It might turn out that the adoption of the agreement on the extension of the Protocol was a facing saving agreement for the EU. It was also able to skilfully negotiate an 8 year second commitment period in which it does not have to take significant actions to reduce emissions. The EU only agreed to 20 per cent emission reduction target of 1990 levels, 2013–2020, and not the more ambitious 30–35 per cent demanded by developing countries as well as some in the environmental movement. This 20 per cent is in line with EU domestic target and at least 18 per cent of which has already been achieved. So in effect the EU will not have to do much more during the 8 years. In fact by the early 2014 the EU was already claiming to have over achieved on its reductions commitment. There is also no comparability of even these minimal efforts agreed to for non-Kyoto Parties such as the US and renegades such as Japan and Canada.

An inconvenient truth is that the proposed new instrument to be negotiated by 2015 and enter into force in 2020 will effectively replace the Kyoto Protocol should it come into force in time. If not, there will be a gap in the climate change regime, especially between 2018 and 2020. It, hence, then should not be a surprise that there has been tremendous foot-dragging by developed-country Kyoto Parties in ratifying the second commitment period. (As of mid-October 2014, the only Parties who have ratified the second commitment period are developing countries – who have no mitigations reduction commitment under the Protocol.)

1.3 Global climate protection policy and gender: gender-blind or male-biased?

Since the coming into force of the UNFCCC (1992) and its associated Kyoto Protocol (1997), there have been growing efforts by gender equality and women's empowerment advocates, both at the governmental, inter-governmental and non-governmental levels working to ensure that climate change policies, decision-making, and initiatives at the global, regional and national levels are gender responsive.

The effort to secure consensus on the inclusion of references to gender and women and related priorities within the substantive negotiations agenda of the UNFCCC, including in the main negotiations texts and, especially with regard to adaptation, mitigation, capacity building, Reducing Emissions from Deforestation and Forest Degradation (REDD) initiative and the Green Climate Fund, was a hard fought for set of gains by the 'the women and gender constituency', which was only recently recognized.[23] This effort led by a wide range of women's non-governmental organizations, individually and jointly as members of the GGCA[24] was also backstopped by support from a high profiled trio of women leaders. At COP 16 (Cancún 2010) had a triplet of high powered women leadership with the Executive Secretary of the UNFCCC (Christiana Figueres, Ambassador Patricia Espinosa, Minister for Foreign Affairs, Mexico and the President of COP 16/CMP 6 and Ambassador Dessima Williams, the Grenadian ambassador to the UN and Chair of the over 40 member grouping of the Alliance of Small Island States). This trend of women at the top continued with COP 17 (Durban) with the transfer of leadership of the COP Presidency (COP 17/CMP7) to South Africa, with Minister Maite Nkoana-Mashabane, Minister of International Relations and Cooperation, South Africa, picking up the mantle. A trend that was only broken with the assumption of the COP presidency by H.E. Abdullah bin Hamad Al-Attiyah of Qatar, Doha (COP 18/CMP 8). In addition to the women leaders of the UNFCCC process, there was support by Mary Robinson,[25]

Connie Hedegaard, EU Commissioner for Climate Action, and Michelle Bachelet, Executive Director, UN Women, and members of the Network of Women Ministers of the Environment.

The effort to engender global climate policy regime has increased intensely over the last 5 years culminating at high point before the inception of the post-2012 period (see Boxes 1.2 and 1.3). Gender advocates were successful in leveraging their influence and coordinated lobby skills to integrate at least eight references to women and gender across seven sections of the Cancún (2010) final decisions. The Durban Outcome has 11 explicit references to gender mainly focused on governance features of the GCF, the Standing Committee and the Technology Mechanisms. The Doha COP 18 rendered a decision focused on women's participation as a step towards greater gender equality in climate change policies and programming and agreed to the goal of gender balance in bodies established pursuant to the Convention and the Kyoto Protocol. The decision entitled *Promoting Gender Balance and Improving the Participation of Women in UNFCCC Negotiations and in the Representation of Parties in Bodies Established Pursuant to the Convention or the Kyoto Protocol* will put in place several key actions and changes

The 2012 gender decision built on a decade old mandate from the Seventh Meeting of the Conference of the Parties, Marrakesh, 2001, which adopted the very first UNFCCC decision on gender. This Decision 36/CP.7 noted the importance of women's participation in achieving progress on mitigation and adapting to climate change at all levels.

However, gender activists have noted that progress in implementing the 2001 decision had been slow (WEDO 2012). There has been an average of 30 per cent of women as members of national delegations to the UNFCCC and participation in the annual COP meetings over the last 5 years (see Tables 1.1 and 1.2). Women also continued to be under-representation (below 10 per cent) of women at all levels of COP bodies and boards of UNFCCC.

Research by gender advocates, WEDO and Gender CC for the period 2008–2012 shows that there has been progress in the participation of women over the years with the last COP at 33 per cent (COP 18, Doha 2012) having the highest ever participation, but that women's participation tended to be 'slightly less than at other meetings' in the eighteen UNFCCC formal meetings held between 2008 and 2013,[26] including 5 annual meetings and at least 2–3 inter-sessional meetings per year (WEDO 2012).

In terms of constituted bodies of the UNFCCC women are quite under-represented (Table 1.1). In 2012, women accounted for 4 of the 15 members of the Adaptation Committee, 5 of the 28 members of the Adaptation Fund Board, 8 of 24 members of the Consultative Group of Experts on National Communications. Women also comprise 4 of 20 members of the executive board of the Clean Development Mechanism, 8 of 48 members of the Green Climate Fund (GCF), 2 of 13 members of the Least Developing Countries Export group. Women's under-representation in constituted UNFCCC bodies has continued with even recently created bodies such as the Technology Executive Committee

BOX 1.3 EVOLUTION OF GENDER IN THE UNFCCC DECISION-MAKING

Gender Decision 1.0: The Marrakesh Decision 36/CP.7

The Seventh Meeting of the Conference of the Parties, Marrakesh, 2001 adopted the very first UNFCCC decision on gender. Decision 36/CP.7 noted the importance of women's participation in achieving progress on mitigation and adapting to climate change at all levels.

Gender Decision 2.0: The Durban Gender Decision

The COP 18 Gender Decision 'Promoting gender balance and improving the participation of women in UNFCCC negotiations and in the representation of Parties in bodies established pursuant to the Convention or the Kyoto Protocol' reaffirms the COP decision taken over a decade ago. Despite the COP 7 decision, participation of women in UNFCCC bodies and as Party delegates overall has remained low. The COP 18 Gender Decisions adds new provisions to increase women's participation and gender balance on delegations and to give more attention and resources toward the goal of gender balance.

The COP 18 Gender Decision recognizes that gender balance is but a step towards gender equality, and a means to 'improve women's participation and inform more effective climate change policy' (Paragraph 2). Furthermore, the UNFCCC Secretariat's mandate to compile and report on sex-disaggregated data is driven by the importance of 'tracking of progress made towards the goal of gender balance in advancing gender-sensitive climate policy' (Paragraph 8). Building on the UNFCCC Secretariat's data collection and dissemination mandate to support (1) the goal of 'gender balance in the UNFCCC process', (2) 'gender-sensitive climate policy' and (3) 'capacity-building activities to promote the greater participation of women in the UNFCCC process' (Paragraph 10). The COP 18 Gender Decision sets the stage to strengthen gender balance and women's participation, while linking these pieces tie into the ultimate goals of gender equality and gender-responsive climate policy.

(TEC) and the Standing Committee on Finance (SCF): women were only 2 of 20 members of the Technology Executive Committee and 4 of the 20 members of the Standing Committee on Finance.

Women do only slightly better in terms of their participation in the various negotiating blocs of the UNFCCC (Table 1.2). The participation rate of women over the last 5 years averages 43 per cent for the European Union (EU), 42 per cent for the Alianza Bolivariana de Nuestra America (ALBA), 38 per cent for the Umbrella Group, 31 per cent for the Alliance of Small Island States (AOSIS), 28 per cent for the BASIC – Brazil, South Africa, India and China, 24 per cent for the Group of 77 and China, 21 per cent for the African Group, 20 per cent

> **BOX 1.4 OPERATIONAL PROVISIONS OF THE DURBAN GENDER DECISION**
>
> **Key operational provisions**
> The COP 18 Gender Decision calls for:
>
> - COP 22 review of progress towards goal of gender balance (by UNFCCC Parties and other institutions established under the Convention and Kyoto Protocol) (Paragraphs 4 and 5)
> - UNFCCC Secretariat will collect and report annually on sex-disaggregated data on bodies under the Convention and Kyoto Protocol (including regional bodies and country delegations) 'in order to enable the tracking of progress made towards the goal of gender balance in advancing gender-sensitive climate policy' (Paragraph 8)
> - Gender will be included as a standing COP agenda item to allow the COP to consider the UNFCCC Secretariat's annual reporting (Paragraph 9)
> - The UNFCCC Secretariat to organize an in-session COP 19 workshop on 'gender balance in the UNFCCC process, gender-sensitive climate policy and capacity-building activities to promote the greater participation of women in the UNFCCC process' (Paragraph 10)
> - Submissions from Parties and Observer organizations on 'the goal of gender [. . .] in order to improve women's participation and inform more effective climate change policy that addresses the needs of women and men equally' (Paragraphs 2 and 11).
>
> http://unfccc.int/files/meetings/doha_nov_2012/decisions/application/pdf/cop18_gender.pdf

for the LDCs and 18 per cent for the OPEC group. When looked at in terms of the five Official UN regions, women have high participation rate over the 5 year period from 2008–2012, on delegations from Eastern Europe (46 per cent, 55 per cent in 2012) compared to 40 per cent (51 per cent in 2012) for Western Europe and other, includes the US, New Zealand and Australia, 36 per cent (33 per cent in 2012) for Latin America and the Caribbean, 22 per cent (21 per cent in 2012) for Asia-Pacific and 21 per cent (21 per cent in 2012) for Africa. Women's participation as head of delegation is about 19 per cent (compared to 81 per cent for men) with the highest rate going from 17 per cent (2011) to 23 per cent, a 6 per cent increase in 2012.

The UNFCCC secretariat concept note[27] *Breakdown of the Gender Composition of Constituted Bodies Established under the Convention and the Kyoto Protocol* included information on the representation of women from regional groups and information on the gender composition of Party delegations to sessions under the Convention and the Kyoto Protocol.

TABLE 1.1 Gender composition of constituted bodies established under the Convention and the Kyoto Protocol

Body	Total number of members	Number of female members	Number of male members	Percentage of women
Executive Board of the Clean Development Mechanism	10	2	8	20
Joint Implementation Supervisory Committee	10	4	6	40
Compliance Committee facilitative branch	10	1	8	11
Compliance Committee enforcement branch	10(a)	2 (b)	8	20
Least developed countries expert	13	2 (b)	11	15
Consultative group of experts on national communications from parties not included in Annex I o the Convention	21	11	10	52
Adaptation Fund Board	16	5	11	31
Technology Executive Committee	20 (c)	2	17	11
Adaptation Committee	16 (d)	3 (b)	12	20
Standing Committee on Finance	20	5 (b)	15	25
Advisory Board of the Climate Technology Centre and Network	16	2	14	13

Notes: The gender composition of the constituted bodies varies: while women's representation is as high as 52 per cent in the Consultative Group of Experts on National Communications from Parties not included in Annex I to the Convention, there is a clear gender imbalance in all of the other constituted bodies, with women's representation as low as 11–13 per cent in some cases. Data based on the official UNFCCC Membership Chart of Convention and Protocol Bodies as of June 2013, available at http://unfccc.int/bodies/election_and_membership/items/6558.php. (a) One person has resigned. The actual total number is 9 as at 27 June 2013. (b) The Chair, Co-Chair and/or Vice-Chair of the body are women. (c) One person has resigned. The actual total number is 19 as at 27 June 2013. (d) One person has resigned. The actual total number is 15 as at 27 June 2013.

Source: UNFCCC (2013/4: Table 1)

While the outcomes of both the Cancún and the Durban COPs were significant milestones for women in the UNFCCC process, the work on engendering the climate change governance architecture is still only at the beginning stage. Global climate change policy remains ostensibly gender blind. The climate change policy regime does not specifically address the roles of women and men, their contributions to solving the climate change challenges, or the impacts of climate change on their lives. The uptake of gender issues and concerns are occurring on

38 The global climate change policy environment

TABLE 1.2 Gender composition of party delegates to sessions under the Convention and the Kyoto Protocol

Session	Total number of delegates	Number of female delegates	Number of male delegates	Percentage of women
Eighteenth session of the COP and eighth session of the CPM	5,090	1,497	3,593	29.4
Second session of the ADP	615	218	397	35.4
Thirty-eighth session of the SBI and the SBSTA	1,538	572	966	37.2

Note: The figures shown above indicate that the representation of women is between 29 and 37 per cent at recent sessions under the Convention and the Kyoto Protocol.

Abbreviations: ADP = Ad Hoc Working Group on the Durban Platform for Enhanced Action, CMP = Conference of the Parties serving as the meeting of the Parties to the Kyoto Protocol, COP = Conference of the Parties, SBSTA = Subsidiary Body for Scientific and Technological Advice, SBI = Subsidiary Body for Implementation.

Source: UNFCCC (2013/4: Table 3)

an ad hoc basis, as gender analysis and gender perspective are not integrated into the over-arching policy/negotiations frameworks. The work on engendering climate change finance has yet to begin in earnest.

In the new negotiations era now launched by the Durban Platform and the establishment of a new working group, the Ad Hoc Working Group on the Durban Platform for Enhanced Action, for the period 2012–2015, which is charged with working on all of the issues that had been under the Ad Hoc Working Group on Long-term Cooperative Action (LCA)[28] and the Working Group on the Kyoto Protocol,[29] it is not clear where the directions of the new regime is headed.[30] That will be determined by the negotiations to take place during that time frame. The one clear intention as state above is to 'develop a protocol, another legal instrument or a legal outcome with force under the Convention applicable to all Parties'. Gender advocates are clear that gender equality and women's empowerment should be a fundamental principle and guiding ethos of this new framework. At the same time, they are concerned that if the outcome of the ADP does not result in a significant shift towards sustainable development and equity within the framework of meeting the objectives of the Convention, it will not protect the lives of women and men, especially those in the developing countries.

As within the governmental circles, there is also tension within the gender and climate advocacy circles. The tension is primarily between those who simply want to see gender issues taken on board and mainstreamed within the UNFCCC and those who are in favour of a gender sensitive, pro-development, equitable and just outcome; in a word, climate justice. Thus as with the broader negotiation the context matters and there is great temptation by some parties to use gender in an instrumental way to put pressure on developing countries. But this should be resisted. Gender equality and women's empowerment are fundamental and intrinsically important on its own and have a rightful place in climate governance and its financing; it is not a political football.

Ultimately, from all perspectives, including the gender perspective, the UNFCCC is a science-based Convention. Hence, the decisions of the Parties with regard to the substantive areas to be agreed under the Durban Platform will be informed by the work of the scientific community as expressed through the Fifth Assessment Report of the Intergovernmental Panel on Climate Change (IPCC 2013). The next section will consider the scientific case for climate change protection policies.

1.4 The scientific imperative of global climate protection regime

The current goal of preventing global average mean temperature from increasing more than 2 degrees Celsius (3.6 degrees Fahrenheit) above pre-industrial level agreed by the Cancún climate meeting (2010) is the subject of a great deal of debate.[31] Though based on scientific analyses about the risks of dangerous, irreversible and likely catastrophic change in the climate system and its potential inability beyond that point to support human and ecosystem, the 2 degree stabilisation target often trumpeted as a 'guardrail' between what is an acceptable and what is a dangerous level of CO_2 in the atmosphere (dangerous climate change) is nonetheless a 'normative choice' set by G8 governments as to what level of impacts are acceptable or thought to be tolerable to them; it is not a target set by the science. 2 degrees Celsius is associated with atmospheric concentration CO_2 levels of 450 parts per million (ppm).

The IPCC fourth Assessment Report (AR4, 2007) while warning that a 2 degrees Celsius rise in temperature could have adverse impacts on water, food security, intensifying migration and conflicts, allowed for some time to catch up. The IPCC also argued that a 2 degrees Celsius target may mean a 50 per cent chance of stabilizing the climate. But since the IPCC AR4 Report in 2007, the scientific evidence is much clearer and the scientific community is expressing with greater clarity the resolution of many of the uncertainties and ambiguities of IPCC AR4 about global warming, including showing that it is not slowing (the Copenhagen Diagnosis 2009). This work has closed the research gap since the closed-off period for the work of the IPCC report and is based on the best science supported by US and European institutions and the best from developing countries.

The Synthesis Report of the Copenhagen Climate Congress while recognizing that many nations have committed to a 2 degrees Celsius temperature limit, argues that '(t)emperature rises above 2 degrees Celsius will be difficult for contemporary societies to cope with, and are likely to cause major societal and environmental disruptions through the rest of the century and beyond' (Richardson *et al.* 2009). The IPCC in its 2007 report argued that increase in storm intensity is likely. Global

BOX 1.5 WHAT THE SCIENCE SAYS

Carbon dioxide emissions cannot be allowed to continue to rise if humanity intends to limit the risk of unacceptable climate change. The task is urgent and the turning point must come soon. If we are to avoid more than 2 degrees Celsius warming, which many countries have already accepted as a goal, then emissions need to peak before 2020 and then decline rapidly.

Professor Richard Somerville, Scripps Institution of Oceanography, University of California, San Diego, US

- Every year this century (2001–2008) has been among the top 10 warmest years since instrumental records began. Both the Greenland and Antarctic ice sheets are losing mass and contributing to sea-level rise at an increasing rate.
- The area of summer sea ice remaining during 2007–2009 was about 40 per cent less than the average projection from the 2007 IPCC Fourth Assessment Report.
- Global sea-level rise may exceed 1 meter by 2100. Without significant mitigation, sea-level rise of several meters is to be expected over the next few centuries.
- Global mean air-temperature is projected to warm between 2 and 7 degrees Celsius above pre-industrial levels by 2100. (The wide range is mainly due to uncertainty in future emissions.)
- There is a very high probability of the warming exceeding 2 degrees Celsius unless global emissions peak and start to decline rapidly by 2020.
- If long-term global warming is to be limited to a maximum of 2 degrees Celsius above pre-industrial values, average annual per-capita emissions in industrialized nations will have to be reduced by around 80–95 per cent below 1990 levels by 2050.
- Surging greenhouse gas emissions: Global carbon dioxide emissions from fossil fuels in 2008 were 40 per cent higher than those in 1990. Even if global emission rates are stabilized at present-day levels, just 20 more years of emissions would give a 25 per cent probability that warming exceeds 2 degrees Celsius, even with zero emissions after 2030. Every year of delayed action increases the chances of exceeding 2 degrees Celsius warming.
- To stabilize climate, a decarbonized global society – with near-zero emissions of CO_2 and other long-lived GHGs – needs to be reached well within this century. More specifically, the average annual per-capita emissions will have to shrink to well under 1 metric ton CO_2 by 2050. This is 80–95 per cent below the per-capita emissions in developed nations in 2000.

- 50 per cent probability to stay under 2 degrees Celsius is not enough for a decent chance of success (avoiding dangerous human interference with the climate system).
- 2 degrees Celsius warming threshold could be crossed as early as 2040 unless significant mitigation measures are taken urgently.
- An emissions cut of 40 per cent below 1990 levels by 2020 is needed for industrial countries for a 2 degree Celsius limit.

Source: Copenhagen Diagnosis (2010)

mean warming of even just 1.5–2.0 degrees Celsius still carries a significant risk of adverse impacts on ecosystems and human society (see Boxes 1.4 and 1.5). For example, 2 degrees Celsius global temperature rise could lead to sufficient warming over Greenland to eventually melt much of its ice sheet (Oppenheimer and Alley 2005), raising sea level by over six meters and displacing hundreds of millions of people worldwide. An MIT peer-reviewed[32] scientific study notes that global warming could be twice as bad as previously forecasted as the 'the median surface warming could be as high as 5.2 degrees Celsius between 2091 to 2100, in contrast to earlier predictions of 2.4 degrees Celsius.

These reports point to the urgent need to act to keep the earth's temperature at safe levels for the peoples of the developing countries who are increasingly vulnerable to extreme weather events. The IPCC (2011) Special Report, *Managing the Risks of Extreme Events and Disasters to Advance Climate Change Adaptation*, argues that 'climate change may increase the probability of some ordinary weather events reaching extreme levels or of some extreme events becoming more extreme'. The Report also notes that '(t)here is evidence that anthropogenic influences, including increasing atmospheric greenhouse gas concentrations, have changed these extremes weather events'.

It is also important to recognize that the 2 degrees Celsius is a global mean temperature and that there are regional variations that can be higher than that. This is the case, for example, with Africa which is expected to experience one and a half times as much warming as the global average (IPCC 2007; UNECA 2011). Hence a 2 degrees Celsius global mean average temperature can lead to temperature increase as high as plus 3 degrees Celsius warming for Africa (UNECA 2011). It is widely accepted that even a 2 degrees Celsius limitation will generate widespread losses in food crops and agricultural lands and will contribute to increasing hunger. Research from Stanford University scientists warn that even 1.5 degrees Celsius warning pose dire threat to African food security through drastic reduction in yields of major food crops. Clearly 2 degrees Celsius and above spells serious trouble for the continent of Africa, and most especially the least developing countries who have limited adaptive capacity and limited financial and technological means for climate-proofing and climate resilient activities as well as small island states in the Caribbean (see Boxes 1.6 and 1.7). A target around peaking global emission by even 2050 is

BOX 1.6 CLIMATE CHANGE, ITS IMPACTS AND PROJECTION

Known and growing concerns

Water tables are falling for over 50 per cent of the world population

Record low Arctic sea ice Arctic warming: Arctic summer show retreat of regional ice yearly. The 2012 annual near surface air temperatures over much of the arctic ocean were 1.5 °C (2.7 °F) higher than in 1981–2010 base. Arctic sea ice cover fell to a low of 4.33 million square meters (2.7 million square miles) and 2.38 million square kilometres (1.4875 million square miles less than the 1979–2000 average. Note: as the Arctic warms and ice melts it absorbs rather than reflects heat leading to acceleration of the process.

Increased frequency and severity of extreme weather events

Incidence, onset and severity of: droughts; floods; heatwave; hurricanes and storms; pestilence, weed and infestation

Droughts: droughts have ancillary effects including: lack of rain and associated dust storms, and increase in land subsidence (in Europe): create problems for water management and hydrology. (In France subsidence claim increased over 50 per cent in the last 20 years, averaging $425 million a year.) Droughts have occurred in Europe, South West US and West Africa. Drought in the Horn of Africa killed ten thousand children and pushed families to the brink of starvation (World Vision 2011). Droughts in Europe cost $100 billion in the last 30 years (European Commission 2010).

Heat waves: occurrence southern Europe, Western US. Also associated with wildfire in these places. 'Out of control' heatwaves in Spain, France, Greece and Italy in 2009. Heatwave in Britain in 2010 caused over 55,000 deaths. In 2012 there was record-breaking heatwaves in Australia.

Heavy precipitation, hurricanes, floods and storms: hurricanes have not been proven conclusively to be caused by climate change but experts argue that climate change may increase their severity. ('There appears to be a poleward shift in the main northern and southern hemisphere extra tropical storm tracks'.) Super Storm Sandy Hurricane Katrina left 300,000 homeless in New Orleans and killed 1,200 persons. 2009/2011: floods in Southern India killed hundreds of people and left millions homeless. 2011: over 3,000 person killed by storms and floods in the Philippines; flood in Thailand resulted in the largest insured fresh water loss in history; floods in Mississippi disrupted 13 per cent of US petroleum refinery output which impact the price of petrol. Floods lead to growth in fungal growth and nematodes. In 2012 flooding and landslides in Brazil, Bangladesh and the Philippines. In 2012, England had the wettest year on record. (Europe also had the worst cold snap in decades in that year.)

Pestilence, weed and infestation: extreme weather events encourage the outbreak of diseases and infestations. Earlier springs and warmer weather lead to increase in the insect population and increase weeds. The increase in insects and pathogens that comes with warming results in increased use of pesticides. There are both food security and health effects. In the Southwest US farmers are reported to have lost 64 per cent of soybean crops to invasive weeds. This is coupled with $11 billion a year for weed control spent by the US government. In addition, droughts lead to an increase in locusts and the whitefly population.

2010: National disaster affected over 200 million people and killed 270,000 people and generated $110 billion in damages.

2012 AND BEYOND: Future Shocks

The IPCC warned in a November 2011 report of the frequency of heatwaves which it said would increase by a factor of 10 in most regions of the world if CO_2 and other gases continue to be produces at today's level. The number of heat-related deaths in the city of London is predicted to quadruple by 2080 (Kings College and UK Met Office).

Source: unless otherwise cited: Lloyd's Details 'Growing Impact of Climate Change' as UN Meets, 25 June 2010

still too far away for the comfort and safety of Africa, the coastal cities in Asia and the small island states of the Caribbean and the Pacific's safety.

Ultimately, a rise in global mean temperature above the 2 degrees Celsius target would put the global economy on a dangerous path: many species, human communities and livelihoods will be endangered. Science also argues that temperature rise at or above 0.8 degrees Celsius will melt the Arctic. Anywhere above that may also lead to tipping points (abrupt climate change or crossing critical thresholds) such as the 'disappearance of late-summer Arctic sea ice' or the 'destabilization of the west Antarctic ice sheet', that can generate a cascade of impacts that could be catastrophic.

What science can say with a fair degree of consensus is that based on historical records, atmospheric concentration of GHGs at 280 ppm (the pre-industrial level concentration) can be considered safe. Some scientists, such as James Hansen, argue that 350 ppm marks a dangerous turn for the planet. Since May 2013, there have been signs that we may be steadily crossing into that very alarming territory. Two independent scientific teams, one from the US National Oceanic and Atmospheric Administration (NOAA) and the other from the Scripps Institution of Oceanography, reported that on 10 May CO_2 concentration levels of 400.03 ppm had been measured at the climate-observing station in Mauna Loa, Hawaii.

> ### BOX 1.7 IMPACT OF CLIMATE CHANGE ON AFRICA – AGRICULTURE
>
> Recent scientific information regarding the impacts of climate change on agriculture in Africa
>
> - 1980–2008, due to rising global temperature, global maize and wheat production has already decreased by 3.8 per cent and 5.5 per cent, respectively.
> - Currently at 0.74 degree of warming, African farmers and pastoralists are seeing changes in the timing and severity of rains and in the temperature they and their crops and animals are exposed to.
> - Food production is already threatened by the temperature rise of the last century, and the committed warming due to greenhouse gas emissions of the last decades.
> - With a 1 degree Celsius warming – the level of expected approximately one decade from now – roughly 65 per cent of current maize growing areas in Africa are predicted to experience yield losses under optimal rain-fed conditions; under drought conditions, 75 per cent of areas can expect yield declines of at least 20 per cent for 1 degrees Celsius of warming.
> - At the current rate of temperature increase, global average temperatures will have increased 1.5 degrees Celsius by 2050. Average predicted production losses by 2050 for African crops are: maize 22 per cent, sorghum 17 per cent, millet 17 per cent, groundnut 18 per cent and cassava 8 per cent.
>
> Source: UNECA ACPC and ClimDev-Africa

This is short-term CO_2, but the global average is expected to cross the 400 ppm mark in the next year. This would mean that for every one million molecules in the earth's atmosphere, there are 400 molecules of carbon dioxide. Carbon dioxide (CO_2) concentration in the atmosphere is linked to earth's temperature, so continuing at this rate we will reach to 450 ppm, the ultimate dangerous threshold, quite soon. Thus we are on track for a 3 to 5 degree increase in temperature by the end of the century.[33]

According to climate scientists, global emission must peak as soon as possible (by 2015 or 2017). This will require the setting of stringent global emissions reduction targets and the reversal of current emission trends in both developed countries and developing countries. But the Cancún Agreements will not accomplish any of these. Rather, research shows that, at best, the pledges made by developed countries may lead to a rise of 2 degrees Celsius temperature or even, at worst, a rise of 4–5 degrees Celsius.[34]

Many scientific experts argue that if global warming is to be stopped, global CO_2 emissions must eventually decline to zero and that the sooner emissions stop, the

BOX 1.8 THE CARIBBEAN

The Caribbean is poised to expect annual expected losses from wind, storm surge and inland flooding already amount to up to 6 per cent of GDP in some countries and that, in a worst case scenario, climate change has the potential to increase these expected losses by 1–3 percentage points of GDP by 2030.

Source: 'Economics of Climate Adaptation (ECA) in the Caribbean', the Caribbean Catastrophe Risk Insurance Facility (CCRIF)

lower the final warming will be. Specifically, the global community has the next 10 to 15 years (or, as UNDP so graphically puts, it 100–150 months) to take transformative action to allow global emissions to peak and then decline rapidly to 'have a reasonable chance of avoiding the very worst impacts of climate change'.

At this point, the 2 C degree is an arbitrary target and more aspirational than concrete since no road map is provided for its achievement.[35] Neither the Warsaw (2013), Doha (2012), Durban (2011) nor the Cancún (2010) meetings set a quantitative goal for the peaking of global carbon emissions in 2020. More importantly, the so-called Cancún emissions reduction pledges made by Annex I parties in relation to the temperature target have been shown not to be realistically to even give a 50:50 chances of making the target. The reality is that 'there is no peaking year mentioned in the texts and there was no mention of global emission goal set for 2050' (Carlsen 2010). Many rigorous analyses of the Cancún pledges show that even if it all were fulfilled, it is still likely that the world will not meet the 2 degrees Celsius target and the world is seemingly moving towards a 'much higher increase of 3.2 degrees Celsius' (UNEP 2010 and SEI 2011). In addition, given the loopholes and accounting possibilities (shown in Box 1.9) available to the rich countries many of the pledges will not actually be implemented resulting in not much significant reduction of emissions.

Some scientists also argue in favour of a cumulative Carbon Budget for the world as part of a climate policy agreement: 'Such an agreed global budget could then be distributed among countries, for example, on the basis of equity principles' (WBGU 2009).

For the first time, the IPCC in its AR 5 Working Group I report, has raised the issue of carbon budgets.[36] In this discussion, it is clear that in order to have the likely (66 per cent) chance of meeting the 2 degree goal atmosphere concentration of CO_2 must be at most 450 ppm by 2100. The IPCC discussed different budget pathways, but the reality is that there is only about 800–860 billion tonnes of carbon (GTC) that can be burned. Between 1750 and 2011, about 531 billion tonnes (about 2/3 or 50 per cent) of that amount has already been spent. At the current rate of 10 billion per year, arguably, there is about 25 years left of the budget. Hence, in order to achieved the 2 degree target the world must peak its emission

BOX 1.9 WHEN PLEDGES ARE NOT PLEDGES

Loopholes that can negate Annex I's pledges:

- **LULUCF accounting rules:** Reference levels for forest management accounting/Gross-net and net-net accounting; Article 3.7: 5–6 per cent of Annex I Parties. 1990 levels
- **Market-based mechanisms (i.e., CDM):** Accounting problems–.non-additionality. Approximate scale of CDM loophole: 5 to 8 per cent of Annex I Parties. 1990 levels
- **Surplus AAUs:** Approximate scale of loophole: Around 9 per cent per year of Annex I Parties. 1990 emissions (in an 8-year commitment period). Around 15 per cent per year of Annex I Parties. 1990 emissions (in a 5 year commitment period)
- **International aviation and shipping:** Large emissions from this sector are currently excluded from Kyoto Protocol accounting. Approximate scale of loophole: Around 5 per cent per year of all Annex I countries 1990 emissions (inclusive of the US)

Source: Lim Li Lin (2010)

of carbon dioxide into the atmosphere as soon as possible such that by 2100 the atmospheric concentration level holds at 450 ppm (with 430 ppm or lower preferred).

Up until 2013, there has been no significant discussion about sharing specificities of the limited budget available to humankind. As noted above the negotiations under the rubric of shared vision in the UNFCCC has come to naught with the closure of the AWG-LCA in 2012.

Climate negotiators and members of the UNFCCC clearly accept that human-induced actions that increase GHG concentration into the atmosphere are altering the radiation balance. Therefore climate negotiators are not climate sceptics, deniers or climate doubters. Then what is the obstacle to increased scale of ambition to significantly reduce the amount of anthropogenic GHGs emissions into the atmosphere? What has obstructed and blocked the unconditional renewal of the second commitment period of the Kyoto Protocol, the only legally binding regime for targeted GHGs reductions? And what factors have prevented the full implementation of the Bali Action Plan and Roadmap that proposed remedies for tightening up the loopholes (escape valves) that weaken mitigation efforts as well as proposed to ensure that the US undertook comparable effort in terms of reducing GHGs under the LCA framework as was agreed in the Bali Action Plan (2007)? It is clear from the scientific evidence that the current trajectory and pledges of Cancún will not keep rise in global temperatures below 2 degrees Celsius and that instead it is likely to push temperatures in the range 2–5 degrees Celsius warming by 2100 and is henceforth inviting dangerous or catastrophic climate change (UNEP 2012; World Bank 2013; IPCC 2013).

The reasons for the foot-drag are multiple. Clearly, though un-stated in the public debate, there are countries that may now believe that they can adapt to global warming, and, or, in the long run, they can be saved by technology that will remove the constraint of relying on the existing projected global carbon budget.[37] Current carbon budget analysis and equitable sharing principles of the remaining carbon space, indicate that all developed countries are in deficit which has clear implications in terms of climate debt/climate justice and equitable sharing of the atmospheric space. Thus, overlaying the scientific imperative, climate negotiations are heavily driven and bogged down by national economic and political determined factors.

1.5 The economics of climate negotiation

Climate change raises questions about the present dynamic growth path of both developed and developing countries. Sustainable growth will require a path towards limiting greenhouse gas concentrations in the atmosphere to below 450 parts per million (ppm) and, by at least 2020–2050, cutting global emissions to between 50 and 85 per cent of 1990 levels (Pew 2009; Union of Concerned Scientists 2007).[38] This would help to maintain average global temperature to below 2 degrees Celsius. At the same time, countries such as Bolivia argues for keeping the concentration of GHGs at or below 350 ppm in order to restore the earth's energy balance and stop the melting of the artic. Many scientists such as Hansen *et al.* (2008) agree that 350 ppm is the safe upper limits for CO_2 in the atmosphere.

Dealing successfully with climate change, hence entails radical shifts in rich countries' consumption and production patterns and developing countries' high carbon-dependent growth models. In this context, the nature and scope of economic development must be rescripted. Currently, it is known that at the global level, a one percentage increase in GDP per capita is related to an almost equal percentage increase in emissions per capita (Khor 2010), Sir Nicolas Stern in his 2006 report pointed out that:

> Historically, economic development has been associated with increased energy consumption and hence energy-related CO_2 emissions per head. Across 163 countries, from 1960 to 1999, the correlation between CO_2 emissions per head and GDP per head (expressed as natural logarithms) was nearly 0.9. Similarly, one study for the United States estimated that, over the long term, a 1 per cent rise in GDP per head leads to a 0.9 per cent increase in emissions per head, holding other explanatory factors constant.
>
> (Stern 2006: 179)

The historical correlation between CO_2 emissions per capita and GDP per capita will, however, change depending on the timeframe used and on whether the data is disaggregated or not. For example, South Centre calculations of the correlation between GDP per capita growth and per capita emissions growth for the 15-year period from 1990 to 2005 (as compared to the forty-year period from 1960 to 1999 in the Stern Report) for Annex I Parties was 0.297 (i.e. 1 per cent of GDP growth per capita leads to 0.297 per cent, per capita emissions growth). For developing countries, which comprise non-Annex I Parties, it was 0.73 (i.e. 1 per cent of GDP growth per capita leads to 0.73 per cent, per capita emissions growth), and globally, it was at 0.683 (i.e., 1 per cent of GDP growth per capita leads to 0.683 per cent per cent per capita emissions growth; South Centre 2011).[39]

Unquestionably, given the current historical juncture and the realities of climate change all countries are aware and must consciously choose to take on board the challenges of sustainable production and growth, as much as is possible, within the context and constraints of their economic and social reality. Developed countries must seek to restrain their heavy consumption trajectory so as to conserve atmospheric space that allows for developing countries, with populations still in need of basics goods and services, to continue to pursue a reasonable and sustainable development growth path.

At the macro level, climate change-related phenomena raise questions about agriculture and industrial production sustainability. The issue of climate change-related impacts on food and water supplies are increasingly urgent. Furthermore, climate change can generate systemic disequilibrium and discontinuities in economic growth paths as the underlying structure of the ecosystem may be rapidly eroded.

On the economic front, there is significant adjustment and implementation costs associated with both adaptation and mitigation strategies. These pose serious constraints for economic development in the global south. Governments and citizens must wrestle with the question of how best to address the needs of a growing population and promote economic growth that is environmentally sustainable in the context of rising climate change issues. Hence, the key developmental problematic in the face of climate change is the transformation and growth of the productive sectors of the economy from one that is mainly oriented to fossil-based energy sources towards a low-carbon economy. There are also critical questions about how rapid should the de-carbonization occur and who should pay for it. Clearly, either rapid or slower paced de-carbonization poses significant constraints on economic growth and development in the south. It also has implications for all of the productive sectors of the economy from agriculture, fishery, and forestry to industrial and services which also impinge on trade, development, industrial, gender equality and poverty reduction policies and programmes.

At the same time, not shifting, or seeking to maintain 'business as usual' is not a viable option. Climate change will have adverse impact on the very sectors that most developing economies are concerned with. It is already the case that in the developing countries 70–80 per cent of the damages caused by weather is to infrastructure, compared to 40 per cent in developed countries (Hart 2007). In general richer countries are better able to adapt to climate change phenomena than poorer ones. And in the case of small island nations, they face special vulnerabilities to rising sea levels and damaged ecosystem due to adverse weather events. Thus for these and other developing countries there is no option but to integrate adaptation and mitigation strategies in all aspect of economic and social planning and decision-making.

Developing countries, especially the poorest among them, are extremely vulnerable to the damaging effects of climate change and extreme weather events. According to Maple Croft Climate Vulnerability Index, Bangladesh ranks number 1, with India number 2, Nepal number 4 and Philippines number 6 for the period 2010–2011. On the NGO German Watch's climate risk index, Pakistan for example, with a human development index of 145 ranks number 1 and experiences 5.42 per cent loss in GDP. Due to extreme climate events, the country also faced unprecedented flooding in the southern province of Sindh in 2011, devastating super floods experienced during July/August 2010 and intense heat waves during 2003, 2005, 2007 2010 (53.7°C) and 2014.

Developing countries such as Jamaica, Pakistan and Zambia are plagued by issues of limited basic physical infrastructure, limited access to the technologies needed for climate-proofing, building climate resilience and promoting the transition to low carbon economy (Boxes 1.9 and 1.10). Jamaica and a number of other Caribbean islands (Trinidad and Tobago and St Lucia) are experiencing historic drought conditions in some localities. The phenomenon which is variously identified by officials as 'extended dry season' or very, very dry season (Jamaica), 'prolonged dry season' (Trinidad) or 'dry spells' (Tobago) due to below normal rainfall (relative observed in relation to long-term averages over a 30-year period). However, the situation is being classified, what is clear is that the situation is unprecedented in its scope and persistence, creating water shortage and threatening food production and is becoming a growing and significant economic and social challenge: In July of 2014, Jamaica government officials were contemplating whether to issue permits for the importation of some agricultural products.

These issues – droughts, floods, wildfires etc. – create specific vulnerability and adaptation constraints for different groups of developing countries, even those within the same political groupings within the climate negotiations. Clearly, even developing countries which are small island states have different levels of per capita income (for example, Singapore US$41,122, Jamaica $5,274, Trinidad and Tobago

BOX 1.10 ZAMBIA AND CLIMATE CHANGE

Zambia, especially its southern part, which is most vulnerable to climate change. In the absence of adaptation, rainfall variability could keep an additional 300,000 more Zambians below the poverty line. Furthermore climate variability could cost Zambia US$4.3 billion in lost GDP over the next decade, reducing annual growth by 0.9 per cent (Kabula 2014).

BOX 1.11 JAMAICA AND CLIMATE CHANGE

In Jamaica agriculture is the main source of livelihood of the rural population (which represents ~46 per cent of the total population) and plays a major role in safeguarding food security. Agriculture is primarily rain-fed and impacted by drought and water deficiency hence is vulnerable to hydromet events, there was damage and loss of $23.5 billion since. Additionally, over US$18.6 billion social and economic assets and infrastructure, especially those on the coastal zones, are exposed to hazards.

Source: Bernard (2014)

$15,359 and Haiti $671), different ability to obtain and secure financing (both national and international) to undertake adaptation and mitigation activities.

Even as it is straining under the heavy debt situation, the Jamaican government, as with many other developing countries, must find ways to set aside money for climate change. In the case of Jamaica, this is necessary because of the need to rehabilitate and improve the management of watersheds to reduce downstream run-off and associated pollution and health risks; and to restore and protect the coastal ecosystem so as to enhance natural buffers and increasing resilience.

Given their advance infrastructure, production base and control of technology, developed countries, as a group, can be more sanguine about global warming and their capacity to adapt to warming temperature in the short to medium term (2020 to 2050 +). In the long term (beyond 2091 to 2100) they can focus on engineering technological fixes to the climate challenge.

Developed countries that are generally located in higher latitudes can be comfortable with 2 degrees and above warming. They are confident of their ability to adapt and cope with whatever losses may occur. There will be some damage to their economies but it may be bearable (Cline 2007). But developing countries who are 'generally located in lower latitudes and are already closer to or beyond thresholds' have to be less than sanguine about global warming even up to 2 degrees Celsius. As noted by Cline (2007), 'the damages will be the most severe and begin the soonest where they can least be afforded: in the developing countries'.

More ominous for developing countries is that as the time has passed, since the early 1990s, there is a new reality settling in the awareness of some developed countries such as Canada, the US and Russia: global warming is not completely disastrous for their economies.[40] This may also be the case with northern Europe, but not southern Europe. In the former group of countries, there are clear cases of high benefits if warming is gradual. These benefits exist in terms of agricultural, health, land use and tourism.

Agriculture productivity yield effect of global warming. Cline among others notes that 'a small amount of global warming (in the next two or three decades) might benefit agriculture'. This is true only for the global north. And is due mainly to two sets of factors: the potential yield impact from increased concentrated carbon dioxides in the atmosphere (and carbon fertilization) and longer growing season.

On this point, as noted by many researchers, there is great asymmetry between agriculture in developing and developed countries. In the former, agriculture is the main source of income and livelihood and small loss of agriculture production/productivity due to warming will be a setback for these countries. Most developing countries need to see a decline in GHG now not 2050, 2080 or 2090.

The developed countries that are poised to gain or, lose by a small amount, (if the worst case scenario occurs) can afford to stay on the business as usual track. Some, such as the US and Canada, may even gain additional markets as they can then sell food to the developing countries, who suffer significant agricultural loss (i.e. Africa, India, Central America and the Caribbean).[41] Countries now poised to gain from rising agricultural yield under best case scenario or lose less under worst case scenario include Australia and Canada. It is therefore no wonder these countries seek to opt out or are indifferent to the second commitment period of the Kyoto Protocol.[42]

Land use availability and agricultural production. Countries projected to gain land (for increasing agricultural production area) due to warming of temperature include those in the Scandinavian regions, Russia and North America. But many developing countries are projected to lose land and suffer declining harvests. A number of research studies forecast that developing countries may increase their imports of grain by 25 per cent in the next 80 years (Cline 2007; Mendelsohn 2008).[43]

Health benefits of global warming. While global warming is having deadly impacts on the lives in many developing countries, increasing warming may positively impact many lives in some developed countries. According to the *Financial Times* (2007), 'fewer in the north would die of cold'.[44] This would benefit, for example, the UK and Sweden. Anthropologists, economists, health and demographic researchers such as Peiser (2008), Moore (2008) and others argue that diseases such as the flu strike hardest in winter, not summer.[45] Research in the US also shows that 'a somewhat warmer climate would probably reduce mortality . . . and provide Americans with valuable benefits.[46] 'Global warming can be beneficial for human health in some developed countries, if the temperature rises slowly' (Peiser 2008).[47] It should be noted that if there is a significant and dramatic increase in the warming then the situation could become adverse.[48]

Global warming and tourism. While global warming and associated extreme weather events pose serious economic challenges for small island states such as those in the Caribbean where tourism is heavily dependent on natural resources such as proximity to the sea, it also portends benefit for tourism in countries such as Canada and Russia. Researcher Richard Tol of the Economic and Social Research Institute, Ireland, projects that Canada will see a 220 per cent increase in tourists this century, followed by Russia at 174 per cent.[49] Mendelsohn (2008) points out that there will be increased tourism gains for countries which will outweigh the likely losses from decline in the shortened winter seasons.

The foregoing analysis might explain the apparent lack of a sense of urgency about setting and implementing global emissions targets and a global peaking goal by major developed countries. This new warming may not be all bad awareness and their faith in an eventually technological save, as well as, the overhanging economic and financial crisis can help to explain their foot-dragging about providing the needed finance and technology transfer that they committed to under the UNFCCC in 1992. Unquestionably, other crucially important factors also influence the political weighing of the cost and benefits of adapting and adjusting economies to global warming versus the rather high mitigation costs (and likely growth slowing) impacts of their economies plus the costs of meeting financial commitments and transfer technology to developing countries. The fact that developing countries such as China, India, Brazil and South Africa were able to weather the crisis and have continued to grow is not a minor factor in this debate. Clearly developed countries such as the US and the EU fear the competitive threats of the BASIC countries, most especially China, such that they ignore the fact that on all the objective criteria of global economic analysis these countries are still developing countries with extremely large segments of their population living in poverty.

Both the IMF and the World Bank list China, India, Brazil and South Africa as developing countries. In terms of per capita in GDP (in purchasing power parity$), China at $7,544.2 is ranked 95 out of 184 countries, India $3,408.4 is ranked 129 and South Africa $10,519.0 is ranked 80 out of 184 countries.[50] In terms of per capita emission (2008) the three countries rank 77, 138 and 41, respectively, out of 218 countries.[51] Though their absolute emissions may be high, their per capita emissions are low (China emitting 5.5 metric tons CO_2e per capita, India 1.7 and South Africa 9.0 metric tons CO_2e per person) relative to developed countries such as the US (23.4 metric tons CO_2 per person), Canada 22.9, and Singapore 11.4 metric tons CO_2e per person, and other developing countries (such as Chile 5.4, Gabon 10.2 and Trinidad & Tobago 27.4 metric tons CO_2e person).[52]

It is also the case, that these countries have no significant historical responsibility for the stock of GHG gases contributing to global warming. So China and the rest of the fast growing developing countries may be implicated in terms of current and future flows of emissions but that needs to be balanced against their historical role when apportioning burden sharing of emissions reduction cuts. In either case, as will be seen below, these countries are all involved in extensive efforts to transform the major contours of their economies towards low carbon emission pathway.

Another important factor to be weighed in trying to understand the position of the developed countries in the climate debate is the rising cost of meeting adaptation and mitigation in transforming economic structures to meet climate change. The combined financial resource and investment required for adapting to and mitigation climate change are in the hundreds of trillion dollars with about 40–50 per cent of this required in developing countries. Conservative costing estimation of the amount of finance needed for adaptation and mitigation in developing countries range from $100 billion and $175 billion, respectively, per year, in the next 20 year (World Bank 2011).

Thus the economics of climate change must include a massive transfer of financial and technical resources from developed to developing countries in support of developing countries climate change efforts and consistent with the goals of the convention that '(s)uch a level (meaning the stabilization of GHG concentration in the atmosphere) should be achieved within a time-frame sufficient to allow ecosystems to adapt naturally to climate change, to ensure that food production is not threatened and to enable economic development to proceed in a sustainable manner'. Article 3 of the Convention has quite remarkable principles around equity (Article 3(1)), burden sharing (Article 3(2)) and differentiated responsibility between developed and developing countries were affirmed. Article 3(4) also affirms the right to sustainable development and the essential role of economic development. Furthermore, both the Convention and the Protocol also mandated obligations around of the provision of technology transfer and financial resources to support their adaptation and mitigation strategies.

These were stipulated in Article 4 (3):

> The developed country Parties and other developed Parties included in Annex II shall provide new and additional financial resources to meet the agreed full costs incurred by developing country Parties in complying with their obligations under Article 12, Paragraph 1. They shall also provide such financial resources, including for the transfer of technology, needed by the developing country Parties to meet the agreed full incremental costs of implementing measures that are covered by Paragraph 1 of this Article and that are agreed between a developing country Party and the international entity or entities referred to in Article 11, in accordance with that Article. The implementation of these commitments shall take into account the need for adequacy and predictability in the flow of funds and the importance of appropriate burden sharing among the developed country Parties.

1.6 The politics of climate change negotiations

The UNFCCC, the reigning climate Convention, was negotiated at a time when both Europe and the US were complacent with their economic superiority. Urged on by the urgency of the impending doom of climate change, which was then in its nascent stage of heightened awareness in the international political economy,[53] these countries quite seriously negotiated the Convention and developed the protocol. The negotiators from developed countries were also quite mindful of the role of their economic growth path in creating the factors (fossil fuel burning, clearing and forest and development of cities in the long march to industrialization and economic growth) giving rising to climate change. It is unquestioned that since the nineteenth century the industrialization-led economies of Western Europe and the US have contributed significantly to the increase in the volume of heat-trapping GHGs emitted into the atmosphere. Even today the US has continued to be the world's biggest emitter among the industrialized countries.

During the time of the negotiation of the UNFCCC, there seem to have been a sense of accountability, responsibility (linked to the polluter pays principle) and solidarity with the peoples of the developing countries who would experience and have to adapt to the harshest effects of the growing climate change problem. It is quite remarkable the nature of the climate Convention. Despite the strong almost anti-development stance of the US, Europe and the G77 & China countries were able to enable acceptance of issue such as 'historical responsibility',[54] 'common but differentiated responsibilities' and 'respective capabilities/capacities' as the foundational core principles on which to orchestrated mitigation commitments and actions to stabilizes the earth's climate. The implicit assumption behind the global approach to climate change policy is that 'decision-making rights and benefits' to use the atmosphere belong to the entire global community (Athanasiou and Bear 2005).

The under-girding negotiating philosophy of responsibility, polluter pays and accountability help to facilitate, it would seem, a high sense of trust and a highly open, democratic and transparent process, based on UN principles, at least in the initial years of the Convention. This process and high level of commitment to environmental integrity and climate security was likely what held the glue of the Kyoto Protocol, when after participating in the negotiations of the Protocol, the US abandoned it. Unfortunately, that ethos does not seem to be holding much anymore. Increasingly, since 2007 and culminating into the debacle of the Copenhagen Climate Conference, 2009, there have been increasing north-south tensions, the introduction of in-transparent and undemocratic processes and consequential lack of trust brought into the negotiations arena from other spaces, and a hard winner take all bargaining technique such as was commonplace in the arena of the World Trade Organization negotiations.[55]

All of these factors were dramatically intensified in Copenhagen where the Obama administration's leadership achieved only a political declaration, the so-called Copenhagen Accord out of what was reputed to be a very discordant process which did not follow traditional UN Conference mode of operations. But it is not just the US, both among the Europeans and other industrialized countries such as Canada, Japan, New Zealand and Australia, there would seem to be a new approach – a technocratic, conservative, single under-taking,[56] take-it-or-leave-it mentality have come to dominate the process. The Europeans, for the most part, and with their own self-interests at stake, alternate between blaming and following the US or seem to be otherwise unsure of themselves. Yet in the beginning, they were the stalwart climate change protagonists bringing everyone to a heightened level of concern about the deteriorating state of the climate.

What is clear is that with the exception of grandfathering of the Small Island Developing States (SIDs) and the Least Developed Countries (LDCs), there is not much more sentimentality about development and under-development.

In the current dynamics, the SIDs (negotiation under the umbrella of the Alliance of Small Island States, AOSIS – a coalition of over 43 of these entities mostly from the Caribbean and the Pacific) and the Less Developing Countries are usually ring-fenced from mitigation actions and offered some minimum floor of financing while the rest of the developing countries, many of whom, such as the Philippines, Thailand and El Salvador and Nicaragua suffer from varied aspects of vulnerability to climate change including low level of per capita GDF relative to some of the AOSIS countries, are left to fend for themselves (see Appendix 1.2 for list of country groups within the UNFCCC process).

This point of departure away from the Convention's traditional focus has been on the cards and become more evident after the Poznan meeting (2008). But it was driven home with certainty at the Copenhagen meeting in 2009. Developed countries such as the EU, Canada and Japan had begun to back-track on agreeing to a second commitment period for Kyoto. Though developing countries, who have no mitigation commitments under either the Convention or the Kyoto Protocol, made numerous concessions, including accepting to undertake nationally appropriate policies and actions to reduce GHGs emissions, that would be measurable, reportable and verifiable (MRV) under the nationally appropriate mitigation actions (NAMA) framework, developed countries continuously pushed for these countries to take on more responsibility. Over time, the demands of developed countries and the relative acquiescence of some developing countries was slowly tilting the balance achieved in the Convention by shifting the burden of mitigations reductions unto developing countries. This was occurring even as developed countries were stalling in meeting their own legally binding commitments to both reduce emissions and to provide finance, technology transfer and capacity building support to the developing countries. At Copenhagen, a US-led coalition sought to get developing countries to make quantitative numerical commitments in return for fast start financing. Ultimately, a side agreement, the Copenhagen Accord, involving about 30 countries, was reached wherein some developing countries made voluntary mitigation commitment and developed countries promised to implement $30 billion in fast start financing for the period 2010–2012.

By the time of Cancún (2010), developing countries were being inundated with a series of initiatives that were slowly but surely seeking to transform their voluntary pledges from Copenhagen into a more formal and binding system. Tools such as international assessment and review (IAR) for developed countries, and international consultation and analysis (ICA) for developing (Paragraphs 46 and 66 of the Cancún Agreements) and biennial reports potentially impose even more burden on developing countries and enveloping them into a an increasingly complex and burdensome process of MRV of mitigation actions. This was occurring even as the developed countries were back-tracking on their commitments and taking actions to formalize their own pledge and review system formulated in Copenhagen. Both the EU and the US pushed for collapsing the two-tracked (LCA-KP) negotiating processes of the Bali Action Plan into one track that would work towards a single binding treaty that would include so-called 'major emitters'. This has morphed into the Durban Platform which seeks to include all countries equally, in another legally binding treaty or Protocol, turning the current equity and science based regime on its head.

Thus not only is the shared vision of the Bali Road Map slowly being shredded but there is also certainly threat to the UNFCCC itself. Totally eschewing the Bali bargain and the two track processes set in place, the US is calling for 'symmetry' and a single treaty where all countries are treated the same equally. Since the Cancún meeting, as noted by the African Ministers of the Environment in their 2011 declaration:

> The objective of many, if not most, developed country parties is now to replace the Kyoto Protocol with a single weaker agreement under the Convention . . . This approach, in addition to deviating from the agreement struck in Bali, places at risk the principle of common but differentiated responsibility, limits potential to establish internationally binding mitigation commitments for developed countries, and/or risks establishing weaker but broadly comparable requirements for developed countries, while raising new obligations for developing countries.

So whither the Convention?

The UNFCCC[57] is a lovely little treaty, elegant and based on equity and common but differentiated responsibility (with respect to the rights and obligation between developed and developing countries) and respective capabilities (with respect to burden sharing among developed countries). Its provisions quite clearly and explicitly demarcate between the rights and obligations of developed and developing countries and its preamble stipulate in very clear and straight forward language the historical responsibility of developed countries for the overhang of GHG gases in the global atmosphere and their obligations to lead on actions to reduce and eliminate the human-induced factors that contribute to climate change:

> Noting that the largest share of historical and current global emissions of greenhouse gases has originated in developed countries, that per capita emissions in developing countries are still relatively low and that the share of global emissions originating in developing countries will grow to meet their social and development needs.
>
> (UNFCCC 1992: preamble)

The Convention is quite clear on the respect for difference among developed and developing countries (Article 3.2) and the importance of taking into account different socio economic contexts (Article 3.3) and the right to development (Article 3.4). Article 3.5 is also specific that 'measures taken to combat climate change, including unilateral ones, should not constitute a means of arbitrary or unjustifiable discrimination or a disguised restriction on international trade'.

Furthermore, of the ten commitment provisions (Article 4) only three are explicitly specific to developing countries (Articles 7–9).

> *Commitment 7*: The extent to which developing country Parties will effectively implement their commitments under the Convention will depend on

the effective implementation by developed country Parties of their commitments under the Convention related to financial resources and transfer of technology and will take fully into account that economic and social development and poverty eradication are the first and overriding priorities of the developing country Parties.

Commitment 8: In the implementation of the commitments in this Article, the Parties shall give full consideration to what actions are necessary under the Convention, including actions related to funding, insurance and the transfer of technology, to meet the specific needs and concerns of developing country Parties arising from the adverse effects of climate change and/or the impact of the implementation of response measures

Commitment 9: The Parties shall take full account of the specific needs and special situations of the least developed countries in their actions with regard to funding and transfer of technology.

Article 11 on financing mechanism is quite specific as to the nature of the funds that are expected to support developing countries: 'A mechanism for the provision of financial resources on a grant or concessional basis, including for the transfer of technology, is hereby defined' (art. 11.1).

Clearly the Convention recognizes climate change as a global commons problem and as an environmental issue and a developmental issue. (It is also a social justice and human welfare issues, as will be discussed Chapter 2 below.) It is clear that what is needed as dictated by the provisions of the treaty and science, is a fair, ambitious global solution to deal with the challenges of climate change. It is also clear that for vast swathes of millions of the world's population this must be done in a manner that ensures continuous poverty reduction, sustainable development and gender equality and protect the lives of millions of people worldwide. This seems to be the understanding underlying the negotiation of the Convention and its key defining principles of equity, common but differentiated responsibility. However, now seemingly the Convention, itself, is under threat and its mitigation implementation mechanism, the Kyoto Protocol, is being slowly killed off.

How did this come about? Environmental integrity and equity objectives have given away to political expediency, economic competitiveness and a pernicious blame game; not a genuine search for a common way out of true global dilemma. There is disagreement not about the science, at the heart of the Convention, but rather an attempt to rework the notions of 'equity, and 'ambitious goal' and 'historical responsibility and accountability' embedded in the Convention to the total disadvantages of the developing countries. Much of this is explicitly about sidestepping the legal obligations of developed countries to the developing countries and seeking to escape from their historical responsibility which implies massive financial and technology transfer from the global north to the global south. Unfortunately, this turn-about is occurring under the framework of a call for 'comprehensivity', 'modernity', and 'symmetry' and bringing 'major emitters aboard'. A brigade, ironically, led by a more than major emitter, who is not a party to the Protocol, and one that has consistently maintained that it cannot not abide by binding international mitigations commitments.

There are thus serious political issues underlying this debate. This at one level is a debate about the numbers, and at another level, it signals a clash of paradigms regarding the equitable sharing of the remaining atmospheric space between developed and developing countries. Hence underlying the calls for a new regime are serious issues about carbon budget/carbon equity, climate debt and climate justice and the right to development. Dealing with any or all of these issues poses serious financial and economic adjustment costs for both developed and developing countries. An equity based framework not only posits a massive transfer of finance and technology from the developed countries, but it also has implications for the sharing of the remaining and slowly dwindling atmospheric space.

The developed countries have contributed to well over 70 per cent of the anthropogenic factors contributing to the cumulative stock of GHGs and the consequential global warming now creating havoc in many parts of the developing countries, including the existential threats of life in small island states. It is therefore quite understandable that the developed countries would much rather divert attention from their lack-lustre performance with regard to their mitigation and financial obligation with counter claims of single treaty and bringing 'major emitters' aboard.[58]

It is the numbers!

The fundamental political issue is about the direction the world is headed with regard to responding to, and meeting the climate change challenge in a timely sustainable and precautionary and no-regrets manner. In this negotiation, the quest for environmental integrity seems to revolve around a triplet of numbers: a global temperature goal (and the level of concentration of GHG in the atmospheric critical for ensuring that temperature), a peaking year, a global long-term emissions reduction goal and a clear pathway for scaling-up to achieving the promised $100 billion per year by 2020.

With regard to the temperature goal, science, as noted above, is quite clear and emphatic: a safe level is to keep global temperature rise between 1.5 and substantially below 2 degrees Celsius (or in Cancún parlance, well below 2 degrees Celsius), compared with pre-industrial times. The IPCC (2007) argues that in order to ensure this temperature range the concentration of GHGs in the atmosphere should be around 380 ppm carbon dioxide.

The politics, however, is not so clear. While the Cancún Agreements specified a political 'consensus' temperature target of 2 degrees Celsius, not all countries agree with that target. Bolivia certainly registered its explicit objection to the 2 degrees Celsius target and argued strongly in favour of 1–1.5 degrees Celsius as the acceptable limit. The work of UNEP (2010) shows that with the pledges in the Cancún there will be significant emission gap (gap between emission levels consistent with a 2 degrees Celsius limit and those resulting from the Copenhagen

Accord pledges by 2020). But more ominously, UNEP argue that Cancún pledges will likely result in temperatures of 2–5 degrees Celsius before the end of the century.[59] Since Cancún, over 100 countries, including the African Ministers of the Environment, have called for 1.5 Celsius as the temperature target. Global civil society also seeks a target within the range of 1–1.5 degrees Celsius. Though there is disagreement as to nature of effort that will be required to obtain and maintain 1–1.5 degrees Celsius, it is clear from numerous studies that 2 degrees Celsius spells disasters of different regions such as Africa and Small Island states in the Pacific and the Caribbean. Beyond its political declaration of 2 degrees Celsius as the global temperature goal, the Cancún agreements itself raise the issue of the adequacy of 2 degrees Celsius target but left that decision as a matter for ongoing negotiations (Paragraphs 138–40) which set up parameter for review starting in 2013 and concluding in 2015:

> Paragraph 138, Decides to periodically review the adequacy of the long-term global goal referred to in Paragraph 4[60] above, in the light of the ultimate objective of the Convention, and overall progress towards achieving it, in accordance with the relevant principles and provisions of the Convention; ... and 139 (a)(iv) Consideration of strengthening the long-term global goal, referencing various matters presented by the science, including in relation to temperature rises of 1.5 degrees Celsius.

The second important number for environmental integrity is the year by which global emissions must peak and then start to decrease (the so-called peaking year). As noted above, many scientific researchers argue for peak year of 2015 (as the safest for ensuring 2 degrees Celsius). This is seen as the most ambitious path and is associated with a 61 per cent chance of keeping warming below 2 degrees Celsius (Kartha and Erickson 2011). Other peaking years under discussion in the climate negotiations are 2017 and 2020 (seen as the least ambitious path, with a less than 40 per cent change of keeping warming below 2 degrees Celsius; ibid.). However, there is no political consensus on a peaking year. This may be because the selection of a peaking year is associated with a specific carbon budget and implies a particular level of mitigation burden. Cancún was silent on the matter and the Durban Outcome has left that question open for consideration at future climate change meetings. The Group of 77 and China and other groups of countries have not articulated a shared goal in this regard but seems to signal acceptance of 2015 (for developed countries) and 2020 as the global peaking year for developing countries. But the nature of the emissions reduction cut necessary to achieve this outcome remains unspecified.

The third number is the long-term global goal for aggregate emissions cut (as envisioned under the Bali Action Plan and the LCA track of the Bali Road Map). Here the science argues for 50–85 per cent reduction of global emissions below the 1990 level by the year 2050. Some researchers argue that developed countries should reduce emissions by 25 per cent to 40 per cent below the 1990 level in 2020 and developing countries 15–30 per cent below the baseline in 2020 (den Elzen and Höhne, 2008). As reported by Khor 2010, developed countries are proposing a 50 per cent global greenhouse gas emission cut by 2050 (from 1990 levels) and the G8 proposes that the developed countries cut by 80 per cent.[61] The EU has set in place the operationalization of its own internal 20 per cent cut by 2020 based on 1990 levels and promises a 30 per cent cut conditional on 'an ambitious comprehensive global deal'.

Much of the research on the numbers issue has been undertaken by developed countries' researchers. But at the Durban Conference, path breaking work by developing countries' researchers from the BASIC countries' (Brazil, China, India and South Africa) Expert Group on Equitable Access to Sustainable Development was released. The BASIC's expert group put upfront the fact that the global carbon budget has been almost exhausted and argues that developmental justice is a precondition for high ambition for reduction of emissions globally (Chapter 2 discusses more on this point).

A global goal and peaking year have 'significant implication for developing countries and the future distribution of world emission rights and of world income' (Khor 2010; Kharta 2011). From this perspective, an 80 per cent cut by developed countries would not be a fair or equitable outcome for developing countries, which would have to accept a 20 per cent cut that would be the equivalent of a 60 per cent per capita cut, given their larger relative share of the world population. This would have great implication for their ability to grow, eradicate poverty and provide essential services to their population.[62]

From shared vision to shredded vision?

Until the 'Copenhagen nightmare', as termed by one negotiator, the Bali Road Map (COP 13, 2007) which launched a 'comprehensive process to enable the full, effective and sustained implementation of the Convention, through a negotiation process anchored in the Bali Action Plan. The Bali Action Plan recognized and reaffirmed that urgent emissions reduction needed to be taken to delivery deep cuts in GHG and that this could only occur with significant implementation of the Convention. It also recognized and upheld that economic and social development and poverty eradication are global priorities. This is in conformity with the Millennium Declaration and the MDGs.

In 2000, 189 heads of states, the world largest gathering of heads of state ever, adopted the Millennium Declaration on the key issues of paramount interest to the global community: Values and Principles, Peace, Security and Disarmament, Development and Poverty Eradication, Protecting our Common Environment, Human Rights, Democracy and Good Governance Protecting the Vulnerable, Meeting the Special Needs of Africa and strengthening the UN. The Millennium Summit's greatest achievement was its ratification of eight specific[63] time bound, monitorable, verifiable and reportable goals that encapsulated these overarching and fundamental global and human concerns.

Under the Bali Action Plan, countries agreed to stronger actions on mitigation – developed countries through quantified targets and developing countries through nationally appropriate mitigation actions within the context of sustainable development. Thus the Bali Road Map was built on a well-balanced three pillars approach meant to address the known inadequacies and deficiencies of the Kyoto Protocol: (1) weak mitigation actions; (2) the missing mitigation commitment of a key high emitting industrialized country through comparability of efforts by Parties to the convention who were not Parties to the Kyoto Protocol; and (3) to address complaints that developing countries need to do more in the mitigation area. The Bali Action Plan notes that enhanced actions by developing countries was predicated on supported by finance and technology transfer from developed countries. This three pillar approach, the so-called Bali bargain was agreed to by all Parties, including the US. It was accepted that the US could not make commitments under the protocol so 1b (i) was to ensure that the US undertook comparable measures with the other industrialized countries. The developing countries who have no mitigations commitment under the Convention or the Protocol agreed to undertake mitigation actions that would be measurable, reportable and verifiable in order to promote greater environmental integrity to the system. However, it did not take too long for that bargain to be unravelled.

The great escape[64]

Securing a safe climate future for the inhabitants and species on earth can only be ensured by ambitious and deep emissions reduction. It is developed countries who must make take the lead in making these cuts. The developed countries must both take actions to clean up the environment and reduce and eliminate their reliance on GHGs contributors. They have benefited the most from the using up the earth's atmospheric resources; they have high level of technological know-how for clean, renewable energy and to promote energy efficiencies. Developing countries, as a group have significant ways to go to build their domestic, housing, commercial, social and transportation infrastructure. Their poverty reduction and development are their over-riding priorities. This is recognized in the Convention. At the same time, it is the case that all countries must try to contribute to stabilizing the concentration of GHGs into the atmosphere. So developing countries must also seek to follow a sustainable low carbon pathway. By the time of Durban many developing countries have made voluntary targets for emissions reductions and some are in different stages of implementing through pilots low carbon emissions strategies. But it is widely known that many developing countries can only successfully make the low carbon transition and transformation with financial support and support for clean technological development and transfer.

However, developed countries have not fulfilled either their emissions reductions under Kyoto or the transfer of finance and technology. Furthermore, they are seeking to shift these obligations and responsibility unto developing countries. The Durban outcome is one attempt at achieving this great escape, especially for the US, as it now fully legitimizes the bottom-up voluntary pledge system and threatens to unbalance the delicate balance achieved under the Convention through the principles of Common But Differentiated Responsibility and equity.

Notes

1 Global warming (a rise in the earth average temperature due to a build-up of CO_2 and other gases in the atmosphere) causes climate change. This is quite distinct from short term variation in weather that we observed daily such as hourly changes in temperature, seasonal shifts, wind, humidity, atmospheric pressure, cloudiness, sunshine or normal precipitation. Climate refers to the totality of weather over a long period of years.
2 82 per cent of earth scientists agree that the climate is warming and human activities are contributing to it (Center for Climate and Energy Solutions, formerly Pew: www.c2es.org/facts-figures/basics). 97 per cent of the scientists specializing in studying climate system agree that recent warming is real and almost certainly caused by humans (ibid.). Meteorology, oceanography also agree that the 'there is unequivocal evidence that earth's lower atmosphere, ocean, and land surface are warming; sea level is rising; and snow cover, mountain glaciers, and Arctic sea ice are shrinking. The dominant cause of the warming since the 1950s is human activities' (Wikipedia: http://en.wikipedia.org/wiki/Scientific_opinion_on_climate_change). October 2011, the International Journal of Public Opinion Research published a paper with the survey results from over 400 scientists from academia, government and industry in which 97 per cent agreed that global temperature has risen over the past century and 84 per cent agreed with the ACC tenet. In 2010 the Proceedings of the National Academy of sciences of the US also published a paper which presents reviews of publication and citation of over 1,000 which shows that 97–98 per cent of the climate research most actively publishing in the field, supported the ACC tenet. Naomi Oreskes 2004 study of the scientific literature on climate change argue that there is a scientific consensus on the realities of anthropogenic climate change (Wikipedia, ibid.).
3 Uncertainty is primarily due to 'uncertainty about the future trend of greenhouse gases emission' – a human behavioural issue (CES2).
4 Environmental degradation (GHGs, industrial pollutants, fertilizer run-off etc.) contributes to loss of bio diversity which threatens bird species; other environmental degradation such as depletion of ozone layers threaten plant and animal life; global warming result in life destroying ultra violet rays that also threatens plant life in the ocean and on land. Plant species are also vulnerable to regional temperature change as well as land-use change.
5 The creation of UNEP was a recommendation from the UN Conference on Human Environment in 1972. The UN General Assembly created UNEP that same year. UNEP is headquartered in Nairobi, Kenya.
6 According to Wikipedia, China formal environmental policy actions in terms of establishing environmental protection agencies and putting controls on some of its industrial waste was stimulated by the UN Conference on the Human Environment in 1972. China is also the first developing countries to implement a sustainable development strategy (Wikipedia 2013). The National Development Reform Commission (NDRC) is in charge of UNFCCC matters, including work at the national level with regard to climate change strategies, plans and policies [functions 11-14]. http://en.ndrc.gov.cn/mfndrc/.
7 The Montreal Protocol is an international treaty, ratified by 196 states and the European Union, which is designed to protect the ozone layer by phasing out the production of numerous substances believed to be responsible for ozone depletion. Under the Protocol, which is linked to the Vienna Convention for the Protection of the Ozone layer, countries agree to equitably control total global emissions of substances that deplete the ozone, primarily chlorofluorocarbons (CFCs) and hydrochlorofluorocarbons (HCFCs). It is often hailed as 'perhaps the single most successful international agreement to date has been the Montreal Protocol' (Wikipedia 2012). (The ozone layer is a layer in earth's atmosphere which contains relatively high concentrations of ozone (O3). This layer absorbs 97–99

The global climate change policy environment   63

    per cent of the sun's high frequency ultra violet light, which potentially damages the life forms on earth (Wikipedia 2012).
 8 Both the Montreal Protocol and the Transboundary convention indirectly deals with climate change as some noxious gases are precursors to GHGs and CFCs are themselves GHGs.
 9 Also known as the Brundtland Report (published 1987) which is known for bringing together environment and development as a single issue and stresses the environmental limits to growth both for developed and developing countries. The report posited poverty reduction, gender equity, and wealth redistribution (all human resource development issues) as central to environmental conservation.
10 Climate scientists argue that the climate has warmed over 0.5 degrees Celsius in the past century. 2011 has been noted as the ninth warmest year on record since 1880.
11 At the end of the last Ice Age there was approximately 180–260 part per million (ppm) of CO_2 in the atmosphere. Today it is about 392 ppm. This marks over a 100 ppm increase in 100 years.
12 Roger Revelle and Hans Seuss, both scientists at Scripps Institute of Oceanography in 1957, observed that oceans do not absorbs much of the CO_2 emitted into the atmosphere leaving significant amount of it in the atmosphere which could eventually warm the earth. In 1958, Revelle and Keeling establish the National Oceanic Atmospheric administration to monitor CO_2 from industrial sources and confirmed the trend in rising level of CO_2 in the atmosphere.
13 Climate change is argued to have a significant impact on the life cycle dynamics of vector borne parasites. For example, temperature can speed put the maturation period of malarial parasite inside mosquitos an increase of 5 degrees Celsius, from say 20 degrees Celsius (68 °F) to 25 degrees Celsius (77 °F) reduces the malaria protozoa maturity period by half the time (from 26 days to 13 days; Bueno et al. 2008: 367; McArthur 1972).
14 Relevant provisions of General Assembly resolution 44/228 of 22 December 1989 (UNCED), and resolutions 43/53 of 6 December 1988, 44/207 of 22 December 1989, 45/212 of 21 December 1990 and 46/169 of 19 December 1991 on protection of global climate for present and future generations of mankind; the provisions of General Assembly resolution 44/206 of 22 December 1989 on the possible adverse effects of General Assembly resolution 44/172 of 19 December 1989 on the implementation of the Plan of Action to Combat Desertification;
15 Note that there is a difference between the UNFCCC's definition of climate change and that utilized by the IPCC. The latter defines climate change as a change in the state of the climate that can be statistically identified by changes in the mean and/or the variability of its properties, and that persists for an extended period, typically decades or longer. It refers to any change in climate over time.
16 The Convention reads: *Noting* that the largest share of historical and current global emissions of GHGs has originated in developed countries, that per capita emissions in developing countries are still relatively low and that the share of global emissions originating in developing countries will grow to meet their social and development needs.
17 EIT may use this flexibility to select a baseline for their specific commitment other than 1990, that is, prior to the economic changes that led to big cuts in their emissions. UNFCCC 2002.
18 The US did not ratify the Kyoto Protocol and hence has no obligation under the Protocol. However, it has general reductions and other commitments under the Convention.
19 As of September 2011, 191 countries had ratified the protocol. Overall, about 37 countries committed to reduce four GHGs: Carbon dioxide, methane, and nitrous oxide, sulphur hexafluoride plus two other gases, hydrofluorocarbons and perfluorocarbons.
20 Up until near the end of 2010 countries were assured that this discussion for the second period of the Kyoto Protocol as established under the Bali Action Plan and the two track processes agreed in 2007, then Japan announced that it would not make commitments under a second commitment period of the protocol. Since then other countries: Russia and Canada have also made similar announcement thus putting the Protocol in jeopardy.

64 The global climate change policy environment

In December 2011, Canada announced that it would formally withdraw from the Protocol.
21 During the closing plenary of the Durban Conference this language was modified as a result of intervention by the Indian Minister of Environment and Forests, Ms. Jayanti Natarajan, to replace 'legal outcome' with 'agreed outcome with legal force'.
22 The Durban Decision only 'take[s] note of the proposed amendments to the Kyoto Protocol developed by the Ad Hoc Working Group on the Kyoto Protocol . . .' and further 'take[s] note of the quantified economy-wide emission reduction targets to be implemented by Parties in Annex I'. It also noted the 'intention of these Parties to convert these targets to quantified emission limitation or reduction objectives'. It 'invites' the Parties that have not submitted anything to do so by May 1, 2012. The Decision was awkwardly silent on the refusal of Canada, Japan and Russia to make any pledges in Annex B (as they are legally required to do) for amendment for the second commitment period. (Rather these countries seek to have their pledges noted in the LCA 1b1.) It also does not address the implication and consequence for countries such as Australia and New Zealand who are keeping their options open by listing in the draft Annex B but have conditioned the listing of their pledges 'pursuant to decision 1/CMP.7, para 5 and following the necessary domestic processes and taking into account decision 1/CP.17 and decision on mitigation' (Draft Decision -/CMP.7 Notes (a) and (i), 2011). It further notes the 'intentions' of Annex I parties to convert targets into quantified emissions limitation reduction objectives (QELROS). Nor does the Durban Decision adopt or indicate a plan to adopt proposed amendments; rather, it says with a 'view' to the adopting. These are not language of implementing a legal binding second commitment period or outcome with legal force, but rather best endeavour urgings. It does leave the door open for CMP8 (2012) to confer a legal second period. But the timing does not seem favourable as the Protocol first period expires 31 December 2012. There will not be time for national government to ratify any amendment that would come into force before the expiry date and thus there would certainly be a legal gap. The implication of this gap is not known.
23 The 'women and gender constituency, one of nine 'constituencies' recognized by the UNFCCC Secretariat, hosted a number of daily constituency meetings as well as numerous side-events targeted to negotiators and governmental decision-makers. The women and gender group led by focal point, Gender CC – for women for climate justice, hosts the Women's Caucus which includes the active participation of a number of non-governmental, inter-governmental institutions and universities. The Engendering process was also supported at high level working directly with negotiators and country groups by the Mary Robinson foundation-Climate Justice, WEDO and the Gender focal points of UNDP and IUCN, the latter three are leaders in the GGCA.
24 The GGCA was launched in 2007 as a network of nongovernmental and inter-governmental organizations and UN agencies. It seeks to ensure that all climate change decision-making, policies and initiatives, all levels are gender responsive. Founding members are the United Nations Development Program (UNDP), the United Nations Environment Program (UNEP), the International Union for the conservation of Nature (IUCN) and the Women's Environment & Development Organization (WEDO). The GGCA focus on global and national policy advocacy, capacity building and knowledge generation around the UNFCCC process, www.gender-climate.org.
25 Mary Robinson, the first woman President of Ireland (1990–1997), former UN High Commissioner for Human Rights (1997–2002), and founder and President of Realizing Rights: The Ethical Globalization Initiative (2002–2010). Connie Hedegaard hosted the COP 15 Copenhagen meeting in 2009. She is a former Danish Minister for Climate and Energy and a former Danish Minister of the Environment. Michelle Bachelet is the first Under-Secretary-General of the UN and was the President of Chile from11 March 2006 to 11 March 2010. She was appointed Executive Director UN Women the United Nations Entity for Gender Equality and the Empowerment of Women, in 2010. UN women was created in 2010 as part of the UN reform agenda. It is the merger of four entities: the Division for the Advancement of Women (DAW); the International

The global climate change policy environment 65

Research and Training Institute for the Advancement of women (INSTRAW), the Office of the Special Adviser on Gender Issues and Advancement of Women (OSAGI), and the United Nations Development Fund for Women (UNIFEM).

26 In general there is an annual meeting of the Conference of the Parties (COP) each year as well as at least two inter-sessional meetings per year. The meetings of the COP, which is the highest decision-making body of the UNFCCC, is usually attended by Ministers of the Environment and/or Ministers of Foreign Affairs, depending each country. The annual COP makes decisions on the agreements worked out at technical levels and at intersessional meetings held during the particular year of that COP. In general intersessional meetings are held in Bonn, the headquarters of the UNFCCC, with the exception of 2008 (three such meetings were held: Bangkok, Bonn, and Accra), in 2009, five such meetings: Bonn I, Bonn II, Bonn III, Bangkok and Barcelona; in 2010: four such meetings took place: Bonn I, Bonn II, Bonn III and Tianjin; in 2011, three such meetings were held: Bangkok, Bonn and Panama, and in 2012 only two intersessionals were held: Bonn and Bangkok. Research undertaken by Women's Environment & Development Organization and Gender CC show that the participation of women in national delegations across both intersessionals and annual meetings of the Parties has been consistently holding at around 30 per cent over the period 2008–2012, with the peak participation of average by year of 33 per cent (compared to 67 per cent for men in 2012) and the low of 30 per cent (compared to 70 per cent for male participation) in 2009. In terms of percentage per meeting, the highest participation rate for women on national delegation was 39 per cent (Bangkok 2008) followed by 37 per cent (Bonn 2, 2010). The lowest participation rate per meeting for women was 27 per cent for both COP 15, 2009 and Panama 2011.

The associate annual COP, where decisions are made at the highest level including any agreements worked out at technical level intersessional meetings for these years were: COP 14 (2008)-Poznan with 31 per cent participation by women on national delegations; COP 15 (2009)-Copenhagen with 27 per cent participation rate for women; COP 16 (2010)-Cancún with 30 per cent participation of women on delegations. COP 16 also had a trio of high powered women leadership of with the Executive Secretary, Christiana Figueres, the executive secretary of the UN Framework Convention on Climate Change (UNFCCC), Ambassador Patricia Espinosa, Minister of Foreign Affairs, Mexico and the President of *COP 16*/CMP 6 and Ambassador Dessima Williams, the Grenadian ambassador to the UN and Chair, of the over 40 member grouping of the Alliance of Small Island States. COP 17-Durban 2011 had 29 per cent participation rate for women and, like COP 16, had a large number of women in leadership position, including the Executive Secretary of the UNFCCC, the South African COP Presidency, the EU Commissioner for Climate Change and Amb. Williams. COP 18 Doha witness a reduction in women at the top with the assumption of Qatar as COP presidency. However, the rotation of AOSIS leadership to the Pacific and the assumption of the position of chairperson leave the leadership of the 44 nation group led by another woman, Ambassador Marlene Moses of Nauru. COP 18 had 30 per cent participation of women delegates.

27 *Report on gender composition* Note by the secretariat. Conference of the Parties Nineteenth session Warsaw, 11–22 November 2013 Item 15 of the provisional agenda Gender and climate change FCCC/CP/2013/4.

28 Durban extended the LCA for 1 year 'in order for it to continue its work and reach the agreed outcome pursuant to Decision 1/CP.13 (Bali Action Plan) through decisions adopted by the sixteenth, seventeenth and eighteenth sessions of the COP, at which time' it will be terminated.

29 The Ad Hoc Working Group on Further Commitments for Annex I Parties under the Kyoto Protocol was requested to 'aim to deliver the results of its work pursuant to Decision 1/CMP.1 in time to complete its work by the eighth session of the COP serving as the meeting of the Parties to the Kyoto Protocol'. Durban was the 7th meeting of the CMP.

30 These issues are referenced in the Draft Decision -/CP.17 and on which the decision instructs the new working group 'to plan its work in the first half of 2012, including inter alia, on mitigation, adaptation, finance, technology development and transfer, transparency of action, and support and capacity building, drawing upon submissions from Parties and relevant technical, social and economic information and expertise' (FCCC/CO/2011/L.10, para 5).
31 The world is currently at 0.8 degrees Celsius above pre-industrial temperature.
32 Sokolov, A.P. et al., *Probabilistic Forecast for 21st Century Climate Based on Uncertainties in Emissions (Without Policy) and Climate Parameters* (MIT Joint Program Report 169, 2009). http://globalchange.mit.edu/files/document/MITJPSPGC_Rpt169.pdf
33 For more on the likely devastating impacts of this please see *Turn Down the Heat* (World Bank 2013).
34 Source: Meena Reman, Cancún texts adopted, overriding Bolivia's objections, TWN Cancún Update No. 19; Laura Carlsen, Cancún Agreement Succeeds in Meeting Low expectations. CIPAmericas.
35 A road map would include elements of global reduction targets, peak year in relation to a cumulative carbon budget. See also UNEP's Emission Gap report (2010) as well as the Copenhagen Diagnosis 2009.
36 Carbon budgets associated with different emissions pathways – these are called Representative Concentration Pathways (or RCPs).
37 The IEA identifies three technology pathways, but the record on all three of these so far has been not as accelerated as expected: 1) Energy efficiency improvements: for example in power generation and energy end-use 2) Shift towards lower carbon power generation: for example coal to gas, use of biofuels, renewable energy and nuclear and 3) Carbon capture and storage (PWC 2013). At the same time, the record on decarbonisation has been poor: 'G20 economies decarbonised at 0.7 per cent per year, and over 90 per cent of this was due to energy efficiency changes'(Grant 2013). But it is often pointed out that 'the global economy needs to cut carbon intensity by 6.0 per cent every year from now to 2100' (PWC 2013).
38 Pre-industrial levels of carbon dioxide concentrates in the atmosphere were about 280ppm, (IPCC 2007a). Many experts would like to limit greenhouse gas concentrations to 450 ppm (Pew 2009).
39 Calculated from per capita GDP and per capita emissions data from WRI CAIT version 8.0, at http://cait.wri.org.
40 But, on the whole, moderate climate change of an additional 2 degrees will likely be beneficial for the world, says Benny Peiser, an anthropologist at John Moore University in Liverpool, England (cited in the *Edmonton Journal*, 23 November 2008).
41 According to the International Institute for Systems Analysis – UN, Northern regions such as Britain, Ireland and Spain will also lose good land due to change in rainfall patterns which will bring drier summers. But Scandinavian will gain when the cold northern areas warm up. The Mediterranean is expected to be adversely impacted with 'crippling water shortage and declining tourist arrivals'.
42 Such benefits could well make Canadians feel ambivalent about taking measures to stop global warming, says economist Thomas Gale Moore, a senior fellow at the Hoover Institute (*Edmonton Journal*, 24 November 2008). 'As far as Canada is concerned, over the next century whether it's a 2-degree rise or a 5-degree rise, it's probably going to be beneficial, . . . With global warming, the ocean level will also rise, but this shouldn't be a big issue in Canada, because most of the country's coastal areas are uninhabited, and it won't be significant if some of that land is claimed by the ocean . . . Populated areas will fight back by building higher.' Robert Mendelsohn, cited in the Edmonton Journal 24 November 2008.
43 Cited in the *Edmonton Journal* (2008).
44 Europe to suffer as the world warms up. *Financial Times*, 5 January 2007 www.ft.com/cms/s/0/358a1bd0-9ce9-11db-8ec6-0000779e2340.html#axzz191aefiN8.

45 The argument is backed up by a British study that says that an increase of 2 degrees over the next 50 years will increase heat-related deaths by 2,000 in Britain, but would cut cold-related deaths by 20,000 (Peiser 2008).
46 Regressions of death rates in Washington, D.C. and in some 89 urban counties scattered across the nation on climate and demographic variables demonstrate that warmer temperatures reduce deaths. The results imply that a 2.5 degrees Celsius warming would lower deaths in the US by about 40,000 per year. Although the data on illness are poor, the numbers indicate that warming might reduce medical costs by about $20 billion annually. Utilizing willingness to pay as a measure of preference, this paper regresses wage rates for a few narrowly defined occupations in metropolitan areas on measures of temperature and size of city and finds that people prefer warm climates. Workers today would be willing to give up between $30 billion and $100 billion annually in wages for a 2.5 degrees Celsius increase in temperatures. Thomas Gale Moore 1996, *Health and Amenity Effects of Global Warming*. Hoover Institution and Stanford University.
47 Cited in the *Edmonton Journal* (2008).
48 Though increase warming brings its own challenge, it can be met by the provision of air conditioners, in summers and central heating in winters. Hence what is important is enabling economic growth and rising standard of living.
49 *Edmonton Journal* 2008.
50 IMF WEO (September 2011) and UNstats.
51 Ibid.
52 Data for 2005 and excludes land use change. Source: CAIT, WRI accessed 21 November 2011.
53 The Convention was agreed and adopted by the Intergovernmental Negotiating Committee for a Framework Convention on Climate Change, during its Fifth session, second part, held at New York from 30 April to 9 May 1992. Annex I: Australia, Austria, Belarus, Belgium, Bulgaria, Canada, Croatia★, Czech Republic★, Denmark, European Economic Community, Estonia, Finland, France, Germany, Greece, Hungary, Iceland, Ireland, Italy, Japan, Latvia, Liechtenstein★, Lithuania, Luxembourg, Monaco★, Netherlands, New Zealand, Norway, Poland, Portugal, Romania, Russian Federation, Slovakia★, Slovenia★, Spain, Sweden, Switzerland, Turkey, Ukraine, United Kingdom of Great Britain and Northern Ireland, United States of America. Countries in italics are undergoing the process of transition to a market economy. ★ Countries added to Annex I by an amendment that entered into force on 13 August 1998, pursuant to Decision 4/CP.3 adopted at COP.3. Annex II: Australia, Austria, Belgium, Canada, Denmark, European Economic Community, Finland, France, Germany, Greece, Iceland, Ireland, Italy, Japan, Luxembourg, Netherlands, New Zealand, Norway, Portugal, Spain, Sweden, Switzerland, United Kingdom of Great Britain and Northern Ireland, United States of America. (Turkey was deleted from Annex II by an amendment that entered into force 28 June 2002, pursuant to Decision 26/CP.7 adopted at COP 7.)
54 The concept of historical responsibility in this book generally refers to the contributions made by various countries to the stock of GHGs in the atmosphere. It is often measured in terms of the cumulative emissions by countries and/or groups of countries. A gross approximate can be weighted in terms of a country or group of countries population size relative to their share of the total global population (per capita cumulative emissions). However, scholars are working to refining this. It is currently estimated that since the industrial revolution, developed countries, or Annex I countries with an average share of between 20–25 per cent of the world population, have contributed to about 70–75 per cent of the cumulative emissions and about 69.59 per cent of current concentration of GHG emissions and approximately 75 per cent of the temperature increase, 1850–2007/8 (CAIT-WRI, Tejal Kanitkar *et al.* 2010 and Khor 2010). During the same time period the share of developing countries (non-Annex I), with a population share of about 75 per cent of the global total, was about 28 per cent.

68 The global climate change policy environment

55 The WTO ministerial negotiations process became infamous for its use of so-called green rooms negotiation techniques that selectively and secretly invited groups of countries to form consensus on certain issues, excluding the majority of members. Concern over the disturbing trend moving away from a Party driven process prompted the African Ministerial Conference on the Environment (AMCEN) at its Fourth Special Session (2011) to comment that:

> In many respects, the Climate Change Conference in Cancún helped to reinstate the multilateral process after the Copenhagen Conference, through outcomes under both the Convention and its Kyoto Protocol . . . addressing seemingly 'ripe' issues – such as the establishing of new institutions – in order to rebuild the trust necessary to address more difficult issues . . . At the same time, it raised concerns regarding the transparency and processes that must not be repeated in the future negotiations, such as the tabling of a draft agreement that was eventually adopted at the last hour and put together by the country holding the presidency of the COP. Tackling these issues through a genuinely open, transparent and participatory process in accordance with UN practices must be a central focus in Durban . . .

56 See note 4 above.
57 1992. FCCC/INFORMAL/84 GE.05–62220 (E) 200705.
58 This claim would be more believable if in fact the major emitter, the US, was on board and/or doing its best to contribute to the reduction efforts. Yet, it hypocritically points its fingers at others. The actions of the Obama-led administration in this regard are rather puzzling though not in consistent with their actions in other areas of global governance, such as the WTO, where they are also blocking the process with unrealistic demands of developing countries and the same attempt at obliterating the distinction between developed and developing countries. Being Climate change proponent and in respect for their difficulties at home, the international community has been quite patient with the administration. The expectation is that it would under a tacit understanding of its political reality have a constructive role in the strengthening of the best global architecture with the understanding that it would do its national best and then join in formally at a later date. But that is not what it does; rather it seeks to destroy the architecture to weaken it or rather replace it with a system that is more liken to its national needs not the global needs.
59 The UNEP report concludes that: 'the range of 2020 emission levels from the Copenhagen Accord pledges is consistent with pathways that lead to a likely temperature increases of 2.5 to 5 degrees Celsius up to the end of the twenty-first century.'
60 Para 4 being referred to read as follows:

> Further recognizes that deep cuts in global greenhouse gas emissions are required according to science, and as documented in the Fourth Assessment Report of the Intergovernmental Panel on Climate Change, with a view to reducing global greenhouse gas emissions so as to hold the increase in global average temperature below 2 degrees Celsius above preindustrial levels, and that Parties should take urgent action to meet this long-term goal, consistent with science and on the basis of equity; also recognizes the need to consider, in the context of the first review, as referred to in Paragraph 138 below, strengthening the long-term global goal on the basis of the best available scientific knowledge, including in relation to a global average temperature rise of 1.5 degrees Celsius.

61 From 38 billion tonnes in 1990 to 19.3 billion tonnes in 2050. The G8 (2010) argued that – meaning that developed countries are willing to take an 80 per cent cut by 2050.
62 Remember that the north has already used up more than its fair share of the global emission right to date and is in deficit. Given the global cut of 50 per cent, there would be 19.3 billion tonnes of carbon dioxide equivalent in 2050, then an 80 per cent cut by the north implies use of 3.6 billion tonnes, then developing countries would be left with 15.7 billion tonnes. Ultimately, developing countries would be taking per capita emissions cut below

or the same, (given the base year chosen) as the developed countries. In the case of 100 per cent cut by the developed countries, developing still has to make a 52 per cent per capita cut. A fair cut would be somewhere in the range of 213 per cent by developed countries and cutting emissions to zero and creating sinks to absorb GHGs equivalent to 113 per cent of their 1990 emissions. Note: 1800 to 2050, the world has 600 billion tonnes of emission of carbon (equivalent to around 2,200 billion tonnes of carbon dioxide has its carbon budget. The developed countries have emitted 240 tonnes of carbon, 1800–2008 so they are far above their fair share of 81 billion tonnes. So they have a carbon debt of 159 billion (or 583 billion tonnes of carbon dioxide, from 1800 to 2008 (Khor 2010).

63 The eight Millennium Development Goals (or MDGs), which are to be achieved by 2015, are (please see special insert at end of document for MDG with targets):

Goal 1: Eradicate Extreme Poverty and Hunger
Goal 2: Achieve Universal Education
Goal 3: Promote Gender Equality and Empower Women
Goal 4: Reduce Child Mortality
Goal 5: Improve Maternal Health
Goal 6: Combat HIV/AIDs, Malaria and other Diseases
Goal 7: Ensure Environmental Sustainability
Goal 8: Develop a Global Partnership for Development

MDGs with key targets (1990–2015)

Goal 1: End Poverty and Hunger
Halve the proportion of people living on income of less than $1 a day; Halve the proportion of people who suffer from hunger

Goal 2: Universal Education
Ensure all children – boys and girls alike, are able to complete a full course of primary schooling

Goal 3: Gender Equality
Eliminate gender disparity in primary and secondary education, preferably by 2005, and in all levels of education no later than 2015

Goal 4: Child Health
Reduce by two thirds the under-five mortality rate

Goal 5: Maternal Health
Reduce by three quarters the maternal mortality ratio
Achieve universal access to reproductive health

Goal 6: Combat HIV/AIDs
Halted by 2015 and begun to reverse the spread of HIV/AIDS
Achieve, by 2010, universal access to treatment for HIV/AIDS for all those who need it
Halted by 2015 and begun to reverse the incidence of malaria and other major diseases

Goal 7: Environmental Sustainability
Integrate the principles of sustainable development into country policies and programmes and reverse the loss of environmental resources
Reduce biodiversity loss, achieving, by 2010, a significant reduction in the rate of loss
Halve, by 2015, the proportion of the population without sustainable access to safe drinking water and basic sanitation
By 2020, to have achieved a significant improvement in the lives of at least 100 million slum dwellers

Goal 8: Global Partnership
Address the special needs of least developed countries, landlocked countries and Small Island Developing States
Deal comprehensively with developing countries' debt

64 A description coined by China in describing the attempt by Kyoto Parties to jump ship (Khor 2010).

2
THE ETHICAL, EQUITY AND SOCIAL DEVELOPMENT DIMENSIONS OF GLOBAL CLIMATE CHANGE POLICY

> Temperature rises above 2°C will be difficult for contemporary societies to cope with, and are likely to cause major societal and environmental disruptions through the rest of the century and beyond.
>
> Richardson *et al.* (2009)

> The most severe impact of climate change is being felt by vulnerable populations who have contributed least to the problem. The risk of death or disability and economic loss due to natural disasters is increasing globally and is concentrated in poorer countries.
>
> The Millennium Development Goals Report, United Nations (2010)

This chapter discusses equity and ethics as core principles undergirding the architecture and structuring of the UNFCCC and hence the global climate protection framework, including climate finance. Equity is now acknowledged to be the lynchpin for any attempt to successfully address the climate change issues. However, there are serious contestations about the nature and elaboration of equity including its gender and other social dimensions.

The big picture issues discussed in the preceding chapter have serious consequences for the lives of countless millions of men and women on the ground in developing countries in Africa, Asia, the Caribbean, Latin America and the Pacific. These are the people whose lives are most exposed to the devastating effects of climate change and extreme weather events, and who have the least capacity to respond to the impacts of climate change and climate variability. They also tend to suffer overwhelming, and in some cases irrecoverable, losses and damages given their existing economic state before a climate crisis.

Already it is well known that over 1 billion people live in extreme poverty. The roughly 2.4 billion women, men and children living without reliable access to energy (1.5 billion lack access to electricity) and water are in the developing countries (more than half in Asia). Distinct from the development growth models undergirding the economic growth dynamics of developing countries, about 3 billion people in these countries still rely on traditional forms of fuels such as dung, wood, agricultural residue and charcoal (WHO, cited in UNCTAD 2009). WHO data also shows that in 2003, 74 per cent of the population in developing countries, as compared to 4 per cent of the OECD population, relied on traditional energy sources.

Many of these people, who are women, rural folks, smallholders and subsistent farmers, artisanal fisher folks and coastal dwellers also live in inadequate shelter, lack basic access to sanitation and try to make a living in the most vulnerable areas of their countries. They, as well as millions of their counterparts in the peri-urban and densely packed urban areas of geographically vulnerable countries such as those in Least Developing African Countries and South Asia, Small Islands States of Asia, the Caribbean and the Pacific as well as many countries in Central and Latin America, are also subject to and least able to cope with the devastating effects of sea-level rise, strong winds, floods, storms and droughts.

Thus the global temperature target, peaking year and long-term global goal for emissions reductions are not academic issues incidental to the lives of these girls, boys, women and men. Neither is the question of the actualization of the $100 billion per year by 2020 support to be provided for adaptation and mitigation programmes, projects and policies in developing countries an academic matter to the lives of millions of citizens in developing countries. The setting of the appropriate temperature, the rapid implementation of strategies towards meeting that goal and the equitable sharing of atmospheric and sustainable development space are critical determinants of adaptation requirements and the short term and the long-term prospects for meaningful human economic and social security and the enjoyment of the right to life and sustainable livelihoods with dignity of women, girls, boys and men in developing countries. The availability of adequate climate finance for climate adaptation and protection against loss and damage that does not contribute to rising indebtedness or the shifting of government priorities from poverty eradication and ensuring affordable social services to the financing of climate-related expenditures is of vital interest to the continued progress in women's empowerment, gender equality and gender justice.

These issues are explored in-depth in this chapter. The next section examines the problem that climate change, as an exogenous shock on developing countries' economies, poses for the economic development pathway given the necessity of tackling climate change induced adaptation issues as well as seeking to transform the economy to clean and efficient use of energy. Adaptation imposes a number of constraints on development including the shifting of scare budgetary and domestic resources to climate-proof existing infrastructure as well as to build climate resilient ones while securing access to affordable essential services. What happens when adaptation is not enough? There is the issue of what to do about the losses and damages sustained by the economy as a result of frequent and extreme weather anomalies. Sections 2 and 3 of the chapter tackles head on the ethical issues of in-equality, vulnerability and climate change. The last two sections (sections 4 and 5) continue to delve deeper into the ethical and equity dimensions of climate change by focusing the discussion on the seeming quest by developed countries to legitimize an unjust situation. This occurs in what may appear to be sanitized discussions about emissions gaps in meeting the 2 degree target. But underneath this gap lie other important gaps that will not simply disappear and which are the underlying basis for some of the most serious disagreements between developed and developing countries.

While the emissions gap is readily discussed and widely acknowledged, there is less of an acknowledgement of the development, equity and finance gaps – which constitute the case for a just sharing of the remaining carbon on a preferential basis for all developing countries, including SIDS and LDCs. The question of development space is a fundamental climate (finance) justice. The chapter ends with an overview of the gender and social equity gaps that have long simmered beneath global, regional and national responses to the climate challenges

2.1 The development problématique of climate change adaptation and mitigation

How quickly the temperature target (whether set at 1.5 or 2 degrees Celsius) is achieved has serious material implication for the lives of men and women and children in Africa, Asia and the Caribbean and the Pacific. The setting of a global mean temperature has different implications for warming levels in those regions with rising probabilities of more severe weather events such as droughts, floods and for coastal areas and island, rising sea levels pose serious threats.

The sooner the long-term emissions reduction goal and a peaking year are set and met for developed countries matters for developing countries for sustainable economic development. It has implications for managing the risks of climate change and extreme weather events while attempting to address in a sustainable manner the development deficits that are important for longer term sustainability. The greater the extent to which developing countries must address mitigation actions out of national resources, the lesser the amounts of monies that will be available for adaptation; the more money that has to be spent for adaptation, the less money there may be for meeting social development priorities such as poverty eradication and women's empowerment and gender equality interventions.

The 'numbers issues' discussed in Chapter 1 impact both the quantum and the scale of required financial and other resources. Hence shifting of the burden of mitigation obligations and actions to the developing countries by developed countries has implication at all levels of developing countries' economies. These are not esoteric matters. For citizens of developed countries adjusting to climate change, for the most part, may be a matter of lifestyle adjustments, but this is not the case in any developing countries. For far too many countries, adjusting to climate change is a matter of national survival (for example, the Pacific Island States) and for countless millions of men, women and children in Africa Asia and Latin America and the Caribbean, it is matter of life and death.

Likewise, the financing of climate change, its scale, scope, sources, timely delivery, challenges and constraints have serious implications for poverty eradication, social development and social protection programming in developing countries. To the extent that developing countries either must trade-off national budgetary expenditures from the social sector budgets and channel these funds towards climate change measures, and/or make up for the damages and losses to infrastructure and the livelihoods of women and men caused by climate-related events, this will weaken or retard progress on core development objectives. It will also adversely impact trends toward enhancing social protection and employment generation for women and men living in poor communities. Where the financing of climate change adaptation or mitigation compel developing countries to borrow in order to finance such activities, this will result in rising indebtedness of developing countries. High level of indebtedness will impose further constraints on the fiscal policy space of these countries. Hence progress on promoting gender equality and women's economic and social empowerment may be at risk.

According to the IPCC's special report, *Managing the Risk of Disaster and Extreme Weather Events 2011*, 'from 1970–2008, over 95 per cent of natural-disaster-related deaths occurred in developing countries'. This is compared to the developed countries, where most of the impacts of climate-related events are in the form of property damages. According to WHO, climate change was responsible for around 150,000 fatalities in 2000 (WHO, 2008). The IPCC warns that by 2020, between 75 and 250 million people are projected to be exposed to increased water stress due to climate change and that '*climate-related events* will likely have tremendous negative impact on health systems including causing increases in malnutrition, diseases and injury'.

Almost 18 years after the coming into force of the Climate Convention, increasingly many developing countries are left to rely on 'humanitarian relief to manage climate-related disasters and to absorb the losses and damages resulting from climate and extreme disasters'. It is therefore time, as argued by proponents of the Greenhouse Development rights, that

> the right to development in a climate constrained world ... is tackled head on. ... while people remain poor, it is unacceptable and unrealistic to expect them to focus their valuable resources on the climate change crisis ... others who are wealthier and have enjoyed higher levels of emissions already, must take on their fair share of the effort. ... the global consuming class – both within these countries and especially in the industrialized countries – are the ones who must pay ... were the negotiators to today divide the effort of an adequate global response in a fair way, fully a third of that effort would fall on the shoulders of the US and one-quarter more would go to the European Union.

Undeniably, climate change adds to the multiple challenges facing developing countries. These countries must simultaneously promote economic development that is social development, poverty eradicating and gender equality sensitive while taking rapid and expeditious actions to adapt to climate change and climate variability, build climate resilience and to mitigate climate change. Given developing countries have high vulnerability to climate change risks,[1] there is no option but to pursue both objectives in tandem. Hence both LDCs,[2] such as Bangladesh, Haiti and Mali, lower- and middle-income[3] developing countries in Asia and Latin America (such as India, the Philippines, Thailand, Bolivia, Ecuador, El Salvador and Nicaragua) as well as upper middle and higher-income Caribbean Small Island States (such as, Antigua and Barbuda, the Bahamas and Trinidad and Tobago)[4] will need significant sources of finance and investments. They will need to build climate resilient infrastructure, climate-proof public, private and commercial buildings, build adequate homes for the poor, improve agricultural productivity, ensure irrigation efficiency and make the transformation to a low carbon economy. They will also need resources for enhancing the information and knowledge base of their populations with regard to climate change and its effects as well as to institute early warning systems in flood and disaster prone areas and to raise roads, bridges and other infrastructure in coastal areas. The availability of adequate and predictable short and long-term finance for climate protection activities, therefore, is of paramount importance for developing countries in Africa, Asia, Latin America, the Caribbean and the Pacific.

The 'right to development' assures the importance of developing countries having access to both the necessary atmospheric space and the development space to grow sustainably, to prosper, and to have access to adequate finance for climate-proofing development and covering loss and damages from extreme weather and other effect of climate changes. This should occur through country led/driven adaptation and mitigation measures that support and enhance the process of economic development.

As noted in Chapter 1, on the economic front, there are significant adjustments and implementation costs associated with both adaptation and mitigation strategies. For example, it is estimated that if no action is taken to reduce the impacts of climate change, small island states in the Caribbean could suffer negative impacts to their GDP of 14 per cent by 2025, 39 per cent by 2050, 45 per cent by 2075 and 63 per cent by 2100 (Bueno et al. 2008, cited in Dulal et al. 2009).

Working Group III of the IPCC noted the complex, conflicting and challenging relationship between development and climate change, adaptation and mitigation. It observes that:

> Making development more sustainable can enhance mitigative and adaptive capacities, reduce emissions, and reduce vulnerability . . . Both adaptive and mitigative capacities can be enhanced through sustainable development. Sustainable development can, thereby, reduce vulnerability to climate change by reducing sensitivities (through adaptation) and/or exposure (through

mitigation). At present, however, few plans for promoting sustainability have explicitly included either adapting to climate change impacts, or promoting adaptive capacity. Similarly, changing development paths can make a major contribution to mitigation but may require resources to overcome multiple barriers.

(IPCC 2007)[5]

The key developmental problematique, therefore, in the context of climate change, is a twin one. First, how can developing countries address adaptation and mitigation without sacrificing economic development? Second, which is interrelated with the first, how should developing countries continue to promote poverty eradication, gender equality, social equity and women's empowerment in the face of the high cost of adaptation and mitigation? Explicitly, within these challenges is the issue of how rapidly the de-carbonization of the economies should occur in the transformation from a mainly fossil-fuel based energy source toward a low carbon economy. And who should pay for it.

Development issues must be addressed explicitly and fully within the scope of adaptation and mitigation policies and financing. While development and adaptation are closely linked (Parry *et al.* 2009), mitigation and development can be at odds or antagonistic with each other. Adaptation actions, as noted by the IPCC 2007, have multiple drivers, such as economic development and poverty alleviation, and are embedded within broader development, sectoral, regional and local planning initiatives.[6] Noy (2009) and Bowen *et al.* (2009) argue that there is evidence that higher measures of development indicators such as per capita income, literacy and institutional capacity are associated with lower vulnerability to climate events. Their argument points to an overlap between adaptation and development (Fankhauser 2009), which has led authors such as Schelling (1992) to conclude that 'good development is the best form of adaptation' (cited by Fankhauser 2009: 21). Fankhauser argues that it is therefore 'difficult to delineate where socio-economic development ends and adaptation to anthropogenic climate change begins'[7] (ibid.).

Adaptation, in so much as it, 'involves protection and strengthening of current activities, has more immediate synergy with development, as it often involves protection of public health, conservation of farmland, and improvements in disaster preparedness'[8] (Ackerman 2009: 16). Mitigation actions around renewable energy and new technologies can alter the trajectory of economic development. If its financing evinces trade-off between economic and social development or distorts development priorities, then there are no positive synergies. But if mitigation actions facilitate sustainable development, then there will be significant co-benefits for both the economy and climate change. This positive inter-linkage is advocated for by the IPCC which envisions a two-way intertwine between sustainable development and climate change: 'sustainable development can reduce vulnerability to climate change, and climate change could impede nations' abilities to achieve sustainable development pathways.'[9] Or, as Ackerman so aptly puts it, 'economic development, if carefully managed, can increase resilience, promote adaptation, and reduce climate impacts' (Ackerman 2009: 18).

The reality, however, is vastly different from these expectations. Currently, the financing of climate change is biased towards mitigation projects, adaptation has been left behind and when support is proffered, it seeks to segment or isolate adaptation from development. So contrary to the dictates of the global policy architecture, in practice development and adaptation, in particular, have become contested terrains. The reality is that there is a quite significant adaptation deficit in the actual outcome and patterns of global financial and investment flows. Parry et al. (2009) argues that this adaptation deficit, which is due to low levels of investment, is really a development deficit that needs to be filled as a matter of urgency if climate change goals are to be kept on track (Parry et al. 2009).

So ostensibly, on two grounds climate finance is not the same as traditional development aid. It should not be offered out of charity, humanitarian or security motives but, in the case of adaptation and loss and damage, financing is, in fact, compensation for damage to the climate system caused by the developmental processes of the OECD countries. Second climate finance is also payment for the overutilization of the earth's resources and support for the mitigation actions (sacrifice in development) that developing countries must now endure in order to help to stabilize the climate system, while at the same time eradicating poverty and ensuring access to modern energy services and the resources necessary for the self-realization of the men, women and children in developing countries.

Undoubtedly, many developing countries, particularly in Asia and Latin America, have grown rapidly in the past 20 years and many milestones have been reached: poverty has decreased dramatically in some countries (Bangladesh, China, Rwanda, and Vietnam) and its depth and severity reduced modestly or significantly in others such as Bolivia, Guatemala, El Salvador, Ghana and Uganda.[10] But these successful achievements and forward progress are all under threat with the damaging effects of climate change and variability. Extreme weather such as floods, droughts, and tropical cyclones are now becoming increasingly prevalent in all regions. Already farmers in the southern Indian state of Andhra Pradesh are under threat from inadequate rainfall, which has decimated harvest of groundnut. In the Caribbean, men and women living in rich and poor islands alike such as Trinidad and Tobago, St Lucia and Jamaica are dealing with droughts and dry seasons, and the consequential water rationing, which they hope will only be temporary features of daily life but which may in fact become persistent day-to-day challenges. Further, the World Bank warns that the direct impacts of climate will further impede developing countries' abilities to sustain all MDGs through their indirect effects on education, child mortality, maternal health and women's empowerment.

The extent to which climate change (variability and extremes) can negatively impact the livelihoods, assets and savings of men and women in developing countries depends, in the first case, on the degree and timing of successful mitigation of global emissions, and, in the second case, on the successful implementation of anti-poverty programmes that reinforce adaptation strategies at the economy wide and sectoral levels in developing countries. It is important that the financing of adaptation and mitigation helps to bolster social and economic development, including poverty eradication and the promotion of equity. Efforts to transform economies to low carbon pathways and increasing climate resilience are linked, for developing countries, to the nature scope and scale of financing available both from internal and external sources.

2.2 Inequality, vulnerability and climate change

Unfortunately, due to lack of adequate social and economic development (such as inferior quality of housing, minimal or inferior public health care infrastructure, and high levels of informal and temporary employment and resource dependency) the lives of millions of poor women and men in developing countries are more at risk of the human generated causes of climate change. These are often the women and men with the least stock of assets and access to insurance and other financial instruments to be able to respond effectively in a climate crisis and to resume their normal lives after exposure to droughts, floods and storms (Box 2.1). In times of rising heat or warming episodes poor men and women may not have access to cooling equipment such as air conditioners or refrigeration to help protect themselves and their resources (Bueno *et al.* 2008).

Of the hundreds of people killed during the 2005 South Asia heat waves, most were women and children and poor males, especially farmers and day labourers. These victims of climate-related disaster often die due to lack of available social resources such as clean water or medicine. For example, the South Asian heat waves dried up the available water sources, which were not offset by readily available potable water. Women and children suffered from diarrhoea and dehydration (BBC 2005; Chiang 2007). Poor men, such as rickshaw pullers, daily wage labourers, subsistence farmers and others who worked outdoors, died or became severely affected by heat waves. In addition, cyclones in Bangladesh, earthquakes in China, Haiti and Chile and droughts in India also caused deaths and injuries to millions of rural and urban dwellers in those countries.

Though the majority of deaths and damages occur in the developing world, industrialized countries have also been affected. Super Storm Sandy, Hurricane Katrina and excessive heat waves in Europe and North America have been implicated in the loss of lives and livelihoods. The European heat waves of summer 2003 are reported to have killed between 22,000 and 35,000, many of whom were elderly (Epstein 2005; Kosatsky 2003). Likewise, heat waves in the US (2006 and 1995, Chicago) also killed hundreds of people (IPS 2009).

In addition to causing injuries and deaths, extreme weather events and other climate events such as droughts, desertification, flooding and sea level rises) may leave people homeless and destitute, contributing to the growing challenge of 'climate refugees'. Climate refugees are generally thought of as persons who leave their homes and communities as result of climate induced factors. As such climate refugees form part of broader grouping of what some researchers such as

> **BOX 2.1 CLIMATE CHANGE, POVERTY, VULNERABILITY AND FOOD SECURITY**
>
> Through extreme or prolonged stress, climate variability and change can affect the quality, quantity, and reliability of many of the services natural resources provide. This in turn has a critical impact on food intake, health, and livelihoods of poor people. Climate variability can fundamentally drive processes of impoverishment through direct and indirect routes (IRI 2005).
>
> - *Direct*: Severe or repeated climate shocks can push vulnerable households into a persistent poverty trap when their individual coping responses involve divestment of productive assets such as land or livestock.
>
> - *Indirect*: Climate uncertainty causes inability to anticipate when climatic extremes will occur, which acts as a disincentive to investment, innovation, and development interventions at the same time, poverty increases vulnerability to climate change by reducing options. The poor are typically forced to live in marginal lands (e.g. flood-prone, degraded soil, etc.) and in living conditions which 'are predisposing conditions to ill health'. This includes low quality housing (e.g. lack of screen doors), bad sanitation, and unprotected sources of drinking water, which juxtaposed with under nourishment and deficient health care, makes them highly prone to vector- and water-borne diseases. The poor are generally dependent on subsistence activities involving extraction of natural resources, which are vulnerable to climate change. Most importantly, there is little accumulation of assets to draw on in times of stress.
>
> Source: UNDP (2007)

El-Hinnawi defined as environmental refugees, 'people who have been forced to leave their traditional habitat, temporarily or permanently, because of a marked environmental disruption (natural and/or triggered by people) that jeopardized their existence and/or seriously affected the quality of their life'[11] (WorldWatch Institute and El Hinnawi 1985).

While there is no agreed definition of a climate refugee and there is ongoing debate about accounting for and tracking such persons, it is generally acknowledged in both migration and climate literature that sudden or rapid-onset events (floods, mud/landslide, hurricanes, cyclones, fires and tornadoes) as well as incremental or slow-onset environmental changes (extreme weather, rising temperatures, increased droughts, desertification and sea-level rises) can negatively affect livelihood systems, food production and food security, thereby inducing mobility and changing patterns of migration (Holmes 2008; Everland 2009). Slow onset events may adversely impact the ability to diversify household income. Such events also may cause decline in agricultural yields of farming, loss of herds and lack of access to productive fishing areas (ACCES 2010), while rapid onset events may contribute to dramatic and sometimes irreversible loss of assets and shelter.

Ultimately, whether slow- or rapid-onset, climate change 'reduces resources for livelihood which will lead to conflict (and under certain conditions (such as in the arid or semi-arid areas) may lead to armed conflicts) over remaining resources and, as a result, to intensified (temporary or permanent migration flows' (Ashton 2005). Antonio Guterres, the UN High Commissioner for Refugees, 2009 argues passionately that climate change can enhance competition for resources, water, food, grazing lands and that such competition can trigger conflict. Walter Kälin, the former representative of the UN Secretary-General on the human rights of internally displaced persons (2008), has identified five climate change-related scenarios that may directly or indirectly cause human displacement (Box 2.2). These are useful in elaborating some of the risks and vulnerabilities of climate change for the women and men in very poor developing countries. Box 2.3 highlights some issues around gender and climate refugees.

According to UNHCR over the last two decades the number of recorded natural disasters has risen from 200 natural disasters per year to over 400 per year; and nine out of ten of every such recent natural disaster have recently been identified as being climate-related (UNHCR 2009). Elverland (2009) reported that 20 million people may have been displaced by climate induced sudden onset in 2008 alone. UNHCR reported 36 million in 2009 and the International Federation of Red Cross estimates 25 to 50 million people are climate refugees today. Scientists predict that this number may rise to as high as 200 million by 2050. Worldwide more than one billion people live in low-lying regions (WorldWatch 2013). It is estimated that between

BOX 2.2 CLIMATE CHANGE AND HUMAN DISPLACEMENT

Climate-related scenarios directly or indirectly linked as causal factors in human displacement include:

- Hydro-meteorological disasters (flooding, hurricanes/typhoons/cyclones, mudslides, etc.)
- Zones designated by governments as being too high-risk and dangerous for human habitation
- Environmental degradation and slow onset disaster (e.g. reduction of water availability, desertification, recurrent flooding, salinization of coastal zones, etc.)
- The case of 'sinking' small island states
- Violent conflict triggered by a decrease in essential resources (e.g. water, land, food) owing to climate change.

Source: adapted from Kälin (2008)

> **BOX 2.3 GENDER AND CLIMATE REFUGEE**
>
> Though no rigorous data set has been analysed, it is generally thought that women constitute a high proportion of climate refugees and suffer from particular gender differentiated issues. A 2011 report for the EU Parliament argues that this is because of the gendered impact of climate change and environmental degradation on women in terms of 'their roles caregivers and attitudes that influence family decisions';* access to resources, mobility and other social constraints and biases.
>
> It is also the case as noted by the same EU Parliament Report that women 'are also affected by environmentally induced migration when they are not migrating themselves'. In particular, male out-migration often results in increased workloads for the women left behind.
>
>> The access to financial resources is also a core variable in the construction of vulnerability as this determines the ability to migrate. In many cases climate change affects disproportionally poor agrarian communities which have not the financial means to leave their home or resources may further decline due to climate and environmental change which may result in a decreasing number of people having the ability to migrate
>> (Pratikshya Bohra-Mishra, Ulisses E.C. Confalonieri 2011, pp.74–101; Tacoli 2009, p.4 cited in EU Parliament 2011)
>
> * For instance for earlier evacuation (Hunter and David 2011: 324)

286 million and up to 400 million of these people may be at risk for flooding and storm surges and extreme flooding by 2030, 2060, respectively (IPCC 2014).

Regardless of the debate about classifying, monitoring and tracking climate refugees or their lack of legal status, the reality is that climate change can wreak havoc on the lives of those most vulnerable destroying their assets and lives and livelihood. Climate change also has it most iniquitous impacts on those most vulnerable to its effect either because of economic, gender, other social or ethnic biases and marginalization. This is true for the poorest of the poor whether in a developed countries or developing countries.

In the southern US, Hurricane Katrina devastated the lives of thousands of African Americans and poor white men and women, boys and girls.[12] Box 2.4 highlights some of the challenges and constraints faced by the victims of Katrina. In some cases, the heavy rain that accompanies hurricanes may also trigger mudslides. Hurricane Mitch, for example, killed over 5,000 women, men and children and left about 1.5 million homeless in Honduras in 1998 (USAID 2009) and the 2010 floods in Pakistan left almost 6 million men, women and children homeless.

Rapid onset of reconstruction engenders rapid return of people. After the 1995 Kobe earthquake in Japan: 83 per cent or 250,000 of the 300,000 persons returned

> **BOX 2.4 POOR AND LOW-INCOME BLACKS IMPACTED THE WORST BY HURRICANE KATRINA 2005**
>
> Hurricane Katrina hit the Gulf coast of the US (Louisiana, Texas, and Mississippi) late August 2005. Leaving in its wake:
>
> - Death toll/fatalities of between 1,200 and 1,300
> - Almost $200 billion worth of damage
> - 90 per cent of resident of South East Louisiana evacuated
> - 80 per cent of the city of New Orleans flooded
>
> It created a gigantic humanitarian crisis for thousands of black Americans.
>
> The most impacted were the poor, the elderly and the sick, the majority of whom were black American. Tens of thousands of blacks were marooned in the city after it became flooded (even as a reported hundreds of local school buses parked idly), because they had:
>
> - No personal vehicle (27 per cent of New Orleans without own transportation)
> - No money and no jobs (38 per cent poverty rate, one of the highest in the nation)
> - No social capital
>
> Thousands of black Americans lost everything and had no insurance. Thousands were and remain displaced. ('New Orleans is now at the risk of losing more than 80 per cent of its black population, Brown University)
>
> Source: *Journal of Blacks in Higher Education*

within 3 months of the disaster due to rapid onset of reconstruction. Compared to the 1991 Mount Minatuba eruption in the Philippines: several years after the event people are still in temporary camps or squatter settlements (Castles 2002). These different outcomes occur because developed countries have resources to prepare for and to respond to and recover from the effects of climate change.

The 2011 Human Development Report (UNDP 2010c) shows a direct link between low Human Development Index (HDI) and vulnerability to climate change. It also shows that 'household environmental deprivation in the form of indoor air pollution, inadequate access to clean water and improved sanitation are more severe at low HDI levels and declines as the HDI rises' (ibid.: 4). Poor and marginalized men and women make up the majority of those living in vulnerable areas in low HDI countries.

The IPCC Special Report also points to the critical interaction between social development and vulnerability and exposure to disaster risks: 'Socioeconomic development interacts with natural climate variations and human-caused climate change to influence disaster risk' (IPCC 2011).

TABLE 2.1 Carbon dioxide emissions per tonne per capita, 2009

Country	2009 CO_2 emissions per capita tonnes
World average	4.49
Africa	1.13
China	5.83
Brazil	2.11
India	1.38
Virgin Islands★	113.71
Trinidad & Tobago★	38.88
Singapore★	34.59
Australia	19.64
US	17.67
Canada	16.15
Germany	9.30
South Africa	9.18
UK	8.35
Japan	8.64
Argentina	4.08
Chile	3.96
Bolivia	1.42
Jamaica★	4.29
Ecuador	1.97
Malaysia	5.32
Thailand	3.80
Pakistan	0.77
Philippines	0.74
Bangladesh	0.36
Kenya	11.50
Zimbabwe	10.61
Cameroon	0.40
Ghana	0.34
Ethiopia	0.08
Democratic Republic of the Congo	0.04

Source: data from International Energy Statistics (2011)

Poor men and women, both in the developed countries, and most especially those that live in developing countries, have the lowest carbon footprints. It is the rich countries and rich individuals in developing countries who have benefited most from the factors and processes that have led to the current crisis. The carbon dioxide emissions for India and sub-Saharan African countries average between 0.04 (the DRC) and 1.38 (India) per tonne, per capita in 2009 relative to 17.67, 16.15 and 19.64 for the US, Canada and Australia, respectively (Table 2.1). Likewise, Caribbean countries contribute only 0.2 per cent of global CO_2 emissions but have been suffering from severe extreme weather events resulting in about $11 billion in insured losses in the region in 2008 alone (Bueno et al. 2008).

Undeniably, the growing climate crisis is impacting the lives of the less fortunate the most. There is therefore need for rebalancing. This can only come about through some form of climate equity – climate justice. Globally, as discussed in Chapter 1, it must be the case that the rich countries pay or compensate the poorer countries for their over-use of the atmosphere, since now the poor countries must be involved in the shared burden of regulating GHG emissions by sacrificing some of their growth prospects. For example, reliable access to 4,000 kilowatt hours of energy is correlated with a decent human development. But many Asian people have access to about 2,500 with the poorest having as little access as 400 (World Energy.Org 2011). Sanitation coverage in developing countries rose from 43 per cent in 1990 to 54 per cent in 2008 (World Bank 2010). Currently, about 63 per cent of the world's population now has improved sanitation access , a system that 'hygienically separates human excreta from human contact', such as flush or pour-flush to a piped sewer system, septic tank or pit latrine, ventilated improved pit latrine (VIP), pit latrine with slab or composting toilet (WHO/UNICEF 2012), but the global MDG target (number 7) of achieving 75 per cent coverage of people with improved sanitation access by 2015 will be missed.[13] In sub-Saharan Africa, the proportion of the population with access to improved sanitation rose from 27 per cent in 1990 to 30 per cent in 2010. In South Asia access rose when it rose from 22 per cent in 1990 to 41 per cent in 2010 (World Bank 2010; WHO/UNICEF 2012). Nevertheless, there still remains a significant proportion of people in developing countries without sanitation. Each new extreme event causes backward movement in the efforts to improve the social development conditions in these countries.

Since the absolute trade-off in curtailing development growth by transforming to a low carbon economy may mean doing with less by those who already have less and are living at the margin, climate change poses an enormous challenge to development and poverty reduction (World Bank 2010). As noted by the World Bank, the need to respond to climate change makes development even more urgent, since this is the most effective way to increase climate resilience. Yet climate change also makes development more costly, as additional investments are needed to adapt to climate uncertainties (World Bank 2010). The transformation to a low carbon pathway can occur only if there is a transfer of resources from rich countries to poor countries to facilitate their clean growth and sustainable development (World Bank 2010).

This transfer of resources to developing countries is important not just for mitigation effort but is even more important for undertaking the necessary and critically important adaptation actions for responding to the negative effects of climate change. This transfer of resources from rich to poor countries is necessary because of the scientific evidence that the anthropogenic factors attributed to the climate change problem are the burning of fossil fuels since industrialization. The growth and accumulation of wealth, high standard of living and strong infrastructure that accompanied this process has primarily benefited the developed countries with the losses and high costs of the environmental and other climate-related challenges now being borne by the developing countries. This raises the highly political charged issue of climate debt and climate justice.

Every human being as a matter of birth-right is entitled to his or her fair share of the global atmospheric space. As a result of historical and socio-economic inequality, citizens in developed and rich countries have, as a group, used up more than their fair share of the global atmospheric space and they will continue to have need for more of the remaining share of carbon space.

There is high agreement and 'robust evidence' in the scientific literature reviewed by the IPCC that (i)nequalities influence local coping and adaptive capacity, and pose disaster risk management and adaptation challenges from the local to national levels. It is also the case that these inequalities reflect socioeconomic, demographic, and health-related differences and differences in governance, access to livelihoods, entitlements, and other factors (IPCC 2011).

For example, as pointed out by the World Energy Council,

> On average, the poorest 2.5 billion people in the world use only 0.2 toe per capita annually while the billion richest people use 5 toe per capita per year, which is 25 times more. In terms of electricity consumption, the richest 20 per cent uses 75 per cent of all electricity while the poorest 20 per cent uses less than 3 per cent.

As a result of inequality, undeniably, 'developed countries are often better equipped financially and institutionally to adopt explicit measures to effectively respond and adapt to projected changes in exposure, vulnerability, and climate extremes than developing countries' (IPCC 2011).

Under the Convention, a climate regulation instrument, the underlying basis of which was the active intervention and leadership of the developed countries, developed countries agreed to the fundamental principles of equity expressed in terms of common but differentiated responsibility and respective capacity. While there was some unwillingness and reservation by some countries in the initial discussion, without a doubt the core principles of the Convention derive from the scientific evidence that that shows the historical responsibility of developed countries with respect to the causes of anthropogenic climate change and the economic and political reality of the differential abilities of developing countries to respond to climate extremes and disasters. Developed countries therefore committed to take the lead in reducing their own emissions at home in order to stabilize the climate. They also committed to finance the adaptation needs as well as to take into account the negative effects of response measures on developing countries. They also knew at that time and accepted that developing countries must have the right to development (which is not the same as the right to pollute), the right to secure the basic human security essentials of clean water, basic sanitation, access to clean modern energy services and food security for their population.

This reality has not changed significantly since 1992. Yet today a sort of predatory consciousness has pervaded climate change negotiations. This includes a seeming willingness to let the poor in developing countries sacrifice increasingly more of their development opportunities as well as their entitlements to the atmosphere in order to promote mitigation efforts and maintain the competitiveness of developed countries vis-à-vis the so-called rising growth of some developing countries, namely Brazil, China and South Africa. This is occurring even while the rich countries have not significantly addressed their own lifestyle, consumption and production patterns.

The widely stated intentions of Annex I parties, in particular the US, is to end the distinction (differentiation) now explicit between developed and developing countries in terms of historical responsibility for climate change and the obligations and responsibility for mitigation and initial actions and continuing to stabilize the climate system. The US negotiators who call for 'modernization' of and 'symmetry' in the Convention like to make the argument that differentiation needs to be transformed to account for the fact that developing countries now and in the future will account for the lion share of emissions. The US emphasizes future responsibility, but they ignore the fact that they have yet to honour their obligations regarding responsibility for over 70 per cent of GHG now in the atmosphere, which is creating havoc in the lives of millions of men and women in the developing countries. Furthermore, the US has never accepted to play its role (to undertake comparability of efforts with the Parties to the Kyoto Protocol. Tod Stern, the US climate envoy has argued that 'for differentiation to support our mutual, overarching commitment to ambition, it must be based on the real and material circumstances of countries in the period covered by the agreement – in this case, the 2020s and beyond'. But this is a not a very good argument.

The Convention, its principles and commitment were all based on very real material circumstances arising from the development paths and fossil-fuel utilization of Annex I countries, which led to the present problem. These countries became rich and continue to benefit abundantly and they need to accept their responsibilities. The developing countries, be they the large and growing nations, such as China, India and Brazil or small island states, such as Jamaica and Nauru or LDCs such as Burkina Faso, did not create the problems and they have incomes that are significantly less than the incomes of the developed countries as well as an overabundance of poverty-stricken men and women lacking adequate access to water, sanitation and modern energy services. So if, as the US claims, differentiation between countries and their climate ambitions must be based on the real and material circumstances of countries in the period covered by the agreement, this cannot simply hold for the 2020s and beyond (when developing countries are projected to be the major emitters). The US's energy need, as with the other developed countries, is still reliant on and dominated by strong coal or oil sectors with many states still heavily reliant on electricity generated by energy sourced from coal, natural gas and petroleum.

2.3 Ethical dimensions of climate change policy

Every man, women and child has a right, an entitlement, to atmospheric space. No group of people or country deserve more than others. This fact must register indelibly in the consciousness of those in developed countries that have over-used and damaged the atmosphere leaving the majority of people on the planet with very little remaining atmospheric space to grow. Stern argues that:

> In the case of the ... 'contents of the atmosphere', it is hard to think of an argument as to why rich people should have more of this shared resource than poor people. They are not exchanging their labour for somebody else's and they are not consuming the proceeds of their own land, or some natural resource that lies beneath it.
>
> (Stern 2006)

Presently the top 20 per cent of the world's population absorb 80 per cent of its natural resources (World Bank 2003; World Resource Institute 2009). At the same time, as noted by Fujii (1991) and Bos *et al.* (1994), the developed countries have contributed to '85.9 per cent of the increase in atmospheric concentration of carbon dioxide since 1800, and 73.6 per cent of current carbon dioxide emissions in 1987, while their population share is only approximately 21 per cent'.[14] Despite their obligation to reduce emissions, developed countries have increased their emissions by 11.2 per cent in the period from 1990 to 2007 (Cochamba People's Accord).[15]

This point to a need for reallocation and global distribution of emission rights and obligations as well as compensation for losses and adjustment burdens thereby incurred to those adversely impacted by the resulting outcome. This to some degree is a matter that has been mooted in the negotiations context in the form of equitable sharing of the atmospheric space, carbon debt, 'climate debt' and 'climate justice' in proposals and policy documents by countries from Central America and Asian countries such as the Republic of Bolivia, Malaysia, Paraguay and Pakistan.[16] For well over 10 years many small island nations have been arguing for the recognition of 'loss and damage' as an area of accountability that goes beyond adaptation. They have been calling for an international mechanism on loss and damage. Recognition of this area has been very slow in coming but there was some conditional acceptance of this framework though an unwillingness to see it independently of adaptation (primarily by the US). Despite this the Warsaw International Mechanism on Loss and Damage was launched in 2013. The details are still being elaborating and given the developed countries concern about the liability and financial implications, will likely take another couple of years to conclude.

Inherent in this discussion around North–South imbalance, is that the North pays for and subsidizes the South's climate change transformation to a low carbon economy. It is typically argued that the North should pay the extra cost of climate change mitigation (Athanasiou and Bear 2005). Developing countries have consistently maintained that the developed countries compensate for 'overuse of environmental space' (Athanasiou and Bear 2005). To a certain extent some elements of this argument have been captured quite explicitly in the UNFCCC. The Convention recognized the responsibility of the developed countries for

TABLE 2.2 Comparison of per capita principle, HR and SD approach to equity as aspects of equitable access to sustainable development

Per capita principle	Historical responsibility	Sustainable development
Key focus: Equity and size	*Key focus:* Long lived nature of GHGs★	*Key focus:* Capability and indicators of sustainable development are important.
Justification: Distinguish between nations of different sizes (larger nations need proportionately greater amounts of carbon space) is important.	*Justification:* Current concentration of GHGs in the atmosphere is a result of past emissions since the beginning of the industrial revolution. Current challenges are the result of past interference with the climate system.	*Justification:* Sustainability cannot simply be about pursuing a low carbon pathway of development; it must include eradicating poverty and erasing development deficits.
Features: Equity – Per capita allocation based on cumulative emissions (not flows). Principle of carbon equity in allocating global carbon budget. Share global budget in equal per capita distribution of cumulative emission, inclusive of emissions in the past and future emission	*Features:* Current activities will impact the future climate. Limit to growth (even though necessary will impact developing countries development. Climate change imposes extra burden on developing countries. Developed countries are responsible for this extra burden. Developed countries must take the lead in mitigation effort.	*Features:* Adherence to the principles of the Convention: Article 3.1 – responsibility and capability to protect the climate system and 3.4: Right to development. Mitigation action is based on historical responsibility for emissions and capability to mitigate in terms of GDP and level of development.
Cross-linkages: Historical responsibility – in terms of accumulative emissions of each nation	*Cross-linkages:* Equity – Contribution of parties to global average temperature increases (not just emissions flows) is important	BASIC's proponent: South Africa
BASIC's Proponents: China and India	BASIC's proponent: Brazil	

Source: data from BASIC (2011)

★ As opposed to urban atmospheric pollution or water contamination) – With such cases of short-lived pollutants, emissions is a good measure of both the responsibility of polluters and the level of mitigation needed. But this is not the case with GHGs which can have effects lasting up to 1,000 years.

BOX 2.5 HISTORICAL ACCOUNTABILITY AND HISTORICAL RESPONSIBILITY AND GLOBAL CLIMATE POLICY

> States shall cooperate in a spirit of global partnership to conserve, protect and restore the health and integrity of the earth's ecosystem. In view of the different contributions to global environmental degradation, States have common but differentiated responsibilities. The developed countries acknowledge the responsibility that they bear in the international pursuit of sustainable development in view of the pressures their societies place on the global environment and of the technologies and financial resources they command.
>
> (Rio Declaration, Principle 7)

Why historical responsibility should not be ignored

On the most basic level, science is on the side of historical accountability. It is undisputed that global warming is a consequence of the increased concentration of GHGs in the atmosphere, which is a function of emissions that accumulated over time. To neglect historical accountability is therefore tantamount to ignoring the physical laws that give rise to the environmental problem of global warming.

Ignoring historical accountability would give a retrospective licence to past emitters from developed countries to disadvantage the poorer countries. This would clearly violate Principle 21 of the Declaration of the 1972 United Nations Conference on the Human Environment in Stockholm which postulates that nation-states' 'sovereign right to exploit their own resources' is subject to not causing 'damage to the environment of other states or of areas beyond the limits of national jurisdiction' (Molitor 1991: 83). This principle has been reiterated in the preamble to the UNFCCC (1992).

Historical accountability is supported by the principle of equality of opportunity. The natural absorptive capacity of the planet earth that allows for the decay of a certain amount of greenhouse gas emissions truly belongs to nobody and should therefore be equally assigned to everybody in order to give everybody equal opportunity to benefit from emissions . . . To account for historical emissions ensures equality of opportunity to use the global resource atmosphere, no matter where or when he or she happens to live.

> To ignore historical accountability would mean to privilege those who lived in the past in the developed countries and to discriminate against those who live in the present or will live in the future developing countries.
>
> Eric Neumayer (2000)

climate change. The fact that there was no mandated reciprocal obligations for emissions reductions required of developing countries coupled with mandated obligations around financing and technology to those from the industrialized countries are explicit recognition of the underlying equity and historical responsibility and historical accountability principles.

Equity issues arise from the unequal distribution and utilization of the earth's natural resources and the historical and continuing disparate emissions levels between developing and developed countries, notwithstanding the rising emissions of China, India and Brazil. The specific nature of the historical responsibilities, accountability and obligations continue to be source of tension between the two groups (Table 2.2). The historical responsibility principle was more recently confirmed by the Conference of Parties in the preamble to the section on mitigation commitments or actions of Annex I parties, the decision of the 15th Conference of Parties in Cancún (2010): 'Acknowledging that the largest share of historical global emissions of GHGs originated in developed countries and that, owing to this historical responsibility, developed country parties must take the lead in combating climate change and the adverse effects thereof.'

Historical accountability takes into account historical inequalities in per capita emissions. Implicitly it gives every human being an equal share of the global resource atmosphere, independent of place or time.

In many ways, the UNFCCC seems quite a remarkable document. It completely eschews any retrogressive requirement about 'reciprocity' (same level of effort) wholly and without reservation. (However, increasingly this element is slowing and pervasively creeping into the negotiations, as noted below.) The problems have been in specifying targets and establishing a base year for calculating emissions reductions.[17] Developed countries are relatively comfortable with setting a cut-off date somewhere in the 1990s and putting greater emphasis on 'future responsibility', which necessarily implicates developing countries who still need to grow, while alternating disingenuously between de-emphasizing their own historical responsibility or trying to cap their historical accountability at a mere 'goal of mobilizing $100 billion of long-term finance from various sources' (Cancún 2010). But from a strict equity perspective, 1990s' levels are significantly off the mark if a proper accounting of historical responsibility and accountability is to be taken on board and the question of equitable sharing of the remaining atmospheric space and emission rights justly addressed. It is clear by all the various budgeting approaches (discussed below) that the current emissions reduction (and financing) by developed countries is woefully insufficient to the meet the climate challenges at hand.

The issue of historical responsibility and historically accountability for climate change is central to the discussion and stalemate in the current climate negotiations. It also under-girds the flow of finance and the scale and scope of this finance under the climate change finance architecture. (See Boxes 2.4 and 2.5 for expanded treatment of these concepts.) Explicit issues are of course around the three ethical principles underlying the Convention and which permeate developing countries' position: the polluter pays principle (PPP), the principle of equality and the precautionary principle. These are the critical underpinning of Common but differentiate responsibility and respective capacities that makes for the critical differentiation among UNFCCC Parties in term so of mitigation responsibility and the one-way flow of finance and technology transfer and development.

Under the PPP, which is well established in international and national environmental law and policies, the developed countries have the responsibility to cut their own emissions and undertake the deepest possible cuts as well as compensate the victims (in this case developing countries) for the injurious side-effects of the long march of the developed countries to industrialization. In the global climate policy arena the issue is what is the most appropriate time frame for the period of historical accountability (in other words, as stated by the BASIC experts, 'how to carry forward historical accountability of developed countries for their contribution to the average global temperature increase[18] from an emissions or a carbon budgeting perspective').

Given the urgency of the matter and that scientific studies argue persuasively that time is running out (the remaining atmospheric space is greatly constrained), many scientists, among others, argue in favour of a global carbon budget. But that budget must be equitably determined if it is to be acceptable (WBGU 2009; BASIC 2011). Such a budget must explicitly take into account the historical emissions of developed countries as a starting point. Further, the peaking year for emissions must be different as between developed and developing countries, as the latter as yet to achieve significant social and economic development (South Centre 2010). Developed countries (Annex I) must peak first, drastically cutting their emissions reductions in a sustainable manner, given their financial and technological capacities and capabilities.

There are various approaches around the establishment of a global carbon budget and the apportioning of the remaining carbon space between and among countries and regions. This has to be done equitably. So it is not the case that the remaining carbon space can simply be divided on a per capita or per country basis among countries without taking into account that developed countries have used up more than their fair share of the atmospheric resources. Nor can the developed countries simply choose, as they are wont to do, any arbitrary reductions goal. The residual of whatever such choice is selected must be made by developing countries. This will allow developed countries to claim a greater share of the remaining atmospheric space than they are entitled to. Such a distribution of the atmospheric space will further leave developing countries with even less development space than they have now. This is neither a just or a fair way of allocating emissions rights.

The fact is that given the over-use of the global atmospheric resource, developing countries are not able to take advantage of their entitlement even if accounting wise they are in surplus (as shown in Tables 2.6–2.8 and Box 2.5). There is just not enough carbon space remaining, given past emissions rate and current technological capacities. To date, as noted in Chapter 1, most of the pro-

$$NAI = global - AI$$
$$\downarrow$$
AI = Global − NAI

FIGURE 2.1 Turning around the formula

posed reductions options work to the disadvantage of the developing countries and privileges the developed countries. As argued by the BASIC's expert group, the present formula should be reversed: Annex I should take on the residual after accounting from the total atmospheric space for developing countries' share ('with substantial deviation below baseline and lower assessed stabilization level achieved to avoid the worst impacts') of the remaining atmospheric space (Figure 2.1). It cannot be the other way around in a world conditioned by and committed to the values of equity, human rights and justice.

Many developed countries' proponents such as the German Advisory Council on Global Change (WBGU), tend to favour a more recent starting year, such as the 1990s, for the start period of the historical accounting and some form of discounting. On the other hand, it is in the interest of developing countries to argue for a much earlier date as possible. On an ideal and pure justice perspective, that date should likely be somewhere in the mid-to late 1800s or early 1900s. But political feasibility points to something closer to the modern period as in the approach taken by some of the BASICs' expert group who posit a start date in the 1970s.

WBGU's 2009 report, *Solving the Climate Dilemma: the Budget Approach*, discussed two 'policy options for implementing the budget Approach. Option 1: historical responsibility and option 2: future responsibility. Both have the same ending date, 2050,[19] but different start dates for the budget period, are replicated in Tables 2.3 and 2.4. Option 1 proposes to include developed countries' historical responsibility from 1990–2050 with the justification that 1990 was the year of the first Assessment Report of the IPCC hence that was when all the countries became fully aware of the problem of climate change and its human induced causal factors. Option 2 looks at the budgeting with an eye towards the 'future responsibility' of both developed and developing countries.

Working with the population shares of both groups of countries and a 75 per cent probability of complying with the 2 degrees Celsius 'guard rail' of the Cancún Decision, the total cumulative emissions budget for the period 1990–2050 is 1,100 Gt CO_2.[20] Based on the polluter pays principle, retroactively (for the historical responsibility of the developed countries), and the estimated 2008 emissions of both groups of countries, WBGU estimated the budget life-time for each countries. The data show that the US, Germany and Russia have emitted more than they would have been entitled to and are effectively 'carbon bankrupt'. Japan will also soon exhaust its budget. All developing countries have positive balances in their national budget accounts. However, WBGU argues that this situation would be 'politically difficult to carry through as it would greatly limit the industrialized countries' scope

TABLE 2.3 The WBGU budget approach option 1: historical responsibility, 1990–2050

	Share of world population, 1990 (%)	Total budget 1990–2050 (Gt CO_2)	Emissions (consumption) to date 1990–2009 (Gt CO_2)	Residual (remaining) budget 2010–2050 (Gt CO_2)	Reach of the budget lifetime (years)*
Germany	1.5	17	17	−0.91	−1
US	4.7	52	108	−56	−9
China	22	239	75	164	26
Brazil	2.9	31	6.1	25	55
Burkina Faso	0.16	1.7	0.0090	1.7	2,810
Japan	2.3	26	23	2.4	2
Russia	2.8	31	31	−0.29	0
Mexico	1.6	18	6.9	11	23
Indonesia	3.4	38	4.8	33	88
India	16	175	19	156	103
Maldives	0.0041	0.045	0.0098	0.035	50
EU	8.9	98	81	18	4
World	100	1,100	500	600	20

* Assuming annual emissions as in 2008.

Source: Table 5.3-1, the WBGU Budget Approach p. 26. Assumes 2 degree 'guard rail and historical responsibility 1999–2009 (retroactively) with a start date of 1999 (year of release of AR1 (IPCC). This item is licensed under a creative commons license. Details can be found at http://creativecommons.org/licenses/by-nc-nd/2.0/de/deed.en (Attribution-Noncommercial-No Derivative Works 2.0 Germany).

for action'. They, therefore, recommended that in order to maintain the momentum that is currently emerging in global climate policy, option 2 presents a better option (WBGU 2009: 29).

The second option 'looks forward from today's status quo and is thus oriented to the responsibility of all countries for future emissions'. Thus the same analysis is undertaken, but with the start date and demographic reference date of 2010. Assuming a greater climate risk, a 67 per cent probability of achieving the 2 degrees Celsius target is associated with a budget of 750 Gt (based on the works of Meinshausen et al. 2009 and Le Quéré 2008). Under the new scenario, 2010–2050, and population shares for the year 2010, the situation improves somewhat for the developed countries: all three countries of focus have positive balances but will likely use up their budgeted allotment before the period expires in 2050. As seen in Table 2.4, the US would have about 6 years of budget life-time, assuming it maintains emissions levels as in 2008, Germany 10 years and Japan 11 years, whereas China, India and Brazil would have 24 years, 88 years and 46 years of budget life-time, respectively). In this option, historical responsibility could be taken into account through a lump-sum compensation payment from the industrialized countries to the newly industrializing and developing countries to support adaptation to climate change.

TABLE 2.4 The WBGU budget approach option 2: future responsibility, 2010–2050

	Share of world population 2010 (%)	Budget 2010–2050 (Gt CO_2)	Estimated emission in 2008 (Gt CO_2)	Reach of the budget lifetime (years)*
		Total period		
Germany	1.2	9.0	0.91	10
US	4.6	35	6.1	6
China	20	148	6.2	24
Brazil	2.8	21	0.46	46
Burkina Faso	0.24	1.8	0.00062	2,892
Japan	1.8	14	1.3	11
Russia	2.0	15	1.6	9
Mexico	1.6	12	0.46	26
Indonesia	3.4	25	0.38	67
India	18	133	1.5	88
Maldives	0.0058	0.043	0.00071	61
EU	7.2	54	4.5	12
World	100	750	30	25

* Assuming annual emissions as in 2008

Source: Table 5.3–2, WBGU 2009. This item is licensed under a creative commons license. Details can be found at http://creativecommons.org/licenses/by-nc-nd/2.0/de/deed.en (Attribution-Non-commercial-No Derivative Works 2.0 Germany).

> The CO_2 budgets available for Germany and the EU to 2050 – assuming that the current level of emissions is maintained (Germany: 11 t CO_2 per capita per year; EU: 9 t CO_2 per capita per year) – would be exhausted within 10 and 12 years respectively. In light of this situation, it is clear that the industrialized countries must carry out rapid and comprehensive decarbonization of their economies by 2050 if they wish to present themselves as credible advocates of global climate protection.
>
> (WBGU 2009: 28)

However, since the developed countries would be in deficit for much of the period, WBGU argues that an international emissions trading system whereby these countries could purchase emissions from surplus developing countries such as those in Africa would be the most workable solution.

Overall, this approach of WBGU may not be in the best interest of developing countries for three key reasons. First, back-dating historical responsibility to 1990 is not adequate to cover what would be required under the polluter pay principle. Though going back to 1850 may be political unfeasible, it certainly is more justifiable. If a more recent time period is to be used then the 1970s could be a relatively plausible start date as by then there was considerable recognition of human induced interference with the environment. Second, institutionalizing an equal per capita-based system without adjusting and compensating directly for past emissions coupled with the resort to financial transfer through international emissions trading, as a predominant means of financing adaptation etc., would enforce a reciprocity-based system that would in fact be moving away from equity. Third, though a 67 per cent probability, which carries a greater risk of warming exceeding 2 degrees Celsius, gives more flexibility and leeway for developed countries and they have more lifetime years under this scenario, it would not be in the favour of vulnerable developing countries. As discussed in Chapter 1, developed countries due to their advance level of development may be able to tolerate high levels of warming but most developing countries cannot.

Such a budgeting framework as proposed by WBGU, though ostensibly justified on ethical grounds, would not be in favour of developing countries as in the future (post-2020 period) when their emissions begin to rise even more significantly they would face a greater built-in penalty. This is why historical responsibility/accountability is so critical. As argued by Neumayer (2000) historically accountability is not about laying 'blame or collective moral guilt . . . not even about awareness of harm caused' (ibid.: 188). Rather, it is about 'assigning an equal share of the beneficent existence of the absorptive capacity of nature to every individual, independent of his or her place in either space or time' (ibid.). It therefore has tremendous implication for the future sharing and apportionment of the dwindling atmospheric space (carbon budget). In this regard, Neumayer cautions that:

> While it makes sense for developing countries not to insist on a strict application of equal per capita emission rights with historical accountability now, they would be ill advised to give up their insistence on this allocation rule coming into effect some time not too far into the future.[21]
>
> (Neumayer 2000: 190)

Interestingly enough, though reluctant to operationalizing an effective historical responsibility framework around mitigation, developed countries seem quite willing to passively allow some form of 'allocation proportional to emissions in a specified base year or future business-as-usual projected emissions (a rule known as "grandfathering")' and/or find acceptable 'allocation on an equal per capita basis without historical accountability'[22] (Neumayer 2000). Developed countries also seem to place a high premium on 'future responsibility'. Thus developed countries are quick to point to the future emissions trajectory of China, India, Brazil, South Africa and other middle-income developing countries and would wish to impose ex ante penalties on these countries now without accepting and taking care of their own (ex post) historical responsibility. Thus developing countries would be wise to learn from another of Neumayer's precautionary approach. For, as Neumayer points out, 'right now it is not in the interest of the developed countries to accept the basic validity of equal per capita allocation with historical accountability and the developing countries do not have the bargaining strength to enforce it. But things can change over time (Neumayer 2000: 191).

In contrast to the WBGU approach, the focus of some developing countries' proponents such as the BASIC experts, the Stockholm Environment Institute (SEI) and the South Centre is on ensuring equitable access to sustainable development'. The BASIC experts proposed an alternative framing of the problem that would help developing countries operationalize the principle of equity, common but differentiated responsibility and respective capabilities through a linked dual approach of a 'resource-sharing budget approach' and an 'effort/burden sharing approach' (Box 2.6). Explicitly accounting for historical emissions is critical to this equitable approach in which historical responsibility along with the per capita principle and sustainable development are important and critical for identifying the criteria 'which can be approximated quantitatively . . . (and) forms the basis of calculation to operationalize the two approaches' (BASIC 2011).

The 'resource-sharing' approach presupposes the equitable sharing of atmospheric resource. The BASIC group works with a cumulative global carbon budget of between 1000 and 1440 Gt of CO_2 for the period 2000–2049. Arguing that 1000 Gt CO_2, which has a 25 per cent probability of exceeding the 2 degree is infeasible given that between 2000 and 2007 the world emitted cumulative emissions of 210 Gt CO_2 (excluding land use, land-use change and forestry (LULUCF)), then 1440 GT as the gross amount of carbon dioxide that the world can emit between 2000 and 2049 is seen as 'reachable with substantial effort and has a probability of exceeding 2 degree by 50 per cent'.

Under the 'resource-sharing' approach every country has total entitlement for the period 1850–2049. So the total budget has a historical aspect (1850–1999) and a future (2000–2049). It is also associated with the 2 degrees Celsius temperature target. The budget is allocated based on per capita equal accumulative emissions. Each country's share is allotted based on their relative population size and adjustments are made for their past emissions in order to arrive at the future share of the carbon budget. In this approach, as with the WBGU approach discussed above, developed countries are in deficit for the entire period 1850–2049, with 2000–2049

TABLE 2.5 Cross comparison emission only and double accumulations methods

Country	1850–2005 CO_2 (energy) WRI CAIT (%)	1850–1900 CO_2 (energy + cement) Brazilian proposal (%)
China	8.39	3.05
India	2.22	0.90
South Africa	1.10	0.21
Brazil	0.80	0.32
BASIC	12.51	4.48
Non-Annex I	26.48	10.35
Annex I	73.52	89.65

Source: BASIC (2011). WRI/CAIT represent historical responsibility only with emission; Brazilian with double accumulation. http://gdrights.org/wp-content/uploads/2011/12/EASD-final.pdf Table 1 'actually negative' (BASIC 2011: 10). So developed countries have negative entitlement for the future, while many developing countries have positive entitlement. However, as noted above, these entitlements cannot be fully physically exploited given the highly constrained nature of the remaining physical carbon space.

The 'effort/burden sharing approach' of the BASIC's expert group focus on 'sharing the effort required to reduce emissions compared to future trends' (BASIC 2011: 10). Based on assessment of the future trends of emission growth and the business-as-usual (BAU) trends in emission and IPCC scenarios, it seeks to allocate the effort to get to a desired future emission pathway on the basis of equity.[23] Historical cumulative emissions play a role here but are taken into account through a process that seeks to account for each country's contribution to climate change and the rise in global mean temperature over time and not strictly through the carrying forward of the historical portion of the global carbon budget as in the resource sharing approach. Historical responsibility can be determined by the methodology of double accumulation process.

The basic approach of an equity-based framework for climate change policy is in alignment with the work of the Stockholm Environmental Institute's Green House Development right and the South Centre's Environment, Development, Equity (EDE) approach.

2.4 The emissions, development, equity and finance gaps – the case for a just sharing of the carbon and development space and climate (finance) justice

Most environmentalists and many developed countries are now deeply invested in the paradigm of the so-called emissions gap (the fact that the current pledges of countries to reduce emissions is still significantly below what is needed to meet the 2 degrees Celsius target).[24] It should be recognized that the emissions gap, which is quite a serious matter, is not the result of a quirk of fate but is the result of the past and continuing inaction of the developed countries to undertake meaningful and sustained economy-wide emissions reductions (relative to 1990 levels) within their own countries as well as the failure to urgently finance the transformation of the developing countries to low carbon pathway in any significant way (that is, beyond pilot projects here and there). Now the existence of the gap has become something of a cause célèbrè for beating upon developing countries to 'do more'. But while conventional ethos focuses single-mindedly on the emissions gap, it is often ignored, or benignly neglected, that this emissions gap belies the existence of at least three other gaps: the development gap, the equity gap, and the finance gap. These three are critical to unlocking the discussions about shared vision and achieving targets around emission reduction goals and peaking year. Ultimately these are also the keys to unlocking the Durban Platform Paris 2015 Agreement.

Wrestling with different degrees of acceptance and acknowledgement of these sets of inter-locking gaps are at the heart of discussion among and between countries. Addressing one or another of the gaps is also the subject of arbitrary and selective cross country money flows and divided and rule tactics seeking to break any G77 and China consensus now in play by developed countries. This situation is in many ways reminiscent of another struggle in a far distant era: the struggle for access and control of natural resources, minerals and human resource that led to the Berlin Conference of 1865 when the various European contending powers legalized their control of Africa. So with the dwindling atmospheric space, the race to secure raw material (this is occurring in many space such as the trade and investment agreements including the European Economic Partnership Agreements with African countries) and the issue of global commons.

Developed countries are seeking to rewrite in some cases, and in other cases create, new rules that operate in their favour and which will ultimately preclude developing countries' equitable access to atmospheric space. The developed countries are attempting to reconstitute the rules of the game to suit their interests within a framework that achieves the consent of developing countries – a legitimation process similar to the Berlin Conference of 1865. Before discussing the nature of the gaps, it is worthwhile to contextualize the struggle over addressing them in the contextual framing of history to understand more fully the real underlying dynamics and why resolving the climate issues has seemingly become such an intractable one.

2.4.1 Legitimizing the unjust?

After the conquest of Africa, the various European powers decided to end the internecine and unproductive rivalries between each other and to engender an orderly rules-based process for their colonial empires. Back then no consent of the dispossessed was required.

Although controlling the slave trade and promoting humanitarian idealism were promoted as the focus of the Berlin Conference, the Conference only passed empty resolutions about the ending of slave trade and providing for the welfare of Africa. In truth, the result of the Conference was a method of dividing the continent of Africa between the European powers. The Berlin Act was an important change in international affairs. It created the rules for 'effective occupation' of conquered lands, ensuring that the division of Africa would take place without war among the European powers.[25] What the act did was simply legitimize European control and ownership of Africa and its resources (gold, timber, lands, market and labour power) in support of their development process which necessitated cheap labour, resources and markets. By 1902, over 90 per cent of Africa's land was in the hands of European powers.

Likewise, the call for a new 2015 climate agreement is occurring under a seemingly simple pretext: the world has changed since 1992, there is a need for 'symmetry' and 'fairness' in the form of a new universally instrument applicable to all. This presupposes that both the UNFCCC and the Kyoto Protocol are (a) not universal legally binding instruments and (b) not applicable to all; they are unequivocally both. (The Convention applies to all Parties and it carefully balances rights and responsibilities. The Protocol enables developed countries to undertake their mitigation reductions in developing countries through the Clean Development Mechanism, which was also to contribute to sustainable development in the developing countries.)

What the developed countries now object to is the division of countries into Annex I, those with historical responsibility for climate change, and non-Annex I (the developing countries). The developed countries would like to do away with their financial and technology transfer obligations and commitments under Articles 4.1(c), 4.3, 4.4 and 4.5. But, above all, what they apparently find most objectionable are Article 3, where-in the principle of equity is firmly grounded, and Article 4, in particular 4.7, which unambiguously links the actions of developing countries as being dependent on the extent to which developed countries undertake their commitments to both mitigation and to provide finance and technology for adaptation and mitigation by developing countries. While Article 3 is the foundation and basis for the differentiation between the two broad annexes, Article 4 gives careful balance in obligations and responsibility between developed and developing countries. These two articles if done away with, or are somehow undermined will relieve developed countries, in particular Annex II parties, such as the US and the EU, from any financial and technology transfer obligations to developing countries.

If developed countries are able to escape their obligations and commitments[26] and hence get their way in the current Ad Hoc Working Group on the Durban Platform (ADP) negotiations, under the apparent open and transparent process of the UNFCCC, then, like the Berlin Conference, they will pretty much be given carte blanche to undertake best endeavour, bottom up actions, both in terms of mitigating GHGs and in supporting developing countries. The developing countries would then have acquiesced in relinquishing their right to the equitable distribution of the atmospheric space as well as their moral and legal hold over the developed countries for the provision of support for adaptation and mitigation. They would then be left on their own to deal with the impacts of climate change, SIDS and the LDCs would most likely be grandfathered.[27] The developed countries' climate debt[28] for their over-use of the atmosphere would be wiped away cleanly and legally. But the significant carbon debt of the developed countries is a constraint on the future growth of developing countries. The repayment of this debt can and should be paid in the form of finance and technology transfer.

The claim is usually made that developing countries such as China and India are now major emitters and so equity cannot be the basis for global agreement. By all objective criteria both China and India despite their enviable international surpluses and strong growth rates going into the 2007–2008 financial crisis, are developing countries with a significant portion of their population living at or below international poverty lines and going without access to modern energy services, water and proper sanitation. The same cannot be said for any developed countries today.

The developed countries, which are wealthy, have not stopped growing and are fighting tooth and nail to continue on their growth path without seriously jeopardizing their economies. Nothing in the Durban Agreement puts a stop to that. In fact, countries such as Canada, Japan and Russia have stepped out of the

Kyoto regime. The US has never been on board and thus far it has not implemented a credible national mechanism for climate change. Whereas, all the evidence demonstrates that developing countries such as Brazil, China, India, South Africa and the Philippines are doing so. Despite the fact that they have no legal obligation to do so under the current framework, most developing countries are undertaking mitigation actions and commitment to reduce GHGs and de-link their economic growth from emissions growth through their Nationally Appropriate Mitigation Action (NAMAs). Some of the specificities around different NAMAs are highlighted in Box 2.6.

The fact is that the new Durban mandate does nothing to address the urgent and precarious position in which SIDS and LDCs find themselves. It did not adopt a ratifiable second commitment period with aggressive mitigation reduction commitments; rather, it has kicked this to the post-2015 period. More dramatically instead of bolstering the current system it has set in place the possibility of at least 5 years of inaction. The reality is the Kyoto Protocol is a walking zombie. It lingers on only to sustain the market mechanisms and carbon offsetting projects that benefits the developed countries. In recognition of this reality, the developed countries, particularly the EU, are busily working to establish new market-based mechanisms under non-Kyoto frameworks inside the Convention, independent from it, but, ultimately, these outcomes will be folded into the new post-2015 Durban Platform arrangements which will form the basis of the Paris Agreement, December 2015.

Developed countries are running away from their obligations and hence seeking to rewrite the UNFCCC so that it is be more favourable to them, shifting the burden of mitigation to the developed countries. They also do not want to address the question of long-term finance and technology transfer.

In the current era, the struggle is for the last remaining bit of atmospheric space. (But elsewhere the securing of natural resources continues to play a pivotal role.) This struggle is playing itself out in multiple forums, from the World Trade Organization, the Economic Partnership Agreements now being discussed between the EU and Africa and most recently at the Rio plus 20 Conference in June 2012. Will the Durban Platform be the instrument and Paris (2015) the place where developing countries, in particular Africa, concede their rights and entitlement to the equitable sharing of atmospheric space and to the 'adequate, predictable and sustainable'[29] sources of financing for adaptation, loss and damage and transformation to a low carbon pathway?

2.4.2 Equity and development gap

The current discussion and proposals (under the UNFCCC) regarding reducing emissions and sharing the remaining carbon space is both inadequate to the task of reducing global emissions and unfair to developing countries (South Centre 2010). The various options on the table for emissions reduction will have significant implications for developing countries. In the worst case scenario, developing countries may have to undertake a drastic 50 per cent cut in per capita emission levels.

Given the almost one-to-one link between GDP and emissions this would have serious implications for meeting economic and social development goals.

Unquestionably, there are significant development gaps between developing countries and developed countries. Drawing on work done by the South Centre, a few of the major development gaps include:

- Relative to developing countries, developed countries have far better developed infrastructure such as roads, buildings, factories, power plants, etc., much of which were built cheaply but also were emission-intensive to build because of the use of fossil fuels. This infrastructure reflects high levels of embedded carbon and the carbon debt built up since the industrial revolution.
- Relative to developing countries, developed countries have far superior levels of technology in terms of machinery, knowledge and innovation capability.
- Relative to developing countries, developed countries have greater human and organizational capacity to transform their economies toward low-emissions pathways.
- Relative to developing countries, developed countries have far higher levels of income that also enable them to pay for and be better at the three above factors.

These development gaps vary across the spectrum of developing countries both in terms of income level and regional specificities. But they have one thing in common: the need for means of support: finance, technology transfer and capacity building. For example, a 2011 United Nations University (WIDER) study reports that African countries 'can expect an extra $183 billion bill just to maintain its few paved roads over the next 60 years (or $22 million–$54 million a year) because of the impacts of climate change'.[30] As reported in *The Guardian*, the study results 'show how even the minimum of infrastructural improvement – considered a prerequisite for economic development – will be reined in in poor countries unless money is made available for them to adapt to climate change'.

According to the same UNU-WIDER study, African countries face an average loss of opportunity to expand road networks from a low of 22 per cent to a high of 35 per cent in the central region. This has significant implications for sustainable livelihoods of small farmers and micro and small enterprises, many of whom are women. These male and female farmers and male and female-owned or operated enterprises can benefit from the provision of new and/or improved roads that would provide for better transportation for getting products to markets. Such developments will free, in particular, women farmers from the trap of the monopolistic practice of low farm-gate pricing by middlemen. It will also allow increased access to markets, improved product delivery time and quality at consumer sales points contributing to a higher income for these farmers. Higher income can contribute to better adaptation as well as build up savings for use during times of extreme weather events In addition, woman and girls can have better access to transportation, liberating them from all kinds of gender-related violence.

BOX 2.6 DEVELOPING COUNTRIES MITIGATION UPDATE ON NAMA EFFORTS

China in its NAMA presentation said that NAMAs are in the context of the BAP and in accordance with CBDR. NAMAs are coordinated with sustainable development and poverty eradication goals, and based on national circumstances, priorities and strategies for sustainable development. In that context, China reported that its autonomous domestic mitigation has three pillars: 1) lowering CO_2 emissions per unit of GDP by 40–45 per cent by 2020 with 2005 as base year; 2) enhancing forestry management as sinks; and 3) increasing forest coverage by 40 million hectare. In terms of policy instruments China also has a five year plan for improving energy intensity and saving energy and reducing emission.

Ghana submitted 55 NAMAs after Copenhagen. A NAMA plan is now being developed as well as the development of a low carbon growth path.

India seeks to reduce emission intensity of GDP by 20–25 per cent by 2020 based on 2005 levels. (This excludes agricultural emissions.) India argues that its emissions are likely to be 2.6 tons per capita in 2020, which is low compared to global average of 4.4 tons per capita. Annex I average per capita is 12 tons. India's goal is to lift 470 million people out of poverty, etc.

Indonesia's national emissions target is for 26 per cent reductions through domestically supported NAMA and 15 per cent through internationally supported NAMA.

Peru's deforestation in the Amazon is the main source of its emissions. In 2020 this will be about 47 per cent, with energy consumption accounting for 21 per cent, agriculture for 19 per cent, industry for 75 per cent and solid waste for 6 per cent. Its voluntary mitigation target for 2021 is zero net emission in the LULUCF sectors, 40 per cent from renewable energy sources yielding 28 per cent reduction on 2000 levels.

Singapore pledges 16 per cent and argues that it already working towards achieving 7–11 per cent reduction of GHG emission below BAU levels in 2020. All to be domestically funded.

South Africa pledge 34 per cent deviation below the BAU emissions growth trajectory by 2020 and 42 per cent by 2025. But this is subjected to support of international finance technology via a comprehensive legally binding agreement. A national process is underway on climate policy, utilizing legislation, regulation, economic instruments and action plans on a sector-by-sector basis to build the foundation for a low carbon society.

> Countries that are LDCs (such as **Bangladesh**) are not required to carry out mitigation but may voluntarily contribute, as long as financial and technical support is available and their need for growth, sustainable development and accelerated poverty reduction is not compromised.
>
> Source: *Developing Countries taking Mitigation Actions despite Lack of Support*, Lim Li Lin, TWN Bangkok News Update 5, 6 April 2011. www.twnside.org.sg

In spite of the challenges discussed above, in their willingness to help secure reduction in global emissions of GHGs, many developing countries have been engaged in voluntary national mitigation efforts to tackle climate change. This they do in spite of sluggish or lack lustre international financial and technology support. At the UNFCCC pre-sessional meeting in Bangkok, 5 April 2011, many of these countries show-cased their mitigation activities and progress thus far (Box 2.6). These include the undertakings of countries at varied levels of economic development such as Ghana, India, Peru, St Lucia, Singapore, South Africa, Marshall Islands, Bangladesh and Brazil. In total 48 developing countries have submitted NAMAs. Additionally, countries such as Mexico stated that they are in the process of developing a low emission development strategy.

There is broad agreement that developing countries' pledges amount to more mitigation than developed countries' pledges (Kartha and Erickson 2011).[31] Yet developed countries continue to argue for more commitments from developing countries.

It is without question that the developed countries have over-used their fair share (based on population) of the atmospheric space (Table 2.6). In the first case, they are all in deficit (Table 2.7) and in the second case, there is very little remaining space left for developing countries to grow (Table 2.8). Thus the action to ensure stable climate must be equitable; it cannot come at the further expense of the poor men and women in developing countries, especially those now without access to safe drinking water, sanitation or energy services.

TABLE 2.6 Fair carbon shares and actual emissions of CO_2, 1850–2008 (Gt CO_2)

Group	Cumulative emissions CO_2				
	Actual	Actual share in total (%)	Fair share based on population share	Over-use/ under-use of share	Over-use/ under-use over proportional share
Annex I	878	72	310	568	183
Non-Annex I	336	28	904	−568	−63
World	1,214	100	1,214		

Source: South Centre, 2010

TABLE 2.7 Cumulative emissions: fair shares and carbon creditors and debts: selected countries, 1850–2008 (in billion t or Gt)

Country	CO$_2$ emissions 1850–2008		CO$_2$ debt or credit as of 2008	
	Cumulative	Cumulative fair share		
Australia	13.7	3.8	9.9	Debtor
Bolivia	**0.3**	**1.5**	**−1.2**	**Creditor**
Brazil	**9.9**	**30.5**	**−20.6**	**Creditor**
Canada	25.5	6.4	19.1	Debtor
China	**113.8**	**265.5**	**−151.7**	**Creditor**
France	32.9	16.5	16.4	Debtor
Germany	81.1	23.7	57.4	Debtor
India	**33.2**	**193.1**	**−159.9**	**Creditor**
Japan	45.9	30.1	15.8	Debtor
Tanzania	**0.1**	**4.7**	**−4.6**	**Creditor**
UK	69.8	17.2	52.6	Debtor
US	343.1	61.8	281.3	Debtor
Annex I	878	310	568	Debtor
Non-Annex I	**336**	**904**	**−568**	**Creditor**
World	**1,214**	**1,214**		

Source: South Centre, 2010

Note: * Countries in bold are developing countries. ** Carbon debt refers to the amount by which the country's cumulative emissions exceeded what its cumulative fair share of emissions (based on its population) should have been for the same period 1850–2008. Carbon credit refers to the amount by which cumulative emissions are less than the cumulative fair share for the same period.

Sharing the remaining limited stock of carbon space, 2010–2050 (2–1.5 degrees Celsius)

TABLE 2.8 Allocation for 2010–2050, global budget of 750 Gt CO$_2$* (in Gt CO$_2$)

Group	1850–2008			2010–2050*	1850–2050	2010–2050*
	Fair share emission budget	Actual emissions	Cumulative emission debt	Fair share emission budget	Fair share emission budget	Allocated budget**
Annex I	310	878	568	120	430	−448
Non-Annex I	904	336	−568	630	1,534	1,198
Total	1,214	1,214		750	1,964	750

Source: South Centre (2010)

Note: * Assuming a global budget of 750 Gt CO$_2$ (corresponding to a 67 per cent chance of not exceeding 2 °C by 2050) and a 16 per cent average share for Annex I countries of the global population from 2010–2050. ** Taking into account cumulative emission debt from 1850–2008

The existence of development and emissions gaps mean that any emphasis on a simplistic notion of equity in terms of absolute emission per country, or equal emissions per country, as the basis for sharing of the remaining global emissions/carbon budget is inherently unfair (and locks in economic disparities among countries). Such a starting point can only lead to an inequitable outcome. In the current context, developed countries have used up more than their fair share of atmospheric and development space, contributing to the problem of climate change.[32] This reality has been a big stumbling block in the inability to agree on a global emissions reduction goal or global peaking year.

The question of a long-term global goal for emissions reduction is a critical one. Annex I and developed countries must take the greater cut leaving more space for developing countries. Developing countries would like the developed countries to collectively cut their emission by at least 40 per cent by 2020 (compared to 1990 levels) (Khor 2010). The current pledges of developed countries to date only add up to about 16–23 per cent (excluding the US; UNFCCC 2010; Khor 2010). Furthermore, as noted by Khor (2010); Kartha and Erickson (2011), these aggregates are overstated. Due to the many accounting loopholes, emissions trading, market-based mechanisms and offset programmes available to them, the developed countries commitments will be significantly lower than stated or in the worst case developed countries may even increase their emissions (see Box 1.9 in Chapter 1). In many cases, through market-based mechanisms such as the Clean Development Mechanism and carbon offsets, they can make these cuts in the developing countries but not in their own countries.

Ultimately, a fair climate deal would require drastic emissions cuts by the developed countries and strong action to remove the overhang of CO_2 from the atmosphere plus adequate compensation for developing countries for the rich countries over-use of the atmospheric space. This can be accomplished by financial transfer, technology transfer and capacity building so that developing countries can adapt to climate change impacts and adopt clean and renewable energy pathways to development in the context of adequate economic growth, poverty reduction and provision of water, sanitation and energy to their population. This however has economic implications for developed countries' domestic constituencies.

In the current climate negotiating process, the real realpolitik of managing the costs and expectations of corporations and taxpayers in developed countries is resulting in backtracking from the advance equity position of the Convention. This can be seen in terms of the increasing pressure to obtain emissions reduction (mitigations commitments) from developing countries. There are also attempts by some developed countries to introduce clear differentiation among developing countries for the purpose of imposing reciprocity-based commitments.

If developed countries do not increase their level of ambition for mitigation targets this implies greater commitment and resource mobilization around mitigation on the part of developing countries. This means increased financing and human resource burden on developing countries and it implies that these countries may over-focus on mitigation as opposed to adaptation activities or promoting economic development and the building of the economy so it can arrive at a state where it can be better prepared to meet climate challenges.

The fact that the new disciplines for developing countries (expanded commitments such as nationally appropriate mitigation actions, measuring, reporting and verification (MRV) procedures as well as biennial update reports, international assessment and review (IAR) and international consultation and analysis) are the only pillars still standing of the Bali tripod is alarming.[33] Under this framework, developing countries are now obligated to put forward mitigation plans and targets for climate mitigation to be registered and regularly updated. At the same the developed countries have been negligent in meeting their obligation to provide financing technology transfer and capacity building to developing countries. There is no concrete commitment for future financing other than the often repeated 'goal' of mobilizing $100 billion by 2020. So besides the mitigation gap, discussed above, there is also a financing gap existing now and there will be a financing gap after the so-called financing period 2010–2012.[34] While countries such as the US backed up by the EU and others demand that developing countries' mitigation actions are measurable reportable and verifiable (MRV), there is reluctance by these same countries to subject their commitment to provide finance and technological support to a similar MRV process.

The injustice of climate change lies in one evident fact: the impacts of climate change are real and are most urgently and most devastatingly felt in the developing countries and by the poorest who are the least responsible for creating or contributing to the factors giving rise to climate change. Science has attributed 'climate change' to the emission of GHGs arising primarily from the long march to industrialization and growth of the now rich and industrialized countries of the EU, the US, Australia, Canada, New Zealand and Japan. These countries have grown rich from utilizing fossil fuels, the transformation of rural ecosystem to urban cities and the exploitation of industrial agriculture. They have high income and well developed industries, infrastructures and technologies.

The developing world, long the major provider of natural resources, labour and land that fostered the industrialization of the rich countries, not only have not benefited significantly from the transformation of these resources but now must bear the brunt of the effects of a changing climate. The developing countries must now be the ones to sacrifice their growth potential in order to help to alter the trajectory of rising GHGs and to deal with the reality of limited atmospheric space.

Climate change thus places on developed countries a central responsibility for cleaning up the atmosphere and also to provide support for the losses and damages incurred by the women and men in the developing countries, provide support for their adapting to climate change as well as support the rapid transformation of developing countries' economies to a low carbon, clean energy development pathway.

Fairness, equity and democracy, hence, lie at the heart of global climate change protection policy. But the issues of fairness, equity and democracy also have to do with issues of gender inequality and injustice and the marginalized and heightened vulnerability of Indigenous men and women.

2.5 Emissions gap, development gap, equity and gender gaps

In its fourth Assessment Report, the IPCC flagged issues around equity. Specifically, it made reference to three areas of equity: (1) equity between developed and developing countries 'in the delineation of rights and responsibilities within any climate-change response framework'; (2) 'the need for equity across vulnerable groups that are disproportionately exposed to climate-change impacts'; and (3) 'intergenerational ethics; i.e., the degree to which the interests of future generations are given relatively lower weighting in favour of short-term concerns'. Intergeneration ethic is based on Page (1999, cited in IPCC 2007b). Intergenerational justice has implications for individuals and collectives (for example, indigenous cultures) (IPCC 2007b). The IPCC also flagged the gender aspects of vulnerabilities (Masika 2002) and cited Swart *et al.* (2003) observation that there is the need to describe potential changes in vulnerability and adaptive capacity within the SRES[35] storylines (IPCC 2007b).

All of these issues are now beginning to rise dramatically to the top of the agenda in global public discussions around climate change. Different ones, to different degrees, have made some headway into the margins of climate change negotiation discussions, though none on the formal conference agenda in a significant way. This is the case with the issue of indigenous rights and gender justice.

2.5.1 Indigenous rights

The historical and continuing disenfranchisement and dispossession of indigenous peoples worldwide must be addressed. If climate change adaptation and mitigation strategies focus on disaster management, land-use, afforestation/reforestation and carbon sequestration, and are not properly designed to include equitable benefit-sharing agreements and to address the rights and concerns of indigenous peoples, this is likely to further result in the marginalization of indigenous men and women. Projects and programmes that involve or encroach upon resources such as forests that are normally under the control of, or critical to the livelihoods and lives of indigenous people must be avoided. Indigenous people must be effective participants and decision-makers in the areas that impact them. There is tremendous historical economic and ecological debt already outstanding to indigenous peoples. It would indeed be tragic if in trying to address the problems of climate change, that iniquitous process was furthered.

2.5.2 Women's rights

Increasingly it is being recognized and acknowledged that the gender and social inequality and their relationship to climate change policy responses should also not be ignored in this debate. Women have inequitable distribution of global and national resources that have left them more vulnerable to the effects of climate change than men in their communities. Because of historical gender biases and discrimination, women have less tangible or intangible resources with which to climate-proof and recoup economic and social losses from adverse climate change induced events. Women must face and deal with the adverse challenges of climate change with fewer personal and social resources than their male counterparts. Yet, women are critical actors in managing and maintaining their households, the community, the ecosystems and natural resources. Meeting climate change-induced adaptation and mitigation goals should not come at the expense of gender equality and women's economic empowerment.

Gender issues in the climate protection discussions, therefore, arise from:

- The material impact of climate change (on production, consumption and resources uses) – all have inequalities and injustices dimensions. In the case of gender, there are multiple and interrelated adverse and sometimes disproportional impact on women: (see, for example, women's versus men's carbon footprint, and climate change impacts on pre-existing gender biases and unequal access to resources etc.). It is, therefore, important to understand and addressed gender issues in strategies, policies and measures underlying climate protection policies.
- Voice, Democracy and Representation – women's and men's voices, particularly the poorest and the most disadvantaged, must be central in discussions about the climate crisis, and consequent resource distribution impacts. Considerations of their priorities and concerns in the solutions and policies proposed and developed – in terms of mitigation, adaptation, finance etc., must guide these discussions. The degree to which women's and men's participation and systemic representation (agency) is integrated across all aspects of climate governance is essential to ensure the most fair, equitable and cost effective solutions to the climate crisis.
- Knowledge, experience, insights and capacities for contributing to the way forward requires drawing on all the available resources to which a country has access in a climate constrained world. Women and indigenous peoples, as with other groups that have been historically marginalized, have knowledge, insights and practices that could be integrated in climate protection policies. They also need the upgrading of their knowledge and capacities for ensuring livelihoods, sustainable development and for contributing to local, national and planetary safety.

The United Nations Framework Convention (UNFCCC), unlike a number of multilateral environmental instruments, did not include any reference to gender in its initiating provisions. As a result, there has been ongoing advocacy to mend this deficiency. Since 2001 with a provision on gender and representation in the

Marrakech Decision, the COP has been slowly taking actions towards the goal of gender equality. The Cancún (2010) and Durban (2011) COP Decisions as well as the governing instrument of the GCF all have explicit gender references.[36]

The Doha 2012 Decision marks the high point in this trend by marking a goal of gender balance in representation and establishing gender among the standing items of the COP agenda in the widely lauded Gender Decision entitled *Promoting Gender Balance and Improving the Participation of Women in UNFCCC Negotiations and in the Representation of Parties in Bodies Established Pursuant to the Convention or the Kyoto Protocol.*

The Gender Decision recognizes 'women's equitable participation as a procedural right, while gender equitable outcomes of UNFCCC Decisions would be recognized as a goal in its own right. However the Decision does not address the broader question of women's empowerment and the impact of climate change and climate protection (including discussion around mitigation reductions, loss and damage, financing for adaptation) on this agenda.

Women and indigenous peoples have and are playing proactive role in adapting to climate events and in reducing emissions of carbon. Women and indigenous people historically have been quite involved in the most natural and simplest forms of sequestration – tree planting. They have also used natural plants and resources to protect against landslides and have developed low-cost, effective and efficient sustainable energy farming practice.

Still women, as a group, and indigenous men and women face significant hurdles with regard to climate change. The ability to effectively and successful navigate and overcome these hurdles is driven by two critical and inextricable intertwined imperatives.

The first and primary imperative is to survive. This is a critical underlying issue that must permeate all discussions. Science has shown that wide gaps and low ambition targets associated with the 2 degrees Celsius pathway place an unacceptable risk on vulnerable populations in Africa, Asia, the Caribbean, Latin America and the Pacific. Quite starkly, 2 degrees Celsius is not safe for women, men and children in developing countries. It is associated with threats of ecological disruption and damage, species extinction, social conflicts and the violation of human rights.[37]

The survival and life chance of poor women and men in developing countries as well as those in the bottom fifths in rich countries must be the ultimate barometer of what is satisfactory climate policy outcome. Women's groups and gender advocates therefore must inform discussion not just around the soft issues under the shared vision agenda but must also focus attention on the technical, equity and sustainability issues of sharing the global goal, global peaking and mitigation scenarios.

The second imperative is to thrive. Poor men and women must thrive: live a good and decent life with protection from extreme weather to the highest degree possible. When circumstances are otherwise, they must have the best chance of recovery from these events. These best chances of good adaptation to climate change can best be assured by robust gender equitable and poverty eradicating development strategies and programmes.

Surviving and thriving with climate change require effective sustainable development, which includes attention to ensure the physical infrastructure (access to affordable basics services, transportation, energy and power, and communications system, housing, health and education) both at the country and community levels.

This points to the importance of dealing with climate engendered development issues in the context of indigenous peoples' rights, climate and gender justice. Climate justice[38] fundamentally affirms equal rights to the atmosphere for all human beings. It affirms the right of all people, including the poor, women, rural and indigenous peoples, to a specific set of climate-related rights, including:

- safeguards for the fundamental rights to clean air, land, water, food and healthy ecosystems;
- access to affordable and sustainable energy;
- effective recourse to rehabilitation and the restoration of assets in terms of loss and damage finance.

Gender justice is 'the ending of, and if necessary, the provision of redress for, inequalities between women and men' (Goetz 2003). An essential element of gender justice is the opportunity for women to hold institutions and actors accountable for actions that negatively impact on women's access to resources or negatively impact on their capacity to make choices (Goetz 2003).

Most of the member states, Parties, to the UNFCCC[39] have accepted the responsibility to implement the Convention on the Elimination of Discrimination Against Women (CEDAW) and the Beijing Platform for Action (BfA), and should therefore take measures to ensure that the policies of the climate change financing architecture do not 'aggravate social inequality and marginalization' (BfA).

In addition, the key principles of UNFCCC, which have been repeatedly reaffirmed by subsequent COP Decisions – including the Bali Plan of Action and the Cancún Decisions – are grounded in equity and common but differentiate responsibility. Therefore, within the framework of the Convention and the Kyoto Protocol, there is scope for integrating gender equality and women's empowerment principles. To this end, governments should seek to ensure that adaptation, mitigation, technology transfer and the financing of these actions explicitly integrates gender equality concerns and creates provisions that enable the continued economic and social empowerment of women.

As noted in the Beijing Platform for Action (BfA), 'absolute poverty and the feminization of poverty, unemployment, the increasing fragility of the environment, continued violence against women and the widespread exclusion of half of humanity from institutions of power and governance underscore the need to continue the search for development, peace and security and for ways of assuring people-centred sustainable development.' This is even more important in the context of climate change. As also noted in the BfA, and which is relevant to the climate change challenge, 'the participation and leadership of the half of humanity that is female is essential to the success of that search' (para 19). The Platform also identified three strategic objectives in the critical area of women and the environment:

1 Involve women actively in environmental decision-making at all levels.
2 Integrate gender concerns and perspectives in policies and programmes for sustainable development.
3 Strengthen or establish mechanisms at the national, regional and international levels to assess the impact of development and environmental policies on women.

(WomenWatch Forum)

In conclusion, equity in the allocation of global atmospheric resources must be grounded in distributive and corrective justice. Distributive and corrective justices focus actions on the historical responsibility of developed countries for their past emissions of GHGs which still exist in today's atmosphere and hence is contributing to the current problem. It is also the case that, on a per capita basis, developed countries are still utilizing more than their fair share of the global atmospheric space. Hence financing must be sufficient to enable developing countries to cover the cost of adapting to the adverse effects of climate change as well as to take action to mitigate GHG emissions in the future. Developed countries should also seek to take appropriate actions such as accepting the responsibility to cut their emissions levels commensurate with the existing global atmospheric space, including ending their excessive use of this space. In addition to financial flow there is a responsibility to support technology transfer and to facilitate capacity building around mitigation in developing countries.

There will be many challenges both for developing countries to hold onto the strong equity foundation of the Convention and for gender advocates to deepen and strengthen gender perspectives into the work of the subsidiary bodies, the negotiation agendas as well as within the work of the IPCC and its upcoming Assessment Report (AR5) 2013–14.

Greater and greater emphasis will be placed on national, regional and global climate protection policy architecture to move beyond the simple recognition of the importance of gender equality and women's empowerment but to understand more rigorously the importance of these issues as key drivers of adaptation, mitigation and technology transfer and development. Many developing countries have already, in principle, recognized some aspects of this agenda in their national adaptation plan of actions. Now there will be increased motivation and incentives for developing countries to elaborate with greater specificity in planning and financing on the gender and social dimensions aspect of their climate change planning and implementation both at national level as well as international negotiation mandates.

Notes

1 In general, about 66 per cent of vulnerable countries are Least Developed Countries and the most at risk cities are in developing countries: Dhaka, Mumbai, Manila, Kolkata and Bangkok, with London and Paris being in the lowest risk. On country by country ranking, according to the Maple Croft's Climate Change Vulnerability Index (CCVI) 2014, '(t)he economic impacts of climate change will be most keenly felt by Bangladesh (1st and most at risk), Guinea-Bissau (2nd), Sierra Leone (3rd), Haiti (4th), South Sudan (5th), Nigeria (6th), DR Congo (7th), Cambodia (8th), Philippines (9th) and Ethiopia (10th), which make up the 10 most at risk countries out of the 193 rated by the CCVI. Other vulnerable developing countries the 'extreme risk' category, include: India (20th), Pakistan (24th), Vietnam (26th) and Indonesia (38th). Thailand (45th), Kenya (56th) and China (61st) are classified at 'high risk'. Maplecroft's CCVI identifies climate-related risks to populations, business and governments over the next 30 years. It evaluates three factors: 1) exposure to extreme climate-related events, including sea level rise and future changes in temperature, precipitation and specific humidity; 2) the sensitivity of populations, in terms of health, education, agricultural dependence and available infrastructure; and 3) the adaptive capacity of countries to combat the impacts of climate change, which encompasses R&D, economic factors, resource security and the effectiveness of government.
2 The category of LDCs was officially established in 1971 by the UN General Assembly with a view to attracting special international support for the most vulnerable and disadvantaged members of the UN family. The current list of LDCs includes 48 countries: 33 in Africa, 14 in Asia and the Pacific and 1 (Haiti) in Latin America. LDCs 'represent the poorest and weakest segment of the international community. They comprise more than 880 million people (about 12 per cent of world population), but account for less than 2 per cent of world GDP and about 1 per cent of global trade in goods'. Africa (33): Angola, Benin, Burkina Faso, Burundi, Central African Republic, Chad, Comoros (SIDS), Democratic Republic of the Congo, Djibouti, Equatorial Guinea, Eritrea, Ethiopia, Gambia, Guinea, Guinea-Bissau (SIDS), Lesotho, Liberia, Madagascar, Malawi, Mali, Mauritania, Mozambique, Niger, Rwanda, São Tomé and Príncipe (SIDS), Senegal, Sierra Leone, Somalia, Sudan, Togo, Uganda, United Republic of Tanzania and Zambia. Asia (14): Afghanistan, Bangladesh, Bhutan, Cambodia, Kiribati (SIDS), Lao People's Democratic Republic, Myanmar, Nepal, Samoa (SIDS), Solomon Island (SIDS), Timor Leste (SIDS), Tuvalu (SIDS), Vanuatu (SIDS), Yemen. SIDS. Small Island Developing States. Source: www.unohrlls.org/en/ldc/25/.
3 World Bank (Atlas Method) Classification based on 2011 Gross National Income. Low income: $1,025 per capita or less, lower middle income: $1,026-$4,035; upper middle income: $4,036-$12,475 and high income: $12,476 plus.
4 Income categories are from the World Bank, based on Atlas method: 2011 Gross national income per capita (2008–12): The groups are: low income, $1,025 or less; lower middle income, $1,026-$4,035; upper middle income, $4,036-$12,475; and high income, $12,476 or more. http://data.worldbank.org/about/country-classifications.
5 Parry *et al.* 2007 (WG II 20.3, 20.5, 20.8); WG III 12.2 SPM; WG III 2.1, 2.5, 12.1, SPM.
6 Parry *et al.* 2007 (WG II 1.3, 5.5.2, 11.6, 17.2).
7 Fankhauser (2009) argues that though it is important to delineate between adaptation and socio-economic development, '(s)ocioeconomic trends over the coming decades – population growth, economic expansion, the deployment of new technologies – will affect our vulnerability to climate events and indeed may be shaped by climate conditions. Human activity has always been influenced by the climate conditions people find themselves in. It is therefore difficult to delineate where socio-economic development ends and adaptation to anthropogenic climate change begins' (Fankhauser (2009, p. 21).
8 As Ackerman notes this is a very broad notion of adaptation, but it resonates with the distinctions being made by Parry *et al.* (2009) between hard (structural) adaptation and soft (behavioural or regulatory) adaptation.

9 WG II SPM.
10 For example, Bangladesh experienced a 18 per cent reduction of people living below the upper poverty line, 2000–9, Vietnam is reported to have lifted over 20 million persons out of poverty in a decade and Rwanda data show a reduction in poverty at the national level by 12 percentage points between 2005/06 and 2010/11 (national institute of statistics of Rwanda, February 2012) available (20.09.2012) http://eeas.europa.eu/delegations/rwanda/documents/press_corner/news/poverty_report_en.pdf. The 'depth of poverty' signifies how far the average poor person falls below the poverty line and the 'severity' of poverty takes account of inequality among the poor. Information on other countries: Chronic poverty Research Centre www.chronicpoverty.org/uploads/publication_files/CPR2_Background_Papers_Grant_05_2.pdf.
11 The identification of these persons as refugees is still a matter of debate since they were so identified in the 1970s by Lester of Brown WorldWatch and in 1985 by UN Essen El-Hinnawi. Currently climate refugees do not legally fall under this status of a refugees under the 1951 Geneva Refugee Convention: a refugee is a person who 'owing to well-founded fear of being persecuted for reasons of race, religion, nationality, membership of a particular social group or political opinion, is outside the country of his nationality and is unable or, owing to such fear, is unwilling to avail himself of the protection of that country. Deprived of legal status, climate refugees, many of whom are internal migrants and rural and coastal residents can be sent home or forced into migration.
12 Of the 1.5 million displaced by Katrina, approximately 300,000 is reported to have never returned.
13 According to a WHO/UNICEF Joint Monitoring Programme for Water Supply and Sanitation, the future projected increase in the proportion of people with improved sanitation access will increased only by 67 per cent by 2015.
14 Cited in Neumayer 2000: 190.
15 During that same period, the US has increased its greenhouse gas emissions by 16.8 per cent, reaching an average of 20 to 23 tons of CO_2 per-person. This represents 9 times more than that of the average inhabitant of the 'Third World', and 20 times more than that of the average inhabitant of sub-Saharan Africa (Cochamba Peoples Accord).
16 In this context, developing countries and many in civil society raise the issue of climate debt, which is the sum of 'adaptation debt' and 'emissions debt', regarding the historic responsibility of developed countries to honour their historical responsibilities for global emissions now built up into the atmosphere and their overuse of the global atmospheric space. The Convention notes that the 'largest share of historical and current global emissions of greenhouse gases has originated in developed countries'. In addition, it is noted that almost three quarters of CO_2 emissions from fossil fuels have been emitted by less than one-fifth of the world's population (those living in developed countries). The call by groups such as the People's Agreement of Cochabamba is for compensation and repayment of this 'climate debt' due to the harmful effects of climate change. The adaptation debt refers to the rising level of damage and costs of adapting to climate change. Emissions debt refers to the claim that the 'excessive and historical and current emissions by the developed country are denying developing countries their fair share' of emissions. People's Agreement of Cochabama, the World People's Conference on Climate Change and the Rights of Mother Earth, Cochabamba, Bolivia, 22 April 2010. Please see also various submissions by the Republic of Bolivia, Malaysia, Paraguay and Pakistan to the AWG-KP and the AWG-LCA.
17 A compromise reached thus far on this point was the agreement on the Nationally Appropriate Mitigation Actions (NAMA) 2005, Bali Plan of Action.
18 Brazil in a submission to UNFCCC during the Kyoto Protocol discussion May 1997 made the first ever proposal for using historical responsibility as a basis for the elements of the Protocol. This proposal submitted to the Ad Hoc Working Group on the Berlin Mandate has become known as the Brazilian proposal proposed an objective criterion to share the burden in accordance with historical responsibility of AI countries. It allowed

for periodic updating and reviews (for example, every 5 or 10 years) so as to reflect actual emission pathways, both past and present. Sharing of the burden is in accordance to a countries relative contribution to climate change as reflected in term so induced changes in temperature. p.11 (BASIC 2011) UNFCCC. 1992. *United Nations Framework on Climate Change*. Brazilian Ministry of Science and Technology. November 2002, www.mct. gov.br/clima and UNFCCC 1997 United Nations Framework on Climate Change: Ad Hoc Group on the Berlin Mandate. Implementation of the Berlin Mandate: Additional proposals from Parties – Addendum – Note by the secretariat. 30 May 1997. FCCC/ AGBM/1997/MIS.1/Add.3. November 2002, www.unfccc.int.
19 2050 is generally argued to be the date by which decarbonisation must be accomplished. So globally emissions are zero are tending to zero.
20 Though the recent IPCC report now shows that this budget is greatly overstated and there is significantly less carbon space available, the analysis nonetheless holds.
21 The reason why the developing countries should insist on historical accountability, nevertheless, and not just on an equal per capita rule without historical accountability, is

> twofold: first, the difference between historically accumulated and current carbon dioxide emissions of developed countries is likely to increase in the future. This is because current emissions of developing countries are likely to increase faster than those of developed countries and because of the time lag until this translates into significantly lower cumulated emissions for developed countries. The second reason is that methane, the second most important greenhouse gas after carbon dioxide, has a relatively low estimated atmospheric residence time of 10 years.
> (Smith 1995, p. 24)

> Because developing countries emit relatively more methane than carbon dioxide than the developed countries do, and because of the low residence time of methane, the gap between historical and current emissions will widen if the 'comprehensive' approach is taken. Eventually, therefore, the difference between historical and current emissions will matter.
> (Neumayer 2000, p. 190)

22 'Grandfathering', the first allocation rule, is in the interests of developed or Annex I countries. It allows the continuation of their unequal access to the common resource atmosphere (Neumayer 2000: 188). The allocation (of the rights to emit GHGs) without historical responsibility is the second of three rules discussed by Neumayer. The third is allocation on an equal per capita basis with historical accountability.
23 According to the report: 'the global mitigation burden is defined by the difference between one of the IPCC scenarios (see footnote viii below) and a required global pathway. The area under the required global pathway is equivalent to the future global carbon budget.' In this context, the burden sharing approach 'focuses on the effort required in "bending the curve" of future emissions trends down towards the required pathway'.
24 The United Nations Environment Programme (UNEP) examination of these current pledges found that despite these pledges GHG emissions in 2020 will be 18 to 27 per cent above where they need to be if warming is likely to be limited to 2 degrees Celsius above pre-industrial levels. This corresponds 8–12 billion tons of GHG emissions in 2020 above the level needed for keeping warming to the 2 degree threshold.
25 The Berlin West Africa Conference was organized ostensibly under the banner of ending black and Islamic slavery – the political cover. But the words slave/slavery/slave trade occur only 9 times in the 5,600 word document and in two articles of the over 37 articles of the general agreement which regulated European colonialism and formalized the scramble for Africa. The General Act of the Berlin Conference on West Africa, 26 February 1885 had 14 signatories including to the usually gang of colonial powers: the UK of Great Britain and Ireland, Germany, France, the Austria-Hungarian, Belgium,

Denmark, Italy, Netherlands, Portugal, Russia, Spain, Sweden-Norway (union until 1901), Turkey (Ottoman Empire) plus the US. Critical to this was the rise of competition threat from Russia, the US and Japan. (1) freedom of trade in the basin of the Congo; (2) the slave trade; (3) neutrality of the territories in the basin of the Congo; (4) navigation of the Congo; (5) navigation of the Niger; and (6) rules for future occupation on the coast of the African continent.

26 This would be their best case scenario. But they are seemingly willing to settle for a second level outcome: a subtle, direct or indirect shifting, sharing or discharging these obligations to the emerging economies (China, Brazil, India and South Africa, working their way down to the middle to lower income countries in Asia, Africa and Latin America, who are not LDCs or SIDS).

27 The danger for LDCs is that they can be graduated, whereas SIDS are geographically defined and challenged. Yet, there are still some dangerous pitfalls for high income and high emitting SIDS: Trinidad & Tobago and Singapore, to name a few.

28 As noted above, the total remaining carbon budget available is very small. The developed countries have used more than their fair share: the US has used about 4 times its per capita share and the EU about twice its per capita share. Ultimately, it can be said that the developed countries had access to a line of credit to the atmospheric space that most developing countries do not now have.

29 UNFCCC (2007): Bali Action Plan.

30 Africa, notoriously, has the worst roads in the world because its extremes of sun and rain bake them dry or leave them cratered and impassable for months at a time. The study, which notes that 'the whole continent, which is physically larger than China, western Europe, India and the US together, still only has 171,000 km of all-weather roads – less than a country such as Poland. It argues that every African country will have to pay an extra $22–54m a year just to keep its already substandard road infrastructure in today's condition. The bill to upgrade and maintain Africa's many millions of miles of secondary roads and tracks, which can be expected to deteriorate even further with climate change, is not even considered (United Nations University 2012 cited in The *Guardian*, 15 June 2011 www.guardian.co.uk/global-development/poverty-matters/2011/jun/15/climate-change-cost-poor-countries-billions.

31 The Stockholm Environmental Institute under took a review of four detailed studies of countries' mitigation pledges under the Cancún agreements. The studies reviewed: UNEP, Climate Action Tracker, McKinsey and Jatzo.

32 Khor 2010. Thus, if a level of 1 tonne per capita is chosen as a 'sustainable level' to avoid climate damage, it is conceivable that developed countries can reach that low-carbon per capita level, with technological and other changes, and retain their present level of living, such as $30,000 per capita income or more. Khor also argues that one possible approach is to retain the aim of having an equal per capita emission as a starting point, but to provide countries with coefficients. Thus a country that is much poorer and lacks in infrastructure and technology could have a 'multiplier' of 5 or 10 to apply to its coefficient of 1. In contrast, another country that is very advanced in technology and income could have a coefficient below 1, and may even have a negative coefficient so that it has a target of a negative emission. The coefficient would be a measure of the relative capacities of the countries, in terms of income, infrastructure, technology and human capacity. On the other hand, a country that now has a per capita emission of 1 tonne of emissions or below may retain that level and not be able to climb up the income scale, so that its economic level remains at, for example, $1,000 or less. Also, developing countries that are currently at moderate emission levels of 3 to 8 tonnes per capita would find it difficult to reduce their emission levels while maintaining or expanding their economies through a low-emissions path, as they are lacking in the three factors.

33 This was discussed in Chapter 1: The Bali tripod: Enhance financing, NAMAs (for developing countries) and high mitigation ambition in the context of comparability of efforts by non-KP Parties such as the US.

Dimensions of global climate change policy   **115**

34 As will be discussed in subsequent chapters, the subject of finance is a matter of high tensions in the climate change negotiations. In regard to the promised $30 billion of so-called fast start finance, as the Secretariat Note to the African Ministers' of the Environment (AMCEN) 2011 meeting pointed out, 'there is also increasing concern that the $30 billion in 'fast-start' financing pledged by developed countries in Copenhagen for the period 2010–2012 is being slowly disbursed. . . . The balance of the funds are mainly rebranded grants, loans or other forms of non-additional finance, meaning that developing countries are being asked in the negotiations to take on new commitments that would be financed by funding that in some cases has been redirected away from other development priorities AMCEN 2011: 7).

35 SRES, Special Report on Emissions Scenarios, the IPCC's family of scenarios outlining plausible descriptions 'of how the future may develop, based on a coherent and internally consistent set of assumptions ('scenario logic') about key relationships and driving forces (for example, rate of technology change, prices'). The SRES scenarios are grouped into four categories of cumulative CO_2 emissions (all sources) between 1990 and 2100: low, medium-low, medium-high, and high emissions. Each category contains scenarios with a range of different driving forces yet similar cumulative emissions. IPCC SRES Glossary.

36 Gender equality language in the Cancún Agreements, in particular the outcome of the Ad Hoc Working Group on Long-term Cooperative Action include: the Preamble; I: A shared vision for long-term cooperative action, Paragraph 7; II: Enhanced action on Adaptation, Paragraph 12; III: Enhanced action on Mitigation C, Paragraph 72; III: Enhanced action on Mitigation E; IV: Finance, technology and capacity-building C; Capacity-building, Paragraph 130 and Annex IV: Paragraph 3. (Advance unedited version of Cancún Agreements, from 11 December 2010, Cancún, Mexico compiled by WEDO.org).

Explicit gender language in Durban COP 17 – Outcome of the work of the Ad Hoc Working Group on Long-term Cooperative Action Draft Decision [-/CP.17]: II. Enhanced action on mitigation, F. Economic and social consequences of response measures para 90; III. Enhanced action on adaptation para 103; VI. Capacity-building; Annex VI, para 2: Annex VII Terms of reference of the Climate Technology Centre and Network, para 1, para 4 and 4c; and Gender Equality Language in Durban Outcomes – Green Climate Fund – report of the Transitional Committee Draft Decision [-/CP.17], I, para 3; II, C, para 2; 2, para 11; E, 1, para 21; V, para 31; XIII, para 71. Gender Equality Language in Durban Outcomes – National adaptation plans. Draft Decision [-/CP.17], A, para 3; Annex, B, para 2 and para 3. Gender Equality Language in Durban Outcomes – Nairobi work programme on impacts, vulnerability and adaptation to climate change Draft Decision [-/CP.17], para 4. Gender Equality Language in Durban Outcomes – Draft Decision on guidance on systems for providing information on how safeguards are addressed and respected and modalities related to forest reference emission levels and forest reference levels as referred in Decision 1/CP.16, appendix I. Draft Decision [-/CP.17], para 2. Gender Equality Language in Durban Outcomes – Capacity-building under the Convention Draft decision [-/CP.17] – preamble. Gender Equality Language in Durban Outcomes – Capacity-building under the Kyoto Protocol Draft Decision [-/CMP.7] – preamble.

Explicit gender references in the GCF Governing Instruments: I. Objectives and Guiding Principles, Paragraph 3; II. Governance and Institutional Arrangements, Paragraphs 11 and 21; V. Operational Modalities, Paragraphs 31; XII. Stakeholder Input and Participation, Paragraph 71.

37 2 degree is termed a 'risking runaway climate change'. Bishop Tutu of South Africa argues that a global goal of 2 degrees is to condemn Africa to incineration and no modern development.

38 Climate justice ensures that the adjustment to the climate crisis is borne by those who create it. A varying set of principles has been articulated in this respect. The set present

here draws heavily from the Bali Principles of Climate Justice articulated by civil society coalitions. According to the Global Human Forum, 'climate justice means ensuring that people everywhere are safe from danger and free from suffering due to climate change' ... This means (e)nsuring the poor can live in safety ... providing substantial additional support to these communities, a responsibility that falls to major polluters. The GHF has also articulated a set of climate justice guidelines.
39 Only seven of the Parties to UNFCCC (and the Kyoto Protocol) have not signed and ratified the Convention on the Elimination of Discrimination against Women. These are: Iran, Nauru, Palau, Sudan, Tonga and the US (signed but not ratified). Somali, which is an observer to UNFCCC, is the eighth country to not sign CEDAW.

3
CLIMATE CHANGE, GENDER EQUALITY AND WOMEN'S EMPOWERMENT ISSUES

> The battle to protect the environment is not solely about technological innovation – it is also about empowering women and their communities to hold their governments accountable for results ... Climate mitigation and adaptation strategies must be developed with women, not for them, and women must be involved alongside men in every stage of climate and development policy-making.
> Wangari Maathai and Mary Robinson, *The Huffington Post*, 2010

This chapter undertakes an exegesis review of the gender dimensions of the adaptation, mitigation and technology development and transfer and capacity building components of global climate protection policy. The chapter ends with an initial template for a qualitative gender empowerment risk assessment framework that could serve as the analytical base for the setting of guidelines, checklists and the refinement of gender sensitive indictors that can be useful in expanding climate-related financial and economic resources for poor women and men.

Climate change and climate variability can cause loss of lives, tremendous property and infrastructural damages and retrogression in economic and social development in the global south. Climate-related weather events are also associated with the destruction of women's and men's lives, livelihoods and shelter and the loss of access to biodiversity. In many regions such as in Africa and South Asia, the lives and livelihoods of women are 'tied to natural resource base' (water resource, agriculture, aquaculture, biodiversity, land use and land use change). In these countries, as well as in the Caribbean and other small island states, rising sea levels have implications for women's and men's access to and control over essential commodities, such as food, water and shelter.

The first section of this chapter (Section 3.1) explores the issue of women's and men's vulnerability to climate change. Section 3.2 discusses gender and climate change within the context of the capabilities framework. Sections 3.3 and 3.4 focus on the specificities of gender equality and women's empowerment issues with regard to adaptation (Section 3.3) and mitigation (Section 3.4). The mitigation section further explores issues around women's and men's energy uses and the employment and entrepreneurial opportunities that are possible under mitigation scenarios. Section 3.5 is devoted to exploring women and forests in the form of REDD and other market based mechanisms while Section 3.6 explores issues around gender and technology. Section 3.7 highlights gender issues in capacity building, including access to technology and science. The chapter ends with a tentative gender empowerment climate change risk analytical framework (Section 3.8).

3.1 Gender, climate change and vulnerability

Women and children die disproportionately more than men from extreme weather events such as floods, hurricanes and storms. Evidence from the aftermath of extreme weather events analysed by Neumayer and Plümper (2007) show that 'natural disasters (and their subsequent impacts) on average kill more women than men or kill women at an earlier age than men'. (Hence, as noted by the authors, one of the social consequences of climate change may be, in some societies, a perverse narrowing of the life expectancy gap between men and women by contributing to the lowering of female life expectancy.) Of the hundreds of people killed during the 2005 South Asia heat waves, most were women and children. Women and children often suffer from diarrhoea and dehydration (BBC 2005; Chiang 2007).

The IPCC's Fifth Assessment Report, though affirming the high propensity of women to serious injuries and death from climate-related events, offers a much more nuanced perspective on the gendered mortality effects of extreme weather. It highlights that the mortality of men and women to extreme events varies regionally. For example, it found that males in the US, China and Vietnam seem to be at greater risk of death following flooding. In the latter two cases men died due to rural farming activities and search and rescue and protection of fields during flooding. It further noted that the Paris 2003 heat wave led to 'excess mortality among females overall, ... there were more excess deaths among men in the working age span (25–64)'.[1] (Appendix 3.1 provides more extensive treatment of AR 5 assessment of the published literature on gender and climate change.)

Climate change induced warming or flooding can have very negative impacts on the lives of men and women. Rising temperature lead to more growth and/or shifting of mosquito habitats, while floods and increased precipitation promote new mosquito breeding grounds.[2] The IPCC's Fourth Assessment Report notes that 'climate change is likely to directly impact children and pregnant women because they are particularly susceptible to vector-and water-borne diseases'. Pregnant women are four times more likely to contract malaria than the general population (Bordallo 2008). Furthermore, World Health Organization data show that pregnant women are more susceptible to (and die from) malaria and water borne diseases (WHO 2003). For example, malaria is currently responsible for a quarter of maternal mortality.

These direct impacts of climate change in turn generate highly interrelated chains of cause-and-effect (consequences) linking profoundly and indirectly to areas such as food security, health and economic security. As noted by the World Bank, these events may also 'impede countries' abilities to sustain all the MDGs, through their indirect effects on education, child mortality, maternal health and women's empowerment' (World Bank 2010).

In addition to the direct and indirect impacts, human meso and micro level responses to climate challenges ranging from migration, to increased violence and conflicts over diminishing resources (water, fertile lands and fisheries, Pachauri and Reisinger 2007) to the exacerbation of malnutrition among vulnerable groups, further complicate and compromise the lives of women, men and boys and girls. WHO (2011) argues that the responses to climate change is a function of 'capacities, resources, behaviour and attitudes'.

These factors, however, are all mediated by pre-existing social and gendered norms, values, roles and relationships and the attendant gender biases and gender-based inequalities existing in the economy. The norms and values and the underlying gender system condition men and women's ability and capacities to take precautionary actions, to respond to the immediate threats and to recover and replace damaged or destroyed assets in the aftermaths of particular climate-related events at a given point in time, or over a period of time.

Tables A3.1A and A3.1B, in Appendix 3.1, present a quick snapshot of the various instances where gender issues are introduced in the IPCC's Fifth and Fourth Assessment Reports (2013 and 2007) as well as in the Cancún and Durban texts. Many of the references with regard to adaptation are usually well represented in discussions around adaptation where gender is usually seen as more relevant so the presentation focuses on mitigation and gender linkages to a large degree. As can be seen in the tables, both the earlier and later Assessment Reports focus the gender lens on a broad range of issues, as well as tackle some specific gender issues treated in the various chapters and sections of this book and in each of the thematic areas. These include food security, bio energy and efficient cooking stoves and women's health and time burden, hydroelectricity and women's personal security and the need for mitigation options that are gender neutral. The main drawback is that gender does not make it into the policy discussion nor into the highly influential Summary for Policy Makers. Hopefully, this marks the trail towards a more extensive treatment of gender into future Assessment Reports.

While there is a growing array of climate actions undertaken by non-governmental organizations, international institutions and overseas development agencies focused at the community level, it is often assumed that women's and men's needs are adequately covered, but this is not often the case. Addressing community concerns does not automatically take care of gender or social equity issues. As noted by gender and water activists, this is because although there is a tendency to see communities as collections of people with a common purpose, 'in reality communities are made up of individuals and interest groups who command different levels of power, wealth, influence and ability to express their needs, concerns and rights' (African Water Strategy). Most often those at the lower spectrum, primarily poor women, men and other vulnerable groups, are usually left out or neglected. This unequal power relation often places women in a disadvantaged position. Individual women and women's organizations take part fully in community life where they contribute greatly to the building of social capital but their participation in many aspects of decision-making processes remains weak and their representation at provincial, regional and national levels is still minimal (Oxfam and OECD).

Climate Policy responses at the macro level are determined by the nature and extent of the climate change policy and the concepts, processes and frameworks that enable the identification and implementation of solutions in terms of the globally adopted twin strategies of adaptation (focusing also on vulnerability and resilience of people to climate change) and mitigation (focusing on forest protection and clean efficient and renewal energy) and their associated means of implementation – finance and technology transfer and capacity building. These areas too are impacted by the gender biases and gender inequalities at play in the global, regional, national and local economies. At the same time, carefully addressing climate change can present many opportunities for employment and entrepreneurial opportunities, as well as enhance the lives and living standards of women and men in poor, rural and urban communities. This can be the case if proactive attempts are undertaken with designing, developing and implementing adaptation projects that enhance and ensure food security and access to health care and clean and renewable projects, and ensure access to decent work and opportunities for women as workers and business owners. Unfortunately, this is not yet automatically the case in the current operation of adaptation and mitigation responses to climate change.

On the adaptation side, women participate actively in sustainable agriculture and water uptake for family and community life, on their own account as well as through working on family and other types of farms. Worldwide women are 43 per cent of the workforce in agriculture and over 50 per cent in Asia and Africa (Nellemann *et al.* 2011). In India, women undertake 4.6 to 5.7 times the agricultural work men carry out. In Nepal, the range is skewed even more with women carrying out 6.3 to 6.6 times the agricultural work that men carry out (ICIMOD, cited in Nelleman *et al.* 2011). Yet, they are not the major drivers or beneficiaries in adaptation programmes, policies and projects (IUCN/UNDP/GGCA 2009: 155; UNFPA/WEDO 2009: 4). Additionally, as noted by Achim Steiner of UNEP, 'women play a much stronger role than men in the management of ecosystem services and food security' (Nellemann *et al.* 2011). Women are also more likely than men to suffer from the ill effects of maladaptation in responding to climate change and they are less likely to receive any or adequate compensation for the losses and damages suffered during extreme events or to have adequate recognition of gender-specific needs and priorities before, during and after such events.

A host of factors contribute to women's pronounced disadvantage in adaptation programming and policy-making in developing countries, including: women's systematic lack of access to formal education, their persistent economic poverty, and pervasive gender-based discrimination in food distribution, food insecurity, limited access to resources and, as previously noted, exclusion from policy and decision-making institutions and processes and other forms of social marginalization (Nellemann *et al.* 2011; FAO 2011; World Bank 2010). Sustainable adaptation, hence, must focus on gender and the role of women if it is to become successful (Nellemann *et al.* 2011). (Adaptation and gender issues are discussed in further detail in Section 3.3 below.)

On the mitigation side, women in Africa, Asia and Latin America are noted to have knowledge and high dependence on forests and forest products. They are often at the forefront of conservation of forests as well as in managing forests, agro forests and tree genetic resources. For example, in the work of the Chipko Movement in India in the 1970s, noted for being the original 'tree huggers', these women challenged the extensive logging that was taking place in their communities. Their struggle contributed to major reform in India's forestry laws. Also in the Asian region, the Tebtebba Foundation in the Philippines works to promote indigenous women's as well as men's continued access and ownership rights to natural resources. In the Latin American region there is the long tradition of the Wangki women of Nicaragua who work to prevent deforestation and degradation, which ensures that more carbon remains in the trees and forests and is not released into the atmosphere. In Africa, the most famous of all, the Green Belt Movement, a Kenyan women's NGO that began to plant trees at the grassroots level in 1977 to tackle the problems of deforestation, soil erosion and water scarcity. Led by Nobel Laureate, Wangari Maathai, the Green Belt Movement is hailed for having saved thousands of trees, thereby also preventing deforestation and degradation and helping to preserve the soils in Kenya. Women in forest communities can generate more than 50 per cent of their income from forests, compared with about one-third for men. Yet according to researchers (such as Tinker 1994; Locke 1999; Agarwal 2001; Blessings *et al.* 2006; Jumbe and Angelsen 2007) women do not fare well under forestry co-management and devolution programmes and mitigation oriented programmes. Often, changes in tree cover and loss of access to forests can therefore have a disproportionate impact on women, with indirect impacts on the livelihoods of 5–10 times as many people (CIFOR 2013).

The positive responses to climate change in terms of increasing the provision of clean energy services may potentially vastly improve women's and men's lives, health and morbidity, especially if keen attention is paid also to lessening and ultimately eliminating the burning of unhealthy biomass for fuel and improving domestic and commercial ventilation. Emerging evidence (Box 3.1) is showing that exposure to smoke from cooking is the fourth risk factor for diseases in developing countries resulting in a wide range of illnesses from chronic and acute health effects such as child pneumonia, lung cancer, chronic obstructive pulmonary disease and heart disease, as well as low birth-weight in children born and ultimately to premature deaths.[3] (Further discussion on the gender and social equity dimension of mitigation is undertaken in Section 3.4.)

> ### BOX 3.1 THE GLOBAL BURDEN OF DISEASE STUDY 2010
>
> The study estimates that exposure to smoke from the simple act of cooking is the fourth worst risk factor for disease in developing countries, and causes four million premature deaths per year – exceeding deaths attributable to malaria or tuberculosis. In addition, tens of millions more fall sick with illnesses that could readily be prevented with increased adoption of clean and efficient cooking solutions.
>
> Women in developing countries are also at risk of head and spinal injuries, pregnancy complications, and maternal mortality from the strenuous task of carrying heavy loads of firewood or other fuels. Frequent exposure to cookstove smoke can also cause disabling health impacts like cataracts, which affect women more than men, and is the leading cause of blindness in developing countries.
>
> Exposure to smoke is greatest among women and young children, who spend the most time near open fires or traditional cookstoves tending to the family meal, or schoolchildren who may study by the light of an open flame. Both inhale unhealthy levels of emissions. Rudimentary wood-fired cookstoves and open fires emit fine particles, carbon monoxide, and other pollutants at levels up to 100 times higher than the recommended limits set by WHO.
>
> Source: Global Alliance for Clean CookStoves, www.cleancookstoves.org/our-work/the-issues/health-impacts.html

Both climate change adaptation and mitigation are reliant on the development and transfer of environmentally sound technologies, an area that could ideally help to better promote, enhance and upscale women's knowledge as well as promote their access to agriculture, food security and other technologies. Along with limited land ownership, and lack of access to credit, access to technology is an important constraint on women's productive and entrepreneurial activities. Numerous research highlights that there are gender differentiated perceptions of risks with regard to new technologies (Denton 2002; Richards 2005). There are also gender differentiated patterns to the access and utilization of new innovations. Furthermore, women's innovations in agriculture, food production and water will require nurturing and protection to ensure their sustainability and that women and their families retain benefits during the long term. Opportunities available in energy efficiency and clean and renewal energy arenas may also bypass women business owners as well as poor female-headed households if there is not proactive attention taken by governments and energy suppliers to include women in the value-chain in the development, acquisition and supply of solar, wind and other clean energy technologies. As noted by Dr Asuncion Lera St Clear, Lead Author, of IPCC's Fifth Assessment Report, Working Group, II, clean and renewable energy as well as access to technology when forthcoming to the sectors that women dominate, such as the household, food production and the informal sector, can be of great use to women facilitating their improved health, functioning and greater well-being.

Along with technology, stronger and more deliberately gender friendly support for capacity building and the strengthening of project frameworks will be important in providing women enhanced access to extensions trainings and services in food production and climate resilient agriculture and forest management. Research is showing that comprehensive capacity building in food production, processing and marketing, apiculture and the planting and care of trees helps to empower women to generate an income of their own. Likewise, increased knowledge about climate science and the phenomenon of climate change is an important part of capacity building which is a growing aspect of approaches to addressing climate change for ensuring gender equality and women's empowerment. While there continues to be a disproportionate presence of women researchers in the social and the human sciences, there are even fewer women from developing countries involved in the area of climate science research and development. (The concluding sections of this chapter address the question of gender technology and capacity building in greater detail.)

In order for positive outcomes to occur at the global, regional and national and local levels with regard to climate change adaptation and mitigation, policy frameworks and instruments must be made sufficiently gender-aware and gender sensitive. Policymakers and technical experts working on climate and environmental issues must pay attention to the gendered nature of vulnerability, capabilities and capacities with regard to the design, implementation and monitoring of climate protection policies. They must also become more aware of and more proactive about including gender-sensitive elements that promote and support the preservation and enhancement of women's and men's lives and livelihoods in the face of climate change and climate variability generated events.

Climate change policies, programmes and projects should seek to reinforce the reduction of gender inequality and to enhance the empowerment of women as well as ensure that specific climate resilient adaptation and mitigation programming work to promote gender equality and women's empowerment in each of the specific programmatic areas.

Both targeted gender equality interventions and non-targeted gender equality interventions that benefit the lives of women and girls and contribute to overall community and national resiliency and the development of sustainable growth pathways require deep and comprehensive understanding of the nature and pattern of vulnerabilities that women and men face in different settings as well as the opportunities, challenges and constraints that influence their ability to respond to changing policy dynamics, incentives and signalling. The next section explores these issues in greater detail.

The IPCC, in its 2007 report, identified five key sectors – agriculture, forestry and fisheries, water supply, human health, coastal zones and infrastructure – as critical parameters for adaptation activities (Table 3.1). These sectors are also the

TABLE 3.1 Key adaptation sectors

Sector	Areas/adaptation measures considered
Agriculture, forestry and fisheries	Production and processing, research and development, extension activities
Water supply	Water supply infrastructure
Human health	Treating increased cases of diarrhoeal disease, malnutrition and malaria
Coastal zones	Beach nourishment and dykes
Infrastructure	New infrastructure

Source: adapted from UNFCCC (2008)

sectors that are highlighted among the top categories of the over 400 'urgent and immediate' adaptation projects listed in the 41 plus NAPAs of the least developing countries received by the GEF, an operating entity of the financial mechanism of the UNFCCC. Undeniably, these are also the sectors that are critical for the lives of men and women. Women are very active and perform significant roles in all of the five sectors in all developing countries. Women are also dynamic actors in projects and programmes particularly related to climate change, such as crop and livestock selection, crop shifting and soil preservation and the use of traditional water harvesting techniques and the efficient use of water. Women undertake these as autonomous adaptation activities within women's groups and also within community based adaptation processes.

Climate change related events such as heat waves, cyclones and hurricanes are likely to exacerbate the existing vulnerabilities of women – and create new ones. Loss of livelihood and other weather-related changes, such as decreased access to grazing lands and water resources, increase hardship and exacerbate and reinforce poverty while making it more intractable to reduce or eradicate. Women and men are therefore forced to take defensive survival strategies such as migration or involuntary leave from their homes, villages and localities resulting in displacement, loss of homes and livelihoods.

Women in countries as diverse as Ghana, the Philippines and Senegal have been coping with soil erosion, through crop rotation, mixed crops and shifting cultivation to higher ground (WEDO 2008; Perlata 2008). They have also used stony borders, half-moon canals and open trenches to backtrack shorelines and control and direct water flow and recharge ground water. Women have also drawn on traditional knowledge, information and techniques to undertake small-scale levels of reforestation. In most cases, women have undertaken these tasks on their own, in women's groups and cooperatives, or have initiated the projects and later, with the enrolment of the youths and men in their communities, achieved successful outcomes in adaptation and mitigation projects.

For example, in Senegal, water collection has become a heavy burden on women due to the impact of climate variability on underground water resources

(Ndiaye 2008, cited in WEDO 2008). Rainfall shortage, shorter rain seasons and drought forced women to walk far distances for water. Women have responded by improving their energy and water management solutions, including undertaking their own small-scale regeneration of mangroves and reforesting parts of forests (ibid.).

In the coastal areas of Ghana some women have experienced losses to livelihoods due to declining fish stocks. Climate change, in conjunction with detrimental fishing practices by men and fishing trawlers, have exacerbated gender asymmetries in the fishing sector. This has resulted in the 'loss of income for poorer women (who are in charge of processing, storing and marketing fish catches), increases in the price of fish, and lower levels of protein in diets' (Damptey and Mensah 2005, cited in WEDO 2008). Without the benefit of institutional frameworks and support, women have tracked and monitored dramatic changes in weather patterns over the last 10 years (ibid.).

The literature on women and vulnerability (Swain and Floro 2007; Antonopoulos and Floro 2008; Agarwal 1995) highlights that pre-existing gender-related patterns of vulnerabilities can block women's ability and capacity to effectively engage in eco-friendly technology, natural resource management and early warning systems[4] (Appendix 3.2 highlights nine areas of vulnerability and their climate change linkages). These vulnerabilities range from lack of secure land rights (which is interrelated with access to credits and livelihood), gender gaps in the ownership of productive assets, higher illiteracy rates among women than men, unpredictable and less favourable access to employment and income and inequality in participation in decision-making (FAO 1998). Working Group II of the IPCC presents a box with descriptions of 'how adaptive capacity and vulnerability to climate change impacts are different for men and women, with gender-related vulnerability particularly apparent in resource-dependent societies and in the impacts of extreme weather-related events' (2007b: 730). (This box and its contents, which are also included in a separate document of 'cross sector studies', are reproduced in their entirety below in Box 3.2).

The roles assigned to women and men in society, their differential access to resources, and their different responsibilities and obligations condition their adaptive capacity in the face of climate change. This fundamental reality is not yet well recognized and integrated into climate change policy discourse. The pre-existing gender biases and gender inequities that emanated from these gendered roles, responsibilities and constraints continue to operate in the economy in spite of climate change and its variability. In fact some of these biases and inequities may even be exacerbated by extreme weather events. In turn, these gender realities may have serious implications for the pathways and the ultimate outcomes of climate change policy responses. The IPCC Working Group II cites work by O'Brien *et al.* (2004) that lends some support to this point. Adaptive capacity plays a key role in influencing the outcomes of adaptation or other climate strategy. O'Brien *et al.* locate gender as one of the socio-economic factors that 'influenced the

BOX 3.2 GENDER ASPECTS OF VULNERABILITY AND ADAPTIVE CAPACITY*

Empirical research has shown that entitlements to elements of adaptive capacity are socially differentiated along the lines of age, ethnicity, class, religion and gender (Cutter 1995; Denton 2002; Enarson 2002). Climate change therefore has gender-specific implications in terms of both vulnerability and adaptive capacity (Dankelman 2002). There are structural differences between men and women through, for example, gender-specific roles in society, work and domestic life. These differences affect the vulnerability and capacity of women and men to adapt to climate change. In the developing world in particular, women are disproportionately involved in natural resource-dependent activities, such as agriculture (Davison 1988), compared to salaried occupations. As resource-dependent activities are directly dependent on climatic conditions, changes in climate variability projected for future climates are likely to affect women through a variety of mechanisms: directly through water availability, vegetation and fuelwood availability and through health issues relating to vulnerable populations (especially dependent children and elderly). Most fundamentally, the vulnerability of women in agricultural economies is affected by their relative insecurity of access and rights over resources and sources of wealth such as agricultural land. It is well established that women are disadvantaged in terms of property rights and security of tenure, though the mechanisms and exact form of the insecurity are contested (Agarwal 2003, Jackson 2003). This insecurity can have implications both for their vulnerability in a changing climate, and also their capacity to adapt productive livelihoods to a changing climate.

There is a body of research that argues that women are more vulnerable than men to weather-related disasters. The impacts of past weather-related hazards have been disaggregated to determine the differential effects on women and men. Such studies have been done, for example, for Hurricane Mitch in 1998 (Bradshaw 2004) and for natural disasters more generally (Fordham 2003). These differential impacts include numbers of deaths, and well-being in the post-event recovery period. The disproportionate amount of the burden endured by women during rehabilitation has been related to their roles in the reproductive sphere (Nelson *et al.* 2002). Children and elderly persons tend to be based in and around the home and so are often more likely to be affected by flooding events with speedy onset. Women are usually responsible for the additional care burden during the period of rehabilitation, while men generally return to their pre-disaster productive roles outside the home. Fordham (2003) has argued that the key factors that contribute to the differential vulnerability of women in the context of natural hazards in South Asia include: high levels of illiteracy, minimum mobility and

> work opportunities outside the home, and issues around ownership of resources such as land.
>
> The role of gender in influencing adaptive capacity and adaptation is thus an important consideration for the development of interventions to enhance adaptive capacity and to facilitate adaptation. Gender differences in vulnerability and adaptive capacity reflect wider patterns of structural gender inequality. One lesson that can be drawn from the gender and development literature is that climate interventions that ignore gender concerns reinforce the differential gender dimensions of vulnerability (Denton 2002). It has also become clear that a shift in policy focus away from reactive disaster management to more proactive capacity building can reduce gender inequality (Mirza 2003).
>
> * Reproduced from IPCC (2007: Cross sectoral and Chapter 17, Box 17.5, p.729)

capacity to adapt to changing environmental and economic conditions' (IPCC 2007b: 729).

This recognition simply affirms the findings of over 20 years of empirical research linking gender biases and inequities to the persistence of women's poverty. Poverty and the lack of opportunities have also been synonymous with lack of sustained growth in many poor developing countries. Yet, in spite of the numerous empirical research and that has given rise to voluminous literature on the critical importance of gender equality and women's empowerment to sustainable development, climate change policy and institutional framework remain highly gender insensitive.

Many of the factors affecting women's empowerment and their control over economic and financial resources are well known and have become widely accepted. These factors include gender inequality around differential access to economy, social and physical goods, gender gaps in education, income, time use, and leisure and gender differentiated roles and responsibilities in the household, community and labour markets.

In the MDG-oriented literature, these factors are clustered in terms of their implications for the three operational domains of gender equality and women's human development: capabilities, resources and opportunities and security (UN Millennium Project 2005; Crown et al. 2006; Antonopoulos and Floro 2008; Agarwal 1995; Pearl 2003). Box 3.3 presents more detailed summaries of these clusters of gender equality domains.

The 'capabilities domain' refers to basic human abilities as reflected in education, health and nutrition. The 'access to resources and opportunities domain' refers to equality in the opportunity to use or apply basic capabilities through access to economic assets (such as land, property or infrastructure) and resources (such as

> ## BOX 3.3 THE GENDER EQUALITY DOMAINS
>
> The Millennium Project Task Force on MDG3 expanded gender equality to encompass at least five other goals: (1) equal opportunity, (2) equal ownership and control over productive assets, (3) freedom from drudgery, (4) equal representation in decision-making and freedom, and (5) freedom from the threat of violence.
>
> These dimensions of gender equality can be aggregated in terms of three interrelated and interdependent operational domains of: capabilities; resources and opportunity; and security (Grown *et al.* 2006). The capabilities domain includes all elements that are important and necessary for the well-being of women and girls. Examples of such capabilities include education, health and nutrition. The resources and opportunities domain enables girls and women to contribute maximally to economic and social life. This domain refers to equal access to economic assets, such as land, property, infrastructure and income, and equal access to political participation. The security domain includes factors that will help to reduce women's and girls' vulnerability to violence and conflict. The elements in these three domains are operationalized through seven strategic priorities focused on: (1) providing universal primary and post-primary education for girls; (2) guaranteeing sexual and reproductive health and rights; (3) reducing women's and girls' time burdens; (4) guaranteeing women's and girls and property and inheritance rights; (5) eliminating inequality in employment, gender gaps in earnings and occupational segregation; (6) increasing women's share of seats in national parliaments and local government bodies and; (7) reducing violence against girls and women (UN Millennium Project 2005).

income and employment), as well as political opportunity (such as representation in parliaments). The 'security domain' is defined to mean reduced vulnerability to violence and conflict. Empirical research has also located the gender-differentiated dynamics of these domains across a broad range of human social and economic activities, including agriculture, services, manufacturing, water and energy distribution and use, transportation and disaster management (Antonopoulos and Floro 2008; Agarwal 1994; Pearl 2003).

3.2 Gender, climate change and the capabilities framework

3.2.1 Capabilities

For many women in developing countries climate change is associated with the intensification of food shortage, increased respiratory diseases and exhaustion from travelling further distances in order to securing drinking water and water for other household uses. These factors relate to women's and men's health and morbidity and time-use, and hence climate change poses significant challenges for women's and men's personal adaptability and resilience. The available literature on the social and human costs of climate change points out that women and men living at the margins of poverty or below the poverty line face specific forms of vulnerabilities in terms of lack of access to clean drinking water, inadequate sanitation and water-borne diseases. Therefore, climate change and climate variability – expressed in the forms of drought, floods and storms (by negatively affecting water sources, introducing other contaminants into water and impacting the vector of diseases) – increase women's vulnerability and impose disproportionate amounts of adaptation pressures (both planned and reactive) to secure food, water and housing for their children and extended families, especially elders and themselves.

3.2.2 Opportunities and resources

Climate change and related events such as droughts and floods are associated with the destruction of women's agricultural livelihoods, shelter and access to biodiversities. Climate change may create the need for climate-proofing housing and business establishments. In the case of extreme weather events, households and individuals may need to purchase materials and equipment to rebuild or repair damaged dwellings. They may also need to obtain new appliances to replace lost or damaged household appliances and farm equipment. In the immediate aftermath of climate induced events the prices for these items may be at a premium and credit may be constrained in the short run. In such cases, women are more likely than men to be unable to access credit and must draw down their income and savings. Therefore, climate change may also impact women's access to credit, technology and finance. Depending on the duration and severity of the problem, this may have long-term implications for women's economic empowerment. The IPCC's Working Group II notes that women's relative 'insecurity of access and rights over resources and sources of wealth such as agricultural land can have implications both for their vulnerability in a changing climate, and also their capacity to adapt productive livelihoods to a changing climate' (IPCC 2007b: 729).

3.2.3 Security

Climate change also intensifies the effects of pre-existing gender gaps. First, older forms of information asymmetries such as differential access to crop and marketing information between men and women may be superimposed by new forms of asymmetries. While the old forms of asymmetries led to long-term chronic problems such as endemic poverty, the new forms such as asymmetrical information sharing regarding early warning and disaster preparedness are urgent and immediately life-threatening. This is more likely to be the case in areas where men dominate the public space and therefore have earlier access to, and can act upon, information about pending extreme weather events. Women, if they tend to remain in the household sphere, may not have such information until it is too late to take precautionary measures.

Second, climate change-induced weather events, to the extent that they create homelessness and forced resettlement, adversely impact women's personal security. It is widely reported that rape, sexual assault and other forms of gender-based violence are perpetuated against girls and women, who are forced to leave their homes during climate-related events, and find shelter in refugee camps or other forms of resettlement. As a result of droughts drying up nearby water sources, young girls and women must wander further away from their residences to secure water for their family. They are vulnerable to attacks and harassment.

Third, conflicts over resources, especially water and land, intensify with climate change. Ironically, some of these conflicts are generated as individuals seek to take the opportunity presented by climate change. For example, in the area of carbon offset, with regards to afforestation and reforestation and other land-use changes, the forest and its environment have becoming increasingly valuable resources. This in some cases may lead to women as well as indigenous peoples losing control over land and forests. Many of these changes predispose women to both domestic and community violence.

If climate policies, to adapt to or to mitigate climate change, ignore or benignly neglect gender equality interventions or do not mainstream gender issues into sectoral programmes, projects and policies, they will exacerbate structural gender inequalities, and may potentially further disadvantage women. This will act as a brake on the forward momentum of gender equality and women's economic and social empowerment that the last 20 years of global commitments on gender equality and gender mainstreaming have set in motion. It is therefore imperative that proactive attention, including the necessary remedial measures, is paid to address any adverse gender-differentiated impacts of climate change policy, social and economic response measures, and financing. (These are discussed in Chapters 4–8.) Recognition of the links between gender equality outcomes and successful climate change outcomes might lead to the process of integrating both targeted and non-targeted gender and non-gender equality interventions within the framework of adaptation, mitigation and technological transfer programmes and projects. (The distinction between targeted and non-targeted gender equality interventions is highlighted very clearly in Box 3.4.)

Both the IPCC (2007) and the Stern (2006) reports have systematically stressed the importance that the tools to reduce the adverse impacts of climate change take advantage of opportunities to address development and equity issues. However, the UNFCCC and the climate change regime have tended to overemphasize the role of mitigation and technology as exclusive and first-best solutions to the climate change dilemma. Thus in the design and implementation of climate policy, development and equity concerns have been neglected in favour of pronouncedly mitigation bias. As a result, adaptation, social and gender issues, though critical for both adaptive behaviour and mitigation processes, have been benignly neglected.

> **BOX 3.4 TARGETED GENDER EQUALITY AND NON-TARGETED GENDER EQUALITY INTERVENTIONS**
>
> | Targeted gender equality interventions | Non-targeted gender equality interventions |
> |---|---|
> | Programmes and projects that directly reduce gender inequality and empower women. | Projects and programmes that are directed at improving social development but which have spill-over effects on gender equality. |
> | Examples include MDG3-specific programmes dedicated to improving educational outcomes for girls and women, and gender mainstreaming activities such as gender training and gender focal points in sector ministries. | Examples include the construction of feeder and rural roads, health clinics and water services. |
> | (MDG sectors include: education, health, rural development, slum upgrading, water, sanitation and energy.) | Projects and programmes in these areas will work for the achievement of the MDGs as a whole, and while not directly aimed at gender equality will synergistically promote gender equality and MDG3. |
>
> Source: based on UN Millennium Task Force and Grown et al. (2006)

3.3 Gender and adaptation

The IPCC defines adaptation as 'the adjustment in natural or human systems in response to actual or expected climate stimuli or their effects, which moderates harm or exploits beneficial opportunities'. Adaptation is hence a multidimensional, dynamic, iterative process that involves changes in lifestyle, behaviour and risk management by individuals, households, firms and countries. On a practical level then, adaptation actions can be seen in terms of those actions that (a) are focused on climate-proofing socio-economic activities by integrating future climate risk; (b) actions that expand the adaptive capacity of socio-economic activities to deal with future and not only current climate risks; and (c) actions that are purely aimed at adapting to the impacts of climate change and would not otherwise be initiated (UNFCCC 2008: 26).

Projects that seek to expand the adaptive capacity of socio-economic activities to deal with the future include projects for the management of flash floods, strengthening early warning systems and cultivation of drought areas. The IPCC Working Group II identified the combination of biophysical (i.e., soil quality), socio-economic (i.e. measure of literacy and gender equity) and technological conditions as important issues that influence the capacity to adapt to changing environmental conditions (IPCC 2007b).[5] The IPCC Working Group II also noted that 'the capacity to adapt is dynamic and is influenced by a society's productive base, including natural and man-made capital assets, social networks and entitlements, human capital and institutions, governance, national income, health and technology' (IPCC 2007b; WG II 17.3). Further 'adaptive capacity is intimately connected to social and economic development but it is not evenly distributed across and within societies, and within societies'.[6]

Therefore actions that address 'distinct risks posed by climate change' including, for example, undertaking projects to lower water levels or divert water, should be cognizant of the social dynamics of the area and community in which the project is undertaken if it is to properly meet and ensure adaptive capacity. The same would hold for adaptation actions around a wide range of other activities such as capacity-building, research and assessments (to understand vulnerabilities to climate change and how adaptation can reduce these risk); disaster risk reduction and risk management and specific interventions (e.g. infrastructure or economic diversification). The IPCC's Working Group III highlighted that the 'role of gender in influencing adaptive capacity and adaptation is thus an important consideration for the development of interventions to enhance adaptive capacity and to facilitate adaptation. Gender differences in vulnerability and adaptive capacity reflect wider patterns of structural gender inequality' (IPCC 2007b: 730).

climate-proofing (making the economic and social structures resistant to climate change) is an added dimension to the development planning. It is a direct result of climate change and variability and creates the additional costs of identifying the likely risks of climate-related events to social and economic assets. Appropriate measures must then be undertaken by different stakeholders to guard against or mitigate those risks. Thus, climate-proofing activities would include investments in infrastructure (e.g. airports, sanitation and transport), public health or education, areas that primarily seek to achieve social and economic developmental goals (Table 3.2). Ultimately, adaptation includes actions taken by governments, institutions, firms, households and individuals to climate-proof domiciles, communities and capital stock against the ravages of extreme weather events and to minimize the effects of global warming on human and biological systems. Such actions include changing the mix of crops, plant varieties, livestock and fish species, modifying irrigation and flood control systems, implementing pest and disease management programmes, managing fire, expanding health systems, developing infrastructure relocating and migrating.

A good programmatic focus of adaptation would seek to develop programmes ranging from 'very concrete efforts around decreasing the impact of disasters, ensuring coping and relief strategies for dealing with damages when they do occur to the more complex issue of increasing resilience' (UNDESA 2010). This points to different types and approaches to adaptation including climate-proofing existing infrastructure, community based adaptation and the integration

TABLE 3.2 A typology of climate-proofing by selected sectors and activities

Sector	Typical climate-proofing activities include:
Agriculture and food security	• Tree farming; incorporating different plants and seed variety that can adapt to heat or water stresses, implementing proper drainage and run-off of agricultural land
	• Implementing appropriate land-use planning
Housing and building	• Building or retrofitting offices and dwellings with all-weather materials
	• Strengthening and adapting new buildings to withstand extreme weather events
Health care	• Conducting assessments of climate-related health risks, including vector-borne and water-borne diseases
	• Initiating relevant early warning systems
	• Implementing public education programmes
Roads	• Ensuring proper drainage
	• Modifying infrastructure to accommodate changes in rainfall patterns or drainage run-off
	• Ensuring adequate breakwater and quays
Water	• Building catchment tanks for rainwater

Source: developed from *Climate-Proofing: A Risk-based Approach to Adaptation*, ADB (2005)

of adaptation strategies and measures into the framework of poverty reduction programmes. It is also important to improve the climate resilience of communities, especially those in the rural and agricultural sector as well as those on the coastal areas.

Adapting to climate change challenges therefore will stretch the coping skills of men and women. Adaptation of women and men, as consumers, entrepreneurs, individuals and workers and as heads of households, is a function of multiple interrelated factors including control over land, money credit, health, personal mobility and food and housing security. As indicated above, women, especially poor women, tend to have less control than men over these factors. They are therefore at a significant disadvantage in the face of gender blind and male-biased climate change policies.

One key area in which women are very active is sustainable agricultural.[7] Earlier it was noted that women are strong in food production in many developing countries; they are also likewise involved in the fishery sectors in many countries. Up to 80 per cent of all fish and shellfish caught by local, artisanal fisherfolk in tropical Africa, Asia and the Pacific are cleaned, dried, smoked and marketed by women and children (UNFPA 2009). Research from the International Fund for Agricultural Development (IFAD) also shows 'that over the past 20 years the number of rural women living in absolute poverty increased by 50 per cent from 370 million to about 565 million' (cited in UNFPA 2009). Over the same period, the percentage of rural men in absolute poverty increased by only 30 per cent (ibid.).

In many countries women produce on inadequate land, have irregular or no access to irrigated water and very little access to credit and technology. The FAO notes that although African women dominate food production and comprise 60 per cent of the agricultural labour force, they receive less than 1 per cent of the total credit available to agriculture (FAO).

The gender and agriculture literature (FAO 1993; IPRI 2009; Truitt 1999) indicates that when women have equal access to key farming inputs they are equally as productive as men (Quisumbing 2008). China is a good example of this. Chinese women farmers who have equal access to farm inputs including family labour, adequate amount of land, irrigation, credit, and information and technology are just as productive as men (ibid.). Chinese women also comprise about 30 per cent of extension agents and the government is focused on training more women (ibid.). In comparison only 15 per cent of global extension workers are women (IAASTD 2008). In many developing countries, women in the agricultural sector generally have: (1) unequal access to farm inputs and (2) there are few female extension workers and the male ones tend to bypass female farmers. Furthermore, seminars, trainings and workshops are often scheduled at times of the day that women must perform their household duties. If meetings are held at night, that poses personal security issues for women, who often do not have access to private transport. As a result, women farmers tend to have less access to technology and information that would improve their productivity.

Technological interventions should also focus on improving women's productivity especially in the area of food production. In general, policy makers should ensure that agricultural technologies are targeted to women (within a context that builds on their own traditional knowledge and practices), promote food security and ensure sustainability.

Research shows that women's empowerment promote better health and nutrition of the household as well as more healthy behaviours among household members. For example:

- Studies in Asia show strong links between increase in women's status and long-term and short-term nutritional status of children leading to reductions in both stunting and wasting (Quisumbing 2008). According to Quisumbing (2008), 'the same study estimates that if the status of men and women were equalized, the underweight rate among children under 3 years old would drop by approximately 13 percentage points – a reduction of 13.4 million malnourished children' (ibid.).
- An intensive survey of 278 households in rural Nepal found that when both subsistence production and market production were considered, women, despite having two-thirds less cash income than men, still contributed 15 per cent

more money to the monthly household budget. In general, men spent a disproportionate amount of income from cash crops or wages on relative luxuries, including tobacco, liquor and leisure activities. Women devoted much more of their income to maintaining better nutritional levels and were more likely to set aside extra money for health care and education (UNFPA 2009).
- Quisumbing (2008) reports that a recent IPRI assessment of vegetable and fishpond technologies in rural Bangladesh showed that if agricultural technology is not targeted to women, its dissemination is more likely to benefit men and better-off households. The same report showed that when training and credit are targeted to women, they have greater poverty reducing impact (Quisumbing 2008).
- In Latin America, work undertaken by Truitt (1999) found that 'the presence of women in technical positions on agricultural extension teams enables projects to reach a greater number of female beneficiaries and, through them, to men who had not previously participated'.

Climate and gender sensitive agriculture would involve a shift from energy intensive industrial farming practices towards diversified agriculture that safeguards natural resources and promote agro-ecological practices. Such a shift would include emphasis on community based and traditional regenerative processes such as nutrient cycling, nitrogen fixation and soil regeneration processes. Women and indigenous communities have practised crop rotation that increases soil nitrogen and decreased the need for synthetic fertilizers. They have also incorporated conservation tillage practices and integrated pest management within their mode of operations in the farming sector.

Researchers Perlata (2008), Brody *et al.* (2008) and Parikh (2007) have noted that when it comes to adaptation priorities, women have specific and sometimes different concerns from men. Women's priorities often include crop diversification, skills, knowledge and training on drought, flood resistant crops, and the proper use of manure, pesticides and irrigation. While many of these may be similar to men in the same communities, the nature and scope of how they are presented, accessed and utilized may be vastly different between men and women in those same communities. Therefore, a climate change policy environment that is supportive of women's practical and strategic interests would enhance the value of local innovation and context specific knowledge as captured by participatory research. It would also need to address the obstacles to women's participation, (such as poor infrastructure and limited time), and would also focus on ensuring the availability of new agricultural techniques to women farmers. It would break the constraints on women's adaptation activities by facilitating the cultivation of flood and drought resistant crops which can be harvested before flood season (Perlata 2008; Parikh 2007). This is important especially in Sub Saharan Africa where women make up a significant proportion of food producers. In some countries they produce over 70 per cent of food.

Despite these concerns noted above, and prior to 2010, gender concerns did not shape the design and outcomes of the over 450 NAPAs projects that have been produced by 46 Least Developing countries.[8] Agriculture, forestry and fisheries, water supply, human health, coastal zones and infrastructure are also the top five sectors identified in these 'urgent and immediate' adaptation projects listed in the NAPAs of the least developed countries in Africa, Asia and the Caribbean.[9] But while 90 per cent of these NAPAs are focused on sectoral issues (such as food security – the priority sectors for over one-fourth of NAPA projects) with 10 per cent focused on cross sectoral adaptation needs, they are glaringly absent of gender considerations. This is especially so with regard to the critical areas prioritized in the lists of projects for which funding is sought. About seven countries such as Bangladesh, Burkina Faso, the Democratic Republic of the Congo and Malawi do make reference to gender and women's empowerment concerns in their NAPAs. Box 3.5 presents an overview of the range of gender issues identified in many of these NAPAs. The NAPA presentations of the LDCs also show quite importantly that food security is certainly an area that is central to gender equality interventions. Priorities area number three (water resources) is also critical for men's and women's social reproduction work.[10]

An evaluation report by COWI and IIED (2009) argues that 'by design, NAPAs focused on the grassroots level participation of communities and societies, using a gender-sensitive approach ... (opens) a window for the inclusion of women and men equally in the identification and implementation of urgent and immediate adaptation activities'.

The Cancún Adaptation Framework (CAF) launched in 2010 introduced a new adaptation policy instrument, the National Adaptation Programme (NAP), which will focus on longer term adaptation issues. Box 3.6 highlights selected key provisions in the preamble to the CAF, while Box 3.7 points out the critical dimension of gender and adaptation in new instrumentality of the NAPs. Both the CAF and the NAP, the relationship with pre-existing NAPA as well as the more recent Durban (2012) outcome on adaptation (the gender equality oriented provisions of which are noted in Box 3.8) and their gender dimensions will be discussed further in Chapter 5 on gender and adaptation funding.

3.4 Gender and mitigation

Mitigation refers to actions aimed at reducing GHG emissions and actions that enhance both natural and man-made greenhouse gas sinks.[11] Natural sinks, such as oceans, forests and trees, contribute to the absorption of carbon dioxide; for example, the earth's oceans via living organisms and chemical interactions with the surface of the water), and plants and algae via photosynthesis. Man-made sinks include benign ones such as landfills and organic agriculture and speculative technologies such as carbon capture and storage. Typically mitigation policies and strategies in developing countries are focused on facilitating the transfer to a low-carbon economy. This means addressing 'the large number of human activities, among them, agriculture, deforestation, land-use changes, industrial production, energy generation and end use – that generate [greenhouse gas] emissions' (UNFCCC 2008).

BOX 3.5 SNAPSHOTS OF GENDER-RELATED CONSIDERATIONS FROM THE NAPAS OF THE LDCS

Burkina Faso's NAPA is based on four key economic sectors (namely agriculture, water resources, livestock and forests/biodiversity) and the inclusion of women, the young and low-production farmers was an overriding principle in the NAPA preparation process.

In the Democratic Republic of the Congo, gender-related considerations have been integrated into all stages of NAPA preparation and implementation. Gender-related elements are included as concrete elements within each project/activity (e.g. national workshops must have a 25 per cent representation of women, as a minimum target).

Interventions proposed in Malawi's NAPA include activities targeting women in highly vulnerable situations, including: (a) the empowerment of women through access to microfinance in order to diversify earning potential; (b) ensuring easier access to water and energy sources by drilling boreholes and planting trees; and (c) the use of electricity provided through the rural electrification programme.

Mauritania's first approved NAPA project for implementation has the objective of improving the living conditions and incomes of women and young people in a sustainable way, by developing numerous agricultural value chains.

Nepal performed gender sensitivity analyses of climate change impacts in the formulation of its NAPA.

In Niger, women are the beneficiaries of three livestock/crop farming NAPA projects, one of which includes enhancing women's land use and ownership as an activity. Women were also involved in national consultations on the NAPA.

In Senegal, a NAPA project on water efficiency is aiming at distributing kits based on criteria which include gender. In addition, forestry projects specifically mention women as beneficiaries.

The activities identified in Sierra Leone's NAPA aim to train women in implementing adaptation activities and to undertake sensitization campaigns on the specific climate change impacts on women. The NAPA mentions that it is through the inclusion of women and children that the project will be sustainable.

Source: Cancún Adaptation Framework, Annex II: Gender-related consideration

BOX 3.6 GENDER AND THE CANCÚN ADAPTATION FRAMEWORK

1   The Preamble

2   Para 7. Recognizes the need to engage a broad range of stakeholders at the global, regional, national and local levels, be they government, including subnational and local government, private business or civil society, including youth and persons with disability, and that gender equality and the effective participation of women and indigenous peoples are important for effective action on all aspects of climate change; (Section I. A shared vision for long-term cooperative action,) . . .

3   Para 12. Affirms that enhanced action on adaptation should be undertaken in accordance with the Convention, should follow a country-driven, gender-sensitive, participatory and fully transparent approach, taking into consideration vulnerable groups, communities and ecosystems, and should be based on and guided by the best available science and, as appropriate, traditional and indigenous knowledge, with a view to integrating adaptation into relevant social, economic and environmental policies and actions, where appropriate; (Section II. Enhanced action on adaptation 12) . . .

4   Para 72. Also requests developing country Parties, when developing and implementing their national strategies or action plans, to address, inter alia, the drivers of deforestation and forest degradation, land tenure issues, forest governance issues, gender considerations and the safeguards identified in Paragraph 2 of appendix I to this decision, ensuring the full and effective participation of relevant stakeholders, inter alia indigenous peoples and local communities;

5   Para 130. Decides that capacity-building support to developing country Parties should be enhanced with a view to strengthening endogenous capacities at the subnational, national or regional levels, as appropriate, taking into account gender aspects, to contribute to the achievement of the full, effective and sustained implementation of the Convention, . . .

Source: 1/CP.16 The Cancún Agreements: Outcome of the work of the Ad Hoc Working Group on Long-term Cooperative Action under the Convention. Decisions adopted FCCC/CP/2010/7/Add.1

BOX 3.7 GENDER AND NAPS

II. National Adaptation Plans (NAPs)

Para 3: Further agrees that enhanced action on adaptation should be undertaken in accordance with the Convention, should follow a country-driven, gender-sensitive, participatory and fully transparent approach, taking into consideration vulnerable groups, communities and ecosystems, and should be based on and guided by the best available science and, as appropriate, traditional and indigenous knowledge, and by gender-sensitive approaches, with a view to integrating adaptation into relevant social, economic and environmental policies and actions, where appropriate Draft Decision –/CP.17 National adaptation plans (A: Framing NAPs) . . .

Annex: Initial guidelines for the formulation of national adaptation plans by least developed country Parties B. Elements of national adaptation plans. 2. Preparatory elements

Para 3: In developing NAPs, consideration would be given to identifying specific needs, options and priorities on a country-driven basis, utilizing the services of national and, where appropriate, regional institutions, and to the effective and continued promotion of participatory and gender-sensitive approaches coordinated with sustainable development objectives, policies, plans and programmes . . .

Para 4: Also requests the secretariat to organize, in collaboration with Nairobi work programme partner organizations and other relevant organizations, the following workshops, informed by the information contained in annex I to the report of the Subsidiary Body for Scientific and Technological Advice on its thirty-fourth session1 and subsequent views of Parties, and to include indigenous and traditional knowledge and practices for adaptation and gender-sensitive tools and approaches as cross-cutting issues.

Source: advance unedited version Draft Decision –/CP.17 Nairobi work programme on impacts, vulnerability and adaptation to climate change

BOX 3.8 GENDER EQUALITY, ADAPTATION AND THE DURBAN OUTCOMES

Outcome of the work of the Ad Hoc Working Group on Long-term Cooperative Action Draft Decision [–/CP.17]

III. Enhanced action on adaptation
Para 103. Encourages Parties to nominate experts to the Adaptation Committee with a diversity of experience and knowledge relevant to adaptation to climate change, while also taking into account the need to achieve gender balance in accordance with Decision 36/CP.7;

National adaptation plans Draft Decision [–/CP.17]

A. Framing national adaptation plans
Para 3. Further agrees that enhanced action on adaptation should be undertaken in accordance with the Convention, should follow a country-driven, gender-sensitive, participatory and fully transparent approach, taking into consideration vulnerable groups, communities and ecosystems, and should be based on and guided by the best available science and, as appropriate, traditional and indigenous knowledge, and by gender-sensitive approaches, with a view to integrating adaptation into relevant social, economic and environmental policies and actions, where appropriate;

Annex – Draft initial guidelines for the formulation of national adaptation plans by least developed country Parties

B. Elements of national plans 2. Preparatory elements
Para 3. In developing NAPs, consideration would be given to identifying specific needs, options and priorities on a country-driven basis, utilizing the services of national and, where appropriate, regional institutions, and to the effective and continued promotion of participatory and gender-sensitive approaches coordinated with sustainable development objectives, policies, plans and programmes.

Nairobi work programme on impacts, vulnerability and adaptation to climate change
Draft Decision [–/CP.17]

Para 4. Also requests the secretariat to organize, in collaboration with Nairobi work programme partner organizations and other relevant organizations, the following workshops, informed by the information contained in annex I to the report of the Subsidiary Body for Scientific and Technological Advice on its thirty-fourth session1 and subsequent views of parties, and to include indigenous and traditional knowledge and practices for adaptation and gender-sensitive tools and approaches as cross-cutting issues . . .

Compilation of gender equality texts (direct quotes from text) retained in the advance version of the Durban Outcome

Source: advance version of Durban Agreements, from 11 December 2011, Durban, South Africa. Compiled by Women Environment and Development Organization (WEDO) for Global Gender and Climate Alliance (GGCA)

Similar to adaptation efforts, mitigation actions will entail both technological and behavioural changes. Taking place at the household and private sector levels, mitigation actions and strategies range from the promotion of conservation tillage and control of deforestation, to the promotion of energy efficiency programmes.

For many developing countries the priority areas for mitigation effort are: (1) the energy sector, including activities such as switching to renewable sources of energy, the efficient conversion of fossil fuels to electricity and switching to lower carbon fossil fuels; (2) limiting emissions and enhancing removals by sinks through land use and land use change and forestry (LULUCF); and (3) measures to abate GHG emission in agriculture and waste sectors. These involve projects such as solar photovoltaic (grid and off-grid), wind farms, biomass and micro-and mini hydro plants.

As noted by the UNFCCC Secretariat, in their interim national communications, developing countries reported mitigation measures in the residential and commercial sector such as: improving the efficiency of cooking stoves; promoting more efficient household appliances; enhancing efficiency of lighting; increasing efficiency in the building sector; promoting solar energy for water heating in the residential sector; and implementing demand-side management programmers (UNFCCC 2007).[12] The focus of many African countries is on improving cooking stoves and improving efficient lighting. Mitigation measures in the agriculture sectors related to changes in cattle management practices, rice cultivation and the use of fertilizers. Mitigation measures reported for LULUCF include: the promotion of forest conservation and restoration; afforestation and reforestation activities; improvement of forest management practices and the promotion of sustainable forest development; the promotion of conservation and substitution of fuel wood; and the promotion and development of agro forests (UNFCCC 2007).

All of these mitigation efforts have different challenges with regard to the twofold issues of meeting energy needs and meeting the needs of the climate. There is also the need to be careful in the balancing of equity and development issues within projects and programmes focusing on mitigation. From a gender equity and sustainable development perspective there are ostensibly at least four broad issues that must be addressed: (1) women's and men's energy uses; (2) the role and potential for employment and entrepreneurship for different groups of women and men in the energy and power sectors; (3) the role of traditional mitigation knowledge and practices and (4) a whole range of equity issues around the use, conservation and management of forests. Each of these issues will be touched on briefly.

3.4.1 Women's and men's energy uses

Women and men in the developing countries rely on energy for cooking and other household and farming activities. Good and reliable energy service can save time and potentially improve health. They also rely on varied forms of transportation for meeting personal, household and business needs. For many rural dwellers much of the energy used for cooking and food production is likely to be traditional biomass (wood, charcoal, agricultural residues and animal dung). This form of energy is typically associated with smoke inhalation/indoor air pollution (leading to respiratory disease) and deforestation. Thus millions of women and men can benefit from improved biomass- and solar-powered stoves and equipment. There are also inadequate forms of modern transport for taking goods to markets and for accessing health care and other services. Therefore, there is strong demand for clean and safe modern energy services for lighting, information and communication and production (agro or other industry) and transport.

Rural electrification and securing electricity and other forms of energy to poor urban and peri urban communities is a critical area of demand and a strong pillar in energy policy in many developing countries. This concern raises the issue of how clean and renewable energy can be promoted cost effectively to poor households, rural communities and the micro-small enterprise sectors. However, underlying that concern must be the awareness that even in these contexts, there are gender relations and clean and efficient energy solutions may either alleviate or exacerbate pre-existing gender inequalities with regard to access, ownership, and participation in decision-making and the prioritization of needs in the energy and power sector. In addition to seeking to mitigate GHGs, the focus on renewable and efficient energy that promotes high quality clean combustion must also support gender equitable poverty eradication and ease women's and men's work burdens and improve their access to safe energy and health services and education (Clancy et al. 2011).

A recent background paper for the World Development Report argues that: 'energy services based on modern energy and improved technologies have the potential to positively influence two specific aspects of women's and men's lives: time-use, with its links to reduction in drudgery and improvements in wellbeing, and economic opportunities' (Clancy et al. 2011).

Gender analysis of time-use in Sub Saharan Africa, carried out by the World Bank show that there are 'synergies, and short-term trade-offs, between and within market-oriented and household-oriented activities – economic production, childbearing and rearing, and household/community management responsibilities' which generate 'competing claims on women's labour time' (Blackden and Wodon 2006). Responding to these competitive claims causes women to have heavy work burdens and suffer from chronic shortage of time. As a result, many women in developing countries experience time poverty, which has been linked to women's economic burdens and health status in the literature.

Access to electrification and modern energy services is important for releasing the time constraints that many poor women face in the developing countries. With access to electricity and improved cooking stoves they can spend less time securing fuel wood and water. In addition, labour saving devices help to better meet household activities as well as community activities such as water pumping and grain grinding. Access to such services also helps to improve men's and women's income. Cases studies in Tanzania, Bolivia and Vietnam show that electricity, which also expands the working day, makes it much easier to complete small and medium entrepreneurial activities in the home where women can combine income generation-tasks with household duties (Clancy et al. 2011).

Thus gender sensitive and poverty reduction friendly mitigation effort can have a double transformative effect: it can curb emissions and create better overall economic and social welfare. Other likely gains for women with increased access to clean energy, beyond the health factor of reduced respiratory illness, include the reduction of the burden of carrying wood and other materials for fuel and fire. It is noted that in rural sub-Saharan Africa women have the 'most substantial transport task – they carry water, firewood and crops for grinding, primarily by foot'. Blackden and Wooten cite village transport surveys in Ghana, Tanzania and Zambia which show that women spend nearly three times as much time in transport activities compared with men and they transport about four times more in volume (Blackden and Wooten 2006: 8; Malmberge-Calvo 1994). Clancy *et al.* (2011) argue that one of the main areas of intervention to improve time-saving for women is to address the issue of fuelwood collection.[13] Women could also benefit tremendously from small clean energy powered forms of transportation in rural and peri-urban areas.

Mitigation, in as much as it focuses on large scale, capital-intense energy, manufacturing and commercial activities, has not been seen as an area that is amenable to gender dynamics. Thus there has been a blind spot with regard to the household sector in this area of climate change. However, this blind spot is being marginally transformed towards a greater appreciation of the role of the household, informal and community sectors in both creating mitigation factors as well as being areas for the proactive application of mitigation's technologically-focused applications.

An important area where mitigation efforts can translate into immediate and direct benefits for women on multiple levels is the area of women's cooking activities in the developing world and its association with the production of black carbon (soot/smoke).[14] Due to previous neglect in emissions and mitigation analysis, now common household soot seems to have moved up in importance on the climate change agenda as black carbon, which is a product of incomplete combustion (PICs) or short-lived climate pollutants,[15] is said to contribute to about 18 per cent of global warming (Rosenthal 2009) and is the likely number two leading contributor to global warming. The household sector in developing countries which is still over reliant on traditional unsustainable biomass, should therefore increase in importance in the mitigation arena.

Increasingly, the contribution of black carbon to greenhouse gas reduction is being recognized and it is now being prioritized as a key issue to be dealt with in the mitigation of climate change. This is a promising area that directly links women's issues to the ongoing evolution of climate science and policy. Not only does the recognition of black carbon impact climate change science, but also its amelioration is dependent on women's household role in carrying out family maintenance.

Addressing black carbon will require paying greater attention to mitigation at the household level in order to reduce its release into the atmosphere. So climate science, climate policy and climate change finance must intersect at the level of the kitchen. Prior to this, black carbon was under appreciated as a source of global climate change, so the impact of individual women's activities was confined to the margin of both the scientific as well as the policy arenas.

Reduction in black carbon emissions is now seen as a relatively cheap way to reduce global warming, as it can be accomplished by simply switching to solar and new energy efficient low (or none) soot cooking stoves (GHF 2009; Rosenthal 2009). Advocates focusing on the reduction of soot argue that it is a quick, simple low-hanging fruit.[16] Beyond its cost-reducing effect, eliminating the pervasive presence of mud stoves and soot from women's lives, especially in Africa and Asia, will have tremendous health improving effects on the health status and morbidity of women and children, particularly in girls. As noted by researchers, solar or other forms of energy efficient cookers in 20 million homes at an approximate cost of $20 each will cause less smoke and less fuel use (Rosenthal 2009).

The household sector also plays a role in mitigation financing. Here, financing is needed for mitigative activities such as improving the efficiency of cooking stoves, household appliances and lighting. This type of financing may be small-scale and less profitable or less likely to attract pure market mechanisms. It is also the area most closely related to enabling high quality functioning of women and girls. Hence, a gender-sensitive approach to mitigation financing would ensure that growing streams of funds are tracked into programmes and projects in this sector. Often adaptive and mitigative activities in the household and informal sectors tend to be low cost but may achieve high benefits.

For example, some projects under the reformed methodologies, which seek to enable more support for sustainable development by the Clean Development Mechanism (CDM), are increasingly focusing on providing clean energy solutions for cooking, lighting and off-grid power generation (UNFCCC 2012; GreenStream 2010). (The CDM is a financing mechanism under the Kyoto protocol with the dual mandate of providing developed countries with the option of sourcing low-costs GHG emission reduction projects in developing countries as part of meeting their obligations under the Protocol while at the same time promoting sustainable development in developing countries. Both the CDM's and the CIF's Small Grants Program which is also focused on promoting clean energy at the household and community level are discussed in greater detail in Chapters 4 and 7 of this book.)

3.4.2 Women's and men's employment and entrepreneurship in the renewable energy sectors[17]

The renewable energy sector can produce employment and entrepreneurial activities in areas of energy development, production and transportation. Gender issues arise in terms of 'employment equity and working conditions and women's participation in decision-making (Norad 2010). Particular issues that are now being discussed are the degree to which women are being integrated and finding employment in the clean energy sector. This includes their emersion and enrolment in skill building programmes in all levels of the six renewable sectors identified by the IPCC (solar, wind, hydro, geothermal, ocean and biomass-bio energy). Though there is a tremendous amount of research on the mitigation potentials of each of the sectors, there is insufficient research on the gender dimension of these sectors as well as with regard to the petroleum and oil sector. The Norwegian aid agency Norad has recently commissioned a six country study exploring issues such as the development of a technical skills base and best practices in relation to the integration of gender equality in clean energy and petroleum.[18] In terms of entrepreneurship women seem to be more involved in micro-hydro power and agriculturally related modern biomass areas. However these are areas that are under-researched.

3.4.3 The role of traditional mitigation knowledge and practices

Far too often it is the case that many resources are spent on expensive highly technology oriented projects with little focused attention paid to less expensive and socially oriented activities including the practices of indigenous peoples and women. Attention in the area of mitigation must also seek to understand and enhance women's role in ensuring energy supply and security at the household level (World Bank 2009). Greater attention should also focus on women's and men's roles in the domestic economy that can have global benefits. Such activities include (1) the promotion of renewable energy through enhanced development of bioenergy (for example, Jatropha oil for cooking, lighting and power); and (2) women-led and community-led agricultural and village-driven activities around afforestation, reforestation and biogas/waste management. A close examination of Box 3.9 will show that many such 'small-scale activities' can generate cost effective mitigation benefits as well as social and development benefits.

Many of these methods appear simple and do not carry the cache of high technology efforts that are to be found in the Clean Development Mechanism arena or carbon capture and storage technology and conventional offset projects. But they avoid many of the issues of corruption and lack of real mitigation or sustainable development benefit that is now becoming a challenge within the global carbon market. (These are discussed more in Chapter 6 on mitigation financing.)

3.5 Gender and equity issues around the use, conservation and management of forests

Forests and trees capture and store carbon. They also support water catchments, regulate weather and biodiversity as well as provide food and livelihoods for countless thousands of indigenous men and women and their families who depend on them. The destruction of global rainforests through the burning and clearing of forests for a variety of reasons including timber, agricultural expansion and human

> **BOX 3.9 SMALL-SCALE AGRICULTURAL ACTIVITIES AND COST EFFECTIVE MITIGATION**
>
> - Changing crop mixes to include more plants that are perennial or have deep root systems increases the amount of carbon stored in the soil.
> - Cultivation systems that leave residues and reduce tillage, especially deep tillage, encourage the build-up of soil carbon.
> - Shifting land use from annual crops to perennial crops, pasture and agroforestry increases both above- and below-ground carbon stocks.
> - Changes in crop genetics and the management of irrigation, fertilizer use, and soils can reduce both nitrous oxide and methane emissions.
> - Changes in livestock species and improved feeding practices can also cut methane emissions.
>
> Ways to overcome the drawback of tracking agricultural mitigation activities of women and other small farmers:
>
> - Promising technologies exist to reduce the cost of tracking the performance of agricultural mitigation programmes:
>   o Satellite imagery can be used for frequent, high-resolution land cover imaging.
>   o Inexpensive standardized methods are available to test soil carbon.
>   o Simple assessment methods can adequately quantify the effects of management technologies on methane and nitrous oxide emissions.
>
> Innovative financing instruments to promote agriculture impact in the area of mitigation:
>
> - Land retirement contracts.
> - One-time payments for physical infrastructure investments that have long-term mitigation effects.
> - Payments for institutional innovations that encourage mitigating behaviour in common property resources.
>
> Source: adapted from G. C. Nelson, IFPRI May 2009

settlement has created the problem of deforestation and forest degradation. This degradation and deforestation of tropical forests (including peat and wet lands) contributes to 12–15 per cent of global GHGs emissions each year.[19] The solution to this problem has been to arrest deforestation and promote forest preservation through reforestation and afforestation

Initiatives to Reducing Emissions from Deforestation and Forest Degradation (REDD) are now being discussed and implemented worldwide in countries as varied as the US,[20] Indonesia, Brazil and Mozambique. As presently being articulated, policies and measures under REDD include payments for environmental services, agricultural intensification and sustainable forest management.

A global REDD initiative for developing countries has been established to offer positive incentives in the form of financial transfer to developing countries in order to slow down their rates of deforestation and forest degradation. REDD came into being as a result of deliberations of COP 13 (Bali 2007), and is part of the Bali road map. It builds on an initial proposal by Papua New Guinea and the Coalition of Rainforest Nations[21] 2005 (COP 11) to make forests valuable by offering financial incentives to leave trees standing and rewarding countries for not cutting down their forests.

In the run up to the Copenhagen (2009) meeting, attention focused on a third dimension of forest preservation: that of enhancing forest carbon stock through emphasis on sustainable forest management and afforestation. This third dimension is now being promoted as REDD Plus (REDD+).[22] Under REDD/REDD Plus industrial countries that create carbon emissions pay poor nations to maintain and preserve their forests, either by paying into a fund or by purchasing credits (pollution allowances) from them on the carbon markets (Butler 2009; UN REDD 2009; GFC 2009). Since then a series of pilot projects focused on building the capacity of developing countries to reduce deforestation and degradation etc. has been centred on the UN REDD, which is the collaboration of UN agencies (UNDP, FAO and UNEP)[23] in implementing the REDD mechanism.

The period 2009–2012 were the preparatory stages for REDD Plus while full implementation began in 2013. The preparatory work focused on building the capacity of governments to prepare and implement national REDD Plus strategies. This should include the active involvement of all stakeholders including indigenous people and forest dependent communities. Funding towards National REDD Plus readiness strategies can occur under the UN REDD, the World Bank's Forest Carbon Partnership Facility and the Forest Investment Partnership or another voluntary mechanism. A second phase[24] would involve support for land reform and forestry laws, sustainable forest management initiatives, and payments for environmental services to local communities, indigenous peoples and other parties. According to Butler the 'funding would be performance-based and come from a global fund financed by voluntary donations, auctioning of emissions allowances, and possibly fuel and carbon taxes in some countries (2009). The third phase would include compliance-grade monitoring, reporting, and verification of emissions against agreed reference levels[25] (Butler 2009). Forest conservation and tree plantation projects also receive funding through voluntary carbon markets.

Forest negotiations were also part of the Long-term Cooperative Action under the Convention (LCA) process. One positive outcome of Copenhagen was the $3.5 billion pledge by the governments of Norway, Japan, the US, UK, France and Australia for the 'immediate establishment of mechanisms including REDD Plus'.

148 Climate change and gender equality

Further discussion on the evolution of REDD/REDD-Plus mechanism will likely be finalized in the post-2012 period.

Challenges and constraints around REDD include:

- The criticism that rich countries are able to buy part of their emissions obligation instead of cutting their own emissions – so called 'green washing'.
- Equity and Community Development: the risk that the benefits and costs of REDD related initiatives will not be shared equitably with the Indigenous Peoples and local communities that have historically been responsible for the conservation and sustainable use of large tracks of forests and other carbon-rich ecosystems.
- Methodological issues around carbon measurement and monitoring.
- Lack of hard target to reduce deforestation (proposals are for 50 per cent by 2020, 25 per cent from current levels by 2015 and elimination by 2030.
- The issue of permanency (the integrity of forest carbon stocks and the capacity of a forest to retain carbon in the future).
- Implications for food sovereignty and loss of alternative sources of jobs and income.
- Impact on traditional biodiversity related knowledge.

Apart from the general challenges outlined above, REDD and related mechanisms, to the extent that they rely on a market-based mechanism, the carbon market, imposed some specific equity issues, including:

- Impact on men and women who have no legal land tenure.
- Impact on men and women who are unable to afford the expenses involved in the preparation of environmental impact assessments, the delivery of environmental services.
- Implications for men and women who are not able to meet the range of quantifiable qualification criteria and the provision of upfront and operational finance and risk insurance.
- Privatization of both knowledge and communal lands.
- Risk of the substitution of monoculture timber plantation versus biodiversity-friendly economic activities such as bee-keeping.
- Increased global 'landgrabbing'.

3.5.1 Gender issues and REDD/REDD-Plus

Women are vital for the conservation of forests around the world (Aguilar *et al.* 2007). Yet an analysis by the Global Forest Coalition of the impact of market based mechanisms on REDD type initiatives argues that the 'position of women within the communities was also affected, as women's interests are more likely to be overlooked in commercial transactions normally closed by men (even in communities where women previously had responsibility for matters related to forests and biodiversity). The report further notes that 'women have a serious disadvantage with the monetization of forest and related products'. This is so for two primary reasons. In the first case, women's traditional activities (child care, household management, procuring clean water etc.) are not rewarded in monetary terms. Second, women are generally the poorest of the poor and hence among those who depend on the forest and will suffer more from the loss of the multi-functionality of forests (GFC 2009).

Given the large number of case studies that argue that 'social exclusion seems to be the rule, rather than the exception, in carbon sequestration projects, and other approaches putting in place payments for environmental services' (GFC 2009), then it is important that a priori gender equity considerations are built explicitly into REDD programmes and projects. This is certainly likely with UN REDD given that it is supposed to be based on the five interrelated principles (articulated by the UN Development Group (UNDG): Human-rights-based approaches to programming, gender equality, environmental sustainability, results-based management and capacity development (UN REDD).

Gender equality is a central pivot of these principles. Furthermore, to the extent that gender equality priorities and commitments are integral to national development planning process into which the REDD strategy is supposed to be integrated then the more likely it is that there will be gender sensitive women-friendly empowerment outcomes. The ultimate justification for integrating REDD strategy into national development process, according to UN REDD, is to ensure that carbon savings are not made at the expense of other national priorities (i.e. poverty reduction, job creation, biodiversity conservation, human rights etc.).

Gender and women's effort are critically important in many developing countries for sustainable forest management (reducing harvest rates and harvest damage). Gender concerns and priorities should be an essential core of initiatives designed to improve forest governance arrangements, strengthen capacities and means for forest law enforcement, encouraging adoption of reduced impact logging, strengthening forest conservation programmes. Women's and men's different constraints, challenges and opportunities to respond effectively to new opportunities must be the grounding for the development of community-based small-scale forest enterprises in the area of wood and non-wood forest products and improving forest fire management systems (paraphrased from UN REDD 2009).

Unfortunately, as noted by UN REDD (2009), 'REDD schemes do not automatically guarantee a capacity to link carbon sensitive policies with pro poor and environmental policies (for income, employment generation, for asset/rights/biodiversity preservation and for social/cultural cohesion).' However this does not mean that gender equality outcomes cannot be integrated into the policy framework prior to implementation or (next based as part of outcome assessment of result based management frameworks. Since it is widely acknowledged that 'REDD induced changes to legal frameworks that regulate incentives, rights, financing options (including taxation) and practices do not necessarily ensure equitable delivery' (UN REDD), then it is already predisposed to transforming legal and institutional policy process. Certainly women's rights, particularly as they relate to the use and ownership of forests and forest-related products, are an important set of rights that must be bolstered and safeguarded. Finally, gender-sensitive indicators must be one of the pro-poor co-benefit indicators anchored within the REDD benefit distribution systems (UN REDD 2009).

Unfortunately, the myths of the male farmers, the male business owner and the male head of household continue to dominate the imagination of climate change policy decision-makers. In the case of REDD programming, it is important to undertake gender and social impact assessments in order to ensure that women and indigenous groups do not lose ownership or usufruct rights to their traditional land or land to which they have historical access. Great care and attention must be paid to ensure that women and poor men receive their equitable share in the benefits to be derived from community resources. This can be ensured through community benefit sharing agreement and gender sensitive property rights arrangement. They should also be protected from disproportionately shouldering the burden of any adverse costs of projects funded under REDD and other related projects, which involve land use or land use change and forests for reforestation, afforestation or for carbon offsetting projects.

National governments should also enact appropriate legislations for regulating private sector initiatives that impact on poor women's and men's access and ownership of land, access to water and other economic resources. Careful monitoring of the issues of resource conflict and the dispossessing and takeover of land ('land-grabbing') from vulnerable groups for the purpose of partaking in the lucrative carbon markets is essential.

In order to mitigate climate change, women and indigenous men and women, should not unfairly and without just compensation lose control of land and forests. In order to prevent such occurrences, there will likely need to be structural and institutional changes, including land reform that goes beyond western conceptions of property titles. In some cases, conventional entitlement processes have been associated with further marginalization of women and the dispossession of families from land. Land reform must therefore be undertaken in a gender-sensitive negotiated process between men and women stakeholders in the community. It must also take into account different forms and dimensions of the existing inequities and accounting for both distributive and corrective justice. Thus there have to be some social and gender justice preconditions that must be settled on prior to the operations of programmes under REDD and/or similar mechanisms. Ultimately, the underlying principle must be: do no harm. At best, such projects should aim to enhance women's and men's economic and social status.

Unfortunately, it is the case that the greater issue with regard to climate change and humanity is its untoward effect on human economic, social and health systems. Thus more focused attention must be paid to securing women's and men's lives and livelihoods and the earth's atmosphere. Since in many developing countries, as repeatedly pointed out in this book, women are at a disproportionate disadvantage with regard to the negative impacts of climate change and climate variability, it is important to explicitly face the challenges that have life impairing effects. Specifically, the frequency of adverse weather events such as floods, droughts and heat waves, linked to warming trends, presents new categories of risks for women that may exacerbate older forms of vulnerabilities and in some case create newer varieties.

Undeniably, the current scale and scope of the climate change challenge will demand massive upscaled and large scale mitigation effort and clean and renewable energy technologies will play a large role in this. At the same time, it is important to also recognize support and seek to upgrade and leverage existing and traditional methods that enable mitigation and to provide greater access to modern energy services to populations presently lacking those services; and promote poverty eradication. In order to be more effective for sustainable development and the empowerment of women, there needs to be better linkage between adaptation and mitigation. Drexhage (2006) argues that effective linkage of the mitigation and adaptation agendas should fit the best practice/no-regrets approach ('policies that provide benefits whether an abrupt climate change ultimately occurs or not'; National Academy of Sciences 2007).

According to the Pew Center 'the 'no regrets' options are steps to reduce GHGs that would pay for themselves even without a climate change policy' (Pew 2009).[26] These can be accomplished by addressing conservation, sustainable livelihoods and natural resource management (ibid.). Drexhage also suggests that decentralized renewable energy in rural areas can contribute to both mitigation and adaptation.

Most mitigation projects are connected to voluntary market-based instruments, whereas there may be beneficial outcomes to gender equality and sustainable development if there were more of a mixed basket of instruments including carbon taxes and emission permit auction. As we will see below these mechanisms have clearly differentiated impacts for gender and social equity.

3.5.2 Gender and global mitigation policy

The state of the arts in mitigation policy with regard to developing countries is the nationally appropriate mitigation actions (NAMA) vehicle through which these countries submitted their 'plans to limit the growth of their emissions, with appropriate and adequate support from industrialized countries in the form of technology cooperation, finance and help in capacity-building' (UNFCCC 2011). These NAMAs originally evolved under the Bali Plan of Action and have since been formalized by the Cancún Decision.

In addition to reporting on mitigation measures in their interim/national communications, as per the Cancún Decisions, these NAMAs, particularly those that require international support (such as technology, finance and capacity building) will be inscribed in a formal international registry to be maintained by the UNFCCC secretariat. Cancún also promised to strengthened support for the preparation of such plans. Non-support actions will also be inscribed in the registry but in a different section.

Developing countries are also required to 'increase reporting of their progress towards their mitigation objectives'. A process of international consultation and analysis of these biennial reports will be established. Developing countries are encouraged under the agreement to draw up low-carbon development strategies or plans.

However none of these policy instruments and frameworks is gender sensitive. In a number of workshops on mitigation as noted in the reports of the chairs of SABSTA, some developing countries point to the need to distinguish energy use in households from the industrial sector, as their characteristics 'are very different'. They also emphasized the need to support biomass energy development, 'as it can play an important role in sustainable energy development, and, thus, climate mitigation'. It was also pointed out that climate mitigation needs to be integrated into, and be consistent with, broader sustainable development objectives (SBSTA[27] 2004). These are good steps along the way to transforming the approach to mitigation towards one that is more amenable to gender and social equity sensitization. Another significant marker along the way was the inclusion of gender references in the mitigation section of the Cancún and Durban Decisions.

A third area that is also amenable to gender sensitization is around the issue of economic and social consequences of response measures. In recognition of the fact that in implementing actions that reduced emissions there may be negative economic or social consequences for some developing countries there has been an item under discussion in the negotiations called *Economic and Social Consequences of Response Measures*. The Cancún Decision established a forum and a work programme to address these issues. Under Section II:(F), para 90 urges Parties to give full consideration to the positive and negative impacts of the implementation of response measures to mitigate climate change on society and on all vulnerable groups, in particular women and children.

Box 3.10 identifies some critical areas where climate changes impacts, and the policies designed to address these impacts will need to be prioritised as areas of attention, if the women empowerment and gender equality impacts of climate change and climate variability are to be dealt with in a way that helps to further, rather than obstruct, the achievement of these goals and agendas. In each of the areas listed in Box 3.10 the issues of technology and capacity building stand out, both individually and inter-connectedly. Access to technological resources goes hand in hand with capacity building to both enhance the use and application of the technology and access to new equipment and knowledge helps to promote women's awareness, skills and resourcefulness with regard to adaptation and mitigation. Capacity building is important on its own for issues such as improving women's knowledge and skills with regard to early warning information, disaster preparedness and management. We now turn to examine the issue of gender and climate change technology.

BOX 3.10 FURTHER IDENTIFICATION OF WOMEN-SPECIFIC CLIMATE CHANGE VULNERABILITIES

1   Further identification of women-specific climate change vulnerabilities:

  (a) Cross-regional comparisons in term of six specific areas: nutrient capacity and women's health; women's domestic burden and increased hardships; women's reduced ability to provide self-protection; religious and social dogma concerns; lack of education; and unequal power relations;
  (b) Gender audits of vulnerability and assessment methodologies and
  (c) Programmes and projects to decrease women's and girls' vulnerability to climate change effects.

2   *Gender, land-use and forestry (deforestation, afforestation and reforestation)*: This should be contextualized with awareness of traditional knowledge and women's challenges and constraints concerning intellectual property rights with regard to land-use and forestry management know-how.

3   *Gender climate change and sectoral issues*: agriculture (food security, adaptation and traditional knowledge/intellectual property); water, health, sanitation and livelihood; clean energy, energy efficiency and renewable energy – all with an awareness of the issues of traditional knowledge and women's challenges and constraints around women and intellectual property rights. Some critical areas that needed to be further developed include:

  (a) Gender and climate-induced human displacement, migration and conflict;
  (b) Gender, climate change and the household and informal economies;
  (c) Gender and climate change economics;
  (d) Gender, climate change and trade;
  (e) Gender climate change and domestic investments and FDI;
  (f) Gender and proposals for post-2012 negotiations.

3.6 Gender and technology transfer and development

The development (or acquisition), deployment, diffusion and transfer of technology to control greenhouse gas emissions are critically important for both adaptation and mitigation in developing countries. Successful adaptation and mitigation of climate change in priority sectors such as agriculture, fishery, forestry, coastal zones and health require relevant adaptive technologies. The adoption of relevant technologies is also important for systemic observation and monitoring of climate change and the prevention and protection against national disaster.

In order to contribute to gender equality outcomes, technology development should focus on areas that help to ease women's time burden, scale up their economic activities and promote their human development. Examples include solar or wind powered water pumps for the drying of agricultural products, which in many developing countries is a female-dominated activity. Even as countries seek to upgrade to capital-intensive technologies (for example, carbon capture and storage, nuclear energy, clean fossil fuel generation and biofuels) they should ensure that the technologies are appropriate to the needs of different social groups.

Women in many countries, whether in the household, informal or formal business sectors, face substantial barriers to entry and adoption of technology. Barriers include informational/knowledge, credit, finance and investment gaps. Often, women's – more so than men's – acquisition of technology is blocked by upfront purchase prices or administrative costs. Many women who operate across all three sectors (household, informal and formal economies) may be unaware of the availability of new technologies and their relative costs and benefits.[28] Men tend to be more up-to-date on acquisition and diffusion of new technology. Even when women are aware of new technologies, they may not be able to make the transition due to their generally limited income and capital base. These cases of informational and initial capital bias can be overcome by having special or thematic windows within the funding mechanisms or by having funds specifically dedicated to capacity-building and knowledge sharing among similar cohorts of male and female actors.

Technology transfer and cooperation is also linked to financing. It is important to focus such support on technology that is gender, social and development friendly and that protects the web of life and promotes ecological security. This includes paying particular attention to protecting traditional knowledge and seeking to improve and enhance its effectiveness through gender-sensitive approaches to traditional knowledge and gender-aware benefit sharing agreements. For example, rainwater harvesting, recharging of ground wells and facilitating sustainable agriculture and development are critical to women's involvement in food production and food self-sufficiency. However, these areas tend to be time consuming and impose a heavy care burden on women and girls. Technological support would be beneficial in reducing women's time burden as well as increaseing their productivity.

3.7 Gender and capacity building and access to the 'science'

It is widely recognized and much discussed both in climate negotiations, advocacy and research that the capacity to deal with climate change involves having the knowledge tools and resources to deal with adaptation and mitigation but that these are not enough. It is also important to building public support and understanding of the issues as well as enhancing or building local scientific expertise to deal with the challenges of climate change – its predictions, early warning and impacts. As hopefully demonstrated in this chapter this is also important for women's empowerment and gender equality. Therefore in addition to support for concrete projects on the ground, it is import to promote the ability of individual women, women's organization and gender machineries in developing countries to better take part in local and national processes that identify, plan and implement capacity building in adaptation and mitigation efforts to address climate change.

As noted by the UNFCCC secretariat, greater attention hence needs to be paid to ensuring that education, outreach and empowerment process reach out to women to build their capacity to engage at individual institutional and systemic levels related to climate change (UNFCCC 2014): 'The specific needs, conditions and constraint of different groups of women should inform the priorities and initiatives'. The secretariat also point out that it is important to 'launch projects and programmes to build the capacity and improve the involvement of women scientists in research and systematic observation, including meteorological, hydrological and climatological services'.

More women need to be involved in the areas of work of the IPCC and other such organizations, as can be seen below in the very rough snapshot of the distribution of IPCC contributing authors, lead authors and review editors in Table 3.3). Women tend to be quite under-representative especially in the areas of working group I (which assesses the physical scientific aspects of the climate system and climate change) and working group III (which assesses options for mitigating climate change through limiting or preventing greenhouse gas emissions and enhancing activities that remove them from the atmosphere). See also Box 1.1 on IPCC in Chapter 1.

TABLE 3.3 Distribution of authors by gender and developing countries for IPCC AR5 (2013)

WG	Total	Women		CLA	Women	LA	Women	RE	Women
WG I	255	47 (18%)		29	3 (10%)	176	34	50	10
DC/EIT	60			2		48		10	
WG II	308	86 (27%)		64	13 (20%)	178	55	66	18
DC/EIT	115			26		76		22	
WG III*	235	35* (23%)		35 (20%)	7	200	37	38	11
DC/EIT									
TOT									

Source: author's own. CLA: Contributing lead authors, LA: Lead authors, RE: review editors. WG I and WG II distributional profiles are taken directly from the IPCC sites, www.climatechange2013.org and http://ipcc-wg2.gov/AR5/, respectively. * For WG III no gender distribution was specified, but rough calculations by the author, based on chapter profiles which presented photographs of CLA, LA and names of RE, are presented here for initial comparison. Please also see http://mitigation2014.org/

3.8 A tentative qualitative gender empowerment climate change risk analysis framework

A gender climate risk and vulnerability assessment framework provides an opportunity to clearly identify the risks that climate change poses for women's social and economic situations, and provides the appropriate visibility so the risks can be fully addressed. Such a framework can be developed or grafted on to one, more or all of the numerous emerging climate risks and vulnerability approaches. One such easily amenable approach is Hart's (2007) qualitative climate risk analysis applied to infrastructure finance risk assessment.[29]

Hart defines climate risk as 'several kinds of weather-related risks that are caused by or correlate with an increase in the frequency and/or severity of weather events beyond their normal ranges as a result of anthropogenic induced climate change' (2007: 18). According to Hart, climate risks are threefold: (1) volatility in short term weather patterns, (2) increased severity and likelihood of catastrophic events and (3) longer term gradual warming that leads to desertification, impacting biodiversity and water resources.

The possibility of greater volatility in short term weather patterns that may induce heat waves or heavy rain will impact on women's health and productivity in the household and market. Increasing severity and likelihood of catastrophic event such as storms, floods and hurricanes poses significant impact for women's land use (access to food), security and shelter. This can lead to relocation and involuntary abandonment of dwelling and other properties, loss of equipment as well as the threat of loss of life. Longer-term weather trend of gradual warming (increase in global mean temperature) portends further loss of biodiversity, desertification, and dramatic shifts in agricultural and disease patterns, declining availability of water and changing sea levels. This has implications for all of the events under the second risk but necessitates longer-term planning for both enhanced adaptation activities and mitigation. All three forms of climate risks have the potential to adversely affect the adaptation resilience and the financial status and needs of women and men in communities, more so those in communities (i.e. coastal areas) with extreme exposure to adverse weather events.

Drawing on the emerging gender and vulnerability literature discussed in earlier sections of this chapter, it is possible to develop a rich gendered and well contextured qualitative risk assessment framework. Adapting the qualitative infrastructure finance climate risk assessment framework proposed by Hart (2007) to take account of gender dimensions allows for the further disaggregation of the three broad risk areas (and a reduction of Hart's 14-item matrix[30]) into seven risk assessment categories: (1) supply risk, (2) market risk, (3) operating risk-cost/losses, (4) social and personal security risk, (5) domestic/time burden risk, (6) recovery risk and (7) participant risk. These risk categories and their likely economic effects are presented in Table 3.4. The economic effects can serve as key entry points and the basis for claims on both public sector financing and options for private sector financial opportunities.

Climate change and gender equality 157

TABLE 3.4 A qualitative gender climate risk assessment for climate change financing

Category of risk	Description/likely effects
Market risk	Price or demand changes for food and input. Food in-security and livelihood loss
Supply risk	Supply interrupted; decrease access
Operating risk-cost/losses	Loss of assets including shelter
Social and personal security risk	− Health/wellness disparity − Information gap − Mobility and public space constraints − Relocation − Rise in violence − Increase exposure to sexual abuse and harassment
Domestic/time burden risk	Increased care and other workload
Recovery risk	Impaired ability to recover assets and resources after catastrophe
Participant risk	Financial stability, asset holding/management. Credit worthiness. Inadequate administrative and technical capacity.

Source: based on Hart (2007)

3.8.1 Supply risk

Supply risk represents the potential for disruption of supply or demand and cost of input due to a climate event. It is anticipated that climate risk will increase supply risk and disrupt supply channels (Hart 2007). For example storms, floods and hurricanes may damage homes and businesses and destroys harvests and livestock. This will negatively impact economic activity and the livelihoods of men and women. In some countries, women may face disproportionately more negative impacts than men from weather events such as floods, because of their over-reliance on food processing, cattle, and chickens for their cash income (Khondker 1996). The impact of climate change in the agricultural sector will negatively impact food security imposing additional burdens on women, who are primarily responsible for maintaining food supplies in many households. From the vantage point of gender and indigenous men and women, an emerging and unique form of climate risk may be disruption, due to offset programmes, which leads to loss of access and control of land, as occurred in the Mt. Elgon debacle and is reported to be on the rise due to monetary incentives around afforestation and reforestation. There is some concern that REDD Plus, if not properly managed and implemented, could exacerbate these negative effects.

3.8.2 Market risk

Market risk may be more applicable to entrepreneurs and smallholders. However, market risk and supply risks are interrelated as extreme weather events will tend to drive both in the same direction. In the case of market risk, the primary effect will be on price and demand conditions. Climate risk will likely decrease the availability of locally relevant inputs, increasing the price of inputs and final goods. From the vantage point of smallholders, the change in demand conditions may be both advantageous and disadvantageous: While prices may increase, demand may not be forthcoming and, or, there will be competition from imports.

From the household side, rising prices of basic goods and services present hardship for women, who must manage the shortfall income against rising prices. In terms of mitigation, households may experience rising costs in the purchase of energy efficient appliances, heating and energy bills for weather-related events such as heat waves etc. Female-headed households, which tend to have lower income and less access to resources than male-headed households, in some countries may be at a disadvantage with regard to the purchase or repairs of such household items or with meeting the additional cost of heating or cooling that may be associated with extreme variability in climate.

3.8.3 Operating risk

Operating risk raises the issues of data gathering regarding adaptation, mitigation, technology and finance. It underscores the need for resilient and climate-proofed dwellings and business establishments. It also highlights the importance of insurance products to offset the increased risk of flooding etc. Climate change and adverse weather events increase the cost of housing and community infrastructure and overall cost of living, especially in vulnerable areas. With regard to data gathering, there may be an information cost premium for many women, who are not always connected to the main flow of information about new technology, adaptation or mitigation programmes. Most often, women, because of household duties, are unable to participate in informational and extension type training that takes place during the daytime when they must perform livelihood or farming work. Women may also not be able to travel far distances or in the late evening to access information and training about financial, technology or other opportunities that may be available to support the climate-proofing of their dwelling and livelihood activities. Women may also suffer from premium bias with regard to insurance products to transfer risk of crop and other losses due to climate change and climate variability.

3.8.4 Social and personal security risk

Social and personal security risk, time burden risk and recovery risk are this book's proposed new additions to Hart's framework. From the purview of gender analysis, social risk covers a broad range of gender related phenomena including: nutritional capacity and health; lack of education; the influence of religious and social dogmas and unequal power relationships. According to del Ninno *et al.* (2001), women in many poor economies are generally more calorie-deficient than men and suffer from chronic energy deficiency. This poor health and caloric deficiency make women vulnerable during climate induced catastrophes (del Ninno *et al.* 2001). Climate risk compounds the problem of lack of education that affects poor men and women. Because of women's lower levels of education (i.e. knowledge about technology and other information) in many poor and vulnerable countries, women and girls suffer from reduced 'ability to access information, including early warning mechanisms and resources, or to make their voices heard' (Islam 2009) in climate change and disaster risk reduction planning.

In some cultures, religion and social dogmas place taboos on females and males cohabitating in the same public space or unaccompanied single women participating in the public domain (Masika 2002: 5). This places women in an extremely vulnerable position during extreme weather events (Masika 2002: 5). Women are likely to suffer increased mental strain, and bear the brunt of certain social constraints; for instance, they are shamed by using public latrines, or being seen by men when in wet clothing (Rashid and Michaud 2000). The social and institutional barrier of women's mobility also keeps them in vulnerable positions as they may not be able to move easily to find alternative sources of livelihood and income.

Unequal power relations between women and men[31] impact women's differential and lesser access to environmental resources and opportunities for income diversification, all of which intensify climate change (Islam 2009). This has implications for critical matters such as accessing quality of housing, and building material and the location of dwelling. For example, power dynamics may underlie whether women's houses are located on raised grounds or less attractive (in terms of adaptation to climate risk) areas.

With regard to personal security (self-protection), women face risks of bodily injury during climate and weather events. Women and girls are also subject to sexual harassment and rape due to further distances needed to fetch water while at their permanent residential areas, during relocation or at shelters. As noted by researchers such as Islam (2009), post-disaster mortality, injury, and illness rates are often (but not universally) higher for girls and women.

3.8.5 Domestic and time burden risk

Domestic and time burden risk are quite strongly connected to social risk. In the first case, many poor women in developing countries must spend more time on the search for food, fuel and water, especially if warming events intensify water scarcity and dry up nearby water sources. Evidence from the literature suggests that droughts and floods increase women's domestic burden. Women must expend more energy and time sourcing water from faraway places while still maintaining their customary domestic workloads. According to Islam (2009) 'workload changes increase women's responsibilities in the domestic sphere, paid workplace, and community through the disaster cycle of preparation, relief, reconstruction, and mitigation'. When there are girl children of the appropriate age in the household, they may support the women of the housing in carrying water. Ultimately, intensified domestic load and time burden may exacerbate women's physical and mental stress.

It is important to note that there is an implicit technology risk that is cross cutting across the seven climate risk areas. This technological risk is assumed to be a decreasing one and thus may act as a leveraging factor within the framework. The technology risk may be positive if technology supports care services and, if, after its costs of implementation are accounted for, it delivers net benefits to the household or business sector. It is assumed that technology has beneficial effects on productive and care activities and thus on the domestic and time burden of the women and girls in the household. Time burden can be reduced by the availability of technological innovations in milling and processing of grains and nuts, cooking, and heating as climate change mitigation and adaptation projects are implemented.

3.8.6 Recovery risk

Recovery risk covers a range of losses to individuals, households and businesses. It is a particularly relevant concept for poor female-headed households whose loss of assets are often not visible in statistical damage estimation and often ignored in governmental assistance measures. Women and female-headed households are likely to experience full or partial loss of essential household durables (including utensils) that they are unable to recoup in a short or medium time frame. Women, especially those in the agricultural sector, may lose livelihood and income sources on a permanent basis depending on the nature of the damage and the permanency of resettlement efforts. Furthermore, as noted in the literature, many female-headed households face social issues around the resettlement and the rebuilding of homes and community that impact their health and wellbeing. Women with micro and small business are also likely to lose their inventories of goods. Since these may also tend to be quite small in volume and value, they may not be eligible for grants or other compensation, where these exist. Often, women may not have adequate documentation to verify assets or insurance protection.

3.8.7 Participant risk

Participant risk covers issues such as financial stability, credit worthiness and inadequate administrative or technical capacity. Women suffer from significant bias in the financial market. Many times, because of the precarious nature of their income sources, some women may lack the kind of income stability that is important for financial stability. Their lack of property rights may also impede access to loans (outside of microfinance) and may also impact their ability to develop and meet creditworthiness criteria. They may also suffer from informational and premium bias with regard to life and other forms of insurance. Women's micro

TABLE 3.5 Climate change and gender operational domains plus finance-related issues

Capability and security-related impacts/challenges	Resources and opportunity (economic resources)	Resources and opportunity (financial impacts/resources)
Climate change		
FOOD/HEALTH and NUTRITION	Safety nets	Asset valuation effect
Food insecurity/malnutrition	Access to inputs etc. (fertilize)	Access to credit
Food shortage (higher rate malnutrition)	Land tenure/security	Insurance
Ill-health/morbidity/ maternal and infant deaths	Literacy/education and training	Savings/wealth effect
Time burden (increase)	Livelihood	Pension etc.
Family planning/antenatal care/home deliveries	Employment	Access to finance
Access to health care	Access to social services	Subsidy
Increased respiratory diseases	Social protection	Household budget effect
Stress-related illness/ exhaustion (travel further for water or fire wood)	Social insurance	Adaptation finance needs
Increase in water borne-diseases	Access to housing	Mitigation finance needs
Heat related mortality; heat stress	Real Wage/disposable income	Technology transfer
Workload increase	Housing/land	R&D
New skill set for survival (tree climbing and swimming)	Information asymmetry in the transmittal of warning	
EDUCATION	Hazard management	
Challenge for girls due to need to travel longer distance for water etc.	Disaster preparedness and management	
SECURITY	Control of early warning system	
Increased potential for conflict	Weather-related hazard	
Increased violence against women	Training and cap. building	
Increased risk of sexual harassment and violence		

enterprises also suffer from lack of proper administration in terms of management of records and accounting. Often because of their cash flow, size of operations and rate of turnover, women-owned enterprises may not be able to hire or have access to ancillary management support staff.

Gender advocates should focus attention on threshold issues such as the financial, time and physical resource costs of adapting to, and mitigating climate change that are incurred by particular groups of women (for example, agricultural food producers and fisher folks). In this way a climate risk assessment framework can be used to make these costs more visible. This can help to provide the basis for securing funding for gender equality objectives and women's economic empowerment in the context of the emerging climate change financing architecture.

The next three chapters explore the different types of financing that are currently available in the global economy for dealing with climate change. Interest is centred on whether or not and to what extent women, as a group, have equitable access to these funds as their risk profiles may be worsening due to increased risk of loss or injury to their lives and the likely shrinking existing bundle of economic and social assets.

Notes

1 These deaths it is argued were possible due to differential exposure to heat in occupation settings. Fouillet *et al.* 2006 cited in IPCC 2014.
2 Climate change induced warming can lead to wider transmission of malaria; 'rising temperature extends the habitats of the mosquitoes that carry the malaria parasite, shifting the boundaries of latitude and altitude for malaria transmission – for example, many highland areas in Burundi, Kenya and Uganda that have historically been classed as malaria-free are now experiencing epidemics' (Sulaiman 2007). Floods and higher rainfalls are associated with new breeding grounds for mosquitoes in Mozambique and droughts in sub-Saharan Africa lead to declining water levels and rising stagnant pools of water. Sulaiman, Suad 2007 *How is climate change shifting Africa's malaria map?* SciDevnet 1/8/07.
3 The Global Burden of Disease Study 2010.
4 Please see list of references in this document.
5 WG II, chapter 17, p.726.
6 Parry *et al.* 2007 (WG II 7.1, 7.2, 7.4, 17.3).
7 According to the International Assessment of Agricultural Knowledge, Science and Technology for Development (IAASTD) 2008 and TWN 2009, there is a two-way relationship between climate change and agriculture. Agriculture contributes to climate changes (due to industrial, energy intensive and monoculture type farming practices) that focus on irrigation, chemical pesticide, synthetic fertilizers, hybrid seeds and herbicides that lead to 'collateral damages to the environment, soil degradation'. These impact the resources that are critical for storing carbon such as forests and other vegetation (TWN 2009). Climate change impacts agriculture through increased climate variability and extreme weather events that destroy crops and impair the natural resource base of agricultures.
8 There are over 49 LDCs; with the exception of Somalia all are parties to the UNFCCC. Forty-one countries have completed preparation of their NAPAS. Six countries are still in the preparatory phases (Angola, Chad, Myanmar, Nepal, Timor Leste and Togo) and two have not started (Equatorial Guinea and Somalia).
9 Thus far about 385 of these projects have been costed at over USD 800 million (UNFCCC 2008).

Climate change and gender equality 163

10 Terrestrial ecosystem is priority area number two.
11 Sinks are reservoirs that accumulate and store carbon-containing chemical compounds.
12 Section VI: Priorities for mitigation and adaptation as reported by developing countries under the Convention.
13 It should be noted that in some countries men are responsible for firewood collection. Evidence from research by Cooke *et al.* 2008 shows that 'fuelwood collection is not necessarily always a female task'. In countries such as Ethiopia, Madagascar, India, Nepal, Vietnam and Indonesia both men and women collect, and on some occasions men and children are the primary collectors (Cooke *et al.* 2008 cited in Bäthge 2010 and Norad 2010). Further the study shows that the determination as to who collects fuelwood in the household is a matter of prioritization around the timing and clustering of economic activities and the minimization of the costs of doing particular types of activities. Hence, '(c)hildren can be allocated fuelwood collection duties during labour-intensive periods of the agricultural cycle, such as harvest time'. The household decides 'who will collect and at what time in a manner that minimizes the cost to the household' (Cooke *et al.* 2008, p.113, cited in Bäthge 2010 and Norad 2010).
14 The IPCC (2007) glossary defines black carbon as the 'operationally defined species based on measurement of light absorption and chemical reactivity and/or thermal stability; (it) consists of soot, charcoal, and/or possible light-absorbing refractory organic matter'. In the developed countries the main source of black carbon is diesel fuels. But in the developing countries it is produced from the burning of wood, animal dung, vegetable oil and other biomass fuels. V. Ramanathan and Greg Carmichael found that 'black carbon soot, from burning wood and other biomass, cooking with solid fuels, and diesel exhaust has a warming effect in the atmosphere three to four times greater than prevailing estimates' (Nature Geoscience 1, 221–7, March 24, 2008). According to Ramanathan and Carmichael, *black carbon* emissions arising from: (1) 'cooking with biofuels such as wood, dung and crop residue', 20 per cent of the total, (2) 'fossil fuel combustion (diesel and coal)', 40 per cent of the total, and (3) 'open biomass burning (associated with deforestation and crop residue burning)', 40 per cent of the total. They argue that 'soot and other forms of black carbon could have as much as 60 per cent of the current global warming effect of carbon dioxide'. Ramanathan and Carmichael also argue that 'over 400,000 annual fatalities among women and children are attributed to smoke inhalation during indoor cooking', especially in Asia.
15 Other short-lived climate pollutants (SLCPs) are methane, tropospheric ozone, and hydro fluorocarbons (HFCs). These SLCPs, which have their relatively short lifespan in the atmosphere have now been upgraded as climate threats by the IPCC in its fifth Assessment Report (AR5) and hence, are now the focus many activities at the global level.
16 Soot is sometimes considered as a low hanging fruit. See Rosenthal (2009) and GHF (2009).
17 This topic is beyond the scope of this book but an in-depth treat of the subject is offered by Clancy *et al.*, as well as commissioned work by the Norwegian aid agency Norad., *Progress Report Gender Mainstreaming in Norad's Energy programme* 2010, and a 2010 working paper for GTZ by Sandra Bäthge, *Climate change and gender: economic empowerment of women through climate mitigation and adaptation*.
18 Please see Progress Report on Gender mainstreaming in Norad's Energy Programme 2010.
19 The IPCC 2007 Report has established the official benchmark of forest degradation to contribution to GHG emission at 20 per cent. This figure was based on 1990s data. In 2009 scientists (van der Werf *et al.* 2009) using 2008 data re-evaluated this figure to between 12 per cent and 15 per cent. It is important to note that the 12 per cent does not reflect a decline in deforestation but rather in industrial emissions from burning fossil fuel (Van der Werf *et al.*, 2009).
20 US: The American Climate and Energy Security Act (ACES, House of Representative June 2009). Brazil: The Juma project in the Amazonas state, Brazil (which has been

164 Climate change and gender equality

awarded the Climate, Community and Biodiversity Alliance's Gold Standard for its safeguards). In Mozambique, the Nhambita project a carbon finance initiative.
21 The Coalition for Rainforest Nations is an intergovernmental organization established by forested tropical countries (such as Argentina, Ecuador and Ghana) to collaboratively reconcile forest stewardship with economic development The coalition also involves partnership with Industrialized Nations that support fair trade and improved market access for developing countries.
22 CDM allowed for afforestation (planting of new lands) and reforestation projects, but not for 'avoided deforestation'.
23 With the cooperation of the Forest Carbon Partnership Facility (FCPF), Forest Investment Programme (FIP), UNFCCC and the GEF.
24 Based on the 'the phased approach proposed by the Coalition for Rainforest Nations and presented in the Meridian report for the Norwegian government' (Butler 2009).
25 According to Butler (2009), 'it would likely be financed by the sale of REDD units within global compliance markets or a non-market compliance mechanism. Supporters of the phased approach say it accommodates both fund- and market-based mechanisms, includes provisions for indigenous people, offers flexibility allowing countries at different levels of capacity to participate, and considers many of the outstanding concerns for REDD.'
26 Examples of likely 'no regrets' policy options include: switching from coal-burning to other fuels, which can also have benefits in reducing health or environmental effects of emissions and improving water, land and air quality (National Academies of Science 2007).
27 The Subsidiary Body for Scientific and Technological Advice of the UNFCCC.
28 It is important to acknowledge that these barriers and challenges around technologies at the micro level also exist at the country level for many poor and developing countries. As noted by the UNFCCC: 'The biggest barrier to technology transfer identified was the lack of financial resources. High investment costs, prohibitive prices acting as a deterrent to widespread use, subsidies and tariffs were also considered important economic/market barriers. Other important barriers included a lack of information and awareness regarding environmentally sound technologies (ESTs) (for example a lack of information on the technical performance of ESTs and on means to acquire them). The measures identified by Parties to address barriers were most commonly: regulatory and policy measures; measures to increase access to information and build awareness; or economic and market measures' (2007). The point being made here is that women will still be underserved in these countries if specific attention is not paid to the particularly gendered constraint they will face with the acquisition and deployment of technology that does occur through the different financing and capacity building funds becoming available at the country level.
29 Hart applied qualitative climate risk analysis to the Infrastructure Finance Risk Assessment Framework of Tinsley 2000. Tenley developed a 15-item framework: 1) Supply risk: supply interrupted or input price increase, 2) Marketing risk: price or demand decrease, 3) Foreign exchange risk: mismatched revenues and cost due to currency fluctuations, 4) Technology risk: technology failure or inefficiency, 5) Operating risk: failure in management performance(management capacity)/increase cost of inputs, 6) Environmental risk: environmental liability or regulation, 7) Infrastructure risk: inter connections to other critical infrastructure, 8) Force Majeure risk: acts of nature (storms, fire earthquakes), acts of man (riot, war) and impersonal acts (financial system collapse), 9) Completion Risk: construction delay/overruns/defects, 10) Engineering risk: failure in engineering analysis, design and data, 11) Political risk: war unrest, nationalization, regulation (creeping expropriation). Change in government, environmental activism, corruption), 12) Participation risk: competency/financial stability of participants – project sponsors, lenders, equipment vendors etc., 13) Interest rate risk: float interest loan, 14) Syndication risk: lead banks' ability to sell portion of loans to other banks and 15) Legal risk: enforcement of contract (Hart 2007; Table 4.1).

30 Hart revised and reformulated Tinsley's assessment framework into a 14 itemed qualitative climate risk assessment matrix. He introduced new categories of risks such as management capacity risk, Capital market/finance risk and Governance risk. He also transformed or separated out some of Tinsley risk categories. For example, environmental was transformed into environmental regulations. All items were embedded with climate risk analysis. Hence supply risk now represents new technology rare materials/energy/weather disruption of supply chain/carbon credits. Market risk was revised to cover climate affects short and long-term/changing consumer attitude and preferences. Reputation risk for emissions/environment. Technology risk includes accelerate new carbon neutral technology. More complex carbon neutral technology. Hart's final matrix (Table 4.2): 1) Supply risk, 2) Marketing risk, 3) Technology risk, 4) Engineering, 5) Infrastructure risk, 6) Environmental regulation risk, 7) Political risk, 8) Legal risk; 9) Force majeure risk, 10) Operating risk, 11) Management capacity risk, 12) Capital market/finance risk, 13) Participation risk and 14) Governance risk.

31 In a more complex and nuanced development of this framework this subcategory could potentially hold its own as a key climate risk category. This is quite possible under some reformulation combining management capacity/operational risk and political risk maybe under the heading: Power and Decision-Making Risk. Since the framework presented here is but a first round approximation and requires further thinking through and validation it is kept very simple.

4
THE GLOBAL CLIMATE CHANGE FINANCE ARCHITECTURE

> There is a lot of international talk about climate change funding for local communities and especially for women, but not much is actually happening.
> Ange Bukasa of Chezange Connect, The Democratic Republic of Congo*

This chapter explores the dynamics and operations of the global climate change finance architecture, including its principles, norms, finance instruments, mechanisms and funding apparatuses both those under the Framework Convention as well as multilateral and bilateral sources of finance outside of the Convention. The growth of these instruments and mechanisms is, however, not simply technical or mechanical financial engineering processes but rather the outcomes of deeply (and sometime polarizing) political tensions between developing and developed countries. These tensions are underpinned by the development and social challenges of managing climate change outcomes faced by developing countries as well as the commitments of developed countries to undertake significant economy-wide emissions and the resulting implications for production and consumption patterns in these countries. Both groups of countries must negotiate agreements on the best way forward in attempting to cope with the growing global climate crisis. Thus climate change finance negotiations are not simply about the numbers – the quantum of money, though the numbers are of immense importance as we will see below.

The chapter therefore first explores the background issues pertaining to the flows of climate finance, including definitional issues as well as the historical and contemporary challenges that drive these flows. Section 4.3 explores the normative, political and legitimation issues surrounding the scale, scope and sources of climate finance, while Section 4.4 outlines the distinctive features of climate finance. It distinguishes between the nature and scope of the financing of adaptation and mitigation strategies as well as discusses the different actors, instruments and frameworks involved in climate finance. Section 4.5 explores the numbers issues in details. It delves deeply into the debate about the mismatch between the scale of financing offered by developed countries versus the needs of climate finance of developing countries, as presented in various estimation methodologies and approaches. Section 4.6 looks closely at the operations of publicly financed funding mechanisms and institutions that play a determining role in climate finance. It has three parts. The first part explores the UNFCCC Financial Mechanism set up under the Convention to receive and disburse funds from developed countries to developing countries. It discusses the specific funds and funding instruments operated and utilized by the Global Environment Facility (GEF), such as the Least Developed Country Fund and the Special Climate Change Fund, as well as the Adaptation Fund. The second part explores the most recent operating entity of the financial mechanism, the Green Climate Fund (GCF), created in 2011–2012 and assorted climate-related vehicles set up under the Convention in the post-2010 period. Chapter 5 tackles the role of the World Bank, the regional development banks, such as the Asian, African and Caribbean development banks, and bilateral finance mechanisms, respectively, in the flow of climate finance. It also explores the role and operation of the market for the buying, selling and trading of carbon permits and other GHGs permits in order for key actors to meet either their voluntary or binding emissions reduction commitments. This is the carbon market and the activities of so-called flexible market-based mechanisms such as the Clean Development Mechanism which allows for the operations of mitigation projects in developing countries that allows for the off-setting the cost of (more costly) mitigation in developed countries. The chapter ends with a state of play of climate finance projected up to the 2015 period.

4.1 Climate finance: definition, historical background and contemporary challenges

The UNFCCC in Articles 4 and 11 defines and specifies the nature and scope of the finance and its preferred source as well as establishes a Financial Mechanism to enable delivery of monetary flows from developed countries to finance climate-related policies, programmes and projects of developing countries. This is commonly referred to as climate finance. Beyond that, there is no internationally agreed definition of the term climate finance (AGF 2010; Buchner *et al.* 2011; OECD 2011). Many researchers focus on quite broad and varying operational definitions of climate finance in terms of the global flow of finance and investments oriented towards climate change activities (IPCC 2013; Corfee-Morlot *et al.* 2009; Buchner *et al.* 2011; Clapp *et al.* 2012).

Both Corfee-Morlot *et al.* (2009) and Clapp *et al.* (2012) make a distinction between what they identify as 'climate finance' or 'climate-specific finance' as flows of resources that target low carbon or climate resilient development and 'climate-relevant finance' as flows of resources that have climate change outcome (which may be negative or positive). Both types of flows involve public and private capital flows from developed countries to developing countries. This type of climate finance is argued to be more consistent with the kind of support for mitigation and adaptation actions that the Convention envisions, while climate-relevant finance is reflective of a much broader flow going to support economic growth and enhance the profitability of the private sector. This so-called climate-relevant finance (Buchner et al. 2011) would include all forms of finance instruments (grants, loans, capital and investments), public and private, externally as well as domestically generated. But all these forms of related climate finance will not necessarily reduce vulnerability or reduce emissions; many of these general flows of finance may also lead to the accumulation of debts by poor developing countries for financing adaptation and mitigation activities. This type of finance would be contrary to both the spirit and the intent of the Convention.

Climate finance, under the climate change Convention, and in this book, is more narrowly conceptualized as the flows of publicly generated funds flowing from developed countries to developing countries for the financing of climate protection policies with the aim of fulfilling the objective of the UNFCCC. This climate finance has a much narrower scope and clear level of obligations and commitments by developed countries to developing countries, than is commonly used in the climate finance literature.

Climate finance is specific to supporting developing countries to achieve their obligations with regards to three-fold objectives of the UNFCCC, in the context of common but differentiated responsibilities and equity:

1 Stabilization of GHG concentrations in the atmosphere . . . prevent dangerous and anthropogenic interference with the climate system.
2 Ensure food production (and food security).
3 (Enable) sustainable development.

This kind of climate finance is expected to be proffered in the form of grants and concessional loans, not highly debt creating instruments; it is quite distinct from traditional development finance or overseas development assistance that flows from developed countries to developing countries. While the latter (development finance) derives from the foreign policy, humanitarian and charitable impulses of developed countries, the former (climate finance) is a response to a global commons problem (anthropogenic climate change) which has been scientifically linked to the actions of developed countries in promoting their economic development processes since at least the late 1700s. Climate finance is hence a global public good.

Thus climate finance is linked inextricably to the issue of historical responsibility for climate change by developed countries. As noted in Chapter 2, the developed countries have used more than their fair share of the atmospheric space leaving very little remaining space for developing countries to grow. Developing countries with millions of poor men and women living with little or no access to clean energy sources and inadequate infrastructure will need to build climate resilient infrastructure and adopt cleaner sources of energy, which are currently more costly than the more readily available and cheaper fossil fuels. This rising cost to the development enterprise must be offset by support from developed countries. It is in this context that under the Convention, developed countries are committed to providing flows of finance to support developing countries' mitigation and adaptation actions, including technology development and transfer. What was not specified or agreed was the scope, scale and magnitude of this flow and the nature of the burden sharing between the developed countries (Annex II Parties). In subsequent COP Decisions, including under the Copenhagen agreement (2009) and Cancún (2010), Durban (2011) and Doha (2012) and Warsaw (2013), developed countries have reaffirmed this commitment, especially through the Copenhagen fast start financing initiative and their commitment towards 'a goal of mobilizing $100 billion per year by 2020'.

Within the context of the ongoing climate negotiations, there has been recognition of a structural deficiency in the sourcing and delivery of climate finance. Repeatedly COP Decisions (Bali 2007, Copenhagen 2009 and Cancún 2010) have tried to address this issue. The Bali Action Plan (2007, 1/CP13) reinforced developed countries financing commitment and called for 'enhanced action on the provision of financial resources and investment to support action on mitigation and adaptation and technology cooperation' (para 1(e)), as well as 'improved access to adequate, predictable and sustainable financial resources and financial and technical support, and the provision of new and additional resources, . . .' (para 1(e) i). At the 2009 Copenhagen meeting of the COP, a group of about 30 developed countries coalesced around a US-led initiative of realizing approximately $30 billion in finance between 2010–2012. This initiative was termed Fast-Start Finance (FSF, see also Appendix 4.2).

> The collective commitment by developed countries is to provide new and additional resources, including forestry and investments through international institutions, approaching USD 30 billion for the period 2010–2012 with balanced allocation between adaptation and mitigation. Funding for adaptation will be prioritized for the most vulnerable developing countries, such as the least developed countries, Small Island Developing States and Africa.
>
> (Para 8, 2/CP 15 2009, The Copenhagen Accord)

A year later, the 2010 Cancún Agreements (para 95 1/CP.16) formalized the collective commitment by developed countries to provide new and additional funding for the short- and longer-term, with balanced allocation between adaptation and mitigation, to developing countries (Buchner et al. 2011). It emphasized that this flow of fund is to be scaled-up, new and additional, predictable and adequate, taking into account the urgent and immediate needs of developing countries that are particularly vulnerable to the adverse effects of climate change (para 97). Cancún also reaffirmed developed countries' commitment to 'a goal to jointly mobilise US$100 billion annually by 2020 from a wide variety of funding sources, including public and private, bilateral and multilateral, as well as alternative sources of finance'. The funding will aim to help developing countries adapt to and address the impacts of climate change and to pursue actions that will bring them towards a low-carbon future (Buchner et al. 2011).

In the present historical juncture of financial, economic and sovereign debt crises (particularly in the Europe zone, but also in some developing countries, most notably the Caribbean region), public finance is indeed under stress. It is therefore understandable that developed countries may find the challenge of dealing with untold trillions of dollars of finance for climate change, both for national efforts as well as for the global cooperative effort, to alter the present global warming trajectory, daunting. But the unfolding epic global catastrophe of an ever warming world must be dealt with. The rich industrialized countries have the obligation to finance climate change actions in developing countries that will help to protect and enhance the lives of men and women and children and to ensure the safety of the planet for future generations, both in the developing and the developed countries.

When the banking/financial crisis dramatically unfolded, in 2008–2009, the developed countries immediately galvanized their resources to protect the financial system including utilizing national lender-of-last-resort activities, which for the US alone is reported to be between $7.77 trillion and $29 trillion dollars.[1] Correspondingly, governments in the EU spent upwards of €4.5 trillion (equivalent to 37 per cent of the region's output to stem the bank inspired financial crisis between 2008 and 2011). Additionally, developed countries, in particular the US, broke their long standing resistance and supported the strengthening of the global financial safety net by allowing a general allocation of Special Drawing Rights (SDRs) by the International Monetary Fund (IMF). (SDR is an international reserve asset, created by the IMF in 1969 to supplement its member countries' official reserves.[2])

For the first time in 28 years a third general allocation of drawing rights was permitted, which, coupled with a special one-time allocation of SDRs to new (since 1981) developing country members of the IMF, provided an additional $250 billion equivalent of SDRs.[3] Thus it is clear that despite present circumstances, when the political will is present, the resources can be found with quite urgent timing. If we are at all serious about the climate challenge and the present catastrophic course on which the global economy seems to be set, then the resources must be found. As the late Hugo Chavez of Venezuela is noted to have said, '(i)f the climate were a bank, they (the rich governments) would have already saved it'.[4] The reality is that the science is now clearer than ever that warming of the climate system is 'unequivocal', 'human influence is clear' and projections of the future of climate change indicate that limiting climate change will require 'substantial and sustained reduction of GHG emission' (IPCC 2013). Hence urgent action must be taken to decarbonize the world economy and to promote adaptation and climate resilience in developing countries to address the impacts of the already high degree of committed warming of the atmosphere.

A way forward out of the present climate finance challenge is to recognize two important realities: (1) the urgency of the situation (the longer the wait the more the costs will rise for both adaptation and mitigation as well as 'loss and damage'[5] and (2) climate change finance cannot be undertaken in a business as usual manner, as with traditional development financing; nor can the situation be fixed by simply shifting the developed countries' obligations to the developing countries, or by relying solely on the private sector. Developed countries must end the protracted debate and stop ignoring historical responsibility for contributing to the climate problem by fully implementing, wholeheartedly, mitigation strategies at home and begin to stipulate how they plan to scale up climate finance in the long term after the 2015 period.

Undoubtedly, developing countries, especially major economies, such as Brazil, China, India, Indonesia, Mexico and South Africa, who are members of the Major Economies Forum on Energy and Climate,[6] must shoulder the consequences of their current and future emissions. And, many developing countries are doing just that. Developing countries' combined pledges in their various nationally appropriate mitigation actions (NAMAs) far outweigh those of the developed countries' Cancún pledges for ensuring the 2 degree climate stabilization target.

Though many of the NAMAs are conditional on external financial support, a significant number of countries are budgeting these actions within their domestic budgetary frameworks. Already many developing countries are expending significant amounts of their domestic resources on responding to adaptation climate-related challenges, which currently account for about 70–80 per cent of the resources allocated to climate change (relative to mitigation of 20–30 per cent) by some developing countries in the Asian region (UNDP 2012). This is quite different from the global average for donor-driven international climate finance where over 90 per cent is dedicated to mitigation with a miniscule share to adaptation. Bird et al. (2012) in a review of the public expenditure on activities that are related to climate change in developing countries in Asia and the Pacific, found that 'climate relevant' components of the national budget with relevance to climate-change mitigation or adaptation outcomes accounted were substantial as proportions of the budget as well as proportions of GDP. Climate relevant expenditure as a proportion of total expenditure and GDP ranged from 2.7 per cent of total budget (and 0.5 per cent of GDP) in Thailand to 16.95 of budget and (3.1–6.9 per cent of GDP) in Cambodia.[7] The authors also estimated the relative proportions of these expenditures that were contributed from domestic resources and from externally provided resources over a 3-year period, 2009–2011. Bangladesh had the highest per cent (77 per cent) of climate relevant expenditures that were domestically sourced with 23 per cent externally sourced – loans and grants. Whereas, Cambodia, Nepal and Samoa had a high proportion of their climate relevant expenditure sources externally (87 per cent, 56 per cent and 59 per cent, respectively).[8]

For the Philippines, noted for being the third most highly vulnerable country to climate-related extreme events, things are not so fortunate. In the first case, as Philippines government officials highlighted, 'more funds have come into the country for mitigation efforts instead of adaptation programmes and projects'. Worse, finance for adaptation activities has come in the form of loans. According to the World Bank, for the Philippines, between 2008 and 2012, climate appropriations increased by two and a half times in real terms and on average 26 per cent annually, outpacing the growth of the national budget (around 6 per cent). Climate appropriations are about 2 per cent of the national budget in 2013, compared with less than 1 per cent in 2008. Climate appropriations are funded largely from domestic sources with development partners funding flood control management.[9]

The World Bank recommends that countries, especially highly vulnerable countries, target 2 per cent of their budget for climate change (World Bank 2013). Countries such as India, which is spending over 2.6 per cent of its GDP to deal with challenges of climate change, in 2014 had to create an adaptation fund (of INR 7 billion (US$1.1 billion)).[10] Elsewhere, others such as China, in responding to extreme weather events is reported to have cost the economy more than 200 billion Yuan ($32 billion) annually in direct economic damage. It is projected that China, which now has a current account expenditure of an estimated $13.5 billion will need at least $24 billion per year for adaptation actions by 2020. In Africa, for example, Kenya's cumulative spending and commitments between 2005 and 2015 for projects classified as having a significant 'climate change component' was $2.728 billion. Kenya now faces investment costs required to adapt to climate change impacts and to implement the low carbon development of about $12.76 billion from 2013.

Many developing countries simply cannot afford to carry the burden of mitigation and adaptation in addition to meeting the costs of the loss and damage caused by extreme weather events, while growing their economies to satisfy the demands of the millions of poor and vulnerable women and men within their borders. There is a need to work cooperatively, to globally transform the current approach to climate change and its financing. Unfortunately, the climate finance discussions, especially those around accelerating and scaling up the flow of long-term finance for adaptation and mitigation projects in developing countries are driven by simplistic mantra-like expressions exhorted by developed countries: climate finance must be 'transformative', 'scarce public finance' and 'leveraging the private sector'. There is a certain amount of dissonance in the set of most oft repeated mantras that dominate the climate finance debate (see Box 4.1).

The dissonance in the mantras in the universe of climate finance are reflective of the clash between the traditional 'aid paradigm' of development finance automatically applied to climate change and the transformative 'responsibility and equity paradigm' that is the hallmark of the approach to climate finance that underlies the UNFCCC (Articles 4 and 11.1). The traditional aid paradigm is based in the ethos of solidarity, doing good and humanitarian support for developing countries. Hence, unilateral public flows from developed countries' governments to developing countries' governments are seen as primarily a voluntary effort and is also more often than not driven by national competitiveness and foreign policy concerns. However, climate finance is not this. Climate finance is a legally binding obligation accepted and agreed to by developed countries under the framework convention.

BOX 4.1 CLIMATE FINANCE 'MANTRAS'

The most often repeated mantras that dominate the climate finance debate include:

- *Climate change is urgent and urgent actions needs to be undertaken now!* (Yet, there are lengthy and interminable delays in getting the means of implementation to developing countries and in mitigating GHG gases in the atmosphere without conditional pledges linked to 'other' countries' actions.)

- *Climate financing by the GCF must be transformative!* (Yet, OECD countries continue the 'aid paradigm' in sourcing and delivering 'climate finance': there is nothing transformative about that, nor in seeking to primarily fund the private sector. After over 3 years, the GCF remains uncapitalized.)

- *Public finance is scarce!* (Yet, the 'scarce public finance' is not dedicated to meeting the urgent and immediate adaptation needs of the least developing countries and to support loss and damage, but to 'attract' private capital, such as the institutional investors with $83 trillion of assets under management, investment funds (the top 10 hedge managers' combined income in 2012 was $9.75 billion) and FDI (currently about $1 trillion (2013). Clearly these actors are not in need of money to undertake activities they deem as profitable.

- *Leveraging the private sector!* (Maybe if the mantra is repeated enough private finance will magically resolve a problem that is in part a result of market failure. Private capital is driven by profit not environmental integrity and the safeguarding of community and natural resources; it is not much interested in adaptation. It is conveniently forgotten or left unstated just how much work (beyond so-called 'enabling environment in developing countries') will be needed to get this in the right direction.)

- *Paradigm shift and transformative!* (This mantra is most often repeated with respect to long-term climate finance and in the context of the Green Climate Fund. Yet proponents continue to rely on outdated 'aid donor-driven paradigm' and the transformative element they usually identify is the role of the private sector.)

Though in 1992, with the signing of the UNFCCC and in subsequent COP Decisions (Bali 2007, Copenhagen Accord 2009, Cancún 2010), developed and developing countries have agreed radical points of departure from business-as-usual development finance, the reality is a far different thing. Back home in the capitals Washington, D.C., London, Paris and Berlin, seemingly the corresponding behavioural and operational shift that is required to implement the agreed provisions of the Convention is not forthcoming. Rather, the inherent conflict between the responsibility approach and the entrenched old business-as-usual aid paradigm results in rigidities, inertia and actions that lead to dismaying and disappointing results. This dissipates confidence and trust in multilateral agreements.

This is an important backdrop in trying to understand the climate finance debate. Since 2009, developed countries have steadfastly resisted elaborating a pathway for securing the goal of mobilizing the $100 billion per year by 2020. There are also continued contestations over the delivery of the $30 billion fast start finance and even greater perturbations about the lack of funding for the GCF. From this vantage point, it is quite perplexing how the global community is likely to meet the (conservatively estimated) $70-100 billion per year estimated as required for adaptation needs in developing countries much less the seemingly herculean challenge of achieving the $1 trillion to $5 trillion cost tag for the transformation to low carbon resilient development now being projected by the International Energy Agency and the IPCC 2013 among others.

The reality is that the stranglehold of the 'aid paradigm' on developed countries' decision-makers' consciousness is a critical factor obstructing both the flow of climate finance, its scaling-up as well as creating and maintaining the current impasse in resolving some of the technical issues around the operational definition and measurement, verification and reporting (MRV) of climate finance. The 'aid paradigm' is in direct contrast to the more transformative 'responsibility-collective and collaborative paradigm' embedded in the Framework Convention and so well-articulated by the *Delhi Vision* (2012, with regard to the financing of the GCF).

The aid paradigm is in direct conflict with four undeniable facts: 1) Climate change is a global problem, the underlying condition of which is the accumulation of anthropogenic GHGs arising from the fossil-fuels-based industrialization of the OECD countries;[11] 2) Climate change is a global commons problem; 3) Climate Finance, as one of the key pillars of global climate policy, is a global public good; and 4) climate finance is a legally binding obligation of Annex II developed countries Parties (Article 4.3, UNFCCC).

Unfortunately, the 'aid paradigm' in which developed countries do not accept responsibility for causing the underlying problem and hence view their financial support from the prism of 'doing good', 'solidarity', and a donor-recipient framework, continues to pervade the climate finance arena. As a result, developed countries, as noted by the Delhi Vision, continue to determine the quantum, modalities, extent of concessionality of funding, priorities and delivery channels. Additionally, this framework is dominated by a governance structure in which decision-making is heavily weighted in favour of the 'donors' (Delhi Vision). There is also a conditional approach to financing which is currently evolving into an almost single-minded focus on outcome or result based approach to financing climate actions in developing countries. The developed countries have also continued to preserve this outdated model by their persistence in by-passing the Convention's financing mechanism and their insistence on utilizing their traditional bilateral channels.

Such a donor-driven approach to climate finance is contrary to both the spirit and the legal framework and the commitments of Annex I (which have historical and moral responsibility for anthropogenic climate change) and Annex II countries (which have the legal responsibility to provide climate finance, including for technology transfer countries) signed under the UNFCCC. In the face of this reality, the perpetuation of the aid paradigm in the sourcing and delivery of climate finance has led to the growing problems of insufficiency, inadequacy and underdelivery of finance, the fragmentation (and associated high cost) of delivery mechanism, distortions of priorities and distrust between developed and developing countries. This situation has also resulted in political intransigence in defining climate finance and in elaborating a systematic common frarmework for assessing, monitoring, evaluating and resolving the challenges around sourcing and delivering of climate finance. Climate finance continues to be treated as voluntary and hence determined by the strategic needs of 'donor' governments, divorced from the climate financing needs of developing countries.

The alternative is the responsibility paradigm embedded in the Convention, which is grounded in the responsibility for climate change. The guiding principles are fairness, equity, legal commitments and the Needs Based Approach. A critical element of this transformative approach is to include the needs and perspectives of those most affected by climate change into climate finance decision-making. This includes the integration of gender perspective into climate finance governance.

As noted by the Delhi Vision, in this approach, the quantum of contribution is explicitly based on responsibility and capability (it is not discretionary). Activities, priorities, modalities, extent of concessionality of fund are collectively agreed between source and destination countries. And, as with the Adaptation fund and now the GCF, there is an agreed balance in terms of representation between developed (source) and developing (destination) countries in the Funds' governance structure: decision-making is, hence, fair and transparent. It would not be surprising if the resistance of developed countries to contribute their publicly generated funds as well as commit a significant proportion of the promised $100 billion to the GCF, is not, partly due to the recognition of the less than full control over decision-making that they can exercise in the institution, as well as the drive to redirect public money to their private sector.

The continued intransigence of developed countries in providing a pathway for the actualization of the $100 billion per year by 2020, a significant portion[12] of which is expected to go to the GCF is now also rearing its ugly head in the continued stonewalling of the mobilizing and provision of resources to the GCF as agreed in 2009 and 2010.[13] The GCF was operationalized in 2011 with the agreement on its governing instrument and the fielding of its board members as agreed by developing countries and developed countries in Durban. In 2013 the GCF was headquartered in South Korea and now has transitioned from an interim secretariat to its own independent secretariat with an executive director. Yet there continues to be contestations raised by developing countries' parties and their supporters as to whether the fund has been operationalized. This then provides one of the growing rationales for delaying commitment of resources to the fund for the implementation of the financing of programmes, projects and policies in developing countries.

Even as there is foot-dragging around making adequate[14] commitment to the fund, developed countries governments continue to fund multilateral entities such as the World Bank's CIF despite the existence of a sunset clause[15] in that fund's mandate that provides for its cessation of operation when a new financial mechanism has been operationalized under the UNFCCC. In addition, developed countries seek to impose a string of conditionalities to their funding to the GCF such as weighted voting which if accepted will make the GCF just another fund such as those that currently exist and which do not serve the needs of developing countries. The GCF may hence not be the 'transformative' game changer it was once envisioned to become. Additionally, developed countries, through a web of consultants and think-tanks are proposing their bilateral entities as well as the multilateral development banks as the key channels of delivery for disbursement of funds under the GCF. Furthermore, developed countries are also seeking to ensure the unmitigated access of their private sector to the resources contributed to the GCF.

These actions and proposals by developed countries with regard to the function of the GCF have implications not only for the reduction of the actual flow of funds to developing countries to finance national climate change adaptation and mitigation projects, hence dissipating climate actions, but may have reverberations for the multilateral trade system where subsidies are heavily contested and certain kinds of subsidies are prohibited. With the channelling of funding redirected via the GCF to the companies of the US, Japan, UK etc., this may act as a pathway for the indirect subsidization of environmental goods and services that may otherwise not be available under multilateral and plurilateral trade rules.

Ultimately, the sourcing, allocation, disbursement, funding modalities and type of coverage of climate finance have significant importance for women's and men's economic and social empowerment in developing countries. Climate finance is important for greening public transportation, and enabling the accessibility for individuals, households and businesses to clean energy and promoting their responsibilities for energy efficiency, waste handling and sustainable consumption (Lethbridge 2011; Walby 2013). Climate strategies that call for radical emissions reductions and societal transformation will impact men and women differently.

Economy wide, sectoral activities and policy commitments to reduce emissions and transition to low carbon paths that underlie nationally appropriate mitigation actions (NAMAs) have implications at individual, household and firm levels and have different burdens and benefits, and implications and consequences for men, women, female headed/male headed households, women/male farmers, and women and men-owned and operated micro-, small- and medium-sized enterprises (MSMEs).

The current imbalance in the funding for adaptation (relative to mitigation) puts women's lives and livelihood in severe jeopardy as it means that national governments will be forced to use scarce national resources or borrow from incurring debt services, either of which ultimately impacts and enforces a trade-off between allocation to the social sector and other forms of tax expenditures and direct spending or tax credit on mitigation expenditures or debt services. In the worst case scenario, adaptation activities may be short-changed leaving vulnerable communities of women and men to fend for themselves during times of extreme weather events.

A gender perspective on the climate finance architecture, its normative values, funds and instruments, mechanisms and thematic and programmatic approaches is, hence, important for ensuring appropriate flows of funds that meet both gender-equality interventions as well as non-gender equality interventions that affect the household and care economies and provide for reducing the burden of adaptation for women and men.

The dangerous undertow in climate negotiations and in particular with regard to finance is the competitive dynamics of a set of countries historically used to being in economic dominance and who now find their economies caught in the throes of financial and economic uncertainties with at best lacklustre to dismal growth and rising economic insecurity. This is coupled with the so-called 'rise of the South' premise (the rapid growth of so-called emerging economies such as Brazil, China, India and South Africa).[16]

Finally, a second important factor contributing to the stalling climate negotiations and which under-girds the mobilization and delivery of climate finance, is that due to their own foot-dragging, both in terms of addressing climate change in their domestic economies and in providing the financing to developing countries to undertake radical change from the business as usual path, since 1992, the cost of climate change has been rising dramatically. These countries, therefore, see themselves exposed to meeting undetermined and rising trillions of dollars for climate damages. In a sense, then, the Cancún $100 billion per year by 2020 goal, cited above, can be seen as an attempt to limit or put a cap on these obligations.

It has been repeatedly pointed out by researchers, non-governmental climate actors and developing countries that both the fast start finance initiative, which was widely welcomed by all stakeholders, and the $100 billion pledge (of which many remain sceptical) are not based on any substantive groundings, either on the needs of developing countries or requirements behind the science of ensuring the 1.5 to 2 degrees Celsius temperature target guardrail. Enabling and ensuring a transition towards clean energy and low carbon development pathway and holding a global mean temperature rise significantly below the 2 degree goal will require quite radical global and national emissions reductions, which have significant cost implications. According to the CERES and the International Energy Agency, 'to have an 80 per cent chance of maintaining this 2 degrees Celsius limit, an additional $36 trillion in clean energy investment will be needed through 2050 – or an average of $1 trillion more per year compared to a "business as usual" scenario over the next 36 years' (CERES 2014).

Climate finance and the architecture for enabling the sourcing and delivery of funds to developing countries is thus evolving in a highly charged political context of assessing causes and consequences, and responsibility and accountability for the factors contributing to the accumulated levels of GHGs and the consequential damaging effects on the earth's system. These issues of historical responsibility and accountability are often juxtaposed, sometimes mis-leadingly and always confusingly to the issue of the present and future responsibility of actors, agents and countries for climate change.

For example, the US while rejecting any notion of historical responsibility is quite vocal in asserting the current and future responsibility of developing countries, primarily China, for their growing emissions. It has called for 'symmetry' and 'fairness' in the context of the current and future climate negotiations and would like to do away with common but differentiated responsibility or at least reinterpret it to something more to its liking. In both the fast start finance initiative (FSF) and the long-term finance issue, the US has not fully entered into the discussion of appropriate burden sharing among it and its cohorts of Annex II countries, though it has provided $7.5 billion, or about 20 per cent of the global self-reported total flows of FSF (Jones *et al.* 2013; US 2012) that effort, for which it does and should take credit.[17] Both the US and the rest of Annex II have, however, been unwilling to discuss anything to do with the sourcing of the $100 billion per year by 2020 pledge other than to painstakingly argue for a stronger role for the private sector in generating the scale-up of climate finance.

Nearly always missing in discussion and research on climate finance is the explicit taking into account of the inequalities and injustices of the impact of climate change and hence the need for paying particular attention to how climate finance is targeted beyond the broad categories of small island developing states (SIDS) and the least developed countries (LDCs). Rarely are gender and the concerns of indigenous and ethnically marginalized groups considered relevant in decision-making about climate finance. These issues are much more comprehensive than the narrow focus on special groupings of countries within the developing world currently being adopted by developed countries. It also can lead a focus by developed countries on climate finance targeting and allocations geared to selected groupings of countries that simply works to create political division and polarization within the developing world and that is oriented towards seeking outcomes in climate negotiations that work to the benefit of the rich countries. For example, the EU

Global climate change finance architecture **179**

works assiduously to court the Alliance of Small Island States (AOSIS). Connie Hedegaard, EU environment commissioner in a statement as well as tweeted in the waning of the Durban meeting 2012 bragged that the LDCs, AOSIS and the EU were united in the desire for an ambitious outcome in Durban. When at the 2013 Warsaw climate meeting, Japan broke its commitment to the 2020 reduction target, it also offered more climate finance money to SIDS and LDCs. (An offer that was reportedly publicly rebuffed by some SIDS countries – rejecting it as an attempt to buy their acquiescence with Japan's actions.) Many African and SIDS delegations felt that this was a way to lessen their condemnation of Japan for its decision to increase its emissions.[18]

The next section explores the context underlying the tensions and debate over climate finance, including its potential for diverting conventional overseas development assistance, especially away from its traditional focus on gender equality, poverty and social development towards climate protection.

4.2 Climate change finance and the UNFCCC – normative, political and legitimation issues

As noted in earlier chapters, under the Convention and consistent with the principles of equity, polluter pay and common but differentiated responsibilities, there is an explicit demarcation between two groups of countries which goes beyond the simple division of developed and developing countries. The countries with responsibility for historical emissions are identified as Annex I Parties and those who have little or no responsibility for historical emissions as non-Annex I Parties. Annex I Parties include developed countries and countries under-going transition to market economies. These Annex I countries (industrialized countries[19]) agreed to adopt national policies and take the lead on measures to mitigate climate change. Annex II countries (a subset of Annex I, mainly members of the Organisation for Economic Co-operation and Development, OECD[20]) have committed to support the costs of the developing countries as they put in place measures to meet the obligations under the Convention. Specifically, these countries agreed to provide 'new and additional financial resources to meet the agreed full costs incurred by developing countries in complying with their obligations under Article 12, Paragraph 1 (Art. 4.3, and Kyoto Protocol 11.2)'.[21]

Non-Annex I Parties, including all developing countries as well as high income and developing countries members of the OECD, such as Singapore,[22] Chile, Mexico and South Korea, have no obligations for mitigation under the Convention, but can take voluntary GHG emissions reductions actions with support of finance and transfer of technology from developed countries. But over the years, developing countries have increasingly accepted to take on more mitigation actions, including, under the 2007 Bali Action Plan, wherein they agreed to undertake nationally appropriated mitigation actions (NAMA) 2008 Bali Action Plan (UNFCCC 2008). NAMAs specify the voluntary GHG reduction mitigation activities to be undertaken which will achieve deviation from the business-as-usual emissions in developing countries. These NAMAs, which are not the subject of mitigation commitments and can be project and/or economy wide based, are also to be supported with finance, technology transfer and capacity building resources (16/CP.1, para 50). (NAMAs are discussed further in Chapter 7 on mitigation finance.)

The obligation of Annex II countries to provide finance for developing countries is primarily what distinguishes climate finance from development finance, which is primarily a voluntary-quasi-humanitarian-foreign policy-economic interest based effort. Developed countries that are listed under Annex II of the UNFCCC are obliged under Article 4.3 to provide new and additional financial resources to developing countries that would:

- meet the agreed full costs for the preparation and submissions of developing countries' national communications;
- meet the agreed full incremental costs (including for technology transfer) of developing countries to implement their obligations under Article 4 of the Convention. 4.1. (See also Box 4.2.)

Additionally, such developed countries as are listed in Annex II of the UNFCCC also have, under Article. 4.4, the obligation to 'assist the developing country Parties that are particularly vulnerable to the adverse effects of climate change in meeting costs of adaptation to those adverse effects'. Financing flows under the UNFCCC from developed (Annex II) Parties to developing countries pursuant to Articles. 4.3, 4.4, and 4.5, are supposed to be primarily 'on a grant or concessional basis'[23] (South Centre 2011).

In general the funds to be provided by Annex II Parties (hereafter developed countries) to Non-Annex I Parties (hereafter developing countries) are to be new, adequate, additional, appropriate, equitable and predictable.

- *Adequate*: Funds are to be available to carry out the actions that are needed to meet and mitigate climate risks and in line with the objectively determined needs of developing countries for adaptation, mitigation and technology transfer.
- *Additional*: Funds are to be new and additional to existing commitments to increase ODA flows. (Many researchers argue that 0.7 per cent GNI should be the appropriate reference point of benchmark for determining additionality.) There should be no diversion of funds from traditional flows of ODA or sector of aid spending (i.e., health or Education).
- *Appropriate*: Funds should be compensatory in nature in line with the polluter pays principle. The polluter pays principle implies that the party responsible for producing pollution is responsible for paying for the damage done to the natural environment. Funds, hence, should not be in the form of loans.[24]

> **BOX 4.2 ANNEX II FINANCIAL COMMITMENTS UNDER THE CONVENTION**
>
> In terms of the scope of financial support, under the Convention, developed countries have agreed to provide agreed full incremental costs for cooperation in preparing for adaptation to the impacts of climate change; full incremental costs for cooperation in developing appropriate plans for costal zones, water and agriculture and protection and rehabilitation of areas affected by drought, desertification and floods; and full incremental costs for formulating and implementing national and regional programmes containing measures to facilitate adequate adaptation and assist particularly vulnerable developing countries in meeting the costs of adaptation to adverse effects. They are also committed to providing support for enabling activities, including the preparation of national communications.
>
> In the area of mitigation, developed countries have committed to provide agreed full costs for formulating and implementing national and regional programmes containing measure to mitigate climate change and by addressing emission by sources and removal of sinks of all GHGs as well as to provide agreed full incremental costs for cooperating in the conservation and enhancement of sinks and reservoirs of GHGs including biomass, forests, oceans and other ecosystems.
>
> With regard to technology development and transfer, developed countries have committed to provide agreed full incremental costs for cooperating in the development and transfer of technologies to mitigate climate change in all relevant sectors (including energy, transportation, industry, agriculture, forestry and waste. Other areas in which developed countries have agreed to provide financial support to developing countries include: communications, capacity building and other actions.

- *Equitable*: Based on the principle of 'common but differentiated responsibility and respective capacity'.
- *Predictable*: Funds should be available (on a long-term and guaranteed basis) so as to enable long-term planning.

Despite these seemingly clear guiding principles and agreed commitments that determine the framework for climate change finance, since the entry into force of the Convention, there has been persistent, pervasive and protracted wrangling over finance between the developed and the developing countries. Developing countries point to lack of access to needed finance, imbalance in accessing finance for adaptation actions relative to mitigation actions, overly burdensome criteria and the imposition of onerous co-financing requirements by funding implementing agencies and climate funds.

Civil society groups in the Asian region have also called attention to the perverse over reliance on lending instruments offered to poor developing countries as part of climate finance packages by, for example, the World Bank as well as some bilateral lenders.[25] These challenges not only erode the core equity basis of the Convention but may have impeded some developing countries' capacity to undertake meaningful adaptation and mitigation actions, while imposing heavy debt burden on others, such as the Philippines, as they seek to take adaptation actions.

At the same time, developing countries' mitigation actions, such as GHG emissions and removals at national, sectoral and project levels, which were put forward in the NAMA and were expected to be purely voluntary are to be subjected to processes of transparency and emerging frameworks of measurement, reporting and verification (MRV). This so-called MRV focuses on the 'the measurement of emissions/removals or other performance metrics of NAMAs, reporting on those outcomes, and domestic verification of the emissions/ removals or other metrics' (submission by the Umbrella Group countries to the UNFCCC[26]). Despite a lack of common understanding of the purpose or functions of MRV, it is argued to include specification of underlying assumptions, methodologies and GHGs inventorying. The outcome of MRV should prepare for yet another obligation of reporting, the biennial update reports (BUR) containing updates of national greenhouse gas inventories, including a national inventory report and information on mitigation actions, needs and support received. These BURs are themselves to be the basis of technical experts' analyses of the information contained there-in under the process of International consultation and analysis (ICA), (the Cancún Agreements, 1/CP.16). Finally, NAMAs are to be subjected to a NAMA registry which will record information on NAMAs seeking international support. All of these instruments of reporting obligations impose additional burdens in terms of technical expertise for measuring, report preparation, capacity building for undertaking investigations and developing and managing technical tools. These will have high costs implications for developing countries. Developing countries have also taken on additional requirements as noted in Paragraphs 33, 54 and 60 of the Cancún Decision (1/CP.16) and Paragraphs 33, 38 and 41 of the Durban Decision (2/CP.17).

Developed countries are very active in promoting and constructing a comprehensive framework for assessing the mitigation actions of developing countries, including detailed processes of measurement, reporting and verification (MRV) of support (both those domestically support through a country's own generated resources as well as for those seeking international support). However, developed countries have been less proactive in establishing a similar comprehensive and transparent framework for monitoring the financial and technical support to be provided by them to the developing countries. Almost 18 years after the entry into force of the UNFCCC, the flows of both finance and technology transfer have not been significant or adequate to meet the most conservatively estimated needs

Global climate change finance architecture **183**

of adaptation and mitigation for developing countries. (This issue is discussed in detail in Sections 4.5 and 4.6.)

The issues underlying the seeming intractable debates between developing and developed countries' Parties about what is to be financed and how much under the climate change umbrella are complex, conflictual and difficult to unravel. In the first case, there is no agreed standard as to what climate finance is and what type of support should be counted as such. Second, there is no consistent, robust and comprehensive system internationally for measuring reporting and verifying climate finance support (OECD 2011).

Reporting on climate support occurs primarily through the National Communications reports and the biennial reports of Annex II parties that are made to the UNFCCC. There is also reporting of climate support through the OECD Development Assistance Committee (OECD-DAC). But while the UNFCCC Secretariat compiles and synthesizes national communications reports, there is no in-depth and comprehensive analysis of them. There is no thorough analysis of the information provided in a clear, easily comparable and transparent way. The UNFCCC does not track and assess the financing information provided in national communications and the biennial reports. According to the UNFCCC's Standing Committee on Finance, information in these documents is for purposes of transparency as to how, when and for whom funds are provided (SCF 2014).

While the OECD-DAC is increasingly tracking climate finance, there are still many limitations on this effort. Presently, the OECD-DAC reporting framework tracks mitigation and adaptation finance under its Rio Markers.[27] But the focus has been on bilateral ODA for mitigation (since 1998) and with similar work on adaptation only beginning in 2010. There is some work in progress on tracking both bilateral non-ODA flows as well as multilateral ODA flows for mitigation and adaptation (OECD/Benn 2011).

Discussions around the costs of adaptation and mitigation activities are usually circumscribed by the nature and extent of investment and financial flows as well as by the determination of what are the relevant sectors to be considered and the ultimate effects of these flows. The lacunae in defining and establishing systematic processes for the treatment, measuring and facilitation of climate flows makes it difficult to track flows and assess progress. Yet answers to these questions are important for mobilizing and analysing the effectiveness of adequate flow of funds to developing countries through the financing architecture. The foundational elements towards a more rigorous system for defining, measuring and verifying climate finance exist within the normative framework established under the Convention. However, these seem to pose challenges (including tacit acceptance of historical responsibility, some loss of control over discretionary power over how the financing is utilized) for the major contributors to climate financing activities in developing countries. Hence the perpetuation and continuation of the status quo, which no one believes is entirely useful or sustainable towards achieving the agreed objectives of global climate protection policies.

4.3 The normative and governance dimension of climate change finance

Climate change financing is grounded in three interrelated pillars: climate change science, the UNFCCC policy framework and the dynamics of global finance.

4.3.1 Climate science

Climate science determines the objective parameters that will guide the flow of finance and investment for climate change. Scientific experts' views and recommendations as to the critical actions and pathways that the global community should or must take in order to ensure the successful achievement of the goal of the Convention, which is the 'stabilization of greenhouse gas concentrations in the atmosphere at a level that would prevent dangerous anthropogenic interference with the climate system'. Science states the parameters that will determine the scope, scale and speed of the transformation. Scientific understandings are conveyed into climate (finance) policy discussion through the interventions of the IPCC periodic assessment reports. The recent IPCC Assessment Report (AR 5, 2013) will have tremendous bearing on the progress and outcome of the ongoing Durban Platform negotiations. Ultimately, of course, economic and social priorities will contribute to the penultimate determination of the politically feasible responses and associated response measures that countries will or should take. The IPCC and other scientific reports impact the negotiations directly through expert meetings and workshops that convened with the Parties at both the inter-sessional climate meetings and the annual end of year meeting of the COP. The Convention's subsidiary bodies are the Subsidiary Body for Scientific and Technological Advice (SBSTA) and the Subsidiary Body for Implementation (SBI). SBSTA and SBI are also in charge of collaborating with external scientific bodies such as the IPCC on the latest scientific findings, as part of the mandated review of the adequacy of the 2 degrees goal and actions currently underway to meet that goal. Part of this work is being undertaken under the framework of the Structured Expert Dialogue (SED).[28] For the first time ever the IPCC Assessment Report has examined the issue of climate finance, as a standalone item in Working Group III, Chapter 16, *Cross-cutting Investment and Finance Issues*, and has also considered the costing of adaptation and mitigation in Working Group II, Chapter 17, *Economics of Adaptation*.

4.3.2 Climate policy

The UNFCCC with its principles and provisions with regard to the financing for climate protection is at the base of the evolving international climate change finance regime. The UNFCCC is quite clear that the financing and technology transfer that are necessary for implementing the actions and obligations of developing countries and thus enabling the successful achievement of the goal of the Convention must come from Annex II countries, primarily OECD countries (South Centre 2011). The developed countries are responsible for providing developing countries with finance and technology transfer necessary to meet adaptation and mitigation costs.

BOX 4.3 EVOLUTION OF CLIMATE FINANCE UNDER THE UNFCCC

Pre-UNFCCC: Under the 1972 Stockholm UN Conference on Human Environment states have recognized that 'financial and technological assistance as a supplement to the domestic effort of the developing countries ... is a pivotal component to avoid negative effects of human development on the earth system environment'.*

1994: UNFCCC Article 4(3) and (4). And **Article 11** (para 1) Financial Mechanism: A mechanism for the provision of financial resources on a grant or concessional basis, including for the transfer of technology, is hereby defined. It shall function under the guidance of and be accountable to the COP, which shall decide on its policies, programme priorities and eligibility criteria related to this Convention. Its operation shall be entrusted to one or more existing international entities.

Kyoto Protocol 1997: Direct implementation and financing of emissions reduction projects in developing countries through its Clean Development Mechanisms targets for global emissions of GHGs – limited the permitted emission of countries; created market-based financing mechanisms to help countries meet emissions targets: Emission trading-carbon markets, CDM and Joint Implementation. (KP: assign burden of financing clearly and unambiguously to developed countries to provide new and additional financial resources to meet the 'agreed full costs' incurred by developing countries' parties.)**

Buenos Aires Plan of Action 1998: Global Environment Facility (GEF) on behalf of the UNFCCC responsible for managing the funding activities supporting adaptation in developing countries, specifically Transfer of Technology and Capacity building. GEF was set up as trust fund administered by the World Bank to provide funding to the 4 Rio Conventions: Convention on Biodiversity, Stockholm, CCD and, ultimately, the UNFCCC.

2001: UNFCCC establishes the Special climate change fund (voluntary contributions beyond regular GEF replenishment) – from 13 participants and the Least Developing Country Fund (LDCF) to finance project related to climate change adaptation, technology transfer and capacity building. Also agreed to setting up the Adaptation Fund.

2007 COP – Bali Action Plan (BAP, COP 13): To accelerate global response to climate change by specific action to mobilize increase funding and enhance development assistance for climate change; finance identified The *Bali Action Plan* agreed to in 2007 at the thirteenth COP (COP 13) identified 'financing' as a key component in reaching a future global agreement on climate change.

2009/2010 Copenhagen Accord: Short term or Fast Start Finance Initiative $30 billion per year for three years, 2010–2012 and Long-term financing (goal to mobilize $100 billion per year by 2020). (Effectively a side agreement reached among 30 or so parties.)

2010 Cancún Agreement: Legitimized the Copenhagen accord under the Convention and hence can be seen as the first actual quantification of the financial obligation of developed countries for climate finance: $30 billion in Fast-start Finance, 2010–2012 and a commitment to a goal of mobilizing $100 billion per year by 2020 it also establish a Green Climate Fund and a Standing Committee.

The Cancún Decision COP 15:
Paragraph 95: Takes note of the collective commitment by developed countries to provide new and additional resources, including forestry and investments through international, approaching USD 30 billion for the 2010–2012, with a balanced allocation between adaptation and mitigation; funding for adaptation will be prioritized for the most vulnerable developing, such as the least developing countries, small island developing States and Africa';

Paragraph 97: 'Decides that, in accordance with the relevant provisions of the Convention, scaled-up, new and additional, predictable and adequate funding shall be provided to developing countries Parties, taking into account the urgent and immediate needs of developing that are particularly vulnerable to the adverse effects of climate change';

Paragraph 98: 'Recognizes that developed country parties commit, in the context of meaningful action and transparency on implementation, to a goal of mobilizing jointly USD 100 billion per year by 2020 to address the needs of developing parties'.

2011: Durban Decision operationalizes Green Climate Fund and the Standing Committee for Finance as well as the instituted a Work Programme on Long Term Finance.

2012: Doha Climate Gateway extended the Work Programme on Long Term Finance for 1 year to end and **LTF to** identify pathways for mobilizing scaled-up finance to reach the 100 billion target by 2020; and initiated the 5th Review of the Financial Mechanisms; invited developed countries submit before the next Conference information on their strategies for mobilizing scaled-up finance. Work programme on long-term finance during 2013 provided for the mechanism of a high-level roundtable on finance is planned for COP 19/CMP 9 in Warsaw so that ministers can provide general guidance on the scaling up of finance

2013: Warsaw Instituted a High level ministerial Dialogue on Finance, the Work programme on Result Based Finance to progress the full implementation of the activities referred to in Decision 1/CP.16, Paragraph 70, and 'Requests the GCF, when providing results-based finance, to apply the methodological guidance consistent with Decisions 4/CP.16, 2/CP.17, 12/CP.17 and _/CP.19 to _/CP.19, as well as this Decision, in order to improve the effectiveness and coordination of results-based finance'. The Standing Committee on Finance to 'in the context of the preparation of its biennial assessment and overview of climate finance flows, to consider ongoing technical work on operational definitions of climate finance, including private finance mobilized by public interventions, to assess how adaptation and mitigation needs can most effectively be met by climate finance, and to include the results in its annual report to the COP' (Paragraph 11 of that Decision).

* Declaration of the UN Conference on the Human Environment, 16 June 1972, UN Doc. A/CONF.48/14/Rev.1 (1973), reprinted in (1972) 11 ILM 1416, Principle 9, cited in Nafo 2012; ***Kyoto Protocol to the United Nations Framework Convention on Climate Change*, Tokyo: 11 December 1997 entered into force on 16 February 2005, UN Doc. FCCC/CP/1997/7/Add.1, Dec. 1/CP.3 Annex-I, Article 12.

The legally binding provisions of the Convention and the subsequent decisions by the COP over the ensuing years since the Convention entered into force have established the broad normative and operational contours of the international climate change finance architecture. These decisions have been arrived at through multilateral negotiations and cooperation between developing countries and developed country Parties. (See Box 4.2 for an overview of the evolution of such decisions on climate finance.) Starting with the Convention itself, COP decisions have launched a specific Financial Mechanism (Article 11) populated with funding entities which is complemented by a plethora of dedicated climate change finance instruments and mechanisms created by developed countries that have been shaping the international climate change architecture.

The Bali Action Plan (2007), which attempted to further consolidate the financing dimensions of the Convention by calling for enhanced action on financing, reaffirmed that the foundational core of the Convention in all its dimensions is the principle of equity and common but differentiated responsibility and articulated a core set of principles for guiding, measuring and monitoring the flow of climate change finance, as highlighted above.

Climate change finance is in many respects quite different from the broader global finance or development aid framework. First, as noted above, the climate change finance regime currently in place is governed by a specific normative framework emanating from the principles of the Convention, therefore its scope and scale are impacted by the ongoing negotiations parameters established within that framework. Underlying that framework are the principles of equity and compensation-based support for developing countries to address the impacts of climate change (especially with regard to adaptation finance and newly emerging discussion around 'loss and damage'). Second, a critical requirement is the need for a dedicated stream of public financial flow that is primarily grant or concessional finance.

4.3.3 Global finance

Broadly, climate change finance, like the global financial system under which it is evolving, is constructed around at least three broad areas: financial management, financial markets and investments. It has the added aspect of a stream of fiscally generated public funds as its foundation. The key actors and institutions in climate finance are, for the most part, the same as those in the global financial markets: public and quasi-public institutions and private individuals and institutional players, such as commercial banks, insurance companies, hedge funds, money market funds and pension funds. The main asset forms are grants, concessional loans, non-concessional loans, equity shares, bonds (increasingly so-called green bonds are gaining currency), commodities, and derivatives (options, futures and swaps) and wan guarantees. (See Boxes 4.4 and 4.5.)

A key difference between the climate change finance and the global financial regime is the specific nature of the primary activities each undertakes. Climate change finance mechanisms such as the Clean Development Mechanism's portfolio are primarily based on greenhouse gas emissions, and thus the key asset in which instruments are likely to be traded, valued and weighted is 'carbon' as the euphemism for GHGs reduction objectives, specifically, carbon credits/offsets (Box 4.4).

In the climate arena, financing risks are those around the likely under-delivery of carbon credits for compliance and/or to insure against climate risks (such as frequent and destructive adverse weather conditions and their impact on commodities, buildings and equipment). Additionally, unlike global finance, which is dominated by private sector players and market-based activities, climate change financing is a mixture of active government (bilateral institutions) and international quasi-governmental institutions (for example, UN agencies and multilateral development banks) and market and non-market-based mechanisms.

Another key difference separating climate finance from global finance is the obligation to pay attention to issues of geographic balance, the balance between finance for adaptation and finance for mitigation, equity and the targeting of finance to particularly vulnerable groups of countries such as small-islands states, low lying and mountainous regions. Increasingly, gender and climate justice activists are seeking to widen the scope of equity in the context of climate finance to take into account issues of gender inequality and women's empowerment and the role contribution of indigenous peoples. The gender dimensions of global finance and its impact on the climate finance are discussed in Chapter 5. The next section briefly explores the nature and dynamics around the financing of adaptation and mitigation, including of actors, instruments and frameworks.

BOX 4.4 THE NUTS AND BOLTS OF CLIMATE CHANGE FINANCE I: USEFUL TERMS

- *Angel* – An angel investor or angel (also known as a business angel or informal investor) is an affluent individual who provides capital for a business start-up usually in exchange for ownership equity. Angel investing is a component of the venture capital model. Venture capital tends seek investments in entities at a later growth phase of a business entity than angel investors.

- *Bonds* – A (debt) investment through which an investor loans money to an entity (corporate or governmental) that borrows the funds for a defined period of time, of projects and activities, at a fixed interest rate.
  So-called Green bonds enable capital-raising and investment from capital markets for new and existing projects with environmental benefits (CBI).

- *Commodity(ies)* – A basic good that is interchangeable with another. Traditional commodities include grains, gold, beef, oil and natural gas. New age commodities are financial products such as foreign currencies and indexes and carbon/carbon offsets.

- *Derivative* – A financial instrument that is derived from some other asset, index, event, value or condition (known as the underlying asset).

- *Options* – A guarantee of the right to purchase or sell allowances at a fixed price within a defined period of time; and

- *Forward* – The purchase of emission allowances to be supplied in the future at a fixed price.

- *Futures* – A financial contract obligating the buyer to purchase an asset (or the seller to sell an asset), such as a physical commodity or a financial instrument at a predetermined future date and price.

- *Loan guarantees* – A loan guaranteed by a third party, in case of a default.

- *Hedge Funds* – Investments are pooled and professionally and aggressively managed speculatively and flexibly to generate maximum return on investment. Managers utilize a wide range of investment strategies including leverage, long and short and derivatives positions in domestic and international markets.

- *Money Market Funds* – An investment fund that holds short term (less than one year) high quality securities, liquid debt and monetary instruments. It emphasizes low risk low, return investment and high safety and accessibility of funds.

- *Pension Fund* – A fund established by an employer to facilitate and organize the investment of employees' retirement funds contributed by the employer and employees.

- *Swaps* – The exchange of payment obligations so that different allowance currencies can be exchanged.

- *Venture capital* – Wealth available for investment in new or speculative enterprises.

Source: adapted from Investopedia.com

BOX 4.5 GREEN BONDS

Green Bonds enable capital-raising and investment from capital market for new and existing projects with environmental benefits (CBI).

Currently most green bonds are issued by Development Finance Institutions, who tend to have strong credit rating to issues bonds, i.e. raise debt from the capital markets and can do so for green investment objectives.

Key green bond actors and frameworks include the World Bank Green Bonds, IFC Green Bonds, the AfDB Green Bonds, The Climate Bonds Initiative, and the Green Bonds Principles.

Corporations such as GDF-Suez and EDF have now also begun to issue their own green bonds, with or without any financial institution. Financial institutions also are increasingly becoming strong actors in the Green Bond area. In January of 2014, Bank of America, Merrill Lynch, Citi, Crédit Agricole Corporate and Investment Banking and JPMorgan Chase released the Green Bond Principles – a set of guidelines for issuers of green bonds. It had by July 2014 signed by at least commercial and investment banks including BNP Paribas, Daiwa, Deutsche Bank, Goldman Sachs, HSBC, Mizuho Securities, Morgan Stanley, Rabobank and SEB.

These Principles, which were developed with guidance from issuers, investors and environmental groups, will serve as voluntary guidelines on recommended processes for the development and issuance of Green Bonds and encourage transparency, disclosure and integrity in the development of the Green Bond market. The Principles focus on four key areas – use of proceeds, project evaluation and selection, management of proceeds, and reporting. They are designed to provide issuers with guidance on the key components involved in launching a Green Bond, to aid investors by ensuring the availability of information necessary to evaluate the environmental impact of their Green Bond investments and to assist underwriters by moving the market towards standard disclosures which facilitate transactions (press statement on GBP). Under the GBP, 'each issuer is responsible for defining the investment criteria included in their Green Bonds', JP Morgan Chase.

Criticisms and caution with regard to Green Bonds and the GBPs by climate finance advocates:

- Green bonds can be a positive way to raise money for the right projects – especially when initiatives/issuances have clear standards and definitions of what is meant by 'green' and follow best international practices with regard to social and environmental safeguards, not simply on the basis of CO_2 avoided.
- The money raised can go to a general pot and be spent on any type of project.
- While the Green Bond Principles are a good start in the right direction, they are only broad recommendations, not commitments.
- There is a lack of clarity over what projects can be considered 'green'; there are neither agreed rules nor standards among these institutions/ initiatives on what qualifies as 'green'. Each one has its own set of guidelines, standards, defining what projects are acceptable to earmark as 'green' when issuing a debenture.
- There have been clear example of problematic UK-financed projects where environmental standards fall short, such as Jirau Dams and GDF Suez pipeline projects.
- There are other more innovative ways that green bonds could raise additional capital for green/climate finance, and one example is that of the IFFIM and GAVI, whereby governments do 'commit' to long-term finance, but rather than pay cash into the mechanism they agree to underwrite the mechanism. Under IFFIm raises finance (over $4.5 billion) for immunization programmes by issuing bonds in the capital markets and so converts long-term government pledges into immediately available cash resources. The long-term government pledges will be used to repay the IFFIm bonds.

Source: Climate Bond Initiatives, Friends of the Earth, press statement

4.4 Distinctive features of climate change finance

The broad objectives of the current climate change financing regime are to promote and ensure adaptation and mitigation activities. Thus the goals of climate change financing are ostensibly at least twofold: 1) to mitigate climate change (reduction of GHG emissions) and accelerate the transition to low carbon economy and 2) to manage the risk of climate change induced weather events – so as to prevent and minimize loss of lives and livelihoods and damages to infrastructure and capital stock. But while mitigation, within the UNFCCC framework, includes clearly 'defined objectives, measures, costs and instruments, this is not the case for adaptation' (IPCC 2007). There are obvious developmental dimensions to adaptation which tend to create some tensions and concerns for developed countries that fund adaptation projects and programmes. For example, development financing is normally required to promote and build up the current level of housing stocks and infrastructure. The nature and magnitude of these expenditures are known and can be planned for with financing from traditional development financing sources. Adaptation financing to a certain extent can contribute to these areas but it is not expected to substitute for development finance.

Adaptation has both known and unknown financing challenges. Known financing challenges are related to the requirements for climate-proofing existing structures, which imply additional (or incremental) costs that must be added to the costs of preparing for, in anticipation of future, as yet unknown, climate events (resilience). Unknown adaptation financing challenges include the cost of dealing with the aftermaths of extreme climate-related weather events (i.e., disaster management), which can be anticipated but cannot be known with certainty. It is clearly quite difficult to unbundle these multiple aspects of adaptation. It is also quite clear that women's and men's lives and livelihoods in developing countries are critically dependent on the nature and extent of adaptation costs and its financing in the immediate and medium term outlook.

Fundamentally, climate change finance encompasses the roles and actions of public and private sector financial institutions and financial decision-makers with regard to intermediating among contributing and recipient governments, savers and investors, lenders and borrowers. The aim of intermediation is to manage the risk of adapting to climate change induced weather events (including addressing the loss and damages associated with these events) and the reduction of GHGs into the atmosphere.

With climate change, the risks to be mitigated, or offset, or to take speculative positions with regard to, by individuals and firms, are climate risks such as adverse weather conditions (floods, droughts and storms). This involves the innovation of creative forms of traditional instruments such as bonds (catastrophe and green bonds) and derivatives (weather derivatives) and various forms of climate risk insurance. The main novelty in climate change financing is the emergence of a new commodity around which a major part of private climate and investment flows are increasingly centred – emissions reductions or removal, or simply, 'carbon'. Hence, the emergence of a distinctive type of financial market, the carbon finance/market in which different types of financial instruments, products and services that lead to climate change mitigation and adaptation are traded (UNEP 2009). The terms carbon offsets, carbon credits and cap and trade are now ubiquitous in the global financial markets. (See Box 4.6.)

Investment opportunities in the climate change financing environment are primarily in the areas of energy efficiency, renewable and clean energy and carbon financing. There are also investment opportunities in adaptation financing, but with the exception of infrastructure investment/financing this area is often seen as less profitable, hence it is primarily funded by public funds.

BOX 4.6 THE NUTS AND BOLTS OF CLIMATE CHANGE FINANCE II: CARBON FINANCING

- *Cap and trade:* The government sets an overall emissions cap (limit) and issues tradable permits to firms that allow them to emit a specified amount of GHGs. Companies with excess allowances can sell these permits.
- *Carbon credit:* A permit that allows the holder to emit one ton of *carbon* dioxide.
- *Carbon market:* A trading system through which entities buy or sell units of reduction credits for greenhouse gas emissions.
- *Carbon offset:* Allows purchasers to neutralize the carbon dioxide produced from their businesses and everyday activities – their 'carbon footprint' – by supporting a variety of emissions reduction initiatives (sourced from external projects).
- *Carbon tax:* A tax on energy sources which emit carbon dioxide.
- *CERs:* Certified emissions reduction. 1 CER is created when 1 tonne of CO_2 is prevented from entering the atmosphere.
- CO_2e: Carbon dioxide equivalent– measuring units for GHGs
- *Clean Development Mechanism:* The CDM allows emission-reduction projects in developing countries to earn certified emission reduction (CER) credits, each equivalent to one tonne of CO_2. These CERs can be traded and sold, and used by industrialized countries to a meet a part of their emission reduction targets under the Kyoto Protocol (UNFCCC).
- *Emissions trading (or carbon trading):* A market-based approach to achieving environmental objectives that allow those reducing greenhouse gas emissions below what is required to use or trade the excess reductions to offset emissions at another source inside or outside the country. In general, trading can occur at the intra-company, domestic and international levels. Under Article 17, Kyoto Protocol, countries that have emissions units to spare (emissions permitted but not used) can sell this excess capacity to countries that are over target. *Emissions trading units in the carbon markets:*
    - o AAUs: Allowance Assigned Units: Emission quotas assigned to Annex I/Annex B countries under Kyoto Protocol. These can be directly trade on a bilateral basis under International Emission Trading.
    - o CERs: Certified Emission Reduction (generated by CDM projects)
    - o ERUs: Emission Reduction Unit (generated by JI projects)
    - o EUA: European Allowance Units (generated in the EU ETS)
    - o RMU: Removal unit (on the basis of LULUCF activities such as reforestation, i.e. the development of domestic sinks).

In the carbon market, there is a demand for carbon delivery that is guaranteed and the monetization of forward contracts. The unit of currency is the price of carbon, expressed in terms of certified emissions reductions (CERs), assigned amounts units (AAUs) or emissions removal units (ERUs). (These instruments, which are used to deliver carbon credits are further defined in Box 4.4.) Suppliers of carbon credits have carbon dioxide emitting facilities, emission-reduction purchase facilities, or they supply emission reduction projects or, are owners of carbon rich projects. The nature of the facilities, carbon market and the marketing of carbon emissions through cap and trade and the price of carbon will be discussed more in depth in Chapter 9.

Flexibility, liquidity and protection against climate risk/loss are sought by individuals, companies and countries. Analyses of risks, gains and losses are performed by academics, NGOs, banks and development and other financial intermediaries, brokers and traders. Both global finance and climate change finance also depend on the evolution of a range of financial technologies, accounting and payment transactions flow, financial statistics and financial instruments.

Chapters 6 and 7 will present in-depth treatment on the flows of finance for adaptation and mitigation considering the gender dimensions of these flows. Chapter 8 will provide expanded treatment of the carbon market. We move now to explore the tensions ridden area of the mis-match between the scale of finance currently provided by developed countries and the estimation of the requirements or needs for adaptation and mitigation project financing by developing counties.

4.5 The scale, scope and needs for climate change finance

The predictable availability of a large-scale flow of funds that is equitable, non-debt creating and easily accessible to the broad and highly differentiated groups of countries (from Least Developing, Small and vulnerable, Low- and middle-income to high-income) countries is inextricably linked to the faithfulness of developed countries in following through on the financing and transfer of technology commitments they made under the UNFCCC and its Kyoto Protocol.

There are multiple and varying attempts at estimating the costs of adaptation, mitigation and technology transfer and development in the coming years, both globally and in developing countries. The UNFCCC's secretariat estimates climate-related financial flows of 0.5 to 2.3 per cent of global GDP in 2030 and 1.1 to 1.7 per cent of global investment in 2030. The Group of 77 and China developing countries argues that the level of new funding through the finance mechanism of the Convention, from developed countries, be set at 0.5 per cent of the GNP of those countries, as an initial minimum, and which should be additional to existing official development assistance flows. In 2009, the African Group argued in favour of financing equivalent to 5 per cent of developed countries' GDP. Other researchers, including the South Centre and the United Nations Department of Economic and Social Affairs, posit a financial transfer to meeting developing countries' climate financing needs of $600 billion a year in 2020 and over $3 trillion in 2050. As noted by Harvard University researchers, 'this is an unprecedented implicit wealth transfer form developed to developing countries, if developed countries are to fully compensate developing countries for their mitigation activities up to 2020 under a global emissions reduction target of 50 per cent' (HPICA 2009). Appendix 4.1 presents an overview of global cost estimates as well as selected estimates for developing countries for adaptation and mitigation.

The estimates by developing countries seems more in line with top-down estimation results, which for mitigation alone vary from $290 billion (for the generation of new energy plants, energy efficiency and a small proportion for agriculture ($20 billion) and forestry to $1,100 billion per year for mitigation in in developing countries in all sectors (UNDESA 2011).

Top-down estimates for adaptation financing requirements vary widely and are at best unreliable and, at worst, seriously under-estimate the amount needed to help developing countries to avoid or adjust to the factors that cause harm to people, ecosystems and infrastructures arising from climate change and climate variability. At the low end, the UNFCCC Secretariat estimates that between $28 billion and $67 billion is needed annually by 2030 to help developing countries to adapt; in the middle there is Oxfam's estimate of $50 billion each year and at the high end there is the UN Human Development Report estimate that $86–109 billion is needed annually by 2015 (2007). Recently (2010), World Bank estimates for adaptation range from $75 billion to $100 billion per year. But even this has been critiqued for under-counting or ignoring important sectors and the cost of residual damages. More realistic estimates of adaptation costs, which take into account factors such as ecosystem services and residual damages from natural disasters (estimated at about $150 billion and $300 billion per year, respectively, for developing countries) argue in favour of adaptation costs of about $582 billion per year.[29]

In terms of strictly climate change financing, Asia is estimated to require $130–225 billion in total for adaptation and mitigation per year by 2030 (CDKN 2010). Africa will require over $120 billion per year by 2050 for climate resilient development, including indicative costs of roughly $18-35 billion for adaptation, $13-26 billion for mitigation and $82 billion (from external sources) to cover the MDGs, coastal protection measures and disaster response (African Progress Panel 2010/2014, UNEP 2015). An additional $55 billion of resources will be needed to mend Africa's current energy investment gap (Progress Panel 2015). The Latin American and Caribbean region will need a similar financing quantum: $58 billion to $101 billion per year by 2030 for financing climate change mitigation and adaptation (CDKN 2010).

Furthermore, the Asian region alone will require between $1–32.4 billion for additional investment to adapt infrastructure to climate change risk in 2030. The UN Millennium Project argues for $2,000 billion (without high-income Asian nations) over 10 years to meet the MDGs (also supported by the 2009) report of the International Strategy for Disaster Reduction (ISDR 2009) as about what is needed in order to reduce the deficit in disaster-risk avoidance and risk reduction (cited in Parry *et al.* 2009). These figures do not include assessment from the potential new sets of goals and targets presently being devised under the Post-2015 Development Agenda (which review and revise the MDGs) and the Sustainable

Development Goals (from the post-Rio plus 20 outcome). These new frameworks are more than highly likely to include stand-alone goals on climate change and climate-related areas.

The results from bottom-up financial assessments for climate change studies show the enormity of the financing challenges faced by developing countries in responding to climate change. Both India and China have been the subjects of independently undertaken assessments of mitigation financing needs for transition to a low carbon pathway. The Centre for Science and the Environment in India studied India's six most emission intensive sectors (power, steel, aluminium, cement, fertilizer and paper) and reported that the additional cost of generating power from renewable technologies in a low carbon strategy over business as usual until 2030–2031 is approximately $203 billion or about $10 billion a year. (This is roughly about the same amount that developed countries contributed through the UNFCCC mechanism for all developing countries 2005–2010 as well as the average yearly amount for the fast start initiative, 2010–2012.) The 2009/2010 China Human Development Report (UNDP 2009) also undertook a scenario-based evaluation of China's low carbon development option. It found that in order to meet the ambitious emission abatement pathway, China would have to invest upwards of $355 billion a year (depending on the selected emission ambition pathway).

Results from the National Economic, Environment and Development Study (NEEDS) for the climate change project, undertaken under the auspice of the UNFCCC Secretariat show that for the eleven countries (Costa Rica, Egypt, Ghana, Indonesia, Jordan, Lebanon, Maldives, Mali, Nigeria and the Philippines) participating in the study the estimated short-term (2020) and long-term (2050) costs for mitigating GHG emissions range from $45 million to $33.01 billion with adaptation costs ranging from $161.5 million to $20.69 billion. The NEEDS study also shows that while many developing countries such as Nepal, the Philippines and India are increasingly allocating funds in their national budgets for climate change initiatives, climate finance flows from external sources are of critical importance. This is especially so for the scaling up of adaptation and mitigation measures in developing countries, which require large investment. However, as noted by the UNFCCC Synthesis Report on the NEEDS study, the existing (and prospective $100 billion per year by 2020) resources on the table are inadequate to address this need.

These figures do not include the financing for social protection (measures such as universal basic old age and disability pensions, basic child benefits and universal access to essential health care) that will help poor men and women to decrease vulnerability to events and the pervading conditions that can threaten their lives and livelihoods. Social protection availability can help poor men and women and indigenous communities better meet their daily lives as they adapt to, recover from and rehabilitate their personal, household and community stock of assets that are 'damaged or lost' during extreme weather events.[30] Research on the costing of social protection measures in developing countries such as Burkina Faso, Ethiopia,

Kenya, Nepal, Senegal and Tanzania show that it can be as much as 1–1.5 per cent of GDP (ILO 2008).

It is acknowledged, as discussed earlier, that climate change has adverse impacts on the development of infrastructures, food production and livelihood strategies. Therefore, finance geared for adaptation must also seek to emphasize the promotion of food security and climate resilient livelihoods as well as address barriers to gender equality as they relate to vulnerability and adaptive capacity. This enhanced adaptation must be a key pillar of financing strategy. Finance for mitigation must also seek to integrate measures that are pro-poor, employment generating outcomes and promote social protection; it must be socially aware.

Ultimately, the adequate and the right balance (as between enhanced adaptation finance and socially aware mitigation finance) can only be delivered once all the various gender and social dynamics are also integrated into needs and vulnerability assessment studies and estimation modelling. How financing is provided and accessed has important equity implications. Hence the source of climate finance and the nature of its delivery mechanisms are important for meeting the goals of the Convention and for ensuring the lives and livelihoods of hundreds of millions of men, women and children.

4.6 Sources and delivery mechanisms of global climate change finance

The issues of the scale, scope and sources of financing needed for adaptation and mitigation of climate change remain a matter of high tension in the climate change negotiations. As discussed in the preceding section, there is a wide universe of climate finance instruments including ODA, foreign direct investment, debt creating instruments, such as loans, and guarantees and offsets (in the carbon market). These instruments, however, do not all exactly fit the conceptualization of climate finance under the UNFCCC, because they all will not satisfy the obligations of developed countries as described under Articles 4 and 11 of the Convention. The range of instruments that most clearly meet the requirements of the Convention includes primarily public funds such as grants, grant components of loans and possible subsidy component of loans. (In general, loans must be paid back.)

4.6.1 How much is flowing where and how?

Research on the amount of climate finance flowing globally and between developed and developing regions give quite different and contradictory pictures.[31] The aforementioned IPCC AR assessment reports that there is limited evidence and high agreement that the total climate finance currently flowing to developing countries is estimated to be between $39–120 billion USD per year (2009, 2010, 2011 and 2012). Of this, public climate finance is estimated at $35–49 billion (2011/2012 USD) (medium confidence). Yet, the climate finance reported by

Annex II Parties to the UNFCCC averaged nearly $10 billion per year from 2005 to 2010 and between 2010 and 2012 and the 'fast-start finance' (FSF) provided by some developed countries amounted to over $10 billion per year.

The different estimates of aggregate climate finance between the two studies of the CPI and the OECD that are the basis for the IPCC analysis as well as other research findings is, partly due to, the lack of clear definition of what counts as climate finance, compounded by the lack of a clear and transparent system (including accounting and methodology) for measuring, verifying and tracking climate finance. In addition, lack of uniform or agreed and common official definition and method for assessing 'new and additional' flow of climate finance increases the risk of double counting across financing flows (OECD 2011; Haites 2011; UNFCCC 2011).[32]

Buchner et al. 2011, who produced the CPI research output, note that the US$97 billion total includes some developing countries and domestic sources and that not all of the amounts included in their assessment can be defined as additional to the climate finance available prior to the Copenhagen Accord (2011). Clapp et al. in their OECD report, caution that the estimated range they present depends upon a simple methodology, which 'adds' different types of climate finance, from grants to non-concessional development finance and private capital. This aggregate figure, they argue 'has a significant degree of uncertainty, given the potential for double-counting across several of the sources, and does not take into consideration which flows might count as "additional"' (OECD 2012, p.11).

Both the CPI and the OECD numbers reflect a significant portion of private sector investment in the form of direct equity and debt investment,[33] $37–72 billion (OECD) and $55 billion of CPI. With the public sector contribution accounting for significantly less than the private contribution, both studies account for $15–20 billion (OECD) and $21 billion (CPI). But not all of this public sector attribution is for dedicated climate change activities.

The picture presented also connotes a fairly liquid flow of climate finance to developing countries, significantly more than what most developing countries convey that they are receiving to the UNFCCC. These studies would seem to give a false sense of what is actually available for countries to fund national adaptation and mitigation plans. According to OECD, many developing countries' adaptation projects are unfunded (only a few have been funded) and no technology need assessments (TNA) identified have been funded (OECD 2012).

Dedicated climate change finance from developed countries to developing countries that meet the parameters specified under the Convention is not very easy to assess. The UNFCCC to which Annex II parties must report their contributions and support to developing countries through the vehicle of their national communications report, argues that it is difficult to determine accurately the actual flows of finance due to data gaps and inconsistencies (UNFCCC 2011). Though the UNFCCC has a reporting format, it is not used by many countries. Contributing countries insisted on utilizing their different approaches, different reporting periods, time scales (year, several years, multiyear or other) and currencies. The US dollar is the expected reporting currency but most countries report in their own national currencies. Reporting contributing countries also report using different sectoral categories and tabular and textual formats. Ultimately, according to the UNFCCC, these differences in reporting create problems for robust aggregation of data in order to gain understanding of the overall trends (UNFCCC 2011).

According to currently available information from across a wide variety of sources, such as the UNFCCC, OECD, the World Bank and Climate Funds Update, Annex II parties contributed $59.4 billion between 2005–2010 and another approximately $30 billion in fast start financing for the period 2010–2012. It is estimated that less than 10 per cent (approximately $3.3 billion spent dollar – an average of 0.6 per cent per year over 6 years) of this reported contribution flowed through the Convention financial mechanism.[34] This amounts to about $10–15 billion per year flowing as grants and concessional loans from developed to developing countries through bilateral, multilateral channels and the purchase of CDM credits (OECD 2011; Haites 2011). Most of this finance funds mitigation projects.

Overall, the aggregate amount of finance provided by developed countries is quite small relative to the developing countries' adaptation and mitigation needs. The World Bank argues that 'the resources committed cover just 5 per cent of the needs of developing countries' (World Bank 2011). The OECD argues that:

> The limited data available suggest that the climate-related financial resources for mitigation are of the order of USD 14 to 21 billion per year, mostly through the purchase of CDM credits and bilateral assistance. Only the adaptation funding provided through multilateral funds is known. It is of the order of USD 100 to 200 million per year. The number of projects that cannot obtain funding is a good indicator of the substantial shortfall in international financial support for adaptation.
>
> (OECD 2011: 6)

Therefore on any metrics, though developed countries have mobilized a growing stream of finance to meet their obligations to developing countries under the UNFCCC, these amounts have been (and continue to be) insufficient to the financing needs of developing countries to deal with the climate change crisis. As a result, there have been tremendous pressures from developing countries, civil society activists and researchers for the scaling up of climate change finance to developing countries to meet both the general commitment by developed countries as well as the specific requirements of new and additional flows in excess of existing flows. Given that the mitigation actions of developing countries are dependent on the extent to which they receive finance and technology transfer from developed countries (Article 4.7 of the Convention), coupled with the new reality that the urgency of the climate change crisis requires rapid actions by all countries, the need to rapidly upscale climate finance is paramount.

However, the challenges surrounding the quantum and scale of financing for climate change needs in developing countries is only part of the climate finance story. There are also outstanding issues about the performance, efficiency and efficacy of delivery mechanisms and the obstacles developing countries face in attempting to access the available funds they distribute. In many cases, the funding is supply driven and not in line with the needs of the 'demandeurs'. There are also growing concerns about the efficiency and results based management of the funds once allocated and disbursed to developing countries.

These issues continue to plague the climate negotiations and are sources of tensions between developed and developing countries in the discussions around the business model of the newly created GCF and calls for the up-scaling of medium and long-term climate finance flows under the Convention.

Currently, developing countries face a climate change financing architecture that is multi-layered, fragmented and grounded in a complex intertwine of funds, mechanisms and instruments, each with a complicated layering of access and distribution frameworks. At its core is a network of publicly financed, multilateral sources, some under the UNFCCC framework but with the bulk operating outside that framework, through multilateral channels, such as the World Bank and its network of regional development banks. Bilateral government funds implemented through various development cooperation entities, including national development banks also form part of this complex weave of climate finance providers. These actors are complemented by the activities of private sector actors involved in the operations of market-based mechanisms such as the Clean Development Mechanism, set up under the Kyoto Protocol, the private Carbon market, and firms involved in the flow of traditional FDI type activities in predominantly mitigation projects.

The remaining sections of this chapter will explore in detail the operations of these different layers of the climate finance mechanisms. The driving question is: *How is current climate finance delivered now and into the future?* The next section focuses on funds operating under the UNFCCC's financial mechanism elaborated in Article 11 of the Convention.

4.7 The operations of funds under the UNFCCC

The UNFCCC at its inception established a clear and transparent framework for the distribution and delivery of climate finance to developing countries to support their adaptation and mitigations actions. This framework is grounded in the establishment of a Financial Mechanism 'for the provision of financial resources on a grant or concessional basis, including for the transfer of technology, is hereby defined' (Article 11 Paragraph 1). Article 11 further stipulates that the Financial Mechanism 'shall function under the guidance of and be accountable to the COP, which shall decide on its policies, programme priorities and eligibility criteria related to this Convention. Its operation shall be entrusted to one or more existing international entities . . .'

Today there are two independent operating entities of the Financial Mechanism, the GEF, which operates a network of about three climate funds and subfunds, and the recently created GCF (created by the 2010 Cancún Decision, fully established but not yet fully operational in 2013). The COP is to be assisted with the workings of the Financial Mechanism and the rationalization of climate finance flows under the Convention by a newly created body, the Standing Committee on Finance (also decided at Cancún).

4.7.1 Funds under the Global Environment Facility

The COP entrusted (since 1994) the GEF as an operating entity of the Financial Mechanism (Article 11) of the Climate Convention (Article 11). The GEF serves on an ongoing basis, subject to review every 4 years. It was expected to provide financial resources on a grant and concessional basis, including for the transfer of technology, and is to function under the guidance of, and be accountable to, the COP, which should decide on its policies, programme priorities and eligibility criteria related to the Convention. Initially, GEF disbursed funding for its climate change focal area through the operations of its Trust fund, but over the years the COP have established a set of funds (the Adaptation Fund, the Least Developing Countries Fund and the Special Climate Change Fund), specifically for increasing the flow of financing under GEF for adaptation and mitigation actions in developing countries as well as to accelerate the transfer of technology between developed and developed countries and technology development within developing countries. As noted above, in 2011 the COP approved the governing instrument of a second operating entity of its Finance Mechanism, the GCF.

The rest of this section will discuss in detail the operation of the various funds under the UNFCCC, including the GCF. The gender dimensions, though at times alluded to here, will be discussed more fully in the subsequent chapters dealing with the specific impacts of the operations of the funds and instruments in the areas of adaptation, mitigation, capacity building and technology.

4.7.1.1 The Global Environment Facility

The GEF was established in 1991 under the World Bank as a $1 billion pilot project with the 'mission to transform the market development paths of eligible countries into trajectories with lower GHG emissions in the energy, industry, transportation and land use sector' (Hosier 2009).[35] The GEF, which later became an independent entity with the bank as its Trustee, is a multi-Convention financing mechanism that also operates as the financial mechanism for a number of environmental conventions, including the Convention on Biological Diversity. GEF funding operations are carried out through a number of implementing agencies – the World Bank, the United Nations Development Programme (UNDP) and the United Nations Environment Programme (UNEP) – and a web of executing agencies, (since the 1990s) – the four regional development banks (the Asian Development Bank and the Inter-American Bank granted direct access to

GEF resources in 2002, and the African Development Bank gained direct access in 2004), the Food and Agriculture Organization (FAO), the International Fund for Agriculture and Development (IFAD) and the United Nations Industrial Organization (UNIDO).

The GEF is funded through a 4-year replenishment cycle which is based on voluntary contributions. It is now in its sixth replenishment cycle (1 July 2014–30 June 2018).[36] Contributors are primarily OECD countries but some developing countries such as Brazil, China, India, Nigeria and South Africa pledged funds for GEF's fifth replenishment period.[37] GEF's financing facility vis-à-vis climate change is two-fold. It consists of the GEF Trust fund and assorted portfolios of special funds. The Trust Fund focuses on GEF's climate change focal areas. (Contribution to the Trust Fund is on a pre-defined basic burden sharing basis.) The Trust Fund requires that projects meet agreed incremental costs – that is the cost of a measure that exceeds what would have been adopted for environmental protection which would have been put in place without any global environmental concern (Boissan de Chazounne 2013) – for delivering global environmental benefits.

4.7.1.2 The GEF Trust Fund, the Strategic Priority for Adaptation and the Small Grants Programme

In addition to managing funds directly under the guidelines of the Convention, the GEF also operates its own climate change related funds (under its Trust Fund) that support the objectives of the Convention. Several rules and principles apply to the GEF Trust Fund, such as incremental costs financing,[38] and the requirement for contribution to global environmental benefits, and the application of the resource allocation framework (RAF[39] since 2005), now the system for transparent allocation of resources (STAR). STAR includes the use of social economic development indicators in the prioritizing of the allocation of GEF-5 resources within its focal areas.

In response to concerns from developing countries about GEF's lack of funding for adaptation and under the COP guidance in 2004, the *Strategic Priority for Adaptation* (SPA) was developed to pilot an 'operational approach to adaptation'. It funded pilots, demonstration adaptation projects that are based on country needs and which yield global benefits (such as reduction in greenhouse gas). According to GEF, 'activities financed under the SPA priority were to generate real adaptation benefits on the ground' (GEF 2008). GEF's Report on SPA to the Council (2008) shows that with a pledge basket of $50 million, the SPA has funded about 22 projects totalling $49,983. The SPA primarily financed biodiversity (40 per cent) and land degradation (34 per cent) and international waters (12 per cent) projects; it also funded so-called cross sector projects (13 per cent) which included activities such as market led small holder development (Mozambique), strategies for the improvement of traditional crops and livestock (Namibia) and community based adaptation programmes in Bangladesh, Bolivia, Jamaica and Niger etc. (GEF 2008).

The SPA is now completed, with its $50 million in resources allocated to about 26 countries in Asia and Latin America and the Caribbean.

Some climate change adaptation projects are also funded under the umbrella of the Small Grants Programme (SGP) GEF administers with the United Nations Development Programme. The SGP, which was established in 1992 to support community based climate change and environmental projects in developing countries with up to $50,000 as well as to provide technical support. The SGP is meant for countries with little capacity (mainly small island developing countries and least developed countries). It operates across GEF's focal areas (such as water supply and water related infrastructure). The SGP is designed to be a very flexible programme that is responsive to the needs of developing countries. Since 1992, it has disbursed funding of about $365.8 million, about 20 per cent of which is for adaptation efforts. According to UNDP, the implementing agency for the SGP, the 'programme has paid special attention to local and indigenous communities and gender concerns' (UNDP 2009a).

GEF's climate change portfolio covers the priority areas of adaptation, mitigation, development, technical transfer, capacity building, enabling activities, public awareness and other reach (Art 4 (8h)). Since its inception as an operational entity of the Financing Mechanism of the Convention, the GEF has supported 639 mitigation projects in 156 developing and economies in transition countries with $4 billion, mostly under its GEF Trust Fund. Additionally it has leveraged nearly $27.2 billion from a variety of sources including GEF Agencies, national and local governments, multilateral and bilateral agencies, the private sector, and NGOs (GEF 2013). Roughly 33 per cent of these mitigation projects are in Asia Pacific with 21.9 per cent in Africa, 19.6 per cent in Latin America, 19.6 per cent in Eastern Europe and Central Asia and 5.5 per cent allotted to 'global projects' (GEF 2013). Over 50 per cent of these projects (in terms of funding) are for energy efficiency and renewable energy projects with the remainder for projects such as sustainable urban transport and land use, land-use change and forestry (LULUCF).

Countries that participate in the GEF climate change funding processes are expected to prepare a series of national communications vehicles that involve stocktaking on their climate change needs and priorities (see Box 4.6). Proposals for funding must include indicative co-financing amounts. GEF runs country programmes in countries such as Indonesia (where it has over 14 projects) and mainly operates via the World Bank, Bangladesh ($8,540,000 grant for Rural Electrification and Renewable Energy Development) and China (since 2009).[40] In China, GEF's small grants programme has provided grants of US$1,050,000 to over 22 community groups in 14 provinces in 2010. Overall, the Asian region accounts for approximately 26.4 per cent of GEF's mitigation funded projects with Latin America and Africa averaging 20.9 per cent and 13 per cent, respectively.

The GEF utilizes a number of assessments and implementing instruments in administering its various funds. These included the earlier (2007) use of the resource allocation framework (RAF, incorporating a benefit index and a

BOX 4.7 NATIONAL COMMUNICATIONS

Pursuant to UNFCCC, Article 12, countries are in various stages of preparing initial and national climate change communication strategies, which are funded through 'enabling activities' under the GEF (thus far $200 million for over 139 countries). Each country's national communications are to be receive full cost funding up to $500,000 for preparation of national communications. These national communications outline a country's priority issues for dealing with climate change. They have a five-year cycle. As of June 2011 143 non-annex I countries have received financial support for the preparation of national communications.

Developed countries that are listed under Annex II of the UNFCCC are obliged under Article 4.3 to provide new and additional financial resources to developing countries that would meet the agreed full costs for the preparation and submissions of developing countries' national communications.

performance index to allocated funds to countries[41]); the NAPAs (for the least developing countries, under LDCF); national communications support programme and, national capacity self-assessment-NCSAs (UNDP and UNEP). The GEF argues that it does not fund projects through loans and its loans are linked to investment projects, which are part of its programme. However, GEF projects have a co-financing element.[42]

To date, GEF has systematically prioritized mitigation funding in terms of the following strategic objectives: (1) the promotion of energy efficiency in residential and commercial building; (2) the promotion of energy efficiency in industrial sectors; (3) the promotion of market approaches for renewable energy; (4) the promotion of sustainable energy production from biomass; and (5) the promotion of the management of land use, land use change and forestry as a means to protect carbon stock and decrease greenhouse gas emissions.

GEF's fifth phase (GEF-5) has committed approximately $1.3 billion (of its $4.34 billion funding) to its climate change focal area during this period (2010–2014) (Table 4.2). It has also revamped some of its policies including the substitution of the new STAR allocation framework and doing away with the RAF, and the development of procedures to better serve developing countries. According to GEF, its GEF-5 strategy in the climate change focal area will draw on past experience and will be guided by three principles:

1   responsiveness to Convention guidance;
2   consideration of different national circumstances of recipient countries;
3   cost-effectiveness in achieving global environmental benefits.

In addition to upgrading its climate change focal areas, GEF introduced new policy changes to adapt to the demands of developing countries. These include featuring somewhat more attention to direct access, country-driven strategy and replacement of the much critiqued RAF (instituted during GEF-4) with a new approach, the System for Transparent Allocation of Resources (STAR). STAR is the mechanism that is utilized in order to determine the amount of resources that a given country can access in a replenishment period. It is based on three key indices all of which rely on the World Bank's Country Policy and Institutional Assessment and the bank's IDA resources allocation frameworks: the revised Global Performance Index (GPI), the revised Global Benefit Index (GBI) and Gross domestic product (GDP) per capita. Though argued to be significantly different from the troubled RAF system, only the GDP variable is new and is has the least influence, while the other two (the GPI and the GBI) are simply the revised versions of what was in the RAF and the country scores carry the same weight as in the RAF.[43] The GDP based index and the revised global performance index are meant to take account of the barriers to generating global environmental benefits in the poorest countries.

With regard to its climate change portfolio, the GEF is expected to operate within the institutional framework of international climate change policy under UNFCCC and is supervised by the COP and the Subsidiary Body on Implementation (SBI). Hence, the GEF is technically responsive to the Convention and policy guidance of the COP, although functionally independent of the World Bank (from which it also receives administrative support) and under the authority of its main governance organs – the GEF Assembly and the GEF Council (its executive organ), the GEF's policies and procedures are more closely aligned with the World Bank. It does not operate under the authority of the COP.[44]

Over the years since its inception as an operating entity of the finance mechanism of the Convention, developing countries have persistently registered dissatisfaction with the GEF, through the COP.[45] The sources of dissatisfaction are primarily over inadequate flow of resources and the long and complex approval process – it takes 66 months' lapse between entry of a concept into the pine line and initiation, tensions over the GEF definition and use of 'incremental cost' and 'additionality'.[46]

Another source of tension between the GEF and the developing countries lies in the fact that the GEF's funding is traditionally conditional on projects' capacity to deliver global benefits. Adaptation activities do not inherently have direct global benefits. A further complaint of developing countries is that the GEF requirement of co-financing penalizes poor and least developed countries and restricts their ability to undertake both adaptation and mitigation. These problems were heightened with the introduction of the GEF's highly critiqued resource allocation framework (RAF, introduced in GEF-4) 'wherein funding is determined by a country's potential to generate global environmental benefits and its capacity to successfully implement the GEF projects' (CR 2010).

> **BOX 4.8 GEF PROJECT CYCLE**
>
> The GEF project cycle, which is not a true cycle but consists of GEF decision points in the cycles of the GEF Agencies, is notoriously slow. It takes 6 months before at least half of the project concepts are accepted and are taken up in a work programme of the Council. It takes another 20 months for at least half of the approved project concepts to be fully prepared and achieve CEO endorsement. Only half of the CEO-endorsed projects start within 5 months after that. All in all, it takes 2.5 years for half of the concepts to become a reality on the ground. At that time, the other half of the concepts remain stuck at various decision points. Implementation takes 5 years on average, and is often extended by another 1.5 years.
>
> Source: Fifth Overall Performance Study of the GEF (OPS5, 2014: 11)

Evaluations of the GEF over the years have confirmed these challenges and reported on the lengthy delays in project preparation and approval. For example, one evaluation reported that 'GEF's activity cycle was not efficient and that the situation had grown worse over the years' (GEF 2007). An evaluation commissioned by DANIDA found that the time needed for a project to be identified, prepared, approved and launched increased through the various replenishment periods (from 36 months in the first replenishment period to 50 months in the second and 66 months in the third replenishment.[47] Despite repeated evaluation findings validating this one and subsequent attempt to reform GEF's project cycle GEF's evaluation Office's most recent fifth Overall Performance Study of the GEF (OPS5, 2014) notes that although the approval of project has accelerated, the project cycle is notoriously slow, 'project cycle reform has failed and there is need for another reform' (GEF 2014: 11; see also Box 4.8).

The GEF's own funding would seem to offers some constraint on its effective delivery of funds to developing countries. Many researchers argue that the timing and the size of GEF's 4-year replenishment cycle has created some challenges for it in terms of its ability to effectively and efficiently disburse funding. This, along with GEF's cumbersome management, its resource allocation framework and project cycle frameworks,[48] have been identified as major bottlenecks for developing countries' access to its fund.

Over the years, the Conference of Parties has elucidated new provisions and tightened up financing mechanisms and processes in its periodic guidance to the GEF. This also occurs through GEF's 4 yearly replenishment cycles. Between 1995–2008, the COP has adopted 160 decisions giving guidance to the GEF (OECD 2012). There have been long running tensions between the COP and the

GEF over the implementation, or lack, thereof, of COP guidance. COP sets of guidance have tended to focus on dealing with the slow and cumbersome funding process that negatively impacted the responsiveness, efficacy and efficiency of the flow of climate finance to developing countries.

As a result of these and other related issues, the COP, therefore, created the Least Developed Countries Fund (LDCF, 2001) and the Special Climate Change Fund (SCCF 2001), the Adaptation Fund and most recently the GCF (2010–2011) (Table 4.1). Both the SCCF and the LDCF target projects with 'clear development objectives', such as ensuring food security, access to water for drinking and irrigation, disaster prevention, and control of diseases spreading because of climate change, such as malaria and dengue fever (GEF 2009). Unlike the GEF Trust Funded activities, the SCCF and the LDCF focus on primarily meeting local benefits and do not have to satisfy 'global environmental benefits' requirements (such as reducing the vulnerability of coral reefs, international water and land degradation). However, both the LDCF and the SCCF suffer from the problem of limited funding and sustainability issues in meeting the climate change needs of developing countries. Until fairly recently, gender issues were not a high priority in the allocation of GEF funding. However, according to the GEF, currently 'all adaptation projects and programmes financed under SPA, the LDCF and the SCCF

TABLE 4.1 UNFCCC adaptation funds classification at a glance

Fund	Special Climate Change Fund (SCCF) since 2004	Least Developed Country Fund (LDCF) since 2002	Adaptation Fund (AF)
Instrument/ Feature	RAF/STAR	NAPA	(Kyoto Protocol)
Amount	Pledged: $328 million (GEF 2013)[a]	Pledged: $748.1 million (GEF 2013)[b]	$205 million (donations)[c] $190 million (CER proceeds) (Trustee Report on status of resources 3/2014)

Notes: a. 15 contributing participants: Belgium, Canada, Denmark, Finland, Germany, Ireland, Italy, the Netherlands, Norway, Portugal, Spain, Sweden, Switzerland, the UK and the US. b. From 25 contributing participants: Australia, Austria, Belgium, Canada, Czech Republic, Denmark, Finland, France, Germany, Hungary, Iceland, Ireland, Italy, Japan, Luxembourg, the Netherlands, New Zealand, Norway, Portugal, Romania, Spain, Sweden, Switzerland, the United Kingdom and the United States of America. c. World Bank is interim Trustee. Data for end December 2013. The four largest donors are: Sweden, Spain, Germany and Switzerland. The key holders of CER inventories are: China, India, Republic of Korea, Brazil and Mexico.

Source: based on UNFCCC/CP/2011/7

share the same guiding principles of country-drivenness, replicability, sustainability, stakeholder participation, and a specific focus on gender' (2013).

4.7.1.3 The Least Developed Countries Fund

The Least Developed Countries Fund (LDCF) was established in 2002 'to support projects addressing the urgent and immediate adaptation needs of the least developed countries (LDCs) as identified in their National Adaptation Program of Action (NAPAs)' (GEF 2009). The objective of this fund is to help Least Developed Countries such as Bangladesh and Haiti finance the 'the additional costs' arising from the special needs of these countries under the Climate Convention. Additional cost is 'the cost imposed on vulnerable countries to meet their immediate adaptation needs' (GEF 2009). NAPA preparations are to be funded on an 'agreed full costs' basis. Each LDC was to be given $200,000 to prepare its NAPA. Since 2003, the LDCF has supported the preparation of 50 NAPAs (49 completed as of June 2014).

The LDCF has now moved into operationalizing the second phase of the NAPAs. With this funding, there is the associated requirement of incremental cost and co-financing from the recipient government. Funding is for projects that are above the development baseline, and hence presupposes the existence of prior streams of development financing. In a sense then, the presumed pre-existing development financing is itself 'de facto co-financing on the ground' (GEF 2009). Countries are expected in their proposal to include indicative co-financing.

A main challenge with the LDCF is that finance for the fund, itself, is greatly constrained and unpredictable. Presently, the level of funding is also insufficient to cover an individual country's entire NAPA-indicated needs; rather the LDCF tends to cover only a few projects of the over four hundred projects submitted. The LDCF was established on the stipulation of funding the 'agreed full costs' of the preparation of NAPAs, not necessarily the full cost of implementation of all of a country's NAPA priority projects. Access to the fund is available for relatively small amounts and is based on non-direct access. According to the GEF's 2013 Report to the COP, the LDCs have exhausted the resources available to them to-date.

The National Adaptation Program of Action (NAPA) is the key instrument for the allocation of funding under the LDCF. NAPAs are developed through a two-step process starting with Preparation which focuses on the identification of the urgent and immediate needs of countries and culminating with Implementation (the approval of projects and the mobilization of resources).[49] Box 4.9 presents an overview of the NAPA process while the gender dimensions of NAPAs will be discussed in Chapter 6 on Adaptation Finance.

BOX 4.9 THE LDCF APPROVAL PROCESS FOR NAPA PRIORITY

The NAPAs were designed and conducted to identify the top priority urgent and immediate adaptation actions. These actions once identified were then put forward to the LDCF for funding by the GEF Agency together with the LDC. Approximately USD 3.5 million was made available to each country as the LDCF contribution to the implementation of NAPA priority projects, irrespective of the timing of submission of projects for funding. This limit has now been removed. The LDCF approval process for NAPA priority projects consists of the following two steps.

- *Step 1: Project Identification Format (PIF) approval:* PIFs can be submitted on a rolling basis. LDCF administration review of the PIF takes place within a maximum of 10 days. Upon clearing for LDCF Council approval the PIF is posted on the GEF website for 4 weeks for review by the LDCF Council on a 'no objection basis'. Following clearance for Council approval, the project is eligible for a project preparation grant (PPG). Once the PIF is approved by the LDCF Council, the proposed funding is reserved.
- *Step 2: CEO endorsement requests*: CEO endorsement requests can be submitted at any time no later than the date indicated in the PIF and approval letter. CEO endorsement requests, based on a fully developed project document, are reviewed and endorsed by the GEF Secretariat on a rolling basis. After a 10 day review period in the Secretariat, projects are either endorsed by the CEO (subject to four weeks of LDCF Council review), or returned to the relevant Agency with indication of issues preventing recommendation for CEO endorsement.

The time from submission of the first PIF to the CEO endorsement/approval has taken on average 607 days. (The Bangladesh project took 772 days, Bhutan 576 days and Cambodia 646 days.)

Projects undergoing CEO endorsement usually takes about 22 months. (Part of the challenge in the length LDCF cycle is the process of incremental cost assessment (which is less demanding here than with other GEF programmes.)

NAPAs themselves are implemented in two stages: Stage 1: NAPA preparation, completion and submission of NAPAs. Stage 2: project preparation and the implementation of priority projects.

Countries have technical support for their NAPAs through UNDP, UNEP or the World Bank. Most Asian countries have tended to utilize UNDP technical support in the preparation of their NAPAs.

Source: DANIDA

> **BOX 4.10 COUNTRIES WITH COMPLETED NAPAS AND APPROVED NAPA IMPLEMENTATION PROJECTS**
>
> *Countries that have completed their NAPAs (as of June 2013):*
>
> Afghanistan, Angola, Bangladesh, Benin, Bhutan, Burkina Faso, Burundi, Cambodia, Cape Verde, Central African Republic, Chad, Comoros, Democratic Republic of the Congo, Djibouti, Eritrea, Ethiopia, the Gambia, Guinea, Guinea Bissau, Haiti, Kiribati, Lao People's Democratic Republic, Lesotho, Liberia, Madagascar, Malawi, Maldives, Mali, Mauritania, Mozambique, Myanmar, Nepal, Niger, Rwanda, Samoa, São Tomé and Principe, Senegal, Sierra Leone, Solomon Islands, Somalia, Sudan, Timor Leste, Togo, Tuvalu, Uganda, United Republic of Tanzania, Vanuatu, Yemen, and Zambia.
>
> *Countries with approved NAPA implementation projects (as of May 2012):*
>
> Afghanistan, Bangladesh, Benin, Bhutan, Burkina Faso, Burundi, Cambodia, Cape Verde, Central African Republic, Chad, Comoros, Democratic Republic of the Congo, Djibouti, Ethiopia, Gambia, Guinea, Guinea-Bissau, Haiti, Kiribati, Lao PDR, Lesotho, Liberia, Malawi, Maldives, Mali, Mauritania, Mozambique, Nepal, Niger, Rwanda, Samoa, São Tomé and Principe, Senegal, Sierra Leone, Sudan, Tanzania, Timor-Leste, Togo, Tuvalu, Vanuatu, Yemen and Zambia.
>
> Source: GEF May 2012

4.7.1.4 The Special Climate Change Fund

The Special Climate Change Fund is more long-term and comprehensive in scope and coverage than the LDCF. It was established in 2004 to cover adaptation and mitigation as well as technology transfer. The SCCF addresses issues of long-term planned adaptation response to climate change (SCCF-a), technology transfer (SCCF-b); (c) energy, transport, industry, agriculture, forestry and waste management; and (d) economic diversification. (The operationalization of the latter areas (c and d) is in process since COP 12).

The Special Climate Change Fund, like the LDCF, is also a voluntary fund that relies on donor contributions and targets projects with 'clear development objectives' such as ensuring food security, access to water for drinking and irrigation, disaster prevention, and control of diseases spreading because of climate change, such as malaria and dengue fever (GEF 2009). Both funds were also created by the COP to scale up and expedite the delivering of financing responsive to the needs of developing countries impacted by global warming.

According to Climate Funds Update, all projects must have two of the following three activities: i) the integration of climate change risk reduction strategies, policies, and practices into sectors; ii) the implementation of adaptation measures;

and iii) institutional and constituency capacity building and awareness raising (Mitchell and Huq 2008). SCCF eligible projects do not need to meet global environmental benefit criteria. But SCCF projects must be activities that are in response to global warming (i.e., adaptation increment') and must meet the 'additionality' (means additional to Business as Usual, BAU, – social and economic development and poverty eradication) requirement. Such projects, therefore, cannot be part of the 'development baseline' (what would have occurred in the absence of climate change). Adaptation 'activities financed under the fund will seek to assist the most vulnerable countries and those within a country with the greatest need'. Activities will therefore seek to recognize the link between adaptation and poverty reduction (Decision 12).

The SCCF is open to all developing countries.[50] Developing countries in the Asian region have a total of nine projects through SCCF and in terms of project size they account for $44.1 million, 31 per cent (the largest part) of SCCF funding.[51] Co-financing is also much higher in Asia than in other regions ($382 million versus $274.9 million in Africa.[52] This may be because co-financing under the GEF is heavily nationally government driven. According to the SCCF Evaluations report, other GEF fund sources account for about 36 per cent of co-financing and national governments provide 44 per cent with the private sector and NGOs contributing a negligible amount of 1 per cent each (GEF 2011). The ADB contributes to co-financing of regional SCCF projects such as to the project *Pilot Asia-Pacific Climate technology Network and Finance Center*. This project is implemented by UNEP with the ADB as the primary co-financing entity contributing 67.6 million (or 80 per cent of the $83.8 million in co-financing of the project (GEF 2011).

As with the LDCF, the SCCF suffers from the problem of limited funding and sustainability issues in meeting the climate change needs of developing countries. In 2006, the SCCF received its first voluntary contribution and approved its first projects.[53] Since then, however, as repeated in each status report to the GEF council, later the LDCF/SCCFF Council, the funding has been quite limited relative to its mandate and the needs it is meant to address. The GEF estimates that the need for SCCF adaptation funding is about $500 million for 4 years (GEF 2010).

Lack of funding activities originally envisioned to be financed under sectoral cluster (SCCF-C) and economic diversification for fossil fuel dependent economies (SCCF-D) led to those programmes not been implemented.[54] The GEF argued that funders had reservations about these aspects of the SCCF and therefore did not support it.

Under the Technology Transfer Programme (SCCF-b), funding of $50 million with $15 million coming from the SCCF-B and $35 million from the GEF Trust Fund (GEF 2011) has been available. This is under its Poznan Strategic Program on Technology Transfer.[55] Since 2009, the GEF has added a global project for Technology Needs Assessment (TNA) which will provide targeted financial and technical support to assist developing countries in carrying out improved TNAs in 24 low- and medium-income countries. This is within the framework of Article 4.5 of the UNFCCC (DANIDA 2009; GEF 2010). The GEF also supports Technology Centers and a Climate Technology Network; it is to support piloting and innovative projects for technology transfer and financing, including four regional climate technology transfers (GEF 2013). But even this is too small in size and scope to meet the tasks. There is therefore much more needed for scaling up.

4.7.2 The Adaptation Fund

The Adaptation Fund was established in 2001 and was officially set up in 2007 under the Kyoto Protocol to finance concrete adaptation projects and programmes in developing countries. (The Protocol also established three market-based mechanisms, the Clean Development Mechanism (CDM), the Joint Implementation mechanism (JI) and Emissions Trading to help developed countries meet their emissions targets. These market-based mechanisms have become the keystones for the evolution of the carbon market.) The Adaptation Fund, which became operational in 2009, is financed through a 2 per cent levy on the proceeds of Clean Development Mechanism's projects as well as from other sources. The monetization of Certified Emission Reductions (CERs, since 2009) currently totals about $190 million, as of March 2014, with contributions from developed countries to date totalling $205 million (Trustee Status of Resource Report, March 2014). As of the end of December 2013, the Adaptation Fund has been in dire straits with the collapse of the carbon market, including the CDM, and the adverse decline in the price of carbon. Things do not look promising for the Fund. In 2013 the Adaptation Fund's board engaged in a $100 million fund raising strategy in order to fund vetted projects in the pipeline. In addition to the fall in the prices of CERs, since 2011 the EU decided to source only from LDCs – a political decision that, though with good intention, may not automatically help the LDCs, who are the ones most in need of adaptation funds and who are also not the most likely source of CER inventories given the low mitigation potential and low uptake of CDM projects in LDCs.

The strategic priorities of the Adaptation Fund, as spelled out by the CMP, are twofold: (a) Assist developing country Parties to the Kyoto Protocol that are particularly vulnerable to the adverse effects of climate change in meeting the costs of adaptation; (b) Finance concrete adaptation projects and programmes that are country driven and are based on the needs, views and priorities of eligible Parties (para 5, AF 2009 and 1/CMP.3, Paragraphs 1 and 2) (see Box 4.11).

The Adaptation Fund finances the full cost (the costs associated with implementing concrete adaptation activities that address the adverse effects of climate change) of country-driven concrete adaptation projects and programmes that reduce the harmful effect of climate change and which explicitly aim to adapt and increase climate resilience.

The Adaptation Fund Board (AFB), which was established at COP 13 as the operating body of the Adaptation Fund, is comprised of 16 members and 16

BOX 4.11 THE ADAPTATION FUND

The Adaptation Fund was established to finance concrete adaptation projects and programmes in developing countries that are Parties to the Kyoto Protocol. The Fund is to be financed in part with a share of proceeds from Clean Development Mechanism project activities. The share of proceeds amounts to 2 per cent of certified emission reductions (CERs) issued for a CDM project activity.

As of 2007, decisions of the COP of the Kyoto Protocol (CMP 3), the operating entity of the Adaptation Fund shall be the Adaptation Fund Board with GEF providing secretariat services and the World Bank as trustee of the Adaptation Fund on an interim basis. These interim institutional arrangements will be reviewed by the CMP after three years. The Board is composed of 16 members and 16 alternates and its meeting will take place at least twice a year in the country hosting the UNFCCC secretariat.

An adaptation programme is a process, a plan or an approach for addressing climate change impacts which goes broader than the scope of an individual project. (The Board will provide further guidance on the adaptation programmes, its aims and objectives in the future on the basis of lessons learned (para 11).) Eligible Parties to receive funding from the Adaptation Fund are understood as developing country Parties to the Kyoto Protocol that are particularly vulnerable to the adverse effects of climate change including low-lying and other small island countries, countries with low-lying coastal, arid and semi-arid areas or areas liable to floods, drought and desertification, and developing countries with fragile mountainous ecosystems (para 10).

According to the Draft Provisional Operational Policies and Guidelines for Parties to Access Resources from the Adaptation Fund (September 2009, Para 10):

> A concrete adaptation project is defined as a set of activities aimed at addressing the adverse impacts of and risks posed by climate change. Adaptation projects can be implemented at the community, national and transboundary level. Projects concern discrete activities with a collective objective(s) and concrete outcomes and outputs that are more narrowly defined in scope, space and time.

alternates: Non-Annex I countries, Least Developed Countries (LDCs), Small Island Developing States (SIDS), and regional constituencies. The board works under the authority of, and is accountable to, the Conference of Parties. The AFB is supported with interim secretariat services by the GEF and Trustee services provided by World Bank, as acting trustee. Both institutional arrangements are on interim basis.

The Fund is the only operational climate fund with direct access modality (eligible Parties can submit their projects directly to the AFB through an accredited National Implementing entity. Its modalities are deliberately simplified: it allows eligible Parties to submit their project proposals directly to the Adaptation Fund Board, and offers host countries the flexibility to access funds directly, to use the services of a multilateral entity, or to nominate an appropriate regional or sub-regional entity to support them (South Centre 2010). The key implementing and Executing Entities of the Adaptation Fund are National Implementing Entity (NIE) and Multilateral Implementing Entities. National Implementing Entities (NIEs) are those national legal entities nominated by Parties that are recognized by the Board as meeting the fiduciary standards established by the Board. Currently 15 countries have been approved for direct access to the Fund's resources: These accredited NIEs include Belize, Benin, Chile, Costa Rica, Jamaica, Jordan, Morocco, Senegal, Rwanda, South Africa and Uruguay. Regional and sub-regional entities and accredited multilateral entities (MIEs) include agencies such as the World Bank, the African Development Bank (AfDB), the Asian Development Bank (ADB), the International Fund for Agriculture and Development (IFAD), the United Nations Educational, Scientific and Cultural Organization (UNESCO), the United Nations Development Programme (UNDP), the United Nations Environment Programme (UNEP), the World Food Programme (WFP) and the World Meteorological Organization (WMO).

The Adaptation fund is not meant to be dependent on voluntary contributions; its primary revenue source is generated from CDM project activities. However, the volume and value of CDM projects and the monetized CERs from these projects are unpredictable and volatile in an unstable carbon market. Currently that market is experiencing over supply of both CERs and EAUs which is depressing carbon prices. Hence funding of the Adaptation fund as it is linked to the movement of the carbon market has suffered from the inherent instability of that market. The Fund which has had a great start and as of February 2013, approved 25 concrete adaptation projects and allocated $175 million in grants geared towards increasing the adaptive capacity of vulnerable communities is now facing funding constraints as the source of its income is drying up due to the partial collapse of the carbon market and limited contributions received from developed countries' contributors. (The AFB set a $100 million fundraising target for the end of 2013.)

In the final analysis, the network of funds under the UNFCCC, 20 years after the Convention came into force, has yet to mobilize and disburse significant flows of finance and investment that could implement the actions and goals of the Convention. The GEF's climate change funds all suffer from the same problems, to a greater or lesser degree, of inadequate funding to meet the needs of developing countries. The Funds are also plagued with high levels of bureaucratization, lack of transparency and complexity which impede the review and processing of countries' project documents through the pipeline. There are also persistent issues of lack of capacity building and inattention to critical social dynamics such as gender inequality.

TABLE 4.2 Overview of the first generation climate funds under the UNFCCC's financial mechanism

Description and date of creation or arrangement	Fund/ operational-ization	Governing and ownership	Trustee/Sec	Distribution channel or primary allocation mechanism
An operating entity of the Financial Mechanism (1994)[a]12/CP.2	GEF – climate climate change focal area of the GEF Trust Fund (1994) (MOU 1996)	GEF Assembly/ Council COP accountability	World Bank (WB)	RAF up to 2010/STARR (since 2011)
Sub fund COP 7 (2001 5/CP-7)	LDCF (2002)	GEF/COP guidance LDCF/SCCF Council	GEF/WB	GEF's operational policies, procedures and governance structure NAPAs
Sub fund COP 7 (2001 7/CP.7)	SCCF (2004)	GEF/COP guidance LDCF/SCCF Council	GEF/WB	GEF's operational policies, procedures and governance structure
COP 7 (2001)	Adaptation Fund (under the Kyoto protocol, 2007)	Adaptation Fund Board/ COP	GEF (interim) WB (acting)	Direct access

Note: a. 9/CP1 and 12/CP 2, 12/CP 3,1996 pursuant to Article 11.3 of the Convention

In the case of the LDCF, all these factors have contributed to lags in project implementation, so that that by 2009, only one project (Bhutan) out of the over 426 projects that were highlighted in developing countries national adaptation plan of actions was under implementation. The Evaluation reported pointed out that Bangladesh and Cambodia experienced great delays in obtaining funding support from the Fund.

The most recent Evaluation report noted that:

- The time from submission of the first PIF to the CEO endorsement/approval has taken an average 607 days.
- When the starting point is calculated from the date of NAPA completion, the time spent on preparation is: Bangladesh – 1135 days, Bhutan – 675 days, Burkina Faso – 509 days, Cambodia – 727 days, and Samoa – 1166 days.
- Projects currently undergoing CEO endorsement review are already close to the 22 months.

At the end of 2010, over 5 years after many LDCs had earnestly mobilized their economies and citizens around the preparation of NAPAs and had diligently identified immediate and urgent priority areas and detailed actions for adapting to climate change, the NAPAs are just beginning their implementation phase. Forty-one countries have finalized NAPAs; but LDCs many can only get one or two of their urgent priorities funded. Many of these problems are the result of contributing countries underestimating the cost of adaptation and their unrealistic expectations that the money they were putting into the LDCF would fund the project (Evaluations Office 2010). But there were only enough contributions to fund the preparation of the NAPAs themselves. As noted above, the LDCF has $85 million (with indicative co-financing of $162 million from other sources). But it is estimated that the projects prioritized in the NAMAs would cost between $800 million and $1.93 billion (UNFCCC up to $1.7 billion, DANIDA $1.5 billion and LEG the higher range, for the 48 NAPAs).

The slowness in the implementation of NAPAs and the chronic lack of financial support to the LDCF has led to a tendency towards projects and not programmes or economy wide efforts. As a result, the usefulness of the NAPAs is being questioned. It has been argued that contributing countries do not rely on the NAPAs and there may be a lack of coherence between NAPAs and other development plans at country level – this may have occurred through the over-reliance on foreign consultants, as opposed to involving the public sector and building national capacity (GEF 2010). More damning, as argued by the evaluation of LDCF, the NAPAs may have implicitly led to significant under-estimation of the true cost of climate change adaptation (DANIDA 2009).

In 2005, there was heightened discussion within the governance structure of the SCCF itself resulting in the Council remarking that:

> The situation of the SCCF remains critical. With about only $60 million for Adaptation worldwide and a demand of over $100 million per year from vulnerable countries, the fund cannot meet the existing demand for projects that address adaptation. The pipeline is currently frozen (. . .)
> (Highlights of the Council's discussions, LDCF/SCCF Meeting of 17 November 2007, Paragraph 5)

Now well over 6 years later, the situation has not changed much as the GEF evaluation Office Report notes that dispersal of funds ($127.5 million) even for its flagship window the SCCF-A is relatively low. The SCCF which is supposed to respond to the needs of developing countries is dispensing fewer funds than the LDCF's $415 million (which covers only 48 LDCs). Not only do the LDCs require assistance for adaptation, they also need financial and technical resources for mitigation and transforming their commercial and residential structure towards energy efficient energy uses. More importantly they also need funds to significantly reduce the energy poverty in the economies. Thus the SCCF is also important for all developing countries. Yet, it remains underfunded relative to its broad scope.

In the short to medium term, the Adaptation Fund would have been expected to become increasingly more active in funding project proposals that will greatly benefit developing countries. But since funding for the AF is dependent on the activities under the Kyoto Protocol which has still not been legalized for the continuation of the second commitment period, there is a dark cloud hanging over the future of the fund. In the present environment, there is no certainty with respect to future CER prices and hence the Adaptation, as with other UNFCCC funds, faces a precarious future. Even if its future becomes more tenable, the Adaptation Fund will not address issues of renewable energy, energy efficiency and technology transfer as these are more in the mitigation frameworks.

The pervasive, persistent and chronically unresolved challenges that developing countries face in accessing GEF's climate change resources led the COP to create other funding instruments, which the GEF also administers, as outlined above. Despite this, developing countries, as a group, have continued to express repeated frustrations with the flow of climate finance under the GEF. The challenges with GEF as experienced by, especially the poorer, developing countries, include, burdensome co-financing requirements, heavily loan driven funds, long and unproductive lags in the review and approval of proposals as well as in the delivery of programmatic financing. GEFs also had inherent structural problems with the funding of adaptation projects, which are seen to delivery benefits primarily at the national level and hence argued to provide little global co-benefits.

GEF's constraints with regard to delivering effectively and efficiently apparently stemmed from its lack of independence of the World Bank in terms of its legal status and influence of the World Bank's economic and policy frameworks. Hence the COP sought to avoid this entanglement by creating another fund, the Adaptation Fund and ultimately a second operating entity under the Financial Mechanisms, the GCF in an attempt to distance UNFCCC generated climate funds from the World Bank's governance and which would be more clearly under the authority of the COP. It was hoped that these funds would have wider latitude in funding the adaptation needs of developing countries and would be more responsive to the control and direct access of developing countries.

However, the developed countries were reluctant to give control fully to the COP, so in both the case of the Adaptation Fund and the GCF, the World Bank continued as Trustees to the Funds. In the case of the GCF, to be discussed below, the developing countries were offered no choice on the trusteeship, the World Bank was offered that role as a fait accompli in the Cancún Decision (2010). After a long protracted battle (at the Durban COP 2011), in which developing countries members of the G77 and China (quite a rare occurrence) raised objections to the GEF's involvement, ultimately, in order to obtain agreement on the approval of the Funds' governing instruments, they reluctantly agreed to the GEF playing a role as part of the interim secretariat of the GCF. Developing countries, however, insisted that the GEF shared this role with the UNFCCC secretariat and that the permanent trusteeship of the Fund would be determined by an open competitive bidding process (as had been stipulated in the Cancún Decision and in the articles of the governing instrument of the GCF, designed by the Transitional Committee). Developing countries also reaffirmed that, as also stipulated in the governing instruments of the GCF, there would be an independent secretariat (independent of the GEF and the World Bank) created for the GCF within a year and half of its operation.

In the case of the Adaptation Fund, things did not work out as the developing countries wanted and through a variety of circumstances and internal dynamics, the World Bank remains as the interim trustee of that entity.[56] It remains to be seen how the power dynamics will work in the case of the GCF, and, if ultimately, the developing countries are indeed able to obtain agreement for an open competitive bidding process for the position of the trustee of the fund as indicated in the governing instrument and reiterated in the Covering document that the COP approved, and if that process will indeed lead to an entity other than the World Bank as trustee.

Thus all three of the three existing operating climate funds under the UNFCCC have issues of the predictability and sustainability of resources to finance climate actions in developing countries. These problems of the existing funding instruments under the Financial Mechanism of the Convention point to the need for more predictable and reliable sources of climate financing, as required under the Convention. Undeniably, there is therefore need for a broad spectrum fund that is active, well-endowed and focused on meeting the comprehensive needs of developing countries, with respect to responding effectively to climate change in the context of sustainable development.

This need for a more effective and dedicated climate change fund is the imperative behind the drive to create a second generation global GCF, under the financial mechanism of the Convention. This outcome was finally realized in 2010–2011 with the establishment of the GCF and related entities, the Standing Committee on Finance and the establishment of a Work Programme on Long-term Finance.

4.7.3 The Green Climate Fund

Cancún (2010) established the Green Climate Fund, to be designated as an operating entity of the Financial Mechanism of the Convention under Article 11, with arrangements to be concluded[57] between the COP and the GCF 'to ensure that it is accountable to and functions under the guidance of the Conference of the Parties, to support projects, programmes, policies and other activities in developing country Parties using thematic funding windows' (para 102). The GCF will support projects, programmes, policies and other activities in developing country Parties using thematic funding windows.

The governing instrument (GI) of the GCF was approved by the Durban Decision (2011). The GI along with the COP guidance determined that the GCF is administered by a 24-member board (12 from developing countries and 12 from developed countries – serving a term of 3 years with eligibility to serve additional terms). The board guided by the governing instrument and the COP Decision is in charge of selecting the headquarters, executive director and designing and implementing a business and resource mobilization model for the full operationalization of the Fund.

The board at its second meeting in October 2012 selected the Republic of Korea as the host country[58] for its secretariat and at its fourth meeting in Songdo, ROK in June 2013, appointed Ms Hela Cheikhrouhou of Tunisia as the Executive Director of the GCF. These were crucially important steps towards the full operationalization and the capitalization of the Fund. The board and the executive Director then began the process of setting up the Fund's independent secretariat and phasing out the current interim co-secretariat arrangements with the GEF and the UNFCCC secretariats. (Though developing countries and most civil society organizations were unanimous in not wanting the GEF's secretariat to administer the new fund, they met adamant opposition from developed countries, most especially the US. During the final hours of the Durban meeting (2011) a compromise was reached that led to the co-secretariat arrangement between the GEF and the UNFCCC secretariat on an interim basis and 'no later than by the nineteenth session of the Conference of the Parties' (2013), 3 CP 17 Paragraphs 18 and 19.)

The Fund's board, which was under the inaugural leadership of Australia and South Africa as co-chairs (for 2012–2013) and led by Germany and the Philippines (2014),[59] must also begin the process of phasing out the GCF interim 3 year trustee arrangement with the World Bank. As with the GEF secretariat arrangements, the World Bank Trusteeship of the Fund did not meet with the approval of many developing countries as well as civil society organizations, given the problematic relationship with previous years of climate financing delivery and the issue of conflict of interest with the World Bank's CIFs.[60] But, the developed countries were adamant on the World Bank's involvement and many developing countries' delegates felt that there was no real choice in the matter if they wanted to get the Fund established. The expectation is that the Fund Board will seek to terminate this arrangement in favour of an open competitive transparent bidding process as agreed in the GCF governing instrument, which was approved by the COP.

The GCF is designed to have initial thematic funding windows (currently for adaptation and mitigation for which there should be balance allocation of resources), and is expected to also ensure adequate resources for capacity building and technology transfer and development. The board has authority to add, modify and remove windows as it deems appropriate. At its fourth and fifth meetings, Songdo, ROK, June 2013 and Paris, France, October 2013, the board began intense discussion on the business model of the Fund including issues of its objectives and guiding principles, structure and organization, financial instruments, country ownership, access modalities and the private sector facility.[61] The business model of the fund will 'promote a paradigm shift towards low emission and climate-resilient development pathways'.

Though the business model discussion has focused on the demand and operational side of the Fund's activities, to the dismay of developing countries and civil society organization there has not yet been any discussion on the resource mobilization model of the fund. The seventh board meeting, Songdo, ROK May 2013, completed the eight essential requirements set by the developed countries as the pre-condition for discussion on initial resource mobilization. Yet, approximately two years after the Decision was taken to establish the GCF, a year after its approval the GCF as an operating entity and up to seven board meetings later the Fund remained uncapitalized.[62] This is quite distinct from the capitalization of the World Bank's Climate Fund which received pledges of over $6 billion while still in the proposal and planning stage. As of April 2015, approximately $10.2 billion has been pledged over four years to the GCF. The Secretariat had projected $15 billion but had to lower that expectation and declare a success in the initial resource mobilization by the end of 2014.

Needless to say there is a great deal of concern by advocates of the GCF that, despite promises of the GCF as the main mechanism through which the promised $100 billion per year by 2020 would support climate mitigation and adaptation activities in the developing countries, it will remain an elegant well built but under-resourced shell. This is not a promising start.

There are concerns that the protracted delay in funding the GCF by developed countries is meant to extract the maximum concessions that they were not able to achieve during negotiations in the UNFCCC from developing countries through the board process. These concessions would include the enhanced environment for making the Fund both attractive to the international private sector (as a source of climate finance and investment) as well as making the entity more like the World Bank.

The GCF has a private sector facility through which developing and developed countries' private sectors can access the fund's resources for mitigation and adaptation activities in developing countries. It is expected that the facility will also promote the participation of private sector actors such as SMEs, especially female-owned and operated businesses, including local financial intermediaries from developing countries, especially from SIDs and LDCs.

Developed countries, especially the UK, US and Japan, would like to see a strong and significant role of the private sector in the Fund. But developing countries are concerned that the funding process may be held hostage to them agreeing on an expanded role for the private sector (and may be even an autonomous private sector facility), through which the money meant for developing countries would be funnelled through the international private sector of the developed countries and not reach the needs of developing countries.

Despite all of these undercurrents, nonetheless, there is great expectation for the Fund: that it will upscale adaptation financing and provide greater access through a direct access modality to all developing countries. Access to the GCF, as with the Adaptation fund, is through National, regional and international implementing entities that are accredited by the Board. National designated authorities can also make recommendations to the board for funding proposals in the context of national climate strategies.

Much of the optimism about the Funds, despite the protracted wrangling about its business model, apart from the potential for it to undertake significant high impact large scale funding of climate initiatives in developing countries, lies in the potential of its two unique features, as an operating entity of the Financial Mechanism. These two unique features of the GCF are the explicit gender sensitivity and the commitment to environmental social and safeguards.

The governing instruments of the GCF commit the board to 'taking a gender sensitive approach in its funding for adaptation and mitigation' (Section 1), call for 'due consideration to be given to gender balance' in the selection of board members and take 'into account geographic and gender balance in the staffing of the secretariat as well as 'address gender aspects' in providing simplified and improved access to funding, including direct access. However, this auspicious gender sensitive beginning, the first for a climate change fund, has dimmed with the selection of a board comprised of only 5 women of the 24 members (and three women among the 24 alternates). This does not add up to equitable representation of women of the governing body, nor does it reflect the aspiration for the Fund to have diversity in leadership and decision-making as anticipated by gender advocates as well as others in civil society (WEDO 2012). The board since its fifth meeting has begun to address the issue of implementing the fund-wide gender sensitization of the GCF. (This process and the future prospect for gendering the fund are discussed in Chapter 8). The Governing instrument also commits the board to adopt best practice environmental and social safeguards, 'which shall be applied to all programmes and projects financed using the resources of the Fund' (Section X, Governing Instrument, GCF).

Another important and somewhat unique feature of the GCF is that developing countries can access the fund directly without requiring the intervention of multilateral or regional entities such as UN agencies. This direct access feature though noteworthy is not new as it was pioneered, within the climate change context, by the Adaptation Fund. But it nonetheless is an important and highly desired feature by developing countries which can accredit their own national entities to intermediate with the Fund as the direct feature is elaborated and implemented by the Board. It is anticipated that this direct access to modalities is amenable to meeting the concerns of poor communities and women's groups as with regard to adaptation, mitigation and technology development and transfer.

4.8 UNFCCC mechanisms to support coherence, rationalization and the scaling up of long-term finance under the convention

While the climate change finance architecture is slowly evolving there is as yet no systematic framework for (1) enabling a consistent and rigorous definition of climate finance with methodologies for measuring, reporting and verifying the flow of funds for adaptation and mitigation projects in developing countries and (2) for ensuring a predictable flow of funds beyond the conclusion of the fast start finance period 2010–2012. The Conference of the Parties has tried to rectify some of these issues by one framework and a mechanism of sort.

The matter of long-term finance (beyond 2020) is being addressed by the recently created work programme on long-term finance[63] which thus far consists of a number of workshops (Bonn, June 2012 and Cape Town, October 2012) and webinars etc. The COP also established a subsidiary body, the Standing Committee on Finance to help it understand better the terrain and operationalization of climate finance, specifically those flows under the convention as well as global flows that aim at supporting climate change, more broadly.

4.8.1 The Standing Committee on finance

The Standing Committee was established through the Cancún Decision (2010) to assist the COP 'in exercising its functions with respect to the Financial Mechanism of the Convention in terms of improving coherence and coordination in the delivery of climate change financing; rationalization of the Financial Mechanism; mobilization of financial resources and measurement, reporting and verification of support provided to developing country Parties'. The Committee is expected to help to improve the efficiency and efficacy of climate finance and to assist the COP, and by extension the GCF, with the rationalization and mobilization of long-term finance under the framework of the Convention.

COP 17 in Durban (2011), further defined the roles and functions of the Standing Committee, including the decision that it shall 'report and make recommendations to the COP, for its consideration on all aspects of its work'. The Durban Decision also elaborated the functions and modalities of the committee, including that the membership of the committee to comprise of 'ten members from Parties included in Annex I to the Convention (Annex I Parties) and ten members from Parties not included in Annex I to the Convention (non-Annex I Parties), including two members each from the Africa, Asia-Pacific, and the Latin America and Caribbean States, one member from a small island developing State and one member from a least developed country Party'. (Annex I Parties comprise developed countries and economies in transition while non-Annex I Parties are developing countries.)

The Standing Committee on Finance is now fully operational as the 20 board members (10 from Annex I countries – those parties with responsibilities for historical emissions and 10 from non-Annex I countries – those parties with little or no responsibilities for historical emissions, including two from each UN regional group, one each for SIDs and the LDCs and two for NAI as determined by the Group of 77 plus China) recently had their series of meeting during which the committee has consolidated itself (through 2012–2013), designed and implemented its work programme in which it has finalized a draft arrangement on the arrangement between the COP and the GCF and organized successful forums. Its attention is now focused on preparation of its annual report for the COP, the relationship between the Subsidiary bodies, the Adaptation Committee, the Technology Executive Committee and other committees; draft guidelines for the arrangements between the COP and the Standing Committee; guidance to the GEF and initial guidance to the GCF.

The Standing Committee on Finance is also expected to contribute to the review of the Financial Mechanism in line with the decision of the fourth COP to review the Financial Mechanism of the Convention every 4 years in accordance with Article 11.4 of the Convention. Previous reviews have been conducted through the subsidiary body on implementation; the most recent was completed at COP 16. The fifth review of the Financial Mechanism is forthcoming. At COP 16, Parties requested the SBI to initiate the fifth review of the Financial Mechanism at its 37th session and to report on the outcome to COP 19. The main objective of the review is to 'examine how to facilitate consistency in financing activities and improve the complementarity of the Financial Mechanism with other sources of investment and financial flows, including relevant sources and means of financing.

The Standing Committee on Finance will have to delve into the issue of the measurement, verification and reporting (MRV) of financial support. Ecuador in accordance with Paragraph 122 of 2/CP.17 has submitted a proposal for the Standing Committee to undertake MRV of climate finance to developing countries. This proposal has wide support from many developing countries who are strongly in favour of guidelines to address the need for accurate accounting of the provisions of funds from developed country parties to developing country parties in order to assess compliance with the finance obligations for mitigation, adaptation, technology transfer and capacity building. These countries seek to ensure robustness and transparency of the Financial Mechanism of the Convention.

The Standing Committee on Finance, like the GCF and the Work programme on long-term finance, must also focus its attention on the mobilization of public and private sector funding and investment, including facilitation of climate friendly investment choices (Bali Action Plan 1(e)(v)). The SCF successfully issued its first Biennial Assessment and Overview of Climate Finance flows in 2014, which essentially confirms the discussion of the previous sections of this chapter. It is now working on the methodologies for reporting of financial flows.

4.9 The way forward on climate finance in the UNFCCC

More rigorous scrutiny of Fast-Start Finance, which, arguably, has many lessons for the provision of long-term finance, requires at least a common definition as to what constitute climate finance and how and what is to be measured and assessed as 'new' and 'additionally' climate finance. As of yet, there are no common definitions for these concepts within the context of climate change. More rigorous scrutiny and a framework of assessment require a set of common reporting parameters and methodology that ensures the accountability, comparability and transparency of climate financial flows to developing countries. The important lessons from the Fast-Start Finance period point to critical issues that must be better understood if financial flows are to address the needs of developing countries.

In this context the ongoing work by the UNFCCC secretariat to open up the black box of estimating finance and investment requirements for adaptation and mitigation by developing countries through bottom needs assessment processes could be a useful activity in the quest to scale up and mobilize finance and investment for climate change under the UNFCCC. Such efforts along with plans for e-forums and workshops envisaged by the Standing Committee and the Long Term Finance work programme, if rigorously pursued, in the right quantity, geographic balance among different groups of countries and eliciting genuine participation from a wide spectrum of citizens, most especially consultations with youths and women's movements, businesses, farmers and workers associations and with indigenous peoples could be good steps towards ensuring adequate finance to meet developing countries' needs.

It is clear from the IPCC WG2 report and other independent analyses that the near term promise of $100 billion currently on the table is insufficient to meet the climate change financing needs of developing countries.

Climate finance scaling up must hence be commensurate with the financing needs of developing countries for adaptation (which is dependent on the magnitude of climate change impacts, the level of acceptable risks and the timing of adaptation actions) and mitigation. There is also need for coherent and rigorous consistency and agreed applied definitions of climate finance, clear methodologies for data collection and reporting of information and transparent rules for measurement.

While recognizing the constraints around traditional sources of public funds in the developed countries, this does not absolve them of their commitment under the Convention. At a minimum, the $100 billion should be met and there is a clear need that this should come from public sources. Developed countries' Parties may seek alternative finance to enable them to provide initial and ongoing funds, for example, to the GCF over the years. There are many pathways to do this, including carbon taxes, financial transaction taxes, the redirection of fossil fuel subsidy, the auctioning of domestic emission permits and the use of Special Drawing Rights. During the financial crisis, within a 5-month period, developed countries mobilized $250 billion of SDRs about two-thirds of which accrued to them (and currently remain utilized) with the remainder for the developing countries (even the IMF has mooted the idea of using SDRs in the context of climate change financing). Undoubtedly, there are many issues around these instruments, including the issue of the incidence on developing countries, but there are also clear strategies for addressing these providing that there is the political will to do so.

It is also clear that the private sector plays an important role in addressing the climate change challenge. It is currently undertaking significant investments in climate change mitigation and will likely continue to do so.

Obviously, governments, both in developed and developing countries, must seek to elicit greater private sector participation in climate change mitigation and adaptation projects and financing through as many channels as possible, always ensuring to take the necessary actions to ensure coherence with national climate change policies and programmes. They must also take measures to ensure environmental integrity and to safeguard the interests of the poor, especially poor women and indigenous people and ethnic minorities.

However, as noted by the trade union movement, such as the ITUC, there must be some clear principles around public–private sector partnership as it relates to climate finance including, that (1) private sector finance should add to (complement) not substitute for public climate finance, (2) fair-risk sharing, (3) the preservation of public interest and public services, (4) leveraging is not transformed into subsidies for bankers and hedge funds, and (5) no over-reliance on large scale project which marginalize the role of micro, small and medium-sized firms in developing countries. There must also be careful distinguishing between 'productive risk' and 'speculative risk' in the case of governmental measures to mitigate private investors' risk. Both developed and developing countries will need to undertake measures at home to create the conducive institutional conditions for enhancing the flow of private sector investment into adaptation and mitigation projects.

In conclusion, scaling up of long-term finance is an interactive process in which it can be expected that there will be financial flows for developing countries' adaptation and mitigation projects, including for the financing of technology transfer will be ratchet up for the immediate period 2013–2015 by at least the level of fast start finance that would be a minimum of $30 billion plus per year, to $60 billion per year in the post-2016 period trending up towards the attainment of the goal of $100 billion per year by 2020. The post-2020 period should witness dramatic scaling of both public and private investment towards meeting the assessed needs of upwards of $1–5 trillion dollars, which many researchers noted will be needed for clean energy alone.

Undoubtedly, finance is the main driver of the 'contributions' or potential and actual climate actions of developing countries. So the predictability and adequacy of climate financing is crucial in influencing what agreements are to be reached for the pre-2020 and post-2020 periods. From this vantage point, the GCF should receive initial mobilization of upwards of $15–30 billion with a steady commitment of predictable funding for at least the first 5-year period.

The majority of developed countries based on their biennial report to the UNFCCC in the 2013–2014 period,[64] characterize long-term finance in terms of private sector investments in developing countries (with public finance seen as an inducement to catalyse investments from the private sector). The counterview is that the $100 billion should be public finance to address the urgent and immediate adaptation needs of developing countries, build climate resilient infrastructure, support loss and damage and ensure energy security and access and availability of poor women and men in developing countries. This can be supported by additional efforts to mobilize private capital, over the long term, accumulating towards the $1 trillion to $3 trillion discussed in the climate finance literature. This view point is supported by many civil society organizations working at the grass root level addressing issues of poverty, food security, disaster support as well as the global trade union movement.

Features of the new CF paradigm:

- Ethical framing: 'doing good' (versus equity, fairness and legal commitment/responsibility).
- Conditional funding approach (versus needs based approach).
- Private sector/leverage driven: emphasis on leveraging private finance and mitigating risk (versus climate objective, environmental integrity).
- Innovative financing (versus grantsand concessional loans).
- Effectiveness (this can be a good trend, but depends on the grounding for effectiveness: if it is in terms of achieving the overall goals of the convention and meeting national priorities, that is good, but if measured in terms of number of investment grade or bankable projects or the degree to which developing countries enable the private sector then it could be problematic).
- Selective targeting: narrowing of the framing of *particularly vulnerable* to just SIDs and LDCs ... But Convention has a wider definition which includes: 1) low-lying; 2) other small island countries; 3) countries with low-lying coastal, arid and semi-arid areas liable to floods, drought and desertification; and 4) developing countries with fragile mountainous ecosystem. Further, Article 4 refers to providing 'financial resources to developing country Parties'.

This new framing for climate finance will be at odds with the commitment of Developed countries and developing countries particularly,

> Article 4.7. *The extent to which developing country Parties will effectively implement their commitments under the Convention will depend on the effective implementation by developed country Parties of their commitments under the Convention related to financial resources and transfer of technology and will take fully into account that economic and social development and poverty eradication are the first and overriding priorities of the developing country Parties.*

The principles that are supportive of gender integration in climate finance include:

Sufficiency: substantial and enough (towards and beyond $100B)
Predictability (generated in a stable and predictable way as much as possible
Equity: reflecting Historical responsilbty and capacity to pay
Additionality: 'new and additional to existing aid commitments
Verifiability: collected and disbursed in a transparent and verifiable manner

Second order criteria

Efficiency – economic efficiency
Ease of implementation: readily implemented
Co-benefit: positive development and environmental impacts

From the purview of the responsibility paradigm, presented in the beginning of this chapter, the following are the essential dimensions that must undergird the scaling up of climate finance:

1   the agreed goal to keep temperature below 1.5–2 degrees Celsius (in the context of ongoing UNFCCC review process);
2   the level of actions by developing countries is critically linked to the level of support provided by Annex II;
3   sufficient and adequate funding for developing countries' needs as expressed through the NAPAs, NAPs, NAMAs, preparation for NDCs etc.;
4   ensuring new and additional, predictability, adequacy, sustainability of climate finance, including addressing the issue of incidence with regard to innovative finance;
5   finance is delivered through mechanisms that ensures country ownership, direct access, and promote gender equity in the distribution of finance flows and, with the majority of funding delivered through the Convention's finance mechanisms (such as the GCF, the Adaptation Fund);
6   bridge the gap between results-based funding approach (RBA) and needs-based funding approach (NBA). RBA – focuses on outcome alone biased towards MIC – larger and with better capacity (public, private and civil society sectors) also not clear for adaptation generally. NBA is more important for ensuring sustainable flow of climate finance to the different groups of countries identified in the Convention to have equitable access to funding: LDCs, SIDs and Africa;
7   finding ways to address or prevent the persistent problem of pledges that do not get transformed into deposits and disbursements;
8   ensuring multi-stakeholders (especially, women's groups, youths, community and indigenous people's organization) engagement to ensure transparency and accountability, as well as environmental integrity and social and environmental safeguards;
9   a political process and agreement to clarify and ensure acceptance (and implementation):

    (a) progress on the technical work around climate finance definition and MRV of support;
    (b) increased and improved information on climate finance needs of developing countries;
    (c) ensure adequate tracking of climate finance (both public and private);

(d) addressing the fragmentation of existing architecture and between sources and delivery channels of funds: bilateral institutions, UNFCC Financial and Mechanism and about subfunds (AF, LDCF, SCCF, and GEF trust fund), and non-UNFCCC agencies: MDBs and separate UN agencies.

Notes

* Women excluded from climate change projects in Africa, UN experts warn. Kristin Palitza, *The Guardian*, 28 June 2011. See www.theguardian.com/environment/2011/jun/28/climate-change-environmental-sustainability.
1 Bloomberg Magazine's analysis shows a cost of $7.77 trillion, based on information received under the Freedom of Information Act, FOIA (2011), Neil Barosfsky, the inspector general for the US's Treasury Trouble Asset Relief Program, argues for $23.7 trillion, while a recent study of the raw data released under the FOIA by Felkerson (2011) show that that the cumulative commitments by the US Federal Reserve, including asset purchase plus lending, is $29 trillion.
2 The SDR is an international reserve asset, created by the IMF in 1969 to supplement its member countries' official reserves. Its value is based on a basket of four key international currencies: the US dollar, the Euro, the British pound, and the Japanese yen. The change in the allocation of SDRs was further complemented by expansion of the New Arrangement to Borrow mechanism (the IMF principal credit line) from SDR 34 billion (US$53 billion) to SDR 367.5 billion (US$576 billion) to boost resources for crisis resolution (IMF 2012).
3 The general allocation of SDR161.2 billion (approximately $250 billion) occurred 28 August and the special allocation of (approximately $34 billion, 9 September 2009, increased the total amount of SDRs from SDR 21.4 billion (pre-2009) to around SDR 204 billion (equivalent to about $310 billion), converted using the rate of 20 August, 2012), IMF 2012 and Obstfeld 2011. General allocations of SDRs have to be based on a long-term global need to supplement existing reserve assets. According to the IMF, '(d)ecisions on general allocations are made for successive basic periods of up to 5 years, although general SDR allocations have been made only three times': allocated and distributed in 1970–1972 (period of the collapse of the Bretton wood system) for a total amount of SDR 9.3 billion and 1979–1981 for SDR 12.1 billion, giving rise to cumulative SDR allocations of SDR 21.4 billion (about $47 billion (at today's prices) prior to 2009), (IMF fact sheet 2012 and Ambrose and Muchhala 2010). The special one-time allocation of SDR 21.5 ($34 billion) was a result of the coming into effect of the fourth amendment to the Fund's articles of agreement which allowed for the approximately one-fifth of members of the Fund, who had joined since 1981 and had never received any allocations of SDRs, to obtain their allocations. The implementation of the amendment had been delayed by the US Congress (Ambrose and Muchhala 2010).
4 Quoted verbatim from simultaneous interpretation of Chavez's speech at the Copenhagen Conference. Chavez said he say something to that effect on the placards carried by young people outside the Conference center. Hugo Chavez, Venezuelan President, said, 'In the streets they are saying the following: if the climate was a bank, you would have already saved it. And I think that's true. If the climate was a big capitalist bank, you would have already saved it. You, the rich governments' (http://therealnews.com). This is also the title of a publication by Chavez and Fidel Castro published in 2010 by the Socialist Alliance National Office.
5 Loss and Damage (associated with climate change impacts) is the phrasing used in the UNFCCC negotiations context. After initial resistance it is now widely accepted within the negotiations and there are different approaches to exploring the topic. COP 18, Doha 2012, mooted the creation of an international mechanism for loss and damage for discussion at future meetings of the COP starting with the 19th meeting in Poland 2013.

Global climate change finance architecture **229**

The Polish Meeting launched the creation of the Warsaw International Mechanism on Loss and Damage. Discussions are now at preliminary stages about the set up of the mechanism and its possible governance structure. At this time the mechanism is completely de-linked from the issue of climate finance.

6 These six large developing countries along with the 11 major developed countries of Australia, Canada, the European Union, France, Germany, Italy, Japan, Korea, Russia, the UK, and the US formed the Major Economies Forum on Energy and Climate (MEF) MEF in March 2009. According to its website the MEF 'is intended to facilitate a candid dialogue among major developed and developing economies, help generate the political leadership necessary to achieve a successful outcome at the annual UN climate negotiations and advance the exploration of concrete initiatives and joint ventures that increase the supply of clean energy while cutting greenhouse gas emissions'. (Chile and Mexico though still categorized as developing countries are members of the OECD.)

7 Nepal (6.7 per cent of Budgetary outlaw and 1.8 per cent of GDP), Bangladesh it is 5.5–7.2 per cent of budgetary Outlaw and 0.9 per cent of GDP, for Samoa climate relevant expenditure is 15 per cent of budget and 6 per cent of GDP, (UNDP 2012 and Bird et al. 2012).

8 The author cautions that due to differing definitions of outlay items as well as 'climate relevant', these percentages cannot give reliable cross country comparison information.

9 Domestic resource on average has 82 per cent of climate expenditures in four separate departments (DPWH, DENR, DOE, PAGASS, 2008–2011). World Bank, Overview of CPIER of the Philippines, Getting a grip climate change and the Philippines. www.worldbank.org/en/news/press-release/2013/06/26/philippines-new-study-says-fully-integrating-climate-change-agenda-in-government-planning-budgeting-will-boost-country-s-resilience.

10 Current Government expenditure in India on adaptation to climate variability exceeds 2.6 per cent of the GDP, with agriculture, water resources, health and sanitation, forests, coastal zone infrastructure and extreme events, being specific areas of concern.

11 The accumulation of GHG, which remains in the atmosphere contributing to global warming, is noted by the Preamble to the Convention – to be due to the actions of developed countries (Annex I parties) in the long historical march to industrialization and economic development. As a result of these past emissions the world is already committed to several decades of warming. (Preambular text from the Convention: *Noting that the largest share of historical and current global emissions of greenhouse gases has originated in developed countries, that per capita emissions in developing countries are still relatively low and that the share of global emissions originating in developing countries will grow to meet their social and development needs.*)

12 The Cancún Decision agreed to by both developed and developing countries specifies that a significant portion of the $100 billion should go through the GCF. The AGF of the UN Secretariat estimates that up to 60 per cent of the $100 billion can come from public sources while the remainder from private sector and various innovative sources of financing.

13 The COP in Decision 1/CP.18 para 67 has requested that developed countries indicate in their biennial reports to the secretariat their 'strategies and approaches for mobilizing climate finance'. However, the majority of the reports speak about past efforts and where they do address the future of scaling up they characterize long-term finance in terms of private sector investment in developing countries (with public finance seen as an inducement to catalyse investments from the private sector). In general, Parties have provided information on their current policies, programmes and priorities with very little clear specification as to future evolution towards scaling up. There is not much information provided on actions and plans geared to mobilize additional finance other than the focus on enhancing enabling environments to finance and private sector investment. There is also not much information provide on how parties will work to are ensuring the balance between adaptation and mitigation. As a result there is not much

clear information on the quantitative pathway to mobilize climate finance from the different sources for the post-2020 period. COP 19 requested developed country Parties to prepare biennial submissions on their updated strategies and approaches for scaling up climate finance from 2014 to 2020, including any available information on quantitative and qualitative elements of a pathway, including information:

- to increase clarity on the expected levels of climate finance mobilized from different sources;
- on their policies, programmes and priorities;
- on actions and plans to mobilize additional finance;
- on how Parties are ensuring the balance between adaptation and mitigation, in particular the needs of developing countries that are particularly vulnerable to the adverse effects of climate change;
- on steps taken to enhance their enabling environments, following on from the report of the co-chairs of the extended work programme on long-term finance.

14 There are of course differences of opinion as to what 'adequate' commitment means. But developing countries of the G77 and China have proposed that initial resources to the GCF of up to $15 billion and recommends a pathway for scaling up long-term finance of a minimum of $10 billion for 2013 (the same as fast start finance), $16 billion for 2016 scaling up too $100 billion per year by 2020.
15 CIF sunset clause.
16 The proclaimed rise of the South seems to lie in the fact that 3 years ago in the throes of the worst financial and economic crisis countries such as China, India and Brazil and a few others were weathering the crisis much better than the north. But today that is clearly not the case, growth is decelerating for all three of the big leaders of the so-called Rise. Second, there are also predictions that 'the combined economic output of three leading developing countries alone – Brazil, China and India – will surpass the aggregate production of Canada, France, Germany, Italy, the UK and the US by 2050 (UNDP 2013). But closer examination of the data by Akyuz 2011, 2012 and Montes 2012 show there is evidence of slow down for China and collapsed growth for India and South Africa – with worsening current account deficits, while Brazil's and other 'risers' in Latin America growth was driven by the commodities boom so they remain vulnerable to shifts in the commodities market. The boom did not necessarily change long-term structural and productivity trends. This raises questions of sustainability as these countries have a continuing dependence on factors in the North. The North still dominates on most metrics including power and decision-making.
17 The US reported that it provided $2 billion of FSF in FY10, $3.2 billion in FY11, and $2.3 billion in FY12, totalling $7.5 billion for the full three-year FSF period. Of this total, $5.8 billion (78 per cent) is described at the level of a programme, project, or fund in the US FSF reports, while another $1.2 billion was identified through other sources, including the Voluntary REDD+ Database and the US Foreign Assistance Dashboard. (Jones et al. (2013) and www.state.gov/e/oes/climate/faststart/c48618.htm.)
18 Japan announced that it would cut its 2020 carbon reduction target hence weakening its climate change commitment: it rolled back on a benchmark commitment to cut greenhouse gas pollution 25 per cent by 2020 based on 1990 levels. A new target was ushered in to reduce greenhouse gas pollution 3.8 per cent by 2020 based on 2005 levels. That amounts to a 3 per cent rise on 1990 levels, effectively annihilating Japan's climate ambition. At the same time it announced extra funds for climate.
19 Annex I countries include approximately forty countries: Australia, Austria, Belarus, Belgium, Bulgaria, Canada, Croatia, Czech Republic, Denmark, Estonia, Finland, France, Germany, Greece, Hungary, Iceland, Ireland, Italy, Japan, Latvia, Liechtenstein, Lithuania, Luxembourg, Monaco, Netherlands, New Zealand, Norway, Poland, Portugal, Romania, Russian Federation, Slovakia, Slovenia, Spain, Sweden, Switzerland, Turkey, Ukraine, United Kingdom, United States of America.

20 Annex II countries (23 developed countries) include: Australia, Austria, Belgium, Canada, Denmark, Finland, France, Germany, Greece, Iceland, Ireland, Italy, Japan, Luxembourg, Netherlands, New Zealand, Norway, Portugal, Spain, Sweden, Switzerland, United Kingdom, United States of America. Turkey was removed from the Annex II list in 2001 at its request to recognize its economy as a transition economy, Wikipedia 2009. Under the Kyoto Protocol, Annex B is Parties with quantified emission limitation or reduction commitment (percentage of base year or period). These are primarily the same as those in Annex I of the Convention.
21 Article 4, Paragraph 3, the UNFCCC Convention under the Kyoto Protocol. Article 4, specifically 4.3, 4.4, 4.5, and Article 12 para 1 address the commitment by the developed country signatories to the Convention to provide the necessary finance and technology transfer and development (Article 4.5) that support the actions of developing countries parties in meeting the goals of the Convention as they both adapt to climate change and undertake mitigation actions consistent with their poverty, social and economic development objectives. Article 4, 3–4: 3. The developed country Parties and other developed Parties included in Annex II shall provide new and additional financial resources to meet the agreed full costs incurred by developing country Parties in complying with their obligations under Article 12, Paragraph 1. They shall also provide such financial resources, including for the transfer of technology, needed by the developing country Parties to meet the agreed full incremental costs of implementing measures that are covered by Paragraph 1 of this article and that are agreed between a developing country Party and the international entity or entities referred to in Article 11, in accordance with that article. The implementation of these commitments shall take into account the need for adequacy and predictability in the flow of funds and the importance of appropriate burden sharing among the developed country Parties. 4. The developed country Parties and other developed Parties included in Annex II shall also assist the developing country Parties that are particularly vulnerable to the adverse effects of climate change in meeting costs of adaptation to those adverse effects. 5. The developed country Parties and other developed Parties included in Annex II shall take all practicable steps to promote, facilitate and finance, as appropriate, the transfer of, or access to, environmentally sound technologies and know-how to other Parties, particularly developing country Parties, to enable them to implement the provisions of the Convention. In this process, the developed country Parties shall support the development and enhancement of endogenous capacities and technologies of developing country Parties. Other Parties and organizations in a position to do so may also assist in facilitating the transfer of such technologies.
22 Singapore, with a per capita GDP per capita of (current) US$51,709, 2008–2012 though high income, is not a member of the OECD. http://data.worldbank.org/indicator/NY.GDP.PCAP.CD.
23 Article 11.2.
24 The polluter Pay Principle: 'implies that the cost incurred from any form of pollution should be the responsibility of the polluter in order to ensure that the environment is protected for present and future generations. The PPP is widely acknowledged as a general principle of International Environmental Law and is frequently mentioned in Multilateral Environmental Agreements (MEA)'. ISS and OECD.
25 See for example, Storm on the horizon? Why World Bank Climate Investment Funds could do more harm than good. Nora Honkaniemi, European Network on Debt & Development (EURODAD 2011).
26 Canada, Japan, New Zealand, and the US. http://unfccc.int/files/cooperation_support/nama/application/pdf/mrvumbrellagroupandusa.pdf.
27 The OECD DAC/Creditor Reporting System is recognized as the 'authoritative source for internationally comparable statistics on aid flows' with the CRS as 'the most comprehensive dataset on climate-change-related aid today' (Benn 2011). According to Benn 2011, the Members of the Development Assistance Committee (DAC) report their aid activities to the OECD Creditor Reporting System (CRS) database and are requested

232 Global climate change finance architecture

to indicate for each aid activity whether or not it targets climate change mitigation or adaptation as a principal or significant objective. Under the Rio framework, the climate markers were established in close collaboration with the UNFCCC Secretariat (Benn 2011). There are two broad categories: 1) Aid in support of climate change mitigation which is defined as activities that contribute to the objective of stabilization of greenhouse gas (GHG) concentrations in the atmosphere at a level that would prevent dangerous anthropogenic interference with the climate system by promoting efforts to reduce or limit GHG emissions or to enhance GHG sequestration. (*Article 2 of the UNFCCC*); and 2) Aid in support of climate change adaptation which is defined as activities that aim to reduce the vulnerability of human or natural systems to the impacts of climate change and climate-related risks, by maintaining or increasing adaptive capacity and resilience (Benn 2011).

28 One dedicated forum where this kind of discussion is being underway is through the Structure Expert Dialogue (SED). The goals of SED are twofold: 1) to assess the adequacy of the long-term global goal to the extent possible, the light of the ultimate objective of the Convention and on the basis of the IPCC's AR5 WG I; and 2) to assess the overall progress made so far towards achieving the long-term global goal, as well as the projected progress, including the likelihood of meeting and maintaining the goal; and to share lessons learned on the effectiveness of the support provided.

29 Though running into the hundreds of billions, the adaptation cost is still only double the current estimated $100 billion per year flow of overseas development assistance. As noted by Oxfam this figure must be assessed in light the fact that many governments and citizens in developed countries devote relatively equivalent amounts on ordinary and extra ordinary expenditures during a given year. For example, Oxfam notes that, at the high end, the US government spent $378 billion for the Iraqi war in 2007, and European spending on passenger flights and air freight at $128 billion was less than the low bound of the projected adaptation costs (Oxfam 2007).

30 This usage of the term social protection draws on the definition of Davis *et al.* (2008): Social protection describes all initiatives that transfer income or assets to the poor, protect the vulnerable against livelihood risks, and enhance the social status and rights of the marginalized. Social protection also includes employment guarantee schemes.

31 The Climate Policy Initiative 2013 global landscape of climate finance report argues that global climate finance flows have plateaued at USD 359 billion, or around USD 1 billion per day, which the report argue is far below even the most conservative estimates of investment needs. The vast majority of the USD 39–62 billion in North-South flows originated from public sources. For example, the two most recent comprehensive studies of the issue, on which the IPCC assessment is based, the report of the Climate Finance Project Initiative 2011 (Buchner *et al.* 2011) and the OECD's Tracking Climate Finance (Clapp *et al.* 2012), which include a subset of the same authors across both research works, present estimates of $97 billion and $70–120 billion, respectively, per year, of annual flow of climate finance and for the period 2009–2010. For 2011/2012 Buchner argues that $120–140 billion reported as flowing to developing countries. Buchner *et al.* (2013). See Appendix 4.1 – Unravelling the climate finance jigsaw.

32 The UNFCCC Secretariat's report points out that countries have different or no method for assessing the newness or additionality of their contributions. It noted that the UK's reference point is the target of meeting the 0.7 per cent of GNI of ODA by 2013, while others referenced agreements under the Convention, such as the Bonn Agreements, still others, such as Norway and Switzerland, present their own individual baselines for measuring new and additional (UNFCCC 2011).

33 CPI research is quite confusing and problematic it simply muddies the water. After the dramatic featuring of $97 billion a year flow it turns out that most of this investment (with ownerships interest), approximately $74–87 of the $97 billion and $56 billion are in the form of market rate loans. As noted in the report the $97 billion also includes south–south climate flows as well as domestic climate financing in developing countries.

Global climate change finance architecture **233**

Hence this does not contribute meaningfully to discussion of the scope and magnitude of climate finance in the UNFCCC process.
34 This is a contribution reported as required by Annex II parties in the 5th National Communications report to the UNFCCC.
35 The GEF which is a multi-convention financing mechanism started life as a $1 billion 3-year pilot project (1991–1994) by a World Bank resolution 91–5). It received its first pledge of support from the French Government (pledge of 900 million French Francs for 3 years) and later support from Germany. Bossion de Chazounne (2003) argues that the GEF was mooted as a solidarity mechanism to get the support of developing countries to address the global problem but it was developed in a way that pre-empted other proposals or the creation of financial mechanisms under UNCED.

In 1992 its structure was modified according to the Agenda 21 (the UN action plan of the 1992 UNCED), the UNFCCC and CBD. It was restructured on a legal basis in March 1994 with 73 states as members and with Executing Agencies the UN Food and Agriculture Organization (FAO), the UN Industrial Development Organization (UNIDO), the African Development Bank (AfDB), the Asian Development Bank (ADB), the European Bank for Reconstruction and Development (EBRD), the Inter-American Development Bank (IDB), and the International Fund for Agricultural Development (IFAD).

The GEF is controversial animal, for the most part, supported by Europeans who desired to see it mature as key (unitary) financing mechanisms to address global environmental problems, but really only tolerated by the US who viewed it as a temporary mechanism that would be integrated into the World Bank's environmental programme. This tension has remained. The DCs as a group have resisted the ideas mooted since UNCED and UNFCCC for green climate funds. But even with the agreement to the GCF that tension of the role of the GEF and the bank still dogged the design and full operationalization of the Fund with the EU led by France promoting the GEF and the US's ultimate desire is that the World Bank would be in charge.
36 Pilot Phase 1991–1994 $1 billion; GEF-1 – 1994–1998 $2.023 billion; GEF2 1998–2002 $2.023 billion; GEF 3 2002–2006 $3 billion; GEF 4 2006–2010 $3.13 billion; GEF 5 2010–2014 $4.25 billion. Replenishment is for projects with global environmental benefit. Climate change is one of its focal areas. For example of the amount receive for GEF 5 only $1.3 billion was agreed to be channelled for climate change projects. The maximum amount a country can access is US$ 2.4 m, this is equivalent to an average of US$600,000 per year. Deals with countries that have individual allocation of US$43.1 million to US$150 million.
37 Negotiations for GEF 6 replenishment which raised pledges of $4.43 billion for funding beginning 1 July 2014 and ending 30 June 2018 concluded April 2014.
38 Under the UNFCCC, the Kyoto Protocol, and the GEF, eligible developing countries may receive grant funding for the 'agreed full incremental costs' of measures taken to implement their commitments (WRI 2009). 'The concept is designed to limit and add leverage to grants made for global environmental purposes by providing a means for distinguishing between the additional, incremental costs of building a global environmental benefit (such as decreasing greenhouse gas emissions) into a development investment, and a business as usual investment made for domestic benefits (ibid.).
39 The RAF was introduced to increase the predictability and transparency of GEF's resource allocation (UNDP 2008). The amount that each eligible country can expect from the GEF is specified at the start of the 4-year replenishment period with an update in the middle of the period. Each country receives a minimum allocation of $1 million with a maximum allocation of 15 per cent of the resources available. Within that range the GEF Benefits Index and the GEF Performance Index are used to determine the resources allocated to each country (UNDP 2008). The GEF Benefits Index measures the potential of a country to generate global environmental benefits, and the GEF Performance Index measures a country's capacity, policies and practices relevant to successful implementation of GEF programmes and projects. The GEF Performance Index relies on World Bank

Country Policy and Institutional Assessment data (GEF 2007). In the GEF 4 climate change focal area, 46 countries have an individual allocation ranging from USD 3.1 million to USD 150 million. The remaining 115 countries may seek project financing from a total group allocation of USD 148.6 million. China, India and the Russian Federation received the largest allocations under the RAF formula, followed by Brazil, Mexico and South Africa and a group of countries that includes Argentina, Egypt, Indonesia, the Islamic Republic of Iran, Kazakhstan, Malaysia, Pakistan, Romania, Thailand, Turkey, Ukraine and the Bolivarian Republic of Venezuela (GEF 2007).

40 As of 1 April 2010, there were 2,610 projects listed in the GEF database, of which 665 were 'closed' or 'completed'; 1,200 were 'under implementation' or had been 'approved by the implementing agency'; and the remaining 745 were in a pre-approval or endorsement stage. Congressional Research Service 2010.

41 GEF two indices are GEF BI and GEF PI. GEF BI – measures the potential of a country to generate global environmental benefits. For climate change, GBI weights the baseline emission of a country with the carbon intensity adjustment factor. It excludes greenhouse gas emissions from land use change and forestry. GEF PI – measures a country's capacity to implement GEF programmes and projects. It is based on the World Bank's Country Policy and Institutional Assessment (*CPIA*) data.

42 Co-financing is 'financing mobilized from sources other than the borrower or project sponsors to augment its own assistance, with funds from *commercial financial institutions, official funding agencies* and *export credit agencies*' (ADB 2009).

43 Country score = $GPI^{1.0} \times GBI^{08} \times GDP^{-0.04}$ where GPI: global performance index, GBI: global benefit index; and GDP per capita nominal GDP (please also see endnotes 22 and 24).

44 The GEF is governed by the GEF Assembly which meets once every 3 years and reviews policy, the GEF Council which meets semi-annually and develops and adopts decision around evaluation and operations. It has an independent secretariat headed by a CEO and is supported by a scientific and technical advisory panel (STAP).The Secretariat and CEO are accountable to the GEF council as are the Implementing agencies, with regard to their GEF funds.

45 The COP has given 160 articles on guidance to GEF in its decisions over the years. In 2004, alone there were 48 of these articles (GEF 2010).

46 'GEF's grants cover the "incremental" or "additional" cost of "transforming a project with national benefits into one with global environmental benefits".' Incremental cost calculations have also been used as preference in project selection. Historically, GEF's implementing agencies have had difficulty producing a coherent methodology for calculating incremental cost, slowing the rate of project development. Congressional Research 2010.

47 Another evaluation of GEF 'found that the GEF's project preparation cycle was not cost effective and that longer preparation time did not result in better projects and that too much energy was spent on obtaining quality on paper but with limited value added'.

48 A new project cycle was implemented in 2007 under GEF-4, introducing the PIF CEO approval process and replacing the Project Development Facility with the project preparation grant.

49 According to Climatefunds Update (2009), 'The steps for the preparation of the NAPAs include synthesis of available information; participatory assessment of vulnerability to current climate variability and extreme events and of areas where risks would increase due to climate change; identification of key adaptation measures as well as criteria for prioritizing activities; and selection of a prioritized short list of activities. The development of a NAPA also includes short profiles of projects and/or activities intended to address urgent and immediate adaptation needs of LDC Parties.

50 Progress Report of the Least Developed Countries FUND (LDCF) AND the Special Climate Change Fund (SCCF). GEF/LDCF.SCCF.9/Inf.3 20 October 2010 (LDCF/SCCF Council Meeting, 18 November 2010) and GEF 2011. Evaluation of the Special

Climate Change Fund (SCCF) October 2011 (unedited version of final report) GEF. Evaluation Office.
51 Most SCCF projects are located in Africa (12 projects) but Asia's 9 projects are larger in size and twice as large. Africa accounts for $37.3 million of SCCF funding and more beneficiaries. Latin America and the Caribbean have a high number of projects (7) accounting for approximately $37.1 million and The SCCF portfolio is also funding 7 projects in Latin America and the Caribbean and 4 projects in Europe and Central Asia and 3 projects on the global level. Additionally, co-financing is higher in Asia than in Africa.
52 The Evaluation Report notes that co-financing in Africa is about only half of that in Asia if the World Bank's Green Wall initiative in Nigeria (which account for about $80 million of Africa's co-financing) is excluded. The World Bank's nine SCCF projects' allocation (which account for 38 per cent of SCCF portfolio and $52 million) also generate the largest amount of co-financing (30 per cent), an average of $34.3 million per project. The average size of a World Bank SCCF project is $5.8 million. In contrast, UNDP, the next larger SCCF project implementer agency of GEF's 10 implementing agencies, with 16 projects (equivalent to 37 per cent of SCCF' portfolio allocation) generates co-financing of $16.5 million. The average size of a UNDP project at $3.4 million is much smaller than the bank's (GEF 2011: 20).
53 Evaluation of the Special Climate Change Fund (SCCF) October 2011 (unedited version of final report) GEF. Evaluation Office.
54 GEF (2011). As noted in the report, it was the intention of the COP as stated in 7/CP.7 that the SCCF finance activities in four fields: a) Adaptation to support the implementation of adaptation actions in non-annex I parties; b) Transfer of technologies to focus on support to the transfer of environmentally sustainable technologies, concentrating on, but not limited to, technologies to reduce emissions or atmospheric concentrations of greenhouse gasses, in line with the recommendations from the national communications, technology needs assessments (TNAs) and other relevant information; c) Support six specific sectors, Energy, transport, industry, agriculture, forestry, and waste management; d) Economic diversification for fossil fuel dependent countries: activities to assist developing countries whose economies are highly dependent on income generated from the production, processing, and export or on consumption of fossil fuels and associated energy-intensive products in diversifying their economies. Source: In July 2010, the LDCF/SCCF Council requested the GEF Evaluation Office to undertake an evaluation of the SCCF. This was undertaken May–September 2011. Please see *Evaluation of the Special Climate Change Fund* (GEF/LDCF.SCCF.11/ME/02).
55 According to Decision 2CP 14 (2009), launching of a policy initiative for the further Development and Transfer of Technologies. The programme included three funding windows aimed at: (1) Conducting Technology Needs Assessments (TNAs); (2) Piloting technology projects linked to TNAs; and (3) Disseminating GEF Experience and successfully demonstrated ESTs.
56 At the COP 18 (2012) meeting developing countries opted to continue the interim institutional arrangements and were not willing to mandate the World Bank as permanent trustee until they are sufficiently assured that there is no other institution that could provide the same services as the bank in a cost effective manner (Adaptation Fund NGO Newsletter No 5. February 2013).
57 Despite a long and tense debate between developing countries and primarily the US over the nature and degree of the relationship between the COP and the GCF, a draft agreement was concluded between the Standing Committee and the co-chairs of the board of the GCF to be approved by the COP at COP 19 (2013). (The US with a few other developed countries wanted an arms-length distance between the two arguing that they were two independent bodies. Developing countries were of the view that since the COP created the GCF the COP should have some measure of control and accountability over the GCF as stipulated both in the governing instrument of the GCF and the COP Decision approving the GCF.)

58 The City of Songdo, South Korea successful competed against five countries to host the entity (Germany, Mexico, Namibia, Poland, South Korea and Switzerland).
59 According to its governing instrument, two co-chairs of the Board will be elected by the Board members from within their membership to serve for a period of 1 year, with one being a member from a developed country Party and the other being a member from a developing country Party.
60 The CIFs have a sunset clause which enables closure of funds once a new financial mechanism (such as the GCF) becomes effective under the UNFCCC regime. Many developed countries and some civil society organizations therefore argued that there was a conflict of interest in the World Bank as Trustee and its staff being involved in the setting up of the GCF. (The Transitional Committee mandated to design the GCF was supported by a Technical Secretariat Unit which was made up primarily of World Bank Group staff.) In addition, during the design of the Fund, many developing countries pushed for the GEF, which many also view as a World Bank aligned entity, to administer the GCF. It was felt that the new Fund though it was to be transformative and function in manner different from the existing funds was being engineered by the developed countries to be exactly the status quo. This became even more evident when countries such as the US and the UK among others sought to prevent the GCF from having its own independent juridical personality and legal capacity that would enable it to have independent exercise of its function, which would make the GCF just like the GEF, which derives its legal personality/status from the World Bank. *Some 115 non-governmental organisations (NGOs) have urged governments to 'sunset' the World Bank's Climate Investment Funds (CIFs) and instead, redirect their funding to the new Green Climate Fund (GCF), and make it fully functional as soon as possible.* SUNS #7355.
61 Other issues for consideration in the business model of the fund include its policy on the participation of advisers in board meetings, the development of a communication strategy and the relationship with the UNFCC and external bodies. The Governing instrument as well as the COP Decision established a number of parameters which are to be the basis on which the business model is to evolve.
62 The idea of the GCF was actually mooted in 2009 at the Copenhagen meeting of the Parties. As reported to the third board meeting (Berlin, March 2013), the Green Climate Fund Trust Fund, established by the World Bank, as the Trustee, received a total pledge of $8.11 million from approximately eleven contributing countries. Most all of this will go towards the operational cost of the Fund. As of 31 December 2012 the GCF Board had approved funding from the GCF Trust Fund totalling USD 8.3 million, in respect of administrative budgets of the GCF to support the activities of the GCF Board, interim secretariat and interim trustee from January 1, 2012 to December 31, 2013. Trustee Report to 3rd Board Meeting, Berlin, March 2013.
63 The Work Programme was initially agreed COP 17 (2011) and co-chaired by Norway and South Africa. It was extended at COP 18 (2012) with new co-chairs, the Philippines and Sweden who will report at COP 19 (Poland 2013). The 2012 Work Programme was implemented through two in-session workshops on long-term finance, July and October 2012; two web-based seminars (webinar), September 2012; and an E-Forum.
64 In general, Parties have provided information on their current policies, programmes and priorities with very little specification as to future scaling up. There is not much information provided on actions and plans geared to mobilize additional finance other than the focus on enhancing enabling environment to finance and private sector investment. There is also not much information provided on how Parties will work to ensuring the balance between adaptation and mitigation. As a result, there is not much clear informant or the quantitative pathway to mobilize climate finance from the different sources for the post-2020 period. In this context, some Parties also pointed to the need for a better definition of climate finance (addressing definitional and measurement issues); but there are no specific proposals for doing this. A few Parties also mooted muted the idea of working towards the next generation of climate finance instruments.

5
THE STATE OF PLAY OF BILATERAL AND MULTILATERAL AND MARKET-BASED CLIMATE FINANCE

This chapter, which is the logical complement to Chapter 4, focuses on the funding arrangements, institutions and instruments operating outside the UNFCCC. These are primarily bilateral and multilateral funds, many of which involve the World Bank and its regional networks of development banks and bilateral institutions of developed countries, which channel the mega portions of climate finance to developing countries. As with the operations of the carbon market and the flexible market-based mechanisms allowed under the Convention, multilateral and bilateral climate finance raise serious questions of access and equity both from gender-equity and climate-justice perspectives.

At the same time that the Convention's inspired climate financial architecture has been evolving, developed countries have also established a variety of climate funds and funding mechanisms outside the framework of the Financial Mechanism of the UNFCCC. These funds and funding mechanisms include bilateral funds such as Japan's Fast-start Finance (initially, the Hatoyama Initiative (2008)) and the Cool Earth Partnership (2008–2010), the Global Climate Change Alliance (the European Commission), the International Climate Fund (the UK), the International Climate Forest Initiative (Norway) and Germany's International Climate Initiative. Developed countries, in addition to their own sui generis funds, also channel resources through multilateral (the World Bank) and regional entities such as the African and Asian development banks. This is allowable under Article 11.5 of the Convention, which allows for developed countries to provide, and developing countries to avail themselves of, financial resources related to the implementation of the Convention through bilateral, regional and other multilateral channels.

However, these other tracks of climate finance which dominate the flow of financing for climate change do not satisfy the requirement to provide funding to developing countries to meet their obligations under the convention. Such flows of funds are expected to be channelled through the Convention's financial mechanism and they have, as noted before, specific constraints – they are expected to be primarily grants and concessional loans, which are adequate and predictable and, as a result of Cancún, balanced between adaptation and mitigation as well has geographically balanced.

However, given donor preference for bilateral and multilateral institutions such as the World Bank Group, the largest flows of international climate change finance tend to go through vertical funds, global programmes/global funds (World Bank 2010). The MDBs allocated annually on average $44.7 billion of climate finance in 2003–2007. The World Bank manages a number of climate funds including the $7 billion CIF and its Forest Carbon Partnership. A large part of mitigation-oriented financing flows through the Clean Development Mechanism. The African Development Bank administers the Congo Basin Forest Fund (CBFF) and the European Investment Bank does likewise with the EU Global Energy Efficiency and Renewable Energy Fund.

These non-Convention funds tend to be supply-driven and fragmentary and are often not in line with the needs of the developing countries as articulated either under the Convention or in the context of national priorities and concerns as regards climate change adaptation needs. As noted by the World Bank, such funding instruments are burdensome and have highly complex institutional arrangements (World Bank 2010). They, as argued by the bank, tend to contribute to growing fragmentation and create problems for country-driven adaptation and development process and hence may be a drawback to effectiveness and sustainability. Thus by circumventing the Convention's financing mechanism, these vertical funds have created challenges for developing countries to access funds for climate change activities, especially adaptation.

The manner in which developed countries have approached climate finance, geared to meet their commitments under the Convention, is quite a dramatic departure from the approach they espoused in the development finance context, where there has been, at least at the level of rhetoric, much emphasis on the key principles of Ownership, Alignment, Harmonisation, Managing for Results and Mutual Accountability. These principles were agreed under the 2005 Paris Declaration on Aid Effectiveness and reaffirmed in the Accra 2008 High Level Forum and the 2011 Busan Partnership on aid effectiveness. Under the Paris and the Busan agreements, developed countries all agreed to 'harmonise and align aid delivery' by eliminating duplication and aligning aid with (developing countries') national priorities.[1] Ownership was specified to mean that 'Partner countries exercise effective leadership over their development policies, and strategies and co-ordinate development actions'; alignment meant that 'donors base their overall support on partner countries' national development strategies, institutions and procedures', and harmonization suggested 'use of common arrangements or procedures by donors'. Ironically, the developed countries also agreed to 'a harmonised approach to environmental assessments' – something which they have seemingly studiously avoided incorporating into their climate finance frameworks.

Paradoxically, though developed countries seek to treat climate finance as aid, they resist applying the same standards that they are promoting in the aid context.

Ironically, the developing countries who resist the idea of climate finance as aid, and hence are allegoric to the direct carryover of the Paris Principles into the UNFCCC finance architecture, would nonetheless want to see more national ownership of climate flows rather than the current pattern of contributing countries selecting what projects and programmes they would fund, hence distorting national climate change efforts.

The rest of this chapter continues the exploration of the specifics of the mechanism for the delivery of climate finance to developing countries. It has three parts. Part 1 examines the second and third layers of the global climate change finance architecture: the activities of multilateral and regional actors (Section 1), the nature and scope of bilateral climate finance (Section 2) and bilateral financial actors, instruments and mechanisms to complete the discussion on the flow of climate finance available to developing countries. Part 2 examines the role, scope and efficacy of flexible market mechanisms, such as the Clean Development Mechanism, in the delivery of climate finance to developing countries.

Part 3 examines how the carbon market contributes to climate finance.

5.1 Non-UNFCCC multilateral funding channels and the flow of climate finance to developing countries

5.1.1 The World Bank

The World Bank Group performs multiple functions and plays a significant role in climate change financing. It provides direct financing for adaptation and mitigation. It is an implementing agency for UN funds (such as the GEF) and it is the Secretariat for climate change funds, such as the Climate Investment Fund, and a Trustee (which holds, manages and disburses finance) for climate funds such as the Adaptation Fund. It is also the interim Trustee for the new GCF.

The Bank is also involved in energy sector lending and leverages funds for energy projects. According to Hosier (2009), the World Bank Group has access to four key climate change mitigation finance tools: (1) the GEF, (2) regular financing (for renewable and energy efficiency programmes) through its networks (the bank/IBRD, MIGA, IFC and IDA),[2] (3) the Clean Technology Fund, and (4) Carbon Financing. The GEF, the CTF and Carbon Financing are the key mitigation financing mechanisms that are important for helping the World Bank meet its mitigation goals of helping developing countries undertake 'nationally appropriate mitigation actions in the context of sustainable development' without compromising growth by transferring finance and technology from developed countries in a 'measurable, reportable and verifiable manner' (Bali Plan of Action; Hosier 2009). Its mitigation financing tools are also complemented by adaptation financing tools under the Strategic Climate funds.

Since October 2008, the World Bank's climate portfolio has operated under the Strategic Framework on Development and Climate Change (SFDCC). Under

SFDCC there two broad groupings of funds: the bank's second generation CIF[3] (July 2008) and the Strategic Climate Fund (SCF).

The CIF is jointly developed and implemented with the networks of multilateral and regional development banks (the African Development Bank, the Asian Development bank, the Inter-American Development Bank and the European Development Bank). The family of CIF, which inter-mix development finance and climate change financing, seeks to promote international cooperation on climate change and support progress towards the future of the climate change regime. The CIF has a sunset clause which will allow for its closure subsequent to the coming into operation of the GCF. However, there is a great deal of scepticism that this clause will be implemented any time soon.

The specific mission of CIF is to provide scaled-up financing to demonstrate, develop and transfer low carbon technology with a significant potential for long-term GHGs emission (Hosier 2009). Its major subcomponent is the Clean Technology Fund (CTF) ($5.5 billion) which is focused on mitigation-oriented funds for low carbon energy projects or energy technology that seek to reduce emissions and promote energy efficiency in buildings, industry and agriculture. It provides concessional financing to middle-income countries. CIF and the Strategic Climate Funds with pledges of over $8.1 billion are disbursed through MDBs in order to 'support effective and flexible implementation of country-led programmes and investments (CIF website; World Bank).

The Special Climate Change Fund (SCCF) has a much broader and more flexible scope. It provides adaptation and mitigation funds that aim to make development planning more resilient. SCCF currently has three subcomponents: the Pilot Program for Climate Resilience (PPCR) ($1.2 billion), the Forest Investment Program (FIP) and the Scaling up Renewable Energy Program (SREP).

PPCR, which is in effect the bank's version of an adaptation fund, promotes capacity building to 'integrate climate resilience into development plans' (Climate Investment Funds 2015). It also provides funding for public-private partnerships through budget support and sector wide approaches. Funds are to be blended with national finance. The FIP seeks to promote reductions in deforestation. SREP provides financing to pilot new development approaches or to scale-up activities aimed at a specific climate change challenges. It is designed to also ensure and promote sustainable development and poverty reduction.

The World Bank also engages in carbon market development and carbon trading. It undertakes purchases of carbon credits in the Clean Development markets and has developed $2 billion in 10 carbon funds including the Forest Carbon Partnership Facility (FCPF) and the Carbon Partnership Fund (CPF).

5.1.2 Regional development banks and climate finance

Existing regional climate-related financing arrangements in Asia, Africa and the Caribbean tend to revolve around each region's respective regional bank: the Asian Development Bank (ADB), the African Development Bank (AfDB), the Inter-

American Development Bank (IDB) and the Caribbean Development Bank (CBD). Regional development banks have complemented their development financing with climate change financing portfolios, including implementing several dedicated funds for financing climate change adaptation and mitigation. As yet there are no significant autonomous dedicated regional climate finance institutional arrangements in any of the different regions or sub-regions of the developing countries. However, three global regions have some form of catastrophe risk insurance scheme. The oldest is the Caribbean Risk Insurance Facility (2007) – a multi-country risk pool for Caribbean governments, which now has created a small grants programme. Five Pacific Islands are now collaborating in a Pacific Catastrophe Risk Insurance Pilot (as of 2003). Since 2014, there is also the African Risk Insurance Pool, also involving five countries on drought-related issues.

Increasingly, regional development banks are integrated in the global climate change financing governance system: almost all are implementing agencies with the GEF, and all are in partnership with the World Bank under the CIF. Developed countries are also channelling funds directly into these banks as they also develop their own approaches to financing adaptation, mitigation and technology development strategies, projects and programmes based on the particular specificities of their region. In many cases, because of their regional and development focus and closer links with member countries in their location, RDBs are better able to respond to both country- and regional-specific needs. They also might be less constrained than the GEF by the requirement of ensuring global benefits.

The African Development Bank, for example, recently implemented the African Water Facility and the ClimDev-Africa Initiative, both of which focus on the critical issue of decreasing climate change risks and sectoral vulnerabilities of the agriculture, water resources and food security and infrastructure development in Africa. The Asian Development Bank also has two programmes, the Poverty and Environment Fund and the Water Financing Partnership Facility (WFPF) that explicitly link climate change financing with poverty reduction and sustainable development. The Inter-American Development Bank is focused on its climate focal area flagship Sustainable Energy and Climate Change Initiative while the Caribbean Development Bank concentrates part of its climate-related activities on disaster risk management.

5.1.2.1 The African Development Bank

The African Development Bank (AfDB) has a clear and explicit strategy to mainstream climate change financing into its programming. It has developed the Climate Risk Management and Adaptation strategy whose focus is on accelerating progress towards eradicating poverty and contributing to sustainable improvement in people's means of subsistence.

As part of its climate policy framework, the African Development Bank (AfDB) is focusing its climate change related financing portfolio on addressing 'Africa's identified climate change risks in vulnerable sectors by improving land-use, water conservation, infrastructural development ... and capacity enhancement'. The AfDB has six specific climate programme areas or 'financing partnerships': (1) the Africa Carbon Support Program – a technical support and capacity building programme to assist African institutions and governments in accessing the carbon market; (2) the aforementioned African Water Facility (focused on strengthening water management and governance in the region); (3) the Congo Basin Forest Fund (for sustainable management of forests and ecosystem); (4) the Clean Energy Bonds; (5) the Sustainable Energy Fund for Africa (providing support to promote development of the clean energy market in Africa); and (6) ClimDev-Africa[4] and ClimDev-Africa Special Fund to promote investments that strengthen the generation, dissemination and use of climate data and information across Africa with the aim of enhancing climate-resilient development in Africa. Of these six core climate programmes the two with the most explicit focus on gender and social equity are the African Water Facility (AWF) and the Congo Basin Forest Fund.

The African Water Facility, in operation since 2006, is an initiative of the African Ministers' Council on Water. Hosted and managed by the AfDB, the AWF focuses on mobilising resources for water and sanitation congruent with attaining the successful achievement of the Africa Water Vision (2025) and the MDGs (2015). Though operating at the level of influencing African countries and regional organizations' capacity to govern water resources as well as seeking to strengthen the financial base of these entities, the AWF also proactively works to mainstream gender, and social equity concerns are mainstreamed into its key areas. This is important given Africa has the lowest total water supply coverage of any region in the world; more than 300 million people in Africa do not have access to safe water and some 313 million have no access to sanitation.

The main goal of the Congo Basin Forest Fund of the AfDB (since 2008) is to slow the rate of deforestation and reduce poverty among forest dwellers and to contribute to a reduction in greenhouse gas emissions while maximizing the storage of carbon. Its key thematic areas are forest management and sustainable practices; livelihoods and economic development; monitoring, assessment and verification; benefits from carbon markets and payment for ecosystem services; and capacity building in reducing emissions from deforestation and degradation (REDD) (see chapter seven). The Fund has recently completed its second call for proposals (2009–2010) and the governing council of the Fund has endorsed 12 project proposals from NGOs (for about €11.2 million), 13 project proposals from governments (€52 million in total). (The first call for proposals in 2008 resulted in 15 projects for about €15 million being considered for funding.)

The AfDB Sustainable Energy Fund for Africa was initiated in 2011 and focuses on private sector development of 'smaller-size renewable energy and energy efficiency players'. Its focus is on building the clean energy market in Africa. While one of its dual strategies is to support SMEs along the renewable energy and energy efficiency value chain as producers, distributors, suppliers and consumers of climate-friendly energy, it has no explicit gender and social equity focus, and is the smaller of its two financing windows, $30 million, on a mixed grant and equity investment basis, versus $75 million on a grant basis for presumably medium-size enterprises for the development and design of renewable energy generation and distribution projects. SEFA does have a thematic focus on increasing rural access to clean electricity in order to support the increase of employment levels. It has an explicit focus on targeting rural and peri-urban communities with inconsistent or no access to energy. This fund is not fully operational and its governance structure is in formation

5.1.2.2 The Asian Development Bank

The Asian Development Bank (ADB), for example, is very involved in supporting both financial and technical analysis of adaptation efforts in the region. It is a major supplier of co-financing to Asian countries.

In 2010, the ADB approved 36 technical assistance programmes and grants, plus 20 investment projects related to climate change adaptation. It argued that this was a 30 per cent increase in the number of technical assistance and grant projects and a 100 per cent increase over 2009 levels in the number of loan projects related to adaptation. But the bulk of its climate change related involvement is with mitigation. Since 2008 the ADB has been increasing its support of projects with 'environmental sustainability as a theme'. By 2010 it had approved 53 projects totaling $4.9 billion under this area which increased its support of such projects by 35 per cent between 2008 and 2010. It invested in renewable energy sources such as wind, solar and hydropower energy. According to the ADB (2011), climate change is recognized as an issue in all its Country Partnership Strategies – India, Pakistan, PRC and Sri Lanka – in terms of renewable energy and energy efficient technologies (and in the case of Sri Lanka – adaptation as well). For example, the ADB is very involved in supporting both financial and technical analysis of adaptation efforts in the region. It is a major supplier of co-financing to Asian countries.

To date, the ADB climate change related portfolio includes programmes focused on mitigation and adaptation such as (1) the Clean Energy Program; (2) the Energy for All Initiative; (3) the Water Financing Program; and (4) the Poverty and Environment Program.

The ADB points out that 'while global financing arrangements are necessary to address climate change, regional financing arrangements play an equally essential role'. The ADB highlights three key reasons for the importance of regional financing arrangements for climate change: (1) regional collective action and specialization in order to confront the regional dimensions of climate change; (2) local knowledge, proximity and operational advantage; and (3) potential for additional resource mobilization.

The need for adaptation and mitigation in Asia has some features that are quite distinctive from other regions such as Africa and the Caribbean. A good example is the existence of transboundary river basins (57 in total[5]). This poses serious risks and heightened vulnerability to cross-border flooding and insecurity of water supply. Thus Asian groups of countries within the region may need to undertake joint financing for some projects. Second, Asia has high dependence on coal (relative to, say, Africa), so it will need to investment heavily in alternative sources of energy, which is quite expensive. The ADB report flags, for example, carbon capture and storage and argues that countries in the region may need financing for these kinds of technologies. Third, there is regional specificity with regard to the melting of the Himalayan glaciers that, as noted by Sharan, will 'mainly affect Asia, and not be confined to the boundaries of one country' (2008). These regional impacts and regional public goods require regional actions supported by international finance. This points to the importance of regional financing of climate change in addition to multilateral and country-based actions and financing. The ADB also notes that while mitigation relates to global public good, adaptation activities are more likely to have regional co-benefits.

5.1.2.3 The Inter-American Development Bank

In Latin America and the Caribbean area, the regional development banks in the regions are increasingly focusing their attention on the key climate issues of adaptation and vulnerability reduction through portfolios that seek to ensure climate resilience. The Inter-America Development Bank (IDB), has been involved in a number of climate-related funding areas through financing of hydropower, wind power and geothermal, in addition to improved energy efficiency in power transmission, renewable energy, land use, land-use change and forestry (LULUCF), agriculture and livestock, water resource management and sanitation. Since 2003, the IDB began incorporating the climate change mitigation and adaptation dimension in its programmes, and mobilized Bank resources and multi-donor funding for technical assistance. The IDB, which is a GEF executing agency as of 2004, formally recognized climate change as a priority in its Ninth General Capital Increase, or GCI-9 (IDB 2010). It supports a climate change adaptation and mitigation agenda and sustainable and renewable energy in LAC as a high priority. IDB identifies the protection of the environment, response to climate change, and the promotion of sustainable energy and food security as priorities.

Since 2011, it has sought to enhance its work in climate change by developing a new climate change strategy (CCS) for adaptation, mitigation, technology transfer and renewable energy within Latin America and the Caribbean. According to the IDB, the objective of the CCS is to contribute to low carbon development and address key vulnerabilities to the consequences of climate change in LAC. It therefore serves as a guiding instrument to scale-up the IDB's support for actions to mitigate and adapt to climate change and sustainable and renewable energy in the region (IADB 2011).

Like the AfDB, above, the IDB also is concerned with funding sustainable energy and climate change – the Sustainable Energy and Climate Change Initiative (SECCI) – and has a unit on this focal area, the Sustainable Energy and Climate Change Unit (ECC, since 2009). The SECCI and the ECC unit focus on ensuring alternative energy, sustainable agriculture, climate-friendly transportation and climate-resilient resource management in the context of ensuring economic viability, social equity, and environmental integrity. The SECCI is also built on four strategic pillars of renewable energy and energy efficiency, sustainable biofuel development, access to carbon markets, and adaptation to climate change.

BOX 5.1 SUSTAINABLE ENERGY IN THE ADB FRAMEWORK

Sustainable energy refers to a sector approach that seeks to: (i) promote universal, reliable and affordable access to energy services; (ii) support the long-term sustainability of energy projects, meeting current and future demand; (iii) ensure quality and promote economic efficiency in the provision of the energy services; and (iv) contribute to the reduction of environmental impacts, including climate change

---

5.1.2.4 The Caribbean Development Bank

Given the high vulnerability of Caribbean countries, the Caribbean Development Bank (CDB) has particularly focused its climate change portfolio on the issue of disaster risk management and climate change adaptation. It had a disaster risk management intervention programme (and operational guidelines, since 1998) long before its explicit climate change adaptation programme came on stream in 2008. The Disaster Management Strategy and Operational Guidelines (DiMSOG) was enhanced as a cross-cutting theme in its 2005–2009 Strategic Plan and as a strategic theme in the seventh cycle (2009–2012) of its Special Development Fund. The CDB argues that 'over the period 1998–2008, CDB's assistance to its Borrowing Member Countries (BMCs) under the NDMSOG amounted to 11.37 per cent of the bank's total lending and technical assistance. The CDB has been consistently enhancing and building the synergy between the Disaster Risk Management (DRM) and Climate Change Adaptation (CCA) agendas by enabling countries to minimize losses by integrating CCA and DRM into development strategies so that they can assess potential risks in their development planning processes and allocate resources for risk reduction and at the same time reduce their vulnerability to climate change. The CDB offer Borrowing Member Countries three specific financial instruments to assist them in their economic, social and environmental recovery, while also reducing vulnerability: the emergency relief grant (ERG), the immediate response loan (IRL), and the rehabilitation and reconstruction loan (RRL).

The specific focus of the Climate Change and Adaptation focus area is to integrate CCA considerations into sustainable development strategies with support provided for: (a) preparing and adopting national climate change strategies and adaptation plans; (b) mainstreaming CCA into sectoral policies, strategies and plans; (c) building community resilience to adapt to climate change.

The CCA is complemented by the Climate Resilience Strategy (CRS) 2012–2017 which is based on five guiding principles: Regional Action, Country Ownership, Selectivity and Focus, Partnerships, and Monitoring and Reporting.

5.1.3 Summary of regional and multilateral banks climate finance

In many cases, because of their regional and development focus and closer links with member countries in their environment, these banks may be better able to respond to both country and regional needs. They also might be less constrained than the GEF to the requirement of ensuring global benefits.

Regional financing arrangements can mobilize additional resources within the specific region, given countries are committed to and have higher levels of participation in decision-making at regional level financing arrangements than those that are global level. Regional financial arrangement can also catalyse bilateral flow (given donor geographical preference ordering) and private sector actions.

However, the reality is that regional financial arrangement may also suffer from the same problems that now beset the current international architecture: fragmentation, heavily loan-based funding, co-financing requirements[6] etc.; regional financial entity may also have the effect of crowding-out of funds to national governments. Therefore, any regional financing arrangement must necessarily play a complementary and supplemental role to the ability of countries to directly access international climate finance in their efforts to implement the UNFCCC. Countries' access to international climate finance must not be mediated by regional financing architecture.

5.2 Bilateral climate change finance

In addition to multilateral funding processes, there is a strong and growing web of bilateral climate change funding from donor governments that both underscores and reinforces the activities of multilateral development banks. Most bilateral climate funding (about 85 per cent) is accounted for from ODA and comes from OECD countries (Atteridge et al. 2009). According to the OECD, which through its OECD-DAC Creditor Reporting System, has been tracking mitigation-related aid since 1998 and adaptation-related aid since 2010, total bilateral flows for adaptation and mitigation was about $23 billion in 2010, of which adaptation represents between $3 billion and $9 billion with mitigation accounting for between $13 and $18 billion (OECD 2011a, b).[7]

Examples of climate-related bilateral funds include America's Africa Clean Energy Finance Initiative, Germany's International Climate Initiative, the UK's International Climate Fund, France's Global Environment Facility and Norway's support for REDDplus (Table 5.1).

Bilateral funding for delivering climate finance to developing countries is available in a wide range of financing instruments such as credit lines (loans and soft loans), debt, equity, and grants.[8] According to a recent review of the bilateral funding institutions and climate finance, such flows of funding, in contrast to multilateral funding, tend to 'conceptualize adaptation quite narrowly, focusing mainly on addressing some of the direct impacts of climate change and rather less on actions which reduce human and/or natural system vulnerability to climate change impacts' (Atteridge et al. 2009).

Bilateral mechanisms have advantages and disadvantages vis-à-vis multilateral mechanisms. In the first place, these mechanisms are providing direct funding for adaptation; bilateral funds tend to more directly mainstream adaptation into development assistance,[9] for example, by focusing on screening projects and assessments for climate change risks. Second, they are expected to meet the guidelines and requirement of the Paris Declaration.[10] So bilateral flows whether for climate change or Conventional ODA should be country owned and hence in accordance with national social and development priorities.

The main advantage of bilateral funding, is that it is likely to offer more flexible access to funds. Bilateral funding, may, therefore, be more amenable to

TABLE 5.1 Bilateral funding for climate change

Name of fund	Country/source	Amount	Funding for . . .
Cool Earth Partnership (2008–2012)	Japan	$10 billion (grants and $8 billion preferential interest loans, PIL)	$2 billion for access to clean energy, and $8 billion PIL for mitigation projects
Climate and Forest Initiative (2008–2012)	Norway	$2.2 billion (grants)	Mitigation projects
International Window of the Environmental Transformation Fund (2008–2010)	UK	$1.18 billion (grants and loans)	Adaptation and mitigation (allocated mainly through World Bank's CIF)
International Climate Initiative	Germany	$764 million (10 per cent to be raised from EU-ETS)	Adaptation, mitigation – general
International Forest Carbon Initiative (2007–2011)	Australia	$129 million (grants)	Mitigation – REDD
UNDP-Spain MDG Achievement Fund (2007–2010)	Spain	$90 million (grants)	Mitigation and adaptation
Global Climate Change Alliance (2007–2011)	European Commission	$76 million (grants to most vulnerable states)	Adaptation, mitigation – REDD, mitigation – general

Source: World Bank (2010a); UNDESA (2010)

customization and fine-tuning to meet local needs, including gender sensitization. The funding can be appropriately targeted to the needs of the most vulnerable and towards the household and communities sectors. Bilateral funders may also tend to have a keen understanding of local constraints; they can also utilize local consultation frameworks that are already in place in the domestic environment (Actionaid 2007).

Unlike multilateral assistance, bilateral assistance may be quite volatile in that it is short term and susceptible to political cycles in donor countries. Projects are also likely to be small-scale and isolated as opposed to being pooled and used cooperatively among groups of funders. It is however, this characteristic of small scope that may make bilateral funding attractive for community and women's groups projects.

Contradictorily to what was positively cited above, a major drawback of bilateral funding may be its close linkage with developmental assistance, which may lead to easy blending of both into the ODA stream of financing. This complicates the requirement of 'additionality'. It may also divert aid into climate change financing at a time when there is even more need for spending on specific poverty and gender equality issues. Because of the likelihood of this kind of slippage, bilateral donors, such as the Canadian government, have implemented legislation that promotes the financing of 'just, equitable and human rights based development assistance that addresses climate change adaptation' (CCIC 2009). This allows for the identification of contribution to climate change adaptation or mitigation (and allows tracking of the additionality) as distinct from current and future ODA increases (CCIC 2009).

A cursory review of the geographical distribution of bilateral climate change related mitigation aid, based on 2008–2009 commitments, in constant 2008 prices, shows that more than half of the aid is allocated to Asia, with India (14 per cent), Indonesia (9 per cent), China (7 per cent), Thailand (16 per cent) and the rest of Asia (16 per cent) accounting for approximately 62 per cent of the total flow of bilateral aid.[11]

5.3 Flexible market-based change finance mechanisms

Under the UNFCCC and, in particular, the Kyoto Protocol, Annex I and Annex B – countries with reductions obligations under the Protocol – agreed to reduce their emissions of GHGs to meet aggregate reduction of 5 per cent below 1990 emissions. Each country, or Kyoto Party, has Allowance Assigned Units (AAUs) to meet for the first compliance period, 2008–2012. The specific obligations and targets were set in the form of reductions of carbon dioxide equivalent (CO_2e). The Kyoto Protocol also sanctioned 'offsets' meaning that parties with reductions obligations are able to source these reductions from external projects, usually by supporting offset reductions projects in developing countries. This occurs under the Clean Development Mechanism (Article 12). Parties also have recourse to low-cost mitigation potentials among one another through the Joint Implementation mechanism (Article 6). The International Emission Trading (IET) provides for trading of allowances between Kyoto Parties (see Box 5.2).

5.3.1 The Clean Development Mechanism

The Clean Development Mechanism (CDM) is a market-based mechanism developed under the Kyoto Protocol which allows developed countries' institutions to implement emissions reduction projects in developing countries, for which they earn certificate of emission reduction credits which they can use or trade. Each CER that is sold to firms or governments in the developed countries (to be used to meet national emission limitation commitments under the Kyoto Protocol) is equivalent to one tonne of CO_2. Under the CDM developed countries' entities facing high emissions reduction costs at home can sponsor carbon reduction projects (such as clean energy – i.e. fuel efficient cook stoves, afforestation/reforestation and rural electrification activities) in developing countries, thereby earning tradable credits, approved units called certified emissions reduction units, CERs,[12] (World Bank 2009; UNEP 2009). Developed countries' entities who are unable to meet (or have exceeded) their emissions quota can offset their emissions by buying CDM-generated credits in the open market (Boxes 5.3 and 5.4). Hence, in practice, the CER plays a dual role of both offset and credit (UNEP 2008a). After going through a process of project design and validation CDM projects that are approved by host governments through a designated authority are registered with CDM Executive Board (Box 5.3). These projects then undergo a process of verification, certification and issuance of CERs by a DOE. All projects must be assessed and measured in order to ensure they produce 'authentic benefits' and are genuinely 'additional' activities (that is activities that would not otherwise have taken place).

The CDM has a fairly narrow range of project types including renewable energy (its largest, at 71 per cent both in terms of numbers and volume), industrial gas projects and projects that focus on methane emission or improvement in energy efficiency. The CDM has over 200 methodologies[13] that are used to set the baseline emission that is the reference for measuring emissions once projects are implemented. Initially, CDM's methodological approach focused on projects but since 2007 there has been attention to a programmatic focus wherein developers can aggregate or place under one 'umbrella' a set of project activities through the mechanism of a programme of Action (PoA), or programmatic CDM. This allows for more financing of small-scale and community-based activities and more beneficial impact of CDM at the micro and meso levels of the economy.

The vitality of the CDM is linked to targets set under the Kyoto regime; while there was certainty about those targets for the first commitment period (2008–2012), since 2012 there are no precisely set targets, and hence there is much uncertainty in the market. In addition, due to years of complaints about the complicated methodologies of the CDM as well as the high transaction costs of both making proposals and implementing projects, there have been many questions raised about the effectiveness and efficiency of the CDM in driving the reduction in GHG as well as in promoting sustainable development in developing countries. The modification of the CDM approach to include the aforementioned CDM (PoA)

> **BOX 5.2 MARKET-BASED MECHANISMS UNDER KYOTO**
>
> - **Emissions trading:** Emissions trading, as set out in Article 17 of the Kyoto Protocol, allows countries that have emission units to spare – emissions levels that are allocated to them, but not used – to sell this excess capacity to countries that are over their targets. Thus, a new commodity was created in the form of emission reductions or removals. Since carbon dioxide is the principal greenhouse gas, people speak simply of trading in carbon. Carbon is now tracked and traded like any other commodity. This is known as the 'carbon market'.
>
> - **The Clean Development Mechanism (CDM):** defined in Article 12 of the Protocol, allows a country with an emission-reduction or emission-limitation commitment under the Kyoto Protocol (Annex B Party) to implement an emission-reduction project in developing countries. Such projects can earn saleable certified emission reduction (CER) credits, each equivalent to one tonne of CO_2, which can be counted towards meeting Kyoto targets. A CDM project activity might involve, for example, a rural electrification project using solar panels or the installation of more energy-efficient boilers.
>
> - **Joint Implementation (JI):** The mechanism known as Joint Implementation, defined in Article 6 of the Kyoto Protocol, allows a country with an emission reduction or limitation commitment under the Kyoto Protocol (Annex B Party) to earn emission reduction units (ERUs) from an emission-reduction or emission removal project in another Annex B Party, each equivalent to one tonne of CO_2, which can be counted towards meeting its Kyoto target. Joint Implementation offers Parties a flexible and cost-efficient means of fulfilling a part of their Kyoto commitments, while the host Party benefits from foreign investment and technology transfer.
>
> Source: UNFCCO database

is supposed to expand the reach of CDM 'from industrial scale facilities to the household levels activities' and thereby to help to enhance the sustainable development benefits of the CDM, including poverty eradication and gender equality.

As of October 2013 the CDM has registered over 7300 projects in 89 countries. It has delivered more than 1.38 billion tonnes of emission reductions. It has also leveraged over $315 billion in capital investment (UNFCCC 2013). Between 2002–2008, the CDM reportedly leveraged over $100 billion for climate-friendly projects (GreenStream 2010). In November 2011, there were 3,583 CDM projects with proceeds from sale of emissions credit totalling about $1.5 billion in the primary

BOX 5.3 STEPS TO ISSUANCE OF CERS

1. Project design culminating in project design document (PDD)
2. Project validation
3. Host country approval (national approval via DNA)
4. Registration with CDM Executive Board
5. Implementation and monitoring (by DOE)
6. Verification/Certification/Issuance of CERs (by DOE)
7. Sale of CERs

BOX 5.4 CDM AT WORK

The CDM, which operates under the oversight of the Conference of the Parties/Meeting of the Parties (COP/MOP), is the world's largest carbon offset market. The CDM operates by accrediting projects 'in developing countries to earn certified emission reduction (CER) credits, each equivalent to one tonne of CO_2 ... These CERs can be traded and sold, and used by industrialized countries to meet a part of their emission reduction targets under the Kyoto Protocol' (UNFCCC).

The CDM operates on the basis of 'additionality' – additionality in two senses: 1) the reduction of GHG emissions below what they would have been in the absence of the project and 2) provision of new funds for investment into CDM projects rather than the diversion of development aid into such projects. Additionality raises the issue of the baseline (foundation for calculating emissions credits and/or determining if funding is additional).

The day-to-day operation of the CDM is carried out by the CDM Executive Board, which had registered over 7,828 projects, in 108 countries, by September 2014. The CDM is reported to have contributed to both reduction in global CO2 and sustainable development in developing countries. However, since 2012, there has been a decline in the number of CERs issued and a drop off in new projects registration due to the fall in carbon price and uncertainty about the second commitment period of the Kyoto Protocol.

CDM market and $18.3 billion in the secondary CDM Market. This was down from 2009 ($2.7 billion primary CDM market) and 59 per cent lower than 2008's proceeds from the sale of emission credits from over 4,000 CDM projects in the pipeline.[14] This amounted to $6.5 billion (which was also 30 per cent down from $7.4 billion in 2007[15] (World Bank 2011; New Carbon Finance 2009). The combined value of both the primary and secondary CDM markets is relatively small when compared to the hundreds of billions that flows into the broader carbon market.

As a climate change financing mechanism, the CDM is expected to benefit developing countries in at least three specific ways: (1) promote capital investment in clean, renewable and efficient energies; (2) increase the flow of environmentally sound technology transfer; and (3) potentially generate beneficial change in land uses. It is also potential source of additional cash inflow (through the sale of CERs) on the open market. It is anticipated that domestic firms in countries such as India, a country projected to garner up to 30 per cent of the value of the CDM market, may generate as much as $8.5 billion by 2012. Given the expiration of the first commitment period and the lack of implementation of a second commitment period, there is weak demand and a decline in demand for certified emission reductions in the carbon market which threatens the CDM.

5.3.2 Joint Implementation and emissions trading

Each developed country with reduction obligations has the option to also engage in emission reductions programmes with two or more other developed countries, especially 'economies in transition' with reductions commitment under the Protocol. In this case of Joint Implementation, there is a transfer from one country to the other. So unlike the CDM, which is generating additional emission reductions, under the Joint Implementation, the total level of authorized reductions do not change. The host/seller country simply issues a certificate which deducts from the buyer/investors emissions. The unit of exchange with regard to Joint Implementation activities is the emission reduction units (ERUs). In either the case of the CDM or the JI process, parties are in effect offsetting or neutralizing their carbon consumption in one place with reduction activities in another location.

The development, gender and social dimensions of the CDM and the carbon market in general will be discussed fully in Chapters 7 and 9 on mitigation finance and the carbon markets, respectively.

5.4 The carbon market and climate finance

UNFCCC-Kyoto's triplet of flexible market-based mechanisms (CDM, the JI and the IET) played a critical role in catalysing the market for carbon (or emissions) trading. These flexible mechanisms are critical pillars undergirding the carbon finance aspect of the climate change finance architecture. These mechanisms create significant pathways for the participation of governmental and inter-governmental institutions in the climate change finance, particularly, with regard to allowance-based (i.e., EU-ETS) and project-based carbon offsets (i.e., CDM and JI). The role of government and public financial mechanisms will be discussed in Chapter 8. Now we turn to highlight the operational dynamics of the growing carbon market and its potential for financing climate protection policies in developing countries.

The establishment of emission reductions targets and emissions trading (through CDM, JI and IET), which was part of the compromised attempt to secure developed countries' agreement to reductions obligations under the Kyoto Protocol, has led to the emergence of carbon as a new, internationally traded commodity. Emissions allowances and project-based emissions reduction are the key commodities around which trading has emerged in the carbon market or carbon finance. Carbon offset credits are derived from projects that are designed to reduce, avoid or sequester GHGs. Carbon allowances are created by fiat (rules) and are earned by not emitting GHGs.

Carbon financing is the broad framework that makes carbon credits a commodity. Emissions reduction credits and offsets are the key instruments that allow companies to emit a certain amount of carbon into the atmosphere. In the carbon market they are transacted in terms of various currencies, such as Assigned Allowance Units (AAU), Certified Emissions Reductions (CERs) in the CDM market, and Emission Reduction Units (ERUs) in the JI arena, defined in the different types of carbon markets (Box 5.4). Irrespective of the particular instrument at trade, each entitles the holder to emit one unit of CO_2 equivalent (Hart 2007). Thus the instruments are fungible[16] (interchangeable), with each other for meeting emissions reduction goals (Hart 2007).

The carbon market constitutes the purchasing and selling of GHG emission allowances/carbon credits and emissions offsets in order to enable countries, companies and individuals to meet their (compliance or voluntary) GHG emission obligations (UNEP 2008: 12). A primary function of the carbon market is to reduce the transactions costs associated with emissions reductions and to ensure efficiency in the distribution of emissions resources. It sets the price of carbon and provides financing for emissions reductions activities that facilitate the lowest cost transformation to low carbon economy. Its pricing mechanism is supposed to act as a signal to investors and help to guide investment decisions in support of adaptation and mitigation of climate change.[17]

As a result of the Kyoto Protocol commitments to set a maximum amount of emissions per compliance period, and then allocate allowances to regulate emitters, the European Union established the European Union Emissions Trading System (EU-ETS) in which emission permits (called EUAs) are assigned to different companies. At the end of the compliance period each emitter must surrender allowances equal to their allotted allowances. If the total emissions during a period exceed their AAUs, the emitter must purchase additional allowance. If total emissions are lower, the emitter may sell excess AAUs (Hart 2007: 167–8). Purchase and sale of assigned amount units (AAUs), CERs and RMUs – issued to countries participating in the development of domestic sinks – are transacted in the EU-ETS market. This market operates as both a spot and a futures/forward market.

The European Union's Emission Trading System, together with the Kyoto Protocol's flexible mechanisms comprise a sort of 'flexible cap and trade' system because it has both national limits on emissions as well as emissions trading (IFPRI 2008). These two constitute the two key pillars of the international emissions trading system. Together they form the compliance part of the market in which regulatory-based credits are generated. A third pillar of the international carbon market is the voluntary market comprised of retail schemes and over the counter transactions by companies and individuals who seek to mitigate their own generation of greenhouse gas emissions. The instruments or price in this market is simply 'exchange allowance' or 'exchange offset'. The Chicago Climate Exchange (CCX), in which participants have voluntary but binding commitments, was a dominant player in this market.[18] According to the World Bank, UNEP, and UNCTAD, the most popular projects include renewable energy (such as hydroelectric dams), energy efficiency projects and forestry projects. Many large corporate entities tend to be involved in transactions around energy efficiency and wind turbine projects (World Bank).

These markets have different emissions abatement costs, diversity of contracts, and are expected to improve the cost-effectiveness of climate change mitigation because they allow firms to cut emission in the most cost-effective manner possible. The EU-ETS accounted for over 70 per cent of emissions and 80 per cent of value in the global carbon market value in 2007. Credits sanctioned under CDM generated 13 per cent of the market in 2007. While the compliance market involves transactions covering all CDM and JI processes, the non-compliance or voluntary market involves transactions with entities that operate in exchanges such as the CCX, where the currency of account and trade is the Carbon Finance Instrument Contract (CFI), and retail schemes that sell emissions to individuals and companies such as Ford, Cargill, IBM and Intel who are 'seeking to offset their own carbon emissions footprint' (IFPRI 2008). These entities may include banks, credit card companies and private equities. But there are increasingly questions raised by key stakeholders as to whether the market, as it is presently evolving, can achieve these results in a manner that is timely and consistent with the global climate policy goals.

Emitting entities with Kyoto compliant or voluntary greenhouse gas emission reduction obligations are allocated carbon credits and/or carbon offsets and may undertake carbon transactions. These transactions (trade in carbon offsets or trade in emissions reductions) can occur either on the primary market where carbon is transacted for the first time) or in the secondary market (where individual or repackaged carbon is sold for the second or subsequent time). The carbon finance market provides the secondary market for liquidity, value and credit that helps to validate the carbon market. In this market companies and individuals are able to trade and speculate on the values of carbon instruments through various carbon/climate exchanges as well as the over-the-counter (electronic) market.

Without the possibility to transform carbon credit into cash flow (obtain liquidity) and protect against (longer term) risks in the futures market, the carbon market would not be very dynamic. According to the World Bank, carbon finance 'increases the bankability of projects by adding an additional revenue stream in hard currency, which reduces the risks of commercial lending or grant finance'. 'Carbon finance', the bank continues, 'provides a means of leveraging new private and public investment into projects that reduce greenhouse gas emissions, thereby mitigating climate change' (World Bank 2009).

Quite apart from the issue of how allowances are distributed, free, as in the EU-ETS, or through some auctioning mechanism or cap and trade and system that is being proposed elsewhere, there a number of challenges the market must resolve. First, carbon offset projects must meet the test of 'additionality'. Projects must demonstrate that they indeed 'create GHG savings which would otherwise not have occurred' (FOE 2009). This is the case for CDM and JI projects which must be verified by the CDM Executive Board before CERs are issued. This makes the process very time consuming and burdensome. There is also a moral hazard problem with regard to the methodologies and outcomes of verified offsets and the emerging issue of 'shoddy' offset projects that do not contribute to greenhouse gas emissions (Chan 2008). The offset test is simply difficult to overcome. The US General Accounting Office has noted that 'it is not possible to ensure that every CDM credit represents a real, measurable, and long-term reduction in emission'.

Second, the rent-seeking behaviour of speculative traders and some hedge funds may give rise to greater than normal price volatility in the carbon market. This behaviour of extracting uncompensated value from others without making any contribution to production is being increasingly argued to underlie the operations of many carbon trading funds. These funds seemingly are set up by investors simply to make a profit (Chan 2008). Chan argues that less than one-third of carbon funds have been established by companies to help them comply with carbon caps.

Third, is the issue of the 'unintended effect of fluctuation in the price of carbon on income distribution and poverty' (Ackerman 2008). Ackerman has argued that fluctuation of carbon prices impacts on related factors such as energy costs which have a disproportionate impact on those with low income. This is because the poor and vulnerable spend a larger share of their income on energy and transportation services. Therefore, variability in carbon price has a regressive effect on income distribution.

The market also has a twofold social function. It should support sustainable development and it should also benefit the poor in the developing world. Discussion on climate change has shifted away from earlier assumption of climate change as only an environmental issue. Today climate change is a broad development issue that must be tackled within the frame of poverty eradication and social justice (UNEP 2008; Gomez 2007). Thus equity and co-benefits of development have taken centre stage in the current negotiations. This is a rejection of the so-called trade-off between efficiency and equity. The new framework envisions no meaningful trade-off between the speed of the transformation to low carbon, development and social development. The two are inextricably interwoven. The solution to the climate change challenge cannot be found by further disadvantaging poor and marginalized women and men in developing countries. Development, gender equality and social justice cannot be sacrificed because of climate change. All must be careful and successfully managed together.

The old logic behind the present 'offsetting' model that dominates current climate change financing was in principle based on a double bargain. Economic and environmental efficiency would be achieved by reaching for the 'low hanging fruits' of cheaper and more efficient emissions reduction in the developing countries in direct exchange for financing for adaptation, mitigation, and the financing of the transfer of technology between developed and developing countries. The new technology and improved infrastructure would ease the transition to low carbon economy (Gomez 2007). But the industrialized countries would also undertake measures to reduce their own domestic emissions. They as well owe a climate debt to the developing countries for their historical and continuing over-use of the global atmospheric space. This debt would be covered by an enlarged pool of financing that would enable the adaptation and economic development of developing countries, including poverty eradication. Central to poverty eradication and social development are gender equality and social justices. This is the other side of the bargain that has now come unglued. It was also a significant source of tension in the lead up to both the Copenhagen (2009) and the Cancún (2010) COP negotiations. It cannot be the case, as pointed out by Gomez (2007), that the current offset sponsored neutrality granted to the industrialized countries simply acts as a kind of 'papal indulgency to expiate the sins of the rich countries for the destruction of the atmosphere'. There must be effective rebalancing and equity-based adjustments.

The carbon market has, on all accounts, been quite successful in that it has advanced steadily and is now valued at approximately $142 billion in 2010 (as compared to $144 billion in 2009). It was worth $123 billion in 2008 (World Bank 2011; New Carbon Finance 2009. It was expected that market-based mechanisms would help to foster the efficient allocation of carbon financing across sectors and countries. This has not occurred. For example, most the CDM's projects are in China, with a large continent such as Africa playing a miniscule role (IFPRI 2008). For example, Sub-Saharan Africa received only 1.4 per cent of all registered CDM projects. This situation did not occur because Africa lacked mitigation potential. In fact, IFPRI reports that the mitigation potential of Africa in forestry, agriculture and avoided deforestation are 14, 17 and 29 per cent of global total, respectively. So Africa's potential in a large range of areas such as crop land management, hydro power and waste management are underutilized.

In the 7 years since its operationalization (in 2006), the CDM has successfully leveraged the carbon finance market and is credited with producing low-cost emissions reductions. Despite its success as a market mechanism, it has not delivered on the goal of contributing to sustainable development. Many researchers raise serious questions about the nature and extent of the CDM's impact on sustainable development (both in terms of its direct and indirect benefits; Oslen 2006; Brown *et al.* 2004; Boyd 2006). Proponents of CDM argue that the CDM has been quite successful as a market-based mechanism and has in fact accomplished what it was meant to achieve (Stehr 2008; Olsen 2006; Murphy *et al.* 2008).

The allowance-based transactions market such as EU-ETS, though it operates a flexible trading regime, has not resulted in significant reductions of GHGs. It suffers from the over-allocation of allowances, volatility in prices and rising electricity costs. Project-based transactions markets, such as CDM and JI, suffer from chronic delivery challenges. It is also a well-acknowledged fact that CDM procedure and delivery is complex and unduly burdensome with high start-up costs. All of these challenges with market-based carbon financing have raised questions about over reliance on the market to solve mitigation challenges and still less to confront adaptation issues. This has prompted a recognition that the carbon market, though necessary, and its pricing of carbon, even when appropriately determined, are not enough, either for the adoption of low carbon technology or for meeting the needs of developing countries, as a whole (Ackerman 2008). Thus there are also non-economic and non-price determinants of emissions that must be considered (Stern 2006; UNDP 2007; Ackerman 2008).

With the ending of the first commitment period of the Kyoto Protocol in 2012 and the resulting uncertainty about its continuation, the carbon market crashed in 2012 with CERs, which were trading at 4 euros at the beginning of the year, selling for a mere 1 euro by the end of the year. Currently, the supply of CERs exceeds the demand for CERs, with the result of a slow down in the development of new projects. At the same time, countries outside the Eurozone and North America are developing their own carbon markets.

We now turn our attention to focus more specifically on the operation of financing instruments, funds and modalities for adaptation, mitigation and technology transfer and their impact on and contribution to gender equality and women's empowerment in their relevant range of operational scope. The next chapter addresses the challenges of adaptation financing for gender equality, while Chapter 7 focuses on the financing of mitigation and technology transfer.

Notes

1 Under the Paris Declaration 2005, developed countries agreed to scale up more aid and committed to

   (i) strengthening partner countries' national development strategies and associated operational frameworks (for example, planning, budget, and performance assessment frameworks);
   (ii) increasing alignment of aid with partner countries' priorities, systems and procedures and helping to strengthen their capacities;
   (iii) enhancing donors' and partner countries' respective accountability to their citizens and parliaments for their development policies, strategies and performance;
   (iv) eliminating duplication of efforts and rationalising donor activities to make them as cost-effective as possible;
   (v) reforming and simplifying donor policies and procedures to encourage collaborative behaviour and progressive alignment with partner countries' priorities, systems and procedures; the Busan Partnership for Effective Development Cooperation 2011 reaffirmed these and other principles;
   (vi) defining measures and standards of performance and accountability of partner country systems in public financial management, procurement, fiduciary safeguards and

environmental assessments, in line with broadly accepted good practices and their quick and widespread application.
2 IBRD: the International Bank for Reconstruction and Redevelopment (the bank), which supports middle-income countries with market value loans, is also an implementing agency under the GEF. MIGA: the Multilateral Investment Guarantee Agency insures foreign capital (lenders and foreign direct investors) in developing countries. Through MIGA the bank is able to leverage additional financing for energy projects: IFC: the International Finance Corporation is the private sector arm of the World Bank; it provides financing to the private sector. IDA: the International Development Association provides subsidized loans to low-income countries.
3 The CIF is a $6.1 billion (pledges) investment programme comprised of two trust funds, the Clean Technology Framework (CTF) and the Special Climate Change Framework (including PPCR, FIP and SREP for low-income countries), administered by the World Bank. It was established in 2008 to support developing countries' transition to low carbon, climate-resilient development by providing loans, grants, equity stakes, guarantees and other support in order to promote the development of climate-related interventions in key sectors. Technically, it is supposed to have a limited lifespan, through a sunset clause, which allows for phasing out of these funds pending the development of a multilateral financing mechanism under UNFCCC. It originated out of the collaboration (May 2008) between the UK government (Environment Transformation-International Window), the Japanese government's Cool Earth Partnership and the then proposed US Clean Technology Fund. CIF were meant to 'bridge the gap in finance between present obligations and post-2012 global climate change agreement' (US Congressional Research 2011).
4 ClimDev-Africa is a joint programme of the African Development Bank, the African Union Commission (AUC) and the United Nations Economic Commission for Africa (UNECA). The Special fund is one of three cornerstones, the other two are the Africa Climate Policy Centre (at UNECA) and the Climate Change and Desertification Unit (at the AUC). The programme essentially aims to promote science-informed and evidence-based policy, planning, and practice for sustainable climate-resilient development by creating and strengthening the knowledge (science and analysis) frameworks to support and integrate the actions required to address climate change and promote sustainable climate-resilient development across Africa.
5 According to the World Bank, the continent has some of the largest river systems in the world cutting across national borders; the Indus (China, India Pakistan), the Ganges (India and Bangladesh) and Brahmaputra (Tibet, India and Bangladesh), the Mekong (China, Burma, Laos, Thailand, Cambodia and Vietnam), and the Red River (China and Vietnam). See also Cooley *et al.* (2009). The IMO points out that the number of forced climate migrants (those forced to leave their countries temporarily or permanently) by 2050 globally could range from 25 million to 1 billion people. Unquestionably, a large proportion of these will be in Asia (Brown 2008).
6 The ADB argues that it 'uses a variety of financing instruments to support clean energy projects including grant funding for studies and project preparation, lending and risk enhancement, upfront purchase of certified emission reduction credits, and, where necessary, donor-funded grant components of investments to buy down the cost of projects' (p.34, 2011). It 'uses concessional funds to catalyze much-needed clean energy investments in the region and leverages additional resources from the private sectors' (ADB 2011).
7 Though there is no international agreement as to what should be counted (OECD 2011a), the OECD-DAC has been measuring what it identifies as 'climate change-related aid in terms of the Rio Markers on Climate Change Mitigation and Adaptation (designed based on input from aid providers with UNFCCC secretariat and other users of the system'. The Rio Markers cover about 90 per cent of aid flows from OECD and multilateral organisations (2011a). The CRS marks each aid activity that serves climate objectives as either principally or significantly targeted at mitigation or adaptation. The ranges

Bilateral and multilateral climate finance 259

presented here reflect those flows identified as a principal and significant objective. For adaptation only $3 billion is identified as 'the principal objective. The $9 billion is an upper boundary and includes about $5 billion that is both adaptation and mitigation.
8 For example, the German Development Bank (KfW) indicates their climate-related financing disbursement breakdown to be roughly 25 per cent equity, 18 per cent grants and the remaining 57 per cent as soft loans (Atteridge *et al.* 2009).
9 Mainstreaming adaptation would, for example, focus on screening projects and assessments for climate change risks. Two examples are DFID's disaster management programme in Bangladesh 2006 and, in the case of the USAID, four pilot projects: Honduras (coastal development), South Africa (water resource infrastructure), Mali (agriculture) and Thailand (rural livelihood).
10 The Paris Declaration on Aid Effectiveness (2005) is an international agreement to which over one hundred Ministers, Heads of Agencies and other Senior Officials adhered and committed their countries and organisations to continue to increase efforts in harmonisation, alignment and managing aid for results with a set of monitorable actions and indicators (OECD). The Paris Declaration is grounded in the five key principles of: 1) Ownership – developing countries set their own strategies for poverty reduction, improve their institutions and tackle corruption; 2) Alignment – donor countries align behind these objectives and use local systems; 3) Harmonisation – donor countries coordinate, simplify procedures and share information to avoid duplication; 4) Results – developing countries and donors shift focus to development results and results get measured; and 5) Mutual Accountability – donors and partners are accountable for development results.
11 The remainder was distributed across the rest of the world: Africa 20 per cent, America 7 per cent, Europe 6 per cent, Oceania and unspecified 14 per cent. In terms of sectoral distribution bilateral aid was disbursed for transport (30 per cent), energy (28 per cent), general environment protection (21 per cent), forestry 9 per cent, water 6 per cent, other 6 per cent. Source: March 2011, OECD-DAC.
12 CERs have been issued since October 2005; they are issued for 'verified emission reduction achieved since January 1, 2000'.
13 There are currently (2010–2013) about 200 methodologies – classified by scale and sectoral scope – under which developers can implement projects. Please refer to CDM Methodology Book.
14 *Forbes Magazine* 28 April 2008. In 2006 there were 1,468 CDM projects in the pipeline, equivalent to the 215 Mt CO_2 eq annual emissions reduction. Each project achieved about 85 per cent of the projected emissions reductions. (China dominates the CDM market accounting for over 53 per cent of the estimated annual emission reduction project that entered the pipeline in 2006.) The estimated revenue from the sale of CERs from CDM projects registered in that year was $1–1.5 billion per year. The estimated revenue from the sale of CERs generated by CDM projects in the pipeline was about $1 billion higher. This estimate revenue was generated from about $7 billion worth of capital invested in registered projects. The amount of capital to be invested in projects entered in the pipeline was $26.4 billion in 2006. (Fifty per cent of this capital was invested in unilateral projects by the host country proponents. That is to say that the project proponents bore all costs before the selling of CERs. India has the most unilateral projects, 33 per cent, China 20 per cent, Brazil 11 per cent and Mexico 6 per cent). The accepted minimum expected price of CERs in 2006 was $10.40–12.40 or €8–9. The actual trading price of issued CERs was $17.75.
15 This is a shift away from its rising trend since 2005, which peaked at $7.4 billion, a 50 per cent increase in value over 2006, and tripling its value from 2005 (UNECA 2009). According to New Carbon Finance (2009), this reduction in value of the CDM market was 'driven by a smaller number of carbon credits entering the UN crediting approval process in 2008 than in 2007. In 2007 new additions to the approval process included some very large industrial gas projects (HFC, N2O). 2008 saw more projects entering

the pipeline but was characterized by a higher number of smaller projects (mainly renewable energy and energy efficiency)'.
16 Like commodities, options and securities are fungible assets.
17 Key determinants of price in the carbon market includes: risk allocation factors, nature of the experience and credit worthiness of the project's sponsor, the viability of the underlying project, the nature of the contract structure (stipulations as to upfront payment and penalties for non-delivery), and the nature of host country support and cooperation etc.
18 The now defunct CCX operated as a comprehensive cap and trade programme with an offsets component in North America between 2003 and 2010. The company which was operated by Climate Exchange PLC actively traded in the emissions of six GHGs, through an allowances system that it generated, known as Carbon Financial Instruments (CFIs), to meet emission reduction commitments from October 2003 until July 2010. Due to inactivity in the US Carbon market, the firm which was acquired by Inter-continental Exchange ended mandatory trading in carbon credits (CFIs) (Wikipedia 2011). In June 2011, under the ICE banner, CCX launched the Chicago Climate Exchange Offsets Registry Program to register verified emission reductions based on a comprehensive set of established protocols (www.theice.com/ccx.jhtml accessed 30/12/2011).

6
GENDER AND THE STATE OF PLAY IN ADAPTATION FINANCE

> Of the millions of dollars spent on climate change projects in developing countries, little has been allocated in a way that will benefit women. Yet, in Africa, it is women who will be most affected by climate change.
>
> Kristin Palitza, *The Guardian*★

This chapter discusses the constraints, challenges and opportunities presented by the different sources of funds dedicated to financing adaptation activities in developing countries. It argues that adaptation funding is a critical concern for women's and men's practical and strategic gender interests.

The financing of climate protection policy affords the global community an opportunity (through a potentially massive transfer of wealth from the North to the South[1]) to deal with long-standing equity issues, including gender inequality and other forms of social injustice. These inequities and injustices are at the root of the vulnerability and over-exposure of millions of men and women in developing countries to climate change. Nowhere else in the global approach to climate change is this issue of equity more relevant and pressing than in discussions around climate change financing and specifically with regard to the financing of adaptation. Yet, at present, neither the adaptation policy framework nor its finance adequately and comprehensively addresses gender and women's empowerment issues. There is great scope for engendering and making development-friendly the UNFCCC's Cancún Adaptation Framework as the focus of global climate policy-making shifts into negotiations around the New Durban Mandate which will ostensibly define climate change policy and financing for the foreseeable future.

Within the framing of adaptation, a central equity issue that must be squarely confronted and more than adequately addressed is the underlying, pre-existing and continuing economic and social gender asymmetries and biases that predispose women in developing countries to poverty and which can exacerbate women's vulnerability to climate risks. Only when gender issues are fully integrated into adaptation analyses, risk assessments and policy frameworks will there be a significant shift in funding towards projects and programmes with an explicit gender and women's empowerment focus.

Section 6.1 highlights the over-arching gender issues that are critical to the framing of adaptation policy frameworks. Section 6.2 weighs in on the discussion around the problematisation of adaptation within the climate finance discussions and points to the implication this has for promoting gender equity and women's empowerment in the context of climate change. Section 6.3 discusses gender and the state of play in adaptation finance. Section 6.4 ends the chapter with a tentative approach to a gender empowerment climate risk analytical framework that can be used to probe issues of vulnerability and resilience, and provide elements for a gender-sensitive adaptation finance template as well as for the emerging area of loss and damage.

6.1 Critical gender issues in climate change adaptation

While decisions of the COP of the UNFCCC have endorsed the principle of 'targeting towards the most vulnerable', as noted by Garnaud (2009), there is no refinement as to who exactly these are, relative to 'countries, regions, villages or individuals'. In practice, since the context of global climate change negotiations and policy setting takes place among countries, there has been much work (though not without controversies) on how to operationalize the different vulnerabilities of different groups of countries (such as Least Developed Countries and Small Island Developing States, countries seemingly the most vulnerable to climate change[2]) to cope with climate risks and climate change physical impacts. For example, indices such as Oxfam's Adaptation Finance index and frameworks such as the Green Development Rights (by EcoEquity and the Stockholm Environmental Institute) seek to identify, quantify and measure the nature, degree and scale of rights, obligations and responsibilities with regard to burden sharing for mitigation and access to financing of climate changes (TERI 2008). But unless actions are explicitly taken to understand and address the inherent gender biases and gender discriminatory norms operating within the institutional and policy frameworks of climate change financing, the activities of women and women's groups in developing countries will remain underfunded, at best, or, at worst, will suffer from benign neglect. This will seriously adversely impact upon countries' and society's ability to respond to and to successfully mitigate climate change as well as build resilience towards such change.

The IPCC defines adaptation as 'adjustment in natural or human systems in response to actual or expected climatic stimuli or their effects, which moderates harm or exploits beneficial opportunities.[3] Beyond this technical definition, adaptation can be looked at, in practice, as a collection of coping strategies, with each strategy focused on a particular threat (CSACC 2012). These strategies are undertaken by individuals, or communities in response to climate change. Whether of the slow-onset variety, or extreme weather events, climate change impacts life-dependent sectors of the economy: agriculture and food production, forestry and fisheries, health and water supply. Apart from killing, maiming or injuring children, women and men, extreme weather events have their next most damaging effects on infrastructure, especially in developing countries, including farm lands, housing, educational and health facilities. Climate change (and environmental degradation) also raises the issue of land use, and land-use change and economic and social resource distribution among women and men and among different communities (PCFS 2012).

However, it manifests itself, in a particular time period, or, a specific location, one thing is certain: women and men have different capabilities, opportunities and access to resources to deal with the climate change's adverse impacts on the availability of food, fuel, water, homes and livelihoods. Women, as a group, relative to men, as a group, have different possibilities for recovering from frequent and intensive periods of droughts, floods and hurricanes.

Adaptation is of pressing concern in developing countries and it is of paramount importance for women's and men's lives. Adaptive activities (for example, climate-proofing agriculture and buildings, both residential and commercial; promoting water conservation and efficiency, pest and disease management; and fire management) are critical to sustainable development. The IPCC noted that adaptation actions have multiple drivers, such as economic development and poverty alleviation, and are embedded within broader development, sectoral, regional and local planning initiatives.[4] Gender equality and ensuring women's and men's equitable access and ownership of economic and social resources is also an under-recognized driver of adaptation. Addressing women's and men's poverty at the root is the ultimate determination of enhancing adaptive capacity.

Women are dynamic actors in projects and programmes, particularly related to adaptation, such as crop and livestock selection, crop shifting and soil preservation, the use of traditional water harvesting techniques and the efficient use of water. Women, as the managers of household energy and water supplies, must adapt to the changing climate conditions. Women, as farmers and major producers of food, must also adopt production and growing practices that ensure food security, in spite of climate change. These activities are all interlinked to the five key adaptation areas (agriculture, forestry and fisheries, water supply, human health, coastal zones and infrastructure) identified by the IPCC and are the areas of cost estimation exercises (UNFCCC 2007, 2008). Yet assessments of countries' vulnerability to climate change rarely focus on gender dynamics in the sectors being assessed or pay attention to how economy-wide policies provide opportunities, challenges and constraints that can help or retard women's and men's adaptation activities due to the underlying gender norms and biases in the economy.

The critical gender issues in adaptation include limited ownership of assets and other resources, limited access to technology, capacity building initiatives and finance as well as the lack of, or inadequate, attention to gender and women's issues in national and global adaptation policy frameworks. The underemphasis of adaptation and the consequent imbalance in the financing of adaptation relative to mitigation activities is also of serious concern to gender advocates as it may impose constraints on the funding of gender equality and women's empowerment interventions. Reports form climate finance monitoring and tracking organisations such as Oxfam, the World Resource Institute and the Climate Funds Update show that only 17 per cent of publicly sourced climate finance goes to adaptation. Climate Funds Update reports that the special funds tracked by it dedicate the majority (about 77 per cent) of their resources to mitigation. Elsewhere, it is highlighted that the multilateral development banks devote over 80 per cent of funding to mitigation,[5] and about 56 per cent of OECD donors' climate finance is devoted to mitigation, with about 19 per cent going to projects combining adaptation and mitigation.[6] Of the approximately $30 plus billion of fast start finance only about $6.3 billion went to fund adaptation activities, though the Cancún Decision prescribed a 'balance between adaptation and mitigation'. Globally, taking into account both private and public sectors' spending on climate projects and programmes, only about 6 per cent was devoted to adaption. This short-changing of adaptation may be shifting with the decision by the board of the GCF made at its sixth meeting (2014) to aim for a 50:50 balance between mitigation and adaptation over time. However, there are questions about just how this commitment will be implemented. This is an issue that is of course critical to women in developing countries. The Fund's operationalization of one of its gender-sensitive commitment under its governing instrument may yet contribute to making this an effective and sustained pathway for GCF financing to developing countries, both within the Fund's private sector facility as well as across its thematic and sectorial areas. But this will mean that the GCF as well as other funding entities that focus on adaptation financing must grapple with and deal with gender-based constraints, adaptation programming and finance.

Gender-based constraints to effective adaptation can best be examined from a sectoral perspective. The next section will attempt to highlight the interactions between sectoral impacts of climate change, resource flow and gender issues.

6.1.1 Gender challenges in adapting to food production and food and water security threats from climate change

Forecasts for Africa point to 75–250 million people facing water stress by 2020 (Nomura 2012). Water stress will have serious implications for agropastoralists and small farmers who rely on rainwater; it will also be accompanied by a serious decline in the land available for farming thus likely contributing to the projected decline in agricultural production using rainwater by 50 per cent by 2020 (Nomura 2012). According to IFAD, 500 million smallholder farmers provide up to 80 per cent of food to Sub-Saharan Africa and some parts of Asia, (IFAD-ASP 2012). Thus climate change and its variability pose a threat to food security. Already it is known that many small farmers are food insecure, highly exposed to climate change and rely on climate-sensitive natural resources for livelihood[7] (IFAD-ASP 2012; FAO 2012). Women make up a large share of food producers, as smallholders and as agricultural workers (more than 50 per cent in Africa and more than 44 per cent in East Asia and the Pacific (CFS 2011)). Hence climate change will negatively affect women's ability to produce food, their livelihoods, their health and their nutrition status.

Women in agriculture suffer from lack of secure tenure, intra-household inequities in labour allocation, resource access, ownership and control in the household economy.[8] This is relevant to climate change adaptation because these inequities negatively affect women's ability to undertake sustainable adaptive activities. The Committee on World Food Security (CFS) argues that insecurity of tenure results in lower investment and potential environmental degradation. Lack of secure tenure means that the necessary investment or actions that would help to nurture and preserve soils may not occur or not to the extent needed. CFS 2012, notes that in Ghana the primary investment in land is fallowing. But longer fallow means loss of land when tenure is insecure, and shorter fallow means lower yields.[9] 'Those with less political capital in a village have less tenure security and as a result leave their land fallow for a shorter period' (Goldstein and Udry 2005 cited in GFS 2012). CFS argues that 'women have less political capital, lower tenure security and [will tend to] sacrifice profits per hectare with shorter fallows' (CFS 2012).

Research by Udry et al. (1995), SOFA (2010) and CFS (2011) demonstrates that yield differences between women and male farmers would disappear if households reallocated total household inputs in an optimal way across male- and female-managed plots of land. The result would likely increase farm output by 10–20 per cent (Udry et al. 1995, cited in CFS 2011).

These research findings confirm that inequities in access to resources such as seeds, fertilizers, extension services and technology are also barriers to women's adaptive capacity in agriculture. Often extension services by-pass women outrightly or inadvertently if service providers do not recognize women's time and mobility constraints. Since dissemination of technology sometimes also occurs through extension services, women are doubly disenfranchised by gender biases, with negative impact on climate change adaptation efforts. Women will also suffer more from the impacts of extreme events which destroy their crops, especially those crops that are in storage, awaiting further processing ('Men's crops are produced with a commercial orientation and are often sold almost immediately as harvested'; CFS 2011: 5).

Women are also active, but under-recognized and under-resourced, in the fishery sector. For example, women living on the coastal areas of Ghana, who have experienced the deleterious impact of chronic changes in climate on their livelihoods in the fishing sectors, have also observed the disturbing ongoing effect of climate change phenomena in their communities. Using their informal, historical, social and cultural knowledge of the atmosphere of the coastline and the behaviour and character of fish, they have anticipated the dire consequences of the resulting shallowing of water for fish breeding (http://www.wedo.org/wp-content/uploads/ghana-case-study.pdf). In response, the women in Ghana (as well as in Senegal) have developed their own informal saving schemes and have organized themselves into cooperatives to finance boats that can venture into deeper waters for viable fish catches. In an enhanced adaptation framework, there should be emphasis on ensuring women's access to aqua-farming and other resources geared towards maintenance of fishery resources.

In farming areas groups of women have undertaken similar activities to learn and share options for mitigating the harmful effects of GHGs by embarking on 'household modernization' projects, including the purchase of butane stoves (Mensah-Kutin 2007, cited in WEDO 2008). Women, as the managers of household energy and water supplies, must adapt to the changing climate conditions.

Currently, some women undertake autonomous adaptation activities within women's groups and also within community-based adaptation processes. Women are also undertaking adaptation and mitigation responses to climate change out of their own individual and family resources.

Mitigating or countering climate change trends will therefore require gender-sensitive approaches that assure women's rights to resources, especially in order to improve agriculture in developing countries. Women also need enhanced provisioning of technologies for agricultural production as well as water conservation. Provision of these services should build on women's accumulated traditional knowledge and practices. There is also need for support of women farmers to nurture and nourish soils, undertake pest control, sustain diversification of flora and fauna and continue processes moderating microclimates in their surroundings. Women and other small farmers will also need support to relocate to more productive areas and to conserve seeds in seed banks as well as storage for protecting harvests.

These adaptation activities clearly will require a significant amount of aggregated finance to be directed towards the key adaptation sectors and to be equitably distributed to take into account and accommodate the gender-based differences in men's and women's adaptation needs. However, currently there are significant barriers to the aggregate flow of finance towards adaptation projects and programming in developing countries thus constraining the space for gender-sensitive adaptation. The next section explores the central theme in the problematization of adaptation in climate protection policy discussion and negotiations and probes the challenges this poses for engendering adaptation and its financing.

6.2 Gender and the adaptation deficit debate

As noted in Chapter 4, adaptation financing is quite controversial. There are issues of significant shortfall in adaptation with regard to the level of investment needed to adapt to climate change (the adaptation deficit) and debate over the measuring and costing of adaptation activities. Overall, there is a great mismatch between the demand for and the supply of funds for adaptation strategies. The World Bank estimates that between 2010 and 2050 approximately $70 billion to $100 billion a year will be needed to adapt to a 2 degrees Celsius warmer world. This makes average annual adaptation cost about $10 billion a year. Typical adaptation costs for many countries include protecting against storm surges and sea level rises and climate-proofing infrastructure. (Box 6.1 presents an overview of basic elements of adaptation costs.) But current funding for adaptation is about one-tenth of that. The Bank estimates that total climate change funding is about $10 billion a year with adaptation receiving about $1 billion of that amount (IPCC 2013; Atteridge *et al.* 2009; World Bank 2010). Though funding for the fast start finance was promised to be 'balanced between mitigation and adaptation', the share of funding so far pledged for adaptation is only about 19 per cent (or approximately US$4.8; Project Catalyst 2010; World Bank 2010).

Until fairly recently, there was the pervasive tendency of developed countries to treat adaptation as distinct from development. But increasingly that unhelpful firewall between adaptation and development is slowing giving way. The IPCC argue that 'although linkages between climate-change adaptation and sustainable development should appear to be self evident, it has been difficult to act on them in practice' (2007b). The World Bank recently declared that it is 'building a shared consensus that climate change is a development issue. Ackerman makes an even more stark pronouncement when he argues that 'the climate crisis is also a crisis for development' (2009: 3). Nonetheless, there remains confusion about the nature of adaptation and significant misperceptions of it, at the global level, as lacking significant global benefits and hence, as the responsibility of developing countries. Wheeler and Tiffin (2009), however, convincingly argue that '(c)limate change is an exogenous shock to the economy'. Adaptation and mitigation are the

---

BOX 6.1 BASIC ELEMENTS OF ADAPTATION COSTING

- Protecting coastal zones against rising sea levels and storm surges – $30 billion per year for a medium sea level rise, and $45 billion for more extreme sea levels.
- Adaptation of water supply and flood protection, up to $19 billion per year.
- Protection against extreme weather events, $7 billion.

Current levels of ODA $108 billion 2010

Adaptation burden (annual adaptation cost as a share of GDP, 2010–2050, per region):

- The East Asia and Pacific region: equivalent to 0.1 to 0.2 per cent of GDP.
- Sub-Saharan Africa: between 0.5 and 0.7 per cent of GDP.
- Small island states: 1 per cent of their GDP.

Source: World Bank (2010)

BOX 6.2 STRUCTURAL DIFFERENCES BETWEEN ADAPTATION AND MITIGATION POLICY AND FINANCING REGIME

Adaptation	*Mitigation*
• No adaptation regime	• A coherent mitigation and legal regime: the Kyoto Protocol with clear objectives (Article 2*) – stabilization of GHGs concentration; reduction of GHGs
• No formal definition or objectives under the convention (Burton 2004) – adaptation means many things, a range of definitions (UNDP 2008)	
	• Mitigation baseline
• No adaptation baseline; no measure; no targets; no schedules	• Clear Funding Regime: the CDM
	• Post-2005: REDD, REDD Plus
• Until 2010 no clear funding regime	

Series of growing number of ad hoc measures since 2005:

- Mainstreaming of adaptation into development
    o NAPAs/NAPs/LEG
    o *Funds*: LDCF, Adaptation Fund (under Kyoto Protocol, operationalized in 2007)
    o Bali (2007) enhanced Actions for Adaptation
    o Nairobi Framework (COP 10)/Adaptation Framework (Cop 16, 2010)
    o Adaptation Committee
    o Adaptation learning Mechanisms (ALM)

*The ultimate objective of the Convention as stated in Article 2 is the 'stabilization of greenhouse gas concentrations in the atmosphere at a level that would prevent dangerous anthropogenic interference with the climate system'.

Source: Burton (2004); UNDP (2008)

responses. There are obvious qualitative differences between the two responses. In contrast to mitigation, adaptation has elements of both public and private good (Calloway 2004, cited in Wheeler and Tiffin 2009). If adaptation is perceived as a public good, 'the market will not provide a welfare maximizing response to exogenous shock'. Hence, there is an imperative for government interventions to improve welfare (Wheeler and Tiffin 2009).

From the inception of the convention there has been a differential treatment to adaptation. While there are many structural elements built for supporting mitigation, the adaptation framework has been evolving on an ad hoc basis. (Box 6.2 compares the structural elements of both adaptation and mitigation as they have evolved during the UNFCCC processes.)

Regardless of the apparent convergence of thinking on the synergies between adaptation and development, there is the still the problem that 'there is an unacceptably large and growing adaptation deficit' (Burton 2004). There is also an extremely large adaptation financing gap relative to finance for mitigation. This financing gap has been a source of tension between developing and developed countries regarding the flow of finance and investment into adaptation strategies.[10] The fact is that climate change adaptation is an additional financial burden on developing countries and it has to be financed.

There are also tensions about the appropriate sources of funding for adaptation. Most developing country proponents argue that financing for adaptation should be primarily public finance and non-debt creating as the need for adaptation arises from the effects of global warming, a calamity to which developing countries as a group have contributed very little in terms of the present stock of GHGs most pronouncedly identified as the sources of the crisis. In this context, adaptation finance, in as much as it imposes extra costs on economic development, should be seen as compensatory finance. On the other side, there is the view that adaptation, like mitigation, should be financed through the private sector and market mechanisms including the carbon market.

There are different perspectives on this. Ackerman (2009) argues that adaptation 'cannot be addressed through carbon markets'. While it would be appropriate to expect the market and market-based mechanisms to generate anticipated results in the area of GHG emissions reduction and the transformation to low carbon economy, which are highly profitable activities, it may be unrealistic to expect them to adequately finance adaptation, which is less a profit-making enterprise. In any event, the climate change financing regime is set up to facilitate the flow of finance and investment from developed to developing countries as well as through market mechanisms such as the carbon market.

Ambiguities about the operational definition of adaptation dominate attempts to estimate adaptation costs and properly plan for it. The IPCC points out that 'while mitigation within the UNFCCC includes clearly defined objectives, measures, costs and instruments, this is not the case for adaptation' (IPCC 2007b). Part of the explanation for this is that, of course, as noted above, there are obvious developmental dimensions to adaptation, for example, the current level of housing stock and infrastructure, which are known and which are expected to be covered by traditional development financing. But there are other aspects to adaptation. These relate to climate-proofing existing structures, which implies additional costs that must be added to the costs of preparation, in anticipation of future, as yet unknown, climate events (resilience). Box 6.1 presents the core elements of adaptation costing as well as a summary of the adaptation cost burden per region. It shows high-budget adaptation elements for slow-onset events such as sea level rise including the protection of coastal zones, as well as lower costing for extreme weather events. However, predicted rise in the frequency and intensity of extreme weather events foreshadows dramatically rising costs for adaptation as well as for loss and damage. The regional adaptation burden for East Asia could consume up to 0.2 per cent of its GDP. Actions to address rising sea levels alone will cost around 5–10 per cent of Africa's GDP (Nomura 2012). Appendix 6.2 delves more deeply into the challenges of costing adaptation.

There is also the cost of dealing with the aftermath of such extreme events, such as disaster management and loss and damage. It is clearly quite difficult to unbundle these multiple and interrelated aspects of adaptation. UNFCCC (2008) estimate about $200 billion a year as the cost of damage from present extreme weather. Parry *et al.* argue that this $200 billion (though significantly under estimated) is the amount of inadequate adaptation. They (along with Wheeler and Tiffin 2009) further argue that this adaptation deficit is equivalent to a development deficit. This adaptation deficit will only grow with the trend of increased extreme weather events. Munich Re notes that there was a total of 950 natural catastrophes in 2010 (nine-tenths were weather-related events – storms and floods), making 2010 the year with the second-highest number of natural catastrophes since 1980 (Munich Re 2011).

According to UNFCCC (Table 6.1), the annual adaptation financial and investment flows needed will be $49–172 billion for the five key adaptation sectors indentified by the IPCC.[11] The UNFCCC estimates are, however, contested as significantly understating the amounts needed for adapting to climate change.[12] Table 6.2 displays at least five different cost estimates of the public sector cost of countries' response to climate change and climate variability such as extreme weather. (Appendix 6.1 explores in great detail the factors underlying the different estimations, which are relatively important in the perpetuation of gender asymmetries and vulnerability.)

Building health, water, energy and transportation infrastructure to meet the needs of populations living with high levels of lack of access to basic social development goods has been traditionally supported by overseas development assistance flows. Adding the additional task of climate-proofing these infrastructures, as required by the fact of climate change, now may mean that increasingly overseas development assistance (ODA) funds are being used for climate-related activities as there is no limitation to the use of ODA funds for climate-related activities (Michaelowa and Michaelowa 2005).[13] But as argued by Michaelowa and Michaelowa (ibid.), ODA should be used specifically for the core development and social objectives (education, health care and poverty reduction) for which it was originally intended and

TABLE 6.1 Total adaptation costs (additional annual investment needed/financial flows) by sector in US$ billion per year by 2030

Sector	Global cost (2005) US$	Developing countries cost	Developed countries cost
Agriculture	14	7	7
Water	11	2	9
Human health	5	5	Not estimated
Coastal zones	11	7	4
Infrastructure	8–130	6–88	2–41
Total	49–171	22–105	27–66

Source: UNFCCC 2007/2008

TABLE 6.2 Comparison of estimations of adaptation costs in developing countries, per annum (2010–2015 and 2030)

Source	US$ billion	Key elements/basis*
1 World Bank (World Bank) 2006	9–41	Cost of climate-proofing FDI, GDI, ODA flows
2 Stern 2006	4–37	World Bank 2006 with update and slight modification**
3 UNFCCC 2007	$27–66 (developing)/ $49–171 (globally)	World Bank 2006/for 2030
3 Oxfam 2007	>50	World Bank 2006 plus extrapolation of costs from NAPAs and NGO projects
4 UNDP 2007	86–109	World Bank 2006 plus costing of Poverty Reduction Strategy (PRS) and better disaster response

Notes: FDI: foreign direct investment, GDI: Gross domestic Investment, ODA: overseas development assistance; NAPA: National Adaptation Program; PRS: Poverty Reduction Strategy.

Source: Agrawala and Fankauser (2008), comments from Parry et al. (2009)

not relied on for indirect contributions to climate policy. While, as noted by Michaelowa and Michaelowa, electrification of a community may result in improved learning, lower drop-out rates, and in higher enrolment, it will not contribute to outcomes such as an increased supply of teachers, a reduction of repetition rates or the provision of school meals.

Diversion, substitution or reorientation of global overseas development assistance (ODA) – by developed countries to developing countries – from development objectives to climate change, in particular mitigation programmes, can have adverse implications for poverty reduction and overall development strategies. Brown et al. (2010), argue that reorientation of ODA towards climate policy objectives tends to move resources from education and health sectors in addition to the Aid for Trade policy area. They also point out that reprioritising aid from poverty and other social development objectives to climate change may result in less aid flows to Africa with aid shifting more towards South Asia, Latin America and the Middle East in an attempt to meet projected future adaptation needs. Thus any significant shift or repackaging of ODA towards prioritizing climate change mitigation activities may impact negatively on poor communities and on women's, girls', men's and boys' access to education, health care and economic opportunities.

Rapid financing and the front loading of investment is urgently needed by all developing countries in order to climate-proof development, to make the transition to a low emission economy and to minimize and offset the damages and losses from the unavoidable impacts of climate change (UNDESA 2011). The report on *Economics of Climate Change in South East Asia* argues that implementing climate change mitigation and adaption measures requires investment, technologies and know-how and financial resources. It pointed out that for Southeast Asia, many mitigation and adaptation technologies are still relatively costly to deploy (ibid.: 202). This is certainly applicable to the rest of Asia-Pacific, Africa and Latin America and the Caribbean. An African Development Bank study concludes that adaptation costs in Africa will be in the region of US$ 20–30 billion per annum over the next 10 to 20 years (African Development Bank 2011). The bank argues that this is an 'amount which is on top of existing development and poverty alleviation needs, which could be in the order of US$ 70 billion to meet the MDGs (African Development Bank 2011).

Adaptation financing presents some nuanced possibilities with regard to enhancing poverty reduction approaches. Adaptation projects financed by ODA may have fewer negative impacts on poverty reduction as adaptation measures such as increasing resource capacity, research on crop varieties and changing farming practices to enhance yields have great synergy with development, though they may not automatically improve outcomes for poor men and women without proactive efforts. Adaptation projects, such as the provisioning and ensuring of clean water can result in decreasing incidences of vector borne diseases (dengue fever or malaria) and hence will be highly beneficial to pregnant women and young children. Better availability of clean drinking water will also reduce women's and girls' work in securing fresh water for household activities. Other adaptation measures which promote better access to quality health care will also improve the health and functioning of girls and women. As noted by Michaelowa and Michaelowa (2005), in case of sickness, girls are often sent to the doctor at a later stage than boys, sometimes too late.

Top-down as well as bottom-up needs assessment and climate change impact studies from across many developing countries all point to the same realities: dealing with climate change challenges will require trillions of dollars of financing. Who will pay the costs of mitigation and adaptation in developing countries? What will be the forms and channels of finance that is to be made available? How will it be distributed, measured and accounted for?

From the point of view of gender equality, women's empowerment and social development, the debate about adaptation, its role in climate change and the development process and the potential of diversion of ODA into adaptation financing is not to be taken lightly. It is critical that these issues are resolved and the adaptation/development deficit is fully funded (to paraphrase Parry *et al.*). The need to improve infrastructure, public health and disaster preparedness, though they are non-gender equality interventions, are centrally important to women's and men's social reproduction roles and care activities. Having access to good roads and bridges that allow mobility during floods or other extreme events is a matter of life and death to women who must shepherd not just themselves but children and the elderly through times of disasters. Access to hospitals and clinics to secure medical attention for oneself and other members of the household within a reasonable distance are critical to the mental health as well as the time burden of women in poor, low- and middle-income countries.

Although there are many unresolved questions about its framing, there is no question that adaptation is a priority for almost all developing countries. In many respects it is a matter of life and death for countless millions of women, men and children in these countries. It is important that gender analysis and perspective undergirds these frameworks. The next section looks at the process of engendering adaptation frameworks.

6.3 Engendering adaptation framework and policies – NAPA, NAPs, CAF and CBA

Gender inequality is critical in the assessment of adaptive capacity. The status of women's economic and social resources and assets must be an important element in promoting climate resilience and in the determination of specific development areas and activities to be climate-proofed.

The Bali meeting (2007) as well as the Cancún meeting (2010) put a renewed focus on adaptation as a critical strategy for dealing with climate change in developing countries. The high point of this is the Cancún Adaptation Framework and the introduction of National Adaptation Programmes. Though analyses of the fast start finance initiative up to the 2011 midpoint still show imbalance between funding for adaptation relative to mitigation, nonetheless the present conjuncture which is focused on discussions around long-term finance up to 2020 and beyond, presents strategic opportunities that are being utilized to ensure that financing mechanisms provide sufficient funding for adaptation. The newest financial mechanism under the Convention, the GCF's governance document and the Durban Outcome, which operationalized the Fund, both have significant gender equity provisions. Therefore the post-2015 period is a critical time for ensuring equitable flow of funds to women's and men's activities in communities, taking account of their different abilities to respond to the opportunities, challenges and constraints posed by climate change.

6.3.1 The Global Adaptation Policy framework and gender

Since the Bali meeting (2007), adaptation has now fully emerged to join mitigation as a high priority in global climate change policy. Cancún (2010) identified adaptation as one of the five key building blocks (along with shared vision, mitigation, adaptation, finance and technology) of a future climate change agreement (UNFCCC 2010:7).

Currently adaptation is increasingly being structured under the Cancún Adaptation Framework which envelopes the previous ad hoc frameworks that support adaptation in the global climate regime. These include:

- *The Nairobi Work Program*: This is a 5 year (2005–2010) programme, focused on assisting countries to better understand impacts, vulnerability and adaptation to climate change to respond to climate change on a sound scientific, technical and socio-economic basis, taking into account current and future climate change and variability. It provides a structured framework for knowledge sharing and collaboration among Parties and organizations (UNFCCC 2010:4).
- *The Bali Plan of Action*: This emphasized 'enhanced action on adaptation', which includes consideration of risk management and risk reduction strategies as well as disaster reduction strategies for developing countries most vulnerable to climate change.

The Buenos Aires work programme on adaptation and response measures focused on regional adaptation priorities through the convening of national workshops on adaptation in the UNFCCC geographic regions to facilitate information exchange and integrated assessments within and between regions, and to help identify specific adaptation needs and concerns.

Arguing that '(a)daptation must be addressed with the same priority as mitigation and requires appropriate institutional arrangements to enhance adaptation action and support' the Cancún meeting called for enhanced action on adaptation. It hence established the Adaptation Committee to 'promote the implementation of enhanced action on adaptation in a coherent manner under the Convention', a work programme for loss and damage and a process for the implementation of national adaptation plans for medium and long-term adaptation needs and the development and implementation of strategies to meet those needs. (NAPs, which focus on the medium and long term, are distinct from NAPAs which focus on urgent and immediate adaptation needs.) The Durban Meeting agreed the modalities for the operationalization of these institutional features of the Cancún Adaptation Framework.

Building on the outputs of the national adaptation programme of action (NAPA) and their sectoral prioritization, under the Cancún Adaptation Framework LDCs as well as other developing countries are now in the process of formulating national adaptation plans (NAPs) focused on 'identifying medium and long-term adaptation needs and developing and implementing strategies and programmes to address those needs'.[14] The focus of both NAPAs (which continue to pinpoint urgent and immediate adaptation actions) and NAPs (which centre attention on long-term adaptation issues) is to build adaptive capacity and resilience as well as to 'climate-proof' development against climate change.

Recently, gender has been included as one of the 10 guiding elements to be emphasized in NAPAs/NAPs.[15] Annex II of a November 2011 Technical Paper on NAP produced by the Subsidiary Body on Implementation of the UNFCCC focused on the integration of gender-related considerations in identifying and implementing medium-and long-term adaptation activities. The Annex which cites numerous reports from the UN Commission on the Status of Women and the United Nations Entity for Gender equality and the Empowerment of Women (UN Women) argues that:

> Integrating a gender perspective into medium- and long-term adaptation is therefore necessary to ensure that adaptation activities undertaken by the least developed countries (LDCs) will not exacerbate gender inequalities and will ensure women's equal participation in the decision-making and implementation phases of adaptation. It will lead to better adaptation and more resilient communities.

Appendix 6.1 of this book, presents an overview of the integration of gender in the negotiations framework and agreements on the Cancún Adaptation Framework, the NAPs and the Durban Outcome. The Annex II of SBI's 2011 Technical Paper on NAP also includes a listing of the elements that should be central to both NAPAs and NAPs programming. (These are reproduced in Boxes 6.3 and 6.4.)

6.4 Gender and the state of play with adaptation finance instruments and mechanisms

Climate change finance presents new opportunities, challenges and constraints for women and men in developing countries. This is consistent with the IPCC's argument that climate change can create economic benefits as economic structures are redesigned to meet climate challenges. The opportunities at this point in time have not been greatly explored and depend to a large extent on the positive spillover from the presumed wider economic benefits associated with potentially increasing streams of financial and investment flows into adaptation and mitigation activities. This is likely to occur, it is argued, primarily through expenditure on infrastructure, equipment and buildings and on the deployment of clean, renewable and efficient energy technologies.

Finance is also needed for the systematization of traditional and emerging indigenous adaptation and mitigation technologies within and across coastal, rural and peri-urban areas of developing countries. Thus women's groups will require

> **BOX 6.3 STRATEGIC ELEMENTS FOR GENDER MAINSTREAMING FOR THE ENHANCEMENT OF CANCÚN ADAPTATION FRAMEWORK**
>
> 1 *Further identification of women-specific climate change vulnerabilities*:
>
>   (a) cross-regional comparisons in terms of six specific areas: nutrient capacity and women's health; women's domestic burden and increased hardships; women's reduced ability to provide self-protection; religious and social dogma concerns; lack of education; and unequal power relations;
>   (b) gender audits of vulnerability and assessment methodologies; and
>   (c) programmes and projects to decrease women and girls' vulnerability to climate change effects.
>
> 2 *Gender, land-use and forestry (deforestation, afforestation and reforestation)*: This should be contextualized with awareness of traditional knowledge and women's challenges and constraints concerning intellectual property rights with regard to land-use and forestry management know-how.
>
> 3 *Gender climate change and sectoral issues*: agriculture (food security, adaptation and traditional knowledge/intellectual property); water, health, sanitation and livelihood; clean energy, energy efficiency and renewable energy – all with an awareness of the issues of traditional knowledge and women's challenges and constraints around women and intellectual property rights. Some critical areas that needed to be further developed include:
>
>   (a) gender and climate-induced human displacement, migration and conflict;
>   (b) gender, climate change and the household and informal economies;
>   (c) gender and climate change economics;
>   (d) gender, climate change and trade;
>   (e) gender climate change and domestic investments and FDI.

access to growing streams of climate change financing at global, regional and national levels. But, given the complex nature of the instruments of the various climate change funds and their complicated applications processes, which are discouraging to even many developing countries governmental institutions, women's and community groups may have difficulties accessing such funds.

In the first instance, these funds are oriented towards capital-intensive and large-scale technology projects, some of which (increasingly with a number of CDM and REDD projects) are now proving to be less effective and less efficient in generating anticipated greenhouse gas emissions reductions. These projects also

BOX 6.4 USEFUL STEPS FOR INTEGRATING GENDER-RELATED CONSIDERATIONS INTO THE MEDIUM- AND LONG-TERM ADAPTATION PROCESS

- Understanding the disproportionate burden of climate change on women and the most vulnerable groups and communities;
- Undertaking gender-based vulnerability assessments and integrating gender perspectives into adaptation and risk assessments;
- Publishing and widely disseminating sex-disaggregated data and gender-differentiated information, and the outcomes of the assessments;
- Consulting women, women's groups and the most vulnerable in the planning of medium- and long-term adaptation, and ensuring that representatives from these groups are included in decision-making processes, including by integrating targets for participation;
- Ensuring that gender-related considerations are taken into account in capacity-building, education and training activities;
- Disseminating and utilizing lessons learned and best practices in the mainstreaming of gender-related considerations, including from the national adaptation programme of action (NAPA) process;
- Ensuring synergy between national adaptation planning and implementation and relevant international institutional arrangements that have a focus on gender;
- Ensuring that the specific departments in charge of gender- and women-related affairs are consulted in the preparation and implementation of adaptation activities;
- Ensuring that reporting guidelines include guidelines for reporting on gender- and vulnerability-related considerations;
- Including criteria for evaluating the integration of gender-related considerations in the monitoring and evaluation processes.

Source: Annex II: Gender-related considerations in medium- and long-term adaptation, UNFCCC/TP/2011/7

do not adequately support many of the adaptation strategies which are important for men and women's lives and livelihoods.

In the second instance, the high upfront costs and intensive application processes of climate change financing mechanisms, is both a disincentive and acts as a barrier to entry for women's and community groups to access such funds. Therefore, under the current climate change financing regime, women, as a group, relative to men, would seem to not have easy and sufficient access to funds to cover weather-related losses, or to adaptation and mitigation technologies services.

In general most climate change funds and instruments discussed in the preceding two chapters, with a few exceptions, such as the Small Grants Program and the Community Development Carbon Fund, are designed for large-scale, well-capitalized projects focused on the reduction of GHGs and the enhancement of skills. Large-scale programmes tend to have access to or employ many different types of professionals who are versed in climate science, grant writing and business administration fundamentals necessary for implementing and running such projects. They are therefore able to navigate the pathways of applying for, registering and undertaking the monitoring and evaluation processes that are inherently part of funding processes. It is difficult for women's groups, who are generally more involved with smaller-scale activities with few if any ancillary staff, to pursue time-consuming applications processes and implement the burdensome requirements that tend to accompany the application processes of such funds. So ultimately, the delivery mechanisms of climate change financing may not be very conducive to the existing level and scope of operations of women-run entities either in the farming, business or household sector.

The GEF small grants programme as discussed in the preceding chapter is focused on supporting sustainable livelihoods and, as such, gender, being a core goal of sustainable development, is emphasized. Gender is one of the main criteria underlying consideration of the approval of grants in the SGP. The roles of women and men are also central to the initial stages of the project conception, approval and implementation. Overall the SGP documents the contribution of women to projects. In order to build women's capacity to access climate finance, the SGP also conducts 'proposal writing workshops' as well as 'accepts project proposals in local languages and in oral format' thus increasing the opportunity for women to access climate finance. A gender specialist is required to be included in the voluntary national steering committee that makes decisions on grants.

Gender inequalities in socio-economic, political and cultural norms drive adaptation. But gender dynamics were understated and under-recognized within NAPAs. However some gender aspects are beginning to be included in the emerging area of NAPs. As the next frontier in climate policy is pursued in 2015 and beyond, there is much work to be done elaborating the vulnerability and risks that men and women face in developing countries and elaborating policy frameworks and instruments that more fully integrate gender and women' empowerment perspectives. In this context, there will be need for carefully calibrations between adaptation and mitigation policies and outcomes. The two can be seen as the two blades of a pair of scissors working in tandem to prevent and reverse drastic climate change events.

Adaptation financing instruments include: (1) a variety of market-based instruments such as those for moderating risks (insurance-index and catastrophe bonds; and foreign direct investment); (2) non-market (or fund-based) mechanisms financed through fiscally generated revenues which are passed through multilateral financing entities approved under the convention, as well as climate-related overseas development assistance (ODA) from bilateral donors through specific programmatic frameworks; (3) grants and levies, contributions (primarily aid-based funds); and (4) domestic national fiscal incentives. Most current multilateral funding instruments for adaptation, with the exception of the Adaptation Fund, are expected to consist of ODA-type bilateral donations that are primarily grants or concessional flows. Both these and national funds are traditionally generated from fiscal sources such as taxes and customs duties – and are discretionary in nature.

Since 2010, the current operating entity of the Financial Mechanism of the UNFCCC Convention, the GEF and its managed financing instruments have begun to explicitly include gender analysis and gender equity considerations within the structure of their modalities and mandates.[16] The GEF itself is still at a nascent stage of engendering its own policies and processes. Its gender mainstreaming attempt is being fostered by: (1) a 2009 self-assessment, *Mainstreaming Gender at the GEF*, which showed that only 68 out of 172 of its projects had examples of gender mainstreaming; (2) a 2009 *Fourth Overall Performance Study*, which also focused on gender-mainstreaming evaluation of the GEF; and (3) an *Updated Results-Based Management Framework*, undergirding both the LDCF and the SCCF, which now have at least two indicators disaggregated by sex (UNDP/GGCA 2011).[17] In practice, however, the World Bank and UNDP, the two key agencies of the GEF in implementing funds to LDCF and SCCF, are the conduits relied on for gender mainstreamining. As noted by UNDP/GGCA, the GEF's new endorsement templates and review criteria for the LDCF and SCCF, which place a strong emphasis on gender equality issues, reflect progress towards incorporating a gender perspective throughout the two funds (2011). Though women may have undoubtedly benefited from the two funds, it is not clear what proportion of funding disbursements have significantly impacted either targeted or non-targeted gender equality interventions.

6.4.1 The Least Developed Country Fund (LDCF) and gender

As of October 2011, the LDCF has received pledges of $460 million for adaptation grants (GEF Progress Report 2013). Thus far there are thirty-three 'CEO endorsed/ approved' projects that are moving to the implementation stage. There has not been a thematic approach to LDCF funding (GEF Progress Report 2011). But that does not preclude gender equality interventions from becoming a priority area. This is especially so in light of the fact that the UNFCCC COP Decision 28/CP.7 'identifies gender equality as a guiding principle for NAPAs' and the Least Developed Countries Expert Group (LEG) annotated guidelines on NAPA preparation stating that 'women need to be recognized as key stakeholders in consultations and decision-making' (COWI and IIED 2009).

As noted by COWI and IIED (2009), 'By design, NAPAs focused on the grassroots level participation of communities and societies, using a gender-sensitive approach . . . [which opens] a window for the inclusion of women and men equally in the identification and implementation of urgent and immediate adaptation activities' (UNFCCC/TP/2011/7).

The LDCFs prioritize a broad range of sectors that support livelihood projects and programmes which are crucial to women's social well-being. It is therefore essential to identify the key issues that are critical for women's economic and social empowerment in order to improve the understanding of NAPA official decision-makers with regard to how LDCF supported adaptation actions can best address gender equality issues and women as agents of adaptation (COWI and IIED 2009). Gender equality and women's empowerment issues are slowly being integrated into the NAPAs; Biagini 2014 shows that as of April 2009, 38 countries mentioned gender inequality as an issue in their NAPAs. These groups of countries include Bangladesh, Niger and Burkina Faso. Bangladesh, which signalled gender as a vulnerability factor related to livelihood, lists gender equality as an activity selection criteria. In its NAPA, Bangladesh wrote that 'Poverty reduction and security of livelihoods with a gender perspective has been ranked as the most important set of criteria for prioritization of adaptation needs' (p.23). It proposed 15 projects that include women among the beneficiaries.

Niger in its NAPA recognizes that women are more vulnerable as a result of poverty and proposed three livestock/crop farming projects in which women are beneficiaries. Women were also reported to have been consulted in the preparation of the NAPAs. Women were also involved in project activities in management committees for cereal banks, fodder banks and distribution of resistant crops. Burkina Faso's LDCF project, according to Biagini (2014), was designed with gender considerations from inception and involved the full participation of women in the NAPA steering committee. In addition, women were also included in training for climate-resilient technologies.

Currently the LDCF result-based management includes the consideration of socioeconomic and gender issues, and it is anticipated that over time the goal of gender equity will become part of the project design requirements as well as part of the project review criteria for both the LDCF and the SCCF.

Increasingly, gender issues and women's empowerment concerns are being integrated into the three pillars of LDCF/SCCF adaptation strategy: (1) increasing adaptive capacity, (2) decreasing vulnerability and (3) promoting technology transfer. Under the rubric of increasing adaptive capacity three outcome areas have four specific gender dimensions including 'vulnerability and risk perception index, disaggregated by gender', 'capacity perception index, disaggregated by gender', 'targeted population awareness of predictive adverse impacts of climate change and appropriate responses, disaggregated by gender' and 'per cent of population affirming ownership of adaptation processes, disaggregated by gender'.

With regard to the adaptation and technology transfer pillar, which seeks to promote the transfer and adoption of adaptation technology, there are similarly two gender-focused indicators: 'per cent of targeted groups adopting transferred adaptation technologies by type, disaggregated by gender' and 'strengthened capacity to transfer appropriate adaptation technologies, disaggregated by gender'. As can be seen, this is at a very rudimentary level of gender disaggregation without analysis as to the constraints and challenges around men and women's access to the transfer and development of technology and how to mitigate these issues so as to promote more uptake of technology by women.

6.4.2 The Special Climate Change Fund (SCCF) and gender

The Special Climate Change Fund is a voluntary fund that relies on donor contributions. As of October 2011, the SCCF made a funding decision to expend $128.6 million on projects and project preparations (GEF 2011). Under its adaptation programme, it has approved 39 projects with 17 in implementation phase and two completed projects (GEF 2011; SCCF website 2011). Like the LDCF, the Special Climate Change Fund (SCCF) targets projects with 'clear development objectives', such as ensuring food security, access to water for drinking and irrigation, disaster prevention, and control of diseases spreading because of climate change, such as malaria and dengue fever (GEF 2009). Unlike, the LDCF which addresses immediate and urgent adaptation needs of the vulnerable countries, the SCCF is more long-term and comprehensive in scope and focus. It, hence, covers adaptation, mitigation as well as technology transfer. But SCCF projects must be activities that are in response to global warming (i.e., 'adaptation increment'). COP9 programmatic guidelines for the SCCF stipulates that activities to be funded should be country-driven, cost-effective and integrated into national sustainable development and poverty-reduction strategies (Decision 5/CP.9(b)).[18] These stipulations ostensibly provide strong grounding for the consideration of gender-sensitive frames. In addition, paragraph 41 of the programmatic guidelines, recognizes that 'climate change impacts fall most heavily on those least able to respond, and often on those that contributed very little to its causes'.

Only two of the three vehicles for project development and implementation that the SCCF framework utilizes in its decision-making process are on track to significantly integrate gender and priorities and concerns, the NAPAs and the national communications. Under its technology transfer programme, SCCF-B, there are three approved projects totalling $14.335 million. All available SCCF-B funding has been programmed (SCCF website 2011). To-date its Technology Needs Assessment (TNA) has not been gender sensitized.

In the case of both the SCCF and the LDCF, it is critically important to ensure that targeted gender equality priorities and concerns are integrated into the design and implementation of these funds. For example, with regard to food security, there must be a focus on ensuring that women farmers have access to extension training and programmes and have the necessary support for climate-proofing their farms and other livelihood activities. This would include ensuring access to climate-proofed feeder roads, storage facilities and transportation for their crops and equipment.

Great care must also be taken to ensure that food security does not translate into exposing domestic markets to cheaper imports simply by measures such as simply reducing tariffs. Instead, concentrated efforts should be made to ensure domestic and local food production, storage and stock-piling through gender-sensitive efforts to increase the productivity of female and male small-farmers. Such actions should focus on building on their traditional knowledge to increase yields and promote the resilience of domestic agriculture to climate-related events.

However, any advocacy strategy must be mindful that the long-term sustainability of the LDCF and the SCCF are uncertain given the rising numbers of alternative adaptation instruments that are being created both inside and outside the framework of the Convention. Many of these instruments, such as the Adaptation Fund, are also sensitive to the needs of Least Developed Countries (COWI and IIED 2009). What will likely have a long life-span are the NAPAs and NAPs which have seemingly become important to the climate policy of LDCs. Hence more proactive attention should focus on engendering the NAPAs (as well as the NAPs and national communications processes). Though NAPAs are not a financing mechanism, per se, they are an important adaptation-related financing vehicle which indicates the nature and scope of funding the LDCs would need regardless of the source of funding.

6.4.3 The Adaptation Fund and gender

The Adaptation Fund, as noted in Chapter 4, is an autonomous ('self-standing'), direct access fund established under the Kyoto Protocol designed to finance concrete adaptation projects and programmes[19] based on the 'the needs, views and priorities of developing countries'. It is funded through a 2 per cent share of the proceeds of all Certified Emission Reductions issued under the Clean Development Mechanism projects. The Fund has built into its operational structure the financing of small projects and programmes up to $1 million as well as regular projects and programmes in excess of $1 million.

The Adaptation Fund, though it emphasizes funding for projects and programmes that take into account development strategies and poverty-reduction strategies, originally did not specifically reference gender as a cross-cutting variable. Presumably, the extent to which national development and poverty reduction strategies are gender sensitive will influence the nature and extent of the flow of funds towards gender equality interventions, but this cannot simply be assumed. However, its 2011 Operational Policies and Guidelines flag the 'needs of the most vulnerable communities' as an aspect of its project criteria review (Decision B.14–15/1 2011). In expanding on the definition of vulnerable communities, women are included in the category of the vulnerable and there is a requirement for sex-disaggregated data for some indicators (GEF 2011b; UNDP/GGCA 2011).

Given the nature of this fund, it is very important that more comprehensive gender-sensitive criteria and guidelines are integrated into the Adaptation Fund itself and that gender perspectives also inform the Fund's resource allocation decision-making. This will entail elaborating and engendering the vague resource allocation guidelines of Paragraph 8 of the strategic priorities, which currently read: 'In developing projects and programmes, special attention shall be given by eligible

Parties to the particular needs of the most vulnerable communities.' Gender criteria and guidelines also must be integrated into the Adaptation Fund Project Review Criteria, in particular under item 2 (Project eligibility criteria). A set of gender-sensitive questions should be included in the Criteria, such as: 'Does the project provide economic, social and environmental benefits? And, 'has special attention been given to the particular needs of the most vulnerable communities?'

6.5 Gender empowerment and climate risk assessment

GEMCRA framework presented in Chapter 3 of this book is useful for guiding and prioritizing policy actions for identifying and designing adaptive actions. The seven risk assessment categories of the GEMCRA frameworks show that it matters what sectors are fully or partially included or excluded in the estimation of the cost of adaptation. Underestimation of adaptation can impact the flow of funding for priorities that are important for the financing of gender equality interventions.

For example, under the 'social and personal security risk category' it is clear that in the area of human health the underlying measures utilized in the UNFCCC adaptation costing estimations, which currently are linked to child health care (in terms of 'climate-change-related cases of diarrhoeal disease, malnutrition and malaria in 2030)', are inadequately assessed (Parry et al. 2005). Apart from the fact that as discussed by Edejer et al. (2005) and Ebi (2008) child-related factors accounted for in the UNFCCC cost estimates are greatly underestimated,[20] the focus on child health alone excludes other areas relevant for women's practical gender needs and thus significantly underestimates the health costs of adaptation. It does not explicitly factor in the costs of women's health.

As was noted in earlier chapters of this report, climate change increases vulnerability of both women and children, and women are high users of heath care systems. Natural disasters pose particular risks for pregnant, post-partum and lactating women (UNFPA 2010; WHO 2011). As a result of these and many other factors which are discussed in great detail in Kovats (2009) (and summarized in Box 6.5), there are significant underestimation biases in the assessment of health costs for adaptation purposes.

The recent 2011 tropical storm in the Southern Philippines destroyed over 22 village health centres and impacted 12,000 pregnant and lactating women. Maternal deaths at 355,000 per year (99 per cent of the global total) are still high in developing countries, particularly LDC.[21] The horrific situation of maternal deaths should indicate a need for some sensitivity analysis with regard to its drivers and their inclusion in costing exercises. Currently, human health costs in estimation sets also do not include key health adaptation cost elements such as the cost of improving or modifying health protection systems (i.e., infrastructure, training new health care workers, increasing laboratory capacity or the cost of heat wave warming systems) (Parry et al. 2009). Including these issues as part of health costs in adaptation estimation would undoubtedly raise the estimated costs of the health

284 Gender and state of play in adaptation finance

BOX 6.5 ELEMENTS OF HEALTH ADAPTATION COSTS

According to Kovats, health adaptation costs include:

- costs of improving or modifying health protection systems to address climate change, for example expanding health or vector surveillance systems – this includes the costs associated with building new infrastructure, training new health care workers, and increasing laboratory and other capacities;
- costs of introducing novel health interventions (e.g. heat-wave warning systems);
- additional costs for meeting environmental and health regulatory standards (e.g. air quality standards, water quality standards);
- costs of improving or modifying health systems infrastructure, for example adapting hospitals to hotter summers;
- occupational health costs, for example measures to prevent the adverse impacts of increased heat load on the health and productivity of workers;
- costs of health research on reducing the impact of climate change, for example evaluation studies;
- costs of preventing the additional cases of disease due to climate change as estimated by scenario-driven impact models (UNFCCC's estimation is based on this set of variables).

Source: Kovats (2009)

---

sector and may promote more financing for adaptation expenditures and activities that improve women's and men's well-being, lives and livelihoods. In addition, access to public outreach and early warning saves lives of women, men and children and prevents illness.

The case of Fiji, where as a result of the activation of early warning system, the lives of many children may have been saved, is very illustrative of this point. The IPCC (2007) highlighted the importance and relevance of seasonal forecasts to increasing resilience to climate variability, including to weather disasters. The IPCC presents the following example:

> The Pacific ENSO Application Center (PEAC) alerted governments when a strong El Nino was developing in 1997/1998, that severe droughts could occur, and that some islands were at unusually high risk of tropical cyclones (Hamnett, 1998). The interventions launched, such as public education and awareness campaigns, were effective in reducing the risk of diarrhoeal and vector-borne diseases. For example, despite the water shortage in Pohnpei, fewer children were admitted to hospital with severe diarrhoeal disease than

normal because of frequent public-health messages about water safety. However, the interventions did not eliminate all negative health impacts, such as micronutrient deficiencies in pregnant women in Fiji.

(IPCC 2007: 416)

Adaptation funding is also needed to provide gender equality interventions and to promote women's empowerment. This is a two-way interchange. Gender equality and women's empowerment can enable better adaptive capacity. Better awareness and capacity also enable more effective and sustainable support for mitigation. So from the point of view of gender, poverty eradication and human development, adaptation must promote development, and development must promote adaptation. In the first case, adaptation promotes development by enhancing and protecting current achievements. It also establishes pillars for anticipating and responding to future climate events. In the second case, development promotes adaptation when it develops resilience to climate change, or when 'climate-change adaptation is mainstream(ed) within development activity' (Agarwala 2005, cited in IPCC 2007b). Ultimately, as argued by Ackerman, 'economic development, if carefully managed, can increase resilience, promote adaptation, and reduce climate impacts' (2009: 17).

At this particular historical juncture, adaptation and development are the two sides of the same coin. In the middle, the stuff holding the sides together, are in

BOX 6.6 SOME CRITICAL QUESTIONS TO BE POSED FOR ENGENDERING ADAPTATION FINANCE FLOWS

What kinds of adaptation readiness or capacity-building programmes and projects are needed for women-owned and operated businesses as distinct from men-owned businesses?

Who are the normal targets of adaptation and mitigation capacity building and technical assistance? How are they integrated in these programmes and projects?

To what extent are the needs, priorities and concerns of micro, SMEs and women entrepreneurs taken into account into the design, planning and implementation of adaptation and mitigation projects and programmes as well as access to available technology and know-how?

Answering the above questions will point to what kinds of supportive policies at national and sector levels are important for creating and enabling conditions for women and men to adapt to climate change and to deal with loss and damage due to extreme weather events. This should include mechanisms to promote more gender-sensitive expenditure allocations for skill development and skill upgrading, day care and family assistance.

fact the labour power, capability, health and wellbeing of children, men and women. Adaptation measures and its financing will therefore need to integrate gender equality, women's empowerment concerns, poverty reduction and human development strategies in order to ensure sustainable development and climate protection.

Notes

* Women excluded from climate change projects in Africa, UN experts warn. Kristin Palitza, *The Guardian*, 28 June 2011. See www.theguardian.com/environment/2011/jun/28/climate-change-environmental-sustainability.
1 If the South is fully compensated for their required mitigation up to 2050 (with global targets of 50 per cent) this could be as much as $400 billion per year in 2030 or $3 trillion in 2030, not including adaptation funding (Jacoby et al. 2008). This is also likely if ODA flows meet their 0.7 per cent target plus the addition of new climate-related ODA flows.
2 Many SIDs, especially those in the Pacific, face existential and sovereign crises as their geographic space could ultimately be inundated with sea water. LDCs are poor in terms of modern capital and investment flows. But most LDCs are in Africa and a recent study on vulnerability shows Africa to be at particular risk and likely the World's most vulnerable region, (Maplecroft's Climate Change Vulnerability Index, CCVI, 2012 – used by USAID and others.) The CCVI assesses each country's vulnerability in terms of three factors: *exposure* (i.e., temperature, rainfall and susceptibility to damage caused by cyclones, typhoons, flooding, sea level rise etc.), *sensitivity* (calculation of severity in the event of damage based on population pressure, infrastructure development, state of conflict, agricultural dependence etc.) and *adaptive capacity* (calculation of capacity to absorb and recover from damage). Exposure, sensitivity and adaptive capacity had weights of 50 per cent, 25 per cent, 25 per cent, respectively. According to CCVI, 13 African countries are in the top 20 of highly vulnerable countries and regions: Zimbabwe (3), Sierra Leone (4), Madagascar (5), Democratic Republic of the Congo (8), Malawi (9), Ethiopia (11), Guinea-Bissau (12), Swaziland (14), Uganda (15), Lesotho (16), Gambia (17), South Sudan (18), Mozambique (7); 5 Asian countries: Bangladesh (2), Cambodia (6), Philippines (10), Nepal (13) and Myanmar (20); and 2 Latin American countries: Haiti (1) and Guatemala (19). Many coastal cities in Asia and Africa are vulnerable to rising sea levels and floods.
3 IPCC Glossary. It also goes on to specify various types of adaptation can be distinguished, including anticipatory (proactive – before climate change impacts has been observed), autonomous (spontaneous – response to climatic stimuli that is triggered by ecological changes in natural systems and by market or welfare changes in human systems) and planned adaptation (the result of a deliberate policy decision, based on an awareness that conditions have changed or are about to change and that action is required to return to, maintain, or achieve a desired state).
4 Parry et al. (2007).
5 Joint MDB Report on Mitigation Finance 2011 and Joint MDB report on Adaptation finance.
6 Data for 2011 based on using Rio Marker analysis for Adaptation and Mitigation.
7 Small-scale farmers, fishers and foresters are 75 per cent of the world's one billion hungry (FAO 2012).
8 Women are less than 20 per cent of landholders in all developing countries, about 15 per cent in sub-Saharan Africa, a bit over 10 per cent in South and South East Asia, about 5 per cent in North Africa and West Asia and less that 5 per cent in Oceania (SOFA 2011, cited in CFS 2011). Deere and Doss (2006) indicate that women are just 5 per cent of registered landowners in Kenya, 15.5 per cent in Nicaragua, 22.4 per cent in the Mexican ejidos and 10 per cent of households in Ghana.

9 The argument is that fallowing land is a delicate balance, with longer fallows potentially leading to loss of land when tenure is insecure but shorter fallows leading to lower yields. Goldstein and Udry (2005) demonstrate that those with less political capital in a village have less tenure security and as a result leave their land fallow for shorter periods. In addition, within households, profits per hectare of a maize-cassava intercrop from similar plots vary according to individual and length of fallow, CFS 2011, p.4.

10 Ackerman 2009 argues that 'adaptation cannot be entirely local, since it often involves national-scale political and economic changes designed to reduce poverty and vulnerability to climate damages. In the agricultural sector, which will be hard hit by climate change, adaptation is not only a matter of farm-level decisions, but increasingly depends on national governments, agri-business strategies, and trade policies' (2009: 8).

11 The range is so large due to the role of infrastructure which can account for three-quarters of the costs of adaptation, especially in developing countries.

12 Overall UNFCCC underestimates adaptation costs by a level of between 2 and 3 for included sectors. The UNFCC estimates are the equivalent of financing 2–3 Olympics; it is only double the current flow of ODA.

13 This assessment by Michaelowa and Michaelowa (2005) is based on their reading of the OECD DAC 2002 use of 'additionality which only excluded CDM activities which governments use directly to purchase CERs', Dutschke and Michaelowa 2006, p.9.

14 Under the Cancún Adaptation Framework, a process was established to enable least developed country Parties to formulate and implement national adaptation plans. This process will build upon their experience in preparing and implementing national adaptation programmes of action, as a means of identifying medium- and long-term adaptation needs and developing and implementing strategies and programmes to address those needs. Medium- and long-term adaptation activities are viewed as those that will follow a structured process aimed at reducing vulnerability to climate change in the LDCs by building adaptive capacity and resilience and 'climate-proofing' development against current and future climate change, UNFCCC FCCC/TP/2011/7.

15 The ten guiding elements as listed are: (1) A participatory approach involving stakeholders; (2) A multidisciplinary approach; (3) A complementary approach that builds on existing plans and programmes; (4) Sustainable development; (5) Gender equity; (6) A country-driven approach; (7) Sound environmental management; (8) Cost-effectiveness; (9) Simplicity; and (10) Flexibility, based on country-specific circumstances (FCCC/TP/2011/7).

16 It must be noted that since 2008 there has been a passive recognition of the importance of gender, but proactive incorporation of making the funds gender-responsive only began in 2010. In 2010 Revised Programming Strategy for the LDCF and SCCF stated that the funds will 1) encourage implementing agencies to conduct gender analyses; 2) require vulnerability analyses to take gender into account; and 3) integrate gender as appropriate in all results frameworks and in updated operational guidance materials.

17 COP guidance to the GEF has so far been gender-neutral. It has focused on requesting GEF to support the preparation and implementation of NAPAs, in the case of the LDCF (of which 45 of the 48 have been completed). LDCF finances the most urgent and immediate needs.

18 This is also reinforced in para 40: 'Activities to be funded will: (a) be country-driven, cost-effective and integrated into national sustainable development and poverty-reduction strategies; and (b) take into account national communications or NAPAs and other relevant studies and information provided by the Party'. Paragraph 41 also recognizes 'that climate change impacts fall most heavily on those least able to respond, and often on those that contributed very little to its causes. Adaptation activities financed under the fund will seek to assist the most vulnerable countries and those within a country with the greatest need. Activities will therefore seek to recognize the link between adaptation and poverty reduction'.

19 According to the operational policies and Guidelines of the Operational Fund Board, a concrete adaptation project is defined as a set of activities aimed at addressing the adverse effects of climate change and builds in climate change resilience. An adaptation programme is a process, a plan or an approach for addressing climate change impacts which are broader than the scope of an individual project.
20 Edejer *et al.* (2005) and Ebi (2008) argue that the annual per capita cost of providing food to improve child health in Africa has been estimated to be much higher (cited in Parry *et al.* 2005). Thus they 'estimated that including such costs would increase the adaptation cost more than 10 fold' (Parry *et al.* 2009).
21 Six LDCs, namely Afghanistan, Bangladesh, Democratic Republic of the Congo, Ethiopia, Sudan and the United Republic of Tanzania, and five other developing countries, Indonesia, Kenya, Nigeria and Pakistan, accounted for 65 per cent of all deaths (WHO 2011).

7
GENDER AND THE STATE OF PLAY IN MITIGATION FINANCING

This chapter explores the nature and scope of present flows of mitigation financing as it relates to gender and social development issues. Attention is focused on how well or not these flows are attuned to ensuring equitable and affordable access to clean energy and the overall empowerment of female entrepreneurs in the clean and renewable energy sector.

This chapter reviews the evidence on the flows of mitigation finance through both the UNFCCC channels described in Chapter 4, the non-UNFCCC channels and the flexible market mechanisms and the carbon market described in Chapter 5. It also discusses the effectiveness and social and equity dimensions of forest conservation and Sustainable Forests management issues under 'reducing emissions from deforestation and degradation' (REDD+) initiatives in developing countries. It argues that mitigation funding streams present more challenges for integrating a gender perspective; but that through focused attention on the provision of clean energy and on engendering mechanisms such as the Clean Development Mechanism and Reducing Emissions from Deforestation and Degradation, there is scope for redirecting the focus to community-based and women's empowerment programmes.

Though some mitigation activities, such as small-scale renewable energy projects and projects that enhance access to electricity and clean energy may benefit poor women and men, mitigation measures are not automatically synergistic with poverty reduction. In some cases, renewable energy projects that, for example, improve rural electrification, may improve agricultural productivity and can have positive effects on the quality of education and learning activities in schools and homes while clean energy projects lead to a decrease in life threatening indoor air pollutions (Michaelowa and Michaelowa 2005). But unfortunately, many high profiled mitigation projects do not bring clean energy to rural households or address their needs. For example, the Clean Development Mechanism literature shows that CDM projects tend to benefit rich farmers and urban dwellers more than rural populations (Brown *et al.* 2010).

The rest of this chapter develops these issues in greater detail. Section 7.1 discusses the landscape of mitigation finance. This is followed by Section 7.2 which explores the gender issues in mitigation finance by examining in details the operation of the GEF's mitigation oriented funds as well as the World Bank's CIFs. Section 7.3 investigates the role and scope of flexible market-based mechanism, the Clean Development Mechanism and carbon finance and gender. The section concludes with a brief overview of the growing role of microfinance in the mitigation arena and highlights the likely gender implications. Section 7.4 wraps up the chapter with a brief overview of the gender issues in the financing of environmentally sustainable technology development and transfer as well as capacity building with regard to mitigation finance.

7.1 The landscape of mitigation finance

Multilateral and bilateral approaches to mitigation financing for developing countries cover two broad areas: mitigation actions (specific support for decreasing GHG reductions in the developing countries) and mitigation support (technology and capacity building). Since Bali (2007) there has been a great deal of emphasis on a new mitigation-funding initiative (the reducing emission for deforestation and degradation, REDD) and two new mitigation climate change financing related vehicles: the nationally appropriate mitigation actions (NAMA) and the framework of 'measurable, reportable and verifiable' (MRV) actions (para 1(b)(iii), Bali Action Plan).

Mitigation is heavily dependent on multilateral fund based mechanisms, proceeds from the carbon market and private sector financing activities such as foreign direct investment. Hence, the key mitigation financing instruments are the price of GHG emission and taxes, fees and levies on carbon-based inputs for production and consumption. The price for GHG emissions is the key mitigation pillar along with the Clean Development Mechanism and the Carbon market. These mechanisms place a value on specific activities – such as cap and trade or emissions allowances. Developing countries also have access to funding mechanisms including grants and concessional finance through multilateral and bilateral sources.

Mitigation financing tends to focus on creating incentives for consumers, individuals, households and producers to reduce GHG emissions and to encourage the transition away from fossil-fuel based production and consumption activities. The financial mechanism and the set of evolving funds under the Convention as well as other multilateral funding sources are the means to secure the financing of mitigation activities in developing countries. This has to date been conditioned on co-financing flows from national budgets, overseas development assistance (ODA), the regional development banks and the private sector. The financial market and the private sector are anticipated to play increasing roles in mitigation financing. However, this is not without controversy.

The household sector also plays an important role in mitigation. Here, financing is needed for mitigation activities such as improving the availability and efficiency of energy to communities and households, including clean and health protecting cooking stoves, other household appliances, lighting and personal transport services. This type of financing may be small-scale and less profitable or less likely to attract pure market mechanisms. It is also the area most closely related to enabling the high quality functioning of women and girls in least developing countries. Hence, a gender-sensitive approach to mitigation financing would ensure that growing streams of funds are tracked into programmes and projects in this sector. Often adaptive and mitigative activities in the household and informal sectors tend to be low cost but may achieve high mitigation benefits.

The financing mechanisms for promoting mitigation focus on providing financial and investment flows to offset the costs or to provide incentives for mitigation strategies and activities. Investments primarily flow into the seven key sectors identified by the IPCC as major contributors to the production and release of GHGs: (1) energy; (2) transportation and its infrastructure; (3) residential and commercial buildings; (4) industry; (5) agriculture; (6) forestry; and (7) waste management (IPCC 2007, p.105).[1] Within this framework there are also investment flows to projects and activities aimed at preventing deforestation and supporting afforestation and reforestation.

Finance and investment are expected to flow from developed countries, through a variety of instruments and mechanisms, to implement emission reduction or removal projects in the developing countries. An important mitigation financing mechanism for facilitating this flow is the Clean Development Mechanism (CDM), a market-based mechanism to promote the reduction of emissions by Annex I countries of the Convention/Protocol and to support the sustainable development of developing countries. It provides countries with emissions obligation a flexible way to meet part of their emissions reductions target, under the Kyoto Protocol, through emission reduction (or emission removal) projects in developing countries. Such projects earn certified emission reduction credits (CERs) that can be traded and sold, and used by Annex I countries.

Since 2008, a market-based mechanism, to promote the reduction of emissions from deforestation and forest degradation (REDD) was launched by the UN as the UN Collaborative Programme designed 'to assist forested developing countries and the international community to gain experience with various risk management formulae and payment structures' (UN 2009). Though REDD initially focused on avoiding emissions from deforestation and degradation of forest, the framework was upgraded (since Bali 2007 and formally by Cancún 2010) to include the role of conservation, sustainable management of forests and enhancement of forest carbon stocks in developing countries. It also became known as REDD+. Though a final mechanism is not yet agreed under the UNFCCC, there are numerous REDD+ projects outside the framework of the Convention. For example, Norway is known to be a big supporter of REDD+ working with forest abundant nations such as Indonesia, Papua New Guinea and others in the Rainforest Coalition of Nations.

Mitigation finance and investment also flow through a variety of channels, such as the Global Environmental Facility, the World Bank and its collaborative network of regional banks and UN agencies. Private sector entities and meso level institutions such as foundations and international organizations also contribute to the flow of mitigation financing through the private markets. Increasingly, large commercial banks, hedge funds and institutional investors, key actors in the global capital markets, are engaging in mitigation financing and related activities.

The key international funds for mitigation financing include the Small Grants Program (SGP), some aspects of GEF's climate finance portfolio, bilateral funds such as Japan's Cool Earth and other funds as discussed in Chapter 4. A significant portion of multilateral publicly generated mitigation funding flows through the World Bank and its web of regional development banks and implementing agencies. As will be discussed in Chapter 8, the private sector also plays a significant and growing role in mitigation financing through traditional forms of investments in clean energy as well as through activities in the carbon finance, offset and capital markets.

The UNFCCC estimated that the global amount of additional financial and investment flows needed in order to reduce carbon dioxide equivalent (CO_2 eq) emissions by 25 per cent below 2000 levels in 2030 will be approximately $200–210 billion (UNFCCC 2008). But recent work by the International Energy Agency indicates that at least $5 trillion additional investment is required to 2020 in the energy sector only, to limit warming to two degrees Celsius (IEA 2013). Hence as with the adaptation estimates, there are a range of competing estimates for mitigation financing (Table 7.1). The scale, scope and delivery methods of mitigation finance are extremely important for supporting developing countries' contribution to the global reduction of GHGs, within the context of sustainable development.

TABLE 7.1 Global mitigation cost estimates

	Estimate	Costs basis
UNFCCC	$200–210 billion	Annual cost to cut emissions by 25 per cent below 2000 by 2030
(Developing countries)	($82–87 billion)	2030–2040 at 55 0 pmp
IPCC (AR4, 2007)	< 0.6–3 per cent	Cost as a percentage of world product in 2030 at 445–535ppm
Stern (2006)	1–2 per cent	Annual investment costs as a percentage of world product 2050 at 500–550 ppm

Notes: 2009: Total climate finance for developing countries over 2010–2020:US$ 180 bln to US$ 250 bln p.a. *or* 0.5 per cent of OECD GDP UNFCCC, IEA, McKinsey http://sitesources.worldbank.org/EXTCC/Resources/BBkfastFinance250409.pdf. Current Dedicated Resources Cover less than 5 per cent of the Needs

Source: data from UNDESA (2010); UNFCCC (2007); World Bank (2009)

In the area of mitigation under the UNFCCC, developed countries have committed to provide 'agreed full costs' for formulating and implementing national and regional programmes containing measures to mitigate climate change and by addressing emissions by sources and removal of sinks of all GHGs. They also agreed to provide 'agreed full incremental costs' for cooperating in the conservation and enhancement of sinks and reservoirs of GHGs including biomass, forests, oceans and other ecosystems. Financing for mitigation, as with adaptation, must also cover the transfer and development of environmentally sound technologies to facilitate adequate and timely adaptation and mitigation to climate change. In this respect developed countries have also committed to provide 'agreed full incremental costs' for cooperating in the development and transfer of technologies to mitigate climate change in all relevant sectors (including energy, transportation, industry, agriculture, forestry and waste management) as indicated by the IPCC, as well as to support the enhancement of developing countries' endogenous technologies and capacities.

In this context, it is important that there is adequate flow of mitigation finance and investment into developing countries, especially those which still have significant shortfall in infrastructural development and ensuring the flow of energy service to their citizens. The incidence of adaptation to the climate change and hence the scope and scale of financing required by developing countries is inextricably linked to the global goal and the mitigation actions taken by developed countries. The earlier wide-scale and massive greenhouse gas reduction occurs, the less the need for adaptation activities and hence the lower the cost of adaptation. Too low of a global spending on the additional investment need for the transformation to low carbon economy or inequitable sharing of the burden of meeting the additional expenditure for mitigation-related expenditure by developed countries implies that developing countries must make up the shortfall. As noted before, these shortfalls have real impacts on the lives and livelihood opportunities of the men and women and children in the developing countries.

7.2 Gender issues in mitigation finance

Mitigation financing typically occurs in a context in which, even when it does consider women, they are seen as 'vulnerable groups' instead of major environmental and agricultural producers or other actors; the myth of the male farmers, the male business owner and the male head of household continues to dominate. It is therefore important to undertake gender and social impact assessments in order to ensure that women and indigenous men and women do not lose ownership or usufruct rights to their traditional land or forests and lands to which they have historical access.

In addition, care and attention must be paid to ensure that women and poor men receive their equitable share in the benefits to be derived from community resources. This can be ensured through community benefit sharing and gender-sensitive, context specific property rights arrangements. Governments should carefully monitor resource conflicts, dispossessions and land takeovers to protect vulnerable groups' ownership of land, access to water and other economic resources.

In order to protect women from losing access to land without just compensation, structural and institutional changes will be needed, including land reform that goes beyond western conceptions of property titles. In some cases, conventional entitlement processes have been associated with further marginalization of women and the dispossession of families from land. Land reform must therefore be undertaken in a gender-sensitive negotiated process between men and women stakeholders in the community. It must also take into account different forms and dimensions of the existing inequities and accounting for both distributive and corrective justice. Thus there has to be social and gender justice preconditions that must be settled on prior to the operations of programmes under REDD and/or similar mechanisms.

The remainder of this section will attempt a gender analysis of a few of the key mitigation funds and instruments presented in Chapter 4 such as the Small Grants Program, the World Bank's CIFs, specifically the Clean Technology Fund, the Scaling UP Renewable Energy Program in Low-income Countries (SREP) and the Forest Investment Program (FIP). The chapter ends with a brief look at the National Communications reporting mechanism whereby countries report their climate change activities to the UNFCCC.

7.2.1 The GEF climate change mitigation activities and gender

The GEF has been the sole functioning operating entity of the Convention's financial mechanism from 1991 to 2014. It funds climate change mitigation projects mostly through its climate change focal area Trust Funds. As of 30 June 2013, the GEF has funded 639 projects on climate change mitigation with $4 billion GEF funding in 156 countries (GEF 2013). Energy efficiency and renewable energy projects account for more than 50 per cent of all projects in terms of funding, with sustainable urban transport and land use, land-use change, and forestry (LULUCF) projects making up the remainder.

Over that time, gender integration and attentions to the impacts (positive or negative on gender equality and women's empowerment) have been ad hoc and piecemeal with inadequate attention paid to these issues. This has been so despite the 1996 Public Involvement Policy of the GEF, which called for public participation, including both women and men, in every step of the GEF project cycle and operations (GEF 2012). GEF has, however, increased its attention to gender issues both in its corporate identity and its programmes and projects. In 2008, it undertook a comprehensive review of gender mainstreaming in GEF projects that 'highlighted the link between gender equality and environmental sustainability' and made recommendations for GEF to strengthen gender mainstreaming. The Fourth overall performance study of GEF (OPS4 2010), conducted in 2009, also facilitated this process with its recommendations, hence by GEF's fifth implementation stage (2010–2014) there was substantial progress in the implementation of gender mainstreaming, including the designation of a gender focal point. In May 2011, GEF adopted a gender mainstreaming policy which was immediately enforceable (it will be reviewed in 2015). Since 2011, the GEF has also undertaken regular gender review and monitoring of its portfolio.

However, the Fifth overall performance study of GEF (OPS5 2014) noted that though 'gender is a highly important dimension in the GEF theory of change, as it is one of the main avenues by which to achieve behavioural change that will lead to broader adoption of sustainable solutions to global environmental problems', GEF still has limited capacity development within the secretariat for gender mainstreaming (GEF-IEO 2014: 62). It further notes that there are no guidelines for mainstreaming gender into project activities (OPS5, GEF-IEO 2014).

OPS5 technical document on gender mainstreaming highlighted that out of 281 projects completed since OPS4 (2010) about 124 did not consider gender and were not expected to do so but only 44 of the remaining 157 projects successfully mainstreamed gender into the design and implementation, while 59 projects mentioned gender, but did not incorporate it in the activities. The residual 43 projects self-identified as 'gender not relevant'. The OPS5, however, noted that on subsequent reviews, gender was indeed relevant to these projects. This omission, it argued, 'may have led to unintended negative gender related consequences' (GEF-IEO 2014: 62).[2] These findings among others led the OPS5 review to conclude that despite significant improvement and implementation of the recommendations of OPS4, there was need for further deepening and capacity building in moving forward the gender mainstreaming agenda. It specifically recommended the adoption and implementation of a gender action plan on gender mainstreaming.

According to the GEF report, *Roadmap for Gender Equality*, during the GEF 6 period (July 2014 to 20 June 2018) there will be the development of a Gender Plan of Action to further integrate gender consideration into GEF's operations which will provide a concrete road map to implement the gender policy on gender mainstreaming during the coming years (p.8). The fivefold stepwise action planning includes mainstreaming gender into GEF project cycle, gender analysis, gender screening, the development of gender sensitive indicators and ensures GEF's agencies compliance with the GEF gender policy on gender mainstreaming.

7.2.1.1 The Small Grants Programme (SGP) and Women's Empowerment

GEF's Small Grants Programme (SGP), which is implemented by UNDP, channels grants of up to $50,000 directly to NGOs, community based organizations (CBOs) and indigenous peoples to undertake environmental projects (GEF/UNDP 2012). After now 20 years (1992–2012) in operation, with climate change accounting for 18 per cent of its portfolio, the SGP has supported more than 2,600 community-based climate change mitigation projects in terms of renewable energy, energy efficiency, sustainable transport and carbon storage, totalling $71 million. During this time the programme is reported to have also leveraged approximately $52 million in cash co-financing, and $42 million in in-kind contributions.

BOX 7.1 EVOLUTION OF GENDER MAINSTREAMING AT THE GEF

- **1996 (April):** the Public Involvement Policy (PIP) adopted. The PIP calls for public participation, including both women and men, in every step of the GEF project cycle and operations.
- **2008:** the first comprehensive review on gender mainstreaming in GEF projects, report, *Mainstreaming Gender at the GEF*. The review highlighted the link between gender equality and environmental sustainability; the scope, content, and depth of gender mainstreaming in GEF projects across all focal areas; and future steps to be considered to strengthen mainstreaming gender at the GEF.
- **2009:** Overall Performance Study (OPS4 2009) recommendations (background document–OPS4 Technical Document No. 9: Gender Mainstreaming in the GEF) and other reviews.
- **GEF-5:** progress in establishing operational systems for gender mainstreaming during. Gender focal point designated (OPS5 notes that this is a half-time position.
- **2011 (May):** Adopted Gender Mainstreaming Policy. Entered into force on adoption; to be reviewed in 2015: regular gender review and monitoring of the portfolio. OPS5 noted still limited capacity development within the secretariat and no guidelines for mainstreaming gender into project activities.
- **GEF-6:** will develop a *Gender Plan of Action* to further integrate gender consideration in GEF operation; will provide a concrete road map to implement the GEF Policy on Gender Mainstreaming during the coming years.

The SGP, which is now in its fifth operational phase, was not designed with specific gender equality objectives, but now according to GEF/UNDP evaluation report it 'devotes particular attention to local and indigenous communities and gender concerns' (GEF/UNDP 2008, 2012). Poor communities receive 72 per cent of its projects (an increase over the 57 per cent in earlier phases of the programme). As its climate change portfolio tends to support 'better living and working conditions in households and communities', the SGP has undoubtedly contributed to the factors that decrease women's time burdens and improve their health, thus enhancing the empowerment of women in the communities in which it serves. By 2013, 26 per cent of the SGP grants are targeted to women and according to the GEF/UNDP women participate in the implementation of many of its other non-gender equality targeted grant projects as members of local community. Indeed some of its funded programmes (such as the training of women as solar engineers, support for tree planting and fuel wood plantations)

> **BOX 7.2 GEF-6: TOWARDS THE GENDER PLAN OF ACTION AND THE FUTURE OF GENDER MAINSTREAMING AT GEF**
>
> - Concrete road map to implement the GEF Policy on Gender Mainstreaming during the coming years.
> - A step-wise approach in achieving its goal and objectives on gender mainstreaming plans: plans for an interagency working group consisting of GEF Agency gender focal points and other experts to exchange ideas and practices to develop the *Gender Plan of Action*.
> - Five-fold action elements in preparation of the plan:
>   - Mainstreaming Gender in GEF Project Cycle, including Gender Analysis, Gender Screening, and Gender Sensitive Indicators
>   - Mainstreaming Gender in GEF Program Strategies
>   - Knowledge Management and Lessons Sharing on Gender Mainstreaming
>   - Ensure GEF Agency Compliance with the GEF Policy on Gender Mainstreaming
>   - Strengthen Results-based Management on Gender Mainstreaming

would appear to directly promote gender equality, while others may have indirect gender effects.

The SGP now has a global gender mainstreaming policy, which promotes gender equality and women's empowerment as well as mainstream gender in community based environmental initiatives at the national level.[3] Under its global approach, gender is integrated into country policy strategy, and country programme support team supports all NGOs and CBO partners to consider gender in designing and implementing projects (GEF/UNDP). A 2008 evaluation of the SGP, undertaken by both the Evaluation Units of the GEF and UNDP, found that women are a priority group for the SGP in almost all countries reviewed.[4] In Senegal, women are almost 60 per cent of the SGP grantees.

Ultimately, only a proper gender and social impact assessment can ascertain the nature, duration and effectiveness of such benefits.[5] This has been an area for advocating the integration of gender-sensitive and women's empowerment objectives, tools and analysis, in addition to up-scaling the financing that goes towards mitigation projects in communities and localities and which are undertaken directly by affected communities as opposed to non-governmental organizations.[6] (Boxes 7.4 and 7.5 highlight some of the gender empowerment dynamics of the SGP programming.)

Because of its structural predisposition towards communities, vulnerable groups and the poor, the SGP stands out as a financing mechanism that supports women's

BOX 7.3 SMALL GRANTS PROGRAMME AND GENDER

The SGP was launched in 1992 with the aim of supporting the activities of nongovernmental and community-based organizations in developing countries in GEF focal areas while generating sustainable livelihoods. It is now in its fifth operational phase (2011–2014) and has added capacity development and sustainable forest management to its menu of operations.

- Gender is one of the main criteria considered for the approval of grants.
- Gender balance is a prerequisite to participate in the initial stages of project conception, approval and implementation.
- Needs assessment is done at the project development phase and is used to define the roles of women and men early in the project.
- SGP documents the contribution of women to project.
- SGP National Steering Committees employ checklists and criteria to assess and screen projects for how they mainstream gender.
- SGP holds 'proposal writing workshops' and accepts project proposals in local languages and even in oral formats through participatory video proposals, thus encouraging maximum participation by women, indigenous peoples.
- SGP encourages women stand-alone projects in line with the GEF focal areas.
- National Steering Committees – a voluntary body that makes all decisions on grant making – are required to include a gender specialist.

Sources: Bonizella (2011); Biagini (2014)

BOX 7.4 GENDER EMPOWERMENT AND THE SGP

Gender Empowerment and the SGP – insights from case snapshots

According to SGP literature, a quarter of all SGP grants specifically target gender matters and privilege the participation of women and gender based projects have enabled women to gain greater autonomy together with the collective responsibilities that come with acquiring experience and leadership (as in 'most SGP projects afford women and men the opportunity to work together as equals and to benefit equally from projects').

Women's empowerment in SGP programming is linked to: promoting women's leadership and involvement in decision-making about the development of their communities, shared participation in mitigation efforts and increasing skills and ability to take advantage of new opportunities and reducing factors contributing to women's and men's ill health and lack of safety. This involves activities such as training women for so-called green jobs, increasing access to solar energy clean cook stoves and providing resources that reduce the exposure of women and girls in seeking to provide water and fuel woods for their individual, home and community uses. A few examples of such projects and efforts are abstracted from GEF/UNDP 2012, *Twenty years of Community Action for the GEF* Report.

- The promotion of community solar energy through gender empowerment. 43 women solar engineers provide clean, low-cost solar energy in poor off-the-grid communities. Women from communities in Benin, Bhutan, Burkina Faso, Cameroon, Chad, Ethiopia, Ghana, Kenya, Mozambique, Niger, Rwanda and Uganda are trained by the Barefoot College (India) in partnership with the SGP, to install, maintain and repair solar panels, batteries. Not only do the women earn income (from these green jobs) but communities and households benefit from the installation of solar lighting in schools, hospitals, food processing etc. and there is environmental benefit in the mitigation of CO_2 emissions (due to fall in for example kerosene consumption), air pollution as well as reduction in deforestation (due to reduction in firewood consumption).*
- Women are empowered through increased bio mass fuel efficiency. 700 women trained to install 1000 improved (fuel efficient) cook stoves in households in Tsirang, West-central Bhutan. This has helped to reduce stress of fuel wood shortage, reduced women's burden of collecting wood and helped to ease prolonged exposure to smoke and indoor pollution. (Reduction of approximately 3,800 tons of fuel wood per year or 6,954 tons of CO_2 equivalent.)

* It is reported that for Mozambique, annual kerosene consumption fell by 27,375 liters and annual firewood consumption by 91,250 metric tons UNDP/GEF 2012. This resulted in an overall decrease of 82,125 kg in Co_2 emissions per year. In both Ghana and Benin UNDP/GEF report that some communities replaced 95 and 50 per cent of kerosene lamps with solar powered lighting, respectively and communities in Niger and Benin were able to eliminate kerosene lamps completely (UNDP/GEF 2012).

empowerment. Unfortunately, this is not unambiguously the case with other financial frameworks such as the wider GEF programming, discussed above, or the CIFs, under the rubric of the multilateral development banks to which we will turn to exploring.

7.2.2 The World Bank's climate financing programme (the CIFs)

In general, climate change multilateral funds such as those falling under the World Bank's ambit tend to be more pooled and cooperative (harmonized) and less volatile[7] than bilateral funds which are not stable or predictable. However, they also may be less sensitive to gender, pro poor and pro-development objectives because until fairly recently their focus was on the ensuring global benefits of climate change through emissions reductions project financing. Development, as such was not a key priority of climate change funding. Thus the World Bank Group's climate change financing for mitigation is not particularly pro-poor or gender equality oriented. Despite the bank's claim to be a 'gender equality bank', and its highly vaunted research on gender growth and development, its climate change funds are constructed around social and gender neutral or biased technological and other imperatives.

In 2008, the World Bank Group's climate change strategy shifted from a focus on mitigation under the Clean Energy for Development Investment Framework (CEIF 2007) to also include adaptation and mainstreaming climate change into development under a new approach, the Strategic Framework for Climate Change and Development (SFCCD). The SFCCD leveraged a set of CIFs, the Clean Technology Fund and the Strategic Climate Fund, which offers financing geared to scaling up low carbon technologies, forest protection and the promotion of climate resilient development planning. Financing for these climate initiatives are through blended grant and concessional loan financing and risk mitigation instruments that incorporate private sector actors. Hence, under this framework, developing countries may incur rising debt servicing obligations in order to fund adaptation and mitigation efforts. From a broad equity perspective, this would seem to be in conflict with the polluter pays principle that underlies the normative framework of climate change financing. More importantly, from a social and gender perspective, further indebtedness and the absorption of the current streams of official development assistance may crowd-out social development and gender equality intervention focused spending.

Until 2010, CIF's more mitigation-oriented programmes (the FIP and the SREP) lacked clear processes for accountability with regard to gender and social audits.[8] While gender was included among a list of other dimensions of climate change to be considered within the SFCCD, gender concerns did not show up in the important areas of finance mobilization and technology deployment (Gender Action 2010). Under the Strategic Environmental and Social Assessment (SEA), now in place, there would seem to be an attempt to pay more attention to 'the social effects': '(s)ocial effects are being fully enhanced and any potential negative effects are being monitored and managed appropriately' (SEA 2011). As noted by the SEA,

> Social and gender co-benefits do not occur automatically when clean technologies are implemented, with the exception of shifting from biomass solid fuel use in households to cleaner energy services. The latter has a direct impact on women and children's health, as well as women's time/productivity. Other clean technology/renewable energy projects/programs/plans need to be designed in a 'pro-poor way' for social and gender co-benefits to be realized.

BOX 7.5 THE CLIMATE INVESTMENT FUNDS SINCE 2008

The two Climate Investment Funds (CIFs) are the Clean Technology Fund (CTF) and the Strategic Climate Fund (SCF).

The CTF is a multi-donor trust fund (since 2008). It finances scaled-up demonstration, deployment and transfer of low-carbon technologies for significant greenhouse gas (GHG) reductions within country investment plans. The SCF finances targeted programmes in developing countries to pilot new climate or sectoral approaches with scaling-up potential. The focus is on large-scale Renewable energy (such as solar, wind, geothermal, biomass, waste to energy and hydro-power), energy efficiency (appliances and bulbs) and transport projects (mass transport and hybrid vehicles), district heating and smart grids, initiated at the country level.

Targeted programmes under the SCF include:

- The Forest Investment Program (FIP), approved in May 2009, aims to support developing countries' efforts to reduce emissions from deforestation and forest degradation by providing scaled-up financing for readiness reforms and public and private investments.
- The Pilot Program for Climate Resilience (PPCR), approved in November 2008; its objective is to pilot and demonstrate ways to integrate climate risk and resilience into core development planning, while complementing other ongoing activities. (The PPCR is adaptation focused and hence was discussed in more detail in Chapter 6.)
- The Program for Scaling-Up Renewable Energy in Low Income Countries (SREP), approved in May 2009 and effective as of December 2009, is aimed at demonstrating the social, economic, and environmental viability of low carbon development pathways in the energy sector. It seeks to create new economic opportunities and increase energy access through the production and use of renewable energy.

Nonetheless, gender analysis and concerns were not integrated into the key areas and committees that govern the CIF's mandated legally binding obligations (Gender Action 2010).

A Strategic Environment, Social and Gender Assessment of the Climate Investment Funds' documentation was undertaken and the report made available in October 2010.[9] The report argued that gender concerns are not adequately addressed in programmes such as the CTF and SREP.

7.2.2.1 The Climate Technology Fund and gender

The Strategic Environmental and Social Assessment (SEA) notes that the Clean Technology Fund (CTF), which is the most advanced of the three targeted programmes under the SFCCD, does not discuss social and gender issues in detail in its investment. But given its mandate the Strategic Environmental, Social and Gender Assessment (SESGA) (2010) argues that 'there is still a great opportunity to increase and maximize social and gender co-benefits as CTF projects are prepared'. The CTF finance is focused on promoting energy efficiency, power generating and urban transportation technologies in developing countries. The implementation of these projects are generally known to produce environmental co-benefits (reduction in local pollutant emissions) that are directly correlated with reduction in GHGs. While as noted in the SESGA, 'social and gender co-benefits do not occur automatically when clean technologies are implemented', hence, pro-poor and gender friendly clean and renewable technology projects and programmes should be designed that take these issues more directly into account (ibid.). The SESGA further recommends the gender and social costs of CTF can be better taken into account by more focused attention on the positive impacts of the introduction of new technologies in terms of four areas.

The CTF can maximize social and gender co-benefits by improving the development impact of projects and investment plans particularly with regard to the poverty alleviation aspect of the development impact.[10] But other critical aspects such as energy security and access and local industrial development are critical for women's empowerment. For example, as pointed out in the SESGA, many countries' investment plans submitted to the CTF include bus rapid transit system which is correlated with jobs, reduction of transportation time and costs. But the 'poor' will only realize these benefits if the 'BRT [Bus Rapid Transit] scheme covers low-income areas and fares are affordable'. Likewise the (employment and market expansion) benefits for small-scale renewable energy schemes will only be realized if local people are given job opportunities and training (SESGA). Here, best practise can be seen in the SGP, where deliberate efforts were made to train women as solar engineers and to repair equipment for RE technologies. So as with the SGP, the CTC investment plans and projects, can target women and vulnerable groups with the skills and capacity building in order to improve the odds of them benefitting from the implementation of clean energy projects. Finally, these projects must have state of the arts gender analysis at sector and economy wide levels and must implement environmental and social (including gender) safeguards in order to increase gender and social co-benefits.

Subsequent to the 2010 SESGA, in 2013, on the instruction of the administrative unit of the CIF, the Global Gender Office of the International Union for the Conservation of Nature (IUCN) undertook a gender review of the CIF.[11] With regard to the CTC, the review team examined 16 endorsed investment plans.[12] They found that only one out of four investment plans referred to gender in the text. These were the investment plans of Chile, India, Nigeria and the Philippines which were a post-2009 cluster of countries investment plans.[13] In these three countries, women were mainly identified as 'stakeholders' (three out of four countries) and as a 'vulnerable group' in one country (Nigeria) (IUCN 2014: 63). In only one case, India, there was the involvement of the national women's machinery. But no women's organizations were engaged as stakeholders in any of the four countries (ibid.). Overall, of the majority of the 16 IPs (87.5 per cent) did not include gender indicators, nor did the majority of the IP mentioned national gender policies in any of the documentation.[14]

The Review also pointed out that of the sixteen investment plans only seven included finance instruments[15] as one of the programmes or projects and only one of the financing documents mentioned gender or women. 'Gender' or 'women' was also not mentioned in the other sectoral areas that the investment plans were dedicated to such as transport, wind, solar, geothermal and energy efficiency, including district heating.[16] Furthermore, according to the gender review of the CIF, only two of the sixteen investment plans assessed explicitly earmarked resources for the promotion of gender equality (the Philippines and India).

According to a 2013 CIF evaluation of the 35 proposals submitted to the CTF Trust Fund Committee, 15 identified an explicit poverty related impact and only 9 explicitly mentioned gender or gender equity; 6 of the 35 describe an impact on gender equity issues.

7.2.2.2 Forest Investment Program and gender

The Forest Investment Program (FIP) supports developing countries' efforts to reduce emission from deforestation and forest degradation by providing scaled-up financing for readiness reforms and public and private investments (SESGA 2010: 1). A critical feature of FIP is the emphasis on the promotion of sustainable forest management (that leads to emission reduction and the protection of carbon reservoirs). FIP is supposed to take into account country-led priorities and strategies for REDD+ and work towards 'transformation change in the forest sectors or sectors affecting the forest'. To this end FIP, which is still in early stage implementation (as of 2010), should focus explicitly on socio-economic objectives (as co-benefits – biodiversity, protection of the rights of indigenous men and women and local communities and poverty reduction), vulnerable populations such as Indigenous men and women and other forest-dependent communities.[17] The FIP should also take into account consultative processes and environmental and social assessment and safeguards, including ensuring equitable benefit sharing arrangement with local communities.

FIP has a dedicated mechanism to provide grants to Indigenous men and women and local communities to support their participation in FIP investment strategies, programmes and projects (SESGA 2010: 25). FIP's foundational documents, including its Operational Guideline and Financing modalities and Investment Criteria, also target 'the promotion of gender equality' and social sustainability as aspects of its expected co-benefits. Though the design document makes it very clear that FIP

TABLE 7.2 At-a-glance view of social and gendering potentials with the CIFs

Social and gender approach and instruments of CIFs	Gender and social dimensions can be included through Strategic Environment Assessment (SEA) and Policy SEA*: dashboard of indicators for each CIF programme linking to technology, environmental, social and gender aspects. Involve consultation and participatory framework. Problematic features: bio fuel production and FIPs programmes – Impacts agriculture and land access issues Monitoring tool: Result Framework				
	Funds				
	Clean Technology Fund (CTF)	Scaling up Renewable Energy in low-income Countries (SREP)	Pilot Program for Climate Resilience (PPCR)		Forest Investment Program (FIP)
Co-benefits built in or that can be easily adapted to provide positive gender and social dimensions.	Focus: low carbon development and technology. Environment co-benefits (reduction in local pollutant emissions) correlated with reduction of GHG	Reduce pollution, increase energy security, enterprise creation and increased social capital. Design document makes reference to greater involvement and empowerment of women and other vulnerable groups Potential for increase employment vis-a-vis small-scale renewable energy services for women as a co-benefit			(Similar to REDD+): biodiversity conservation, protection of the rights of Indigenous people and local communities, poverty reduction and rural livelihoods enhancement. Grants to Indigenous people and local communities
Instruments and approach for engendering	Does not discuss social and gender dimensions in detail in investment plans	Operational guideline	SEA in the Preparation of Strategic programme for climate resilience (SPCR)*		
	Opportunity to increase and maximize social and gender co-benefits in CTF projects from the preparation stage	Can highlight gender co-benefits and request appropriate analysis and gender sensitive consultative approach in the development of SREP investment plans	Dialogue framework potential pathway for increased social and gender concerns		

* SEA (Strategic Environment Assessment and most particularly in Policy SEA). The SEA involves consultation and analysis. *Drawback*: sometime is a parallel activity as opposed to a building block. Adapted from: SCF/TFC.6/Inf.2. 29 October 2010.

investment plans, programmes and projects at all levels should 'be designed with the effective participation of all relevant stakeholders ... including particular groups that are historically marginalized such as ... women and mentions women's groups as a specific category of stakeholders', gender dimensions is under developed in the FIP framework. In terms of social economic objectives, the SESGA review explored eleven potential dashboard indicators for the Forest Investment Program, which included only two with gender identified as a category to be considered: indicator #7 (percentage income change and employment for women and men in rural areas) and indicator #11 (forest/land area cleared for biofuel production). While the other indicators in this are technical in nature regarding specific mitigation parameters such as percentage change in forest cover and percentage change in hectares of forest that are degraded, indicator #4 (percentage of communities/ households with clear titles over forest land/clear rights) and indicator #6 (level of community participation in land-use planning, forest management and monitoring) should be also engendered. The number of female and male-head households with titles to land or over forest land and the nature of male and female participation in land use planning and management are important variables, both to establish baseline date, to assess before and after gender dynamics and to improve the flow of resources to rectify gender imbalances detected.

The FIP does not have a similar dedicated grant mechanism or funds earmarked for the promotion of gender equality and women's empowerment as it does for the Indigenous Peoples and local communities. But as noted by the IUCN gender review, women and women's organization (presumably indigenous women) will have input with regard to how the Dedicated Grant Mechanism will function. In this regard, the FIP differs from other formalized REDD plus programmes such as UN REDD, which focus more closely on gender barriers such as land tenure and property rights.

In terms of the funding or financing of FIP projects, as with the CTC and SREP, women generally tend to be missing and gender issues evaporate. Of the four endorsed investment plans for the FIP, reviewed by IUCN by end 2013, though each integrated gender at different levels, none earmarked specific resources for the promotion of gender equality and women's empowerment.[18]

7.2.2.3 Scaling-up Renewable Energy in Low-income countries (SREP) and gender

SREP (effective since December 2009) aims at 'demonstrating the social, economic and environmental viability of low carbon development pathways in the energy sectors' co-benefits include reduced local pollution, increased energy security, enterprise creation and increased social capital. Hence the focus is on the production and use of renewable energy in the context of creating new economic opportunities and increasing energy security. The SREP targets 'the greater involvement and empowerment of women and other vulnerable groups' (SESGA 2010: vi). The SESGA points to the potentially greater co-benefit of increased employment, particularly for women and linked with small-scale renewable energy services. However, the SREP design document is deficient in spelling out how to maximize or realize these gender co-benefits. More seriously, the document does not include the awareness stated by the SESGA team that 'gender aspects are fundamental to achieve the technological shift in the case of certain household-level renewable energy services such as those for cooking' (ibid.: 30).[19] The review also points out that small-scale renewable energy service products offer considerably more opportunities for the employment (of women) than grid-connected renewable applications' (p.30).

The SESGA argues that there is 'huge potential for certain social and gender co-benefits from SREP technologies if investment plans include considerations of poverty reductions. However, disappointingly, the SESGA only flagged one indicator with a gender component in the matrix of six potential dash board indicators for the SREP: Indicator #5 integrated a gender component – percentage of total energy sector employment working in RE (renewable energy), (women/men).

The IUCN review of the SREP found that two phases of the SREP – phase 1 on preparation of IP and phase 2 on implementation of IP – were not significantly different in the uptake of gender issues. As of March 2012, five countries IP have been endorsed: Ethiopia, Honduras, Kenya, Mali and Nepal. 100 per cent of countries mentioned gender but each had different approaches ranging from women as 'beneficiaries' (mentioned in 80 per cent of the IPs) and women as 'beneficiaries and a vulnerable group' in 20 per cent of IPs (Mali). Ethiopia seemed to have the involvement of its gender machinery (the Women and Youth Directorate of the Ministry of Water and Energy) and will have an important role in the performance of the SREP with regard to gender issues. Kenya's IP is aligned with its gender audit of the energy policies and programme and with national climate change response strategy. As with other CIFs' mitigation programmes, the SREP did not earmark any funds for the promotion of gender equality and women's empowerment. But all of the investment plans had at least one gender indicator per component or within their results framework.

The IUCN gender review findings are affirmed by the 2013 Evaluation of the CIFs. Though the Evaluation did not undertake a gender analytic review, it did emphasize the 'development impacts and beneficiaries' of the CIFs programme. It also included 'exhibit boxes' on gender issues drawing on the ICUN gender review. The evaluation noted that the SREP has lived up to one of its key design principles: that it should 'seek wider economic, social and environmental co-benefits, particularly greater involvement and empowerment of women and other vulnerable groups' (CIF 2014: 55; SREP Design document, June 2009). However, at the same time the evaluation noted that in regard to energy access, the SREP is 'practically overlooking the opportunity to use off-grid photovoltaics (PV) for productive applications'. This has implications for accelerating access to clean energy such as clean cook stoves that are of importance to women and households. It also has implications for expediting the number of women entrepreneurs in the sector. The report noted that PV system 'require[s] viable business opportunities with adequate access to markets and working capital to thrive.[20] Thus given gender dynamics, without proactive support more women's SMEs will be less attracted to this area.

Overall, with regard to gender and the CIF's mitigation focused finance areas, as noted in the CIF gender review, there needs to be strengthening of the gender-responsive approach of the CIF. This can occur via mainstreaming gender and promoting gender equality goals into policy, programme support, analytical work, monitoring and reporting and knowledge sharing and learning across programme nodes as well as across institutions.

The CTF is important for enabling women to be better integrated into the adoption of technologies for harvesting resources (biomass, sun, wind and river water) in many of these areas and in some countries women already are involved to different degrees. There are also gender differentiated risks and vulnerabilities with these areas (males are more prone to accidents in wind harvesting and women are vulnerable to loss of access to land which may be converted for large hydro projects). There needs to be equitable treatment in the approach to indirect and direct employment potentials and opportunities in the transformation and production, sales and distribution and growth of RE value chain.

Currently, worldwide men dominate the renewable energy sector occupying approximately 79 per cent of the jobs with women at 21 per cent. The gender gap in renewable energy is even worse for subsectors such as biofuels (where the male:female employment ratio is 90 per cent:10 per cent), Concentrated Solar Power (CSP) (89 per cent:11 per cent), biogas (86 per cent:14 per cent), geothermal (85 per cent:15 per cent), modern biomass and small hydro (both at 81 per cent:19 per cent each).[21] The gap is relatively less so with solar PV (69 per cent:31 per cent), solar heating and cooling (77 per cent:23 per cent) and wind power (75 per cent:25 per cent). The highest gender disparity in employment is in the large-scale hydro power (95 per cent: 5 per cent). Women are disproportionately favoured in traditional biomass where they hold 75 per cent of positions relative to 25 per cent for males.

Programmes such as SREP are important for supporting women's basic needs for cooking, lighting, power and transport as well as their productive activities and growing women's and household income. The SREP programme can contribute more toward improving understanding of gender equality and equity in renewable energy. More work needs to be undertaken to accelerate women's access to assets, finance, products, technology and labour markets and entrepreneurship. Specifically, there is need to accelerate women's access to and role in renewable energy, mini grids and employment and women's entrepreneurship along the renewable energy value (supply) chain. There is also need for better information and analysis on gender and energy efficiency with regard to district heating.

In the case of the FIP, there needs to be specific focus attention on gender and REDD+ with emphasis on better understanding issues of tenure, rights and benefit sharing (and revenue streams) and their relationship to the promotion of gender equality and women's empowerment. Table 7.3 presents a brief overview of opportunities, challenges and constraints of mitigation finance on gender equality and women's empowerment.

TABLE 7.3 Overview of opportunities, challenges and constraints of mitigation finance on gender equality and women's empowerment

Mitigation financing covers: renewable energy technologies and projects, wind energy, solar energy, small-scale hydro power, bio mass, including biofuels, geothermal, energy efficiency and cleaner energy technologies or cooking; and forest management (REDD and forest investment). Mitigation finance can support women's empowerment and gender equality through (need for gender analysis to ensure maximum benefit and minimum negatives for women and men given their different roles, needs and priorities)

	Activities and opportunities	Enhance positive by:	Reduce negatives by:
Employment effect	Maintenance and manufacture of RE components etc. (such as solar power systems)	Training women for jobs, e.g. electricians, installers, technicians and researchers	Ensuring women have equal access to jobs at all levels
	Off-grid projects	Small business development skills	Ensuring credit availability and gender sensitivity skill and training
	Micro hydro schemes can help to improve productivity for small farmers	Capital for women MSMEs in the manufacture and distribution of solar and other equipment	Ensuring hydro schemes are located where women need them
Health effect (reduction of pollution and improved air quality at work and at home)	Electricity	Expansion of electricity to rural areas, subsidization and feed-in tariff rebates etc.	Ensuring women and men in communities have access to clinics and medical services that operate with clean and efficient energy services.
	Clean cook stoves	Subsidization of cook stoves etc.	
	Occupational health		
Wellbeing and social reproduction effects	Electricity and lighting	Improving electricity coverage in rural and peri-urban areas.	Improving access to basic social services for low-income women and men
	Transportation	Ensuring low-income men and women have access to affordable mass transit that operates where when and how women and men need it for their critical activities.	Community participation in management of small-scale renewable energy
	Micro hydro schemes can help with access to drinking water and water for household uses		
	Cleaner technologies or cooking		

Mitigation finance can adversely impact women's empowerment and gender equality through:

Land use change (Lack of landownership and property rights denies women equal access to compensation. Resettlement (likely in the case of geothermal projects) may lead to disempowerment and material impoverishment of women (Koenig 1995: 22–27, 2001:54) in SCF 2010).	Women, in particular, older women may lose job from one site to another	Community participation in management and in decision-making about resettlement, if necessary Safeguards	Ensuring women's access and effective participation in community processes Ensuring women benefit from grants and other resources for forest. Forest
REDD+ ad forest management projects can adversely impact forest dependent communities, livelihoods and use-rights and practices; relegate Indigenous people to 'unproductive forest lands'	Increasing revenue flow from projects	Community participation in management of forest and natural resources Dedicated mechanism to provide grants to indigenous and local community people	Ensuring women's access and effective participation in community processes Ensuring women benefit from grants and other resources for forest.

Source: adapted from SCF/TFC.6/Inf.2. 29 October 2010

7.2.2.4 Governance and gender participation in CIFs

According to the CIFs gender review, no women's group was consulted in the preparation of: the CTC and SREP Investment plans. Among constituency groupings of CIFs' observers, though there is recommendation to consider gender, regional balance among other proviso, males tend to dominate across observer groups such as the private sector and investment plans. Women dominate among CSO observers. In terms of monitoring and evaluation, the review found that there are no indicators focused on women's empowerment or gender equality in the results framework document. Further the 2013/2014 CIFAU M&E work plan does not include any tasks/deliverables associated with addressing gender or vulnerable populations. However at the programme level (investment plans), according to the review, the revised framework proposes that 'a gender impact indicator should be developed for each project/programme' (SREP and PPCR).

Ironically, though multilateral climate financing institutions, such as the World Bank, have clear gender policies and women's empowerment precepts in their broader organizational frameworks, these tend to evaporate with regard to climate change financing portfolios, despite the SEA. Evidence of this can be seen in the bank's and the European Bank for Reconstruction and Development-funded BTC oil pipeline in Azerbaijan, Georgia and the Sakhalin Island (Sakhalin II oil and gas project). This project is identified with increasing overall poverty, hindering women's access to resources, and increasing still births, prostitution, and a significant rise in trafficking of women, HIV/AIDS and other STIs (Gender Action 2009; Bacheva et al. 2006).

Engendering World Bank Climate Change financing should be relatively straightforward with strategically gender focused advocacy that builds on the World Bank Group's well developed work on gender analytical tools such as the PRSP, its Gender Action Plan: Gender as Smart Economics, periodic country gender assessment (CGAs) and the integration of gender indicators in the corporate Development Outcome Tracking system (DOTs) initiated by the International Financial Corporation. The World Bank has consistently articulated a gender equality agenda, including among other things, a gender chapter within the scope of the Poverty Reduction Strategy Papers. In 2012, its flagship World Development Report was devoted to the theme of gender equality and development. Given these activities focused on engendering the development, there should be not much difficulty in elaborating a gender sensitive framework within CIF operational domains. But there has been. But this state of affairs is changing. The Bank has produced a policy brief on gender and climate change (2011) and according to the CIF 2010 SEA, the World Bank is in the process of ensuring that by FY14, 100 per cent of projects will carry out a gender analyses to identify gender based constraints needs and priorities and if the analysis identify high levels of gender gaps that can be addressed by the project, gender-responsive actions and gender indicators will be included in the design for monitoring progress. This is particularly with regard to the sectoral areas of urban, energy, water, transport, agriculture, environment and social sectors. The report also points out that the bank is in the process of establishing indicators for monitoring gender indicators (SCF/TFC 2010: 20, footnote 2).

The gender analytical, operational tools (i.e., sector tools) and diagnostic tools (such as gender sensitive indicators) that the World Bank incorporates into its GAP and PRSP frameworks are important entry points for including gender consideration in country, bilateral and other multilateral development bank's strategic framework and work programmes. It is therefore imperative that attempts are undertaken to ensure that these analyses and tools permeate the climate change financing operations of the bank and its group of collaborating partners.

7.2.2.5 The Gender Action Plan (GAP)

Gender Equality as Smart Economics, 2009–2012, (GAP-GSE) instituted by the World Bank since 2007 and endorsed by the G-8 Heiligendamm Summit, could be quite an effective tool for engendering the broader areas of climate change financing. With GAP-GSE, the bank has been seeking to integrate gender issues in the economic sectors and to leverage additional financial and productive resources for women's economic empowerment (World Bank 2009). According to the bank, preliminary results indicate that 'gender issues have informed 45 per cent of all lending operations in fiscal year 2008 (as compared to 35 per cent in 2006)' (Wieczorek-Zeul 2009). It is important to note that the largest increase has been in the economic sectors, private sector development and infrastructure as opposed to the traditional gender sensitive areas of education, health and social programmes (ibid.).

The DOTs system has also been reported to allow the IFC to more systematically track the gender and development impacts of its investment portfolio. There is also quite advanced work by the Millennium Task Force on gender equality targeted objectives within the framework of MDG3. This, coupled with the emerging set of recommendations for engendering climate change by gender advocates, provides significant scope for a comprehensive approach to integrating gender issues and concern with the framework, processes and mechanisms of climate change financing under both the World Bank and the GEF.

These advances in gender tracking systems and gender action planning within the context of multilateral financing institutions such as the World Bank Group bode well for the adaptation of processes and mechanisms for integrating gender concerns and priorities into climate change financing. Some multilateral development banks, such as the Asian Development Bank, for which the World Bank is key reference, have also begun to integrate similar gender sensitive approaches to their lending portfolio, including their approach to climate change financing (Box 7.2).

It would appear that the Asian Development Bank is very active with regard to gender sensitizing its funding process and programmes. The Bank is leveraging gender equality based inputs to foster successful achievement of poverty, human development and environmental outcomes. This approach of the ADB bolsters one of the key propositions of this book, which is that integrating gender analysis, perspective and gender tools (such as gender audit, gender impact assessment and gender action guidelines) will generate tremendous positive dividends for successfully achieving climate change goals. A synoptic review of some of the ADB's and other regional banks emerging practices in this regard are presented in the table below. Their activities could serve as gender sensitive models for the global climate change financing institutions, funds and mechanisms.

Along this line, structured and incentive based programmes could be designed and implemented that aim to enhance and build on women's and men's capacity and skills in areas such as forest inventory, sound forest land use and management. Another approach would be to develop projects and programmes that attempt to address the underlying causes as well as the direct drivers of de-gradation and de-forestation in particular areas. In this way also local and traditional knowledge by elder women and men can be valued and drawn into the process of climate change knowledge building and sharing for future sustainability.

Unfortunately, far too few of the more richly endowed financing instruments, particularly those in the strategic area of mitigation, do not encourage the effective and democratic participation of female and male stakeholders. Rather, they tend to be top-down processes. For example, the application and review processes of most funds are quite complex, and given the high level of segmentation of funds, do not encourage or facilitate easy non-governmental access. This is especially relevant for very small and under-resourced NGOs in developing countries. Thus, there is an institutional bias in favour of northern-based NGOs that operate relatively large and well financed operations. Hence it is an understatement to argue that within these frameworks, the voice, priorities and concerns of indigenous people and women are often the last heard and the least responded to. There are many programmes operated by many NGOs and there is no doubt that they have benefited the poor, especially women and that, compared to many governments they consult with local and community groups. This is fine. But it does not compensate for the problem that there is structural bias and imbalance within the framework of climate change financing as with development cooperation financing that favours northern based NGOs, who are then enabled to facilitate processes of partnership with southern groups. This state of affairs also pertains to the carbon market.

The demand side of climate change financing is primarily based on national, regional and international climate change policy. The key demands are for sectoral areas such as energy, agriculture, forestry and the health sectors, including weather-related agricultural losses, finance for mitigation and adaptation technologies. In the area of mitigation, the key demanders of funded activities are developing countries, who make this demand primarily through the preparation of NAMAs, national Communications and their participation in range of mitigation focused projects such as low emissions development strategies. Now have a brief look at the instrument of national communication through which countries report on their mitigation actions as well as the financing of those actions in developing countries.

BOX 7.6 GENDER SENSITIVITY OF THE ASIAN DEVELOPMENT BANK

- Policy on Gender and Development (1998).
- Integration of gender equality considerations in the design and implementation of investment projects.
- Capacity development and activities which directly benefit women.
- External Forum on Gender and Development.
- Loan projects implementing quality gender action plans (GAPs)

According to the ADB, Loan projects implementing quality gender action plans result in:

- increased participation by women in loan activities, (particularly through community-based organizations);
- more equitable access to project and programme resources, including skills training, technology, and government services;
- improved practical benefits for women such as increased income, greater financial security, and more livelihood options;
- progress toward gender equality, including changing decision-making patterns in the household, membership in and leadership of community-based organizations, and increased mobility.

Source: adapted from various ADB publications (2005 and 2009)

BOX 7.7 BEST PRACTICE TIPS FOR INTEGRATING GENDER INTO LENDING/INVESTMENT PROGRAMMES

- Implement gender action plans into rural development projects. Such projects achieve the most comprehensive results;
- Avoid delaying the implementation of gender action plans in such projects.
- Proactively include gender provisions in human development loans. For example, loans that focus on improving women's health and educational status). Such provisions will generate practical benefits.
- Without gender action plans, such projects will make little progress toward strategic changes in gender relations.
- Ensure that governance policy loans include significant gender provisions and gender equality tranche release conditions achieved are important.

Source: drawn from Gender Briefing, ADB (2009)

7.2.3 National communications strategies and gender

Pursuant to UNFCCC, Article 12, countries are in various stages of preparing their national climate change communication.[22] According to the UNFCCC, a national communication is a report that each Party to the Convention prepares periodically in accordance with the guidelines developed and adopted by the COP. National Communications outline a country's priority issues for dealing with climate change. These National Communications have a five-year cycle and can also double as national planning tools for addressing climate change issues within the context of national circumstances at national level; they are also useful for determining needs and attracting financing support for domestic efforts to facilitate adaptation at national or sectoral levels. National Communications are funded through 'enabling activities' under the GEF, and supported on an agreed full-cost basis through expedited procedures with up to $405,000 (UNFCCC). Thus far $200 million has been utilized over the NatComs of 139 countries. While many Annex I Parties (developed countries) are in their fourth to sixth National Communications, most non-Annex I parties (developing countries) are now in their first through third National Communications.

From the vantage point of developing countries, National Communications must be contextualized within existing frameworks for the achievement of national and sustainable development objectives, while simultaneously responding to climate change (South Africa 2004). National Communications must also be consistent with national priorities including poverty eradication and gender equality. In general, National Communications cover a broad range of topics including GHG inventories, vulnerability and adaptation, mitigation analysis, technology needs assessment, integrating climate-change considerations into development planning, education and public awareness-raising Capacity building needs and technical assistance and financial needs (UNDP 2011). Ideally, National Communications should be developed through a process of consultations with key stakeholders, including gender machineries and women's organizations. These periodic reports on a country's climate change strategies, involve reporting on the country's vulnerability and capacity to adapt to and to mitigate possible changes in climate (Warrick 2000).

Gender analysis and women's empowerment perspectives could be included as strategic and integral value-added elements embedded in the vulnerability and adaptation assessment frameworks. This will allow for identifying the gender differentiated risks and vulnerabilities in the medium to long term for health, basic needs and livelihoods of men and women. These tools should also focus attention on women's and men's roles in the domestic economy that can have global benefits. Such activities include (1) the promotion of energy efficiency, through transition or fuel switching from traditional biomass fuel to modern cooking fuels; (2) the promotion of renewable energy through enhanced development of bioenergy (for example, Jatropha oil for cooking, lighting and power); and (3) especially with regard to natural resource and ecosystem management such as women-led, village-driven activities such as afforestation, reforestation and biogas/waste management. In this context, advocacy effort should be directed at ensuring that gender considerations are included in the guidelines for preparing National Communications.

These guidelines for the 3rd and 4th National Communications rounds have now been established. Further, advocacy should be directed at the GEF to provide funds under its enabling activities to move resources so as to encourage thinking about gender differentiated strategies and to promote capacity building that has local, national and global impacts.

Giving the periodic characteristics of National Communications, there is much scope and timing to include gender perspectives in the National Communications of different countries. Given also that these processes are for the most part shepherded by UNDP and UNEP, there is potentially the opportunity to more rigorously create the environment for inclusion of gender mainstreaming considerations within future National Communications strategies. Financing for these activities could potentially come from the GEF Country Support Programme, which 'is a capacity-building project that supports training, outreach etc.'.[23]

The next section investigates the role and scope of flexible market based mechanisms, the clean development mechanism, and carbon finance and gender. It concludes with a brief overview of the growing role of microfinance in the mitigation arena and the likely gender implications.

7.3 Flexible market-based mechanisms, CDM-carbon financing and gender

Under the Kyoto Protocol, industrialized countries were to be supported in achieving their emissions reductions target through access to cost minimizing project based instruments such as the Clean Development Mechanisms (Article 12, Kyoto Protocol) and the Joint implementation (Article 6, Kyoto Protocol). (A third (non-project-based) mechanism, emissions trading (Article 17, Kyoto Protocol), will be discussed in the next chapter.) These mechanisms would allow industrialized countries to undertake emissions reduction efforts in developing countries that would be counted as part of the industrial countries' reductions targets. Such emissions reduction projects were to achieve two results simultaneously: (1) they would transfer technology and finance to developing countries that would help to support their transformation to low carbon pathway; and at the same time (2) allow developed countries to continue to emit carbon dioxide at home by lowering emissions elsewhere in the world.

The logic behind CDM is that the cost of adopting or updating new technologies in industrialized countries is much higher for those countries' business entities than that of supporting the developing countries in updating their outmoded (and highly polluting)[24] factories and equipment. Developing countries would be supported with urgently needed capital, know-how and technologies with regard to renewable energy and energy efficiency. These so-called flexible mechanisms were seen as key to global emissions reduction and the promotion of sustainable development. The mechanism was simple: developed countries financed emission reductions or prevention (mitigation) projects in developing countries for which they received or bought certificates of emission reduction (CER) which gave them the right to emit more.

However, the flexible mechanisms of the Kyoto Protocol such as the Clean Development Mechanisms (CDM) have yet to yield significant sustainable development benefits. There is increasing effort being placed on promoting gender equality and women's empowerment benefits from the operations of CDM projects, especially with regard to programmatic CDM. Despite the predominance of gender mainstreaming in many national development and poverty reduction plans and across donors and UN agencies' mandates, there have only recently been attempts to integrate gender assessment in national CDM strategic documents and approval frameworks. As of yet there are no gender guidelines, checklists or gender impact assessment approaches into the activities around CDM and related publicly operated financial mechanisms.

7.3.1 The Clean Development Mechanism (CDM), sustainable development and poverty

The CDM as a market-based mechanism was established as a bridge between the priorities and concerns of the developing countries for sustainable development and those of the developed countries for flexibility and cost effectiveness in how they meet their emissions reductions targets under the Protocol (Fichtner *et al.* 2002; Grubb and Vriliger 1998). With these twin objectives, the CDM was envisioned as a win-win scenario (Matsuo 2003). The developing countries expected that the CDM would generate sustainable development benefits including investment flows and transfer of technology as well as contribute to poverty alleviation (Kaupp *et al.* 2002; Bhandoni 2002). The developed countries sought a mechanism that would allow them to avoid making the hard political decisions of imposing burdensome and costly emissions reduction requirements on their commercial and residential sectors (Gomez 2007). For these countries, the CDM, as a market-based mechanism, would allow them to alleviate the high costs (both political and economical) of sectoral and economy wide adjustments at home; as their firms could offset domestic emissions by sourcing low-cost emissions reduction projects in developing countries (ibid.). Thus the Brazilian inspired Clean Development Fund (which included a penalty for Annex I non-compliance) was transformed (with the intervention of the US) into a market-based mechanism.[25]

Starting out with the idea of creating a fund for adaptation, financed through fines for non-compliance (the CDF), the developing countries ended up with the CDM, a market based mechanism to meet developed countries obligations in which adaptation became a likely by-product (Stehr 2007). The developing countries, nonetheless, seem to have welcomed the CDM. Having no binding emissions reductions commitment under the Protocol, the developing countries were primarily interested in financing their adaptation cost of adjusting to climate change within the context of successfully growing and developing their economies in a sustainable manner. Adjusting to climate change, while also implementing strategies, programmes and projects for the transformation to a low carbon economy, implied multiple layers of costs that could not be financed domestically alone. Furthermore, the problem of climate change was induced by the long industrialization process that had primarily occurred in and benefited the rich and transitioning economies. Therefore, as recognized in the Convention and the Kyoto-Protocol, the developed countries had a responsibility for financial and investment flows, which may be partly accomplished through the CDM.

However, the seeming smooth transformation of the Clean Development Fund into a market-based mechanism (the CDM), centred around the profit motive and grounded in market dynamics of supply and demand, turned out not to be as seamless as it was originally thought. The problem was that the recalibration/ transformation ignored, left ambiguous or paid in-attention to a few critical elements that would later turn out to be chronic sources of ongoing tensions between the two sets of Parties. Most ignored (and glaringly so) was that the centrepiece of the entire edifice, the pricing mechanism, in this case the price of emissions reductions, or CERs, was an inherent source of tension/conflict in successfully meeting the conflicting goals of low-cost (cheap) emissions reduction and the high cost development co-benefits. A related issue was the lack of anticipation of the likelihood (and its untoward effects) of 'some degree of competition among non-Annex I countries to attract CDM investors'. In this context Olsen (2006) argues that countries may create incentives that are set too low for sustainability. This would create a 'race to the bottom' with negative impacts for overall GHG reductions (ibid.).

BOX 7.8 THE CDM

'[...] the CDM has encountered a number of challenges and weaknesses, including unequal regional distribution of projects, concerns about environmental integrity and technology transfer, complex governance procedures, and questions about the CDM's contribution to sustainable development.'

Source: UNEP (2008c)

Left ambiguous and vague by the Parties to the Protocol was the concept of sustainable development. It was left to be decided by each government, specifically, through the Designated National Authority (DNA). Though seemingly a quite democratic approach, this left many loopholes in the definition and determination of a critical concept to the CDM process. Sustainable development simply broadly encapsulates a set of broad issues including social, poverty alleviation, rural development and environmental sustainability. The working definition pivots around whatever the DNAs accepted and affirmed as being in the context of their national development plans. Thus, there is at present, within the framework of the CDM, no standardized or clear definition for comparability across countries. Sustainable development has thus become a contested term both between developed and developing countries as well as among different sectors of stakeholders in developing countries (Brown and Cobera 2003; Liverman and Boyd 2008). Regardless of the specific element of sustainability that is at the point of enquiry, as will be discussed below, it is widely acknowledged that the CDM has not been successful at catalysing it. The reality is that while emissions reduction is an established goal of the CDM system, sustainable development is only its aspiration.

The lack of clarity around sustainable development also infected other aspects of the CDM architecture. Many other key institutional and procedural elements were likewise benignly neglected or under-developed. These include the compliance mechanism, the criteria for 'additionality' and the baseline for assessing it, and burden sharing. The vagueness around these issues has led to ambiguities in the formal procedures of CDM and has impacted its functioning.[26] These outstanding issues necessarily became the problem children of future COP decision-making, including COP 18 (2012).

7.3.1.1 On the positive benefit side

Proponents of the CDM credited it with making some general beneficial contributions to development. Important among the list of its positive impacts on development are its contribution to the adaptation funds as well as other development funds (UNEP 2008c). It has also been effective in introducing structural change in some sectors in some countries (Americano 2008). This has occurred, for example, with the promotion of clean and renewable energy technology and the resulting de-carbonization or change in the carbon intensity of some sectors in Brazil, for example (ibid.). Brazilian case study research by Americano (ibid.) highlighted that the CDM has contributed positively to waste management, local environmental sustainability and the management of animal waste. This reportedly has positive spill-over on people's health. In the area of waste management, the CDM has been instrumental in catalyzing a 'sanitary revolution' in the Brazilian context, in which, waste is now seen as a financial resource. Landfill projects have also had a positive impact on sanitation. It has decreased the risk of underground water contamination and is associated with a decrease in the pathogenic vectors linked to animal manure. This is argued to have led to an improvement in local environmental sustainability. Furthermore, the CDM projects in some countries such as Brazil and China and India have also generated a strong increase in the numbers of small hydro power and generally contributed to the production and distribution of affordable electricity (UNEP 2008c).

7.3.1.2 On the negative side

Despite these apparent contributions, there is still a significant body of evidence pointing to a pervasively negative impact of the CDM on sustainable development (Olson 2006; Brody *et al.* 2008). Much of the on the ground work shows that in seeking to enable lowest cost emissions reductions, the CDM process ensured a focus on end-of-pipeline projects such as large gas and brownfield sites (landfills and industrial production). While these are cheap sources of emissions reductions and hence have large global benefits, their overwhelming dominance of the CDM market may crowd-out other projects with co-development benefits. Projects such as alternative energy production and hydro-flurocarbon emissions reductions project are a large proportion of CDM approved projects. They also are large sized projects which account for 54 per cent of CDM project portfolio. It is argued that these projects have low co-development benefits. Roberts *et al.* (2009: 5) argue that there is a bias towards 'supply side' energy sector CDM projects and low levels of investment for high development dividends and high GHG emissions reduction potential 'demand side' energy efficient projects such as urban transportation, urban development and infrastructural projects, especially with regard to electricity generation.

These biases and lopsidedness in the focus and outcomes of CDM projects contribute to the emergence of three specific types of gaps and at least two types of distributional imbalances. The triple gaps are: the co-benefits gap, the adaptation gap, and the technological transfer gap. The dual distributional imbalances are both geographical and sectoral. The latter two will be discussed first for ease of presentation.

7.3.1.3 The CDM and the adaptation-mitigation gap

Brown and Vignori (2008) argue that carbon based adaptation raised only 1 per cent of total project costs in developing countries (OECD/ODI 2008). This adaptation-mitigation gap is very much a structural bias issue in terms of the CDM. The entire architecture of the CDM was focused on ensuring environmental sustainability. The primary goal at the level of the carbon market is mitigation through offsetting reduction of GHGs. If all the bias was to work in favour of the developing country, it would work to help them become more environmentally sustainable. Adaptation or adjustment to climate change is not a priority in this. Thus any divergence between global benefits and development benefits will worsen the adaptation mitigation gap. Adaptation then has to be proactively overlaid on the architecture of the CDM (through, for example taxes, special fees or levies) in order to influence its functioning to include adaptation issues. Currently, the key link is the adaptation levy of 2 per cent on CDM which finances the Adaptation Fund. As a result of low intensity of adaptation financing via CDM, there are a number of proposals for up-scaling adaptation financing through the carbon market. An interesting proposal in this regard, put forward by Pakistan, is that JI and IET are treated like the CDM, as additional vehicles for raising the Adaptation fund levy to 3 per cent (Brown and Vignori 2008).

7.3.1.4 The technological gap

Technological transfer is central for development. It is also expected from the CDM process. The CDM is also expected to play a key role in technological innovation. The projects that are ultimately approved by the CDM executive board and DNA should in principle include a wide range of technologies. In this way, it is argued the CDM can spark technological innovations in developing countries. There is, however, the contrary view that indicts the CDM for potentially displacing homegrown technology. This can for, example, occur through the pressure the market imposes to buy low carbon technology from the developed countries.

7.3.1.5 Sectoral imbalance

Within the CDM markets there is excess demand for some sectors and insufficient demand for others. Some researchers have argued that the CDM has encouraged the practice of investors 'exhausting the cheapest means of emission reductions and leaving the more expensive ones for later, when developing countries will have to make commitment'. This shifts the burden to the poor countries and creates further inequity in global climate change financing and climate policy. Del Rio (2005) argues that:

> The deployment of renewable electricity Clean Development Mechanism projects may provide substantial local economic, social and environmental sustainability benefits to host countries. However, in spite of these advantages, a wide array of barriers prevents the realization of these projects. They compete with other CDM options that lead to cheaper greenhouse gas emissions reductions but that do not provide as much opportunity for sustainable development in developing countries. Taking into account that, in contrast to greenhouse gas benefits, sustainability benefits are not valued in the market place, Article 12 of the Kyoto Protocol envisaged two objectives for the CDM (cost-effective emissions reductions and contribution to sustainability). However, this market mechanism might be leading to a market failure.

7.3.1.6 Geographical imbalance

Most CDM projects are located in Asia and to a lesser extent in Latin America. In particular, China, India or Brazil between them host around 70 per cent of all registered projects. Africa accounts for only 4 per cent of CDM projects (UNFCCC 2009). As of December 2011, Africa hosts 205 Projects with 75 registered projects. African countries with registered CDM projects include Egypt and Morocco (17

Gender and state of play in mitigation financing **321**

projects) each, Nigeria (13), Tunisia (5), and Kenya (22), Uganda (14) each, and South Africa (58) (UNRISO 2011). UNECA notes that as of April 2009, 23 African countries submitted a total of 102 CDM projects in the CDM pipeline (UNECA 2009). According to the UNECA a 'number of factors explain Africa's low share of CDM transactions ... (including) ... barriers related to CDM procedures and modalities; coverage of CDM; financial, institutional and capacity barriers in host countries; and, the fact that greenhouse gas emissions in Africa, with possibly the exception of South Africa and Nigeria, are low' (UNECA 2009: 3).

To date, 31 Least Developed Countries (LDCs) and 28 Small Island Developing Countries (SIDs) have no CDM projects in the pipeline. LDCs account for a total of 89 projects in the pipeline with 35 registered projects totalling 1,264k CERs for 2012. For 2012, SIDS have 31 projects in the pipelines and 10 registered projects, totalling 8,215k CERs.

7.3.1.7 The co-benefits gap

Arguably, this is the main gap on the discussion table for the post-2012 period. It is reflected primarily as the divergence in benefits between the rich countries and the developing countries that springs from the management of the former's mandated obligations under the Convention. Instead of the expected synergies between the dual aims of CDM (emissions reduction/global benefits and sustainable development), there has instead been a trade-off between carbon benefit and non-carbon benefit. The benefits of CDM have been lopsided between sustainable development and emissions reduction strategies.

CDM appears to works well as a true market mechanism is meant to, but it trade-offs sustainable development. The result is a co-benefit gap. The co-benefit gap is itself, a complex interplay of at least three underlying equity issues: global, social and gender inequities. Divergences of the benefit path of a critical financing mechanism such as the CDM away from sustainable development, as an accepted pillar of global climate change policy, has a number of adverse implications for both national and global social and economic development. These social and economic development objectives are critical issues around which the global community has cleaved a consensus on poverty, gender equality, development. This consensus is encapsulated in the eight MDGs, which now underpins the global climate debate. The Convention and Protocol both raised and affirmed at least two of the equity issues identified here as part of the legitimate concern of global climate policy under its purview. The third issue, that of gender equity arises from the central concern of this book.

7.3.1.8 The global equity gap

Both the Convention and the Protocol mandated that the flow of financing and investment would be from the developed country to the developing countries. Both also mandated technological transfer and cooperation. The CDM promised to deliver on both of these. However, after many years of operation, there appears to be a widening gap between the promised global benefits (which are seemingly on track) and the co-development benefits (which seemed to be off track). Increasingly, evidence from research on the CDM, points to a negative impact of the CDM in both the areas of sustainable development and technological transfer (UNEP 2008c). Some researchers and practioneers, further argue that the foreign investment dividend is also likely to prove disappointing (Lütken 2008; Maosheng 2008). Others raise questions about the mitigation impacts of the CDM, arguing that it has had negative impact on energy, mining and domestic technology.

The reasons offered for this pattern of high global benefits and low co-development benefits are at least threefold: the market dynamics, structural bias in the CDM architecture and the functioning of the CDM.

First, the rationality and impact of the carbon market predisposes market actors to behave in ways that are not inherently conducive to promoting sustainable development. Investors are not motivated by equity (Olsen 2006: 10). They seek the cheapest emission reduction project and thus are subject to reaching for 'low hanging fruits' (ibid.). Profit maximization will enforce a trade-off by foreign investors between profit and sustainable development objectives (Kim 2003; Humphry 2004; Olsen 2006). So the demand will be for offset projects that yield low-cost emissions. The price mechanism will work to stimulate demand for so-called end-of-the pipeline. So the direct benefits to sustainable development may not be as large as had expected. Emphasis on lower price of carbon has predisposed investors away from higher cost (but high sustainable development benefit) activities such as forest and renewable energy projects (Olsen 2006: 13). As result of the combination of these two broad factors, the CDM does not drive sustainable development. These issues raise questions about whether the carbon market can provide sustainable development.

A second set of factors behind the gap between global benefit and sustainable development is deeply structural deficiencies within the CDM's architecture. These deficiencies such as ambiguity around sustainable development, the compliance mechanism and burden sharing have worsened the trend of low sustainable development of the CDM. As indicated above, the definition of sustainability has been left to in the purview of each country's Designated National Authority (DNA). But as noted by Olsen (2006) and others, DNAs often have little bargaining power over sustainable development objective criteria, given the global scope of the investor's choice versus the choice of locals (Olsen 2006: 10). Investors can shop around for projects that are more desirable to their bottom line.

Another dimension of the structural bias in the CDM architecture lies in terms of what is excluded from its operational scope. Primary among the missing or excluded are broader conceptualization and operationalization of conservation and forestry projects. At its inception, forestry was not included, but the Marrakech (2001 meeting) allowed for the inclusion of afforestation and reforestation under land use, land-use change and forestry (LULUCF). However, such projects operate under severe constraints that detract from their marketability. In the first case, there is a cap or limit on the amount of carbon that can be credited to sink projects (1 per cent of the base year). Second, credits are temporary. Forestry and forest projects are identified as having a very high contribution to development and are important for poverty alleviation and other development benefits to the local people. Thus the exclusion of a wide range of forest activities and the constrained threat on the allowed components are contributing factors to the lack of development co-benefits for least developed countries. This is especially so with regard to Africa. The development of REDD is expected to compensate for this gap in the CDM market.

7.3.1.9 The social equity gap

Social equity is the second inequality identified with CDM. Evidence from the literature points to insignificant impact of CDM on poverty eradication and a likely adverse impact in terms of rising inequality between different groups in some economies. Brown *et al.* (2004) argue that due to lack of effective institutions for 'mediating different and unbalanced stakeholders' interests, CDM projects may exacerbate social inequalities'. Since the market mechanism cannot mediate social inequality, they argue that it is imperative that there is a framework for ensuring equity, including mechanisms for benefit sharing and a 'cross-sector, cross-scale' (politically oriented) institution to manage this process (Olson 2006: 10).

Social equity is also a cross country phenomenon in the CDM discussion. It is acknowledged that wealthy countries' entities have a tendency to 'cherry pick' the cheapest (low hanging fruit) emission reductions. Hence they leave the most expensive adjustments, which will have to be met by developing countries, for a later date. This pattern create a future burden (debt), that must be shouldered monetarily and with regard to adapting to adverse impacts of climate change, on poor men and women in developing countries. The persistency of this issue has led a number of researchers and practioneers to call for the process and/or mechanism that '(d)ecouple sustainable benefits from carbon credits in order to prioritise economic concerns, (and) separate the goals of community development from carbon contracts' (Olsen 2006: 10; Nelson and de Jong 2002; Brown and Adjer 2004; May and Brody 2004).

7.3.1.10 Gender equity

From the point of view of gender equality and women's empowerment, there is some caution to the approach of having market-based mechanisms, such as CDM, as well as non-market based mechanisms, especially if these are only focused on promoting de-carbonization of the economy and not proportionately on sustainable development. These mechanisms must also be guided by gender equality objectives and be formulated in terms of a comprehensive set of strategic programming geared at eliminating gender inequality and promoting women's social and economic empowerment.

Given the aims of the CDM, it is important to pose the question: What were the realized gains for women in terms of employment, affordable and efficient energy supply, and health and entrepreneurship? There is not a significant body of research on the CDM and women. What were the sustainable development criteria? Was gender equality or women's empowerment concerns factored into their framing of sustainable development? As presently constructed, is the CDM a worthwhile mechanism that could promote gender equality?

There is no clear set of answers to these questions. There cannot be without more systematic gender focused research on the issue.

The market works best when market participants exploit the lowest prices/costs, with other things equal. But as noted by (Olsen 2006), in the case of the CDM, other things are not equal. Sustainable development is traded-off and all things are not equal in terms of the social and economic situation of women and indigenous people. So the typical 'low hanging fruit' mentality and the drivers of the current approach to the CDM market do not work for sustainable development, poverty eradication or gender equality. Given that the CDM emphasizes large-scale suppliers of renewable energies, women-owned and other small-scale enterprises or households, where women predominate may receive only a small percentage of CDM projects (Zuckerman 2008). Evidence from case studies on the operation of CDM projects at local and community levels demonstrate that the beneficiaries of these projects are far too often 'the middle income and farmers with property rights to natural resources'. As a result, 'poor household and female headed-households with no land titles are left out' (Olsen 2006: 10; Brown and Corberra 2003; Brown *et al.* 2004).

The recent reform of the CDM to programmatic CDM seems to have some potential for meeting sustainable development objectives. Because the CDM has not fulfilled on its goal to promote sustainable development, it would be hard for there to be discernible gender equality or empowerment for large groups of women in the relevant country context in which CDM projects operate. This is not to say that small groups of women have not benefited at all. This has simply not been objectively investigated. There is a double-bind. Would gender equality consideration or, a set of gender sensitive criteria in the project design documents (PDDs), or gender sensitization of the designated national authorities (DNAs) have led to different outcomes?

For example, Alboher (2009) undertook a systematic review of 1,548 project documents registered with the CDM executive board as of 31 March 2009. She found that only a small minority (about 16 per cent) had any reference to gender or women, and an even smaller set (less than 3 per cent) had substantial gender interventions (indications that the project would benefit women) beyond the intermittent use of the word 'gender' or 'women' in the document. As recently as June 2012, only 5 of 3,864 CDM projects listed gender issues in project documents.

Alboher also argued that it was difficult to ascertain whether any project contributed to women's empowerment. This was, in part, due to the lack of gender disaggregated data and, in greater part, due to the absence of any verification, monitoring and evaluation process. Although 15 of 44 countries investigated included an aspect relating to gender equality or women's empowerment in their national requirements for CDM project, there is no way of accounting for the substance of those gender aspects and if and how they were implemented. Alboher argues that in the absence of monitoring requirements for projects' impacts on sustainable development, in the same way there is for their contribution to emissions reductions, the alternative is to undertake on-site evaluation.

This suggests a systematic approach to monitoring and certifying gender equality criteria or women's empowerment outcomes of projects. Relevant examples include the Clean Clothes, Fair Trade or other campaign/processes. Alboher flags the Gold Standard, a voluntary, NGO-backed labelling scheme for promoting sustainable development in CDM projects as a potential near-term vehicle for incorporating meaningful gender criteria.[27]

Alboher posited that there could be synergies with the search for a meaningful way to ensure gender equality outcome of CDM projects with the emerging concerns and actions presently being undertaken by some developing countries' governments to deal with the lack of co-sustainable development benefits. Most of these actions are remedial, after implementation, but, nonetheless are a step in the right direction. They also have elements that can be used in advocacy towards a post-2012 gender sensitive, development-friendly CDM. Alboher references two broad approaches that could be useful for incorporating gender equality objectives: taxation and earmarking.

Some governments are considering the imposition of a special 'sustainability tax' on projects that earn high returns but show no sustainable development. Revenue from the sustainability taxes could be used to invest in projects that promote women's empowerment and development within the host country (Alboher 2009).

A more recent research project on the CDM and women was undertaken by GreenStream Network Plc on commission by the Ministry of Foreign Affairs of Finland to examine the sustainable development benefits of the CDM from the gender perspective and to explore the potential of the CDM to promote gender equality. Starting from the assumption that given its sustainable development mandate and that gender equality was a core sustainable development objective, the CDM has large and untapped potential to promote gender equality and women's empowerment, GreenStream developed a CDM Gender Spectacle Tool with which to screen potential gender positive local impacts of CDM project type and activities in host countries (GreenStream 2010). GreenStream use this mechanism to test the implicit assumption of the gender neutrality of the CDM. Its finding was that the CDM was not gender neutral. To the contrary, GS found that: a) some CDM projects have contributed to gender equality; and that b) there was at least a threefold entry point to stimulate the gender benefits of CDM.

GreenStream focused on three areas of enquiry: (i) whether and to what extent CDM projects offer opportunities to generate positive gender impacts; (ii) identification of project types which promote these opportunities; and (iii) consideration of the circumstances that may limit their realisation. It noted that there are quadruple entry points for enhancing CDM contribution to gender equality and women's empowerment: (a) inclusion in host countries' sustainable development criteria, (b) inclusion in investor countries' sustainable development criteria, (c) inclusion in buyers of carbon credit criteria for CDM procurement, and/or (d) the CDM gold standard criteria.

Gender and host countries' sustainable development criteria

Host countries can include gender equality objectives into threefold sustainable development criteria (environment, economic and social). GS argue that the social criteria are the most relevant for assessing impacts on gender equality. It noted that some host countries include a direct[28] (Bangladesh and South Africa) or indirect[29] (Brazil, Thailand and India) reference to gender issues.

Gender and investor counties' sustainable development criteria

Few investor states set additional national criteria for CDM projects they tend to rely on host country assessment. The exception is the Netherlands but it does not include gender in its national criteria. Finland does not have specific National criteria for CDM but CDM projects must fit with its development cooperation objective of which gender equality is a cross cutting theme.

Gender and Carbon Buyers' criteria for CDM

Here the World Bank's Community Development Carbon Fund and the Asian Development Bank give preference to small-scale CDM projects and require improvement of the material welfare of the community but have no specific gender criteria.

Gender and the CDM gold standard

The Gold Standard, as noted above, is a voluntary standard for CDM and the emissions reduction projects for those who want to emphasize sustainable development benefits. It only applies to RE and end-use EE projects. The Gold Standard listed gender issues under its social development criteria, specifically under its human and institutional capacity indicators which flags changes in baseline gender equality in terms of livelihood and education for women, including special schooling opportunities, women specific trainings, awareness-raising. Possible parameters include: female adult literacy rates, change in female earned income, change in number of jobs and position for women and change in decision-making structures at community levels, etc.

'Earmarking CER revenues from projects with few development benefits' is already a practice being implemented in some developing countries to try to ensure sustainable development benefits (Ellis *et al.* 2007, cited in Alboher 2009). For example:

- In South Africa, for those projects which 'record disproportionately high profits from CER revenues' or cannot demonstrate high contributions to sustainable development, 'the South African DNA reserves the right to oblige owners of CDM projects . . . to invest a part of the proceeds in additional sustainable development measures near the project location' (Ehlers and Wiekert 2006, cited in Alboher 2009).
- China has instituted a scheme whereby all CER proceeds are taxed and then channelled into a fund which helps provide loans to project developers and finance CDM capacity building measures (Abele 2008). Projects with high levels of sustainable development benefits such as energy efficiency, renewable energies, afforestation, and methane avoidance or utilization are taxed at a rate of only 2 per cent, whereas those with lower sustainable development benefits are taxed at significantly higher rates: 30 per cent for N_2O projects, and 65 per cent for PFC and HFC projects (Resnier *et al.* 2007, cited in Alboher 2009).

The case of Brazil offers both guidance as well as illustrating some of the limitations to be faced in making the CDM gender and sustainable development friendly (Box 6.4).

Americano (2009) argues that case studies on CDM in Brazil show quite positive results in the area of sustainable development (in terms of health and the expansion of electricity). This was not accidental, but rather by design. The Brazilian Designated National Authorities (DNAs) have specific sets of sustainable development oriented expectations/guidelines that are transparently communicated to the general public in order to ensure compliance and accountability of the project developers to the stakeholders in the locality and sectors in which they operate. It is not clear from the available reports whether the criteria integrate gender considerations. Gender does not appear as one of the five headings which detail the anticipated sustainable development contribution of the project (the social criteria) in Annex III that every 'Project proponents' must prepare as part of the project registration process (Americano 2009).

There are no thresholds, indicators, or measures for these headings. But according to Americano (2009), Annex III is a working tool of the Designated National Authority (DNA), who actively interrogate many aspects of the document with the project proponents. Annex III must be made available to the stakeholder during the validation period and it is posted on the Brazilian CDM web site. The Brazilian process is quite different from some reports from other countries, where the sustainability component appears to be superficially treated. In such contexts, stakeholders report that they are not consulted but surveyed through questionnaires etc. Many poor people, especially women, who cannot read are unable to participate by offering their opinions or sharing their concerns about the proposed projects. These apparently systemic 'exclusionary stakeholder consultation tactics' is highlighted by Alboher (2009), who found that only about 1.8 per cent of the project design documents (PDDs) reported consultation with gender equality advocates.[30]

BOX 7.9 BRAZIL, THE CDM AND SUSTAINABLE DEVELOPMENT CRITERIA

Project proponents have to prepare a document, known as 'Annex III', in which the contribution of the project activity under five different aspects or headings must be explained. These five headings are:

1. Contribution to local environmental sustainability
2. Contribution to the improvement of labour conditions and net job creation
3. Contribution to the distribution of income
4. Contribution to training and technological development
5. Contribution to regional integration and linkages with other sectors

There is no threshold for any of these five aspects or headings, nor any kind of indicator for any of them, nor any measure for all the aspects of sustainable development.

The DNA takes into account the project itself based on the document, which explains the contribution to sustainable development (Annex III) and takes into consideration the whole picture.

In many cases the CIMGC requests additional information and clarification about the contribution envisaged to some of the sustainable development aspects described by the project proponent. The purpose is to make clear in the document the aims of the project proponents, who must make Annex III available to local stakeholders during consultation in the validation period. The document also remains on the Brazilian CDM homepage after the project has been registered. Making Annex III public, with a clear statement of how the project activity contributes to sustainable development, to some extent constrains the project proponents to comply with its promises. The control that the DNA has after issuance of the LoA (Letter of Approval) is very limited. If the project does not comply with the country legislation, it is very easy to stop the activity using domestic law. However, if other aspects, like the number of new jobs created, are not in place as promised in Annex III, nothing can be done about it. In this regard, having Annex III publicly available and associated with the PDD in the Brazilian homepage is one way to ensure that promises are kept.

Branca Americano, Designated National Authority (DNA), Brazil (UNEP 2008)

Ultimately, one avenue for balancing out the CDM co-benefit gap, is for government to seriously rethink and ground sustainable development around measures and indicators (both poverty and gender equality) with built-in compliance measures. Many of these indicators already exist and are amenable to modifications, extensions and adjustments, where necessary. There would need to be a high degree of collaboration among governments so as to preclude corporations and individuals from playing countries off against each other.

There has also been considerable attention on how to balance out the geographical, country, sectoral imbalances within the operations of the CDM. Suggestions and recommendations range from suggestions about lowering transaction cost, building national capacity, especially with regard to Designated Operational Entities (DOEs), managing the market and increasing access to finance, to renegotiating the CDM.

Thus the CDM remains a work-in-progress with its institutional process constantly unfolding since its inception in 1997 and operationalization in 2004. In the interim years, many modifications have been undertaken to its architecture. These have included allowance for some kinds of sinks, small-scale projects and adjustment to the process of rule-making for the compliance mechanism. Most recently the CDM executive board permitted the implementation of programmes of activities oriented CDM, so-called programmatic CDMs, which expand the scope of project developers' options from one single-project at a single site to programme activities with multiple sites and the option for adding in additional sites. COP 7 attempted to address the matter of regional and sectoral imbalance by adopting simplified methodologies and procedures for smaller CDM projects (World Bank 2009). In addition, the intervention of the Gold Standard, a best practice methodology for both Kyoto and voluntary markets, may help to expedite the process of transparency and accountability.[31] However, these internal modifications have not stemmed the calls for reform (from moderate to radical) of the CDM.

External attempts to narrow the sustainable development and equity gaps of the CDMs are being set in place. For example, the World Bank's BioCarbon and Community Development Carbon Funds were created to try to overcome the gap between the CDM's focus on large-scale projects and the excess demand for financing by small-scale projects. The BioCarbon Fund 'aims to deliver cost-effective emissions reductions, while promoting biodiversity conservation and poverty alleviation' (World Bank 2009). The CDCF was instituted in collaboration with the International Emissions Trade Association and UNFCCC to 'support projects that combine community development attributes with emission reductions to create "development plus carbon" credits, and will significantly improve the lives of the poor and their local environment' (World Bank 2009). Though the CDCF focused on integrating community-level projects into the carbon funding scheme and poverty reduction, it was not designed to be gender sensitive. Thus gender priorities and concerns are not critical to its emphasis on promoting capacity building and encouraging investors into funding 'alternatives for carbon investing'.

In the interim and over the years different variants and innovations have evolved around the CDM. Examples of the innovations within the CDM sector revolve around the participation of microfinance institutions, the MDG Carbon Facility and the ADB Carbon Market Initiative. The next chapter will explore the latter two initiatives.

7.3.2 Gender micro-finance and CDM

The CDM has being criticized for inadequate financing and low levels of penetration in the critical areas of poverty reduction and sustainable development. Thus efforts have been made to link the CDM, a market-based mechanism, with microfinance, which has the reputation for linking financial instruments to poverty reduction and sustainable development approach (Stehr 2007). In the context of promoting a more equal regional distribution of CDM projects, the CDM Executive Board has, itself, identified potential synergy between CDM and microfinance activities in least developed countries. According to Stehr (2007) 'the involvement of MFIs in CDM can significantly contribute to enhance the effects of climate protection programmes on poverty reduction and sustainable development'.

For example, MFIs such as ACCION and Grameen have proven to be incredibly scalable, and they can spin off renewable-energy focused businesses (Augustine 2008). Initially, they were largely dependent on the donors and development agencies. But today they are able to use their balance sheet to raise capital. They have had to adjust their interest rate structure to enable them to cover cost of services and today the set interest rate covers cost plus generates returns on investment that are sometimes much higher than commercial financial sectors. Now they are adding renewable energy, environmentally sustainable sanitation and water systems to microfinancing. Additionally, financing mechanisms, such as green investment funds and carbon trading, and risk or index insurance hold promise for both expanding the outreach and enhancing the economic sustainability of MFIs in a climate friendly way.

Under the Clean Development framework, the World Bank, as Trustee for the Community Development Carbon Fund, signed Emissions Reductions Purchase Agreements (an agreement to pay for carbon credits)[32] with Grameen Shakti and the Infrastructure and Development Company Limited (IDOL) for the installation of Solar Home Systems to reduce carbon emission in households in Bangladesh (Financial Express 2007). Under these agreements, Grameen Shakti and IDOL can claim benefits for carbon emission reduction for about 970,000 and 227,000 solar home systems installed in Bangladesh respectively[33] (ibid.). These partnerships increase the web of microfinancing, advance and solidify the climate change activities causes and improve the lot of the poor.

There has not been a comprehensive research and analysis on the contribution of micro credit/finance to poverty reduction or women's empowerment. However, microfinance does have a reputation for credit and bringing finance to those, especially poor women, who were left out of the formal banking system/credit market. Micro-finance has provided financial services to the poor and has proved to be a powerful instrument for enabling some sectors of the lower working classes and the poor to build assets, increase incomes and reduce their vulnerability to economic stress (Augustine 2008; Stehr 2007). Thus there is a strong likelihood of high residual impact on poverty reduction among some households. This would seem to be the case in Bangladesh and India. Whatever the poverty reduction results, micro credit and microfinance is now widely available within and across many developing countries.

With at least 2.4 billion people suffering from energy poverty and an equal amount lacking access to basic financial services, there would seem to be tremendous excess demand for both energy and financial services (UNDP 2006). As a quasi-development strategy, micro-finance has the net benefit of permitting massive outreach, reaching more than 58 million beneficiaries (Stehr 2007). With a network greater than 1,400 MFIs (reported to micro-finance Information Exchange, MIX) and with a growth rate of 30 per cent annually over the past 5 years, micro-finance is expected to have far-reaching impact on poverty.

There has been increasing calling for a new energy model in developing nations to follow a sustainable growth path and draw from clean and renewable sources (UN 2006; Augustine 2008). However, there are barriers to establishing renewable energy projects on both the demand and the supply side at the villages, rural and peri urban areas in low-income and middle-income countries (Augustine 2008). The primary barrier is affordability, many poor men and women cannot afford to pay extra for the environmental services. Thus microfinance would seem to have inserted itself as the bridge between the two as a facilitator of delivery and dispersion of the new energy model.

Demand for improved technologies exists for various client segments, i.e. households, communities, farmers and energy entrepreneurs. These demands can be met if credit/financing is available. On the Supply-side, the issues are more challenging because they involve matching financial products to different clients in context in which MFI have had to undertake minimal credit analysis and are accustomed to short payment cycle. There is concern as to whether the microfinance model can translate into underwriting larger-scale, more complex and longer-term financing instruments. Given the nature of the credit market, can MFI have access to financing on a sustainable basis on large-scale? It is likely that Micro finance institutions (MFIs) can make the adjustment as they have had to adjust and transform themselves over time. According to Augustine (2008), MFIs such as ACCION and Grameen have also proven to be incredibly scalable, and they can spin off renewable-energy focused businesses. Initially, they were largely dependent on the donors and development agencies and development finance institutions for grants and subsidies. But today, many MFs are increasingly seeking to raise capital from the international capital markets through bonds, equity investments, debentures as well as with specially created instruments called microfinance investment vehicle (MIVs). This allows them to widen both their scope of offering their customer base.

MicroEnergy Credits Corporation (MEC) has been quite involved in the carbon market (Augustine 2008). MEC has developed two credit instruments. The first is the Micro-finance-originated Carbon Credits which allows MFIs to generate revenue when they lend for energy systems that create verified carbon emissions reductions for solar PV systems, improved cook stoves and biogas digesters. The second is the Millennium Development Goal (MDG) credits, which allow MFIs to gain MDG Credits when they lend for an intervention that enables an MDG household to meet all or part of an MDG credit. Augustine (2008) highlights that, on both counts, the MFI is facilitating verifiable credit. For example, she notes that, 'MEC provides MFIs carbon revenues on a per-unit basis for each system they finance. This gives them near-term access to finance for the seed costs of starting an energy programme. As their programmes scale up, they can pass on the subsidy to end users which enables them to achieve greater volume by reaching poorer clients' (cited in Augustine 2008).

There are two different approaches to enhancing the capital base of micro-finance (Augustine 2008). One focuses on pooling micro-finance institutions and the other on alliance building or cross sectoral partnerships. Microfinance pooling is an innovative instrument. For example, Citigroup Foundation and the US Agency for International Development provide the funds, while Small Enterprise Education and Promotion (SEEP) Network manages the projects. With a team of six MFIs in Asia and Africa, they entered into partnership to organize and explore potential collaborations and business models which lead to the management of a renewable energy company. This collaboration includes firms such as ACCION, BASIX in India and Equity Bank in Kenya.

In terms of alliance building or cross-sectoral partnerships, there are promising alliances being formed between financial institutions and providers of energy and environmental services. In some cases, these involve cooperatives and others that have the capacity to aggregate demand and organize low-income consumers and communities, including NGOs, to manage more complex initiatives. For example, the alliance between the Self-Employed Women's Association (SEWA) Bank and SELCO-India seeks to meet the energy needs of self-employed individuals and micro enterprises for processing, agriculture and other livelihoods. SEWA-SELCO partnership finances the acquisition of the technology package especially designed by the solar energy company to help low-income women who own solar battery chargers and rent out solar lanterns to vendors in evening markets. The hope for the future is clear – to put households and communities on a clean energy path that allows them to be owners of their own reliable and renewable systems.

The key question is whether the rapidly growing micro-finance sector catalyses low-income clients while contributing to climate change mitigation and adaptation.

Innovative partnerships from both the demand and supply sides have offered a glimpse of the possibilities.

Increasingly, banks and other established financial institutions are beginning to seek coherence and synergy between their micro-finance and environmental portfolios. One such example is Triodos Bank of the Netherlands which has set up links between its micro-finance and environment portfolios. In addition, MDBs, such as the World Bank, are also adapting a similar strategy and linking their climate change portfolio with NGOs and MFIs such as Grameen Shakti.

The World Bank and the Community Development Carbon Fund have a partnership through 'Emissions Reductions Purchase Agreements' with the bank as Trustee for CDCF. Through this initiative, Grameen Shakti and Infrastructure and Development Company Limited (IDCOL) can claim benefits for carbon emission reduction for about 970,000 and 227,000 solar home systems installed in Bangladesh respectively. These partnerships increase the web of microfinancing, advance and solidify the climate change activities causes and improve the lot of the poor.

MFIs would appear to be well entrenched in some developing countries and can reach more men and women in ways that current climate change financing mechanisms, both public and private, cannot (Stehr 2007). It is therefore important that they are integrated and embedded in global climate change financing. Households and micro enterprises transfer CER ownership to MFI by incorporation into the programme. The MFI sells the CERs to carbon buyers and refunds the micro credits with the CER revenues (Obrador 2008).

However, though in many places the client base is predominantly female, micro-finance itself is not particularly gender sensitive and there is no formal incorporation of gender equality or gender empowerment frameworks in its operational domain. So there has to be some focused gender advocacy in this area.

Following on the approach set by the micro-finance sector, proponents of the Millennium Development process are also seeing the utility and profitability of exploiting carbon trading as a way of generating funds for achieving the MDGs. Thus far, the primary mechanism in this approach is through the development of the MDG Carbon Facility.

> Some villagers now use solar for electricity, light, tv and radio and biogas for cooking and heating. They are full owners of their own energy generation, without being susceptible to the price of oil, or the fallibility of the electric grid. And they enjoy the environmental benefits of clean, silent, reliable, continuously renewing energy. As their income increases they are demonstrating a preference to buy another solar panel for a fan or a color TV – rather than switch to a diesel genset, or pay a high connection fee for unreliable grid connected service. Once they are on the clean energy path, there is less incentive to get off it.
>
> (April Allderdice, MEC)

7.4 Gender and the financing of the transfer and development of environmentally sustainable technology

The area of technology transfer to enable both adaptation and mitigation strategies is an area of high tension in climate change financing. Under the UNFCCC, developed countries committed to provide funding for the transfer of environmentally sound technologies to the south. The International Energy Agency (IEA) estimates that roughly $720 billion (at an average of $24–6 billion per year) is needed (IEA 2006, cited in UNFCCC 2007). The deployment of new technologies around biofuels and nuclear energy will require approximately $33 billion, while public energy research and development will require about $20 billion (Stern 2006, cited in UNFCCC 2007). Though the GEF argues that about 80 to 100 per cent of its climate change mitigation funding goes towards technology transfer, only about $10.7 million (under SCCF) is directly available for technology transfer to the developing countries (UNFCCC 2007).

Technology needs assessments (TNAs) and initial national communications (INC) are the two vehicles that are currently used in establishing countries' priority technological options. The key priority mitigation technological options commonly identified in the 23 TNAs and 25 INCs submitted by non-Annex I parties (developing countries), were 'renewable energy generation and energy-efficient technologies[34] such as biomass, mini- and micro-hydropower plants, efficient lighting and water heating, water pumping, solar drying of agricultural products, and efficient stoves'. With regard to technology needs for adaptations, TNAs and INCs identified those in agriculture (such as for tolerant and resistant crop varieties), fisheries (such as micro) and coastal zones (such as indigenous and hard and soft technologies with regard to sea level rise).[35]

Technological interventions should also focus on improving women's productivity especially in the area of food production. In general, policy makers should ensure that agricultural technologies are targeted to women (within a context that builds on their own traditional knowledge and practices) promote food security and ensures sustainability.

Notes

1 The IPCC identified seven key sectors (arranged according to their relative percentage contribution to greenhouse gas release into the atmosphere) they include: energy sources (25.9 per cent), industry (19.4 per cent), forestry (17.4 per cent), agriculture (13.5 per cent) transport (13.1 per cent), residential and commercial buildings (7.9 per cent) and waste management (2.8 per cent), (IPCC 2007, p.105).
2 The OPS5 gender review team seem to have gender expertise not available to the secretariat: 'However, 22 per cent of the CEO-endorsed projects that were rated as gender not relevant are in fact considered gender relevant by the evaluation team of this substudy, which includes gender expertise not readily available to the Secretariat.' OPS5, p.62.
3 The SPG has a global partnership with the Huairou Commission to support capacity development on gender and dissemination of gender-related good practices among SGP countries worldwide (GEF/UNDP 2012).

Gender and state of play in mitigation financing 335

4 Of the 22 countries' strategies reviewed, only one did not consider women to be a priority target group. The report also points out that in some countries local sociocultural factors may constraint women's participation while in others, their participation may be in roles that contribute little to their empowerment (GEF 2008). About 15 per cent of the third operation phase of the SPG grants explicitly target indigenous people (GEF 2008).
5 There few rigorous studies of the gender and sustainability benefits of the SPG. The Almanrio women of Guatemala have developed their own method and instruments for designing, implementing and tracking their projects (cited in GEF/UNDP 2012 see also (López Torrejón et al. 2012).
6 The UNDP GEF report of 2012 highlights that still a lower percentage of grants (39 per cent) but relatively higher than in earlier phases (27 per cent) were awarded to CBOs than the share (60 per cent) awarded to NGOs. (The remaining 1 per cent is awarded to CSOs.) However for some countries such as Costa Rica, the report notes there has been 'a striking shift – from 905 NGO grant recipients in the pilot phase to 905 by the end of 2011.
7 Volatility of bilateral and multilateral flow is a much discussed topic in the economics and development financing literature. There is some confusion as to the degree of differences between the cyclical behaviour of multilateral and bilateral aid flow. But there are quite strong 'empirical regularities' regarding the pattern of aid flow (Robe and Pallage 2000). Four relevant trends for this discussion are that 1) 'aid flows are highly volatile over time (on average, two to three times as the recipient's output', 2) aid disbursements are strongly positively correlated with the donor's output, 3) there is a pattern of aid (both commitments and disbursements) pro-cyclicality, the former more so than the latter, and 4) 'aid disbursement patterns contribute to the volatility of developing countries disposable income' (ibid.). Because multilateral aid is pooled across a number of donors there can be some significant smoothing out of the effect of the cycle of individual donor's budget-business cycle upswings and down swings effects.
8 Conceptual and operational documents linking gender and CIFs include: Gender Mainstreaming Evaluation Synthesis May 2011 (Operations Evaluation Department, African Development Bank Group); Strategic Environmental, Social, and Gender Assessment (SESA), 2010; Gender Policies of the MDBs. The World Bank Group, the African Development Bank, the Asian Development Bank, the Inter-American Development Bank etc.; Gender Mandates of the UNFCCC, Gender Inequality Index for CIF countries and Gender as a driver for transformational change.
9 Strategic Environment, Social and Gender Assessment of the Climate Investment Funds. SCF/TFC.6/Inf.2. 29 October 2010. Discussion in below referred to tables1 and 3. CV: Climate variability, CC: Climate change.
10 The CTF documentation flags that investment plans and proposed projects and programmes will be able to meet a four-fold set of criteria for prioritization: (i) potential for long-term GHG emission savings; (ii) demonstration potential; (iii) development impact; and (iv) implementation potential. Development impact is further defined in terms of 'poverty alleviation, fuel savings, efficiency gains, air and water quality, energy security and access, economies of scales, economy-wide impact, local industrial development potential and environmental co-benefits' (Annex A, CTF key document June 9. 2009) cited in SESGA p.10.
11 The review was carried out under the supervision of the CIF AU and in collaboration with MDBs gender focal points.
12 The 16 country plan (with a total of 22 programmes and projects) are: Chile, Colombia, Egypt, India, Indonesia, Kazakhstan, Mexico, Morocco, Nigeria, Philippines, South Africa, Thailand, Turkey, Ukraine, Vietnam, MENA region (Middle East and North Africa).
13 IUCN notes that: 'The Chilean CIP focuses on increasing the role of women in renewable and energy efficiency industries and including sex disaggregated indicators for employment in the industry.' Gender is mentioned in the Indian CIP the policy and

336 Gender and state of play in mitigation financing

regulatory analysis 'electricity access has very important impact on address gender issues' (p.26) and in the private sector financial intermediation project outlined in the annex of the CIP includes gender. The Philippines references are specific to project delivery commitments to deliver gender action plans in keeping with Asian Development Bank Policies.
14 The two exceptions in both cases were Chile and the Philippines, who both use gender indicators partially) (IUCN 2014: 63).
15 Finance instruments mentioned include concessional financing, on-lending through financial intermediaries to reduce the risks of and improve the capacity for financing energy efficiency measures in households, SMEs and the industrial sectors. The countries are: Columbia, Philippines, Turkey, Thailand, Vietnam, Nigeria and India (IUCN p.65).
16 District heating was part of the IP of Ukraine and Kazakhstan; the plan was to refurnish and renovate these systems and thus improve their energy efficiency. The report noted that though gender was not indicated in the IPs, according to the EBRD in-house or external gender analyses had been under taken, including one by the GEF in the Ukraine (IUCN p.67). See appendix contribution and implication of financing of mitigation projects for women's empowerment for gender impact of district heating.
17 Forest dependent people: forests are the mainstay of their livelihoods so any investment could severely impinge on their use rights and practice.
18 The FIP sub-committee selected eight pilot countries by end of 2013 with a pledge of $639 million: Brazil, Burkina Faso, Democratic Republic of the Congo, Ghana, Indonesia, Lao PDR, Mexico and Peru. Of these the four endorsed IPs are: Brazil, DRC, Lao PDR and Mexico. Lao PDR was the only one that 'recognized women as relevant stakeholders and agents of change (the others name them as 'vulnerable groups' and 'beneficiaries'). It also mainstreamed gender throughout its investment policy (IP). The DRC had a section on gender in its IP. Both Lao PDR and the DRC had the engagement of women and women's organization in the development of the IP. Both Lao PDR and Brazil took into consideration the Cancún Decision relating to gender equality and reflected these under the gender and safeguard considerations (IUCN 2014: 47). Brazil further identified gender as a 'cross-cutting issue' during the design stage of each project, to be carefully analysed.
19 Note that both environmental, social and gender co-benefits are reported to 'automatically accrue in the case of certain renewable energy services such as solar lights, cleaner energy technologies for cooking. But for other RE applications, the project would have to be designed in a proper way if there is a decision to maximize the social and gender co-benefits, as these do not occur automatically. But the SREP is not funding household level interventions so there is a need to specify how the social and gender co-benefits will be realized or maximized (p.30). There is strong need to understand the barriers and constraints to the acceleration of rural electrification to very low-income communities (p.30).
20 The Evaluation Report also flags that many of the methods to finance PV systems are still emerging, such as mobile payment platforms and asset financing structure (p.55).
21 Worldwide, the most RE jobs are in biofuels, followed by solar PV, solar heating and Cooling, then modern biomass and wind power, and biogas. CSP has the least number of jobs. Traditional biomass has the most number of jobs overall (IRENA 2013 and Lallement 2014).
22 Specifically, a national communication is a commitment of each Party (in accordance with Article 12, Paragraph 1, of the Convention) to provide the following elements of information to the COP, as set out in Article 4, Paragraph 1, of the Convention: (a) A national inventory of anthropogenic emissions by sources and removals by sinks of all GHGs not controlled by the Montreal Protocol, to the extent its capacities permit, using comparable methodologies to be promoted and agreed upon by the COP; (b) A general description of steps taken or envisaged by the Party to implement the Convention; (c) Any other information that the non-Annex I Party considers relevant to the achievement

of the objectives of the Convention and suitable for inclusion in its communication, including, if feasible, material relevant for calculations of global emissions trends (UNFCCC). National Communications are important for helping to determine progress in implementing the convention; they are also useful for the GEF to determine the needed flow of financing.
23 The GEF Country Support programme provided to GEF national focal points is being 'implemented to provide support to GEF focal points for activities relating to: training, outreach and information sharing; strengthening country level coordination to promote genuine national ownership of GEF-financed activities; and facilitating active involvement of recipient countries and interested government and civil society stakeholders (UNFCCC 2007).
24 The cost of reducing 1 ton of GHG in developing countries is argued to cost less than in developed or industrialized countries. This is because developing countries tend to have obsolete equipment and older technologies which are often cheaper to replace whereas firms in developed countries need to improve or advance technology which is more expensive. Ultimately, from a global climate perspective it is argue that it does not matter where the GHG abatement occurs (GTZ 2010).
25 This was in the context of debate on clarification of the JI. The G77 sought two key things. 1) Domestic actions from the global north and 2) financial penalty for non-compliance with emissions target. According to Olsen (2006) and Grubb *et al.* (1993) the US saw complementarity with the Clean Development Fund (CDF) and JI, if the penalties on Annex I were allocated (in the forms of investment) to non-Annex I countries. This would also provide a mechanism for the involvement of the private sector. The word penalty was eliminated, contribution to compliance was introduced and the CDM was born (Article 12 of Kyoto Protocol).
26 Liverman and Body (UNEP 2008) note these issues raise questions about the role of the CDM and pose challenges to its core business: emission targets, the beneficial effects on climate and the carbon cycles and technological innovation. Additionality is particularly problematic as it requires establishing the counterfactual (what would have happened in the absence of specific projects or Carbon finance), UNEP 2008.
27 The Gold Standard, a voluntary, NGO-backed labelling scheme, had developed a strategy for recognizing those projects which make certifiable contributions to sustainable development in the host country. The Gold Standard accreditation methodology is built directly into the CDM's PDD, but goes far beyond normal CDM requirements to address a number of the shortcomings that exist within the CDM (Alboher 2009, p.4).
28 Direct gender references include: gender equality (generally as in the case of Bangladesh) or in the context of employment as in the case of South Africa. These gender-specific criteria however tend to have the least or last weighted criteria. For example, for Bangladesh gender issue has 5 per cent weight in the overall assessment (GreenStream, p.19).
29 Indirect gender references include: references to the quality of life of the local people (health safety, employment opportunities and enhancement of stakeholder participation).
30 Alboher study of over 1,500 PPDs showed that 'more than 95 per cent of all projects either provided no evidence of women having been involved, or showed that 30 per cent or less of the consulted stakeholders were women' (2009, p.1).
31 Please refer to footnote vii, above for introduction to the GS: 'Prior to project approval, the Gold Standard mandates a comprehensive sustainability assessment which demonstrates the project's contribution to sustainable development. This begins with a 'do no harm' assessment, meant to ensure that the project does not result in any harmful environmental, social, or economic impacts, and is followed by a detailed impact assessment using the Gold Standard's sustainable development matrix. The approval methodology also includes stringent stakeholder consultation requirements, and stipulates that the sustainability benefits be monitored and verified along with emission reductions' (Alboher 2009, p.4).

32 An ERPA is carbon finance agreement or (contractual agreement) for the purchase of CERs or ERUs. It transfers carbon credits between two parties (a carbon buyer and a carbon seller). It is under the framework of the Kyoto Protocol and regulated by the International Emissions Trading Association (IETA) Source: MDG Carbon facility and Investopedia.com.
33 According to the Financial Express, 'the objective of these two Clean Development Mechanism (CDM) projects is to contribute to sustainable development through the provision of renewable solar electricity to households not connected to the electricity grid and thereby reduce the greenhouse gas emissions by displacing kerosene and diesel use for lighting and off-grid electricity generation. The key components of the solar home systems (SHS) include photo-voltaic panels, fluorescent tubes, batteries, installation kits and connections.
34 According to the UNFCCC (2007), the most commonly identified technologies in these groups related to solar photovoltaic (grid-connected and off-grid), biomass (biodigesters, use of forest waste, rice husks and bagasse), mini- and micro-hydropower plants, efficient lighting and water heating (solar and biomass), water pumping (solar and wind), solar drying of agricultural products, and efficient stoves and ovens (solar, charcoal, biomass and liquified petroleum gas (LPG)).
35 In Agriculture priority technologies were identified for 'crop management with the emphasis on developing and using tolerant/resistant crop varieties, and on efficient water utilization and improving irrigation systems (micro-irrigation, creating networks of reservoirs and water resource management). Forestry technology needs included early warning systems for forest fires and technologies for afforestation and reforestation. In coastal zones, technologies (including indigenous technologies) identified included hard and soft technologies to protect against and accommodate sea level rise' (UNFCCC 2007). According to the UNFCCC (2007), 62.5 per cent of reporting Parties identified needs for adaptation relevant technologies in the agriculture and fishery sector, while 41.7 per cent identified such needs in coastal zone management, 37.5 per cent identified needs in the water sector and 25 per cent identified needs in the health sector. The need for support in the areas of capacity-building, tourism, natural disasters, and systematic observation and monitoring was also identified by Parties.

8
GENDER BIASES AND ASYMMETRIES IN GLOBAL AND CLIMATE CHANGE FINANCE

> The governance of the financial architecture is gendered. It is gendered in several ways in addition to the outcome . . . the principles, aims, practices and knowledge base that underpin their decisions are gendered.
>
> Walby 2013

This chapter discusses the different gender biases that operate in the global financial markets. These biases work to thwart women's access to finance. The chapter makes the case that these biases are transmitted to the climate change finance area where they may have negative effects on women's access to climate change finance.

Before turning to examine the gender dynamics of the private sector and the carbon markets in adaptation and mitigation finance, it is important to have a clear understanding of the role that gender discrimination and biases play in the broader global finance market. This is extremely important in light of the push by developed countries to have the private sector play a more pronounced and pivotal role in financing climate protection in developing countries. This is contrary to the emphasis on public finance in the Convention. The shift towards the private sector in climate financing under the UNFCCC framework had been articulated by developed countries' members of the Transitional Committee[1] set up to design the Green Climate Fund (GCF) as well as those members on the board of the now launched Fund, as leveraging the private sector. This leveraging of the private sector is promoted both as the transformative aspect of climate finance under the GCF and as the principal mechanism for working towards fulfilling developed countries. Copenhagen promised $100 billion a year by 2020, a significant portion of which should presumably flow through the GCF.

During the tenure of the Transitional Committee, developed country Party members waged a protracted struggle against strong resistance by developing countries to create a private sector window whereby the international private sector would have direct access to the resources of the Fund. Ultimately, a compromise resulted in much weaker access modality, the private sector facility[2] through which private sector entities could directly access the resources of the Fund, subject to approval of the national designated authority. Developing countries' board members also expressed a more nuanced view of the private sector that would cover the varying ranges of private sector actors, such as small farmers and women's MSMEs operating in developing countries. But there are concerns by many developing countries and civil society that developed countries such as Japan, the UK and the US, remain determined to advance the private sector agenda way beyond what has thus far been agreed. This is indicated for example in the instance of developed countries. In the first four board meetings of the GCF, on engineering a business model framework, that seems to veer towards a purely finance entity or a Multilateral Development Bank type model, rather than an entity that should focus on climate change and development. Approximately two years after the approval of its governing instrument and full complement of board members as dictated by the COP in Durban in 2012, the GCF remained unfunded, except for operational support for the interim secretariat to carry out the support work of the board.

At its sixth board meeting (February 2014), the developed countries and secretariat document GCF BO6/05 sought to set aside up to 20 per cent of the Fund's resources for the Private Sector Facility (PSF), the board however decided only to 'maximize engagement with the private sector, including through a significant allocation to the Private Sector Facility'.[4]

At its eight-board meeting developed country members of the board of the Fund and the various documents prepared by the Secretariat seemed set to promulgate a system for funnelling money to their private sectors. Led by the US, the 12 developed country board members continue to seek to ensure that the private sector has unfettered access by trying to force through a passive 'no objection' procedure, over the objections of one single of the 12 developing country board members, who explicitly argued for an active 'no objection' process.[5] Under a passive 'no objection' process, if a project application was made to a country and there was no response to that application within a specified time frame, the project would not take place. Developing countries, on the other hand, felt that their best interests would be served by explicit written consent allowing or disallowing such a project if it did not fit into national climate change plans. This they did achieve.

Apart from doubts about whether the private sector can lead on fixing the climate challenge, climate change being a magnificent example of colossal market failure, its potential for ensuring an adequate flow of climate finance to women must be questioned as we will see below. That said, there is no question that the private sector, in its multiple dimensions, from major corporations to MSMEs and small holdings, has a role to play in dealing with the climate challenge. But the private sector does not have a silver bullet; and, when it comes to gender equality and women's economic empowerment, there are significant hurdles to be faced in ensuring women's community-based groups and women's enterprises are able to access adequate finance for projects and programmes.

Without a proper understanding of how and why women are underserved in the global and national banking sectors and the financial markets, which has shunted them to the margin of finance, into microfinance, it will be difficult to ensure that adequate amounts of climate finance flow into women's projects and to women's enterprises. The imperative of climate change and the high cost of adaptation as well as the rising losses and damages associated with extreme weather events demand that women are not yet again shunted to the margins of climate finance.

The global financial architecture and its governance, which has been in place since at least the post-war period, are highly gendered. They are so in terms of the principles, aims, practices, and knowledge base underlying decision-making (Lethbridge 2012) as well as in terms of the outcomes of the policies implemented. The operation of the financial system impacts pre-existing structural gender inequalities and can enhance or worsen the situation for gender equality and women's social and economic empowerment (Antonopolous 2009; World Bank 2009; Young *et al.* 2009, 2010).

Financial decision-making at the macro (policy) and meso (institutional and industry) levels affects the day-to-day realities of women as caretakers of home and community, as workers and as business owners. The Stiglitz Commission, which examined the nature of the financial crisis for the UN General Assembly in 2009, noted that democracy and participation require that the people's whose lives are impacted by financial decisions have their voices, priorities and concerns reflected as part of decision-making. This is certainly the case for women. Currently, it is the male perspective that dominates decision-making in finance.

In exploring the gendered nature of the global financial markets, four specific forms of gender biases have implications for the efficacy and efficiency of climate change finance (van Staveren 2002). According to van Staveren, these gender biases are:

- under-representation of women in financial decision-making;
- increased gender gaps in the economic positions of women and men;
- inefficient resource allocation in financial markets due to gender discrimination; and
- gender-based instability of financial markets.

8.1 The under-representation of women in financial markets

Women's issues are generally marginalized in policy processes with regards to lending, investment rules, and private sector financial activities. The International Finance Corporation argues that women's under-representation in the formal sector is due to legal, regulatory, and sociocultural barriers. Others, such as Stotsky (1996), McCaffery (1997) and van Staveren (2002), argue that public sector financial decision-making, such as tax and interest rate policies, can also have gendered effects, which can impact women's participation in financial markets.

Women are under-represented in key decision-making bodies, including government delegations and community-level planning – this is so in both developed countries and developing countries. In the EU, according to the European Commission, there are no women central bank governors and 82 per cent of key decision-making positions are filled by men[6] compared to 18 per cent by women. Only 11 per cent of European Stock Exchange listed companies' boards are female (Bouchet and Isaak 2011). The situation is even less attractive in the management of these firms with wide gender disparity at the very top where only 3 per cent of such companies have a woman directing the highest decision-making body (EU 2010). The three main financial institutions of the European Union, the European Central Bank, European Investment Bank and European Investment Fund have male leadership and an 85:15 male-to-female ratio (Holst and Schimeta 2012). The EU's Justice Commissioner, Viviane Reding, argues that at the current rate of change, it would take more than 40 years for women to hold 40 per cent of board positions in Europe's publicly traded companies.[7]

In the US, Wall Street is a 'boys club' with no woman chief executive of a major securities firm and no woman in the senior executive position at flagship firms such as Goldman Sachs and Citigroup. There is no woman on the 44-member executive leadership committee at Citigroup and one woman senior executive at Morgan Stanley.[8] A recent report on California Women Business Leaders, undertaken by the UC Davis Graduate School of Management, 'found that women hold less than 10 per cent of the board seats and top executive positions of the state's 400 largest companies representing $3 trillion in market value' (UC Davis 2012). The study noted that this represents a 0.2 per cent annual rate of improvement according to which trajectory women won't achieve parity with men for at least a century.[9]

In developing countries women are also under-represented in finance. For example, in Jamaica, research undertaken in 2008 by the Women's Resource and Outreach Centre and the Canadian International Development Agency, showed that while women have made significant strides in educational and professional development, they represent only 16 per cent membership of private sector boards and 33 per cent on public sector boards.

This situation has prompted the formation of the 51 per cent Coalition: Women in Partnership for Development and Empowerment through Equity. The 51 per cent Coalition advocate for women to comprise no less than 40 per cent of boards in the public and private sectors. This situation is familiar across many developing countries. However, at the same time, over 50 developing countries have had women as ministers of finance and/or ministers of the Economy between 2000 and 2012.[10]

Historically, the participation of women's organizations within the UNFCCC framework has been weak. Women continue to be under-represented in boards, bodies and delegation.[11] Despite the fact that fairly early on (COP 7, 2001), gender equality was recognized as important for adaptation and mitigation (Decision 36/CP7), it was not implemented. Women as a group did not have a significant organized presence at climate change policy gatherings until fairly recently. Though there were strong highly placed women in a number of delegations throughout the period of negotiations, including at Cancún and Durban. At the Doha meeting in 2012, the Conference of the parties made yet another decision to improve the representation of women. As noted in Chapter 3, the COP agreed to the goal of gender balance and the participation of women with a commitment to capacity building to ensure the full implementation of the decision (WEDO 2012).

Nonetheless, it is still the case that women remain under-representative in financial decision-making within the UNFCCC's key finance-related bodies such as the GCF (40 men and eight women), the Standing Committee on Finance (16 men and four women), the Adaptation Committee (11 men and 4 women), the Adaptation Fund Board (24 men and four women), and the CDM (16 men and 4 women), in 2012 (WEDO 2012).

The under-representation of women in the various climate change finance forums is partly due to lack of gender sensitization of male and female leaders and inadequate or no gender analysis and perspectives among women leaders within the negotiations process. It is also due to the fact that despite the representation of some women in key positions, climate change is male-dominated in the climate science and policy communities. As noted by Boyd (2002), 'there is strong patriarchal underpinning of the sustainable development and climate change policy agenda, especially mitigation'. She also argues that 'western ideas of science and development are predominantly driven by "masculine" interest especially with regard to forestry, accounting, agriculture and policy making'. Ultimately, the predominant decision-makers in many climate change institutional processes are men (bureaucrats, technical analysts, NGO representatives, extension workers and influential leaders at the community level (Boyd 2002). According to Denton (2002), men are biased towards providing technical solutions to the climate change problem, and some men have little understanding of or regard for the concerns or interests of women (ibid.). Thus decision-making and policy formulation at environmental levels within conservation, protection and rehabilitation and environmental management follow predominantly male agendas and market-driven notions such as emissions reductions, fungibility and flexible mechanisms (Denton 2002: 1; Boyd 2002).

This problem of women's under-representation in climate governance has prompted the call for more women's representation on the various commissions within the climate change policy environment (Dankelman 2002). The problem is not simply numerical representation, which can be easily fixed; but rather, the lack of gender analysis and perspective integrated into those contexts. This problem of the under-representation of women, the voices, concerns and priorities of especially poor women, permeates climate change financing mechanisms, instruments and processes. To this end, WEDO and the GGCA, with support from the government of Finland and Iceland, has implemented the mechanism of the Women's Delegate Fund to help to increase gender diversity within the UNFCCC process. The programme has so far supported 42 women delegates from 72 countries with training on technical issues, diplomacy, networking, communications and legal and drafting skills (WEDO 2012/2014).

8.2 Global finance, gender gaps and the economic and social position of women

Van Staveren (2002) argues that the globalization of finance has brought some advantages for women, such as increased access to credit (due to increase competition and increases in the credit supply) and increased opportunity for employment (though at lower paid and less protected jobs than men). At the same time, there have been losses for women due to the segmentation of financial markets.

A number of research studies have documented the existence of pervasive 'inequalities between women and men in access to financial services, particularly credit' (Baden 1996; van Staveren 2002; World Bank 1995). Even in the contemporary period, findings from the World Bank's Global Findex[12] show that in developing countries women are 20 per cent less likely than men to have an account at formal financial institutions. In South Asia 41 per cent of men relative to 25 per cent of women have a formal bank account (World Bank 2014). The Findex study also shows that women are 17 per cent less likely to have borrowed formally with the past year (2013). According to Yotopoulos and Floro (1992) and Baden (1996), gender-based segmentation involves distortions, high administrative and transaction costs on the supply side (credit institutions) as well as on the demand side (individual female borrowers as compared with male borrowers) to the detriment of women. Baden argues that these transaction costs limit the net gains from financial transactions for women and make financial services less accessible and more expensive for women. Thus gender segmentation of financial markets creates disadvantages for women.

Women may be negatively impacted by a triple jeopardy: (1) lenders may operate from a risk assessment framework that assigns high probability of default to small producers, many of whom are women; (2) high administrative costs of extending and recovering small loans appropriate to the scale of economic activities by lenders as well as the women themselves enduring high costs in mixing multiple and complex informal lending sources (World Bank 2011); and (3) gender asymmetries in the flow of information about credit markets. Due to incomplete information about women's credit patterns and the reality that women are more likely to be in the category of small producers, these three factors may combine to exclude or crowd out women from existing credit markets. Women's lack of access to collateral may also cause them to be disproportionately excluded from credit markets. As a result of high transactions costs and frequent market failures, financial markets may increase or exacerbate the gap between men and women in terms of access to other tangible resources in the economy.

Research focused on the prevalence of microfinance[13] and its outreach to women indicates that these trends continue to dominate the practice of credit and finance in developing and developed countries (Ameen 2004; Fernando 2006; World Bank 2007). Women account for over 90 per cent of the over 100 million persons living in poverty that are served by microfinance lenders.[14] A World Bank study argues that 'after microfinance, [despite] their excellent repayment records, women are not often graduated to larger individual or business loans beyond microfinance programmes' (World Bank 2008). Perversely, 'the share of women served declines as microfinance institutions diversify or transform into banks'. Hence as noted in the study, 'women are less conspicuous in programmes with larger loan size that could support higher level of business development' (World Bank 2008: 9) Given their predominance in microfinance programmes, women still do not have significant opportunities for building 'physical and reputational collateral' such as credit history. It is the case that though there are now well over 3,300 microfinance institutions (MFIs)[15] serving millions of people worldwide, only a small fraction of credit bureaus (42 of 128 worldwide) cover the MFIs and their clientele. Thus women remain trapped in low-capital activities, which require less fund and with less chance for growth and development (World Bank 2011).

In terms of climate change, there are many gender-based inequities in access to education, training and technology. In general women tend to be under-represented in capacity-building initiatives especially those activities focused on mitigation (Dankelman 2002). Hence, currently, women play a limited role as producers in the formal energy sector and in the formulation and implementation of energy policies. In addition, gender-based inequalities in employment opportunities predominate in areas such as forestry, which employs small numbers of women, mainly in ancillary positions (i.e. as cooks for forestry workers). But women are not well integrated into technical teams, community forest concessions and titling processes which are seen as male domains in many communities.

As noted by Skutsch (2008):

> ... the pool of women professionals in the fields of engineering, energy and other technical areas is small. There are few women who own or are involved and involved in managing large business. Inadequate and lack of financial and management capacity has been the main cause for this imbalance ... Within the climate change negotiations, capacity building has been awarded attention specifically within the context of technology transfer and the flexible mechanisms, particularly CDM. Capacity will be needed to identify, assess, access and assimilate technologies; for CDM, capacity is needed to access and later implement.

On the positive side, financial markets may: (1) enable increased credit, which may benefit women; (2) facilitate rising access to foreign exchange for women through remittances and increased opportunities for women's employment. On the negative, there may be: (3) lack of agency (men may control women's loan proceeds and incomes) – a recent Pakistan study shows that 'although women may have bank accounts in their names, the decision-making authority around use of these accounts often lie with a male relative' (World Bank 2014); 4) a high transaction cost[16] which is associated with the administration of small loan size (which in turn may be linked to women's lack of collateral and/or lack of formal credit history) may limit women's net gains to credit market; and (5) a high degree of gender-based segmentation whereby women are not the favoured targeted group for financial services and are excluded from some preferred categories of services works to disadvantage of women business owners.

In a gender-friendly climate-constrained world, there would likely be tremendous speculative for-profit enterprises and employment/income generation opportunities equally, or equitably available for men and women in pioneering and implementing climate friendly solutions. These opportunities would be generated by the flow of investments into plants and infrastructure development around clean energy and climate-proofing investment activities and likely as well by the continued growth of the carbon finance market. Unfortunately, this may not be the case, as in the current environment, most of the many high-valued/returns, high profit, and high-income activities are likely to be filled by men. These include positions in climate management, carbon financing, carbon risk management, construction and transport sectors.

Thus there needs to be specific skills-upgrading and knowledge-building programmes geared towards women in order to enable more women to take advantage of climate change related opportunities in the medium to long run. Such capacity building and skill development efforts should cut across the thematic areas of adaptation, mitigation technology transfer and financing. They should focus on all levels, from rehabilitative work in home and commercial buildings to infrastructure to technical specialist in carbon risk management. Particular attention should also be paid to building capacities for women to fully participate at all levels of carbon marketing financing instruments and mechanisms. This may mean that some of the funding streams associated with the Convention as well as multilateral development banks may have to be sequestered or redirected towards gender-specific capacity building, education and awareness training.

In the transition towards a gender-sensitive, woman-friendly climate change financing world, the negative attributes of global finance may also be muted or transformed. Consider the operating principle of 'no regrets' that is currently a topic of discussion in promoting resilience and climate-proofing development. The idea is that a set of projects may be considered for implementation, after cost and benefit analysis has been undertaken, even if it is doubtful that the anticipated climate event will occur. This is because these projects would of themselves generate net social benefits, even without the effects of climate change. Gender equality and non-gender equality interventions (as discussed in Box 3.3, Chapter 3) fit this 'no regrets' criterion.

On the grounds of social net benefits, there can be targeted interventions by governments and funding for the development of projects and programmes that seek to eliminate the high transaction costs that women and community groups may face in attempting to access and utilize the financing available within existing finance instruments. Such actions could include initiating the provision of finance to women's groups, women-owned entities and projects through special windows that entertain applications for specific types of gender sensitive adaptation and mitigation projects, discounted premiums on insurance products and the subsidization of the administrative costs of registering projects developed by poor women. Over time, women's access to credit should be mainstreamed. This can be accomplished when financing mechanisms begin to incorporate gender sensitive policies and guidelines into their management structure and into project design, implementation, evaluation and monitoring. It is only through such proactive efforts that the pernicious and pervasive issue of gender bias and segmentation can be eliminated. Additionally, a commercial entity could receive specifically targeted tax write-offs or subsidies for supporting gender-sensitive adaptation and mitigation projects. Likewise, national development banks may have a special gender window utilizing donor-sequestered contributions.

8.3 Inefficient resource allocation in global and climate finance

Well-known rigidities and challenges in the national and global financial markets that block or distort women's access to economic resources, credit and financing in credit and money markets can be detected in the climate change financing arena. The concerns, priorities and issues of women are marginal to the operations of climate change financing decision-makers. Nonetheless, the consequences of decision-making in terms of what projects and programmes are financed and by what means are also borne by women.

It may also be the case that the same types of gender-based constraints (such as inequality in property rights and chronic low income and savings) that create problems for women in the regular financial markets, may also operate in the context of climate change financing. Such constraints are interlinked with discriminatory norms in the financial markets resulting in inefficiency in resource allocation.

According to van Staveren, gender-based constraints (such as inequality in property rights) in the economy are interlinked with discriminatory norms in financial markets resulting in inefficiency in resource allocation in the financial markets. The World Bank notes that 'collateral requirements, high transaction costs, limited mobility and education, and other social and cultural barriers contribute to women's inability to obtain credit' (Holt and Ribe 1991).

Discriminatory norms here are at least twofold: (1) credit institutions assume that women are riskier borrowers than men; and (2) that women borrow primarily for consumption. In fact, the reality is that women tend to have high repayment rates. According to the World Bank, 'experience has shown that repayment is higher among female borrowers, mostly due to more conservative investments and lower moral hazard risk' (World Bank 2007).

Van Staveren notes that 'credit programmes that lend exclusively or mainly to women show repayment levels of around 97 per cent, which is higher than many

> **BOX 8.1 GENDER AND DISCRIMINATORY NORMS IN FINANCIAL MARKETS**
>
> Evidence of discrimination against women entrepreneurs by banks in Europe and Central Asia show that: the probability of receiving a loan is about 5 percentage points lower for female-owned/managed firms than for male-owned/managed firms. This is a large difference, given that only 58 per cent of the loans are approved. Further, female entrepreneurs pay higher interest rates – about 0.5 percentage points more than male entrepreneurs do.
>
> Source: http://psdblog.worldbank.org/psdblog/2009/04/do-banks-discriminate-against-women-entrepreneurs.html#more. Data based on the World Bank's Business Environment and Enterprise Performance Survey data (2005).
>
> Although credit institutions tend to regard women as risky borrowers, the reality is different. In fact, women tend to have high repayment rates. Credit programmes that lend exclusively or mainly to women show repayment levels of around 97 per cent, which is higher than many repayment rates of men (Women's World Banking 1996). Credit institutions also often assume that women borrow for consumption without capacities to repay. Yet when women borrow for consumption purposes, they are often addressing short-term liquidity problems that are solved by long-run cash flows that assure repayment (Baden 1996). Moreover, what seem to be consumer goods may in fact be capital investments that improve women's productivity in the care economy, for example refrigerators or washing machines.
>
> In developing countries, gender inequality, such as women earning lower pay than men and women's lack of ownership of property, contributes to low savings rates, low investment rates, and distorted interest rates (van Staveren 2002).

repayment rates of men' (Women's World Banking 1996). In Bangladesh, Hossain (1988) found that the differential repayment rates between women and men were 80 per cent (women) and 74 per cent (men).[17] Similar findings are documented for Bangladesh in the 1990s and early 2000s (Sharma and Zeller 1997; De Aghion and Morduch 2003), Guatemala (Kevane and Wydick 2001) and Malawi (Hulme 1991). After undertaking an analysis of the 'gender-differences with respect to microfinance repayment rates using a large global dataset covering 350 Microfinance Institutions (MFIs) in 70 countries', D'Espallier et al. (2009) argue that 'more women clients are associated with lower portfolio-at-risk, lower write-offs, and lower credit-loss provisions, ceteris paribus'. The report thus would seem to lend support to the widely held view that women consistently outperform men in terms of repayment.[18]

Box 8.1 illustrates the pervasive nature of gender based discrimination in the financial markets which paradoxically force women entrepreneurs to pay higher interest rates though they have a reputation for high repayment rates. Women are also discriminated against because credit institutions assume that women borrow for consumption purposes and are therefore likely to have trouble repaying (van Staveren 2002). But as noted by Baden (1996), women's apparent consumption goods generally serve dual purposes and are often transformed into capital goods that generate income in the informal and household economy. For example, women often utilize household refrigerators for cooling services for drinks and juices, ice production and sale, and storage facilities either for their own account activities or on a fee-based basis for neighbourhood services. Similarly, women may use stoves and other equipment to informally make and sell cooked goods. These activities, which are based on the fungibility of household appliances into capital goods-on-demand, become even more critical during times of crisis such as those caused by instability in the financial sector and extreme weather events.

A number of researchers (Perlata 2008; Zuckerman 2008; Schalatek 2009) in the area of gender and climate finance have argued that many of the financing mechanisms promoted have gendered inefficient outcomes in that they either (a) misallocate resources by funding projects and programmes that create personal and community damages and reduce access to existing natural resources or (b) impact negatively on critical resources such as water, sewage and housing, thereby exacerbating social issues. In all cases, women are the ones to bear the brunt of the burden as the households adopt coping strategies to deal with declining access. This has been the case for indigenous peoples and some rural communities with regard to forest and land resources. See for example, the case of Mount Elgon National Park, Uganda, where the Benet people were forcibly displaced from lands on which they had historically dwelled and for which many claim title holdings. The people were displaced and the land turned over to a foreign entity who had been issueing carbon 'rights' for tree-planting projects. Similar issues face indigenous peoples in the Amazon region in Brazil and elsewhere.

These scenarios point to the challenges that arise when projects are financed without specific intervention strategies focused on preserving the local infrastructure and in ensuring the access of the men and women living in the affected area. Appendix 8.1 presents a schematic overview of some of the common environment finance tools and their likely impacts.

In order to be efficient and effective for women and indigenous peoples, projects approved for funding should have gender and social guidelines that protect and enhance poverty reduction, social development and gender equality outcomes. Otherwise, there can be disastrous consequences both for women and the environment. Evidence of this can be seen in the pattern of World Bank financing under the Prototype Carbon Finance (PCF 2000), the precursor to the CIFs. The Bank and the European Bank for Reconstruction and Development funded the BTC oil pipeline in Azerbaijan, Georgia and the Sakhalin Island (Sakhalin II oil and gas project). These projects are identified with increased overall poverty, hindering women's access to resources as well as increasing still births and prostitution. In addition, a significant rise in trafficking in women, HIV/AIDs and other sexually transmitted infections are also negative outcomes linked with the projects (Gender Action 2009; Bacheva et al. 2006).

While, under the projects, some women received jobs, in the maintenance sector, most of the jobs went to the traditional demographic group for construction work: young male (Bacheva et al. 2006). Though this was anticipated by the Social Impact Assessment undertaken at the inception of both projects, the social and gender impacts were not planned for. As a result, women were particularly negatively impacted. Elderly women, who were the major group of women landowners, did not benefit from compensation schemes due in part to the nature of customary ownership versus formal titling mechanisms. Many elderly women were displaced. Infrastructure was overwhelmed by the influx of foreign workers. The inflow of workers into the communities severely stressed the local water, sewage and housing infrastructure. The health sector was also overwhelmed by rising HIV positive and TB cases. There was also an alarming increase in stillbirths attributed to air pollution from the burning of oil and the residual smell from charcoal (Bacheva et al. 2006).

These are all factors that raise questions about the much-lauded efficiency of the climate change finance regime grounded in carbon trading and offsets. While the currently evolved CIFs project of the World Bank is not directly implicated in the incidents cited here, there is a great deal of concern by civil society groups, including gender advocates, that there are important lessons to be drawn from these experiences and that the same mistakes are not repeated. The CIFs is notably different from the PCF, in that it does try to integrate gender, albeit insufficiently and inadequately, within its framework. Zuckerman of the NGO Gender Action, in her assessment of the CIFs, found that it did include gender in some broad areas of its strategic framework, but that gender was missing in the critical and legally binding mandates. So for example, in the strategic framework document of the CIFs, gender was listed, among a number of other variables, as one the dimensions of climate change for which there would be support for strengthening technical and policy expertise on development-climate linkages and decision-making capacity at the country level (World Bank 2009: 44, para 3). Gender was also highlighted as an area for which 'good practice guidelines to hep relevant operations account for climate change' were to be prepared. This was in relation to action area 6: step up policy research, knowledge and capacity building – develop and test new analytical tool (World Bank 2009: 32, Annex 3). Gender was also flagged as an important category to benefit from bio energy (World Bank 2009: 24, 49) and the importance of taking into account that 'impacts are often differentiated by gender' was a leader into an entire paragraph that highlighted that women had special vulnerabilities that 'weakens their adaptive capacity' to climate change events. The document further noted that it was important to understand that the scope of health impacts caused by climate change would require addressing differentiation by gender among other things. Table A3:1 on key issues and response (Phase 1) tackles the issue directly by posing the question: How will the World Bank address issues of gender and equity? (World Bank 2009: 72) and indicated that these and other social dimensions issues would be addressed in a forthcoming Social Development strategy update (World Bank 2009: 77).

Gender, as a key variable and category of analysis, and women as key stakeholders, evaporated from the rest of the document, in particular, there was no gender sensitization in key areas such as climate action, mobilization of finance and development and deployment of technology. Key committees such as the Trust Fund Committee, the MDB Committee and the Administrative Unit did not have gender sensitive guidelines or criteria.

Inefficiency in climate financing mechanisms and instruments also occurs in terms of an emerging and ever widening adaptation deficit that has resulted from the operations of the current financing framework. Until fairly recently the focus of attention of climate protection at the global level has been on mitigation creating a shortfall in the financing for adaptation activities. Adaptation activities are very critical to women's social reproduction and productive roles in the current moment. There is a great need for climate-proofing and climate resilience activities at the household and community levels. Unfortunately, these needs tend to be neglected in favour of the development of carbon reduction projects that can yield carbon offset to foreign companies from developed countries.

- Gender based inefficiency in financing, investment and credit flows also impacts macro level variables contributing to losses in real output, productivity growth and ultimately overall economic performances. Van Staveren cites the following two examples drawn from analyses undertaken by the World Bank:
- In Burkina Faso, a transfer of resources (like fertilizer and labour) from men's to women's plots of land within the same household could increase agricultural output by 10–20 per cent (World Bank 1999: 10).
- Research in Tanzania indicates that reducing time burdens of women in the care economy could increase household cash incomes for smallholder coffee and banana growers by 10 per cent, labour productivity by 15 per cent and capital productivity by 44 per cent (World Bank 1999: 20).

Ironically, though climate finance institutions such as the World Bank have clear gender policies and women's empowerment precepts in their broader organizational frameworks, these tend to evaporate with regard to their climate change finance portfolio. Even as the bank is being promoted, by donors and the G7, as the most efficient vehicle for climate change finance, its group of CIFs would seem to be introducing greater fragmentation and inefficiency into the climate change financing environment. First, by introducing a parallel set of instruments for adaptation and mitigation, it is argued that the bank is both diverting funds from the more democratic UNFCCC Convention process towards its own non-transparent and undemocratic governance system as well as exacerbating the fragmentation of climate change finance. This is a direct source of inefficiency in the overall climate change financing architecture.

Second, considering the financing that the CIFs will make available for adaptation and mitigation is more likely to be in the form of loans, as compared to funding under the Convention's financing mechanisms, this will violate the principle of 'common but differentiate responsibility'. It will also weaken the emphasis that the Convention makes on the important leadership role and responsibility of developed countries to finance adaptation and mitigation. Third, the World Bank continues to fund fossil fuels and resource extraction which is contradictory to the goals of GHG emissions reduction. Only about 40 per cent of its FY 2007 portfolio was dedicated to low carbon energy sources. This is another source of inefficiency in climate change financing architecture. Fourth, the bank tends to fund large hydro power projects, which are associated with negative environmental and social costs.[19]

Inefficiencies in the climate financing architecture, such as is argued to exist with the World Bank's CIFs, are problematic for gender equality and women's empowerment. In the first, case funding for CIFs eclipses the amount that is currently available to the Adaptation Fund (established in Bali in 2007). Adaptation is an important area for supporting the life and livelihood of poor men and women in developing countries to cope with adverse weather events. If adaptation financing is driven by loans (and the policy conditionalities that usually accompanies them) then that creates a problem in national government financing that may more negatively impact upon women. Policy conditionalities have undesirable association with negative development, poverty reduction and gender equality impacts. Historically, governments operating under tight budgetary constraints tend to trade off gender equality and other social interventions in their budgeting decision-making in order to finance debt services. Second, if the CIFs focus on large hydro power and high efficiency coal plants then there is less likelihood of women's projects (both adaptation and mitigation) having significant access to these significant streams of funding. Third, the negative environmental and social effects of the World Bank's track record in financing fossil fuel and extractive industries are well known. They have not been good for poor communities and the men and women in them.

The CIFs are but one example of financing mechanisms that can have a potentially strong impact on gender equality. But a similar set of issues are raised by instruments directly under the Convention as well as the implementation of various funding projects under the auspices of partner agencies such as the UNDP and UNEP who are charged with disseminating funding around climate change and adaptation. These agencies and the mechanisms and instruments they create and implement have not always effectively and efficiently followed through on designing gender sensitivity into their programmes and projects at the outset. As a result, there are now some efforts across some programme areas to begin to incorporate gender issues in climate programming including financing. But the work is not widespread or deeply integrative at this stage.

Perlata (2008), in examining gender and climate change finance in the Philippines, argues that the CDM mechanisms 'manifest an inordinate reliance on market based solutions that excluded the poor'. This resulted from CDM processes being cumbersome and costly rendering small-scale projects with strong poverty alleviation impacts unviable and making it difficult for the poor to participate.

However, this does not have to be the case. Gender sensitive resource allocation can lead to improved outcomes for women, if it increases women's access to credit and income, and introduces technology that reduces their time burden. In addition, gender equality in access to resources can translate into productive gains, and increased well-being for women as well as economic growth when these resources receive a market price.

In the area of investment, as can be seen with the climate investment funds, these tend to be sequestered around mitigation projects leaving a financing deficit for adaptation activities. There is therefore greater need for climate-proofing and climate resilience activities at the household and community levels. This is many times neglected in favour of industry or the development of carbon reduction projects that can yield carbon offset to foreign companies from developed countries.

The problem of inefficient resource allocation generated by financial systems also occurs when there is a systematic lack of funding for the development and dissemination of a range of technologies in the areas in which women now use energy (Dankelman 2002). These include household energy, agricultural and food processing, forest management and water pumps in rural areas and energy appliances and processing equipment in peri urban areas. This is especially so in the carbon market, where carbon investors are motivated by large one-off investments in industry and so do not fund the range of technologies that women need to be attractive investment options.

8.3.1 Minding the gaps – regional development banks redirecting finance flow to women

Regional development banks are increasingly stepping into the breach to try to bridge the gender financing gap, especially as it relates to climate change and its financing.

The African Development Bank is working to integrate gender mainstreaming into its Climate Risk Management and Adaptation strategy (CRMA): 'through the focus on gender mainstreaming and women's economic empowerment, the bank is increasingly paying attention to mitigating the effects of climate change on gender equality. In particular, the bank is working with other partners to outline the entry points for addressing gender mainstreaming within the climate change framework'.

The bank's midterm strategy of 2008–2012 and the African Development Fund (ADF) recognized gender equality as a critical development issue to be mainstreamed into key operational plans. The bank's Gender, Climate Change and

Sustainable Development Unit (OSUS) was created in July 2008 in response to the concern for greater focus on results regarding the key cross-cutting issues. The newly created unit would provide visibility and clear lines of responsibility as well as accountability in mainstreaming climate change.

According to the AfDB literature, 'strengthening the OSUS will be an important pre-requisite to delivering the bank's commitment to CRMA'. There is a push for the unit to have at least two dedicated climate change experts. And the bank's environment, social and gender experts will be further trained to enable them to incorporate in-depth climate change management risk analysis into their existing environment and gender evaluation. Nonetheless, the work to make the linkages between gender and climate change visible – and to take practical and strategic gender and climate interest into account in sectors such as energy, water and food within the bank's portfolio – is at an initial stage, outlining the entry points for addressing gender mainstreaming with the climate change framework. Thus far, there is a series of checklists for mainstreaming gender and climate change into Bank operation and projects, such as policy based lending, increasing support to gender-based budgeting, and auditing from gender and good governance check lists.

The checklists seek to monitor the integration of gender issues into all levels of project cycle: from project identification (having good gender analysis, to designing the CRM with women's and men's gender roles and responsibilities in mind); to the project concept note (PCN); to project preparations (with gender issues included in terms of reference and environmental and social integrity assessment and the inclusion of gender experts on the team); to project appraisal (which should include the specification of gender equality results in log frame, the application of gender analysis, the use of gender disaggregate data, the identification of specific action to empower women, gender indicators and the; resource for women in cost tables etc.).

The AfDB gender strategy documents note that:

> The resulting health costs include expenditure on disease control and avoidable treatment services. Water borne and hygiene related diseases also impact productivity. The lack of proper sanitation, both in households and at public places, leads to significant public health consequences and spread of various infectious diseases. Lack of separated toilet facilities for girls and boys at school has often accounted for high drop-out rates among teenage girls, as they are unable to tend to their hygiene needs, properly, during menstruation. Lack of gendered toilet complexes (GTC) at schools, hospitals or market places can also cause problems and discomfort for female teachers, nurses, traders and the general public.

The AfDB effort at gender mainstreaming in its climate change portfolio builds on its Gender Plan of Action and the Updated GPOA which emphasizes the constraints faced by women in accessing safe drinking water and sanitation (Box 8.2 highlights the evolution of the AfDB gender policy framework). In its GPOA the bank pays attention to enabling the provisioning of facilities to deliver such

> **BOX 8.2 THE AFDB GENDER POLICY FRAMEWORK**
>
> The African Development Bank Gender Policy Framework consists of the following policy documents that provide the overarching framework for mainstreaming gender issues into the bank-wide operations:
>
> - Gender Policy (2001)
> - Gender Plan of Action (GPOA) (2004–2007)
> - Updated Gender Plan of Action (UGPOA) (2009–2011)
> - Various gender-related checklists to guide its operations, including those in the water sector.
>
> The Bank's first Gender Plan of Action (GPOA) (2004–2007) aimed: (a) to outline an approach to operationalizing the Gender Policy; and (b) to identify specific activities that would further support gender mainstreaming in operations, such as developing programme tools and strategies, project tools for priority sectors, institutional capacity building and organizational support. A midterm review (MTR) of the first GPOA was undertaken in 2007, providing a synthesis of actions implemented by the bank.
>
> The Updated Gender Action Plan (UGPOA) for 2009–2011 builds on lessons learned from: (i) the MTR of GPOA conducted in 2007; (ii) the Gender Equality Institutional Assessment conducted by CIDA in 2008; and (iii) the conclusions and recommendations of the President's Working Group on Gender.

water and sanitation services that meet the needs of women and girls, especially as it relates to access and location. There is also an attempt to not simply focus on women's domestic needs with regard to water (for cooking, washing and cleaning) but to also emphasize the importance of water for women's productive works in agriculture and animal husbandry. As a result, gender and social equity issues are to be integrated into: (i) water resources management at national and transboundary levels, and (ii) water information management and water information management. The primary methodology of integrating gender and social equity concerns in the AWF as in other AfDB projects are through tools such as checklists and monitoring and evaluations indicators. The Gender and social equity focus on the AWF Management of water resources at national and trans-boundary levels is not yet a significant part of the operational gender mainstreaming effort. It is not clear how the AfDB address gender and social inequalities within the water sector.

Beyond the water sector and the governance sector financing, the AfBD does not have explicit clear and well worked out framework for engender its other climate change funded projects. In the energy sector, for example, there is no checklist. But the renewable energy and energy efficiency operations in the portfolio of the bank will contribute to reducing the burden on women and children in collecting fuel wood and their exposure to indoor air pollution, create employment, reduce the dependency on oil products with its highly volatile costs, and open a window for economic development for the currently unserved population.

As with the African Development Bank, the Asian Development Bank (ADB), long a pioneer in seeking to integrate gender considerations into its operational activities, is also focusing on deepening its gender mainstreaming work. Appendix 8.2 presents greater details on the ADB strategy and approach to engendering its lending portfolio, generally and with regard to climate. Given the poverty focus of its Poverty and Environment Fund, gender concerns and priorities could be more easily mainstreamed into the PEF project. Currently, the Poverty and Environment Fund is the smallest of the ADB's regional funds, but with an added gender dimension it should be possible to leverage funds from bilateral donors and governments. This model could then be replicated in other regions.

BOX 8.3 GENDER AND ASIAN DEVELOPMENT BANK

Explicit recognition should be made of gender in natural disasters. The fatality rates of women in recent major disasters in Asia have been substantially higher than those for men. Women are often more vulnerable due to lower access to and control over key survival and recovery resources, including shelter, transport and food (ADB 2012). Under its technical assistance programme, the ADP is emphasising gender and climate finance issues. It has funded projects to 'harness climate change mitigation to benefit women including efficient bio mass for energy and food security and improving access to low carbon technology and carbon finance. The ADP has also produced a policy brief on gender and climate finance' (see Adams et al. 2014).

The ADB, as indicated in Box 8.3, explicitly recognizes the gender constraints and challenges arising from natural disasters. These are focused on recovery of resources such as shelter and food. The ADB also implements gender equality strategies in its lending portfolio both for capacity building as in the case of projects in Pakistan as well as the provision of diversification crop training programmes in Bangladesh. Snippets on these and other such endeavours are highlighted in Box 8.4.

According to the Inter-American Development Bank (IDB), the promotion of gender and social equity has been a focus on its country strategies and the bank has been proactively funding projects that incorporate gender. Between 1998 and 2001, gender-incorporated projects accounted for about 29 per cent of the share of the bank's portfolio, decreasing to 26 per cent in by the time of the 2002–2005 Women in Development Policy framework. The Gender Equality in Development Unit (GED) in the Sustainable Development Department played a central role in facilitating gender mainstreaming in the bank. According to the IDB's literature, 'priority gender issues were mainstreamed into the lending portfolio, primarily in

BOX 8.4 IMPLEMENTING GENDER EQUALITY STRATEGIES IN REGIONAL DEVELOPMENT BANK PORTFOLIOS – THE CASE OF THE ADB

**Gender friendly input gender empowerment outcomes –
PNG: Bridge Replacement for Improved Rural Access Sector Project**

This project aims to improve the connectivity, efficiency and safety of the rural road network in select provinces of PNG by: replacing single-lane Bailey bridges with permanent two-lane structures on five priority national roads; installing reusable Bailey bridges on rural roads; building the capacity of the Department of Works (DOW) to implement the bridge asset management system (BAMS); and improving road safety awareness in rural areas. The project GAP included gender design features such as: physical designs that facilitated greater access to women on reconstructed bridges; a target to hire at least 30 per cent women for construction work with equal pay for equal work paid directly to them; HIV/AIDS and gender awareness training for construction workers and community members; ensuring Bailey bridges with safety measures for women; targeting at least 50 per cent of women to be engaged in routine maintenance activities; incorporating personal safety concerns of women into road safety education programmes; ensuring at least 50 per cent female representation in the implementation of road safety programmes; and gender awareness training to project staff.

Over 200,000 women affected by the 2005 earthquake in Pakistan participated in skills training and reconstructed 55,000 houses owned by women headed households. These 55,000 female household heads also established their own bank accounts without paying any fee. Eight Women Development Centers and Social Welfare Centers were built in which women were provided with various training.

In an agriculture project in Bangladesh 4,326,020 farmers received crop diversification training to formulate farmer groups, of whom 51 per cent were women. A total of 12,415 farmer groups were formed, of which 51 per cent (6,259) were female. The number of loans and credit disbursed were 329,041 including 167,811 (51 per cent) for females, well exceeding the target of 10 per cent, and with a 99 per cent repayment rate. Asset ownership by women grew by 19 per cent in cash, 5 per cent in land and 5 per cent in jewellery. About 35 per cent reported a reduction in domestic violence, partially attributable to the overall income increase, but also to changing male attitudes to women in the communities (ADB 2012: 5, 9).

> **BOX 8.5 THE IDB'S GENDER AND DIVERSITY FUND**
>
> The IDB's Gender and Diversity Fund is to contribute to the equitable and culturally appropriate development of IDB member countries by fostering gender equality, combating discrimination, and supporting development with identity. The fund will serve three main target populations: women and men in positions of disadvantage resulting from gender-based discrimination and inequality, indigenous peoples, and Afro-descendants (hereinafter, the target populations). Priority areas have been identified for the empowerment of each target population. In addition, cross-cutting areas have been prioritized for all three target populations to address the multifaceted dimensions of discrimination and exclusion that intersect gender, ethnicity and race. Given the scope and reach of the bank's investments in the region, the proposed framework will enable the bank to develop a comparative advantage and pioneer innovative interventions to address gender and diversity issues.

the areas of domestic violence prevention, reproductive health, technical training to improve women's labour market participation, and actions that specifically address issues afflicting afro-descendant and indigenous women'.

Recently, the IDB proposed the Gender and Diversity Special Program and Gender and Diversity Multi-Donor Fund which seeks to establish two funding mechanisms: (a) the 'IDB's Gender and Diversity Special Program' (the 'Special Program'), to be financed with up to US$10 million of resources from the Ordinary Capital of the bank and (b) a 'Multi-Donor Gender and Diversity Fund' (the 'Multi-Donor Fund'), as contemplated in the New Framework for Technical Cooperation (GN-2469–2). Both funding mechanisms will be referred to as the 'Gender and Diversity Fund' (Boxes 8.5 and 8.6). Key issues include women's role in coping with natural hazards and disasters, lack of access to water and forest resources, declining food crop yields and malnutrition, and loss of income generating opportunities, among others.

> **BOX 8.6 THE IDB'S GENDER FRAMEWORK**
>
> The overall IDB Gender Framework, as it is evolving, focuses on concrete measurable outcomes, a gender and diversity special programme and a gender and diversity multi-donor fund
>
> 1   Measurable targets:
>   (a) Expand to at least 75 per cent the share of country strategies that integrate gender issues and actions. (The current level is 50 per cent.)
>   (b) Expand to at least 75 per cent the loans in the social areas that mainstream gender issues. (The current level is 55 per cent.)

(c) Expand to at least 30 per cent the loans in the non-social sectors (infrastructure, modernization of the state, economic opportunities and competitiveness) that mainstream gender issues. (The current level is 14 per cent.)

(d) Introduce gender issues in programmatic lending instruments such as policy-based loans

2 The proposed Gender and Diversity Special Program and Gender and Diversity Multi-Donor Fund seek to establish two funding mechanisms:

(a) the 'IDB's Gender and Diversity Special Program' (the 'Special Program'), to be financed with up to US$10 million of resources from the Ordinary Capital of the bank;

(b) a 'Multi-Donor Gender and Diversity Fund' (the 'Multi-Donor Fund'), as contemplated in the New Framework for Technical Cooperation (GN-2469-2). Both funding mechanisms will be referred to as the 'Gender and Diversity Fund'. Key issues include the women's role in coping with natural hazards and disasters, lack of access to water and forest resources, declining food crop yields and malnutrition, and loss of income generating opportunities, among others.

3 In 2011, the IDB's Board of Executive Directors approved the Operational Policy on Gender Equality in Development and set in motion a process for the preparation of a gender action plan. The Gender Policy will help to 'direct investment in strategic areas of gender equality and women's empowerment', foster 'the addition of gender safeguards to the Bank's current environmental and social impact review of projects in order to prevent or minimize potential negative impacts on gender equality that may result from Bank-financed operations'; and 'help to promote institutional monitoring indicators that will help the IDB monitor and evaluate its progress in implementation of the Policy'. There is no specific climate change component to the GDF, but according the IDB, projects developed under the GDF will support governments' efforts 'to incorporate gender and diversity issues in development programs and projects'.

Though the IDB say that the cross-sectoral nature of climate-related issues requires internal coordination and alignment with the bank's strategies and policies, its funding in the climate change area is not always consistent when it comes to integration of its gender policy. For example, compliance with existing policies and their directives, including the Environment and Safeguards Compliance Policy (OP-703), the Operational Policies on Gender and Equality in Development and the Indigenous Peoples, are key to achieving many of the objectives stated in this CCS.

The IDB's Beyond Banking document promotes its new emphasis on equal banking for gender equality and diversity in financial institutions, promotion of gender equality and diversity, and a line of business that provide support to traditionally unserved minorities, including expanded access to banking for persons with disabilities.

Like it cohorts' banks, the Caribbean Development Bank (CDB) has a clear gender equality policy and operational strategy (GEPOS), approved since 2008. This is not fully integrated into either its Disaster and Risk Reduction or Climate Change and Adaptation-CRS strategies. The Gender Equality (GE) Policy is based on the premise that 'measures which support increased GE lead to economic growth and poverty reduction', and positions the bank 'to be a leading catalyst promoting GE in the Region by working with borrowing members and other development partners in a responsive and collaborative manner to analyse the economic and social causes of gender inequality in order to reduce poverty and vulnerability and to assist all women and men to achieve their full potential'.

According to the CBD, the GE policy intends to achieve the following objectives:

- Reduce economic and social vulnerability by empowering women and men to build and protect their assets, including livelihoods and savings, as a means of building sustainable, equitable communities.
- Strengthen the capacity of all women and men, girls and boys to acquire education, skills and self-confidence in order to access economic opportunities, increased livelihood options and improve their quality of life in the changing global economy.
- Support governance processes in which women and men have equal access to power and authority in society, and effectively influence policies and advocate for their rights.

Based on these objectives, there are eight core commitments, as follows:

1   analyse and address the GE dimensions of economic and social issues in all CDB policies, loans, projects and in the bank's external and internal operations;
2   acknowledge that every policy, loan and project affects men and women differently;
3   implement specific measures to eliminate gender inequalities and disparities;
4   promote GE and empowerment through partnership between men and women;
5   communicate the bank's commitment in the region and advocate for GE in the borrowing member countries (BMCs);
6   promote GE as a means to support sustainable development, and reduce poverty and vulnerability;
7   work in partnership with stakeholders and development agencies; and
8   implement an institutional strategy that sensitizes all CDB staff to GE dimensions in all aspects of internal work relationships and promotes the progressive

incorporation of balanced gender perspectives into management policies, operating style and staff relations. Though the GE policy framework was designed to integrate GE into the bank's Strategic Plan 2005–2009, the Poverty Reduction Strategic Levers and the SDF 7 Themes and the incorporation of GE as a cross-cutting theme in the bank's results-based management (RBM) cascade from 2009 and in the 2011–2014 Strategic Plan.

In October 2010, approval was given by the board of directors to conduct CGAs (Country Gender Assessments) in 10 BMCs over a period of three years. CGAs will provide the bank with a framework and strategic planning base to assist in mainstreaming GE in sector programmes and operations in BMCs.

8.3.2 Insurance and gender in the context of climate change

Increasingly insurance schemes are being proposed as an important adaptation tool. But insurance schemes are not always accessible to women for a variety of reasons, such as lack of funds for premiums or lack of information about availability. In addition, due to prevailing gender asymmetries and biases, insurers may erroneously assess the risk of female insurees, resulting in higher premiums and rejection of such clients for insurance products.

This is particularly important given the growing trend towards risk transfer or absorption mechanisms such as weather-index insurance, as part of the set of risk management oriented adaptation strategies, now being promoted by some donors and climate change finance institutions such as the UNDP, the World Bank Group and USAID. For example, the UNDP[20] is piloting a non-commercial, community-based variant of index insurance. Furthermore, micro finance institutions are also becoming involved in risk insurance and are considering the purchase of such mechanisms as a prerequisite for extending loans to clients (UNDP 2009a).

Risk insurance mechanisms, particularly crop insurance, were traditionally available to wealthy and middle-income farmers and individuals. Risk insurance is being promoted as a climate change adaptation tool that can potentially act as 'a risk transfer mechanism, a mechanism to help people access resources need to escape climate-related poverty and as a mechanism to incentivize risk reduction' (Hellmuth et al. 2009: 99).

While opening up access to these mechanisms may be a step in the right direction, a great deal of care and attention must underlie their design and implementation process. Premiums for any insurance product must be paid out of individual and household current income-expenditures flow. Many women already face income constraints and may not be able to meet the additional burden of paying insurance premiums. Therefore governments considering these measures must pay attention to ensure that the social structure in which poor women and men reside are appropriately climate-proofed so that risk and other forms of insurance serve a residual function and are not the primary or sole mechanisms for dealing with the after-effects of climate events. There is, therefore, much scope for ensuring that insurance risk tools are developed within a framework that is pro-poor and gender sensitive in its design and implementation. Only such a framework will prevent increased financial burden and the further marginalization of poor women.

Gender sensitive risk assessment must be a key condition undergirding the design and implementation of financial risk transfer methods and weather index-based risk management tools as an adaptation strategy. Such assessments must consider critical issues such as:

- How to deal with the problem of asymmetric information between men and women in many communities. How do women and men learn about the existence and nature of insurance products?
- If proposed ideas around 'recovery assistance vouchers' are further developed and implemented, how are women's rights and access to such vouchers assured? What will be the distribution channels for these vouchers if they are given pre or post the weather events? How can women access information about these? Are the end use points for transacting the voucher into goods and services accessible to women directly or do they have to go through intermediaries?
- How to impact insurance underwriters' behaviour so that they do not unfairly discriminate against women?

Local approaches to insurance-based risk management are also being complemented by national and regional initiatives for financial risk management. These range from those that compensate farmers and households directly for damage or loss as a result of climate events. One example of such an approach is the Climatologic Contingency Attention Programme (Programa de Atención a Contingencias Climatológicas, PACC). It is paid exclusively from tax revenues. Other initiatives are focused on country level recovery from climate events such as the Caribbean Catastrophe Risk Insurance Facility (CCRIF), the world's first multinational index insurance. In addition there are various catastrophe bonds also available as climate risk management tools (Hellmuth et al. 2009).

Insurance is not a new issue in climate change finance. It was an item of discussion in the adaptation agenda of the Pozan (2008) meeting and it is likely to become an important element in the post-2012 climate change financing architecture. As noted by Hellmuth et al. (2009), insurance as an aspect of climate risk management has been referenced in the UNFCCC (Article 3.14), the 1997 Kyoto Protocol (Article 4.8), and the 2007 Bali Action Plan (adopted at COP 13). The Bali Action Plan calls for 'consideration of risk sharing and transfer mechanisms, such as insurance' to address loss and damage in developing countries particularly vulnerable to climate change (Decision -/CP.13, Bali Action Plan).

However, insurance as a vehicle for financial asset holding is more known to men than women in developing countries. Research on Ghana by Odura *et al.* (2011: 31) shows that the incidence of ownership of formal savings accounts and insurance is higher for men than for women. There are two explanations for this that may seem applicable across the developing countries: (1) men are more likely to have formal sector jobs that require ownership of bank accounts for wages and salary; and (2) in the case of insurance, formal sector employers and employees are required to make social security contributions.

8.4 Gender and instability in the global financial market implications for women's and men's access to change financing

The global finance market is prone to crisis and instability caused by factors such as extreme risk taking and over leveraged speculative positions taken by key market actors, currency risk, capital flight, fragility and contagion. Currency risk or exchange rate fluctuation causes disruptions in the global financial market and can lead to depreciation of a countries currency relative to, say, the US dollar. This poses three risks. First, depreciating currency can lead to higher food and fuel prices for fuel and food-importing countries. This will impact negatively on the poor (most of whom are women, who are already at low consumption). Second, the government may need to defend the currency to ensure stability in the balance of payment. It will therefore need to use up valuable international reserves that could otherwise have been available to cover necessary imports (such as food and medicines etc.). Third, foreign investors and the local elite may seek to convert local currency into dollars and withdraw these from the economy (the capital flight problem.) In either case both scenarios make the economy vulnerable to, and intensify the problems in the local banking sector and the capital market (the fragility problem). If government have sufficient international reserve and exports are diversified across many markets and international currencies, then the problem in the global financial market may be contained and may not spread indiscriminately into the local economy creating the aforementioned problems (this is the contagion issue). Ultimately, any or all of these risks may be associated with losses in real output, shortfall in government revenues and decreases in government spending. This was a dominant feature of the Asian and other financial crises in the 1990s.

The present global financial crisis (2008–2009) was the result of both market and regulatory failures. The current economic recession is due to systemic failure of economic policy including the exhaustion of monetary policy – without stimulating sustained growth, and the abrupt termination of expansionary fiscal policy. Both of these phenomena have led to a recovery-contraction cycle and likely are only working to prolong stagnation in the real sectors of key economies.

Episodic financial crises negatively impact the supply of credit as well as jobs that could be available to women and men. Past experiences show that financial crises tend to impact women more adversely, than men, in terms of job losses and loss of social services. When governments experience decreasing revenue they are likely to respond by reducing government spending, primarily spending on essential services that are critical for the household. Women and men are also likely to be double negatively impacted by the financial crisis if it impacts the flow of public financing for climate change.

Prior to the financial crisis and the beginning of the economic crisis there were pre-existing structural inequalities in terms of women's access to employment and income (including, gender pay gaps) and women's and men's differential access to social and economic resources and governmental services. These gender structural inequalities, as noted above, can either be exacerbated or lessened by government policy responses in normal times. But in periods of a financial and economic crisis these structural inequalities are highly sensitive to the policy approach adopted.

For example, globally women are known to comprise at least 50.5 per cent (relative to 48.2 per cent for men) of the so-called 'vulnerable employment'. The ILO defines this as 'work where people are self-employed or part of family firms, where labour rights are limited and where workers work long hours, for low pay, in poor conditions, with no social benefits or statutory entitlements' – this includes casual work, zero-hour contracts, abusive fixes and part-time contracts (ILO 2012, cited in Lethbridge 2012). Research by the ILO shows that women during economic crises are 'more likely to be affected by loss of employment or cope with increasing insecurity'.

Women also dominate in public sector employment and hence are the group most likely to be affected by reductions in public sector expenditure. In Ireland women are 72 per cent of the public sector workforce, Spain 54 per cent, Latvia 63 per cent and the UK 65 per cent.

In many developing countries, women are 60–80 per cent of the export manufacturing workforce. Women comprise a large percentage of the export led workforce in Malaysia (78 per cent – garments); Bangladesh (85 per cent – garments); Philippines (+50 per cent – electronics); Uganda (85 per cent – cut flowers); Ecuador (70 per cent – cut flowers); and Thailand (80 per cent – fruit) (World Bank 2009).

Initially, the crisis was modulated by a rapid rise in governmental spending in the form of stimulus packages, at least in rich countries and in some developing countries with sizeable foreign exchange reserves. However, since 2010, the focus of policymakers has been on the monetary side which has worsened some dimensions of the macroeconomic challenges facing developing countries. There has also been the implementation of the austerity policy first in many countries which has implicated social equity and poverty reductions efforts across many countries, including developed countries of Southern Europe.

Women are more negatively impacted by crises-driven responses such as privatization, tax policy such as VAT and budget reduction. Furthermore, the buffer function the care economy (which cushions or tries to soften the negative effects of market disruption on people's lives) is often overwhelmed by financial crises.

Young (2002) argues that since the East Asian financial crises, it has become ever more apparent that women are more disadvantaged by cyclical economic and financial instabilities than are men because of their role in providing care and their socio-economic status. The work of Floro (1992) has shown that financial crises can expose women to economic vulnerability by reducing women's earned income, the assets they control, and their voice in household decisions. This may force some women to bear a disproportionate share of household adjustment costs (Young 2002). Important fallout of the financial crises in Asia, Russia and Latin America has been the obvious connection between international finance and social justice (Young 2002).

The current crisis is having tremendous negative impacts on men's and women's lives. Women are projected to be disproportionately impacted. One estimate suggests that the result of the financial shock will be between 200,000 and 400,000 additional infant deaths per year on average from 2009 to 2015 – or a total of 1.4 million to 2.8 million more infant deaths, if the crisis persists (World Bank 2009). Another analysis of child deaths in 59 developing countries (covering 1.7 million births) suggests that a majority of these deaths will be of girl children (World Bank 2009; UNICEF 2009). Though the data on the impact of the crises on maternal deaths are not yet available, given that there is strong linkages between the critical factors underlying infant mortality (inadequate nutrition and health care, including pre and postnatal/partum care and access to medicines) and maternal deaths, it is anticipated that there is likely to be significant negative impact in this area as well. Overall, according to the World Bank 'the current crisis will reduce women's income in developing countries as a result of losses in employment in export oriented industries, tightening micro-finance lending, and/or drop in remittances' (World Bank 2009).

In the current crisis, austerity-led cuts in the public sector wage bill is also impacting women workers. IMF austerity conditions were implemented by Jamaica, Ghana and Ivory Coast (with most adjustment to occur in the first couple years of the loans). The Ivory Coast's public sector wage bill was kept at 6.8 per cent of GDP and Ghana froze its public sector posts and provided 'lower than budgeted salary increase for health workers', (Osei-Akoto et al. 2009). Jamaica's 2010 IMF loan $1.27 billion was conditional on freezing its public sector wage bill, the legality of which was challenged by its public sector unions. Even though the government lost, the IMF nonetheless refused to make regular loan reviews so no further loan instalments were released which also blocked access to other sources of funding. In 2012–2013 Jamaica in yet another IMF restructured debt effort must also cut expenditures.

Additionally, public sector wage freezes or enforced pay cuts will affect women most severely because they earn less than men and are likely to be on low wages (Lethbridge 2012). The loss of income affects women's control over household income and ultimately negative impact on health, education and poverty reduction.

Employment guarantee schemes which some governments are also implementing to help offset the negative effects on employment tend to target male workers (see for example, the research on Greece contrasting the case of construction and tourism and retail sectors) (Woestman 2010). Turkey is a case where employment schemes support women's entry into the labour forces (World Bank 2011). Increasingly, India and South Africa are both paying attention to the gender dynamics of employment guarantee schemes. But more needs to be done, especially as research shows that 'income transfer to women has greater effect on children's nutritional status as well as for child, especially female mortality' (Baird, *et al.* 2007; World Bank 2009).

The austerity era will also negatively impact on the flow of climate finance for adaptation and mitigation projects in developing countries. The 2007–2008 financial crisis required significant fiscal spending estimated at about 2 per cent of global GDP (IMF 2009), which is about what is needed for global mitigations. According to the IMF (2009), developing countries will need at least $25 billion in 2009 to deal with the effects of the crisis. This will have implications for both global and national expenditures for climate change.

To sum up, with regard to climate change and its financing, the engendering imperative is to ensure that the concerns and priorities of women, especially poor women, move to the centre stage of the financing agenda. This points to both immediate, short term and long-term policy and advocacy agendas. This is a theme that will be further probed in the concluding section of this book. But for now it is useful to note that the process of engendering must also tackle the details and intricacies of specific agenda items as well as traverse the contours of the climate change financing regime with a particular focus and attention to its funds, their instruments and modalities. How are the financial resources generated, managed and distributed? Here the concern is with the mobilization and management of financial resources in terms of predictability and adequacy of public and private flow of funds for gender equality and women's empowerment projects.

Another concern is with the nature of the distributional impacts with regard to adaptation and mitigation mechanisms such as the Adaptation Fund, the Clean Development Mechanism and the reduced emissions from degradation and deforestation (REDD) and the carbon market. Here the concern is with the effectiveness, efficiency and transparency, especially with regard to the criteria of funding mechanisms and formal and informal barriers to entry and exit in the private climate change financing market. Since this a markedly equity-oriented analysis, it is important also to ferret out the nature of eligibility criteria – to what extent they are facilitative of women, especially poor women's participation, or are blocks to entry.

Within the scope and framework of the Adaptation Fund Board, which was established in Bali in 2007 to supervise and manage the Adaptation Fund,[21] governments have accepted that all parties must have ownership and decision-making power. Within this context, it is well accepted that 'skewedness or lack of representation' has implications for 'the prioritization and quality of projects selected, given the weak understanding of issues that underlie developing countries and their concerns' (TERI 2008: 10). However, these principles have not yet been applied to gender equality issues or to the claims of indigenous people.

As will be discussed in the closing chapter of this book, the most recent addition to the global climate finance architecture under the UNFCCC, the GCF, has a mandate for gender sensitization of the Fund's operations and activities. The board is presently in the process of elaborating exactly what this means and how it can be implemented. There is hence much expectation that this is an opportunity to enhance women's access to climate finance in the post-2015 period.

We now turn to examine in greater detail the gender challenges, opportunities and constraints with regard to the private sector and climate finance.

Notes

1 COP 16 – Cancún 2010, which the adopted Decision 1/CP.16, in which it decided to establish a Green Climate Fund (GCF), to be designated as an operating entity of the financial mechanism of the Convention under Article 11, also decided that the GCF was to be designed by a Transitional Committee (TC). The TC comprised 40 members, with 15 members from developed country Parties and 25 members from developing country Parties. The TC was charged with developing and recommending for approval to COP 17 a number of operational documents for the GCF. The TC presented the final report and the draft governing instrument for the new fund at COP 17 Durban, 2011, which adopted Decision 3/CP.17 that approved the governing instrument of the GCF.
2 The GCF governing instrument created a private sector facility that enables it to directly and indirectly finance private sector mitigation and adaptation activities at the national, regional and international levels. As per Paragraph 42 of the Governing Instrument, the operation of the facility will be consistent with a country-driven approach. As per Paragraph 43 of the Governing Instrument, the facility will promote the participation of private sector actors in developing countries, in particular local actors, including small and medium-sized enterprises and local financial intermediaries.
3 According to UNFCCC, Decision 3/CP.17, Launching the Green Climate Fund, Annex, Paragraph 46, the national designated authority will 'recommend to the Board funding proposals in the context of national climate strategies and plans, including through consultation processes. The national designated authorities will be consulted on other funding proposals for consideration prior to submission to the Fund, to ensure consistency with national climate strategies and plans.
4 GCF/B.06/05 Policies and Procedures for the Initial Allocation of Fund Resources and Decisions of the Board – Sixth Meeting of the Board, 19–21 February 2014 GCF/B.06/18 17 April 2014, Agenda item 21 (Meeting of the Board 19–21 February 2014 Bali, Indonesia Agenda item 11: Policies and procedures for the initial allocation of Fund resources, Decision B.06/06 (iv).
5 At the 2011 climate summit in Durban, South Africa, the UN Framework Convention on Climate Change requested the board to develop a transparent no-objection procedure to be conducted through national designated authorities in order to ensure consistency with national climate strategies and plans; a country driven approach; and to provide for effective direct and indirect public and private sector financing by the GCF. Further requests the Board to determine this procedure prior to approval of funding proposals by the Fund. http://unfccc.int/resource/docs/2011/cop17/eng/09a01.pdf.

A no-objection procedure can enable (i) a country to facilitate genuine country ownership and (ii) ensure that the people living within a country, particularly individuals and communities affected by a GCF project or programme, have the right to reject such a proposed activity by a private sector entity. 'The no-objection procedure should function as a mechanism to prevent flawed projects from advancing to the GCF board for consideration. It should serve to filter out projects that are incompatible with national strategies, conflict with better programmes and projects, or impose undue harm or costs

368 Biases and asymmetries in climate change finance

upon host communities and their environment.' The no objection procedure would be the basis on which national designated authorities would explicitly endorse or disapprove of projects versus a process that silence equals consent (Orenstein et al. 2014).

6 The exception in Europe is Norway, which a result of a 2006 legal quota, is approaching gender equality, with 42 per cent women and 58 per cent men on the boards of the largest listed companies.

7 To date the following countries in Europe have instigated quota laws: Norway (has had binding quotas for a number of years, but there are few women below board level across the country's top companies, Iceland, France, Spain, Italy and Belgium (EU 2010).

8 As noted by William Cohan (2012), the smaller boutique firms are no more diverse: Greenhill & Company (one woman as general counsel); Evercore (CEO of equities division); Lazard (zero women in senior positions) and Jefferies (zero woman in senior position). Firms with women in senior positions include: Bank of America (Sallie Krawcheck head of global wealth and investment management division and Barbara Desoer as president of the home loan division); JP Morgan has two senior women executives: Heidi Miller, treasury and securities services business and Mary Callahan Erdoes, head of asset management business. Michel-Henry Bouchet and Robert Isaak 2011, Is the Financial Crisis a Male Syndrome? www.businessweek.com/europe/is-the-financial-crisis-a-male-syndrome-11292011.html; William D. Cohan, 2010. Does Wall Street Need an Estrogen Injection? http://opinionator.blogs.nytimes.com/2010/04/01/does-wall-street-need-an-estrogen-injection/?hp.

9 Key Findings of 2012–2013 Study revealed that: there is only one woman for every nine men among directors and highest-paid executives; only 13 of the 400 largest companies have a woman CEO; no company has an all-female (nor gender-balanced) board and management team; almost half (44.8 per cent) of California's companies have no women directors; and 34 per cent have only one woman director. *Top California Company Leaders Dominated by Men*, UC Davis Study says. UC Davis Press Release, 5 December 2012.

10 Some countries include Argentina, Aruba, Bahamas, Barbados, Benin, Bermuda, Bolivia, Burindi, Chile, Cuba, Costa Rica, Ecuador, Gambia, Guatemala, Haiti, Honduras, Indonesia, Jordan, Lebanon, Liberia, Mali, Namibia, Paraguay, Peru, Sao Tome Principe, Syria, Suriname, Tanzania, Timor Leste, Trinidad and Tobago, and Uganda.

11 For example, the Adaptation Committee, the Adaptation Fund board, the Consultataive group of experts on National Communications, the Executive board of the Clean Development Mechanism, the Least Development Country Fund, and the Technology Executive Committee.

12 Global Findex is a comprehensive database measuring how people save, borrow and manage risk in 148 countries.

13 Microfinance is the supply of loans, savings, and other basic financial services to the poor. (http://cgap.org).

14 Women comprise over 90 per cent of the well-known Grameen Bank, the world's largest microfinance institution.

15 A microfinance institution (MFI) is an organization that provides microfinance services. MFIs range from small non-profit organizations to large commercial banks.

16 Transaction costs in the financial market include the cost of time, effort, and money (including commission fees, contracting, and enforcement) of moving assets from sellers to buyers. These transaction costs may be higher or lower depending on the type of product or service offered and the potential client base targeted (USAID 2005).

17 See the reference below for qualifications on this point.

18 Research by Armendáriz and Morduch (2005) supports this view. However, the evidence is mixed when other factors are included such as geography: institutional scope of the micro finance institutions; whether or not there is systematic outreach to women and other supporting services included in the lending approach; and the nature (coercive effect) of peer pressure in the context of cultural influences (D'Espallier et al. 2009, Rahman 2001 and Todd 1996). For example, there was no significant effect

between gender and repayment in countries such as the US (Tang 2002), Ethiopia (Brehanu and Fufa 2008) and even in Bangladesh (Godquin 2004). For an analysis of possible reasons behind women's high repayment rates please see Fernando (2006), Rahman 2001 and Ameen 2004.

19 As a result of numerous critiques by G77 plus China and civil society, the bank instituted a 'sunset clause that will see them (the CIFs) possibly phased in a post-2012 climate change regime' and have included recipient developing countries on the decision-making structure that oversees the fund. It also makes reference to the UNFCCC process. Critics see these actions as 'superficial' and 'not addressing the deeper issues' of democracy, transparency and undermining of the principles of the Convention (Halifax Initiative 2008 and TWN 2008).

20 'In the context of Tajikistan where financial institutions are still very weak, this can be arranged by taking community-based model, whereby local communities, Microfinance Institutions (MFIs), or Jamoat/Community Resource Centres (JRCs) develop and distribute the product, manage the risk pool, and absorb the risk. As with insurance mutuals (cooperatives), there is no involvement on the part of commercial insurers (UNDP 2009a).

21 The Adaptation Fund has been established by the Parties to the Kyoto Protocol of the UN Framework Convention on Climate Change to finance concrete adaptation projects and programmes in developing countries that are Parties to the Kyoto Protocol. www.adaptation-fund.org.

9
PRIVATE SECTOR CLIMATE FINANCE AND GENDER EQUALITY

This chapter explores the role of the private sector in climate finance, including the operations of market-based mechanisms and the carbon market both within and external to the UNFCCC. It scopes out the implications of these activities for women's multiple economic and social activities, and most especially for women-owned and operated SMEs in developing countries.

There is a growing need for large-scale investment in energy infrastructure, to scale up access to clean modern energy services and to facilitate the rapidly needed transformation to a clean energy and low-carbon pathway for developing countries in order to enable and ensure possibilities for men and women to live secure and dignified lives in developing countries.

The International Energy Agency (IEA) argues that the stabilization of global emissions at 2005 levels by 2050 will require an additional $10.3 trillion of cumulative investment in non-Organisation for Economic Co-operation and Development countries by mid-century, in addition to $7.3 trillion of investment in OECD countries (IEA 2008; HPICA 2009). The IEA is also concerned that if significant shift in investment priorities towards cleaner energy infrastructure does not occur by 2017 there will be a lock-in of carbon-intensive infrastructure that will effectively retard efforts to bring global warming to below the 1.5–2° Celsius limit. Additionally, the UN Secretary General's proposed Sustainable Energy for All (SEA4ALL) initiative is estimated to cost approximately $548 billion per year[1] in order to meet the triple inter-linked objectives of ensuring universal access to modern energy services,[2] doubling the rate of improvement in energy efficiency and doubling the share of renewable energy in the global energy mix by 2030. Both of these set of action agendas rely heavily on the private sector shifting investment priorities towards cleaner and renewable energy. Hence there is clamour for the private sector to be more involved in financing climate change activities in developing countries.

Current private sector investments constitute 86 per cent of global investments and financial flows (Ward et al. 2008; UNFCCC 2007). The private sector also finances over 80 per cent of climate change related activities in the three broad areas of clean energy technology, renewable energy and energy efficiency (UNFCCC 2007). While the private sector is the main investor in energy and agriculture (and infrastructure, mainly through Public–Private Partnerships, PPPs[3]) in developing countries, it has less of a presence in other areas of mitigation and very little independent involvement in adaptation, beyond those activities involving co-financing or significant public lead funding.

Despite these shortcomings, developed countries are pushing strongly for greater involvement of the private sector within the framework of the UNFCCC climate finance architecture. However, measuring and accounting for the flow of private finance from developed countries to developing countries is highly 'uncertain' as accurate data is often unavailable. While researchers such as Clapp et al. (2012) and Stadelmann et al. (2013) provide some estimation of private investment flows to developing countries, there remains very low confidence in the numbers reported by these and other studies that aim to track private climate finance flows. Clapp et al. (2012) using 2009–2010 data estimate private flow at $37–72 billion per year,[4] which is significantly different from that estimated by Stadelmann et al. (2013): $10–37 billion 2008–2011.[5] This private finance flow is part of the $39–120 billion total climate finance flowing to developing countries (2009, 2010, 2011 and 2012) which is widely acknowledged to be inadequate in meeting the needs of developing countries for adaptation and mitigation activities in addressing climate change and in successfully meeting the goal of the UNFCCC.

The Cancún Agreements (2010) formalized the Copenhagen (2009) promised by developed countries to work towards the goal of mobilizing $100 billion annually by 2020 for developing countries. But given that there is need for at least a fivefold multiple of that amount and that the current fiscal pressures on developed countries finance, due to the negative impact of the high burden of the financial crisis on public resources in these countries, there is a great deal of scepticism that the developed countries can or are willing to provide all or most of the promised amount.[6] Attention has hence turned to the potential of the private sector for upscaling financial and investment flows into adaptation and mitigation activities under the post-2012 climate change regime (HPICA 2009) as well as to be a significant driver of the flows of funds into the Green Climate Fund (GCF) thereby fulfilling the promised $100 billion.

This chapter seek to explore the nature of the private sector's involvement in financing adaptation and mitigation projects and programmes in developing countries (Section 9.1) and to highlight the current impacts and future implications for women's economic empowerment and the promotion of gender equity. To this end, Section 9.2 explores in further depth the reality of gender and the conventional climate financing market. Section 9.3 focuses on gender and the carbon market. The concluding section examines the scope of microfinance with regard to adaptation and mitigation financing.

9.1 Debates regarding the role of the private sector in climate finance under the UNFCCC

With an eye on more than $79 trillion[7] of assets held by pension funds, mutual funds, private equity funds, hedge funds and sovereign wealth funds and the presumed high leveraging capability of the private sector actors, developed countries' governments envision the private sector as the key source for helping them to meet their future climate finance obligations under the UNFCCC.[8]

Increasingly, over the years and accelerating after the 2007–2008 financial crises, developed countries have placed great emphasis on the potential of the private sector to be a critical player in climate change finance within the context of the UNFCCC financing architecture. Countries such as the US, the UK and Japan supported by other developed countries, Parties have proposed quite a strong role for the private sector in mobilizing and leveraging funds to the GCF.[9]

In early 2010, the UN Secretary-General established a High-Level Advisory Group on Climate Change Financing (AGF) to 'study potential sources of revenue that will enable the achievement of the level of climate change financing that was promised during the United Nations Climate Change Conference in Copenhagen in December 2009' (AGF).[10] After examining the issue for about 10 months, the panel of experts presented their view that the private sector could provide $200–500 billion for gross annual investment and that $10–20 billion of that could go towards the total of $100 billion Copenhagen-Cancún promised made by developing countries. This amount from the private sector, the AGF argued, could be complemented with direct budgetary contributions of about $60 billion from OECD countries, $11 billion from the multilateral development banks and contributions of $8–14 billion from the global carbon markets to top off the Copenhagen-Cancún promise.

This discussion on the role of the private sector and their involvement in scaling up climate finance, especially with regard to the GCF, became rather tense and pointed during discussions of the design of the governing instrument of the GCF. Developed countries argue that the private sector should be the key source for mobilizing funds for the GCF and advocated strongly for high involvement of the private sector in both the governance and operational domains of the fund. Developed country members on the Transitional Committee (TC), which designed the fund, such as the US, Japan and the UK, advocated strongly for a private sector window within the fund, in the same manner in which there are thematic windows for adaptation and mitigation, and a seat on board for the private sector. The discussion ended in a compromise of sorts. There was a final agreement on a private sector facility as a modality through which the private sector's access to the resources of the GCF would be mediated through the mechanism of designated national authority. It was left up to the board of the GCF to determine the specific involvement of stakeholders, including the private sector, in the ongoing governance of the fund. Notably, there was no window or facility created in the GCF for enabling access and support for technology transfer and development, though this is an obligation for developed countries.

The GCF board was established in 2012 (with 12 members from developed countries and 12 members from developing countries)[11] and since then there has been tremendous lobbying by developed countries for upgrading private sector access to the fund and increasing private sector involvement in the governance of the fund. This emphasis by developed country members of the board of the GCF on the private sector has been a dominant theme of the discussion around the business model of the GCF from its first throughout its eighth board meeting (2012–2014). The developed countries sought to make the private sector facility an autonomous and strong part of the GCF governance,[12] with significant flow of expected funds into the GCF earmarked for the private sector facility. But this was resisted by developing countries, resulting in the board deciding that the PSF will operate as an integral component of the fund. Its purpose will be to also promote the participation of private sector actors in developing countries, including small and medium-sized enterprises and local financial intermediaries.[13] An initial allocations framework paper for the fund prepared for the board recommended that initial 20 per cent of total cumulative commitments to the GCF are allocated to the private sector facility.[14] This was in comparison to a recommendation for an initial 10 per cent target for particularly vulnerable counties, SIDS, LDCs and African states. The final decision of the GCF board on this issue was, in the first case, to 'maximize engagement with the private sector, including through a significant allocation to the Private Sector Facility' and, in the second case, 'aim for a floor of 50 per cent of the adaptation allocation for particularly vulnerable countries, including least developed countries (LDCs), small island developing states (SIDS) and African states (Decision B.06/06, Sixth board meeting February 2014).

Many developing countries, however, while acknowledging that national private sector actors are and will continue to be important players in supporting mitigation and adaptation activities domestically, are nonetheless concerned that the funds that flow into the GCF from developed countries would not go to support developing countries' climate activities, as mandated under the Convention, but would instead be diverted to support developed countries' private sectors. This is a valid concern.

Experiences from private sector involvement in development finance shows that between 2008 and 2009 only 16 per cent of all the International Finance Corporation's investment was directed towards local companies in low-income countries (FOE 2011). Even when the IFC had a specific focus on shifting investment to the private sector in these groups of countries, it did so 'through the financing of OECD based multinational corporations, with approximately 63 per cent of its financing going to these entities' (EURODAD 2010, cited in FOE 2011). Moreover, evidence from the activities of public-private partnership, which has a longer history of linking global private sector entities to development finance, raises questions about their impacts and benefits on the development of small and medium-sized enterprises (SMEs)[15] in developing countries as well as their overall contribution to development. Additionally, the efficacy of private equity funding of projects, though it is argued to have worked well in Asia, has been less successful in Africa (New Energy Finance 2012).

The argument that the high leverage activities of the private sector could radically upscale the public funds to the GCF is an interesting one. But it also raises a number of critical issues that must be carefully and rigorously examined from a gender equality and women's empowerment perspective. These critical issues include the nature of the private sector's involvement in climate financing thus far, the scope and extent of the private sector leveraging factor in enhancing or maximizing existing flows of funds through the current climate finance architecture, or, in the least, in the area of development cooperation, where the idea of public-private partnerships and private sector facilities embedded within ODA funding mechanisms have been in existence for over a decade and half. There is also the issue of the equity and climate justice as well as how best to ensure the environmental integrity of investment and financing projects undertaken by the GCF.

Though recognizing that private sector actors are already involved in many dimensions of the promotion of climate change activities, many developing countries, and civil society at large, remain sceptical about reliance on the sector to finance climate change activities in developing countries, in particular, adaptation activities. This reservation arises from at least five critical concerns.

First, developed countries' governments are the responsible parties for providing financing to developing countries for financing adaptation and mitigation. The private sector has no similar obligation and hence its finance can only complement public flows.

Second, under the Convention, there is explicit recognition that climate change finance would come from public sources, and, in the least, not impose additional burden on developing countries, such as rising debt levels associated with financing that may be loan-driven.

Third, there is a general lack of clarity about the nature of the private sector and its contribution to climate finance. In the discussions thus far, the private sector being referred to seems to be very narrowly constituted as pension funds, hedge funds and big corporations. Developing countries argue that the private sector is more heterogeneous in developing countries, where such entities can range from quasi-state entities (state operated enterprises, SOEs), to farmers, taxi driver associations, cooperatives, and micro-small and medium-sized enterprises (MSMSEs). It is important that these private sector actors have their capacity upgraded and enhanced so that they could be better involved in climate change activities, including taking advantage of climate finance opportunities.

Fourth, the success of adaptation and mitigation strategies in developing countries depends to a high degree on the coordination, coherence and goodness of fit of those activities with national development plans and national comprehensive climate change protection strategies and planning. Financing by the private sector, which is naturally motivated by where profit can best be maximized, may not enable this goodness of fit. Hence, there may be distortions and inefficiencies.

Fifth, the private sector will not automatically finance adaptation activities. Given the already lopsided distribution of climate finance between adaptation and mitigation, over-reliance on the private sector for climate finance under the

UNFCCC may, in the most benign case, continue this trend, and, in the worst case, contribute to the further indebtedness of many poor developing countries, who will have to seek access to capital market (where possible) for financing of adaptation activities. Buchner *et al.* (2013) report a 20:1 ratio between the private sector's financing of mitigation and adaptation activities and that 90 per cent of adaptation financing came from the public sector. According to a 2011 World Bank Group report, private adaptation finance[16] is limited due to market, institutional and policy barriers, which depresses return on investments of adaptation activities, such as infrastructure investments (for example, dams, levees, canals) and particularly for soft infrastructures (for example, watershed management, land use planning and information, and stakeholder engagement) (Miralles-Wilhelm 2012; World Bank 2011).

Sixth, private sector climate finance may also have inherent climate justice, gender and social equity dimensions that need to be more rigorously explored, understood and mitigated, where they exist.

From the perspective of gender equality and women's empowerment-based analysis, it is important to fully understand the role of the private sector in climate change finance and the nature of that relationship with regard to, in the first case, gender equality and women's empowerment initiatives. As discussed in Chapter 8, it is quite well known that women, as a group, face tremendous drawbacks with regard to accessing conventional private sector generated credit and investment flows. Additionally, the funding of adaptation activities, which may be risky for profit maximizing driven bottom lines, and which are nonetheless critical for women's, men's, boys' and girls' wellbeing, lives and livelihoods may be in danger of being underfinanced.

9.2 The nature and scope of the private climate change finance market

The nature, scope, composition and direction of the private sector involvement in climate change are complex and dynamic, and occur at multiple levels. According to Climate Policy Initiative and the IPCC, the private sector already plays a significant role in climate change. The problem, therefore, is not crudely about whether they are involved and should be more involved but the nature and extent to which the private sector can assume the responsibility of developed countries to provide adequate, predictable and sustained flows of climate finance for adaptation and mitigation projects, programmes and policies to developing countries. Additionally, how will the private sector contributions be measured, reported and verified?

The private financial actors who are involved in climate change finance perform similar roles and utilize similar sets of instruments as those in conventional financial markets. There are private sector actors, such as multinationals, who invest in physical assets in agriculture, forestry, mining and industries and who are investing in the adoption of green and clean technologies. These are long-term (direct/equity) foreign investments. Many firms have direct and equity stakes through greenfield investment, as well as mergers and acquisition in climate change and related activities, including the development and production of renewable and efficient energy sources such as biofuels, wind and solar power – solar photovoltaic and fuel cells. Besides energy, firms are also heavily invested in agriculture, manufacturing, transportation and water under the clean energy technology tent, which leads to cross-fertilization beyond bio-based fuels to micro-irrigation systems, distributed energy, renewables, energy storage, advance packaging, hybrid vehicles, lighter materials, smart logistic software, water and wastewater treatment, water recycling desalination and new applications of sensing equipment (Forbes 2012). Some firms, along with venture capital investors, may also invest in embryonic and speculative technologies such as carbon sequestration, capture and storage, which promises to utilize fossil fuels in a low-carbon fashion, and enhanced geothermal systems (EGS) for electricity production (both of these involve subsurface geologic applications).

As with other markets, the key financing and investment activities are in the form of derivatives and forward purchases applied to manage climate risk and greenfield (new) investments, mergers and acquisition with existing firms, and angel or venture capital financing of start-up and mid to late expansion activities for the development and delivery of clean energy technologies (see Box 9.1). These financial and investment flows occur both within and across borders and facilitate investment activities such as building sustainable waste management systems and the creation of wind power farms.

Other private sector actors involved in climate finance, as noted in Chapter 4, are the familiar groupings of companies (such as Cisco, Samsung and Siemens) and financial intermediaries (such as Barclays and Deutsche Bank) that have long been associated with the flow of finance and investment in the global economy. These actors also include utilities, investment banks, insurance companies, bond traders, hedge funds and infrastructure funds

According to Forbes (2008) and the IFC (2009), there are around 50 private equity and hedge funds specializing in climate financing and clean energy. Private equity and venture capital funds accounted for over $6 billion investment in clean energy in 2009 (Bloomberg New Energy and *New York Times* 2010). Over 70 green hedge funds focus attention on alternative energy equity, such as water funds, commodity trading for carbon, and commodity trading for forest products. Hedge funds, in particular, have been big drivers behind the biofuels trading boom[17] (and especially ethanol and its subsequent bust in 2007), the solar energy boom (and mild blowout in 2008) and are emerging as important players in the next boom area: clean water. However, the involvement of these funds in climate-related endeavours is not without controversy. Some hedge fund and other financial market actors have been identified in activities such as large tracts of cross-border land purchase, dubbed as 'land-grabbing' by activists, which has implications both for food security, as well as for women's access to and control over, land in the affected countries (see Box 9.2).

BOX 9.1 CLIMATE CHANGE FINANCING AND CONVENTIONAL FINANCE INSTRUMENTS

Catastrophe bonds: High yield insurance-backed bonds. They allow the holder to raise money during catastrophic events (hurricane or earthquake).

Derivative: A financial instrument that is *derived* from some other asset, index, event, value or condition. Currently, most carbon is sold as simple futures contracts (a type of derivative; Chan/FOE 2008).

Greenfield investments: A form of foreign direct investment where a parent company starts a new venture in a foreign country by constructing new operational facilities from the ground up.

Forwards: The purchase of emission allowances to be supplied in the future at a fixed price. Currently, this is the most common type of market-traded allowance. The market for EUA trades on a forward basis.

Merger and acquisition: A merger is a combination of two companies to form a new company, while an acquisition is the purchase of one company by another with no new company being formed.

Weather derivative: A financial instrument that is used by companies to hedge against the risk of high probability weather-related losses (such as a drier than expected summer).

BOX 9.2 LAND-GRABBING

'Land-grabbing' – a process by which large amounts of capital are invested in the purchase of land for large-scale agricultural production, while the farmers who have worked the land for generations are displaced and/or become renters on land that was once their own (Draitser 2014). Hedge funds, private equity funds and big banks, such as Dutch Rabobank group and Sarasin Bank, purchase large tracts of land for the production of biofuel and storing of physical commodities of food stocks etc. as part of their risk and portfolio management strategy, which seriously impacts on food security and ecological sustainability. It also marks a reinforcement of traditional industrial agriculture (Williams 2014).

An estimated 500 million acres was reportedly bought or leased across the developing world between 2000 and 2011, often at the expense of local food security and land rights (Oakland Institute 2014).

There are also new actors, instruments and institutions such as carbon funds, green bonds and emission-trading exchanges. The US Climate Action Partnership, a coalition of companies that include General Electric, General Motors and Dupont are also active private sector alliances involved in climate-related activities. Developing country private sector players active in these markets are primarily from Brazil, China, India and South Africa. Traditional and new private sector actors are complemented by a growing network of international development agencies, such as the United Nations Development Programme (UNDP), the United Nations Environment Programme (UNEP) and the World Bank. Non-profit, civil society organizations and philanthropic institutions also play active roles as aggregators, consultants and trading agencies.

Some private sector actors may choose to be involved in the purchase and sale of a variety of short- and long-term financial assets. These range from assets such as bonds, loans and stock certificates. For example, private sector actors can chose to purchase generic bonds from multilateral and bilateral development banks who issue such instruments on the capital markets.[18] Other private sector actors are involved in purchasing and selling a variety of climate risk products such as crop insurance, catastrophe bonds and assets that hedge against the future such as weather and index insurance. In addition to conventional financing instruments, there are also new instruments, mechanisms and institutional arrangements that have emerged to specifically address climate change. Primary among these are 'carbon credit', 'emissions trading units' and 'carbon offsets', and the Clean Development and Joint Implementation mechanisms. Recently, the MDBs, such as the World Bank and the Asian Development Bank, along with major commercial banks, have developed green bonds as instruments of climate finance. There is also an increasing push towards the development of more complex insurance instruments such as the catastrophic bonds to fit the profiles of different targeted groups in developing countries, groups of small farmers and groups of small island states.

Insurance is the oldest form of adaptive activity and is an area in which the private sector is well versed. Parametric weather insurance and products that securitize catastrophe risks are also now becoming more available (in mostly pilot or demonstration projects) in about 20 developing countries such as Ethiopia and Malawi.[19] However, there is not much understanding of the challenges and constraints around insurance products for things such as weather, crops and covering climate risks for women small-holders and householders in low-income countries, especially in sub-Saharan Africa.

9.2.1 The private sector and adaptation finance

The role and activities of the private sector in the area of adaptation is not very strong to date and there are great challenges to scaling up private sector adaptation financing. The Institutional Investors Group on Climate Change notes that:

> It is still much less clear how the developing world's enormous need for finance for climate change adaptation can be translated on a large scale into

investment opportunities that generate returns that are attractive to institutional investors. While it is reasonable to envisage large-scale private sector investment in mitigation in developing countries if policy frameworks and other conditions are right, it is likely that adaptation will have to be financed primarily by the public sector for the foreseeable future.

This is because adaptation activities are complex and inextricably intertwined with economic development issues (see Chapter 3). Adaptation finance is aimed at providing support for projects to help the most vulnerable to climate risks. This can occur through up scaling poverty eradication activities and supporting projects that promote economic diversification. These projects and others such as flood prevention infrastructure, climate-proofing health system and ensuring the availability of health-care programmes and national disaster planning, while yielding economic benefits, generally do not: (a) have built-in or inherent global co-benefits (SEI 2011) and so have been relatively underfunded by the GEF; and (b) are not attractive for equity investment. They are not high on the list of high-return profiled activities.

Many adaptation activities are also high risk and low return. These include areas such as water management and improving the vulnerability of coastal areas. Other adaptation activities, such as in the agricultural and water sectors may be attractive for equity investment but present difficult challenges. A primary difficulty in this regard may be the absence of ongoing sustainable revenue streams from which to service debt or the heavy reliance on governmental revenue streams that may negatively impact other flows of government expenditures such as the social sector.

As noted by a Harvard study, adaptation is locational, and therefore requires know-how and technology transfers that enable the flow of research to implement climate resiliency in housing, transportation, agriculture etc. in developing countries (HPICA 2009). There is also need for intensive capacity building and to integrate research into capacity development for adaptation, including among higher education professionals and community groups as well as for policymakers.

Ultimately, the private sector's involvement in adaptation activities has been driven by the need to minimize risk and share cost through ODA and public sector finance (HPICA 2009). The private sector has also focused on climate-proofing its own climate change exposure. SEI (2011) and others have argued that 'there is an emerging market for raising new finance from the private sectors for adaptation as signalled by large institutional investors' but they await the right investment products. Such products will undoubtedly include debt instruments and credit lines that focus on lowering the risk and upfront production costs of investment into adaptation activities. In order to promote reasonable risks and cost sharing, countries such as Germany (through the Federal Ministry for Economic Cooperation and Development, BMZ), Japan (through the Japan International Cooperation Agency) and the US (through the Overseas Private Investment Corporation, OPIC) have encouraged private sector involvement through public-private partnerships in infrastructural and related activities such as sewage projects (pipeline and treatment plants) and the promotion of good water/quality.[20]

Hence, considerable public money must first be present to induce (catalyse) private sector participation, including through cross-subsidization. Cross-subsidization has been found to be key to public-private partnership in developing countries. (See Appendix 9.1 for more on PPPs in the climate change arena.) Governments subsidize the building of plants as well as the cost difference of sewage systems. So PPPs involve significant local government subsidies and cost sharing among stakeholders in order for it to be effective.

Outside of cross-subsidies or publicly supported adaptation projects, one dimension through which the private sector views adaptation as profitable business is the insurance sector.[21] Increasingly, insurance schemes (agricultural insurance) indemnity and/or index-based,[22] sovereign disaster risk transfer,[23] property catastrophe risk insurance,[24] and disaster micro-insurance, as well as weather-based index insurance) that insure against perils such as tropical cyclones, drought, rainfall (excess or deficit) and temperature (low/high), flood, weather etc. are being proposed as important adaptation tools. Thus, there is a growing trend towards risk transfer or absorption mechanisms, such as weather-index insurance, as part of the set of risk management oriented adaptation strategies.[25] However, while ex ante risk transfer instruments are important, they do not inherently promote risk reduction or support management of the physical risks of climate change, which is critical for fostering adaptation to climate change. Currently, less than 15 per cent of insurance schemes have consideration for physical risk or make explicit links to adaptation to climate change (Climate Wise Compendium of Disaster Risk Transfer Initiatives 2012).[26]

Globally, most insurance schemes are focused on more well-off countries, individuals and large business sectors rather than poorer ones. Data provided by Climate Wise show that 20 per cent of insurance schemes are in low-income countries, with the majority in lower-middle- and upper-middle-income developing countries. Additionally, very few schemes insure small and medium sized enterprises.[27] Thus, adaptation remains of low attraction for the international private sector.

From the perspective of thinking about financing adaptation, adaptation must be viewed as a spectrum of activities that integrate addressing the causes of vulnerability, ensuring adequate and timely emergency assistance to improving and making climate-resilient local infrastructure and enabling food security. Adaptation, as with mitigation activities, requires long-term commitment and a comprehensive integrated framework which are not likely through private sector activities or with public-private partnerships, where the profit motive and short-term considerations are the driving motivation.

There is nonetheless considerable scope for the private sector's full involvement in adaptation activities in developing countries. It can provide managerial ability and expertise around institutional processes, and can also provide technology for adaptation projects such as in the construction of watersheds or hydrology.

The private sector can also work to enhance human and physical capital for water areas such as water system, water supply roads and bridges. These initiatives can be financed through their participation in national climate change and development strategies facilitated by the criteria and processes developed through the national designated authorities.

The African Development Bank has identified at least three important areas in Africa that must be scaled up for promoting and engaging business sector applications: investment in information services such as early warning and forecasting systems, risk management, including investment in monitoring and surveillance technologies, and insurance protections such as index-based insurance products (see Box 9.3). The Stockholm Environment Institute (SEI) argues that there is a broad spectrum of activities and roles that the private sector could take on in contributing to the UNFCCC's aim of scaling up, optimizing and shifting adaptation finance (SEI 2011). These range from: (1) managing their own climate exposure (climate-proofing their investment); (2) taking advantage of business

---

BOX 9.3 THE PRIVATE SECTOR AND ADAPTATION IN AFRICA

The private sector at all levels can contribute to shaping sector programmes and research agendas to promote improved knowledge and analytical tools for business and investors.

- *Information services*: investment in reliable information such as early warning for floods,* knowledge bank for local data, monitoring and forecasting systems. This includes computer modelling, remote sensing and decision support systems – all of which have opportunities for business applications.
- *Risk management*: risk awareness, identification and decision-making analysis. Monitoring and surveillance of potential hazards through satellite-based systems can benefit from private sectors investment in technology.
- *Insurance protection:* insurance as a climate change adaptation strategy to protect against energy, food and water shortage. Need local-scale monitoring and research programmes for information to create index-based insurance products. This is most clear in agriculture – a 'typical attest arena for index-insurance products'. Insurance against the impact of climate change in Africa is still an untapped market for many insurance companies.

* It is reported that flood warning can reduce damage by up to 35 per cent (African Union et al. 2010).

Source: African Union et al. (2010)

opportunities in helping others to reduce their climate risks, such as generating new finance for adaptation funding, designing and manufacturing and distributing goods and services (food, fuel and water); and (3) providing risk management tools (insurance). As noted above, managing climate exposure and providing risk management tools are the areas in which the private sectors have a high level of involvement.

There is less powerful effort on generating new finance, with the exception of the clean development mechanism and its link to the Adaptation Fund, as noted above. Outside of the mechanism of ODA leveraged PPPs, various forms of insurance instruments and private sector financing of adaptation may rest largely on forms of finance that are debt (and equity) creating which may not meet the requirement of new and additional. So, ultimately, for adaptation in developing countries, private finance may only act as a gap filler when public finance for adaptation is insufficient (SEI 2011).

9.2.2 The private sector and mitigation

The private sector is primarily involved in carbon mitigation activities in developing countries through its involvement with the Clean Development Mechanism[28] (HPICA 2009), as well as multilateral development programmes such as the World Bank's Climate Investment programmes and national programmes. The Clean Development Mechanism (discussed in Chapters 4 and 7) has been the main vehicle for private sector investment in carbon mitigation. As discussed in Chapter 4, the CDM, however, has limited outreach to the vast majority of developing countries. Hence many poor developing countries are dependent on bilateral and multilateral sources for financing of mitigation activities, with the private sector expected to play a co-financing secondary role.[29] It is hoped that the reform of the CDM to include programming modalities instead of the traditional reliance on a single project can help to increase its spread to poor developing countries and small island states where the scope and range of activities are of a much smaller scale and often fragmented.

A primary function of the carbon market activities, such as those undertaken in the CDM and JI markets are to reduce the transaction costs associated with emission reductions and to ensure efficiency in the distribution of emission resources. There are some questions as to whether the market, as it is presently evolving, can achieve these results in a manner that is timely and consistent with the global climate policy goals. At present, the carbon market seeks to accomplish its goal through at least two types of trading instruments: carbon offset credits and carbon allowances. Carbon offset credits are derived from projects that are designed to reduce, avoid or sequester GHGs. Carbon allowances are created by fiat (rules) and are earned by not emitting GHGs. (There are also voluntary carbon markets, which are discussed below.)

Carbon credits entitle the holder to emit a specified amount of carbon dioxide. Such holders usually receive the credits when they have reduced their GHGs below their emission quota. These credits can be traded domestically or internationally. Emission trading units are the currencies through which emission reductions are traded. They assume different names (i.e. certified emissions reductions, CERs) according to the issuing institutions (i.e. CDM) or the form of the reductions to which they correspond (i.e. RMUs). Carbon offsets 'allow purchasers to neutralize the carbon dioxide produced from their businesses and everyday activities . . . by supporting a variety of emissions reduction initiatives' (Environmental Defence Council 2009). These emission reductions are sourced from external projects (primarily in developing countries where costs are lower and so-called low-hanging fruit can be easily exploited).

New institutional forms include business entities such as carbon offsetting firms that consult on and manage emissions reduction projects and provide offsets to other firms and individuals. Institutional arrangements such as the European Union Emissions Trading System create a market that facilitates emission reductions transactions. These new financing instruments, mechanisms and institutions have contributed to the development of a new dimension to global finance: carbon finance – the 'monetisation of future cash flows from the advanced sale of Carbon Credits to finance projects' (UNEP 2008: 34). Carbon finance transactions occur in the carbon market that is specialized in financing and reducing the risks associated with carbon consumption (emissions) reduction schemes.

The value of the carbon market, which was $142 billion in 2010 (Munden Project 2011), rose to a record $176 billion in 2011 (Reuters 2012). The Munden Project notes that only a small fraction would be available for projects on the ground, and much less to forests and communities. That is because most of the money is going into verification and consultancy services. Currently, the overall value in trading carbon offset in CDM is greater than the primary CDM market (Munden Project 2011). This is projected to be the same dynamics with REDD+ projects and finance. Munden and other researchers assume that a good bit of that money will end up precisely where it started, in developed countries with the kind of large multinational organizations capable of servicing the market (Munden Project 2011).

From the vantage point of developing countries, especially LDCs and SIDS, market-driven carbon financing presents both opportunities and challenges. Opportunities exist in terms of market participants' ability to flexibly respond (in providing financial and technological support) to small-scale projects that would typically be undertaken in these countries by SMEs and which are not readily facilitated by the flexible market-based mechanisms, such as the CDM.

However, SMEs from developing countries are under-represented in carbon financing as sellers, buyers and investors (Kalimunjaye *et al.* 2012; Nath 2009; Sethi 2012; Usui and Martinez-Frenandez 2011; Xulong and Limou 2012). For example, a study by GTZ found that Indian SMEs were only 5 per cent of the total number of the CDM projects for India. Other studies, while noting that carbon finance is an attractive area for enhancing developing countries'

SMEs' contribution to climate change, highlight the challenge they face broadly with financing, and more narrowly with the carbon market.

There are at least two challenges specific to the carbon markets for SMEs. First, the market is relatively new, volatile, complex and disjointed (UNEP 2008). The 'rapid pace of the carbon market's development has rendered it difficult for knowledge to keep pace with the availability of funds, and particularly challenging for sellers to keep abreast of innovations in structuring and contracting CDM [and other types of] transactions' (Streck/UNEP 2008). Thus, the market dynamics make it challenging even for very sanguine players and hence much more mystifying to newcomers on the scene. SMEs from developing countries will definitely be at a disadvantage as compared to more vested institutional players.

Second, there is a high degree of uncertainty, political risk and lack of transparency around issues of pricing and verifying carbon offsets. The major political risks include incomplete institutional arrangements, uncertainty and potential deadlock over key issues in the Convention and in national legislatures. These are interlocking factors – there is still controversy over matters such as auctioning or cap and trade and the reforming of existing mechanisms. This is qualitatively different from conventional commodities markets, and may discourage investors with low risk tolerance.

9.3 Gender and the conventional climate financing market

The private climate change finance market, both in its conventional and carbon market aspects, has a diverse set of actors with different interests and with different risk profiles, who, in an ideal world, can enter and exit any market sector on demand. Many of these participants, such as male- and female-owned enterprises, who play the roles of traditional entrepreneurs, equity or venture capitalists, can chose to nurture and help develop the talents, skills and scale of operations of desired entities.

Currently, there are about 8–10 million formal women-owned SMEs in emerging markets (representing 31–38 per cent of all registered SMEs in these markets; GPFI and IFC 2011).[30] At the same time, women-owned business entities grow at a smaller rate than male-owned entities. A recent report, *Strengthening Access to Finance for Women-owned SMEs in Developing Countries* by the Global Partnership for Financial Inclusion and the International Finance Corporation (2011), noted that though there is high growth potential for women-owned small and medium-sized enterprises, they are constrained by a number of institutional and regulatory factors such as lack of access to finance. This lack of access to financing 'is repeatedly identified as a major constraint to women entrepreneurs' (GPFI and IFC 2011: 3). The report argues that scalable financing models are important to increase the opportunities of women-owned businesses to pursue economic opportunities, invest additional capital, hire more employees and grow their business as part of the process of further developing the private sector in developing countries.

This is particularly important in the climate change area, where many growth opportunities are emerging, consistent with the development and implementation of climate protection policies in many developing countries such as Bangladesh, China, Ghana and India.

As noted by the GPFI and IFC (2011: 6), 'if women cannot access financial resources, they are disadvantaged in their ability to pursue economic opportunities'. In the case of climate change adaptation, this may be a matter of life and death.

Gender constraints and gender gaps play a critical role in influencing women's participation in the climate change finance market at any level. The key to effective participation in the financial market, as elsewhere, is the degree of the development of awareness and acquisition of the language and instruments of the market by participants. From these initial starting points, market participants gain familiarity and expertise over time. Beyond these starting points, access and control over capital and other economic resources will become the determining or constraining factors for deeper and wider levels of participation. Unfortunately, as discussed in Chapter 8, the ability and the capacity to enter and exit the market are also impacted by the nature of gender segmentation and lack of access to and ownership of tangible and intangible resources between men and women.

The private market for financing climate change exhibits the same gender dynamics as traditional financial markets discussed in Chapter 8. Numerous research reports show that women entrepreneurs are more likely to face lower access to finance than male entrepreneurs; they also face less favourable borrowing terms, higher interest rates, are required to collateralize a higher share of loans and have shorter-term loans (GPFI and IFC 2011; Bardasi *et al.* 2007; Demiriguc-Kunt *et al.* 2008; Diagne 2000; Global Entrepreneurship Monitor 2005; Faisel 2004; Rose 1992; ILOAFDB 2004; Goheer 2003; Narain 2007; Richardson *et al.* 2004).

In general, women-owned businesses tend to be smaller firms (they make up 32–39 per cent of the very small segments of firms, 30–36 per cent of the very small SMEs and 17–21 per cent of medium-sized companies).[31] They are also more likely than male-owned SMEs to be in the informal sectors and running smaller firms in the services sectors, with lower value added; they also operated more home-based businesses than men (GPFI and IFC 2011).

Numerous and varied financial and non-financial barriers limit women's access to finance. Explicit financial barriers emanate from gendered constraints operating within financial institutions. These, as noted in Chapter 8, include the perception that women are riskier, higher cost and lower return borrowers, and the fact that credits officers are often risk-averse vis-à-vis women entrepreneurs as a client group. Additionally, as noted by the GPFI and IFC study, 'client profile of banks may not fit women entrepreneurs due to gendered factors such as women lack of mobility or care activities that does not align with accessing banking outlets during the standard hours of operation'. Women also operate small businesses that tend to be involved more with early-stage enterprises and start-ups which are identified by financial intermediaries as high risks (Gajigo and Hallward-Driemeir 2010;

Terrell 2008). In developing countries where financial infrastructure may be limited such that there is lack of credit bureau or women lack property rights and access to collateral, the lack of credit information can thwart women's access to credit. The IFC report noted that 'lack of information between financial intermediaries disproportionately impacts women entrepreneurs' (GPFI and IFC 2011: 7).

Women-owned SMEs are also disadvantaged due to their size, which the business literature argues influences performance and creditworthiness. Women-owned SMEs tend to dominate in smaller firms, service sectors and informal sectors and have lower return and disproportionate burden. The GPFI and IFC report points out that male-owned enterprises do not face the same problem in growing their smaller firms (GPFI and IFC 2011: 8).

Non-financial barriers are mostly those emanating from problems or deficiencies in the legal and regulatory environment and the broader investment climate, such as red tape, lack of transportation and weakness in infrastructure (such as frequent power outages). The IFC study found that 'weak investment climate hit smaller firms harder, impacting women entrepreneurs more as they are less likely to have the resources to address the weakness in infrastructures (for example, own generators). As noted in Chapter 8, women are under-represented among all types of market participants, and there may be a high degree of gender bias and gender asymmetries that inhibit women, as a group, in terms of holders of assets and as institutional players. This situation is presumed to apply equally, if not more so, to the climate change financial sub-sectors such as the carbon market. The reasons for this are at least fourfold.

First, in its early stage, only players with significant expertise and historical attachment to the environmental and financial fields will have a high level of comfortability trading in such a non-standardized product as certified emissions reduction. Historically, the environmental field, as well as the financial areas with the most complex instruments, tend to be dominated by males. For example in the private equity area it is small, male and geographically concentrated (the Diana Project and WAVE).

Second, actors at the governmental, business and NGO levels have been primarily white males who are versed in financial markets and have varying degrees of environmental and climate change expertise.

Third, there is also geographically distributional imbalance, with many of the high value-added professional areas, in the sub-sectors, dominated by individuals and institutions from the rich countries (and increasingly the richer developing countries such as Brazil and China).

Fourth, it is also important to recognize that the climate change area has been increasingly mystified and heavily laden with a scientific shroud, even at the level of financing. This is particularly so with regard to the frameworks of vulnerability and assessment for adaptation and mitigation that tends to undergird this area. As a result, over the past few years, this situation has led to the development of unintentional, but nonetheless, exclusionary effects on different groups, notably women. There are fewer women than men actively involved with carbon-neutral companies, registries and the various carbon funds.

Globally, women business owners tend to concentrate on the services sector.[32] In sub-Saharan Africa, where women-owned businesses account for one-third of all firms and are the majority of businesses in the informal sector, there is some diversity with regard to the location of women-owned enterprises (Bardasi, Blackden and Guzman 2007). In countries such as Angola, Malawi and Mali, women-owned enterprises are more likely to be found in the agricultural and food sectors, while in the Democratic Republic of the Congo, Madagascar, Mauritius and South Africa they are likely to be located in the textile sector. The service sector seems to be an important area for women private sector actors in Gambia, Mauritania, Namibia and Uganda.

It is not yet clear just how much involvement female entrepreneurs in any of these countries have in climate change activities. However, there may be some scope for women through wholly-owned enterprises or through joint ventures with large, male-owned entities, foreign companies or NGOs, to have greater and more sustainable involvement in the key areas of adaptation and mitigation. Involving women in these sectors in ways that generate significant qualitative changes in gender equality and women's empowerment will require financial capital, both for start-up and for ongoing capitalization. This capital should be forthcoming from the private financial climate change market and may be leveraged by substantial public financial mechanisms (see Chapter 10). New entrants will require adequate start-up financing and maturing firms will need ongoing capital infusion.

This start-up capital must be enough to enable the development of general education and the kinds of networking and sharing experiences that will be needed in these new fields. This reality, in the context of women's responsibility for household and gender discrimination in the conventional banking sector, would signify that in order for women to access and develop new forms of enterprises in the climate change sector, they will need to rely on accessing climate change oriented financing, beyond microcredit/finance.

The current level of activities in women's enterprise development across regions (see Table 9.1) indicates a greater capacity for increased involvement in higher-valued commercial activities, employment and training. Table 9.1 also shows the increasing level of female entrepreneurship worldwide. However, due to gender-based constraints, women's businesses tend to be small in size and dominate in the informal sector and home-based businesses (Box 9.5). Though women are increasing their numbers as owners of business globally, they are indeed constrained by low access to credit and unfavourable terms of borrowing (Box 9.5). For example, according the IFC, though women own 48 per cent of businesses they only have 7 per cent of formal credit. Appendix 9.1 presents more information on the financial and non-financial barriers to women's business growth.

Lastly, women's increasing (and often unmet) demand for risk transfers and other services will continue to increase as weather and climate change risks increase. This is true for women as potential customers for risk management tools

TABLE 9.1 Level of female entrepreneurship activity across countries

Country	Percentage of entrepreneurial activity
Philippines	49.9★
US	48
Botswana, Cameroon, Cape Verde and Mozambique	40★★
Thailand	39
Venezuela	30
Jamaica	25
New Zealand	22
China	22
Brazil	18
Australia	15
Greece	13
South Africa	5.5
Japan	4.3
Belgium	1.9★

Source: Global Entrepreneurship Monitor (2005); Bardasi, Blackden and Guzman (2007); this is the percentage of women-owned enterprises with at least 10 employees.

such as casualty, property and crop insurance. Women who are located in high-risk sectors and areas may have need for innovative types of risk-transfer mechanisms.

Weather-related events impact assets and properties in individual women's portfolios, as well as those of households, families and communities. Overall, unplanned climate change related costs can negatively impact project viability and profitability, resulting in decreased income for living as well as for investment and speculation. Hence, women's business, and overall women's priority and gender equality interventions that meet the needs of poor women and men, are likely target sectors for a variety of investor portfolios. Where this financing support is not forthcoming from the private sector, market actors will require incentives from government to undertake more socially oriented financing activities. This is particularly so where the rewards are long-term and not clearly discernible to the immediate bottom line.

It is important that men and women in developing countries have access to the financial and investment instruments of the global private climate financing market, including the carbon finance market.[33] This market is not only growing quite rapidly, but it is also larger than the public financial side of climate change financing in terms of equity and market capitalization. There is also a strong upsurge towards 'carbon competitiveness' as market participants seek increasingly to capitalize on the value of carbon.[34]

BOX 9.4 WOMEN'S SMES WORLD-WIDE GROWTH AND CONSTRAINTS

'Women are more likely than their male colleagues to be in the informal sectors, running smaller firms mainly in the service sectors ... and operate more home-based business than do men' (GPFI and IFC 2011). According to IFC and McKinsey (2011), women enterprises make up:

- 32–39 per cent of very small firms
- 30–36 per cent of SMEs
- 17–21 per cent of medium-sized companies

There are an estimated 8–10 million full or partial female-owned companies, formal SMEs in emerging markets, representing 31–38 per cent of such enterprises in these countries (IFC and McKinsey 2011).

Women-owned businesses represent about 38 per cent of all registered small businesses worldwide. In Canada, women hold ownership in 47 per cent of small enterprises and accounted for 70 per cent of new business start-ups in 2004. In the US, women-owned businesses are growing at twice the rate of all firms and 10.1 million firms are owned by women (75 per cent or more), employing more than 13 million people, and generating $1.9 trillion in sales as of 2008. In China, women own one-third of small businesses, of which 17 per cent have more than 1,000 employees (World Bank 2009).

Source: Strengthening Access to Finance for Women-Owned SMEs in Developing Countries. Global partnership for Financial Inclusion and International Finance Corporation World Bank Group. October 2011.

MSMEs: micro 1–4 employees, very small 5–9 employees, small 10–49 employees, and medium sized 50–250 employees

---

As the agricultural sector is also integrated into the global carbon markets, it is projected to secure net benefits from the presumed ever–growing streams of income. These are likely to emanate from carbon stocks and projected for decreasing GHG emissions (IFPRI 2008). Where these opportunities really do exist, some women and women's groups who are able to take advantage of these may thrive and grow by contributing, in multiple ways, to the development of their communities and countries. But in many situations this may not be the case. There are two reasons for this cautious outlook.

First, as noted in Chapter 8, there are also significant barriers and constraints that will impede women's benefits from some of these income streams. There are also gender biases that may act to block or slow the flow of financing and investment to women. Gender gaps in assets, property rights and access to finance

> **BOX 9.5 WOMEN-OWNED BUSINESSES AND THE GLOBAL FINANCIAL MARKET ENVIRONMENT**
>
> Across regions, women entrepreneurs have lower access to finance than do male entrepreneurs (IFC and McKinsey 2011; Women SME Mapping Exercise 2011).
>
> The IFC notes that in Kenya, 48 per cent of business owners are women, yet they have only 7 per cent of formal credit and own just 1 per cent of land. In Nigeria, women own 25–30 per cent of registered businesses and access 10–15 per cent of bank credit. In Uganda, women account for 39 per cent of businesses with registered premises and 9 per cent of commercial bank credit (www.ifc.org/...WomenEntrepreneursFinance/.../Women+Entrepreneurs+and+Access+to+Finance.pdf).
>
> Surveys show that women entrepreneurs are . . . less likely to take out a loan . . . the terms of borrowing can also be less favourable for women. In general, women entrepreneurs are more likely to:
>
> - face higher interest rates
> - be required to collaterize a higher share of loans
> - have shorter-term loans.
>
> Source: Bardasi et al. (2007)

are significant constraints on women, inhibiting their abilities to accrue an equitable share of the benefits associated with climate change financing.

Second, emerging focus on so-called 'climate smart' agriculture may adversely impact many poor women. Climate smart agriculture tends to focus more on the mitigation aspect of agriculture and may, therefore, detract from the adaptation basis of agriculture for many developing countries in Africa and Asia where agriculture is critical for food security, livelihood and rural development. This tension between the mitigation abatement potential (emission reduction primarily from methane and nitrous oxide) surrounding agriculture which is a preoccupation of developed country proponents and the adaptation focused linked to agriculture has made agriculture a very sensitive subject in the UNFCCC negotiations.

Underlying the climate smart agriculture is the agri-carbon offset, financing from the carbon market, which will purportedly contribute to adaptation and food security as co-benefits. However, many gender advocates are also concern about the potential for carbon-related land-grabbing by high net worth individuals and firms, as well as intense and likely pernicious competition for agriculture by big biotechnology, GMO firms at a high cost to women and other small farmers.

Developing country negotiators are likewise duly cautious about this approach. The Africa Group of negotiators within the context of the ongoing UNFCCC negotiations emphasize the central importance of agriculture for the achievement of social and economic development and poverty eradication in developing countries. This position is supported by the G77, and China seeks to enhance the adaptation of agriculture to climate change impacts, while promoting rural development, and productivity of agricultural systems and food security, particularly in developing countries. This should take into account the diversity of the agricultural systems, and the differences in scale, as well as possible adaptation co-benefits.

Many civil society groups raise concerns about the intrusion of the carbon market and so-called 'market-based' activities in the agriculture sector and its potential to disadvantage small and women farmers rather than benefit them.

9.4 Gender and the carbon market

From the vantage point of gender equality and women's empowerment, the carbon market presents both opportunities and challenges. There is the opportunity for the financing of women's small-scale projects as well as the potential for women to develop and operate in a variety of businesses along the carbon market chain. Another key area of business development aims to support women by helping them to take advantage of on-going streams of revenue from emission reduction activities in the household (such as cooking on a new and improved cook stove). However, the functioning of the carbon offset market linked to the clean cook stove industry does not facilitate this process; it simply alienates women's labour by transferring their property rights, to the actual and future emission reductions, to project developers and other actors along the carbon commodity chain (Wang and Corson 2014). Women could also become professionals in the carbon market as project developers, consultants and investors etc. but this too faces significant challenges.

First, the emissions reduction–carbon relationship is a 'convoluted virtual commodity chain' that is difficult for many people to understand without access to expert knowledge. This also applies to many women who produce carbon credits through cooking-induced emission reductions.

Second, creating and managing a business based on carbon/emission reductions is a complex and challenging process with significant technical and financial requirements associated with developing and registering projects, property rights and measuring and verifying emissions.

Overall, the carbon commodity market is qualitatively different from conventional commodity markets, and may discourage investors with low risk tolerance. Commodity markets also exhibit some degree of obscurity that may discourage such investors, but the case of carbon is quite markedly different. Credits are generated by quantifying emission reductions through slightly unclear, imprecise and often faulty mechanisms such as 'baseline' and 'additionality', which are critical to carbon offsetting and the carbon financing business.

This was highlighted by the UK Financial Services Authority (2008), which argued that '[T]he key differences in the emissions market, compared with other commodities markets, are that it is a politically-generated and managed market and that the underlying [instrument] is a dematerialized allowance certificate, as opposed to a physical commodity. Also, there is a compliance aspect to the underlying market'.

While the nature of the carbon markets and the challenges around political and other risks are not ostensibly gender-specific, they do have subtle gender undertones that can work to the disadvantages of women. Primarily, of course, the pre-existing issue of high degree of unfamiliarity and expertise (identified in the GEMCRA framework in Chapter 3 as the participation risk), that women, as a group, relative to men, as a group, have, with regard to the financial sector, especially those most exotic and arcane aspects of the sector. When this is coupled with women's generally low risk tolerance and lower threshold capital/investment portfolio, it presents quite compelling explanations for women's likely low (relative to men's) attraction factor to carbon financing, at least at this early stage. It must be remembered that both of the latter factors are themselves circumscribed, if not created, by the gendered nature of access to resources and gendered responsibilities for care and domestic work in most all economies.

Women, as a group, are under-represented as investors and financial market institutional players, among the consultants and 'market makers', who are active in climate change financing, and who attend specialized workshops, seminars and conference on the topics.[35] The participation of women investors is smaller than that of men. It is possible that high net-worth women and those heading investment entities may not be involved in the climate financing markets on a comparative level as male-owned entities because of its newness and relatively exotic presentation. Compared with the broader financial markets, which have a system of transparent pricing and standardized elements, the climate financial market, especially carbon financing, is quite obscure and not very transparent. Thus, its appeal to mass flow of investment is only gradually occurring even among traditional male-dominated venture capitalists. Nonetheless, in this context as well, the participation of women investors is smaller than that of men.[36] This situation may be shifting somewhat with the creation of the Cleantech Angel Network of Networks (CANN) under the leadership of companies with high-level participation from women.[37] However, this only applies to the clean energy subsector, much more women investors need to move in the direction of carbon market. The launch of CANN may be just the factor to help catalyse more women investors' participation in climate change financing.

Ongoing research on women and investing points out that woman, though they are under-represented as angel or venture capital investors, are more likely to support the growth of women-run businesses.[38] Studies note that women investors have a 'heightened receptivity to investing in women's owners and pay special attention to women-led businesses' (Kauffman Foundation 2006). Many women angel investors also tend to put in extra time and effort in order to ensure that 'women-led business are not passed over' (Kauffman Foundation 2006). Angel investors tend to provide seed money and support start-up businesses to a greater extent than the wider grouping of venture capitalists, which tend to finance businesses at a later stage.

These demonstrated support of women investors for start-up ventures by other women point to the need for education and outreach on climate change financing targeted to increasing the awareness and knowledge of women angel investors about the opportunities and challenges of underwriting climate change and related products. If successful, these groups of investors may prove to be important sources of financial and investment resources for women's businesses and gender equality projects involved in adaptation and mitigation. Increased flow of such investment would also be useful for leveraging support for increasing the profile of women in the carbon finance sector. Government public financial mechanism within the context of the carbon market will be useful in this context.

In this regard, the increasing participation of UN development agencies such as the United Nations Development Programme (UNDP) in carbon market activities could lead to greater support and enabling of women's greater and effective participation in carbon finance. One such potential example is the United Nations Development Programme (UNDP) Millennium Development Goal (MDG) Carbon Facility.

9.4.1 The UNDP/MDG carbon facility

In 2007, the UNDP established the MDG Carbon Facility ('Mechanism') with the dual purpose of improving access to carbon finance by enabling a wider range of developing countries and project types to participate, particularly in those countries that are currently under-represented in the carbon market, and promoting emission reduction projects that generate additional sustainable development (UNDP 2009a). The facility offers emission reduction projects on a comprehensive 'one-stop-shop' package of services. The UNDP provides project development services, including assistance with project design, validation and registration, as well as assisting in the development of a monitoring system for the emission reductions. The UNDP's specific role in the mechanism is to conceptualize projects that reduce greenhouse gas emissions within the Kyoto Protocol's agreed standards, conduct financial and legal assessments and provide technical assistance in passing the approval procedures under the Kyoto Protocol Clean Development Mechanism (CDM) and Joint Implementation (JI). The UNDP's other task is to ensure the benefits to the environment and broader human development.

The UNDP-Fortis Bank collaboration covers an initial set of Kyoto Protocol projects that will generate carbon credits during the Protocol's first commitment period of 2008 to 2012.

Fortis will purchase and market the project's certified emission reduction credits (UNDP 2009a). The proceeds from Fortis purchases will provide project proponents and their communities with a new flow of hard currency that can finance investment and promote development.

The MDG Carbon Facility Mechanism sought to increase the participation of many countries who previously were constrained by size and absorptive capacity precluded from fully participating in the CDM mechanism. The Carbon Facility aimed at facilitating and enhancing access that would not otherwise take place. In theory, it has huge potential to enlarge the participation of poor countries while promoting and consolidating the Millennium Developments Goals. The facility anticipated generating 15 million carbon credits between 2008 and 2012. For example, if the present value of a unit of CER is $23, then it is expected to generate $345 million (UNDP 2009a).

The advantage of the MDG Carbon Facility Mechanism is that it has the opportunity of really serving as a bridge between developing countries and the global carbon market. It also allows for developing countries, especially LDCs, with little risk and low cost, to experiment and build their capacity and gain proficiency in carbon finance. This is because the financing arrangement allows for advance payments that cover the start-up cost so this is no longer an impediment. The financing agent recoups this payment when the carbon credits are issued, especially as there is a standardized pricing formula for the purchase of carbon credits. Standardized pricing provides price stability, thus allowing future planning and stable growth. In addition, the signing agreement of an Emission Reduction Purchase Agreement (ERPA) between the MDG Carbon Facility project and the financing entity such as Fortis provides a significant asset that can be used by project proponents to secure financing from a third party.

Clearly, the UNDP is playing a critical role in facilitating developing countries in the development of the carbon market. In the short term, its advisory role dominates the process, and in the long run, its development objectives are being solidified. This is being accomplished through the building of institutions whose tasks are to remove policy barriers to climate-friendly technologies and investment, thus laying the foundation for behavioural changes across the political and social strata. The difficulty in securing financing in low-income countries is due to inadequate capital market and low savings. There is also a high degree of centralization and bureaucratic barriers around financing. The facility will work with project proponents and governments to ensure a smooth process for project development and implementation.

The MDG Carbon Facility is structured to accommodate a range of projects with the exception of a few categories that would be seen as antithetical to the aim of the MDGs. These categories are: nuclear energy, large-scale hydropower, geo-sequestration (including enhanced oil recovery), projects dealing with shifting of electric power loads, and the capture and destruction of industrial gases. Beyond this, the facility has cast a broad net that focuses on projects and quality. While there is no minimum project size, projects must be able to cover the minimum recovery cost. Each project is evaluated on case-by-case basis for its overall merits, which may come short in one criterion, yet provide a high MDG impact – and would thus meet the eligibility criteria at the margin. This flexibility is favourable to developing countries given the low emissions generated.

The MDG Carbon Facility was designed to be development friendly; it could also have pro poor benefits. Given its emphasis on the MDG, which includes gender equality, it can be expected that there will be a focus on ensuring a focus on women's empowerment as well as proactive efforts to ensure and promote gender equality in outcomes relative to project size, distribution and benefits. The MDG Carbon Facility is currently involved with the development and distribution of efficient cook stoves in El Salvador and the purification of water to enable rural Rwandans to have access to clean drinking water (project launched June 2011). The Turbo Cocina cookstove is supposed to eliminate the need for over 90 per cent of firewood and eliminate smoke emissions across communities in El Salvador. Both projects will help to lighten the workload of women and men in poor communities and contribute to better health.

The MDG Carbon Facility's website displays the interlinkages between each MDG goal, including MDG3 on gender equality, and the range of activities financed under the project that will contribute to those goals. So, in terms of service delivery, women are projected to be high beneficiaries. What is not quite certain is the degree to which such projects will involve women's participation and eventually enhance their role, contribution and empowerment in the development and implementation of projects either as project sponsors are beneficiaries.

More generally, most potential project sponsors face difficulties in securing long-term project finance, and this often leads to delays or failures. Making carbon finance available upfront could be an important contribution to overall project financing by bringing more projects to fruition, as the MDG Carbon Facility may demonstrate. Project sponsors often require assistance and finance well before they receive payments for CERs delivered under emission reduction purchase agreements (ERPAs). To mitigate this gap, the Asian Development Bank created the Carbon Market Initiative (CMI) in order to help support developing countries in the Asia-Pacific region to tap into the growing global carbon market. With the implementation of the CMI, the Asian Development Bank (ADB) is now playing the role of a broker by mobilizing much-needed upfront finance for CDM projects. The Carbon Market Initiative (CMI) supports the development of energy efficiency, renewable energy and other GHG mitigation projects by providing upfront co-financing for project preparation and implementation. It does so through three major activities; the Asia-Pacific Carbon Fund, the Technical Support Facility, and the Credit Marketing Facility. A fourth programme, the Future Carbon Fund, was announced in July of 2008 and will use carbon credits generated beyond 2012 to provide financing for clean energy projects.

This has started a trend in carbon financing in which a few financial institutions now lend against emission reduction purchase agreements (ERPAs). That is, they use the expected proceeds from CER sales as collateral. ERPAs can help to release the drawback of lengthy time between registration, approval and certification of projects. However, given the perceived risks and the financial sector's relative inexperience with the CDM, such finances are still very limited. Nonetheless, this kind of upfront financing, when carefully weighted to avoid onerous obligations on the seller or future unexpected additional costs, can present opportunities for small-scale actors to be involved in the carbon market. Small-scale projects would also need to be aggregated to generate sufficient volume for such activities. This is the role that entities such as the UNDP and the ADB's initiative can play. Such initiatives, coupled with the use of national governments' regulatory and financial mechanisms, can be useful tools for involving women actors in the carbon market as well as ensuring greater social and economic development benefits. However, there are substantial drawbacks to carbon financing, including the recent volatility of the market and the lack of stability of carbon prices.

9.4.2 Challenges with carbon financing

Apart from the practical issues of gender challenges with private sector-oriented approaches to climate finance, especially with regard to the operation of market-based mechanisms, there are broader and compelling issues about carbon financing and its role in addressing climate change. On many levels, carbon financing may simply allow developed countries to source their carbon reductions in developing countries without making significant changes in their own domestic economies.

There are also numerous equity issues around carbon financing. Some of these challenges have led to the reform of CDM, including the creation of the Programme of Activities (PoA) and Standardized Baseline (SB) modalities in order to enable more sector-wide activities. This reform, however, is itself presumed on the development of new generation of carbon finance mechanisms. But global civil society, including gender advocates, have raised concerns about the efficacy and equity issue of the present carbon market as an approach to addressing climate change.

These concerns arise primarily due to the host of problems with the European ETS and the CDM, such as surplus allowances, profiteering by speculators and companies. All of these raise the central issue of environmental integrity. Many of these underlying challenges around carbon financing have already given rise to systemic overloading and the possibility for collapsing of the market, with the world carbon market suffering setbacks in 2009–2010 period.[39] But there are also growing and potential, though unacknowledged, issues surrounding the evolution and development of carbon derivatives.

Women's groups and some of the NGO communities argue strongly that 'carbon market and market-based tools such as the CDM financing may ultimately become "allusions"'. Penultimately, they argue that the 'most effective way of dealing with reducing GHG emission might simply be through carbon taxes'. Appendix 8.2 examines in greater detail the benefits, opportunities, challenges and constraints around the CDM and women's empowerment.

Many questions abound about the efficacy and effectiveness of carbon trading to solve the climate challenge – to move mitigation at scale. With strong supporters on either side: those who believe that the market is the solution and those who

> ## BOX 9.6 BIOGAS RECOVERY, HEAT AND ELECTRICITY GENERATION FROM EFFLUENTS PONDS IN HONDURAS
>
> This project involves the installation of two biodigesters and a biogas recovery system. The captured biogas from agricultural effluents will be utilized in a gas engine for the generation of electricity for the mill's internal processes and in two boilers for the generation of heat. If the project is successful and there is enough biogas available, ERH is considering the installation of a second generator.

believe the contrary, that the carbon market poses more problems than it offers solutions for dealing with climate change challenges. Even proponents of carbon finance agree that carbon financing by itself will not tackle some significant sources and sinks of GHGs, such as ozone depleting substances (ODSs), peatlands, biochar and black carbon. Nor will it automatically promote gender equality and women's empowerment unless there is proactive focus on emission reduction project types that will focus on providing modern energy services that liberate women and girls from energy provisioning (by reducing the need for collecting firewood, supplies energy to health clinics and for the cooling of vaccines and medicines and help in the substitution of on non-renewable biomass).

Undoubtedly, some carbon-financed projects do benefit women and community. For example, projects like the one in Rwanda that, through the installation of water treatment systems that rely on renewable energy and therefore replace the use of non-renewable firewood for treating water by boiling, help to provide clean water that meets the drinking, cooking, and hygiene needs in the rural areas of the country. Biogas recovery projects that generate heat and electricity from effluent ponds in Honduras are another worthwhile example (Box 9.6). The challenge is that many of these types of projects are small-scale and one-off projects that need to be rapidly scaled up to meet the growing untapped demands. They also raise issues around land management, use and ownership, as well as around the rights of indigenous and other community groups.

Notes

1. The International Energy Agency estimates that $48 billion per year is needed to provide universal energy access by 2030, which is about 3 per cent of global annual capital investment in energy. The cost of doubling the global rate of improvement in energy efficiency and the global share of renewable energy would each cost about $500 billion per year, according to the Global Energy Assessment. www.sustainableenergyforall.org/about-us/faq.
2. The IEA defines modern energy access as 'a household having reliable and affordable access to clean cooking facilities, a first connection to electricity and then an increasing level of electricity consumption over time to reach the regional average'.

3 There are varying definitions of the term 'public-private partnership'. The World Economic Forum offers a formal definition of PPP in terms of the reciprocal obligations and mutual accountability, voluntary or contractual relationships, the sharing of investment and reputational risks, and joint responsibility for design and execution' between a business entity or a not-for-profit civil society organization and a governmental or development cooperation agency. Narrod *et al.* (2009: 10), offer a vision of a PPP as 'a cooperative venture between the public and private sectors built on the expertise of each partner that best meets clearly defined goals through the appropriate allocation of resources, risks and rewards'. Though the term PPP is said to have been coined by the US in the 1970s to reflect cooperation between the private and public sectors, PPPs are more well-known in Europe, where they were launched domestically, especially in infrastructure (waste disposal etc.). In the late 1990s, public-private facility began to pop up in the development cooperation arena as state funds were made increasingly to 'backstop' and 'support' (German) companies and ventures abroad. Today, there are over 1,000 public-private partnerships, on a financial platform of more than 4.5 billion euros servicing projects in over 70 countries in four continents and covering a broad sectoral spectrum (Haupt). For the most part PPPs, which are active in the transport, education and health sectors have been structured to involved mid-size companies in Europe in development cooperation (though they have also involve MNCs such as Daimler Chrysler, Siemens and Volkswagen). USAID's global investment alliance programme involves PPPs.
4 US$ 2009/2010 and date of the same period.
5 US$ 2010 and 2008, using data from 2008 and 2011.
6 During the most recent financial crisis, developed countries also spent in multiples of trillions of dollars rescuing their domestic banking sectors and providing stimulus to their domestic firms. (The world financial crisis has come to $11.9 trillion, equivalent to one-fifth of the entire globe's annual economic output (IMF 2009). This amount includes capital injections pumped into banks in order to prevent them from collapse, the cost of soaking up 'toxic assets', guarantees over debt and liquidity support from central banks. Most of the cash has been handed over by developed countries, for which the bill has been $10.2 trillion, while developing countries have spent only about $1.7 trillion, the majority of which is in central bank liquidity support for their stuttering financial sectors. The UK bailout was £500 billion ($850 billion (October 2008)), with an additional £50 billion in 2009, the US bailout in 2008 was about $700 billion, Germany €500 billion (approximately $680 billion). In comparison, the Marshall plan (1947) was $13 billion over four years (or 5.4 per cent of the US's 1947 GDP. It is indeed the case that the financial crisis and the consequential downturn in global economic performance and the still ongoing banking crisis in the eurozone impose serious constraints on many developed countries' budgets. Additionally, the government debt-GDP ratio is projected to rise to 110 per cent by 2015 (IMF 2010).
7 Globally, these institutional investors collectively manage about $75.9 trillion in assets (thin includes insurance companies $24 trillion, pension funds $22.8 trillion, investment managers $15.4 trillion, non-pension funds $11.6 trillion and foundations and endowments $1.5 trillion). Sovereign wealth funds manage another $3.9 trillion worth of assets (CERES 2014).
8 OECD estimates that less than 1 per cent of pension funds 'assets globally are allocated *directly* to infrastructure investment, let alone to clean energy projects' (Kaminker *et al.* 2012).
9 US Climate Envoy Todd Stern has stated publicly that the US expects that the $100 billion has to be 'much more private than public'.
10 The UN Secretary General Advisory Group on Climate Finance (AGF) established in February 2010 was co-chaired by His Excellency Mr. Jens Stoltenberg, Prime Minister of Norway, and His Excellency Mr. Meles Zenawi, (former Prime Minister of the Federal Democratic Republic of Ethiopia). Other members of the 20-person advisory group

included: the President of Guyana, Ministers of Finance of Mexico and Singapore, Christine La Garde (now Managing Director of the International Monetary Fund), the Managing Director of the World Bank, Sir Nicholas Stern, George Soros, Zhu Guangyao, the Vice Minister of Finance, China and Lawrence Summers (then director of the National Economic Council and assistant to the President of the US for Economic Policy). Part of mandate of the was to develop practical proposals on how to significantly scale up long-term financing for mitigation and adaptation strategies in developing countries from various public as well as private sources. The group concluded that it would be challenging but feasible to mobilize the $100 billion for climate actions in developing countries by 2010 and identified a number of different sources, as identified in the text.

11 The nature of the board also speaks to how selections are made and in ensuring horizontal relationships between developed and developing countries' members of the board.

12 Initial proposals include the PSF as a business unit of the fund, with its own governing body to which the board delegates authority. This option was rejected by developing countries. They opted instead that the PSF would be fully integrated within the organizational structure of the fund.

13 The board also decided that, in the initial phase, the PSF will focus on grants and concessional loans, through accredited national, regional and international implementing entities and intermediaries. Over time, the PSF will draw on a broad range of other financial instruments (inter alia, partial risk and partial credit guarantees, subordinated debt, equity and quasi-equity) and modalities to achieve its objectives, and may work directly with private sector adaptation and mitigation actors at the national, regional and international levels, subject to consideration by the board of a phased approach.

14 Formal microenterprises are those registered enterprises with 1–4 employees. There are varying definitions of SMEs: the World Bank defines SMEs as those enterprises with a maximum of 300 employees, $15 million in annual revenue, and $15 million in assets. The Inter-American Development Bank defines SMEs as having a maximum of 100 employees and less than $3 million in revenue. The European Union works with a broad and comprehensive definition of SMEs: enterprises that employ fewer than 250 persons and have an annual turnover not exceeding €50 million, and/or an annual balance sheet total not exceeding €43 million (in other words SMEs are firms with 10 to 250 employees, and more than €10 million turnover or annual balance sheet total. Some countries such as Egypt defines SMEs as having more than 5 and fewer than 50 employees, Vietnam considers SMEs to have between 10 and 300 employees. Dalberg Global Development Advisors 2011, and European Commission, Enterprise and Industry, 2011. 'Small and medium-sized enterprises (SMEs), SME Definition' http://ec.europa.eu/enterprise/policies/sme/facts-figures-analysis/sme-definition/index_en.htm).

15 Adaptation financing broadly refers to resources that are deployed to support climate-resilient development (World Bank Group 2011).

16 This activity of hedge funding has been identified as having an impact on food security through impacts activities contribution to rising food prices; it is also associated in some cases with land grabbing with attendant consequences on gender inequality and women's empowerment issues.

17 GCF/B.06/05 DRAFT 26 January 2014 Meeting of the Board 19–22 February 2014 Bali, Indonesia.

18 For Example the Swedish bank, SEB, in partnership with the World Bank, issued Green Bonds, which had participation from Scandinavian investors (including pension funds and insurance companies. The partnership raised US$665 million from both public and private investors (SEI 2011). The European Investment Bank (EIB) also raised €3 billion from the capital markets for a facility for energy sustainability and security of supply (2007). Investors also seem to be motivated by 'responsible investment' funds, some of which may focus on climate financing instruments (SEI 2011). The African Development Bank also issued three 'clean energy bonds' in 2010 that specifically targeted investors that are interested in supporting clean energy solutions in Africa. The initial bond,

denominated in New Zealand dollars (109 million) or US $77 million was successful, (AU et al. 2010).

19 A parametric insurance product can be defined as an insurance contract where the ultimate payment or contract settlement is determined by a weather or geological observation or index, such as average temperature or rainfall over a given period or the intensity of an earthquake or wind storm. Parametric insurance payouts are not based on individual loss adjustments, but are determined according to the measurement of a highly correlated index. More than 30 pilot projects are underway in about 20 countries, including Ethiopia and Malawi. In Ethiopia, a risk transfer product was purchased by the World Food Programme to supplement emergency aid. In Malawi, a risk transfer product was purchased by smallholder farmers as part of a loan for an input package that encouraged the adoption of new technologies.

20 Public-private partnerships and renewable resources as well as financing tools tailored for the unique needs of the developing world are all key areas of focus for OPIC. www.opic.gov/blog/opic-in-action/looking-to-rio-connecting-the-dots-between-environment-and-development.

21 And yet, as noted by the OECD, 'insurance companies direct allocations to infrastructure projects remain in the billions of dollars, compared with total industry assets of around USD 19.3 trillion'.

22 Examples of agricultural index schemes include: Index weather crop insurance schemes: Ethiopia (HARITA, Malawi, Thailand); weather-based insurance schemes, India; rainfall insurance schemes for coffee growers, India; index-based livestock insurance scheme, Mongolia; and national agricultural insurance scheme (NAIS), India. Indemnity-based schemes may suffer from limited reinsurance capacity, and the need for regulatory interventions, for example with regard to premium subsidies or mandatory insurance provisions include: the Windward Islands Crop Insurance programme and the livestock insurance programme, Nepal.

23 Sovereign risk transfer schemes (constraints include: require donor support by need for current and historical data ad risk models): the Caribbean Catastrophe Risk Insurance Facility, CCRIF, operational and the natural disasters regional insurance facility for Central America (proposed).

24 Property catastrophe risk insurance tends to have low penetration (due to low risk awareness and lack of information). Examples include: Residential earthquake insurance pool, Taiwan; Algerian Catastrophe insurance pool.

25 The UNDP is piloting a non-commercial, community-based variant of index insurance. In addition, microfinance institutions are becoming involved in risk insurance and are considering the purchase of such mechanisms as a prerequisite for extending loans (UNDP 2009a).

26 Schemes can directly link risk transfer and risk reduction and contribute to adaptation to climate change by fostering the adoption of physical risk reduction measures (contingent on the provision of insurance), or incentivize risk management measures through, for example, risk rating of insurance premiums and/or support capacity building in risk reduction through promoting elements of knowledge sharing and expertise transfer. Such schemes would appear to be more likely with the involvement of public and private financing, which include technical assistance, provision of things such as start-up capital, subsidies and other types of financial assistance. This would be beneficial to MSMEs.

27 Schemes that insure or intend to insure SMEs include the proposed Catastrophe Insurance Pool in Bulgaria, the proposed Southeast Europe and the Caucasus Catastrophe risk insurance facility, the proposed water supply index insurance in the Philippines and the pilot Flood Index (ENSO) insurance in Peru. These schemes, as with agricultural insurance schemes, face constraints and challenges for women and the poor with regard to issues of awareness; information; knowledge of insurance and insurance products;

affordability (of premiums) and indebtedness (if linked to loans); availability of local insurance delivery channels; financial sustainability (rising claim costs).
28 The CDM has been the main vehicle for private sector investment in carbon mitigation (totalling over $33 billion in 2009, of which $6.5 billion was in the primary market and the rest in the secondary CDM market). The GEF has $3.3 billion in climate-related projects since 2009 and is argued to have leveraged an additional $14.4 in co-financing from the private sector, recipient countries and donor governments in developing countries (UNFCCC 2007).
29 Though ODA is only about 1 per cent of global investment, it is 6 per cent of investment in least developed countries (HPICA 2009). Multilateral financing for mitigation occurs mainly through the GEF, with the private sector and bilateral flows of ODA playing a role through co-financing.
30 IFC and McKinsey Women SME mapping exercise 2011 defines women-owned SMEs based on survey definition of whether at least one of the owners is female, or whether any of the females are owners.
31 According to the IFC McKinsey Study 2011, the definition of MSME is as follows: micro (1–4) employees, very small (5–9 employees), small 10–49 employees), and medium enterprises (50–250 employees) (GPFI and IFC 2011).
32 Marcucci (2001), among others, found that in many developing countries 'the highest proportion of women-owned enterprises operate within traditionally feminized sectors such as retail and low order services'.
33 The IFC/World Bank are currently developing a Guide on Gender Sensitive Investment Climate Reforms, which hopefully will underscore both its and the World Bank's implementation of the climate fund under their management. In addition, the IFC and the Inter-American Development Bank are also developing a Collaborate on Access to Finance Study, the Multilateral Investment Fund of the Inter-American Development bank which will focus on outreach to women as well as 'gather data on women-owned enterprises in 6 countries in Latin America in order to better understand the gender implications of accessing financial services by women'.
34 Currently the IFC is involved with an emerging secondary carbon market for CERs in which purchase of forward contracts can be made. The volume of this market is a function of the quantity of CERs issued.
35 This has been determined by informal surveys and interviews with key players at such events.
36 The same reasons offered for the relative under-representation of women in professional aspects of the market apply here as well. Further, its newness and narrowness of instrument for which the risks trends are not quite well-known and transparency challenges make this a relatively high-risk area for women, who have been identified as having lower risk tolerance than men. Third, there is arcane and highly specialized language that may not be so widely known among groups of women investors.
37 Kelly Preston, General partner, CalCEF Clean Energy Angel Fund, and Maggie Jacobberger, entrepreneur director the Keiretsu Forum were two high-profile women involved with this network of networks.
38 For example, American women are argued to 'own about half of [the] country's wealth but, make up no more than eight per cent of angel investors'. This has prompted one researcher to argue that 'increasing the numbers could be a logical way of increasing overall financial and mentoring support for new companies'. These points to the need for education and outreach on climate change financing instruments to target groups of women such as these, both in developing and developed countries.
39 Over the last five years, both the value and volume of the world carbon market have fluctuated up and down like a roller coaster ride. This volatility benefits speculators. There was some turn around starting in 2012 when it was at €56 billion, then in 2013 there was about a 36 per cent decline to €40 billion. Analysts blamed much of the decline on

the European Union's actions to delay (postpone or backload some activities into later years) in order to deal with the surplus of allowances. The EU parliament voted for measures to remove 900 million tons of carbon permits over the next three years and return them at the end of the decades (by about 2020) so as to drain the surplus that was dragging prices down to a record low, Matthew Care Jan 8, 2014 (Carbon Market value to gain 15 per cent in 2014 on EU surplus fix).

10
TOWARDS AN EQUITABLE AND GENDER-SENSITIVE POST-2015 CLIMATE CHANGE FINANCING REGIME

> ... women have the power to mobilize against climate change, but this potential can be realized only through policies that empower them.
>
> Thoraya Ahmed Obaid*

This chapter elaborates a three-pronged approach grounded in the principles of climate justice and gender justice as approaches for dealing with the issues of gender segmentation and gender asymmetries in climate finance identified and discussed in Chapter 8. It links the general equity principles embedded in the normative framework of UNFCCC to the search for gender equity in climate change finance. It concludes by suggesting strategies and tactics towards gender-sensitizing climate change science, policies and its financing architecture. It also provides a series of guidelines for engendering climate change science, policy frameworks and finance.

Climate finance is emerging as a core pillar to be integrated into the new post-2015 climate regime, the Paris 2015 agreement, the elements of which are to be negotiated during 2015. Coming out of the cold, so to speak, with the 2009 Copenhagen pledges of the $30 billion Fast Start Initiative (2010–2012) and the goal of mobilizing jointly US$100 billion annually by 2020 to address the needs of developing countries, climate finance achieved limelight status with the 2014 Climate Summit. At that one-day climate summit on 23 September, the first major gathering of heads of state (120 presidents and prime ministers, including Barack Obama, David Cameron, Dilma Rousseff, François Hollande and Chinese Vice Premier Zhang Goali as well as Leonardo DiCaprio in cameo as UN Messenger of Peace) on climate change since the disastrous Copenhagen meeting,[1] developed countries once again made numerous intimations about commitment to climate finance. In addition, the GCF mooted at Cancún (2010) and approved in Durban (2011) since midsummer 2014 has been in the process of initial resource mobilization with the expectation of significant funds for its initial capitalization from various developed countries (as well as a couple of developing countries or non-annex countries such as Indonesia and South Korea).

The much heralded pledges of $1 billion each by France and Germany with other contributions totalling over $10 billion for the GCF is good, but the reality is that the overall amount is quite small relative to the expectation of a significant proportion of the $100 billion Copenhagen promise. The pledged amount when apprised in terms of the anticipated $15 billion that the Secretariat of the GCF expects and in the context of the climate finance pathway for the pre-2020 time frame of at least $15 billion, 2014–2015, annually ratcheting up to at least $50–70 billion in 2016, scaling up to the $100 billion annually by 2020 that has been advocated for by many country groupings that belong to the group of over 130 developing countries under the umbrella of the G77 and China would seem to come up short. At the same time, back in the halls of UNFCC negotiations, developed countries have made statements that seem to signal a shying away from their finance obligations in both the pre-2020 and the post-2020 work-streams of the Ad Hoc Working Group on the Durban Platform negotiations. As a group developed countries are averse to the inclusion of finance (as well as adaptation, capacity building and technology transfer) as part of the legally binding 2015 agreement, which they see as a purely mitigation agreement.

In the context of ever rising CO_2 emissions and accelerated GHG concentrations in the atmosphere, the world is seemingly hurtling close to breaching the safe threshold (1.5–2 degrees Celsius) beyond which there is risk of catastrophic and irreversible climate change. This is of great concern to gender activists. This concern is further heightened by the IPCC 2014 report highlighting that climate-related impacts are already happening at the current degree of warming of 0.85 degrees Celsius above pre-industrial level with significant adverse effects, and that increasing magnitudes of warming will only increase severe, pervasive and irreversible impacts. This as noted by Dumisani Dlamini (Swaziland), Chair of the Subsidiary Body for Scientific and Technological Advice (SBSTA), 'is an indication that any upper limit of global warming can no longer be seen as a safety warranting guardrail for preventing any dangerous anthropogenic interference' (Chiew 2014). Men's, children's and women's lives in communities across the globe, but most especially in developing countries, are bound by the efforts taken to remain on a 1.5–2 degrees Celsius pathway.

This will require finance and technology development and diffusion transfer on an unprecedented scale. Gender advocates hence recognize and argue, in as much as there is clear need for global action on reducing emissions, that there is urgent need for scaling up climate change finance so it is commensurate with the financing needs of developing countries for adaptation and to avert devastating loss and damage. Men and women in communities in the those countries particularly vulnerable to climate change have great need for new, additional, predictable, adequate public sources of funding, especially for adaptation for poverty eradication, ecosystems, food security and the protection of human health. It is also important that there is in place rigorous systems for measuring, reporting and verifying the support offered as well as the support received.

Gender advocates continue to push forward on the engendering mission for climate change finance that is grounded in inclusiveness, transparency and accountability both at the level of the GCF and elsewhere. Getting climate finance to women on the ground is of the utmost importance.

The rest of this chapter returns to the equity theme elaborated in Chapter 2 and which has been the key interweaving thread of this book to elaborate a three-pronged approach grounded in the principle of climate justice and gender justice as approaches for both dealing with the issues of gender segmentation and gender asymmetries in climate finance identified and discussed in Chapter 8 and a way forward in upscaling the flow of climate finance to women and community groups on the ground in developing countries. The next section explores the urgency of recognizing and addressing the transfer burden associated with climate change on developing countries and most often on the poorest segment of the population in these countries. Section 10.2 explores the necessity of integrating gender justice in the 2015 agreement and its impact on climate finance. It concludes by linking the general equity principles embedded in the normative framework of UNFCCC to the search for gender equity in climate change finance. Sections 10.3, 10.4 and 10.5 suggest strategies and tactics towards gender sensitizing climate change science, policies and its financing architecture, respectively. Each section provides a series of guidelines for engendering climate change science, policy frameworks and finance. Finally, Section 10.6 concludes the chapter by drawing on the Gender Empowerment and Climate Finance Risk Assessment Framework presented in Chapter 3, to pinpoint specific strategic interventions in the three broad areas of the capital market, the carbon market and private sector, and national level interventions.

10.1 CBDR, gender and the transfer burden of climate change

Economic development trajectories in developing countries are preoccupied with the challenges of ensuring local development issues such as basic services, access to energy, food security and employment. The imperative to undertake low-carbon and climate-resilient development requires adopting climate management strategies such as the promotion of clean and renewable energy and the building of climate-resilient water management systems. This seemingly adds yet further layers of demand for scarce resources that may detract from development objectives or in the worst case force a trade-off between the two. This works adversely against meeting development objectives successfully. Yet that need not be the case. Developing countries' governments and citizens may instead opt to integrate climate-proofing (making the economic and social structures resistant to climate change) and low emissions development strategies as essential branches of (or in the least cooperating) development planning.

Addressing the risks of climate-related events to social and economic assets presents both challenges and opportunities. The challenges are in terms of meeting the additional capital requirement and investment cost of transforming institutions and structures to a low or decarbonization pathway and in making the economy climate resilient. But opportunities also exist. Costs can be weighted appropriately and attempts made to factor social dimensions into mitigation strategies and measures so that the synergies between mitigation, adaptation and development goals are successfully promoted. Furthermore, the opportunity to recast the development architecture presents the possibility of accelerating the appropriate measures that must be undertaken by different stakeholders, taking into account their gendered and other social realities, to guard against or mitigate those risks by focusing on ensuring that vulnerabilities in the economy, especially those that impact the poorest communities and the most vulnerable areas of a country, are addressed. Quite often these are the same people, regions and institutions that have received little attention and have been ignored or left behind by rapid growth and development trajectories.

Hence there is the opportunity to balance the equity side of the climate and sustainable development agenda, both as a moral imperative and as a healthy cost, against an effective response to the climate challenge. For example, as noted by UNDP, low emissions technologies can be used to improve access to energy in underserved areas thus both satisfying development outcome and promoting climate resilient development. Additionally, financing energy efficiency and promoting local renewal energy development also ensures energy security, while promoting good ecosystem management can lead to improving water quality, food security and flood protection, all of which are important to the poor (UNDP 2011). Interestingly enough, promoting conservation of the ecosystem and using natural resources sustainably through measures that promote the purification of water and soil stabilization and is mindful of gender and community dynamics can deliver a triple dividend: it meets both adaptation and mitigation objectives, provides good social and equity outcomes and has global co-benefits. This triple bottom line impact, so to speak, makes for attractive financing options through the myriad of international funds and instruments for financing climate change.

The foregoing chapters of this book have clearly identified the gender and social development challenges facing developing countries. In the face of the growing climate change challenges and the ever worsening scientific projections for most regions and subregions in light of the relentless global warming evidence since the IPCC released AR4, developing countries must rapidly accelerate climate-proofing and climate mitigation activities. Fortunately, the key sectors identified by the IPCC for which governments must deploy resources to bolster for climate change are the very sectors that are important for economic and social development: energy services, transportation, building, industry, agriculture, forestry/forest and waste management. Such actions must include greater expenditure on infrastructure (e.g. water distribution and storage systems, sanitation and transport), enhancing public health systems and improving information flow and capacity building among the population. Additionally, such actions must primarily seek to achieve social and economic developmental goals and improve access to essential resources in these countries and enhance the level of development for the men and women in the economy.

The 2011 UNDP Human Development Report (UNDP 2010c) shows a direct link between low Human Development Index (HDI) and vulnerability to climate change. It also shows that 'household environmental deprivation in the form of indoor air pollution, inadequate access to clean water and improved sanitation are more severe at low HDI levels and declines as the HDI rises'. The same holds true for the situation of poor and marginalized men and women in poor countries and who live in vulnerable areas (ibid.: 4).

Thus, as is well known, the costs associated with climate change are likely to be shifted among different groups of countries and between different economic sectors and among groups within domestic economies. A transfer burden of meeting the cost of adapting and mitigating climate change is widely acknowledged to exist between poor and rich countries. Within the framework of the current international climate policy architecture, the rich countries have, in principle, accepted the responsibility for their contribution to global warming and have pledged to finance the developing countries' costs related to adaptation and mitigation. But the reality, as noted in earlier chapters, is that with every meeting of the COP that responsibility is being increasingly eschewed, even as the developed countries increasingly seek to shift the burden of mitigation onto developing countries. The actions of developed countries' Parties to the Convention with regard to finance thus tend to be more aspirational promises and vague commitments rather than real enhanced financial and investment flows necessary to meet the massive scale of climate change mitigation and adaptation activities required in the developing countries.

Transformation globally is estimated to be in the trillions of dollars, with about 50 per cent of that being needed by developing countries, this is not an insurmountable challenge. The world currently spends similar amounts on various forms of expenditures such as military ($1.575 trillion in 2012, equivalent to 2.5 per cent of world gross domestic product[2]), fuel subsidies ($40–60 billion per year) and existing carbon-based investments ($5 trillion invested in fossil fuels currently). The global stock market manages over $178 trillion worth of assets and investment in sustainable energy on a global basis is already trending over $200 billion (2010) and is expected to rise to $500 billion by 2020. The additional investment cost to finance mitigation and adaptation is conservatively estimated to be $200–210 billion globally per year and $28–67 billion for developing countries, respectively per year by 2030 (UNFCCC 2014). Further, the cost of subsidising fossil fuels in developed countries at roughly $40–60 billion per year is quite close to the of the cost of adaptation (even though reports such as UNEP's Adaptation Gap Report (2014) argue that adaptation costs are rising and may be 2–3 times the current estimated amounts). Hence the quantum of financing required by developing countries is certainly within the realm of current expectations and demonstrated capability. Nonetheless, securing the capital required to finance the transformation to low emission climate-resilient economies will not be easy due to the strength of pecuniary fossil fuels and other stakeholder interests. Ensuring that the flow of financing is equitable to poor men and women in communities will also not be easy and will require strong advocacy at all levels.

The question of the issue of equity in accessing finance and the extent to which developed countries are willing to follow through on their obligations is serious. But this question of equity must also permeate into the national and regional level.

Developing countries' governments must also confront and deal with the exact nature of the domestic transfer burden that is associated with climate change impacts and adaptation and mitigation strategies implemented in the economy. Mitigation scenarios tend not to focus on this burden; but the household and community sector, not just the business sector, will have to make significant adjustments.

At the national level, there will be adjustment costs related to resource allocation as well as trade-offs in public financial decision-making with regard to taxation, subsidies and public investments around various adaptation and mitigation mechanisms implemented in the economy. These decisions will have different equity impacts for different social groups, as well as affecting men and women differently, given each group's different location in the economy and their different access and control over financial, economic and information resources. Ensuring and enhancing social protection, gender equity and the empowerment of women must be core elements of these strategies. As the IPCC Working Group II pointed out, the combination of biophysical (i.e., soil quality), socio-economic (i.e., measure of literacy and gender equity) and technological conditions are important issues that influence the capacity to adapt to changing environmental conditions (WG II, Chapter 17, p. 726). The IPCC Working Group II also noted that 'the capacity to adapt is dynamic and is influenced by a society's productive base, including natural and man-made capital assets, social networks and entitlements, human capital and institutions, governance, national income, health and technology (IPCC 2007b; WG II 17.3). Further, 'adaptive capacity is intimately connected to social and economic development but it is not evenly distributed across and within societies, and within societies'.[3]

Therefore actions that address 'distinct risks posed by climate change' including, for example, undertaking projects to lower water levels or divert water, should be cognizant of the social dynamics of the area and community in which the project is undertaken if it is to properly meet and ensure adaptive capacity. The same would hold for adaptation actions around a wide range of other activities such as capacity-building, research and assessment (to understand vulnerabilities to climate change and how adaptation can reduce these risks), disaster risk reduction, risk management and specific interventions (e.g. infrastructure or economic diversification).

There is also need for closer scrutiny of the compatibility of economic approaches to climate change with social protection and gender concerns and priorities. In general economic policy dynamics and mechanisms such as supply, demand factors and technological solutions around clean and renewable energy and the resources and capital needed for adaptation undergird and dominate climate risk and vulnerabilities assessments (Walz and Schleich 2009; Harris 2008). These may therefore, at best, be at odds with the social protections agenda or at worst ignore or project these as trade-offs with efficiency. But this would be a costly mistake for developing countries, most of which have millions of poor and vulnerable men and women living within their borders. Apart from monitoring adaptation and mitigation for transfer burden issues discussed above, in developing countries there is an imperative to undergird and strengthen social protection measures.

Many governments are acutely aware of the need to enhance social protection and productive measures such as employment guarantee programmes. But there may not be the recognition that these are sufficiently important for climate change management. In fact, in the face of climate change there is an even more urgent need for social protection programmes. There is the need for improved and well-funded safety nets to address climate change risks, and to increase risk preparedness and the recovery process.

10.1.1 IMF fiscal policy and budgetary impacts of adaptation and mitigation financing

As climate change intensifies, there may be increasing pressures on domestic budgets for financing adaptation and mitigation actions. Adaptation finance raises particular fiscal challenges, given its marginalization in the overall flow of climate finance. (Adaptation received less than 20 per cent of fast start finance, 2010–2012 and accounted for about 10–15 per cent of climate investment expenditures globally, since the convention has been in force.) Fiscal and financial management around adaptation within countries may require budget contingencies (both as *ex ante* and *ex post* finance) and the financing of reserve funds to deal with disaster risk management, loss and damage and the climate-proofing of infrastructures. Both the IMF and the World Bank have noted that '[F]iscal policy has a critical role to play in mitigating GHG emissions and raising revenues for climate finance, fiscal consolidation and other purposes' (IMF 2012). In the context of the 2015 Paris Agreement and the development of countries' (intended) nationally determined contributions to the global effort to address climate change, there will be greater demands for more ambitious mitigation and adaptation actions. Hence, there will be the need to finance measures such as feed-in-tariffs, investment subsidies for clean energy, tax credits and publicly supported R&D.

These climate-related fiscally generated resources will impact governments' budgetary and expenditure patterns. Attention, therefore, will need to be paid to the fiscal implications of financing adaptation and mitigation and their consequential impacts on gender-sensitive expenditures. There is certain to be some potential synergies and cross-fertilization with gender budget analysis. Climate public expenditure and institutional reviews (CPEIRs) tools may be useful connectors between the two spheres. CPEIRs add a public environmental expenditure review component, and wrestle with identifying and classifying climate-related expenditures in the national budgetary process. Gender-responsive budget analysis will have to confront the challenges of identifying gender-sensitive climate actions and pinpointing the gender dimensions (i.e. the transfer burden) of climate adaptation and mitigation expenditures.

For the most part, some developing countries' governments have focused quite appropriately on economic instruments such as energy or emission taxes, CO_2 emission trading and subsidies to stimulate or discourage the demand for different types of adaptation and mitigation activities. Fundamental economic principles such as efficiency, opportunity costs, marginal costs and marginal benefits, have tremendous weight in the formulation of climate change policy, and impact on financial and investment flows. These, in turn, impact on macro-level variables such as employment, government spending and taxation. They also induce sectoral adjustments to climate change. However, they do not automatically lead to ensuring social protection or promote the sustainability of economic development.

As governments adjust policy frameworks to support the economy or sectors to meet the explicit costs of climate change, economic variables and analyses will determine which industries or sectors will be encouraged to grow and which sectors will shrink (Walz and Schleich 2009). Therefore, attention must be refocused on the limitations of these variables and instruments in terms of their poverty, social and gender distributional consequential effects. Closer scrutiny from a gender analytical and gender justice perspective must be focused on the gendered constraints that will determine the adjustment responses and capacities of individuals, households and businesses to respond to climate change. These adjustment demands and responses will be incentivized by economic mechanisms and instruments in the context of climate policy.

These may be seen as providing a basis for retuning the economy in a sustainable direction that promotes investment in human and natural capital (Harris 2008). They may also provide the basis for a rapid reduction in carbon emissions while promoting investment in human and natural capital (Harris 2008). This is a perfect feedback loop.

10.2 The Paris 2015 Agreement, climate finance and gender justice

The Paris Agreement, currently under negotiation, to be adopted in December 2015 and implemented in 2020, will seek to accelerate ambition and actions on adaptation, mitigation, technology development and transfer, transparency of action and support and capacity building in ensuring the further implementation of the UNFCCC (as mandated by the Durban Platform, 2011). It will also have measures to enhance actions on many of these same elements in the pre-2020 period. There are also expectations that it will include issues of sustainable forest management and agriculture. Thus, the Paris Agreement will have serious implications for the pace, nature, scope and extent of sustainable development in developing countries.

While the Durban Platform mandate calls for all elements to be included in the new agreement, many developed countries have focused on mitigation as the most important or core element of the agreement. Developing countries generally reject this approach and call for parity across all the elements as part of the legal outcome of the agreement (whether in the form of a 'protocol, another legal instrument, or an agreed outcome with legal force'). The Africa Group, in particular, has called for a quantitative global goal on adaptation, in tandem with the current mitigation objective or 'goal' (of reducing GHG emissions and limiting warming to below 2° Celsius).

A global goal on climate change adaptation would consolidate all the different elements of adaptation under the UNFCCC (including NAPAs, NAPs, the Nairobi work programme on understanding impacts, vulnerability and adaptation to climate change, and the Cancun Adaptation Framework)—solidly grounded in the commitment to finance and technology development and transfer under article 4 of the Convention. So instead of continuing to be the stepchild of global climate protection policy, adaptation would take its rightful place as both a local, national, regional global phenomenon with the requisite rights and responsibility with regard to financing and technology development and transfer.

From the vantage point of gender equality and women's empowerment, in the context of climate change, the GGCA, which would help to operationalize and give priority to adaptation both at national and global levels is an important advancement in global climate policy that could provide a crucial lever in securing and promoting benefits for women as well as protect their lives and livelihoods. A global adaptation goal would help to increase awareness and actions to address the adaptation challenges that men and women face on the ground in Africa, Asia, Latin America and the Caribbean. Ultimately, such a goal could help to leverage greater flow of the financing of adaptation projects that would benefit women and men. But in order for such flows of finance to reach women in poor communities in developing countries, the post-2015 agreement itself must promote gender equality and women's empowerment. So gender must be the key issue in both the pre-2020 and the post-2020 component of the Paris Agreement. So far, the tentative half steps with regard to the integration of gender issues into the negotiated draft text does not yield much confidence in the penultimate outcome. On the road to Paris, gender has been raised in the Geneva negotiating text in the preamble, as part of the guiding principles, along with human rights and just transitions etc., and in the general objective section of the document. Gender issues have not yet substantially been incorporated into the 'hard' and operational paragraphs of the text.

Gender justice incorporated into the normative framework of the 2015 climate change policy would ensure that funding instruments and mechanisms are gender sensitive. Hence, gender justice within the context of the climate change policy framework would require institutional 'response and answerability' of the funding mechanisms set up to finance climate change, so that these funds and mechanisms promote equitable distribution of such funds so that they work in the interests of women (paraphrased from Goetz 2003 and 2007).

In the first instance, from the point of view of gender equality, women's empowerment and social development, it is critical that adaptation and development efforts are fully integrated and fully funded. The need to improve and climate-proof infrastructure, public health, and undertake disaster preparedness, though they are often seen as non-gendered equality interventions, is centrally important to women's social reproduction roles and care activities. Having access to good roads and bridges that allow mobility during floods or other extreme events is a matter of life and death to many women who are also responsible for children and the elderly. In addition, early warning systems, access to public outreach, climate and environment-related education at community and household levels saves lives and may prevent some illnesses.

But in addition to these necessary activities, attention needs to be paid to the nature and constraints on the behaviour and activities of women and men on the ground in developing countries as it relates to climate change strategies and the financing of those strategies around adaptation, capacity building, mitigation, and technology transfer and development.

The current climate change financing frameworks, instruments and mechanisms are not gender friendly. Rather, the climate change regime reflects features that have been identified with global finance – a combination of gender-blind, male-biased decision-making, which lead to systematic patterns of gender segmentation and gender asymmetries in the allocation of finance that disadvantages women, particularly poor women. Specifically, when it comes to the existing operations and functioning of climate change financing it is increasingly the case that:

- Women do not have easy or sufficient access to funds to cover weather-related losses or to service adaptation and mitigation technological requirements.
- Many activities normally undertaken by women to protect their livelihoods from climate change induced risk, such as crop rotation, substituting flood and drought-resistant crop varieties and shifting patterns and location of cultivation (Mitchel *et al.* 2007) are not recognized in the global carbon trade market or are overlooked by different groups of funds.
- Where some traditionally women-dominated activities are targeted as an area for speculative investment in the carbon trading market, they are often by-passed because the market tends to require larger economies of scale than traditionally found under management by women. Instead, the benefits generally accrue to large, well-capitalized operations.
- Given the complex instruments of the various climate change funds and their complicated applications processes, women's and community groups may have difficulties accessing and absorbing funds that are destined for large-scale, well-capitalized projects. Many times women-owned entities are unable to meet the upfront costs involved in participating in these processes.

The effect of the operations of some climate change financing instruments may be to further marginalize women and decrease their access to economic resources.

At the national level, this points to the importance of correcting historical issues around land distribution and land reform that leaves women and girls at a disadvantage. It also provides the rationale for 'set-asides' or affirmative action-based programmes in the area of climate change financing. In addition to financial flows, there is a responsibility to support technology development transfer and to facilitate capacity building in developing countries. This also extends to supportive programmes for women and girls around environmentally sustainable information and technology.

Both distributive and corrective justice principles are relevant and important for integrating a gender perspective into climate change financing. Once accepted as part of the climate change policy framework, they offer relatively safe springboards for promoting specific forms of affirmative action scenarios. These include setaside programmes for women, especially poor women, who have historical and continuing disadvantages in accessing and controlling the resources necessary for successfully adapting individuals, households and communities to climate change challenges. Thus, paradoxically, climate change, through the global responses grounded in ethics, human rights and fairness, may offer the opportunity to address past inequities and to improve the economic and social situation of women and other historically disenfranchised groups.

The funds, instruments and mechanisms of the current climate change financing environment originated in and are based on the issues and process identified within the normative and science-based frameworks that govern climate change policy. It is important that there is a process geared towards integrating gender analytical perspectives, tools and methods into both the analytical as well as the normative foundations of climate change policy. In the current conjuncture, both aspects of this endeavour should happen simultaneously with work undertaken to introduce gender equity concerns into the operational level of climate change funds and financing. Thus, there needs to be advocacy and an engendering process at the levels of climate science, policy and finance.

10.3 Engendering climate change science

A starting point towards engendering climate change science is to seek to input gender awareness and sensitization within the framework of a future IPCC Assessment Report as well as the work of the UNFCCC's Subsidiary Body for Scientific and Technological Advice (SBSTA), the Subsidiary Body for Implementation (SBI) and related groups such as the Modelling and Assessment of Contributions to Climate Change[4] (MATCH). Both the SBSTA and the SBI 'work together on cross-cutting issues including capacity building, the vulnerability of developing countries to climate change and adaptive response measures' (COWI and IIED 2009). In this context, there needs to be proactive attention needs to be paid to at least two areas – the knowledge base around climate change science, which itself has multiple dimensions spanning the physical and the social, and enhancing a gender perspective on climate change. The IPCC recognizes gender as a cross-cutting issue in climate change. Work remains to build on this recognition and to deepen its scope and depth in climate policy. This is certainly an area of cross-intersection that could conceivably be part of the unfolding work agenda of the two subsidiary bodies. In principle, a similar entity such as MATCH, based on the processes that led to the formation of this body could also play a significant role in bringing gender out of the margins and into the centre of climate change policy and financing.

First, there should be the encouragement of efforts geared at collecting and synthesizing the available scientific works that examines gender and science with a particular focus on unearthing and eliminating gender biases and gaps in the construction of knowledge and the methodologies of environmental, ecological and climate change. Such works and related references should be made available to the relevant IPCC working groups and committees, SBSTA and MATCH, and directed at the process of preparation for feedback and review of the next assessment report. For example, gender-specific gaps in the previous reports, such as the role of black carbon and traditional knowledge around adaptation and mitigation, should be reviewed and highlighted as appropriate.

Second, there should be a programme of capacity building of female scientists and encouragement of a gender-aware approach to the study of climate science. This should be complemented by the popular translation and transmission of the outputs of the IPCC to the women's movement.

10.4 Engendering the climate change policy framework

The key is to build on the gains already made in Cancún, Durban and The Lima Work Programme on Gender and Climate Change to enhance advocacy on two levels: gender mainstreaming at the institutional level and integrating gender perspectives in discussions, negotiations and policy documents. Gender should be comprehensively mainstreamed into the UNFCCC Secretariat and institutional framework, including all subsidiary bodies and technical areas. This must be complemented by the incorporation of gender analytical tools in the social and environmental assessment and climate risk portfolios of all relevant agencies. Gender policy and gender mainstreaming must also permeate climate change institutions at national and local levels, including closer coordination with national women's bureau and ministries of women's affairs.

Ongoing gender sensitization among civil society organizations working on climate and environmental issues is an important imperative for successful advocacy, monitoring and accountability at the global, regional, national and local levels. In addition, there needs to be gender sensitization in the business and philanthropic communities involved with climate change and related activities.

In terms of policy content, comprehensive reviews of analyses and research on gender and climate change suggested topic areas that are critical points for focused attention, and educational and informational projects include the identification of women-specific climate change vulnerabilities, particular attention to programmatic areas such as land-use and forestry as well as sectoral issues such as agriculture, water

BOX 10.1 FURTHER IDENTIFICATION OF WOMEN-SPECIFIC CLIMATE CHANGE VULNERABILITIES

1. Cross-regional comparisons in terms of six specific areas: nutrient capacity and women's health; women's domestic burden and increased hardships; women's reduced ability to provide self-protection; religious and social dogma concerns; lack of education; and unequal power relations.

2. Gender audits of vulnerability and assessment methodologies.

3. Programmes and projects to decrease women's and girls' vulnerability to climate change effects.

4. Gender, land-use and forestry (deforestation, afforestation and reforestation): This should be contextualized with awareness of traditional knowledge and women's challenges and constraints concerning intellectual property rights with regard to land-use and forestry management know-how.

5. Gender climate change and sectoral issues: agriculture (food security, adaptation and traditional knowledge/intellectual property); water, health, sanitation and livelihood; clean energy, energy efficiency and renewable energy – all with an awareness of the issues of traditional knowledge and women's challenges and constraints around women and intellectual property rights. Some critical areas that needed to be further developed include:
   (a) gender and climate-induced human displacement, migration and conflict;
   (b) gender, climate change and the household and informal economies;
   (c) gender and climate change economics;
   (d) gender, climate change and trade;
   (e) gender climate change and domestic investments and FDI;
   (f) gender and proposals for post-2015 negotiations.

and health. An initial attempt at further decomposition of these three broad areas is outlined above in Box 10.1.

10.5 Engendering climate change finance and architecture

Engendering climate change finance must be leveraged around at least three broad areas: (1) articulating overarching principles for a gender-sensitive climate change financing architecture; (2) synthesizing elements common to all aspects of the financing environment, including requirements for gender sensitization of financing adaptation, mitigation and technology; and (3) securing leverage points around market and non-market financial mechanisms.

Attempting to make the financial architecture itself accountable for and responsive to gender equality and women's empowerment outcomes will also require a three-pronged approach.

First, engendering climate change financing should be leveraged around a set of overarching principles that link gender sensitization to the existing normative framework of the UNFCCC. At the same time, these principles should maintain a focus on promoting women's empowerment in the context of the overriding concerns and priorities for sustainable economic and social development. The set of principles under-girding the climate change policy environment are appropriate grounding for gender sensitization of financial instruments, mechanisms and processes. However, they have not been sufficient to ensure gender equality outcomes of the funding mechanisms. Therefore, two broad groupings of principles should be considered.

The first set of principles are those emanating from the articles of the Convention and which have been reaffirmed and further expanded by subsequent COP Decisions, most recently in the context of the Bali Plan of Action. They are, as discussed above, adequate, additional, appropriate, equitable and predictable.

Adequacy refers to the concern that the financing of climate change adaptation and mitigation should adequately compensate developing countries. Thus, financing should not be in the form of loans or other debt-creating instruments. The principle of additionality refers to the situation that financing for climate change initiatives should be new funds. Hence, these funds should not be counted as part of official development assistance flows. Appropriateness can be related to the polluter pays principle. Equitable is based on 'common but differentiated responsibility and respective capacity', while predictability requires that the flow of funds should be long-term and guaranteed.

This set of principles is relevant to gender equality because they have implications for the state of public financing and budgeting in developing countries. At stake in meeting the climate challenges – absent significant new and relatively unrestrained flow of funds – are dramatic shortfalls in expenditures on, and neglect of, economic and social development projects and programmes.[5] To the extent that governments incur debts, or incur shortfalls in revenue as they attempt to meet climate change requirements, there are likely to be trade-offs between different sectors of domestic budgets. Cuts are most often made in the social sector budget, which impacts on spending on essential public services such as health-care, education and water. 'Appropriateness' and 'equity' in financing at the global level are important for locating and legitimizing gendered claims on the flow of financial and investment resources that are available for climate change. Predictability ensures that governments have long-term access to financing and can have consistency across climate programmes, including gender equality interventions.

The second set of principles is distributive and corrective justice, the right to development, climate justice and gender justice. They relate more directly to the development, gender and social dimensions of climate change. When combined with the principles under-girding the UNFCCC normative framework, these provide a comprehensive set of principles that are both necessary and sufficient to generate gender equality outcomes in climate financing.

Equity in the allocation of global atmospheric resources should be grounded in distributive and corrective justice. Distributive and corrective justice focuses actions on the historical responsibility of developed countries for past emissions that still exist in the atmosphere. Further, developed countries such as the US and Japan are still emitting large amounts of GHGs on a per capita basis. Financing must be sufficient to enable developing countries to engage in adaptation and mitigation efforts. In addition to financial flows, there is a responsibility to support technology transfer and to facilitate capacity building in developing countries.

Both distributive and corrective justice principles are relevant and important for integrating a gender perspective into climate change financing. Once accepted as part of the climate change policy framework, they offer sufficient and compelling rationale for promoting specific forms of affirmative action scenarios. These include set-aside programmes for women, especially poor women who have historical and continuing disadvantages in accessing and controlling the resources necessary for successfully adapting individuals, households and communities to climate change challenges.

The second prong critical for creating a gender-aware and gender-sensitive climate change financing architecture is the integration of gender analysis and gender-sensitive tools into the operational elements of climate change funds. This must cut across all areas and types of funding sources and delivery channels. The incorporation of gender analytical tools of assessment, design, monitoring and evaluation could form the basis of guidelines for the allocation and distribution of funds for communities and women's groups.

In this context, there must be an explicit focus on ensuring the application of a less than burdensome criteria for accessing all funds. Thus, the application, registration, approval, implementation, evaluation and monitoring of all funds should be based on simplified, expedited processes, and upfront costs should be as small as possible. This will afford small projects – especially those operated by women – a better opportunity to access funds. In order to increase national governments' support, there must be a commitment to utilize positive incentives rather than the burdensome and overly-intrusive economic or other forms of policy conditionalities. Governments may then feel less constrained to utilize national revenue to leverage a larger number of women and other small community projects.

Another element that may prove beneficial to women and men, especially those in highly vulnerable areas, is a better balance between adaptation and mitigation in prioritizing funding. In the case of developing countries, especially the least developing countries and small island developing states, there may even have to be a tilt towards more funding for adaptation, even as there are deeper commitments for mitigation at global levels.

Government, through its regulatory and budgetary processes, may be able to provide direct resources to areas where the market would be unable to maximize profit. Government could also utilize a part of the revenue intake from rents imposed on market-based climate change financing activities to promote and ensure the resiliency of the household economy. This could be achieved by utilizing such revenues to subsidize or otherwise support the climate-proofing of community infrastructure such as climate-proofing water catchments and storage.

Governmental financing mechanisms that could help to facilitate greater access to financial resources for women could include performance mechanisms (performance assessment frameworks; results-based management of funding initiatives from a gender perspective). It should be very clear from the outset that this is not lodged in the context of a conditionality framework. Emphasis should instead be placed on positive incentives for funds that finance projects and programmes that enhance gender equality and the empowerment of indigenous peoples.

Engendering climate change financing must also leverage requirements for the gender sensitization of development-friendly adaptation, mitigation and technology development and transfer.

10.5.1 Adaptation funding

A first step in the gender sensitization of adaptation funding may be to ensure effective and balanced participation of women in decision-making. Second, it is also critically important to ensure easy access to funds for care activities that promote sustainability in the household sectors. Even where women have a high attachment to the labour market, they, nonetheless, bear primary responsibility for the care and nurturing of children and the elderly.

In rural areas, women also continue to be primarily responsible for food production, farming and in some areas, informal forestry management. Therefore, financing for adaptation should also focus on:

- Supporting sustainable agriculture and sustainable community development.
- Supporting the planting of crops under trees and a diversified approach to tree planting (as opposed to monoculture tree planting).
- Funding a variety of activities, in particular small-scale and household economy-oriented projects including evaluation of appropriateness of finance instrument and delivery channels that seek to make homes and communities climate resilient.

Third, there should be a process for undertaking assessments of the impact of financed adaptation projects including evaluation of appropriateness of finance instrument and delivery channels on women's empowerment.

10.5.2 Mitigation funding

Approved projects should seek to increase the synergies between mitigation, poverty eradication and women's empowerment. This would require that mitigation projects seek to have high employment effects and that monitoring and assessment for distributional/equity effects are in place. From this background, mitigation projects and programmes should seek to:

- Promote gender equity in supply chains of the clean and renewable energy subsectors as well as integrate them into community programmes.
- Enhance household energy services (such as lighting and cooking).
- Promote the spread and diffusion of technology and small appliances for heating water and appliances such as grinders for small-scale agro- and food processing.
- Promote de-centralized and alternative community-developed energy sources such as modern bio energy (i.e. jatropha oil and oil sourced from non-edible seeds). This form of energy does not have an adverse impact on food security as is the case with biofuels from corn and edible grains.
- Promote renewable energy that enhances rural development.
- Promote the switching/transition from traditional biomass fuels (wood, charcoal and animal dung) to biofuels such as biodiesel (made from the processing of plants) and bio-ethanol from sources that do not impact on food security.
- Promote gender-sensitive village-level projects with high per capita impact (employment and livelihood) over large plantations that are based on an agro-business model. While the former type of project maximizes the result for everyone, the latter tend to lead to optimization for only one or a few.
- Ensure that mitigation projects do not negatively impact, but rather protect land rights, water rights, human rights and the labour rights of indigenous peoples and women.

10.5.3 Technology funding

Technology transfer and cooperation are also linked to financing. It is important to focus such support on technologies that are gender, social and development friendly, and that protect the web of life and promote ecological security. This includes paying particular attention to protecting traditional knowledge and seeking to improve and enhance its effectiveness through gender-sensitive approaches to traditional knowledge and gender-aware benefit sharing agreements. For example, rainwater harvesting, recharging of ground water and facilitating sustainable agriculture and development are critical to women's involvement in food production and food self-sufficiency. However, these areas tend to be time-consuming and impose a heavy care burden on women and girls. Technological support would be beneficial in reducing women's time burden as well as increase their productivity.

The final prong in the engendering of climate change financing is a focus on gender sensitizing market and non-market mechanisms. Here there are four main propositions to be advanced.

First, high-impact gender equality benefits are to be gained from the utilization of a mixed system of tightly regulated market and non-market mechanisms to reduce carbon emissions.

Both carbon markets and carbon taxes can play a role in facilitating the mitigation of climate change in different degrees. Carbon taxes should be explored for their poverty reduction and gender equality impacts. In addition, the auctioning of emission rights, if handled correctly and as a complementary mechanism, could potentially help to finance a wide range of targeted and non-targeted climate-friendly gender interventions.

It is, however, now being documented that 'purely commercial voluntary offset projects have negative impacts on women and indigenous communities' (GFC 2007). The Global Forest Coalition also points out that one of the most insidious threats to forests comes from the clearing of forest and its replacement with industrial tree plantations. In this process, indigenous peoples are displaced from their lands.

Second, investment should be channelled into rural infrastructural development projects such as electrification, sustainable water distribution, and health and sanitation systems.

These are critical for poverty eradication, social and human reproduction, safeguarding maternal health, dealing with HIV/AIDs, and decreasing the morbidity and mortality of women. Water is also crucial for sustainable development that helps to secure environmental protection and food security. According to the UN Task Force on water, water is a 'catalytic entry point for developing countries in the fight against poverty and for safeguarding human health, reducing child mortality and promoting gender equality and protection of natural resources' (UN Millennium Task Force on Water and Sanitation 2005).

Third, investment and financial support should be ensured for projects that increase women's access to resources and that enables women to scale up their entrepreneurial activities.

Help to support the growth and development of women's entrepreneurship is critical. This would include the provision of local and household infrastructure such as clean energy stoves, water pumps and generators powered by bioenergy sources. It will also be important to focus on areas such as childcare infrastructure and information communication technologies.

Fourth, government subsidies and other fiscal measures should continue to be useful sources of funds for small-scale, women-run projects.

Most of the successful small-scale pilot projects in the voluntary offset arena have been sustained by access to public funds via the World Bank or bilateral donors. Private funding has not been drawn to such projects. It is therefore important that the existing financial mechanisms of UNFCCC are reoriented to handle micro, small, and medium-scaled and pooled projects with moderate economies of scale.

The high transaction costs around CDM's process of developing a project design development, meeting the expenses of a Designate Operating Entities and other registration requirements for a CDM project is neither feasible nor cost-effective for most small-scale, women-operated projects. CDM's cumbersome and time-consuming process is not gender or development friendly and needs to be radically reformed.

These challenges point to the need for more well-funded, gender-sensitive mechanisms under the authority of and accountable to the COP of the UNFCCC. Within the existing context of proposals for new funding and the trend of proliferation of special and specific funds by bilateral donors under the ambit of the World Bank, there are both opportunities and challenges. Challenges lie in terms of the nature of these funds and to what degree they impose economic or policy conditionality or imposed significant co-financing requirements. But there may also exist the opportunity for the development of a gender-sensitive multilateral financing mechanism under UNFCCC, quite possibly a window or subwindow under the GCF in a similar manner to the integration of the private sector facility which exists under the GCF. Such a mechanism, since it would focus on meeting the priority needs and concerns of women, could likely promote greater funds towards women's empowerment in the area of adaptation, mitigation and technology. It is also important that thorough social and gender assessments of the likely impacts, and of emerging and new funding mechanisms, especially those focused on global and national taxation measures. In the case of taxation measures, it is important that mechanisms to funnel proceeds from such measures target gender equality interventions.

In the case of insurance, risk management models are not inherently gender neutral and will be implemented in a financial system riddled with gender biases, gender distortions and asymmetries. There is need for gender analysis of such approaches with appropriate safeguards built into climate and related insurance instruments and programmes.

10.6 The Gender Empowerment and Climate Finance Risk Assessment Framework

The Gender Empowerment and Climate Finance Risk Assessment Framework (GEM-CRA) present in Section 3.7 of Chapter 3, pinpoints the kinds of strategic interventions that are needed and can be undertaken with respect to climate change financing. These interventions will need to be undertaken in at least three broad areas: (a) capital market interventions; (b) carbon market interventions; and (c) public-private partnership interventions.

10.6.1 Interventions in the capital market

The private sector is expected to increase investments in the areas of adaptation and mitigation; it will drive innovation in clean energy and other climate-related technologies. Mechanisms and processes need to be developed in order to ensure that gender priorities and concerns are integrated into policies and programmes undertaken in this area. Governments can foster this effort by incorporating a gender-impact assessment approach and gender-response budgetary analysis to subsidies, tax policies, public financing and technical assistance programmes. These efforts could be supported by enforcing gender equality measures in tender and bidding processes in government procurement processes and mechanisms. Gender-sensitive employment, and health and safety regulations in many countries provide appropriate blueprints for the kinds of engendering process that should underlies financial sector regulations.

There is a broad range of financing instruments available for managing climate risk. These include insurance, commodity and weather derivatives, carbon offsets and catastrophe bonds. There is also an emerging set of products that have been redesigned to facilitate adaptive activities and to help modulate risks. These include: risk modelling, alternative risk transfers, reinsurance and micro-finance cross-selling of climate insurance products. In addition, existing and traditional sources of savings and remittances can be uploaded and leveraged to enable increased financing for women and men.

Women farmers and entrepreneurs should have access to these instruments to protect against loss from climate change events. This may require governments or donors to establish pools of funds to subsidize insurance premiums. Small groups of entities could also be pooled in different types of cooperative or collaborative arrangements with start-up funding from larger entities. At a minimum, intense education and outreach programmes are needed to educate and present information on the activities' scope. These activities can be complemented by the implementation of gender impact assessments in order to determine the extent to which different actors are involved in the utilization of the different instruments.

As with the carbon market,[6] grouping together groups of smallholders and households with different income asset thresholds for the purpose of index-based weather-related insurance or other climate risk transfer mechanisms (aggregation) seems to be a trend for facilitating the reduction of climate-related vulnerability and adaptation risks. As noted above, though still in an emergent stage, index-based insurance has pitfalls that may, if left unattended, work against the interest of women as a whole. Given the overwhelming evidence of women's greater losses from climate shocks, it is important to understand and pinpoint whether mechanisms such as insurance and quasi-insurance policies and related products will be beneficial to women. It is also important that these instruments are seen as part of a holistic strategy for dealing with climate risk and shock (Barnett *et al.* 2007). They therefore must evolve within a network of gender-friendly complementary approaches, including technology improvement, livelihood diversification, climate information system and integrating marketing with regard to infrastructure (including communications), storage, transportation and trade policy[7] (Barnett *et al.* 2007).

10.6.2 Interventions in the carbon market

Gender-sensitive interventions can be accomplished in the carbon market in a number of ways. First, through the development of gender-sensitive community benefit-sharing arrangements that take women's and men's gender-differentiated needs, priorities and contributions into account, and that ensure that offset projects are accountable for maintaining and promoting women's interests. Second, through the facilitation of the involvement of women's groups, women farmers and women business owners in establishing carbon offset projects, which could be accomplished, for example, through global, regional and nationally sourced carbon funds that can promote early-stage project development. Such funds can be leveraged by development financial institutions (such as national development banks) that help to pool money to create the fund, act as fund managers, and provide carbon delivery guarantees for women's projects. Any of the items listed here can be undertaken in isolation by carbon finance public financial mechanisms at the national, regional or multilateral level.

10.6.3 Interventions in the area of public finance

The goals of public financing of climate change adaptation and mitigation are to decrease climate risk and better enable countries and the global community to undertake necessary measures in order to secure the health, livelihood and productive capacity of women and men in their economy. Hence, it is important for gender advocates to develop and implement proactive strategies, plans, programmes and projects that are focused on ensuring women's economic empowerment, even as society becomes better able to withstand the rigours of climate change events.

Women are more vulnerable than men because of historical and current gender biases, gaps and discrimination, and the impact of those on access to employment, income, savings, credit, investment and housing. Therefore, there is a need to ensure that adaptation and mitigation funding reaches women in rural, peri-urban and urban communities. Furthermore, programmes and projects should be geared to meet the practical and strategic long-term needs, priorities and concerns of women as individuals, heads and members of households, community care-givers, employees and business owners.

When it comes to climate change financing, women require access to grants and credit to decrease vulnerability; skills to participate in the retrofitting of protective measures and in infrastructure building projects; and micro-finance initiatives that are up-scaled to enable greater investment and credit flows.

All projects (especially water management, disaster risk planning, agriculture and industry upgrade, forest and land-use management, and those that promote renewable and efficient energy) should be designed to meet the needs of men and women in the communities. As much as possible, the resulting activities should draw on women's knowledge and skills, encourage and promote the active and effective participation of women in decision-making, and incorporate gender priorities in social and environmental risk assessment and management.

The GEF and the Green Climate Finance (GCF, whose business model was near completion and is expected to be operational in 2015), both financing entities of the UNFCCC – a UN entity – are obligated to implement and align policies and practices with generally agreed UN conventions and treaty practices, including the Convention on the Elimination of Discrimination against Women. They should also be expected to play, within its scope of operation, a key role in the gender mainstreaming process committed to by the United Nations. Therefore, all policies and programmes should be made gender sensitive. The GEF Board has now adopted a gender policy statement. There should be further lobbying to gender mainstream gender equality goals, objectives, policies and practices across all operational areas of the GEF, and into all its funding mechanisms and instruments.

The GCF is getting off to a better start than the GEF with a mandate for fund wide gender sensitization as part of its core foundation. In the first case, during its design phase, 2011, the Transitional Committee mandated to design the GCF was the focus of a great deal of strategic lobbying by gender advocates and women's groups. As a result, the final operational instruments approved by the COP 17 contains a number of references to gender and women as well as some inclusion of gender priorities and concerns (see Box 10.2). The GCF Board has now adopted a gender policy and gender action plan as part of its business model. Appendix 10.1 presents a brief overview of the key elements under discussion.

Second, the COP also agreed to gender language with regard to the Standing Committee which will oversee the financing and related operations under the Convention (Box 10.2).

Both the GEF and the GCF should be encouraged to implement mechanisms such as a Women's and Girls' Climate Change Empowerment Fund or operational windows with cross linkages to both adaptation and mitigation thematic funding areas. A similar set of actions should be undertaken at the regional level, geared most directly at regional development banks, and regional and national development banks climate change portfolios.

It is also important to ensure that the various emerging catastrophic risk fund initiatives, such as the Pacific catastrophe risk Pool Insurance, as well as the proposed Caribbean variant led by the World Bank, integrate gender components.

Gender advocates and women's groups should also actively engage with regional forums on climate change, such as the Asia Clean Energy Forum, which is convened for and by key decision-makers in the region.

Ultimately, the nature and scope of economic and social empowerment processes must be deepened in order to better meet the new climate risks. There is a great deal of work to be undertaken in first understanding, and then mapping the growing networks of private and public-sector climate change-related financing instruments, mechanisms, funds, facilities, programmes and projects. The end point of such actions would be to develop a proactive agenda geared towards eliminating barriers to entry for women.

Integrating a gender empowerment approach to climate risk assessment (GEMCRA) could be a valuable tool for helping to identify, allocate and mitigate the risks that women face with regard to climate change and to account for gender distortions in the pattern of climate change financing. The GEMCRA approach, as it evolves, could provide a systematic method for identifying and analysing gender-differentiated climate risks. There is also scope for linking with the gendered capability approach or other approaches in order to pinpoint interactions among various groups of risks that reinforce each other in adverse ways for women's empowerment.

BOX 10.2 GENDER EQUITY LANGUAGE IN FINANCE AND FINANCE-RELATED AREAS OF THE DURBAN OUTCOME

Annex VI Composition and working modalities of the Standing Committee

Para 2. The Standing Committee shall be composed of members nominated by Parties for approval by the COP, who shall have the necessary experience and skills, notably in the areas of climate change, development and finance, taking into account the need to achieve gender balance in accordance with Decision 36/CP.7.

Green Climate Fund – report of the Transitional Committee Draft Decision [–/CP.17]

I. Objectives and guiding principles

Para 3. [. . .] The Fund will strive to maximize the impact of its funding for adaptation and mitigation, and seek a balance between the two, while promoting environmental, social, economic and development co-benefits and taking a gender-sensitive approach.

II. Governance and Institutional Arrangements

C. Rules of procedure of the Board

Para 2. Selection of Board members

11. The members of the Board and their alternates will be selected by their respective constituency or regional group within a constituency. Members of the Board will have the necessary experience and skills, notably in the areas of climate change and development finance, with due consideration given to gender balance.

E. Secretariat

1. Establishment of the secretariat

Para 21. The secretariat will be staffed with professional staff with relevant experience. The staff selection will be managed by the Executive Director and will be open, transparent and based on merit, taking into account geographical and gender balance.

V. Operational modalities

Para 31. The Fund will provide simplified and improved access to funding, including direct access, basing its activities on a country-driven approach and will encourage the involvement of relevant stakeholders, including vulnerable groups and addressing gender aspects.

XIII. Stakeholder input and participation

Para 71. The Board will develop mechanisms to promote the input and participation of stakeholders, including private-sector actors, civil society organizations, vulnerable groups, women and indigenous peoples, in the design, development and implementation of the strategies and activities to be financed by the Fund.

A collaborative effort between the broadest possible coalitions of like-minded groups of civil society organisations would be an excellent platform from which to launch a campaign or advocate for gender or women-specific empowerment funds, either cloistered within a set of likely friendly funds (for example, the Adaptation Fund and/or the GCF). This is a matter that could be pursued within the context of the Ad Hoc Working Group on the Durban Platform as an element for finance components of the 2015 Paris Agreement.

Notes

* UN Report: *Women's Profound Role in Averting Climate Crisis* (see www.ens-newswire.com/ens/nov2009/2009-11-18-01.asp).
1. After the widely acknowledged failure of the Copenhagen meeting, where failure to reach a decisive consensus lead to only the Copenhagen Accord, not traditional COP Decision, the heads of state of the major economies, who do not want to be associated with failure, have tended to stay away from annual climate meeting, unless they are the host country.
2. Military spending: 81 per cent of this is concentrated in 15 countries (US 39 per cent, China 9.5 per cent, Russia 5.2 per cent, UK 3.5 per cent and Japan 3.4 per cent) (*Stockholm International Peace Research Institute Yearbook 2013*). The current monetary value of fossil fuels investment as reported by Bloomberg New Energy Finance 2014.
3. Parry et al. (2007) (WG II 7.1, 7.2, 7.4, 17.3).
4. Modelling and Assessment of Contributions to Climate Change (MATCH) is the final evolution of a series of expert group meetings convened by the governments of Brazil, Germany, Ireland and the UK to examine a prior proposal made by Brazil that sought to establish historically based specific emissions reductions target for parties. The scientific and methodological aspects of the proposal were referred to the Subsidiary Body for Scientific and Technological Advice (SBSTA) for further consideration. The SBSTA affirmed the framework and mandated MATCH (SBSTA17, 2002) to examine a proposal made by Brazil (1997) to set differentiated emissions reduction targets for parties according to the impact of their historic emissions on temperature rise. This affirmed MATCH's role and mandated the group to work to 'the aim to improve the robustness of the preliminary results and to contributions of greenhouse gases to climate change and to explore the uncertainty and sensitivity of the results to different assumptions' (MATCH). MATCH seeks to provide clear guidance on the implications of the use of the different scientific methods, models, and methodological choices (FCCC/SBSTA/2002/13, para 28). The submission was made in May 1997; it can be reviewed in FCCC/AGBM/1997/MISC.1/Add.3. Two expert groups were convened between 2001 and 2002 (FCCC/SBSTA/2001/INF.2; FCCC/SBSTA/2002/INF.14; FCCC/SBSTA/2002/L.24). Under the sponsorship of the governments of the UK, Brazil Northern Ireland and Germany (2003), a third expert group resulted in the formation of MATCH. Source: www.match-info.net/.
5. The Economic Commission for Latin America and the Caribbean recently projected that pending 'no international agreement . . . to mitigate the effects of climate change, the cost for Latin America and the Caribbean could be equivalent to 137 per cent of the region's current GDP by 2100' (*Economics of Climate Change in Latin America and the Caribbean*, ECLAC 2009).
6. See, for example, the activities that are undertaken by aggregators of carbon credits on the Chicago Climate Exchange (CCX). Examples of aggregators with insurance framework include Agrosamex (market wealth index insurance to state governments in Mexico and is linked to the natural disaster social fund (Fonden) and Basix India, which intermediates between Indian rural clients and global insurance companies.
7. Specifically, trade regulation and development that seeks to 'transfer risk price through trading across space and time to dissipated supply dispersion due to climate shocks' (Barrett et al. 2007).

11
SUMMARY AND RECOMMENDATIONS

> We know what to do: why don't we do it? The question is, how are we to ensure something is done?
>
> Wangari Maathai*

A robust, fair and equitable international financial system for climate change is of the utmost imperative. The finance that flows through this system must be available by direct access to countries and must be of significant scale to overcome the existing climate finance gap as well as to meet medium-term (up to 2030) and long-term financing needs beyond 2050. Climate finance must also be managed both at the global, regional and national levels to ensure and promote gender equality and the empowerment of women as key actors both in climate protection and sustainable development efforts. It thus must also contribute towards and enhance gender equality, poverty eradication and promote women's empowerment. This is a key element of solving the climate challenge through adaptation and mitigation actions. Given the impact of climate change and climate variability on developing countries, climate change is now an essential factor linking poor and rural women's empowerment in developing countries.

Women's empowerment cannot successfully and sustainably occur without proactive attention to resolving the challenges of climate change. There is substantial intertwining between gender equality, women's empowerment and climate change. Successfully adapting to and mitigating climate change is critically interlinked with the nature and constraints of gender equality in the economy. Where this intertwining reinforces the positive trend towards women's empowerment, climate change financing should provide more resources and open up the process for greater engagement and benefit flow to projects that are gender sensitive. Where this intertwining exacerbates processes that work to the disadvantage of women (such as loss of access and control over land and forest resources), the direction of climate change financing should be altered. This can only occur if climate change finance instruments, mechanisms and processes are made gender sensitive and conducive to the achievement of gender equality and women's empowerment goals.

There is therefore an imperative to create mechanisms and strategies that enhance or moderate the linkages between gender equality and the strategic financing of climate change.

Meeting women's and men's practical and strategic gender needs in developing countries, most especially the least developed countries, should be a significant pathway in the advancement towards achieving effective adaptation to and the mitigation of the critical factors exacerbating climate change. This calls for integrating gender analysis and gender analytical tools into both climate change policy and climate change financing. Reference points for integrating gender into public policy and finance already exist in the form of the gender analytical framework of the poverty reduction strategy paper, the MDGs, gender budgeting exercises, and the gender and governance work of agencies such as UNDP. In addition, the World Bank and a number of regional banks have developed or are undertaking gender mainstreaming initiatives. Drawing on these existing frameworks, enhancing their strong points and building in the processes and mechanisms to mitigate weaknesses based on an elaborated GEMCRA framework can provide significant leverage points for gender sensitizing the current climate change financing architecture.

11.1 Recommendations

The gender and climate change community could offer their own set of complementary finance mechanisms developed through a structured process of consultations (possibly via e-conferencing/webinar or online discussion) and a programmatic agenda based around the following seven elements:

1   Demystifying the concepts and instruments of climate change finance and enhancing the value-added of a gender-sensitive and women empowerment-friendly approach. This can occur through a broad educational process focusing on women's groups, climate change and environment groups, gender machinery, policy makers and at all levels of the institutions in charge of implementing climate change finance initiatives. In this context, gender advocates can build on: (i) the Lima 2014 COP Declaration on Education and Awareness-raising wherein governments, at ministerial and heads-of-state levels, encouraged development of 'education strategies that incorporated the issue of climate change in the curricula and to include awareness-raising on climate change in the design of national development and climate strategies and policies'; (ii) the UNFCC two-year (2015-2016) Lima Work Programme on Gender, which will promote gender balance and achieve gender-responsive climate policy, and (iii) promote the gender dimensions of the social and economic consequences of response measures (implemented to address climate change).

2   A comprehensive global and regional assessment and monitoring project that assess the flows and distribution of climate finance through the various instruments and modalities, multilateral and bilateral, for their impacts on poor women and men in communities in developing countries. This could begin, for example, with a gender-based assessment of the fast-start finance and other climate finance flows. Such analyses could be useful for the work of the Board of the GCF, the Standing Committee on Finance, as well as with the emerging growth of national climate funds.

3   Information and training on techniques and operations to scale-up knowledge and practices with regard to proposals around projects and programmes for gendered climate change financing, both in the public and private sectors.

4   Dealing with the underlying, persistent and pervasive structural issues that are maintaining and exacerbating gender inequalities, asymmetries and biases. This requires a coherent approach that consciously grounds advocacy in the broader framework of sustainable economic development, poverty eradication and rural and agriculture reform. Such an approach should necessarily focus on food sovereignty, livelihood and capabilities measures to reinforce micro-meso-macro linkages. These are issues the gender dimensions of which should feature prominently in the technical papers and the ongoing Technical Expert Meetings (TEMs) of the UNFCCC. Gender should be a cross-cutting element in these discussions, which in 2014 focused on a broad range of issues such as land-use change, forestry and urban environments, but did not significantly consider gender dimensions so important to these themes.

5   Programmes that catalyse and leverage women's and community-based organizations to implement, put to tender and manage climate change initiatives locally, nationally, regionally and globally. This will require carefully designed and well-calibrated programmes to build collaborative mechanisms among women's organizations to bid for and win contracts for managing small to medium- to large-scale climate change initiatives. This will require training on the myriad details of public and private climate change funds as well as lobbying and advocacy of both the private and public sectors for the expansion of financing and credit to women.

6   Proactive actions by gender advocates to secure, at national and global levels, new and increased funding, with special earmarks for women's empowerment and gender equality interventions in the climate change area. This could, for example, be part of the Adaptation Fund, engineered as an embedded thematic funding window of the Green Climate Fund. The flexibility of the AF allows for innovation and creativity, or a separate and autonomous fund modelled on the Small Grants Programme, or a special window within the GCF, linked to existing thematic areas of adaptation and mitigation and the private sector facility, but which could receive specific channelled pledges for women's empowerment.

7   A participatory research agenda focused on generating evidence on the impact of climate change financing mechanisms on women's status. (This could be

complementary to the global development rights framework and assorted gender and social impact assessment frameworks.) Within this context, there could be the development of gender audits of financing projects, gender impact assessments and a process towards the development of gender-sensitive climate change financing indicators. The approach should focus on both *ex ante* mechanisms (around areas identified in proposals, NAPAs and NCs) and *ex post* performance mechanisms (performance assessment frameworks; results-based management of funding initiatives from a gender perspective). NAMAs can be gender sensitized to promote readiness and capacity building for community-based and specific focused gender and women's empowerment projects and programmes geared to promote the climate resilience of household infrastructure, the provision of clean energy and sustainable livelihoods. It should be very clear from the outset that this is not lodged in the context of a conditionalities framework. Emphasis should instead be placed on positive incentives for funds that finance projects and programmes that enhance gender equality and the empowerment of indigenous peoples. There should also be careful attention given to elaborating the specificities of gender-responsive climate actions.

Equitable access to critical financial mechanisms is necessary for women's empowerment and for sustainable climate change actions in the long term. Otherwise, climate change remediable and strategic actions will not be sustainable. Therefore, climate change financing, inasmuch as it seeks to promote global benefits, must also seek to ensure benefits to women and men in the formal, informal and household sectors of the economy. It is also important for climate change finance to focus on transforming and upgrading the livelihoods of women and men on the ground in order to engender the necessary behavioural, institutional and policy changes that are essential to secure climate change objectives.

Note

* 'We know what to do: why don't we do it?' Vidal, J. Saturday, 30 May 2009. *Guardian*. www.theguardian.com/environment/2009/may/30/africa-women-climate-change-wangari-maathai

APPENDIX 1

1.1A Markers along the way towards global environmental and climate protection governance and policy

1948   International Union for the Protection of Nature (IUPN) now the International Union for the Conservation of Nature (IUCN)
1961   World Wildlife Federation (initially created to raise money for IUCN but then went independent).
1962   *Silent Spring*, Rachel Carson – Environmental catastrophe
1970   US Environmental Protection Agency established
1971   Friends of the Earth (NGO)
1971   Greenpeace (NGO)
1972   *Limits of Growth*. Club of Rome – non renewable resources
1972   First World Conference on Environment – UN Conference on the Human Environment, Stockholm: management of the biosphere; 26 principles on environment and development; and led to the creation of United Nations Environmental Programme (UNEP)
1979   World Climate Conference
1985   Advisory Group on Greenhouse Gases – identify key policy issues
1983–1987   World Commission on Environment and Development (Brundtland Commission): sustainable development. *Our Common Future*, report. Formal definition of sustainability and sustainable development.
1988   Conference on the Changing Atmosphere
         Establishment of the Inter-governmental Panel on Climate change (IPCC) by UNEP and WMO
         Developed countries should reduce CO_2 emissions by 20 per cent in 2005 with respect to 1988 levels
1989   The Atmospheric Pollution and Climate Change Ministerial Conference, Noordwijk Declaration on Climate Change, Noordwikj, Netherlands

(meeting of heads of states mooted that developed countries should stabilize CO_2 emissions by 2000 with respect to 1990 levels, and provide assistance to developing countries)

1989   Male Declaration – recognized serious impacts especially for small island countries

1990   Second World Climate Conference – it is possible for developed countries to stabilize CO_2 emissions from the energy sector and reduce these by at least 20 per cent by 2005. Developing countries should use modern technologies.

Establishment of a single inter-governmental negotiation process under the auspices of the General Assembly, supported by UNEP and WMO, for the preparation by an Intergovernmental Negotiation Committee for a Framework Convention on Climate Change (INC/FCC), UNGA res. 45/212, 1990

Precautionary principle should guide action (Declaration of Second World Conference and Economic Commission for Europe (ECE) conference).

Development of political targets (with different target years) for the stabilization of CO_2 emissions at 1990 levels by OECD, except US and Turkey

EC target for stabilization of CO_2 emissions in 2000 with respect to 1990 levels

IPCC's First Assessment Report – AR1 – initial consensus on knowledge of climate change, since then AR2(1996) and AR3 (2000)

1992   Second World Conference on Environment – UN Conference on Environment and Development, Rio – Sustainable development through the integration of environment, social and development concerns. Outcome: 5 multilateral agreements.

1992/4   UN Framework Convention on Climate Change (UNFCCC)

1995   Conference of the Parties (COP1 of the UNFCCC – the Berlin Mandate adopted to promote legally binding reduction commitments.

1997/2005   Adoption of legally binding the Kyoto Protocol

2002   Third World Conference on Environment – UN Conference on Environment and Development, Johannesburg, South Africa.

Source: Gupta, 2010

1.1B Outcomes of the United Nations Conference on Environment and Development (UNCED), earth summit, Rio, 1992, entry into force, 1994

Focus: Sustainable development through the integration and balancing of environment, social and development concerns

Five multi-lateral agreements signed at Rio
Legally binding
- Convention on Biological Diversity (CBD)
- UN Framework Convention on Climate Change

Non binding
- Rio Declaration on Environment and Development: 27 principles to guide international actions on the basis of global responsibility towards sustainable development
- Agenda 21: programme of action for various sectors (included a chapter on the atmosphere).
- Statement on Forest Principles: 15 principles for the protection and more sustainable use of forest resources

Rio outcomes – four MEAs adopted after UNCED, Rio
- Convention to Combat Desertification,
- Rotterdam Convention on Prior Informed Consent Procedure for Certain Hazardous Chemicals and Pesticides in International Trade
- Convention on Persistent Organic Pollutants Stradling and Migratory Fish Stock Agreement.

The five sets of principles of the UNFCCC
1. Principle of Common But Differentiate Responsibilities (CBDR) (with regard to contribution to causing the problem of climate change) and respective capacities (with regard to capabilities to address the problem)
2. Attention to be paid to the specific needs of the particularly vulnerable countries
3. The precautionary principle
4. The right to sustainable development
5. The need to support an open, international economic system (art. 3)

Source: Gupta, 2010

1.2 Country Groupings and Non-Governmental Organisations participation in UNFCCC Negotiations, as of December 31, 2012

1 Country groupings UNFCCC

Each Party to the Convention is represented at sessions of the Convention's bodies by a national delegation consisting of one or more officials empowered to represent and negotiate on behalf of their government.

Based on the tradition of the United Nations, Parties are organized into five regional groups, mainly for the purposes of electing the Bureau, namely: African States, Asian States, Eastern European States, Latin American and the Caribbean States, and the Western European and Other States (the 'Other States' include Australia, Canada, Iceland, New Zealand, Norway, Switzerland and the United States of America, but not Japan, which is in the Asian Group).

The five regional groups, however, are not usually used to present the substantive interests of Parties and several other groupings are more important for climate negotiations. Developing countries generally work through the Group of 77 to establish common negotiating positions. The G-77 was founded in 1964 in the context of the UN Conference on Trade and Development (UNCTAD) and now functions throughout the UN system. It has over 130 members. The country holding the Chair of the G-77 in New York (which rotates every year) often speaks for the G-77 and China as a whole.

However, because the G-77 and China is a diverse group with differing interests on climate change issues, individual developing countries also intervene in debates, as do groups within the G-77, such as the African regional Group, the Alliance of Small Island States, the group of Least Developed Countries and the Like-Minded Group of Developing Countries.

The Alliance of Small Island States (AOSIS) is a coalition of some 43 low-lying and small island countries, most of which are members of the G-77, that they are particularly vulnerable to sea-level rise. AOSIS countries are united by the threat that climate change poses to their survival and frequently adopt a common stance in negotiations. They were the first to propose a draft text during the Kyoto Protocol negotiations calling for cuts in carbon dioxide emissions of 20 per cent from 1990 levels by 2005.

The Least Developed Countries (LDCs) are the 50 countries defined as Least Developed Countries by the UN. They regularly work together in the wider UN system. They have become increasingly active in the climate change process, often working together to defend their particular interests, for example with regard to vulnerability and adaptation to climate change.

The European Union comprises the 27 members of the European Union. They meet in private to agree on common negotiating positions. The country that holds the EU Presidency – a position that rotates every six months – then speaks for the

European Union and its 27 member states. As a regional economic integration organization, the European Union itself can be, and is, a Party to the Convention. However, it does not have a separate vote from its members.

The Umbrella Group is a loose coalition of non-EU developed countries which formed following the adoption of the Kyoto Protocol. Although there is no formal list, the Group is usually made up of Australia, Canada, Japan, New Zealand, Norway, the Russian Federation, Ukraine and the US.

The *Like-Minded Group of Developing Countries* (LMDC) have emerged since Bonn 2012 meeting. The group with a diverse regional and size mixed of African, Asian and Latin American countries such as Bolivia, China, Cuba, Ecuador, Egypt, India, Mali, Malaysia, Nicaragua, Philippines, Saudi Arabia, Thailand, and Venezuela LMDC is a platform for like-minded developing countries to exchange views and coordinate positions on the negotiations under the UNFCCC with the view to strengthening the voice of the developing countries, highlight their common concerns and priorities and contributing to achieving the combined goals of environmental sustainability, social and economic development and equity. The group which sees itself as an intrinsic part of the Group of 77 and China are in line with the principles and objectives of the Group of 77 and China in the climate negotiations.

The Environmental Integrity Group (EIG), formed in 2000, comprises Mexico, the Republic of Korea and Switzerland.

Several other groups also work together in the climate change process, including countries from the Organization of Petroleum Exporting Countries (OPEC), a group of countries of Central Asia, Caucasus, Albania and Moldova (CACAM), and countries that are members of organizations such as the League of Arab States and the Agence intergouvernementale de la francophonie.

The Coalition for Rainforest Nations identify as 'Developing Nations with rainforests' – partnering with Industrialized Nations that support fair trade and improved market access for developing countries. Within the UNFCCC process, they mainly advocate around forests and REDD issues. Catalysed by Papua New Guinea in 2005, they include (on a voluntary basis) Argentina, Bangladesh, Belize, Cameroon, Central African Republic, Chile, Congo, Costa Rica, Cote d'Ivoire, DR Congo, Dominica, Dominican Republic, Ecuador, Equatorial Guinea, El Salvador, Fiji, Gabon, Ghana, Guatemala, Guyana, Honduras, Indonesia, Jamaica, Kenya, Lesotho, Liberia, Madagascar, Malaysia, Nicaragua, Nigeria, Pakistan, Panama, Papua New Guinea, Paraguay, Samoa, Sierra Leone, Solomon Islands, Suriname, Thailand, Uruguay, Uganda, Vanuatu and Vietnam. The most recent grouping, the *Independent Alliance of Latin America and the Caribbean* (AILAC) composed of Chile, Columbia, Costa Rica, Guatemala, Panama and Peru, emerged since Doha (December 2012).

Source: UNFCCC

2 Participation of Non-Governmental Stakeholders in UNFCCC processes

The Rio Declaration of 1992, Principle 10, the principle of public participation, affirms that those who are, or, feel affected by a decision have a right to be involved in the decision-making process. It also recognises that environmental issues are best handled with the participation of all concerned citizens, at the relevant levels. Further regional processes such as the UNECE Convention on Access to Information, Public Participation in Decision-Making and Access to Justice in Environmental Matters (the Aarhus Convention) of 1998 which provide operational criteria for public participation. In this tradition, the UNFCCC provides for public participation under Art. 6 (a) and Art. 4 (1)(i) relating to activities of education, training and public awareness at national level. Specifically, the Convention facilitates the participation of nongovernmental organisations (NGOs) at the meetings of the bodies of the UNFCCC under Article 7, paragraph 6, which provides for the admission of non-governmental organizations to sessions of the Convention bodies as observers.

Hence civil society groups, academic, businesses, farmers, trade unions and other interest groups follow the climate negotiations intently and purposefully. These groups of non-governmental actors seek to influence the process for desired outcome that benefit civil society and the other multitude of stakeholders. The UNFCCC has evolved a formal process for admitting these non-governmental organizations as observers at sessions of the Convention bodies. These groups have also formed themselves into broad and loose clusters of interests and perspectives to avail themselves of this access in a systematic, democratic and fair way.

Initial clusters included the business and industry organizations and the environmental groups. Today there are over 1,400 admitted observer organizations who organize themselves through a focal point system in which they liaise with the UNFCCC Secretariat as 'constituencies'.

Constituencies have grown from two, Business nongovernmental organization (BINGOs) and environmental nongovernmental organizations (ENGOs) to nine 9 approved constituencies: 3) local government and municipal authorities (LGMA) at COP 1, 4); indigenous peoples organizations (IPO) at COP 7; 5) the research and independent nongovernmental organizations (RINGO) at COP 9; 6) the trade union non-governmental organizations (TUNGO) at COP 14.; 7) women and gender non-governmental, Women and Gender, (approved since 2011); 8) youth non-governmental organizations, which includes college students (YOUNGOs) and 9) farmers and agricultural nongovernmental organizations (recognized as a constituency on a provisional basis pending a final decision of their status before COP 19/CMP 9, 2013).

Focal points for the constituencies presently include for: Business and industry non-governmental organizations (BINGO) – the International Chamber of Commerce; Environmental non-governmental organizations (ENGO) – Climate Action Network – International Secretariat; Research and independent non-governmental organizations (RINGO) – Centre for European Policy Studies; Trade Unions non- governmental organizations (TUNGO) – International Trade Unions Confederation; Women and Gender – GenderCC – Women for Climate Justice; Youth non-governmental organizations (YOUNGO) – United Kingdom Youth Climate Coalition

Source: UNFCCC website; UNFCCC NGO Liaison/Database /Constituencies/ March 2013 http://unfccc.int/files/parties_and_observers/ngo/application/pdf/ constituency_focal_point_contact_details.pdf ; and submission Ways to Enhance the Engagement of Observer Organisations Submitted by GenderCC. Women for Climate Justice, on behalf of LIFE e.V., Women in Europe for a Common Future (WECF), and Women's Environment and Development Organisation (WEDO) August 2010. http://unfccc.int/resource/docs/2010/smsn/ngo/207.pdf

APPENDIX 2

2.1 South Centre on equity and fairness in emissions reductions scenario

South Centre research shows that cumulative global emissions have totalled about 1214 Gt in 1850–2008 (table 1.1). Of this total:

- Annex I countries accounted for 878 Gt or 72 per cent of the total. Since their share of world population was about 25 per cent in this period, their fair share of emissions was 310 Gt. Therefore their overuse of their fair share was 568 Gt. This overuse was 183 per cent above the fair proportional share.
- Non-Annex I countries accounted for 336 Gt or 28 per cent of the total. Their fair share of emissions was 904 Gt (given their share of total population of 75 per cent). Therefore the under-use was 568 Gt or 63 per cent below their fair share.
- If a total budget of 750 Gt is taken, and Annex I countries' population ratio to world population is 16 per cent, then the Annex I countries' fair share is 120 Gt. However, to fully discharge its carbon debt (568 Gt) as at 2008, its allocation for 2010–2050 is a negative budget of 448 Gt.
- Developing countries with an average population ratio of 84 per cent would have a fair share of 630 Gt of the total 750 Gt budget. However, since it has a credit of 568 Gt in 2008, its allocation for 2010–2050 would be 1198 Gt.

In order for there to be equity, in order to fulfil the environmental global of global cut of 50–85 per cent, developed countries will have to go into negative emissions so that developed countries can have a decent level of development space (Khor 2010).

Acceptance of a 50 per cent global cut and an 80 per cent annex I (developed countries) cut is equivalent to a specific emissions target for developing countries and would also lock in the whole distribution of the carbon budget and set of emission cuts. This is so since the global emissions cut is made up of Annex I and NAI (developing countries) cuts. So if the global cut is fixed and the lower the AI cut, then the (residual) higher the NAI cut.

The implied distribution of carbon budget between Annex I and Non Annex I countries is unfair. A 50 per cent global cut and 80 per cent annex I cut yields a budget share of 30–35 per cent for Annex I. This is significantly above their 16 per cent share of world population.

Explicitly the developing countries would have an adversely unfair distribution of the 2010–2050 budget and would implicitly write off the 1850–2008 cumulative debt of the developed countries.

This will have significant implications for developing countries. In the worst case scenario, they would have to undertake a drastic 50 per cent cut or half in per capita emission levels. This would increase dramatically under a non-1990 base year scenario. Compared to its 2005 levels, NAI total emissions in 2050 would be 42 per cent below and its per capita emission would be 61 per cent below. Given the almost 1:1 relation between GDP and emission this would indicate drastic cut in gross domestic production in these countries (South Centre, 2011).

APPENDIX 3

3.1 The Intergovernmental Panel on Climate Change (IPCC) Fifth Assessment Findings on Gender – Summary and Overview

The Intergovernmental Panel on Climate Change (IPCC), which regularly assesses the science on climate change and presents its conclusions for climate policy makers to digest and discuss in their decision-making processes about global, national and local climate protection issues, issued its most recent assessment report, the Fifth Assessment Report Climate Change 2014 (AR5). The assessment report covers working by its three working groups: Working Group I: *The Physical Science Basis* (2013), Working Group II: *Impacts, Adaptation, and Vulnerability* (2014) and Working Group III: *Mitigation of Climate Change* (2014) also discussed the subject of gender and climate change a theme which was initiated in AR 4 (2007) as well as discussed in the IPCC's Special Report on Extreme Events (SREX 2012).

The Fifth Assessment Report (2014) has now weighed in with a much more comprehensive assessment of the socioeconomic dimensions of climate change including gender, indigenous peoples and climate change. The gender discussion is spread across a number of chapters, particularly 2 (Integrated Risk and Uncertainty Assessment of Climate Change Response Policies), 11 (Human Health: Impacts, Adaptation, and Co-Benefits), 12 (Human Security), 13 (Livelihoods and Poverty) and indigenous people (especially Chapter 11) in the final output of Working Group II: *Impacts, Adaptation, and Vulnerability*. There are also some isolated references to gender and related issues in Chapters 2 (Integrated Risk and Uncertainty Assessment of Climate Change Response Policies, one reference) 7 (Energy Systems, one reference), 9 (Buildings, multiple references) and 11 (Agriculture, Forestry and Other Land Use (AFOLU, multiple references)) of the final output of Working Group III: *Mitigation of Climate Change*.

Appendix 3.1 presents a sampling of the key reference points on gender in terms of the thematic areas of adaptation, mitigation and technology from both AR4

(3.1A) and AR5 (3.1B). Gender and climate finance related issues, of which there were only a few remarks, will be discussed in Chapter 4 as appropriate.

Overall the main points on gender and climates made in the report are:

1 Gender, along with socio-demographic factors of age, wealth and class, is critical to the ways in which climate change is experienced.
(i) Existing gender inequality is increased or heightened as a result of weather events and climate related disasters intertwined with socioeconomic, institutional, cultural, and political drivers that perpetuate differential vulnerabilities.[1]
(ii) There are significant gender dimensions to impacts, adaptation and vulnerability.
(iii) Discussion of new findings since the cut-off date for AR4, 'based on multiple lines of evidence (in every region of the world) (show) how climate change is differentiated by gender, and how climate change contributes to perpetuating existing gender inequalities'.

2 Overall, the theme of gender discrimination and structural gender inequality as drivers of vulnerability from AR4 was continued. But while AR4 focused on women's relatively higher vulnerability to weather-related disasters in terms of numbers of deaths', AR5 argues that 'the published literature since . . . (then) adds nuances by showing how socially constructed gender differences affect exposure to extreme events, leading to differential patterns of mortality for both men and women (high confidence)'. Table 3.1B shows some of these examples of gender differentiated mortality impacts. Here the new evidence shows how gender roles (such as expectations round heroism) for men can affect their vulnerability. AR5 also undertakes more complex nuancing assessments of the effect of heatwaves/stress on men, women, different age cohorts, marital status and the presence, or the lack thereof, of social networks in reducing or exacerbating men and women's vulnerability to climate-induced heat phenomenon.

3 By far the most interesting points of departure and extension of the gender dimension is the report's insistency that it is important to also explore how women's agency (not just their 'victimness') can also expose them to the adverse effects of climate change.

Moreover, the construction of economically poor women as victims denies women's agency and emphasizes their vulnerability as their intrinsic problem (MacGregor, 2010; Manzo, 2010; Arora-Jonsson, 2011) (Chapter 13, p.13, WG II).

4 Other interesting findings in AR5 with regard to gender and climate change adaptation and vulnerability, are the links highlighted between education/women's literacy and adaptation as well as the link between access to reproductive to health services and climate change mitigation.

For example, the report of Working Group II and III notes:

Education for women and girls and adaptation
  In situation where adaptation is severely constrained by cultural norms and/or a lack of local knowledge and analytical skills as to what actions could be taken ... **Adaptive capacity could be improved through investment in education**, development of local financial institutions and property rights systems, women's rights, and other broad_based forms of poverty alleviation (Chapter 2, p.52, WG III).

  Alongside improving general disaster education (greatly assisted by rising literacy rates, especially among women), the country deployed early warning systems and built a network of cyclone shelters). The context here is Bangladesh's successful achievement of reduction in mortality during the 2007 cyclone Sidr (category 4^2), the country's use of early warning systems was partly credited for this. The report flagged the importance of literacy and education with regard to early warning, noting that: **Early warning systems included high technology information systems** and *relatively simple measures such as training volunteers to distribute warning messages by bicycle* (Chapter 11, p.26, WG II).

  Encouraging gender equitable access to education and strengthening of social capital are among the best means of improving adaptation of rural women farmers (Below et al., 2012; Goulden et al., 2009; Vincent et al., 2010), Chapter 12, p.26, WG II).

Reproductive services and mitigation
  Access to reproductive health services for women is linked not only to slower population growth but to 'associated energy demands'. The report highlights that one *study shows that CO_2 emission would be lower by 30% by 2100 if access to contraception was provided to women who expressed a need for it (O'Neill et al, 2010)*. Providing contraceptive service to meet the unmet need was valid for Sahel region of Africa as well as for the US (where the report argues '*there is unmet need for reproductive health services as well a high CO_2 emission per capital (Cohen 2010)* (Chapter 11, p.35 and 37; Chapter 11, p.35, WG II).

5   Lastly, the report revisited and, in some instances, added new details about the relationship between reducing inefficiency in household cooking which will reduce climate-altering pollutants (CAPs) and women's health and livelihoods. These have co-benefits in that they support GHG mitigation while improving the health of women and men in households, families and communities (reduction of premature deaths). It also highlights issues such as gender differences in displacement from extreme events and the gender dimensions of land rush (such as those generated by the competition for land for biofuel production).

  Large-scale land acquisitions(LSLAs) have also triggered a land rush in LICs, which affects livelihood choices and outcomes, with some distinct gender dimensions (Chu, 2011; De Schutter, 2011; Julia and White, 2012; Peters, 2013). (Chapter 13, p.20, WG II).

  There is growing apprehension that increased competition for scarce land undermines women's access to land and their ability to benefit economically from biofuel investment (Molony, 2011; Ardnt *et al.*, 2011; Chu, 2011; Julai and White, 2012; Behrman *et al.*, 2012; Perch *et al.*, 2012) (Chapter 13, p.20, WG II).

Mitigation efforts focused on land acquisition for biofuel production show preliminary negative impacts on the lives of poor people, such as dispossession of farmland and forests, in many LICs and MICs, particularly for indigenous peoples and (women) smallholders. (Chapter 13, p.3, WG II).

6 A few of the points of departure of gender and climate change flagged by WG II and WG III both of which provides much more comprehensive illustrative cases snapshots from around the world. These departures and extensions include:.

(1) Gender inequality is usually heighted by climate related hazards which creates increased work load (from customary and new roles (arising within the context of climate change such as climate induced male out-migration) that exacerbates or creates vulnerability) (Chapter 13, p.3, WG II).

(2) Climate change impacts gender inequality through livelihoods impact and the 'feminization of responsibility' (for addressing climate impacts). As noted by the report, 'whilst both men and women experience increases in productive roles, only women experience increased reproductive roles (Resurreccion, 2011) (Chapter 12, p.25, WG II).

(3) With regard to gender and vulnerability the IPCC assessment tries to distinguish between two interconnecting gender and vulnerability narratives in the global literature on gender and climate change. The conventional one asserted in AR5 and SREX as well as most of the literature that emphasises women as victims of climate change and an emerging and more compelling narrative grounded in women's and men's agency in responding to the challenges posed by climate change. Though the latter narrative is still developing, it is a more empowering approach, especially with regard to the discussion on women's entitlement and equitable access to finance and technology.

(4) The gendered victim approach has multiple dimensions including those that would seem to predispose women (disproportionately more so than men) as victims of climate impacts including issues of mortality, morbidity/health, occupational hazards and emotional and psychological stress.

Mortality: while worldwide, mortality due to natural disasters, including drought, floods and storms is higher among women than men (WHO 2011), there is variation regionally: US, Canada (Inuits) and Paris (see table A3.1A). Women have restricted mobility and may lack social skill such as swimming or trees climbing, or cultural restriction that cause women to wait in the house (Bangladesh and Nicaragua) (Chapter 13, p.14, WG II). Men have a higher mortality rate when fulfilling culturally-imposed roles as heroic life savers (Rohr 2006, Campbell *et al.*, 2009; Resurreccion 2011) (Chapter 13, p.14, WG II).

Food related Mortality: Nepal – food related mortality is twice as high for girls as for women (13.3 per 1,000 girls) and higher for boys than for men (Chapter 13, p.14, WG II).

Health Status: climate variability amplify food shortage – women consume less food (Lambrou and Nelson 2013). Women suffer from reproductive tract infections and water borne diseases after floods (Neelormi *et al.*, 2008; Campbell *et al.*, 2009) (Chapter 13, p.13, WG II).

Food and nutritional issues:
Lower caloric intake can result in physical stunting among children
The effect of food insecurity on growth and development in childhood may be more damaging for girls than for boys (Cook and Frank, 2008).
Tanzania and Malawi demonstrate how women experience food and nutrition insecurity since food is preferentially distributed among other family members (Nelson and Stathers, 2009; Kakota *et al.*, 2011) (Chapter 12, p.25, WG II).

Occupational hazard: women exposed to hazards indoors and outdoors

El Salvador: increased heat-related deaths (due to kidney failures) among male workers on sugar plantation (Peraza *et al.*, 2012) (Chapter 13, p.13, WG II). Spain: increase cases of heat-related indoor work emergencies among young abled bodied urban men (<50), Garcia-Pina *et al.*, 2008) (Chapter 13, p.13, WG II). Malawi, Kenya, India and Sri Lanka: women tea pickers suffer and die from heat stress as payment by quantity discourage rest breaks – Anecdotal evidence (Renton 2009) (Chapter 13, p.13, WG II).
Bangladesh: out migration of male due to unsustainable rural livelihoods, leave women to face unsafe working conditions, exploitation and loss of respect (Pouliotte *et al.*, 2009) (Chapter 13, p.13, WG II). Note: outmigration of male could also provide opportunities for women to move beyond traditionally constrained roles, explore new livelihood options and access public decision-making space (CIDA, 2002 and Fordham *et al.*, 2011) (Chapter 13, p.13, WG II).

Emotional and psychological distress:
Climate-related disorders can affect women's mental health disproportionally due to their multiple social roles (UNECLAC 2005) (Chapter 13, p.13, WG II). Slow onset climate events, stress and tensions, loss and grief, disrupted safety nets and increased gender-based violence within households (Anderson 2009, Alston 2011, Parkinson *et al.*, and Whittenbury 2013, Hazeleger 2013) (Chapter 13, p.13, WG II).

(5) The gendered agency approach to analysing impacts and vulnerability in the context of climate change adaptation has two interrelated and often intersecting storylines: a gendered livelihood impacts theme and the feminisation of responsibility theme.

The gendered livelihood impacts and vulnerability:
This strand focuses on women's agency in adaptation (and mitigation) and balances out the women as victim emphasis of the gender and vulnerability focus. Snapshots presented show a complex picture of the response pathways of women and men adjusting to a new-climate based reality.

(6) Australia: more regular occurrence of drought has put women under increasing pressure to earn off-farm income, and contribute to more on-farm labor (Alston, 2011) (Chapter 12, p.25, WG II).

> India: more women than men work as wage laborers to compensate for crop losses (Lambrou and Nelson, 2013) (Chapter 13, p.13, WG II).
> Tanzania: wealthier women hire poorer women to collect animal fodder during droughts (Muthoni and Wangui, 2013) (Chapter 13, p.13, WG II).
> Philippines: women farmers who relied on high interest loans were sent to jail after defaulting on debt following crop failure (Perlata 2008) (Chapter 13, p.13, WG II).
> Uganda: men amass land after floods; while droughts reduced women's non-land assets (Quisumbing *et al.*, 2011) (Chapter 13, p.13, WG II).
> Ghana: some husbands prevent wives from cultivating individual plots (in response to gradually shifting rainfall seasonality with adverse implications for women's agency and household well-being (Carr 2008) (Chapter 13, p.13, WG II).

The feminization of responsibility, vulnerability:
This strand shows how climate change creates new roles and added responsibility for women and men, which may be at the disadvantage of women, or could be advantageous in the long run? Once again vignettes are illustrative of the story line.

> Vietnam: increased work load for both partners, contingent on socially-accepted gender roles – men work longer hours during extreme events. women adopt extra responsibilities during disaster preparation and recovery (e.g., storing food and water, taking care of children, the sick and the elderly) (Campbell *et al.*, 2009; Resurreccion, 2011) (Chapter 13, p.13, WG II).
> Cambodia: Khmer men and women accepted culturally –taboo income generating activities under duress, when rice cropping patterns shifted due to higher temperatures and more irregular rainfall (Resurreccion 2011) (Chapter 13, p.13, WG II).
> Nepal: shifts in the monsoon season, longer dry periods, and decreased snowfall push Dalit girls and women to grow drought-resistant buckwheat and offer more day labour to the high caste Lama Landlords, while Dalit men seek (previously taboo patronage protection to engage in cross-border trade (Onta and Resurreccion, 2011) (Chapter 13, p.13, WG II).
> Niger and South Africa: rising male out-migration leave women all agricultural tasks (with limited extra labor) (Goh, 2012) (Chapter 13, p.13, WG II).

Men's migration in Northern Mali, for example, increases the workload of the rest of the family, especially women, and reduces children's school attendance (Brockhaus *et al.*, 2013) (Chapter 13, p.21, WG II).

(7) Findings from WG II (Chapter 11) and WG III (Chapters 7, 9 and 11) that have some implication for gender and mitigation.

Though WG III on mitigation did not present much assessment of the, admittedly, small literature linking gender and mitigation, it does present some findings that have implications for advancing work in that area. For example, the report notes that:

Mitigation pathways in developing countries should address the dual need for mitigation and adaptation . . . Prerequisites for the successful implementation of AFOLU mitigation projects are ensuring communities' engagement, a priori consent of a small holder, and that 'extra effort is required to address equity issues including gender , challenges and prospects (Mbow et al. 2012) (Chapter 11, p.55, WG III).

Special care for small holders and equity issues, including gender, should accompany mitigation projects (Chapter 4, p.60, WG III).

One example produces liquid biofuels for stove cooking while creating, near cities, agroforestry zones with rows of fast-growing leguminous trees/shrubs and alleys planted with annual crop rotations, surrounded by a forestry shelterbelt zone that contains indigenous trees and oilseed trees and provides business opportunities across the value chain including for women (WWF-UK, 2011). The mixture of crops and trees produces food with higher nutritive values, enables clean biofuels production for stove cooking, develops businesses, and simultaneously avoids GHG emissions from deforestation to produce charcoal for cooking (Zvinavashe et al., 2011) (Chapter 7, p.47, WG III). These are practices in developing countries for which women are particularly well-known.

Energy efficiency and reducing reliance on coal for electricity generation not only reduces emissions of greenhouse gases, but also reduces emissions of fine particles which cause many premature deaths worldwide as well as reducing other health impacts from the coal fuel cycle (Chapter 11, p.37, WG II).

In developing countries, inefficient combustion of traditional solid fuels in households produces significant gaseous and particulate emissions know as products of incomplete combustion (PICs) and results in significant health impacts, particularly for women and children, who spend longer periods at home (Zhang and Smith, 2007; Duflo et al., 2008; Wilkinson et al., 2009) (Chapter 9, p.47, WG III).

Efficient biomass techniques for cooking (e.g., biomass cookstoves) can have positive impacts on health, especially for women and children in developing countries (Chapter 11, p.100, WG III).

Notes

1 (*robust evidence*) (Lambrou and Paina, 2006; Brouwer et al., 2007; Shackleton et al., p.12, c13).
2 With Sidr a category 4 cyclone only 3,400 persons were killed in comparison to the deaths of approximately 500,000 people when cyclone Bhola (category 3 in severity) hit East Pakistan (present day Bangladesh) in 1970 and 140,000 deaths in cyclone of similar severity 1991 (Chapter 11, p. 26, WG II).

3.1A: A sampling of the Gender References In the IPCC's 4th (2007) and 5th Assessment Reports (2013/14)

A sampling of the Gender References in the IPCC's 4th Assessment Report (2007)

Adaptation (A)
Chapter 17, Box 17.5, Box 17.
Masika (2002) specifically outlines gender aspects of differential vulnerabilities
Box 8.2, p.398, Gender and natural disaster

A&M

Chapter 18 *Inter-relationships between adaptation and mitigation*
In the Niayes region of central Senegal, the government has sought to promote irrigation practices and reduce dependence on rain-fed agriculture with the planting of dense hedges to act as windbreaks. These have enhanced agricultural productivity.

Windbreaks have been effective in combatting soil erosion and desiccation and have also provided fuelwood for cooking, thus reducing the need for women and girls to travel long distances in a rapidly urbanising area in search of wood. The windbreaks have carbon sequestration benefits but, most of all, they have helped to intensify agricultural production, especially with commercial products, thus boosting the economic livelihoods of poor communities. Thus, what started off as an adaptation strategy has had substantial integrated development benefits by easing deforestation and reducing carbon emissions, as well as addressing gender and livelihood issues (Seck *et al.*, 2005).

Mitigation (M)
Development of hydroelectricity may reduce water availability for fish farming and irrigation of home gardens, potentially adversely affecting the food security of women and children (Andah *et al.*, 2004; Hirsch and Wyatt, 2004). Linking carbon sequestration and community development could generate new opportunities for women and marginal socio-economic groups, but this will depend on many local factors and needs to be evaluated with empirical research (p.770).

WG III
Agriculture
Improved management practices for rice cultivation and grazing land, and use of bioenergy and efficient cooking stoves enhance productivity, and promote social harmony and gender equality (p.726).

Energy efficiency
Important to ensure that low-income household energy needs are given due consideration, and that the process and consequences of implementing mitigation options are, or the result is, gender neutral.

Energy substitution can lower mortality and morbidity by reducing indoor air pollution, reduce the workload for women and children and decrease the unsustainable use of fuelwood and related deforestation. (11.8, 11.9, 12.4, WG III).

Hydroelectricity may reduce water availability for fish farming and irrigation of home gardens, potentially adversely affecting the food security of women and children (Andah *et al.*, 2004; Hirsch and Wyatt, 2004).

Switching from solid fuels to modern fuels for cooking and heating indoors can reduce indoor air pollution and increase free time for women in developing countries.

Linking carbon sequestration and community development could generate new opportunities for women and marginal socio-economic groups, but this will depend on many local factors and needs to be evaluated with empirical research (ch.17, p.770).

Waste management
Chapter 10
Engineered sanitary landfilling with landfill gas recovery:

The social dimension includes issues such as gender equality, governance, equitable income distribution, housing

Technology
Chapter 20 (WG II)
Perspectives on climate change and sustainability
Developing and employing 'eco-technologies' (based on an integration of traditional and frontier technologies including biotechnologies, renewable energy and modern management techniques) is a critical ingredient rooted in the principles of economics, gender, social equity and employment generation with due emphasis given to climate change (Swaminathan, 2005, p.835).

3.1B: A sampling of the Gender References in the IPCC's 5th Assessment Report (2013)

Vulnerability
Vulnerability – Mortality*:
Worldwide women have higher mortality due to natural disasters (flood, storms, droughts) than men (WHO 2011)

Statistical evidence of patterns of male and female mortality from recorded extreme events in 141 countries, 1981–2002 found that disasters kill women at an earlier age than men (Neumayer and Plumper 2007):

Regional variation in gender difference in mortality:
In the United States, males are at greater risk of death following flooding (Jonkman and Kelman, 2005).

Hunan province, China experiences excess of flood deaths among males, often related to rural farming (Abuaku *et al.*, 2009). During the Paris 2003 heat wave, excess mortality was greater among females overall, but there were more excess deaths among men in the working age span (25–64) possibly due to differential exposures to heat in occupational settings (Fouillet *et al.*, 2006).

In Hai Lang district, Vietnam, for example, more men died than women due to their involvement in search and rescue and protection of fields during flooding (Campbell *et al.*, 2009).

In Mexico City women had a higher risk of mortality (due to heat waves) than men, although the reverse was true in Santiago and Sao Paulo (Bell *et al.*, 2008).

Adaptation & Mitigation
Gender dimensions of vulnerability derive from differential access to the social and environmental resources required for adaptation

These gender inequalities manifest themselves in gendered livelihood impacts and feminisation of responsibilities: whilst both men and women experience increases in productive roles, only women experience increased reproductive roles

Women and girls are more likely to become victims of domestic violence after a disaster, particularly when they are living in emergency accommodation, which has been documented in the US and Australia (Jenkins and Phillips, 2008; Anastario *et al.*, 2009; Alston, 2011; Whittenbury, 2013, Box 13–1).

Gender roles affect male and female vulnerability:

Men: expected to be 'brave/heroic' – risky life-saving behaviours

Women: victims of domestic violence in emergency accommodation, lack of skills to swim

*In Canada's Inuit population males are exposed to dangers associated with insecure sea ice, while females may be more vulnerable to the effects of diminished food supplies (Pearce *et al.* 2011). In Bangladesh, females are more affected than males by a range of climate hazards, due to differences in prevalence of poverty, under nutrition and exposure to water-logged environments (Neelormi *et al.*, 2009).

3.2: Sectoral areas of vulnerability for women and climate change*

1. Agriculture: Women are the majority of farmers in many developing countries. They produce more than 50 per cent of food (Africa: 80 per cent, Asia: 60 per cent and South America: 30–40 per cent) (FAO, 2009, 1998, 1995). Many women farmers tend to rely on rain-fed agriculture (Rowling 2007). Women also play a large role in natural resource management and nutrition (FAO, 2003). Women grow process and market food and are responsible for small livestock, vegetable gardens and the collection of fuel and water.

Climate change linkages: Given their involvement in agriculture and natural resource management, women are adversely impacted by climate change. Because of their social reproduction responsibility and gender gaps in economic and social resources, women are usually hardest hit by climate change-induced weather-related events.

Climate change policy implications: Women tend to shoulder much of the burden for adaptation in sub-Saharan Africa and Asia. But because of gender biases and gender gaps in terms of lack of property, credit and inadequate access to extension services, some women may not be able to undertake environmental sustainable farming or to make long-term investment in land rehabilitation.

What are needed in terms of climate policy are adjustment mechanisms that facilitate better women's participation. These include: 1) programmes and projects that enhances women's coping strategies to deal with weather-related hazards; 2) programmes and projects to increase women's role in adaptation and the adaptation of sustainable farm practices; 3) programmes and policies that identify and work to decrease the barriers to women's access to credit and new technologies, extension services and credit facility; and 4) programmes that structure mitigation and adaptation strategies to build on and enhance women's traditional knowledge.

2. *Conflict*: When resources are scarce, there is likely to be increase and intensified competition and conflict. Women and girls generally get caught in the crossfire and are often at the losing end of such conflicts.

Climate change linkages: Climate change policy and projects dedicated to the reduction of GHGs tend to be large-scale and top-down projects. In general, they do not involve much community participation. Many of these projects such as those funded through the carbon markets and other forestry-related projects tend to not address issues of participation and benefit sharing among different stakeholders in the areas in which they are located. They are therefore increasingly associated with conflicts over resources.

Climate change policy can increase gender-based access to resources, decision-making and technology. Climate change policy to reduce climate-generated conflicts should also be in alignment with UN RES 1325 on women, peace and security.

3. *Disaster:* Women and children are 14 times more likely to die from natural disaster than men. Natural disaster leads to both migration and internal displacement, which puts women at great disadvantages and subjects them to personal insecurity and vulnerability to sexual harassment, sexual assault and other forms of gender-based violence. It may also be associated with a rising prevalence of female households.

Climate change policy must be cognizant of these specific gender issues around disaster management and climate refugee resettlements, and include mitigation and adaptation strategies to bolster women's coping mechanisms, and ensure women's and girl's personal security. It must also build in processes for jump-starting and enabling women's quick and sustained recovery from natural disasters by providing security and durable resettlement habitation.

4. *Employment:* In general, women in many developing countries tend to dominate informal sector employment and self-employment. The informal sector economy is most hurt by climate change and weather-related shocks. In the first place, physical structures may be inferior or non existent (individuals may operate stalls or makeshift structures from which they do business). These are the most vulnerable

to destruction during floods and hurricanes. Second, it is highly unlikely that owners/operators have proper storage for their inventories, where these exist. Nor are they likely to have climate risk insurance coverage. Thus once a job or position is lost it will be difficult to regain footing in the future. Women-owner operators of business or workers must recoup and rebuild from their savings or become indebted to family friends, microfinance or money lenders.

Climate change policy must be cognizant of these underlying structural issues and include mitigation and adaptation strategies to bolster women's coping mechanisms, labour rights and protect access to health care for women. Temporary or short grants and other forms of assistance would become necessary. The current work programme on loss and damage now formalized by the Durban Outcome (2010) must integrate gender analysis and gender impact assessment in order to ensure that women benefit from any final agreement in this area in the post 2012 period.

5. *Energy:* In many developing countries, traditional sources of energy (charcoal and firewood) constitute the greater portion of available energy resources (74 per cent, compared to 4 per cent for OECD countries). According to UNCTAD 2009, 'lack of efficient and readily available sources of energy has a disproportionate effect on women for at least two reasons'. First, because women are responsible for household energy resources, mismanaged or scarce energy resources impact women's time burden (Dutta 2003, cited in UNCTAD 2009). Second, the use of solid fuels for cooking and heating causes high levels of indoor air pollution, which, in turn, leads to 1.6 million premature deaths each year – mostly among women and children.

Energy also plays a role as a source of income for many women. Micro-, small- and medium-sized enterprises (MSMEs), especially women-owned ones, are more likely to be involved with heat-intensive (food processing) and light-intensive (home-based) activities that take place during the evening at night, hence the price of energy and lack of adequate energy impacts MSMEs' profitability and safety. MSMEs also tend to be energy intensive and lack access to alternative forms of energy (Dutta 2003).

Climate change policy should seek to support the development of local low carbon energy sources. This could, for example, include access to small grants for research and development or subsidies for transformation to low carbon sources of energy. MSMEs could also be trained for greater involvement in carbon financing through, for example, the MDG Carbon Facility, or Micro finance Carbon and trained in the inter-linkage between micro-finance institutions and clean development mechanism projects. (Please see Chapter 6 for more on the increasing role of microfinance in climate change mitigation.)

6. *Health*: Climate change induced weather events can lead to increased water levels and waterborne diseases. It can therefore have a negative impact on food and malnutrition levels. It can also create or exacerbate respiratory diseases, heat related

morbidity and mortality. It may also increase women's time burden, if women and girls must travel further away from their domicile to collect water and firewood. This increases the stress and exposure to personal insecurity. Furthermore, barriers to women's health care can impact their health.

Climate change policy should focus on reducing the barrier to health care by promoting investment in health care facility and social safety nets. This could be complemented by cash transfers, free health care, and increased public health provisioning. Clean technology that reduces kitchen smoke improves women's health.

7. *Water:* In many developing countries, women have primary responsibility for collecting water, cooking, washing and raising small livestock. Women are also more dependent on natural streams and rainwater than men, who tend to use irrigation schemes. Climate change events that lead to water degradation can increase the time burden of women and girls.

Climate change policy: Since women have key roles in ensuring household water supply, adaptation and mitigation strategies must focus on ensuring more efficient water resource management that saves women time. This means that there must be greater emphasis on scaling up water distribution, protecting and improving local water sources. Gender-friendly infrastructure for water supply, storage and distribution must be a key cornerstone of water management, both for rural and urban areas. Thus planners need to be aware of and design and construct water system so that girls and women can have easy access without the need for male intermediaries.

8. *Transportation*: Women have smaller ecological foot prints than men (Johnsson-Latham, 2007). Men are responsible for the bulk of energy use, carbon dioxide emission and air pollution. There are significant gender differences in transportation that can be exploited for changing behavioural approach to energy use. For example, in some places, men are more prone to using private vehicles where as women, as a group, tend to rely on public transportation. Energy efficient transportation systems which move the most people at a time is quite supportive of GHG reduction.

Climate change policy should ensure effective participation of women's organizations and gender perspectives in decision-making on community planning boards, traffic systems and transportation boards.

9. *Technology*: Women benefit greatly from clean technologies in households, home-based businesses, agriculture and food processing and forestry management (UNCTAD 2009). Women also create and adapt technology that is important for adaptation in rural areas, forestry and agriculture.

Climate change policy: there is a need to engender the Clean Development Mechanism and promote environmentally sustainable technologies that focus on women's priorities and concerns. There needs to be focused attention on exploring the traditional energy sources developed by women as well as increased attention to promoting education and literacy for women with regard to emerging energy efficient alternatives. This should be complemented by the development of rural infrastructure in order to facilitate agriculture production, market access and the distribution of inputs. In this context, rural roads, feeder roads and rural infrastructure have to be developed as a priority area of adaptation/mitigation linked to development planning.

* Many of the key areas identified were adapted from Brody *et al.* (2008).

APPENDIX 4

4.1 Unravelling the climate finance jigsaw

I. Global Mitigation Cost Estimation

1. IEA (2010) 'Blue Map' scenario
   - up to 2030 $750 billion a year
   - 2030–2050 $1,600 billion a year
2. Global Energy Assessment (2011)
   - 2010–2050 $1,700–2,100 billion a year
3. Edenhofer et al. (2009) 'RECIPE'
   - up to 2030 $480–600 billion a year
   - in 2050 $1,200 billion a year
4. Mckinsey (2009) Pathways to a Low-Carbon Economy
   - in 2020 $660 billion a year
   - in 2030 $1,000 billion a year
5. UNFCCC (2009) expert group on technology
   - Global additional financing required:
                             $300 to 1,000 billion a year until 2030
   - Developing country share in costs of technology deployment and diffusion *(excl. research and development)*:
                             $182 to 505 billion a year. +more with R&D+
6. World Bank Development Report 2010
   - Incremental mitigation costs in development countries:
                             $140 to 175 billion a year
   - 'Associated financing needs':
                             $265 to 565 billion a year
7. UNDESA (2011)
   - Global investments for energy transformation
   - Developing country requirements

   Energy transformation: $1,080 billion a year
   Agricultural investment: $20 billion a year

4.ID. Mitigation – Bottom Up Estimates

India (Centre for Science and Environment 2010) – 6 key sectors:
$10 billion a year for power sector alone

China (UNDP 2009) 2010–2050:
$240–355 billion a year

II. Adaptation

1 UNFCCC (2007) developing country needs:
$27 to 66 billion a year

2 World Bank (2010) $75 to ~100 billion a year ($102 b a year for 'wetter' scenario):

East Asia/Pacific	$29 billion
South Asia	$17 billion
Latin Am/Caribbean	$23 billion
Sub-Saharan Africa	$19 billion
Europe/Cent. Asia	$11 billion
Middle East	$4 billion (rounding errors)

3 Montes/South Centre (argue in terms of a 'more realistic estimate of adaptation costs')

Fuller cost: 2.5 times UNFCCC range:
$68–165 billion a year

Ecosystem services:
$65–300 billion a year

one half of maximum:
$150

Residual damage:
$200 billion a year

2/3 of maximum residual damage:
$133

Total $448

or approximately $450 billion a year

Still excluding:
- mining, manufacturing, tourism, etc.
- loss of life, homes, infrastructure, livelihoods

Real world comparisons
- Pakistan 2011 floods 14 million affected:
$10–15 billion for reconstruction (MSNBC)
- Thailand 2011 floods:
$46 billion (World Bank 2011)
- US 2011 Mississippi flooding:
$9 billion (WSJ)
- Growing number of natural disasters and economic loss:
1999: $150 b; 2008: $260 b; 2011: $380 b
(Geneva Report 2011)

- In total Mitigation & Adaptation for Developing Country Needs: $600 to >1,550 billion a year (Mitigation $500 to 1,100 billion a year and Adaptation 100 to >450 billion).

Sources: compiled by Montes 2011 and 2012, South Centre

4.2: Summary of Fast-start Finance and lessons learnt

The Cancún Decision (para 96 – AWGLCA Outcome) further invited the developed countries participating in this short term flow (2010–2012) of climate change finance to developing countries to submit information on the resources provided for the Fast-Start period (2010–2012) as well as provide information on how developing country Parties can access these resources to the UNFCCC Secretariat by May 2011, 2012 and 2013. This was in accordance with the Bali Action plan's call for measurement, reporting and verification (MRV) of finance with regard to supported mitigation actions. The UNFCCC Secretariat was mandated to compile information on financial flows implicated in para 95 into an information document.

By December 2012, 35 contributing Parties including the European Commission have pledged approximately $33 plus billion in Fast-Start Finance money. A tentative assessment of these reports shows that only about fifty per cent have actually been budgeted for by countries and only about 30 per cent has been delivered in some cases.

A summary overview of the flow of financing to developing countries in accordance with the Copenhagen and Cancún Decisions is as follows:

- Australia has reported contribution of $619 million (original pledged amount AU$599 million).
- Canada has reported contribution of $1,217 million (based on total pledge of CAD 1,200 (US$1189).
- Germany $1,585 million (original pledge: €1,260 million). Germany reports all of its contribution is new and additional (1/3 from the auctioning of emissions certificated in Germany). WRI 2012.
- France reported $1,585 (pledge in €1,260)
- Japan reported that it has provided US $9.7 billion of its total pledge of US $1500 billion (as of March 2011).
- Norway reported on its contribution of $1,000 million (of its $1000 pledge).
- Switzerland reported its contribution to fast-start of $147 million (of total of CHF 140 million (US $162 million).
- The United Kingdom reported that it has contribution of $2380 million (original £1500 million (equivalent to $2.4 billion) pledged.) This includes approximately £430 million pledge for the World Bank in 2007. WRI 2012
- The United States has reported $7,500 for 2010–2012.

TABLE A4.1 FSF Pledged and Committed amounts by Major countries, 2010–2012

Preliminary quantitative analysis can also be complemented by historical and current qualitative assessment based on countries' past and present actions across a number of funds, instruments and mechanisms. In this regard, the data shows the following:

- Though under Fast-Start, Japan committed to provide $15 billion over three years (2010–20120, researchers note that approximately $10 billion was previously pledged under the Cool Earth Partnership in 2008. In 2009 it announced the Hatoyama Initiative which increased the total amount to $15 billion. Japan also include export credit and traditional development financing as part of its fast-start contribution (Nakhooda, 2012).

- A significant proportion of the United States 2010 $1.7 billion pledge ($1.3 billion is simply 'aid' and the remainder ($400 million) is also qualified as 'development finance and export credit). The US also include its contribution to the Montreal Protocol since the 1990s as well as its contribution to the Climate Investment Funds (CIFS), since 2008 as part of its fast start contribution (Nakhooda, 2012).

- Canada reported its fast-start finance pledge of $1,217 (original pledge C$1,200) million as new and additional. Yet questions can be raised about whether its GEF $18.5 million contribution was anticipated prior to the signing of the Copenhagen Accord. The GEF amount is also unspecified as to its ultimate destination.

- Norway committed under its fast-start a total of $1,000 billion. Given Norway has fulfilled and exceeded its 0.7 per cent GNI target, can it then be assumed that all of this is new money? In Norway's report, it states that it was factoring its share of contribution to the GEF Trust Fund climate change focal area.

- Switzerland argues that its CHF 140 million ($162 million) is new and additional to Swiss climate financing and ODA of previous years. CHF 15 million of this contribution is earmarked for GEF climate change focal areas and the LDCF/SDCF.

- The UK's total contribution of £1500 is questioned by NGO's such as World Development who points out that portion that at least £430 of this was previously pledged in 2007 (World Development 2007 cited in WRI 2011).

A tentative assessment of the data extracted from country reports by the African Climate Policy Centre of the UN ECA argues that figures up to September 2011 indicate that less than $3 billion of fast-start finance are 'additional' (ACPC 2011). The ACPC examined additionality[1] from the perspective that 'financial resources raised for climate change should come in addition to funding developed countries provide towards progress in meeting their development aid commitment, i.e., the 0.7 per cent ODA commitment'.

There is much confusion about the extent to which the fast-start finance can be said to be successfully implemented. Though countries have complied with the reporting obligation as set out by the Cancún Decision, the reports are presented in a variety of formats, with different interpretations around the key parameter of new, additional. There is also confusion about support for regions as different countries present different regional classifications in their allocations framework thereby creating difficulty in cross regional comparison. Furthermore, countries do not always give transparent information about the instrument of delivery of financial mechanism. A clear and ambiguous distinction is the channel of distribution, this usually quite clearly specified, with a few exceptions. Ultimately, lack of clear and transparent information about how countries measure and allocate their fast-start contribution leads to problems in assessing the successful achievement of the fast-start finance across the critical areas of reference cited in the Cancún Decisions. This situation does not do much to reduce the trust deficit with regard to financing of climate change actions that already exists between developing countries and developed countries over the latter's obligation and commitment to transfer adequate and predictable finance to support developing countries' adaptation and mitigation actions.

Nonetheless, the Fast-Start experience at the mid-point points to a number of useful lessons for the way forward on long-term financing as well as for the successful operations of the new Green Climate Fund and the role of the Standing Committee. These critical lessons include:

- a workable common and agreed definition of what is new and additional finance;
- achieving some degree of clarity about the baseline to be used in assessing additionality;
- a common reporting framework or template that facilitate cross comparisons. This should include requirement for consistency in time period, committed and disbursed amounts, indications of past climate finance, shares of grants versus loans etc.;
- the need for accessible and user-friendly data.

The need for more than a centralized depository, which would seem to be the role of the current UNFCCC finance portal, but rather an objective third party, under the authority of, and accountable to, the Conference of the Party, to help process and analyze the reports in a manner such as the role of the OECD does for development finance.

In their ongoing deliberations on long-term finance, UNFCCC Parties must also take into account in their appraisal of FSF, the real concerns about some countries inveighing one or more of the following sleight-of-hand:

- re-packaging or re-labeling existing funds or previously pledged funds as new flows;
- double counting ODA/ climate finance;
- counting the full value of loans requiring payments as additional financing;
- conflating carbon market finance designed to meet developed countries' own mitigation commitments with financing for developing countries;
- counting the full value of funding through innovative mechanisms to which developing countries contribute; and

- conflating financing provided by developed countries with the financing they mobilized from public and private sources in developing countries.

These concerns, which arise from the nature of the flow of Fast-Start Finance, point to critical elements that must be institutionalized in order to build trust in Parties about the flow of medium and longer term finance for climate change activities. Primarily of course is the need for:

- a definition of new and additional finance;
- an agreed benchmark that allows for rigorous differentiation of new funds and new funding sources (IIED 2010);
- guidelines and criteria for what constitutes sources of eligible climate finance;
- more focused attention on sources of finance that do not have high incidence of burden on developing countries;
- a careful plan for how developed countries intend to realize the commitment to the goal of generating $100 billion by 2020. This should include details regarding the mix of public finance and innovative sources;
- guidelines and criteria for transparency on the remaining FSF flow, and medium and long-term finance;
- a process that leads towards an agreement on the aggregate scale of financial resources needed for adaptation and mitigation objectives;
- criteria for allocation between adaptation and mitigation, regions and countries; delivery mechanisms (UNFCCC focus, bilateral, multilateral etc. channels); forms of delivery and distinctions, such as grants and loans and proportion of concessional financing that is additional; and disbursement; and
- guidance towards a framework for assessing vulnerability,[2] under the Convention and for the purpose of allocating the flow of adaptation financing. Such a framework could be useful at local, national and regional levels.

Ultimately, real transparency and accountability will dictate a common reporting framework for all developed countries vis-à-vis Fast-Start Financing and long-term financing including the institutionalization of an independent third party process for verification and assessment.

4.3: Mending the mid term financing gap

Developing countries with one voice called for concrete specification of the nature and sources of filling the financing gaps to address climate change, which will emerge after the Fast-start Finance period ends in 2012. Developed countries insisted that developing countries will not 'fall off the cliff' as they are committed to financing beyond the 2012 period. Many developing countries countered that they were not so much interested in not falling down but in taking off and building up on the financing needed relatively to the growing set of obligations they have taken on and in helping them meet the challenge of deteriorating climate.

Developed countries also reacted cautiously to a suggestion by AOSIS (viewed favorably by a number of developing countries) for a political commitment to another round of three-year fast start financing as a concrete way of beginning to bridge the widening financing gap.

While the EU appears to be neutral to the AOSIS call for another 3 years fast start financing, the US was emphatic that fast start finance was a specific one-time commitment and would not set precedence. The EU said that with regard to the gap, 'we are not going to fall off a cliff'. It said that the EU had been clear and conscious that climate finance will be required for 2012 and beyond. It said that the EU will work towards a pathway for scaling-up finance to 2020 and that it recognized that public finance is important to the most vulnerable developing countries.

The EU said it was committed to providing its fair share of international public support as well as private and innovative finance. However, private finance will have to play a larger role. The EU said there will be a workshop on long-term finance (LTF) in July and another later in the year which will seek to de-mystify both LTF, public and private finance. The reports from these workshops will go to the COP.

The US also noted that the 2020 goal of mobilizing $100 billion was made in the context of meaningful mitigation actions for 2020. It said that there is symmetry between the finance provision and the mitigation provision for the year 2020. Thus, if developing countries want to have a mid-term finance target then it asked if they were willing to have a mid-term mitigation target?

Many developing countries noted that the $100 billion was inadequate and there were no concrete steps as to how it would be sourced.

The US also said that Fast-start Finance (FSF) was a one-time political commitment (COP 15). It does not set a precedent for increments of 3 year commitment periods. The US said that it was not comfortable with another three year second round of FSF start period (in reference to the Barbados proposal above). The US also noted that the 2020 goal of mobilizing $100 billion was made in the context of meaningful mitigation actions for 2020. It said that there is symmetry between the finance provision and the mitigation provision for the year 2020. Thus it said that if developing countries want to have a mid-term finance target then are they willing to have a midterm mitigation target? Lastly, the US said that though it welcomes the sharing of concerns, there were already two spaces for discussions: the Standing Committee and the Long Term Finance (LTF) work programme both of which have COP agenda items and hence the COP president can create contact group(s) for LTF. It said that these were the appropriate political space to discuss these matters hence there was no need for conclusions from the contact group on these matters. *Excerpted from TWN update.*

Notes

1   It is to be acknowledged that given the insufficiency and vagueness of data offering, determining additionality has to be undertaken with a great deal of caution. Hence the

figure offered here is to be taken as only an indicative reference where country indications are straightforward or explicit. Different researchers as well as contributing countries draw on different framework for determining additionality. Some cast a narrow and specific net while others work with a broad definition. Oxfam, for example, measures additionality as on top of pledged or planned development spending, in particular on top of 0.7 per cent target (where applicable). WRI researchers argue that 'additional refers to the idea that financial resources raised for one objective such as climate change should not substitute or divert funding from another important objective, in particular economic and social development'. Germany argues that 'additional is to the level of climate-related support in 2009 and/or derived from innovative financing mechanisms such as the auctioning of emission certificates in Germany. See also Annex 1 for comparison of additionality metrics.

2 A point also made by Ciplet *et al.*, 2011a.

APPENDIX 5

5.1 The global governance framework for adaptation (1992–2013)

A5.1: Convention articles

The Convention articles 4.1b, 4.1e, 4.1f, 4.4, 4.8 and 4.9
Decisions: 2001, 5/CP.7; 1/CP.10; 2/CP11;
1/CP.16 &-/CP.17

Key Frameworks:
- The Nairobi Work Programme 2005/2006 (2005–2010)
- The Buenos Aires Work Program
- The Cancún Adaptation Framework (2010)

Implementation of Adaptation under the Convention:
- National Adaptations Plan (since 2010)
- National Adaptation Programme of Action (since 2001)
- Adaptation Committee (2010/2011)

Funding Mechanisms (SBI):
- LDCF (2001)
- SCCF (2001)
- Adaptation Fund (2010)
- Green Climate Fund (2010 est.)

Scientific and technical aspect of adaptation: SABSTA

Funding, technology transfer: SBI

A5.2: Gender Equality, Adaptation and the Durban Outcomes

Outcome of the work of the Ad Hoc Working Group on Long-term Cooperative Action Draft Decision *[-/CP.17]*

III. Enhanced action on adaptation

Para 103. Encourages Parties to nominate experts to the Adaptation Committee with a diversity of experience and knowledge relevant to adaptation to climate change, while also taking into account the need to achieve gender balance in accordance with Decision 36/CP.7;

National adaptation plans Draft Decision [-/CP.17]

A. Framing national adaptation plans

Para 3. Further agrees that enhanced action on adaptation should be undertaken in accordance with the Convention, should follow a country-driven, gender-sensitive, participatory and fully transparent approach, taking into consideration vulnerable groups, communities and ecosystems, and should be based on and guided by the best available science and, as appropriate, traditional and indigenous knowledge, and by gender-sensitive approaches, with a view to integrating adaptation into relevant social, economic and environmental policies and actions, where appropriate;

Annex – Draft initial guidelines for the formulation of national adaptation plans by least developed country Parties

B. Elements of national plans 2. Preparatory elements

Para 3. In developing NAPs, consideration would be given to identifying specific needs, options and priorities on a country-driven basis, utilizing the services of national and, where appropriate, regional institutions, and to the effective and continued promotion of participatory and gender-sensitive approaches coordinated with sustainable development objectives, policies, plans and programmes.

Nairobi work programme on impacts, vulnerability and adaptation to climate change

Draft Decision [-/CP.17]

Para 4. Also requests the secretariat to organize, in collaboration with Nairobi work programme partner organizations and other relevant organizations, the following workshops, informed by the information contained in Annex I to the report of the Subsidiary Body for Scientific and Technological Advice on its thirty-fourth session and subsequent views of Parties, and to include indigenous and traditional knowledge and practices for adaptation and gender- sensitive tools and approaches as cross-cutting issues . . .

Compilation of gender equality texts (direct quotes from text) retained in the advance version of the Durban Outcome

Source: advance version of Durban Agreements, from December 11, 2011, Durban, South Africa. Compiled by Women Environment and Development Organization (WEDO) for Global Gender and Climate Alliance (GGCA)

A5.3: Gender and the Cancún Adaptation Framework

1. The Preamble;

2. Para 7. Recognizes the need to engage a broad range of stakeholders at the global, regional, national and local levels, be they government, including subnational and local government, private business or civil society, including youth and persons with disability, and that gender equality and the effective participation of women and indigenous peoples are important for effective action on all aspects of climate change; (Section I. A shared vision for long-term cooperative action).

3. Para 12. Affirms that enhanced action on adaptation should be undertaken in accordance with the Convention, should follow a country-driven, gender-sensitive, participatory and fully transparent approach, taking into consideration vulnerable groups, communities and ecosystems, and should be based on and guided by the best available science and, as appropriate, traditional and indigenous knowledge, with a view to integrating adaptation into relevant social, economic and environmental policies and actions, where appropriate; (Section II. Enhanced action on adaptation 12).

4. Para 72. Also requests developing country Parties, when developing and implementing their national strategies or action plans, to address, inter alia, the drivers of deforestation and forest degradation, land tenure issues, forest governance issues, gender considerations and the safeguards identified in paragraph 2 of appendix I to this decision, ensuring the full and effective participation of relevant stakeholders, inter alia indigenous peoples and local communities;

5. Para 130. Decides that capacity-building support to developing country Parties should be enhanced with a view to strengthening endogenous capacities at the subnational, national or regional levels, as appropriate, taking into account gender aspects, to contribute to the achievement of the full, effective and sustained implementation of the Convention.

Source: 1/CP.16 The Cancún Agreements: Outcome of the work of the Ad Hoc Working Group on Long-term Cooperative Action under the Convention. Decisions adopted FCCC/CP/2010/7/Add.1

A5.4: Gender and NAPs

II. National Adaptation Plans (NAPs)

Para 3) Further agrees that enhanced action on adaptation should be undertaken in accordance with the Convention, should follow a country-driven, gender-sensitive, participatory and fully transparent approach, taking into consideration vulnerable groups, communities and ecosystems, and should be based on and guided by the best available science and, as appropriate, traditional and indigenous knowledge, and by gender-sensitive approaches, with a view to integrating adaptation into relevant social, economic and environmental policies and actions, where appropriate Draft Decision -/CP.17 National adaptation plans (A: Framing NAPs) . . .

Annex: Initial guidelines for the formulation of national adaptation plans by least developed country Parties B. Elements of national adaptation plans. 2. Preparatory elements

Para 3. In developing NAPs, consideration would be given to identifying specific needs, options and priorities on a country-driven basis, utilizing the services of national and, where appropriate, regional institutions, and to the effective and continued promotion of participatory and gender-sensitive approaches coordinated with sustainable development objectives, policies, plans and programmes . . .

Para 4. Also requests the secretariat to organize, in collaboration with Nairobi work programme partner organizations and other relevant organizations, the following workshops, informed by the information contained in annex I to the report of the Subsidiary Body for Scientific and Technological Advice on its thirty-fourth session1 and subsequent views of Parties, and to include indigenous and traditional knowledge and practices for adaptation and gender-sensitive tools and approaches as cross-cutting issues:

Source: advance unedited version Draft Decision -/CP.17 Nairobi work programme on impacts, vulnerability and adaptation to climate change

5.2 Measuring the Cost of Adaptation

There are at least five different cost estimates for Adaptation Costs (Table 5.2 above). All of the different estimation results and so raised many questions:

> What are costs are assessed? How is the measurement determined? Why are they so different? Which would be the most appropriate to reference from the point of view of gender advocacy?

1. What are they really measuring (and why)?

First, these are estimated costs are not actual measurements. They are the result of 'costing exercises'. Second, the estimates are what it would cost countries to respond to climate change and climate variability such as extreme weather; the estimate of the additional annual investment and financial flow needed by a specific year to cover the cost of adapting to climate change and climate variability in five to six key areas in billion of dollar per year in present day values. Third, the reference year: 2015, 2020, 2030, 2050 or 2080. UNFCCC estimates are generally based on the year 2030. It follows TAR 2007 A1B scenario. Years may also differ for sectors: for example, water 2050, Coastal zone 2080 (see IPCC Technical summary of WG II). Fourth, the key sectors usually covered include agriculture, water supply, human health, coastal zones, infrastructure and the ecosystem (see below for details of sector coverage and exclusions). Fifth, these estimates do not cover the private cost of adaptation.

2. How are the estimates obtained?

The base of all the adaptation cost figures is a percentage of current investment that is climate sensitive plus a mark-up factor. The markup factor reflects the cost of 'climate-proofing' these investments. This means the cost of climate-proofing a number of different things: foreign direct investment flows, Gross National Income, Overseas Development Assistance Flows, disaster preparedness and poverty reduction targets. Estimates are based on different data sources including NAPAs (Oxfam) and Poverty Reduction Strategy (UNDP).

3. Why are they so different? Why are the ranges so large?

First, all of the estimates and methodology used have the same starting point: the World Bank approach of 2006. Second, they differ for at least four main reasons:

- the reference year chosen (2015, 2030 or other);
- the sectors included (fully or partially);
- the sector(s) excluded;
- the additional cost or investment needed for adaptation may be calculated differently by different studies. Key is the assumption about investment trends This influences the way investment is costed.

> For example, UNFCCC use the current trends of investment, but critics argue that current investment level is already too low, especially in Africa. It is too low to remove high levels of vulnerability to climate so the

UNFCCC underestimates the need to protect the poor. Alternatively, others such as UNDP, Oxfam and Project Catalyst (2010) assume elevated levels of investment to meet MDGs and protect the poor against vulnerability to climate change. They assume there is a need for higher levels of adaptation funding to meet the existing deficit in adaptation financing and investment. This adaptation deficit needs to be fully funded by fully funding development in order to ensure the achievement of sustainable and equitable development.

Third, the ranges are so large because of the role of infrastructure which can account for up to three-fourths of the costs.

4. What are the most important aspects of estimation elements from the point of view of gender advocacy?

From the point of view of gender it matters what is included or excluded. Underestimation can impact the real flow of funding for things that are important for the financing of gender equality interventions as well as non-gender equality interventions that are critical to women's and men's lives.

Agriculture: agriculture, forestry, fisheries (McCarl 2007). There are at least three distinct costs measured: 1) the extra capital investment at farm level (along the production chain – farms, transport, processing, etc.; 2) lines for better extension services at country level; and 3) the cost of additional global research (new cultivars). The need for gender sensitive approach to analysing item 2 in particular has been discussed in Chapter 3.

Human health: the extra preventive costs for three health issues/ based on the global burden of disease in 2030 (WHO-GDW McMichael *et al.*, 2004 and Cooper, 2006): 1) malnutrition; 2) malaria; and 3) diarrhoea. According to Kovats (2009), 'the total costs were estimated by taking the number of additional cases and multiplying them by the costs of prevention per child, obtained from the Disease Control Priorities in Developing Countries project' (this is based on World Bank 2006 methodology). The linkage to cost per child involves a significant underestimation bias (Ebi, 2007). This does not factor in the cost of women's health care. For example, the horrific situation of maternal health and morbidity issues should also be factored as threshold items along with the factors related to infant care. Accounting for these factors would raise the estimated cost of the health sector.

Currently, human health costs estimates do not include the following other health adaptations: 1) the costs of improving or modifying health protection systems (infrastructure, training new health care workers, increasing laboratory capacity); 2) the costs of heat wave warming systems; 3) the occupational health of care workers (impact by rising heat etc); and 4) the health resources in terms of climate change (see Box 6.3).

UNFCCC estimate health costs of $4–12 billion per year in 2030 (UNFCCC, 2007). The adaptation costs are for preventing the additional climate-change-related cases of diarrhoeal disease, malnutrition and malaria in 2030. The total costs were estimated by taking the number of additional cases and multiplying them by the costs of prevention per child, obtained from the Disease Control Priorities in Developing Countries project (World Bank, 2006).

Infrastructure: In 2006, the World Bank used insurance data to determine the share of climate sensitive investment. Apply increasing percentage on current infrastructural investment to get the additional costs for climate-proofing. Emphasis should be placed on housing and community infrastructure.

Water supply: Here also there is a tendency to overlook soft adaptation issues (such as using water more effectively) and focus on the effect of additional water demand and change in water supply up to 2030 (Kirshen, 2007; UNFCCC, 2007) and up to 2050 due to the long-term nature of investment needs in this area. Gender advocates should lobby on the basis of the higher adaptation cost figure. This is to assume elevated investment to cover adaptation deficit, promote sustainable and equitable development and to protect the poor. In this context, sufficient weight should be given to the value of 'soft' adaptation (such as using water more effectively) and hard adaptation (such as the expansion of a water supply system).

Note: Overall, the UNFCCC estimates underestimate adaptation costs by a factor of between 2 and 3 for included sectors. The UNFCCC's estimates are the equivalent of financing 2–3 Olympics; it is only double the current flow of ODA.

5. So which Adaptation cost figure should be the base of gender advocacy?

Probably not the UNFCCC Secretariat's, which is highly underestimated. The best of the current set of estimates from a gender and women's empowerment perspective would be the UNDP's much wider range, which includes the costing of PRS and disaster management and the second best would likely to be Oxfam's, which includes the costing from NAPA and NGO projects. UNEP's recent Adaptation Gap report, 2014, argues that adaptation may increase significantly beyond these earlier estimates. But ultimately, gender advocates should advocate on the basis of an evolved GEMCRA analysis for paying attention to women's health, maternal mortality, and women's time burden/stress. This would also include advocating for costs that cover all that negatively impact human welfare and not only those that are economically feasible or affordable within given budget costs.

APPENDIX 6

6.1: Key elements of GEF Roadmap on Gender Mainstreaming, 2011–2015

Mainstreaming gender in GEF project cycle, including gender analysis, gender screening, and gender sensitive indicators	*Mainstreaming gender in GEF programme strategies*	*Knowledge management and lessons sharing on gender*	*Mainstreaming ensures GEF agency compliance with the GEF policy on gender*	*Mainstreaming strengthens results-based management on gender mainstreaming*
Practical guidance for the implementation of the GEF Policy on Gender Mainstreaming: Secretariat to work with agency on application of gender analysis by the GEF Agencies at the project preparation phase[1]; development of project frameworks with gender sensitive outcomes and outputs; and gender-sensitive monitoring and evaluation for relevant projects. The Secretariat will prepare a simple and practical gender screening criteria and system at the project concept stage in coordination with the GEF Agencies.	Gender-sensitive approaches and activities incorporated in the GEF-6 focal area strategies GEF. Core gender indicators at the *corporate level*. Core gender indicators in *all focal areas and projects*. All will be monitored.	Interagency working group on gender mainstreaming, including the gender focal points of the Secretariat and GEF Agencies, and other experts, to advance gender mainstreaming in GEF operations and project platform to ensure effective operational coordination, exchange of information and experience among the GEF focal points of the GEF Agencies in relation to the GEF portfolio.[2] An interactive GEF webpage on gender mainstreaming will be developed to facilitate exchange of knowledge and lessons on gender	An assessment of the GEF Agencies on the GEF Policy on Gender Mainstreaming: Agencies met all minimum Requirements the development of a Practical guidance on gender mainstreaming that would apply across GEF Agencies. New entities that apply for accreditation as a GEF Project Agency, the GEF accreditation criteria require that all applicants demonstrate consistency with the minimum requirements of the policy with the same criteria as used to assess existing GEF Agencies.	Strengthen GEF-wide accountability for gender mainstreaming by enhancing gender-specific performance targets at all levels. Corporate level, the GEF Results-based management framework will include a set of core gender indicators to examine concrete progress on gender related processes and outputs. At the project level, the project results framework will include CORE gender-sensitive indicators, and sex-disaggregated data, for relevant projects. Monitored, analyzed, and reported on an annual basis through the AMR exercise and assessed and evaluated

Guidance will be provided on the use of gender-sensitive indicators for all relevant projects.

mainstreaming activities derived from specific programmes and projects.

through the Medium-term and Terminal Evaluations. Project Implementation Reports (PIR), Project Evaluation Reports, and other information from the GEF Agencies will provide important inputs to the analysis and reporting.

Review and mainstream gender in the Monitoring and Evaluation Policy

GEF will incorporate a specific section on gender mainstreaming in the templates and/or guidelines for the Project Identification Form (PIF), CEO Endorsement Request Form, Project Implementation Report, Mid-term Evaluation Report, Terminal Evaluation Report and other relevant documents.

Results Framework for Gender Mainstreaming in GEF Operations

GOAL: Achieve global environmental benefits and sustainable development through gender equality and empowerment of women.

OBJECTIVES:
- project design fully integrates gender concerns;
- project implementation ensures gender equitable participation in and benefit from project activities;
- project monitoring and evaluation give adequate attention to gender mainstreaming.

GENDER INDICATORS

1. Percentage of projects that have conducted gender analysis during project preparation;
2. Percentage of projects that have incorporated gender sensitive project results framework, including specific gender sensitive actions, indicators, targets, and/or budget;
3. Share of women and men as direct beneficiaries of project;
4. Number of national/regional/global policies, legislation, plans, and strategies that incorporate gender dimensions (e.g. NBSAP, NAPA, TDA/SAP, etc.);
5. Percentage of projects that have conducted gender analysis during project preparation.

---

1 In GEF-6, appropriate gender analysis will be undertaken by the GEF Agencies as part of the socio-economic assessment during project preparation, and it will be reviewed before CEO endorsement. Once under implementation, projects under different categories would be tracked and reported against on an annual basis through the AMR using information provided through the annual Project Implementation Reports and other tools.
2 This work will be done in coordination with similar working groups among the gender focal points of the Multilateral Development Banks and UN Agencies.

APPENDIX 7

7.1: Common Environment Finance tools and likely gender impacts

Financial Tools	Sustainable Agriculture	Protected areas	Sustainable forestry	Pro poor energy
Fees				
Loans	Rely on loans and subsidies. Very difficult for women to access both.	Rely on fees and PES. Upfront fees may be a draw back for women.	Rely on Fees and PES. Upfront fees may be a draw back for women.	Rely on loans and subsidies. Very difficult for women to access both.
PES				
MBM/CD;/VER	Rarely used by women			
Subsidies & Grants	Need to be extended to SMEs			
Taxes	Can have better gender disaggregated impact if progressively applied			

Source: adapted from UNDP 2012. MBM: market based mechanism, CDM: Clean development mechanism; VER: voluntary emission reduction; and PES: payment for ecosystem services.

7.2: Best practice example – The ADB gender categories for assessing and evaluation projects in the ADB portfolios

Category I (GEN)	Category II (EGM)	Category III (SGE)	Category IV (NGE)
Gender equity as a theme (GEN): (i) the project outcome directly addresses gender equality and/or women's empowerment by narrowing gender disparities through access to social services (e.g. education, health, and water supply/sanitation); and/or economic and financial resources and opportunities (e.g. employment opportunities, financial services, land, and markets), and/or basic rural and urban infrastructure (e.g. rural electrification, rural roads, pro-poor energy distribution, and urban services for the poor); and/or enhancing voices and rights (e.g. decision-making processes and structures, political empowerment, and grievance mechanisms); and, (ii) the outcome statement of the project design and monitoring framework explicitly mentions gender equality and women's empowerment and/or, the outcome performance indicators include gender indicators.	Effective gender mainstreaming (EGM): A project is assigned EGM if the project outcome is not gender equality or women's empowerment, but project outputs are designed to directly improve women's access to social services, and/or economic and financial resources and opportunities, and/or basic rural and urban infrastructure, and/or enhancing voices and rights, which contribute to gender equality and women's empowerment.	Some gender elements (SGE): a project is assigned 'some gender elements' if it meets either of the following: (i) by its nature it is likely to directly improve women's access to social services; and/or economic and financial resources and opportunities, and/or basic rural and urban infrastructure, and/or enhance their voices and rights (for example education, health, rural development, microfinance, water supply and sanitation, food security, and emergency food and rehabilitation assistance), but that included little, if any, gender analysis and few or no specific design features; and did not meet the EGM criteria, or (ii) is unlikely to directly improve women's access to social, economic or financial resources or opportunities, but significant efforts were made during project preparation to identify potential positive and negative impacts on women. Some gender features are included to enhance benefits to women (for example targets for employment of women in project construction work, provision of equal pay for equal work, information campaigns on HIV/AIDS risk, gender training of executing/implementing agencies, and adherence to core labor standards, especially child labor); and where resettlement is involved includes attention	No gender elements (NGE): a project is assigned 'no gender elements' when it does not include any gender design features.

continued …

7.2: Continued

Category I (GEN)	Category II (EGM)	Category III (SGE)	Category IV (NGE)
The requirements for projects with a GEN theme include: (i) gender analysis conducted during project preparation explicit gender equality and/or women's empowerment outcome(s) and/or gender-specific performance outcome indicators and activities in the project DMF; (iii) a gender action plan (GAP) with gender-inclusive design features, and clear gender targets and monitoring indicators, and/or components to directly benefit women or girls; (iv) inclusion of the GAP in the Report and Recommendation of the President to the Board (RRP) as a linked document and GAP included in the Project Administration Memorandum (PAM); (v) the RRP main text discusses how the project will contribute to improving women's access to or benefits from the project, at a minimum in the Poverty and Social subsection under the Due Diligence section (vi) a covenant or a condition in the policy matrix to support implementation of the GAP or gender-design features.	Requirements for projects with an EGM classification include: (i) the social analysis conducted during project preparation included careful consideration of gender issues highlighting both constraints and opportunities; (ii) specific gender design features are included in the majority5 of project outputs and/or components to facilitate and ensure women's participation and access to project benefits. Most of these outputs/components should have at least 3 gender design features and targets. See examples of gender design features; (iii) gender targets and performance and monitoring indicators in the project DMF 6; a GAP is included as a linked document to the RRP and included in the related PAM; (iv) the RRP main text discusses how the project will contribute to improving women's access to or benefits from the project, at a minimum in the Poverty and Social subsection under the Due Diligence section and, (v) a covenant or a condition in the policy matrix to support implementation of the GAP.	to women in the mitigation/resettlement plans (such as compensation payments to both men and women, joint-ownership of replacement land/housing, restoration of livelihood initiatives for women, and so forth). No Requirements specified.	

Category I is based on ADB's *Project Classification System* (2009; p. 9, available in the ADB portal (http://pcs.asiandevbank.org/pcs-filesetup/). Categories II and III were developed

APPENDIX 8

8.1 Financial and non-financial barriers to women's business growth

Non-financial barriers constraint women SME growth	Financial barriers constraining women's SME growth (barriers to women entrepreneurs access to finance)	
Legal and regulatory environment or quality of infrastructure (this affects all businesses but have different effects on women's and men's businesses)	A. Characteristics of entrepreneurs/enterprise (firm size influence performance and credit worthiness:	B. Incentives tools available to FIs: reluctant to lend to early stage enterprises and start up high risks.
	1. Women tend to own smaller enterprises and informal businesses	Lend to clients whom they know well (credit officers risk averse vis-à-vis women entrepreneurs (they know little about them
Personal characteristics of the entrepreneurs. Differentials in: Education Management Training	Note: Male headed enterprises do not seem to face the same problems in growing smaller firms.	Client profile may not fit women entrepreneurs
Constraints within financial institutions: Little familiarity with cultural barriers preventing interest in female clients Financial infrastructure that limits incentives to reach out to more female clients (lack of credit bureaus or collateral registries)	2. Access to human capital and collateral impact access to loans (women are less likely to receive loans). Women tend to be the least educated entrepreneurs (World Bank, 2004, 2006, 2008)	

Women entrepreneurs say that:

Rehabilitated roads and tracks enabled them to travel farther (77 per cent)
Roads and tracks enabled them to travel more safely (67 per cent) and obtain additional income (43 per cent)

Source: result from Impact survey as noted in GPFI/IFC 2011 p.7 (see http://sitesources.world bank.org/INTGENDER/Resources/PeruRRPFINAL.pdg).

Other impediments: power interruption, limited transportation infrastructure, weak governance, red tape and crime. All these reduce the ability to produce goods and services and to get them to market. For example SMEs are less likely to have their own generators to cope with inconsistent power from the public grid, and are less able to have security services to address losses from crime. Bribes as a share of sales are greater for smaller firms. Since women entrepreneurs have disproportionately stronger presence among smaller business they are specifically affect by these limitation in investment climate.

Weak creditor's rights and lack of credit information can disproportionately affect women, especially if they have little or no collateral or control over assets.

Access to finance can also be blocked by formal gaps in legal capacity and property rights such as inability to enter contact in own name or control property within marriage or to receive equal share of assets in divorce on inheritance. Inability to get national identity document – often a precondition for transactions such as opening a back account.

8.2 Public-private partnerships

Public-private partnerships were developed in the late 1990s as the joint operation of projects between public entities (usually donor government development cooperation entities in the development cooperation arena) and private firms.[1] Through the persistent approach of European donors, PPPs are increasingly becoming a company feature in many low-income countries such as Ethiopia, Bangladesh, Congo, Laos, Madagascar, Malawi, Mali, Mozambique, Nepal, Tanzania and Uganda. There are numerous public-private partnerships in renewable energy that are projected to involve a large volume of private investment (de Nevers 2011). These include the Concentrating Solar Power (CPS)[2] projects in Algeria, Egypt, China, and South Africa etc. Global Climate Partnership Fund (German government and KfW state development bank (seeking to leverage $100 million into $500 million for debt finance to low carbon projects in emerging and middle-income countries (Brown and Jacobs, 2011); and the climate public Private Partnership Fund (CP3) to foster low carbon investment in developing countries.[3]

'Public-private partnership' was coined in 1970s in the US. The mechanism of public-private cooperation was implemented in the UK as Private Finance Initiatives in the 1980s involved in highway construction, mass-transit development, airports etc. It has been widely in use in Europe since the 1990s. It signals cooperation between the private and the public sectors. In Europe, PPPs were active first in infrastructure such as waste disposal. Now they are also involved in transport, health and education. PPP mechanisms in the form of public-private facility began to appear in the development cooperation arena by BMZ by 1996. By 2002 there were 62 projects in sub-Saharan Africa:

- one-fourth in South Africa
- 50 per cent in HIPC
- 40 per cent in African LDCs (Ethiopia, Uganda, Tanzania, DRC)

Some middle-income developing countries are also beginning to explore public-private partnerships as a means for 'effectively sharing relevant risks between the public and private sectors and have a critical role in promoting key investment in large scale infrastructure and clean energy.[4] The South Africa Renewables Initiative (SARI), led by the Department of Public Enterprise and focus on securing funding for its Renewable Energy Feed-in-Tariff, REFIT policy mechanism found that financing gap between the BAU energy tariff and REFIT of 20 per cent in 2020. This gap will need to be financed primarily by (international) public finance resources as there are limited domestic consumers and private sectors to fill it. The expectation is that the funding will come from developed countries as the private sector will not 'invest sufficiently to enable the scaling up of renewable energy. This funding may leverage the private sector support for renewable energy.

PPPs are often praised as the 'best of both worlds' (between public provisioning and private provisioning) and generators of co-investment. But the success of PPP, with its multiple forms and varied funding mechanisms,[5] as a strategy for harnessing the participation of the private sector in development finance has not been fully evaluated. The German Development Institute found that PPPs in Germany have a questionable impact in terms of value for money. In many cases, the private sector reaped 'windfall effects', meaning that they benefitted from profits but actually contributed little to development schemes. Public funding creates a developmental value, which, without the state contribution, is not in reasonable proportion to the developmental benefit. There is also some scepticism about the operation of public-private partnership in poor countries. The German evaluation of German PPP pointed out that German companies prefer 'threshold countries (with safe and big markets) for PPP, not poor countries. Third, PPP are also seen as an alternative method of procurement and are accused of distorting competition. In the latter case, it is argued that PPPs have dominant position relative to local partners in the host economies.[6]

In the UK many PPPs have been found to deliver on time (70 per cent of 114 PPPs, National Audit Office). The mechanism also appears to be highly regarded in Australia and Canada vis-à-vis traditional procurement. However, PPPs are not equally suited to all projects and there can be problems with the over monetization of public assets with these mechanisms. PPPs seems best suited to large scale projects as they involve substantial transactions costs and/or government underwriting which may detract from the claims that it is a good way to transfer risks to private sector partners.

An emerging lesson from PPPs in the development arena and now in climate finance is that what matters most to firms (especially when contemplating investments which are inherently long-lived such as investing in RE and energy efficiency equipment) is stability in regulatory and financial policies and procedures. As noted by the International Chamber of Commerce, '(i)nstitutional structures should help facilitate and enhance private sector capital flow but the key driver is business opportunity which also drives research & development investment'.

478 Appendix 8

To sum up, while PPP may be help to expedite projects and valorise public assets, therefore apparently lessening the strain on the public purse, they are not a panacea and within the context of the GCF will not help to promote greater capitalization. The support for PPPs hence should be a matter left to the national level and should take place in the context of significant gender, social and environmental impact assessments.

Notes

1 See note 9 on page 398 regarding PPPs.
2 The GEF notes that CSP investments in developing countries have had limited success in the past.
3 An initiative involving P8 (12 of the world's largest sovereign wealth funds and pension funds focused on climate related investments); the UK-DFID; the ADB and the IFC dedicated to promoting private sector investment in low carbon infrastructure in developing countries. CP3 brings together private investors and the MDBs to foster investment; the UK Government's Capital Market Climate Initiative (CMCI) also aims at promoting private sector finance for low carbon investment.
4 Countries with national public private policy include: India, Tanzania, Ghana and Angola.
5 For example, PPP as DBO (designed-build-finance-operated and control), ppp-joint venture, public outsourcing-GOCO (government owned and control).
6 In other words, many SMEs are simply co-financed through the development cooperation budget.
7 Equivalent to 0.32 per cent of DAC's combined GNI. DAC members are still far away from meeting the target agreed at Gleneagles. (Denmark, Luxembourg, the Netherlands, Norway and Sweden continued to exceed the United Nations ODA target of 0.7 per cent of GNI). In 2010, the United States, the United Kingdom, France, Germany and Japan were the largest donors of official development assistance (ODA) in terms of volume. EU countries that are members of the DAC provided a combined total of USD 70.2 billion, representing 54 per cent of total net ODA provided by DAC donors. OECD http://oecd.org/document/29/0,3746,en_21571361_44315115_47519517_1_1_1_1,00.html

APPENDIX 9

Progress on the fund-wide sensitization of the Green Climate Fund

At its Ninth Board Meeting, held in Songdo, South Korea, the board of the GCF adopted an interim Gender Policy and Gender Action Plan, which is to be reviewed in three years time.

AGENDA ITEM 23: GENDER POLICY AND ACTION PLAN

22. The Board adopted the following decision: *DECISION B.09/11*

The Board, having considered document GCF/B.09/10 Gender Policy and Action Plan:

(a) *Adopts the gender policy proposed in Annex XIII, acknowledging the progress made in advancing gender balance and gender equality within the context of climate change policies and in line with individual country circumstances, when applying said policy;*
(b) *Also adopts the gender action plan as contained in Annex XIV;*
(c) *Requests the Secretariat to take the necessary measures in order to expedite the implementation of the policy and action plan; and*
(d) *Also requests the Secretariat's Gender and Social Development Specialist to conduct a review of the gender policy and action plan, in consultation with the civil society organizations accredited with the Fund, and to submit an updated version of both by the twelfth meeting of the Board. Members of the Board are invited to submit their comments or additional proposals regarding the current policy and action plan by the tenth meeting of the Board. GCF 2015*, Decisions of the Board – Ninth Meeting of the Board, 24–26 March 2015

Below is a very tentative reflection on the key components of these instruments (referred to as *Annex XIII and Annex XIV*) as were presented by Secretariat of the GCF as the Gender Policy and Action Plan GCF/B.09/10 4 March, 2015.

I. Summary review of the Gender Policy and Gender Action Plan

The Gender Policy and Gender Action Plan are consistent with and the attempt to implement the Board's mandate from the GCF's Governing Instrument to undertake fund-wide gender sensitisation (including its administrative policies and operational modalities, and gender balance).

A. **The Gender Policy** constitutes the overriding policy framework —rationale, objectives, principles and highlights elements of its implementation framework that will guide future board decisions as well of the actions of the Secretariat personnel policies and programme staff work in assessing and evaluating the implementation of the fund's internal and external operation.

Overarching objective: Commitment to contributing to gender equality and equity.

The Gender Policy has six principles:

i. Three-fold commitment: understand gender and climate change issues; adopt tools and method to promote gender equality and reduce gender disparity in climate funding: and measure the outcomes and impacts of the GCF's activities on women's and men's resilience to climate change.
ii. Comprehensive scope and coverage: covers all of the Fund's climate funding activities.
iii. Accountability of all entities that carries out the GCF's mission for gender results; and a redress mechanism for gender-related compliance and grievances.
iv. Country Ownership: working through national designated authorities (NDAs) and focal points – be in alignment with national gender policies and priorities as well as the GCF's gender policy (readiness and preparatory support are to be made available to NDAs and FPs in this context).
v. Competencies: gender balance in all funds operations; secretariat in-house gender expertise at senior staff level; gender and climate expertise in all committees, especially the Accreditation Panel, the Investment Committee, the Risk Management Committee, and the Private Sector Advisory Group (PSAG).
vi. Resource Allocation of the Fund should contribute to gender equality and women's empowerment (including, targeted funding to support women's climate change adaptation and mitigation initiatives).

With the approval of this policy the GCF is now the first such fund of its type to begin its operation with a full-fledged gender equity sensitized approach to climate finance.

Potential desirable areas for strengthening the gender policy:

- Greater attention to women's and men's role in both contributing to addressing climate change and how to better enhance their adaptation, resilience and mitigation responses as actors in communities and the nations—male and female farmers, male and female business owners, especially as Micro, small and medium-sized firms.
- Greater and more deepened discussion on the accountability of the Secretariat and the board for gender-sensitive/equitable output and outcomes.

B. **The Gender Action Plan (GAP)** is for an initial three-year period, 2015–2017 to enable the implementation framework for actions for the operationalization of the gender policy.

The Gender Action Plan has six priority areas:

i. Governance and institutional structure:

- *The Board* approves the Gender Policy, oversees and reviews implementation of the gender action plan at least one per year
- Operational responsibility of the gender policy lies with the accredited entities—implementing entitles (IEs) and intermediaries
- NDAs verify through a no-objections procedure that project proposals are align with countries' gender policies and climate change policies

Secretariat

- Liaise with IEs and intermediaries and provide periodic monitoring and progress reports to the board
- A senior social development and gender specialist in the Country Programming Division will have operational responsibility to manage and implement the Gender Policy and action plan.

The Evaluation Unit provides impact evaluation reports to the board and the Redress mechanism provides reports to the board.

ii. Operational guidelines: guidelines, including socio economic and gender assessments/environmental and social safe-guard (ESS), will be issued to external partners—NDAs and accredited entities and will apply to all the fund's internal activities and entities.
iii. Capacity building: gender training for board and staff.
iv. Outputs, outcomes, impacts and 'paradigm-shifting objectives for monitoring, reporting and evaluation: two specific portfolios are proposed—1) X per cent of adaptation & mitigation (A&M) projects that include gender elements and gender-sensitive implementation arrangement; and 2) portfolio classification system consisting of a project rating at entry for gender sensitivity in order to allow for a global analysis of the portfolio from a gender perspective, effective assessment and proposed corrective action.

v. Resource allocation and budgeting: project approval may consider giving additional weight to projects with well-designed gender elements.
vi. Knowledge generation and communications:

- Documentation of acquisition of knowledge and experiences from the implementation of the GAP;
- Identification of good practices from countries and accredited entities;
- Support knowledge exchanges on gender and climate change finance.

The gender sensitized approach is also to be integrated *a priori* into:

- The results management framework;
- Adaptation and mitigation performance measurement framework;
- The accreditation process;
- The Environmental and social safeguards system;
- All compliance system with regard to project and programme cycle activity;
- Evaluation of impacts and processes;
- Initial investment framework and gender sensitive development impacts.

Tentative Gender and Civil Society and some board members' expectations and anticipated deliverables in the further implementation of both the Gender Policy and the Gender Action Plan are in three broad areas:

Technical requirements:

- Gender disaggregate data;
- Gender indicators (for results and portfolio monitoring);
- Periodic auditing of gender sensitive results (for adjusting policies and accountability and enhancing implementation).

Personnel requirements: Gender and Social Development Specialist to be appointed.

Financing requirements: dedicated budgets for gender-related activities.

II. Strengths and weaknesses of the GAP

Strengths:

- The plan is being put in place at the inception of the fund;
- The plan will be reviewed and adjusted periodically;
- Projects (especially from national entities) will have supporting capacity building and readiness support for NDAs, implementing entities and etc.
- Plan is to be implemented and monitored by GCF and external partners in alignment with the national gender policies and priorities and countries'

climate change programme, (emphasis on country ownership, incentives and not conditionalities or punitive).

Weakness:

- Accountability: the accountability for gender equality outcome must be centred at the fund level, not outsourced to external partners;
- Responsibility for implementing and monitoring the GAP will require more of a team focus, where lead staff are high level and report to the director/or CEO level so as not to have gender issues become marginalised in the fund;
- Administrative and operational guidelines need to be more clear and oriented towards measureable effectiveness. For example. Indicators need to be more specific, rigorous and focused. It must go beyond simply featuring multiple generic toolkits to pinpoint specific indicators for adaptation, mitigation, and technology. Work may have to be commissioned in this regard to meet the fund's paradigm shifting and fit-for-purpose characterization;
- The Indicators highlighted in the GAP as output, outcomes and impact monitoring indicators and reporting indicators are both vague and weak. These should not be taken carte blanche but only as indicative. Much more work needs to be done on this; and
- Resource allocation and budget is underspecified.

BIBLIOGRAPHY

Abele, C. (2008) *CDM Market Brief: PR China.* Cologne: German Office of Foreign Trade. Available at www.gtai.de/DE/Content/__SharedDocs/Anlagen/PDF/CDM/cdm-markt-china-endfassung-english,property=publicationFile.pdf?show=true (accessed 25 March 2009).

Abuaku, B.K., J. Zhou, X. Li, S. Li, A. Liu, T. Yang and H. Tan (2009) Morbidity and mortality among populations suffering floods in Hunan, China: the role of socioeconomic status. *Journal of Flood Risk Management* 2(3): 222–8.

ACCES (2010) *Climate Change and Security in Africa.* Vulnerability Discussion Paper. Available at www.africa-eu-partnership.org/sites/default/files/doc_climate_vulnerability_discussion_paper.pdf (accessed 5 September 2011).

Ackerman, A. (2008) *Carbon Markets and Beyond: The Limited Role of Prices and Taxes in Climate and Development Policy.* Stockholm Environment Institute and Tufts University. G-24 Discussion Paper no. 53. Stockholm: Stockholm Environment Institute.

Ackerman, F. (2009) *Financing for Climate Investments.* Washington, DC: Inter-governmental Group of Twenty-four (G-24).

Ackerman, F., Kozul-Wrigth, R. and Vos. R. (eds) (2012) *Climate Protection and Development.* New York: Bloomsbury Academic.

ACPC (African Climate Policy Centre) (2011) *Report on 'Fast Start Finance' United Nations Economic Commission for Africa,* Addis Ababa.

Actionaid (2007) *Compensation for Climate Change: Principles and Lessons for Equitable Adaptation Funding.* London: Actionaid.

Adams, L., Zusman, E., Sorkin, L. and Harms, N. (2014) *Effective. Efficient. Equitable. –Making Climate Finance Work for Women.* Gender and Climate Finance Policy Brief. Mandaluyong City: Asian Development Bank.

ADB (2005) *ADB Climate-Proofing: A Risk-based Approach to Adaptation 2005.* Mandaluyong City: Asian Development Bank.

ADB 2007 *Energy For All: Addressing The Energy, Environment, And Poverty Nexus In Asia.* Mandaluyong City: Asian Development Bank

ADB (2008) *Asia's Urban Challenges.* Mandaluyong City: Asian Development Bank. Available at www.adb.org/documents/events/2008/adb-urban-day2008/presentation-Climate-Change.pdf.

ADB (2012a) *ADB Guidelines for Gender Mainstreaming Categories of ADB Projects.* Mandaluyong City: Asian Development Bank.
ADB (2012b) *Learning Lessons: ADB's Response to Natural Disasters and Disaster Risks September Independent Evaluation 2012.* Mandaluyong City: Asian Development Bank.
ADB (2012c) *Gender and Development Plan of Action (2008–12) 2011.* Performance Summary. Mandaluyong City: Asian Development Bank.
ADB (2012d) *Gender Tool Kit: Energy – Going Beyond the Meter.* Mandaluyong City: Asian Development Bank.
Africa Group 2012 cited in UNFCCC: FCCC/WAGLCA/2012/CRP.2
African Development Bank (2003) *Poverty and Climate Change Reducing the Vulnerability of the Poor through Adaptation.* Tunis-Belvedère: AfDB.
African Development Bank (2011) *The Cost of Adaptation to Climate Change in Africa.* Tunis-Belvedère: AfDB.
African Progress Panel (2010) *Finance for Climate-Resilient Development in Africa.* Africa Progress Panel Policy Brief. Available at www1.uneca.org/Portals/adfvii/documents/Resources/APP-Finance%20for%20Climate%20Resilient%20Development%20in%20Africa_EN.pdf.
African Union (2010) *The Private Sector Responds to Climate Change.* Issue paper 11, Seventh African Development Forum. Addis Abba, Ethiopia: African Union, African Development Bank, Economic Commission for Africa.
African Water Strategy, *African Water Facility*, Tunis: African Development Bank.
Agarwal, B. (1995) *Gender, Environment and Poverty Interlinks in Rural India: Regional Variations and Temporal Shifts, 1971–1991.* Geneva: UNRISD.
AGF (2010) *Report of the Secretary-General's High-level Advisory Group on Climate Change Financing 5 November 2010.* New York: UN.
Aghion, B.A.D. and Morduch, J. (2003) Microfinance beyond group lending. *Economics of Transition* 8: 401–20.
Agrawal, A. (2001) Common Property Institutions and Sustainable Governance of Resources. *World Development* 29(10): 1649–72.
Agrawal, A. (2003) Common Property Institutions and Sustainable Governance of Resources: Context Methods and Politics. *World Development* 29(10): 1649–72.
Agrawal, A. (2005) *Environmentality: Technologies of Government and the Making of Subjects.* Durham, NC: Duke University.
Agrawal, A. (2008) *The Role of Local Institutions in Adaptation to Climate Change: Social Dimensions of Climate Change.* Washington, DC: World Bank.
Agrawala, S. and Fankhauser, S. (eds) (2008) *Economic Aspects of Adaptation to Climate Change. Costs, Benefits and Policy Instruments.* Paris: OECD.
Aguilar, A. (2007) *Reforestation, Afforestation, Deforestation, Climate Change and Gender.Fact Sheet.* Costa Rica: IUCN.
Aguilar, L., Blanco, M. and Dankelman, I. (2007) *The Absence of Gender Equity in the Discussions on the International Regime on Access and Benefit Sharing.* Discussion document for the Eighth Meeting of the Conference of the Parties to the Convention on Biological Diversity. Gland: International Union for Conservation and Nature.
Aguilar, L., Rogers, F., Pearl-Martinez, R., Castaneda, I., Athanas, A. and Siles, J. (2012) *Gender Review of the Climate Investment Funds.* Washington, DC: CIFs.
Alboher, S. (2009) The Clean Development Mechanism: Ensuring Equitable Access for Women. MA Thesis. Brandeis University, Heller School for Social Policy and Management.
Allderdice, A. (2008) Microenergy Credits Corporation: Catalyzing Clean Energy For The Bop *Augustine, G 2008, April 18* http://csi.gsb.stanford.edu/microenergy-credits-corporation-catalyzing-clean-energy-bop

Allen, M.R., Frame, D.J., Huntingford, C., Jones, C.D., Lowe, A.J., Meinshausen, M. and Meinshausen, N. (2009) Warming caused by cumulative carbon emissions towards the trillionth tonne. *Nature* 458: 1163–6.

Allen, M.R., Frame, D., Frieler, K., Hare, W., Huntingford, C., Jones, C., Knutti, R., Lowe, J., Meinshausen, M., Meinshausen, N. and Raper, S. (2009). The exit strategy. *Nature Reports Climate Change* 30 April: 56–8.

Allison, I., Bindoff, N.L., Bindschadler, R.A., Cox, P.M., de Noblet, N., England, M.H., Francis, J.E., Gruber, N., Haywood, A.M., Karoly, D.J., Kaser, G., Le Quéré, C., Lenton, T.M., Mann, M.E., McNeil, B.I., Pitman, A.J., Rahmstorf, S., Rignot, E., Schellnhuber, H.J., Schneider, S.H., Sherwood, S.C., Somerville, R.C.J., Steffen, K., Steig, E.J., Visbeck, M., Weaver, A.J. (2009) *The Copenhagen Diagnosis, 2009: Updating the World on the Latest Climate Science*. Climate Change Research Centre (CCRC). Sydney: The University of New South Wales.

Alston, M. (2011) Gender and climate change in Australia. *Journal of Sociology* 47(1): 53–70.

Alston, M. and K. Whittenbury (2013) *Research, Action and Policy: Addressing the Gendered Impacts of Climate Change*. Dordrecht, Netherlands: Springer Science.

Amarakoon, D., Chen, A. and Taylor, M. (2003) Climate Variability and dengue in the Caribbean. *AIACC Notes* 2: 8.

Ambrose, S. and Muchhala, B. (2010) *Financial Crisis Generated Significant Support: Using Special Drawing Rights for public investment to promote developments*. Third World Network.

AMCEN (2011) *Road to Durban 2011: Overview of Key Elements in the Negotiations*. AMCEN/SS/IV/EG/2. African Ministerial Conference on the Environment.

Ameen, F. (2004) Loan repayment in the Grameen Bank: The importance of borrower opportunity cost and gender. In I. Hasan and W.C. Hunter (eds), *Research in Banking and Finance 5: Bank and Financial Market Efficiency: Global Perspectives*, pp. 109–36. Bingley: JAI Press.

Americano, B. (2008) CDM in Brazil: Towards structural change for sustainable development in some sectors. In K. Olsen and J. Fenhann (eds), *A Reformed CDM – Including New Mechanisms for Sustainable Development*. Nairobi: UNEP-Risø Centre.

Anastario, M., N. Shebab, and L. Lawry (2009) Increased gender-based violence among women internally displaced in Mississippi 2 years post-Hurricane Katrina. *Disaster Medicine and Public Health Preparedness* 3(1): 8–26.

Andah, W., N. van de Giesen, A. Huber-Lee and C. Biney (2004) Can we maintain food security without losing hydropower? The Volta Basin. In J. Cayford (ed.) *Climate Change in Contrasting River Basins: Adaptation Strategies for Water, Food and Environment*, pp. 181–94. Wallingford: CABI Publishing.

Anderson, D. (2009) Enduring drought then coping with climate change: Lived experience and local resolve in rural mental health. *Rural Society* 19(4): 340–52.

Anderson, K. (2012) Climate change going beyond dangerous – Brutal numbers and tenuous hope. In *Climate, Development and Equity: What Next?* Volume III. Development Dialogue no. 16, September. Uppsala: Dag Hammarskjöld Foundation.

Annecke, W. (no date) *Gender and Climate Change Adaptation*. Available at http://r4d.dfid.gov.uk/pdf/outputs/climatechange/adaptationandbeyond04small.pdf.

Antonopoulos, R. (2009) *The Current Economic and Financial Crisis: A Gender Perspective*. Working Paper no. 562. New York: Levy Economics Institute.

Antonopoulos, R. (2013) *Expanding Social Protection in Developing Countries: A Gender Perspective*. New York: Levy Economics Institute.

Antonopoulos, R. and Floro, M.S. (2008) *Asset Ownership Along Gender Lines: Evidence from Thailand*. New York: Levy Economics Institute.

Arend, E. and Lowman, S. (2011) *Governing Climate Funds: What Will Work for Women?* Washington, DC: Gender Action.

Bibliography

Armendáriz de Aghion, B. and Morduch, J. (2005) *The Economics of Microfinance*. Cambridge, MA: MIT.

Arndt, C., R. Benfica, and J. Thurlow (2011) Gender implications of biofuels expansion in Africa: the case of Mozambique. *World Development* 39(9): 1649–62.

Arora-Jonsson, S. (2011) Virtue and vulnerability: Discourses on women, gender and climate change. *Global Environmental Change* 21(2): 744–51.

Assuncão, J. and Chein Freis, F. (2009) *Climate Change, Agricultural Productivity and Poverty*. Rio de Janeiro: PUC-Riol.

Athanasiou, T. and Bear, P. (2005) Where we stand: Honesty about dangerous climate change and about preventing it. *Foreign Policy in Focus*, 7 December.

Atteridge, A., Kehler Siebert, C., Klein, R.J.T., Butler, C. and Tella, P. (2009) *Bilateral Finance Institutions and Climate Change: A Mapping of Climate Portfolios*. Stockholm: Stockholm Environment Institute.

Aubé, M., Centenera, B. and Bedson, J. (2008) *Future of Micro-finance in Asia*. Discussion Paper. Available at www.bwtp.org/files/Events/AMF2008/Reference%20Documents/Future%20of%20Micro-finance%20in%20Asia%20-%20Discussion%20Paper.pdf.

Augustine, G. (2008) *MicroEnergy Credits Corporation: Greening the Base of the Pyramid*. Available at www.worldchanging.com/archives/007982.html (accessed 1 May 2011).

Bacheva, F., Kochladze, M. and Dennis, S. (2006) *Boom-Time Blues: Big Oil's Gender Impacts in Azerbaijan, Georgia, and Sakhalin*. Washington, DC: CEE Bankwatch Network, Gender Action.

Baden, S. (1996) *Gender Issues in Financial Liberalisation and Financial Sector Reform*. Brighton: Institute of Development Studies, University of Sussex.

Bakker, I. (ed.) (1994) *The Strategic Silence: Gender and Economic Policy*. London: Zed Press.

BalaNath, M. (2002) *Financing Sustainable Economic Development in Asia*. Conference on 'Gender Budgets, Financial Markets, Financing for Development', 19 and 20 February. Berlin: Heinrich-Boell Foundation.

Barber, M.B. and Odean, T. (2001) Boys will be boys: Gender, overconfidence, and common stock investment. *Quarterly Journal of Economics* February: 261–91.

Bardallo, M. (2008) *Malaria and Maternal Mortality: Access of Women to Malaria Prevention and Treatment*. German Foundation for World Population (DSW).

Bardasi, E.C., Blackden, M. and Guzman, J.C. (2007) *Gender, Entrepreneurship, and Competitiveness in Africa*i Africa Competitiveness Report 2007. Washington, DC: World Bank.

Barnett, B.J., Barrett, C.B., Carter, M.R., Chantarat, S., Hansen, J.W., Mude, A. G., Osgood, D.E., Skees, J.R., Turvey, C.G. and Ward, M.N. (2007) *Poverty Traps and Climate and Weather Risk Limitations and Opportunities of Index-based Risk Financing*. IRI Technical Report # 07–03.Lexington, KY: International Research Institute for Climate and Society.

BASIC (2011) *Equitable Access to Sustainable Development: Contribution to the Body of Scientific Knowledge*. Beijing, Brasilia, Cape Town, Mumbai: BASIC Expert Group.

Bäthge, S. (2010) Climate Change and Gender: Economic Empowerment of Women through Climate Mitigation and Adaptation. Bonn: Deutsche Gesellschaft für Technische Zusammenarbeit (GTZ).

BBC (2005) South Asian heat. *BBC*, 6 June.

Beckerman, W. and Pasek, J. (1995) The equitable international allocation of tradable carbon emission permits. *Global Environmental Change* 5: 405–13.

Behrman, J., R. Meinzen-Dick, and A. Quisumbing (2012) The gender implications of large-scale land deals. *Journal of Peasant Studies* 39(1): 49–79

Bell, M.L., D.L. Davis, L.A. Cifuentes, A.J. Krupnick, R.D. Morgenstern, and G.D. Thurston (2008a) Ancillary human health benefits of improved air quality resulting from climate change mitigation. *Environmental Health* 7: 41.

Bell, M.L., M.S. O'Neill, N. Ranjit, V.H. Borja-Aburto, L.A. Cifuentes, and N.C. Gouveia (2008b) Vulnerability to heat-related mortality in Latin America: A case-crossover study in Sao Paulo, Brazil, Santiago, Chile and Mexico City, Mexico. *International Journal of Epidemiology* 37(4): 796–804.

Bellamy Foster, J. and Clark, B. (2012) The planetary emergency. *Monthly Review*, 10 December.

Below, T.B., K.D. Mutabizi, D. Kirschke, C. Franke, S. Siebert and K. Tscherning (2012) Can Farmers' adaptation to climate change be house-hold level variables? *Global Environmental Change* 22(1): 223–35.

Benn, J. (2011) *Climate Finance: OECD DAC Reporting Framework*. September. Paris: OECD. Available at www.oecd.org/env/cc/48762203.pdf.

Bernard, C. (2015) Sustainable Development and Social Planning, Planning Institute of Jamaica. Presentation on the panel 'Preparing and implementing a programmatic approach to climate resilience'. Montego Bay, Jamaica: CIF 2014 Partnership Forum.

Bhatt, N. and Tang, S.Y. (2002) Determinants of repayment in microcredit: Evidence from programs in the United States. *International Journal of Urban and Regional Research* 26: 360.

Biagini, B. (2014) Mainstreaming Gender in the GEF: Good Practices *from the* Climate Change Adaptation Portfolio UNFCCC Climate Talks – June 2011, Bonn, Germany. Available at: www.google.com/?gws_rd=ssl#q=Biagini+%2B+as+of+April+2009+38+countries+mention+gender+in+their+NAPAs.

Biermann, F. (2000) The case for a world environment organization. *Environment* 42(9): 22–31.

Biermann, F. and Simonis, U.E. (1998) *A World Environment and Development Organization: Functions, Opportunities, Issues, Development and Peace Foundation (SEF)*. Bonn: SEF.

Biermann, F. and Simonis, U.E. (1999) The multilateral ozone fund: A case study on institutional learning. *International Journal of Social Economics* 26: 239–73.

Bird, N., Beloe, T., Ockenden, S., Corfee-Morlot, J. and Sáni Zou (2013) *Understanding Climate Change Finance Flows and Effectiveness: Mapping of Recent Initiatives 2013 Update*. London: Overseas Development Institute.

Bird, N., Beloe, T., Hedger, M., Lee, J., Nicholson, K., O'Donnell, K. and Steele, P. (2012) DRAFT. *The Climate Public Expenditure and Institutional Review (CPEIR): Developing a Methodology to Review Climate Policy, Institutions and Expenditure*. New York: UNDP/CDDE/ODI.

Birk, G. (2000) *Owners of the Forest: Natural Resource Management by the Bolivian Chiquitano Indigenous People*. Santa Cruz, Bolivia: APCOB/CICOL.

Blackden, M.C. and Wodon, Q. (eds) (2006) *Gender, Time Use, and Poverty in Sub-Saharan Africa*. Working Paper no. 73. Washington, DC: World Bank.

Blessings, C., L. Jumbe and A. Angelsen (2006) Do the poor benefit from devolution policies? Evidence from Malawi's forest co-management program. *Land Economics* 82(4): 562–81.

Bloomberg (2011) Secret Fed loans gave banks $13 billion undisclosed to Congress. Available at www.bloomberg.com/news/2011-11-28/secret-fed-loans-undisclosed-to-congress-gave-banks-13-billion-in-income.html.

Bloomberg (2013) Private Equity Flees Clean Energy as Investment Falls. Available at www.bloomberg.com/news/articles/2013-01-15/private-equity-flees-clean-energy-as-investment-falls-energy.

Bloomberg New Energy Finance (2014) Fossil fuel divestment: A $5 trillion challenge. Available at http://about.bnef.com/white-papers/fossil-fuel-divestment-5-trillion-challenge (accessed 6 August 2014).

Bohra-Mishra, B. and Confalonieri, U.E.C. (2011) Environmental degradation and out-migration: evidence from Nepal. In Piguet, E., Pécoud, A. and de Guchteneire, P. (eds), *Migration and Climate Change*, pp. 74–101. Rome: UNESCO.

Boisson de Chazournes, Laurence. 2003. The GEF as a Pioneering Institution: Lessons Learned and Looking Ahead. *Working Paper* No. 19, October. Washington DC: Global Environment Facility. Available at www.gefweb.org/Outreach/outreach-PUblications/2003-11WP19.pdf

Bonfiglioli, A. and Watson, C. (2011) *Social Protection and Climate Resilience International Conference: Social Protection for Social Justice*. Brighton: Institute of Development Studies, University of Sussex.

Bonizella, B. (2011) Mainstreaming gender in the GEF: Good practices in the Climate Change Adaptation Portfolio. Presentation, UNFCCC Climate Talks, June, Bonn, Germany.

Bordallo, M. 2008. Malaria and Maternal mortality. Access of women to malaria prevention treatment. Humanitarian Congress, Berlin Oct. 2018. German Foundation for World Peace. Available at: http://humanitarian-congress-berlin.org/files/8113/4158/1381/Bordallo.pdf.

Bos, E., Vu, M.T. Massiah, El, and Bulatao, R.A. (1994) *World Population Projections 1994–1995 Edition*. Baltimore, MD/London: John Hopkins University Press.

Bouchet, M.-H. and Isaak, R. (2011) Is the financial crisis a male syndrome? Available at www.businessweek.com/europe/is-the-financial-crisis-a-male-syndrome-11292011.html.

Bowen, A., B. Chatterjee and S. Frankhauser 2009. *Adaptation and Economic Growth*. Paper prepared for the UK Dept of International Development, Grantham Research Institute, London School of Economics. February.

Bowen, A., Forster, P.M., Gouldson, R., A. Hubacek, K., R. Martin, D.W. Oneil, Rapp, A. and Rydges, J. 2009. *The Implications of the Economic Slowdown For Greenhouse Gas Emissions Target*. Policy Paper. Centre for Climate Change Economics.

Boyd, E. (2002) The Noel Kempff Project in Bolivia: gender, power and decision making in climate mitigation. In R. Masika (ed.) *Gender, Development and Climate Change*. Oxford: Oxfam Publishing.

Boyd, E. 2009 Governing the clean development mechanism: global realities versus local realities in carbon sequestration projects. *Environment and Planning A* 40(1): 2380–95.

Boyd, R. (2011) One footprint at a time. *Scientific American* 14 July. Available at http://blogs.scientificamerican.com.

Bradshaw, S. (2004) *Socio-economic Impacts of Natural Disasters: A Gender Analysis*. United Nations Economic Commission for Latin America (ECLA). Serie Manuales 32. Santiago de Chile: ECLAC.

Brahic, C. (2009) Humanity's carbon budget set at one trillion tons. *New Scientist* 29 April.

Brehanu A. and Fufa, B. (2008) Repayment rate of loans from semi-formal financial institutions among small-scale farmers in Ethiopia: Two-limit Tobit analysis. *Journal of Socio-Economics* 37: 2221–30.

Bretton Woods Project (2011) *World Bank Manoeuvers to Influence Climate Finance Debates*. Washington, DC: BWP.

Brockhaus, M., H. Djoudi, and B. Locatelli (2013) Envisioning the future and learning from the past: Adapting to a changing environment in northern Mali. *Environmental Science & Policy* 25: 94–106.

Brody, A., Demetriades, J. and Esplen, E. (2008) *Gender and Climate Change: Mapping the Linkages – A Scoping Study on Knowledge and Gaps*. Brighton: Institute of Development Studies, University of Sussex. Available at www.bridge.ids.ac.uk/bridge/reports/Climate_Change_DFID.pdf.

Broeckhoven, N. (2012) Gender, biodiversity and climate change: Some aspects of the legal and policy dimension. PhD thesis, Department of Public International Law, Faculty of Law, Ghent University.

Brouwer, R., S. Akter, L. Brander, and E. Haque (2007) Socioeconomic vulnerability and adaptation to environmental risk: A case study of climate change and flooding in Bangladesh. *Risk Analysis* 27(2): 313–26.

Brown, J. and Vigneri, M. (2008) Innovative carbon-based funding for adaptation. In *Increasing Access to the Carbon Market: New Countries, New Sectors*. Geneva: UNEP.

Brown, J., Vigneri, M. and Sosis, K. (2008) Innovative carbon-based funding for adaptation. Available at www.odi.org/sites/odi.org.uk/files/odi-assets/publications-opinion-files/3401.pdf.

Brown, K. and Corbera, E. (2003) Exploring equity and sustainable development in the new carbon economy. *Climate Policy* 3S(1): S41–56.

Brown, K., Adjer, E., Boyd, E., Corberra-Elizalde, E. and Shackley, S. (2004) *How do CDM Projects Contribute to Sustainable Development?* Norwich: Tyndall Centre for Climate Change Research.

Brown, L. (2012) *Rising Temperature Raising Food Prices*. Available at www.earth-policy.org/plan_b_updates/2012/update105 (accessed 30 January 2013).

Bryan, E., Akpalu, W. and Ringler, C. (2008) *Global Carbon Markets: Are There Opportunities for Sub-Saharan Africa?* IFPRI Discussion Paper. Available at www.ifpri.org/pubs/dp/ifpridp00832.asp.

Buchner, B., Brown, J. and Carfee-Merlot, J. (2011) *Monitoring and Tracking Long-Term Finance Support to Climate Actions*. Paris: OECD/IEA.

Buchner, B., Falconer, A., Herve-Mignucci, M., Trabacchi, C. and Brinkman, M. (2011) *Landscape of Climate Finance*. San Francisco, CA: Climate Policy Initiative.

Buchner, B., Herve-Mignucci, M., Trabacchi, C., Wilkinson, J., Stadelmann, M., Boyd, R., Mazza, F., and Micale, V. 2013 *The Global Landscape of Climate Finance 2013*. Climate Policy Initiative. October 2013. Available at www.climate policyinitiative.org.

Bueno, R., Herzfeld, C., Stanton, E. and Ackerman, F. (2008) *The Caribbean and Climate Change: the Costs of Inaction*. Tufts University: North Grafton, MA. Available at www.sei-us.org/climate-energz/Caribbean-full-Eng-lowres.pdf (accessed on 12 March 2009).

Burke T., Ashton J (2005) *Climate Change and Global Security*. Available at: www.open democracy.net/globalizationclimate_change_debate/article_2509.jsp.

Burton, I. (2004) Climate change and the adaptation deficit. In A. French *et al.*, *Climate Change: Building the Adaptive Capacity*, pp. 25–33. Ottawa, ON: Meteorological Service of Canada, Environment Canada.

Butler, R.A. (2009) Are we on the brink of saving rainforests? Available at http://news.mongabay.com/2009/0722-redd.html.

Callaway, J.M. (2004) Adaptation benefits and costs: are the important in the global policy picture and how can we estimate them? *Global Environmental Change* 14: 273–82.

Campbell, B., S. Mitchell, and M. Blackett (2009) *Responding to Climate Change in Vietnam: Opportunities for Improving Gender Equality*. A Policy Discussion Paper, Ha noi, Vietnam: Oxfam and UN-Viet Nam.

Carlsen, Lauren (2010) Worlds Collide at Cancun Climate Talks. *Foreign Policy in Focus*, 27 October. Available at www.fpif.org/articles/worlds_collide_at_cancun_climate_talks.

CAN Europe (2012) *A Recipe for Transparent Climate Finance in the EU*. Brussels: Climate Action Network Europe.

Capoor, K. and Ambrosi, P. (2009) *State and Trends of the Carbon Market 2009*. Washington, DC: The World Bank.

Caribbean Development Bank (2012a) *Position Paper Responding to Climate Change in the Caribbean Development Bank and Its Borrowing among Member Countries*. Barbados: Caribbean Development Bank.

Caribbean Development Bank (2012b) *Status Report on the Implementation of the Gender Policy and Operational Strategy*. Barbados: Caribbean Development Bank.

Caribbean Development Bank (2012c) *Action on Climate Change: Draft Climate Resilience Strategy 2012–17*. Barbados: Caribbean Development Bank.

Carr, E.R. (2008) Between structure and agency: Livelihoods and adaptation in Ghana's Central Region. *Global Environmental Change* 18(4): 689–99.

Carr, E.R. (2013) Livelihoods as intimate government: Reframing the logic of livelihoods or development. *Third World Quarterly* 34(1): 77–108.

Carr, M. (2014) Carbon Market Value to Gain 15 percent in 2014 on EU Surplus Fix. *Bloomberg News* January 8, 2014. Available at www.bloomberg.com/news/articles/2014-01-08/global-carbon-market-value-to-gain-15-in-2014-on-eu-surplus-fix.

Carter, S. and Shaw, E. (2006) *Women's Business Ownership: Recent Research and Policy Developments*. Report to the Small Business Services. Stirling: University of Stirling/University of Strathclyde.

Castles, S. (2002) *Environmental Change and Forced Migration: Making Sense of the Debate*. Geneva: UNHCR.

CCIC (2009) *Financing for Climate Change Adaptation: A Discussion Paper*. Ottawa, ON: Canadian Council for International Co-operation.

Cecelski, E. (2004) *Re-thinking Gender and Energy: Old and New Direction*. Leusden: ENERGIA/EASE.

Center for International forestry Research (CIFOR) (2013) *Gender in the CGIAR Research Program on Forests, Trees and Agroforestry: A Strategy for Research and Action*. Bogor, Indonesia: CIFOR.

CERES (2014) *Investing in the Clean trillion: Closing the Clean energy investment Gap*. A CERES Report, January 2014. Available at http://divestinvest.org/wp-content/uploads/2014/04/Ceres_CleanTrillion_Report_0121141.pdf.

CFS (2011) *Policy Roundtable Gender, Food Security and Nutrition*. 17–22 October. Rome: FAO.

CFS (2011/5) Policy roundtable: Gender, food security and nutrition. Committee on World Food Security: Rome 17–22. October 2011. Available at www.fao.org/docrep/meeting/023/mc065e.pdf.

Chan, M. (2008) *Subprime Carbon: Rethinking the World's Largest New Derivatives Market Friends of the Earth*. Available at www.foe.org/pdf/SubprimeCarbonReport.pdf.

Chan, S. and Pedwell, C. (2008) *Women, Gender and the Informal Economy: An Assessment of ILO Research and Suggested Ways Forward*. Working Paper Series. Geneva: ILO.

Chen, M. and Carr, M. (2002) *Globalization and the Informal Economy: How Global Trade and Investment Impact on the Working Poor*. Working Paper on the Informal Economy, No. 1. Geneva: ILO.

Chhaochharia, S. (2006) *Targeting Women: A Financial Perspective*. IBS Research Centre/Institute of Chartered Financial Analysts of India (ICFAI).

Chiang, S. (2007) Heat waves, the 'other' natural disaster: perspective on an often ignored epidemic. *Global Pulse: AMSA International Health Journal*. Available at www.globaljournalpulse.com.

Chiew, H. (2014) *Views and Approaches for 2015 Outcome/Agreement Remain Divergent*. TWN Bonn News Update No. 10, 4 November. Penang: Third World Network.

Chinowsky, P., Schweikert, A., Strzepek, N., Manahan, K., Strzepek, K. and Schlosser, C.A. (2011) *Adaptation Advantage to Climate Change: Impacts on Road Infrastructure in Africa through 2100*. Working Paper No. 2011/25. UNU WIDER. Available at www.wider.unu.edu/publications/working-papers/2011/en_GB/wp2011-025.

Christianson, G.E. (1999) *Greenhouse: The 200-Year Story of Global Warming*. New York: Walker Publishing.

Chu, J. (2011) Gender and 'land grabbing' in sub-Saharan Africa: Women's land rights and customary land tenure. *Development* 54(1): 35–9.

CIDA (2002) *Gender Equality and Climate Change: Why Consider Gender Equality when taking Action on Climate Change?* Gatineau, QC: CIDA.

CIFs (2010) *Strategic Environment, Social and Gender Assessment of the Climate Investment Funds*. SCF/TFC.6/Inf.2. October 29.

CIFs (2013) *Gender Review of CIF*. Global Gender Office of the International Union for Conservation of Nature (IUCN).

Ciplet, D. et al. (2011) *Scoring Fast-Start Climate Finance: Leaders and Laggards in Transparency*. IIED Briefing Papers. London: International Institute for Environment and Development (IIED).

Clancy, J., Winther, T., Matinga, M. and Oparaocha, S. (2011) *Gender Equity in Access to and Benefits from Modern Energy and Improved Energy Technologies*. World Development Report Background Paper. Leusden: ETC/ENERGIA in association Nord/Sør-konsulentene.

Clapp, C., Ellis, J., Benn, J. and Corfee-Morlot, J. (2012) *Tracking Climate Finance: What and How?* Paris: OECD/IEA.

Clean Energy for Development Investment Framework. Available at http://siteresources.worldbank.org/DEVCOMMINT/Documentation/21289621/DC2007-0002(E)-Clean Energy.pdf.

Climate Investment Funds (2015) *About the Climate Investment Funds*. Available at www.climateinvestmentfunds.org/cif/aboutus.

Climate Funds (2012) *From Principles to Operationalization*. Available at www.gender-climate.org/Content/Docs/Publications/BM1_Gender_GCF_2-pager_FINAL_21Aug2012.pdf.

Climate Knowledge and Development Network (2010) Regional Implications of the Agf Recommendations: Latin America and Caribbean Region. November 2010. Available at http://cdkn.org/wp-content/uploads/2010/12/AGF-Implications-LAC-CDKN-Special-Briefing-small1.pdf.

Cline, W.R. (2007) *Warming and Agriculture Impact Estimates by Country*. Washington, DC: Center for Global Development.

Cohen, M.J. and J.L. Garrett (2010) The food price crisis and urban food (in)security. *Environment and Urbanization* 22: 467–82.

Congressional Research and Leggett, J.A. (2010) *International Finance of Responses to Climate Change*. November 23, 2020. Congressional Research Services Available at www.fas.org/sgp/crs/misc/R41500.pdf.

Cook, J.T. and D.A. Frank (2008) Food security, poverty, and human development in the United States. *Annals of the New York Academy of Sciences* 1136(1): 193–209.

Cooke, P., Koh-Lin, G., and Hyde, W.F. (2008) Fuelwood, Forests and community management-evidence from household studies. *Environment and Development Economics* 13:103–35.

Cooley, H., Christian-Smith, J., Gleick, P.H., Allen, L. and Cohen, M. (2009) *Understanding and Reducing the Risks of Climate Change for Transboundary Waters*. Pacific Institute &UNEP. Available at www.pacinst.org/wp-content/uploads/sites/21/2013/02/transboundary_water_and_climate_report3.pdf.

Copenhagen Diagnosis (2009) *Updating the world on the Latest Climate Science*. Sydney, Australis:The University of New South Wales Climate Change Research Centre (CCRC).

Corfee-Morlot, J. et al. (2009) *Financing Climate Change Mitigation: Towards a Framework for Measurement, Reporting and Verification*. October. Paris: OECD/IEA.

Cornia, G.A., Rosignoli, S. and Tiberti, Luca (2011) *The Impact of the Food and Financial Crises on Child Mortality: the Case of Sub-Saharan Africa*. UNICEF Innocenti Research Centre. Working Paper IWP-2011–01. Available at /www.childimpact.unicef-irc.org/documents/view/id/86/lang/en.

Costello, A. et al. (2009) Managing the health effects of climate change. *The Lancet* 373.

COWI and IIED (2009) *Joint External Evaluation: Operation of the Least Developed Countries Fund for Adaptation to Climate Change*. GEF/LDCF.SCCF.7/Inf.4. 13 October. London: International Institute for Environment and Development.

CSACC (2012) *Achieving Food Security in the Face of Climate Change*. Montpellier: CGIAR.

Cullen, H. (2010) *The Weather of the Future*. New York: Harper.

Cutter, S.L. (1995) The forgotten casualties: Women, children, and environmental change. *Global Environmental Change* 5: 181–94.

D'Espallier, B., Guérin, I. and Mersland, R. (2009) *Women and Repayment in Microfinance*. Agder, Working Paper. Norway: University of Agder. Available at www.microfinancegateway.org/gm/document-1.9.40253/Women%20and%20Repayment%20in%20Microfinance.pdf.

Damptey, P. (2007) *Climate Change and Women's Livelihoods*. Paper presented during the National Forum on Climate Change. Accra.

Damptey, P. and Mensah, A. (2005) *Women and Climate Change in Ghana*. Unpublished research report. Accra.

DANIDA (2009) *Executive Summary of the Joint External Evaluation: Operation of the Least Developed Countries Fund for Adaptation to Climate Change*. GEF/LDCF.SCCF.7/5. 13 October, Washington, DC: DANIDA Evaluation Department and GEF Evaluation Office.

Dankelman, I. (2002) Climate change: Learning from gender analysis and women's experience of organizing for sustainable development. In Masika, R. (ed.), *Gender, Development and Climate Change*. Oxford: Oxfam.

DARA (2012) *Climate Vulnerability Monitor: A Guide to the Cold Calculus of a Hot Planet*. 2nd edition. Madrid: DARA.

Davies, M., B. Guenther, J. Leavy, T. Mitchell, and T. Tanner (2009) *Climate Change Adaptation, Disaster Risk Reduction and Social Protection: Complementary Roles in Agriculture and Rural Growth?* IDS Working Paper No. 320. University of Sussex, Brighton: The Institute of Development Studies (IDS).

Davison, J. (1988) *Agriculture, Women and the Land: the African Experience*. Boulder, CO: Westview Press.

DAW (1999) *World Survey on the Role of Women in Development: Globalization, Gender and Work*. New York: United Nations Division for the Advancement of Women.

DBSA (2011) *Synthesis of Climate Finance Literature: Report of the DBSA*. Pretoria: DBSA.

de Nevers, M. (2011) *Climate Finance – Mobilizing Private Investment to Transform Development*. GEG Working Paper 2011/60. Oxford: The Global Economic Governance Programme, University College. Available at www.globaleconomicgovernance.org/sites/geg/files/Nevers_GEG%20WP%202011_60.pdf.

De Schutter, O. (2011) How not to think of land-grabbing: Three critiques of large-scale investments in farmland. *The Journal of Peasant Studies* 38(2): 249–79.

Del Ninno, C., Dorosh, P.A., Smith, L.C. and Roy, D.K. (2001) *The 1998 Floods in Bangladesh: Disaster Impacts, Household Coping Strategies, and Response*. Research Report 122. Washington, DC: International Food Policy Research Institute.

Del Rio, P. (2005) Encouraging the implementation of small renewable electricity CDM projects: an economic analysis of different options. *Renewable and Sustainable Energy Reviews* 11(7): 1361–87.

den Elzen, M.G.J., and Höhne, N. (2008) Reductions of greenhouse gas emissions in Annex I and non-Annex I countries for meeting concentration stabilisation targets. *Climatic Change* 91: 249–74.

Dennison, C. (2003) *From Beijing to Kyoto: Gendering the International Climate Change Negotiation Process*. Paper presented at 53rd Pugwash Conference on Science and World Affairs – Advancing Human Security: The Role of Technology and Politics. Available at www.pugwash.org/reports/pac/53/dennison.htm.

Denton, F. (2002) Climate change vulnerability, impacts, and adaptation: Why does gender matter? *Gender and Development* 10(2): 10–20.

Demirguc-Kunt, A., Thorsten, B. and Honohan, P. (2008) *Finance for all? A World Bank Policy Research Report: Policies and pitfalls in expanding access*. World Bank.

Diagne, A., Zeller, M. and Sharma, M. (2000) *Empirical Measurements of Households' Access to Credit and Credit Constraints in Developing Countries: Methodological Issues And Evidence*. IFPRI, FCND Discussion Paper No. 90. IFPRI.

Dixit, K. (2009) Small is bountiful in Nepal's energy sector. *Nepali Times*. Available at www.ashdenawards.org.

Draitser, E. (2014) The financial elite and the global land grab. Available at http://journal-neo.org/2014/03/24/the-financial-elite-and-the-global-land-grab.

Drexhage, J. (2006) *The World Conservation Union (IUCN) Climate Change Situation. Analysis. Final Report*. Switzerland: IISD-IUCN.

Duflo, D., Greenstone, M. and Hanna, R. (2008) Cooking stoves, indoor air pollution and respiratory health in rural Orissa. Reprint Series Number 205. *Economic & Political Weekly* 43(23): 71–6.

Dulal, H.B., Shah, K.U. and Ahmad, N. (2009) Social equity considerations in the implementation of Caribbean climate change adaptation policies. *Sustainability* I: 363–83.

Dutschke, M. and Michaelowa, A. (2006) Development assistance and the CDM – how to interpret 'financial additionality'. *Environment and Development Economics* 11(2): 235–46.

Dutta, S. (2003) *Mainstreaming Gender in Energy Planning and Policies*. UNESCAP Project on Capacity Building on Integration of Energy and Rural Development Planning. New York: United Nations.

Duval, R. (2008) *A Taxonomy of Instruments to Reduce Greenhouse Gases and their Interactions*. OECD Economics Department Paper 636. Paris: OECD.

Ebi, K. (2007) *Health Impacts of Climate Change: A Report to the UNFCCC Financial and Technical Support Division*. Available at http://unfccc.int/cooperation_and_support/financial_mechanism/financial_mechanism_gef/items/4054.php.

Ebi, K. (2008) Adaptation costs for climate change-related cases of diarrhoeal disease, malnutrition, and malaria in 2030. *Globalization and Health* 4(9).

Ebi, K., Kovats, R.S. and Menne, B. (2006) An approach for assessing human health vulnerability and public health interventions to adapt to climate change. *Environmental Health Perspectives* 114(12): 1930–4.

Economist (2013) Typhoon Haiyan Worse than hell. Available at www.economist.com/news/asia/21589916-one-strongest-storms-ever-recorded-has-devastated-parts-philippines-and-relief.

Ecosystem Marketplace and New Carbon Finance (2009) Fortifying the Foundation: State of the Voluntary Carbon Markets.

Ecosystem Marketplace Survey of Carbon Offsetting Trends Survey 2008. Available at www.greenbiz.com/research/report/2008/09/24/ecosecurities-and-climatebiz-carbon-offsetting-trends-survey-2008.

Edejer, T.T.T., Alkins, M., Black, R., Wolfson, L., Hutubessy, R. and Evans, D.B. (2005) Cost effectiveness analysis of strategies for child health in developing countries. *British Medical Journal* 331.

Edenhofer, O., R. Pichs-Madruga, Y. Sokona, K. Seyboth, P. Matschoss, S. Kadner, T. Zwickel, P. Eickemeier, G. Hansen, and S. Schlömer (eds) (2011) *The IPCC Special Report on Renewable Energy Sources and Climate Change Mitigation*. Prepared by Working Group III of the Intergovernmental Panel on Climate Change. Cambridge/New York: Cambridge University Press.

Ehlers, C., Wiekert, M. (2006) *CDM Market Brief*. German Office for Foreign Trade.

El-Hinnawi, E. (1985) *Environmental Refugees*. Nairobi: United Nations Environment Programme.

Ellis, J. and Tirpak, D. (2006) *Linking Greenhouse Gas Emission Trading Schemes and Markets*. Paris: OECD.

Ellis, J., Winkler, H., Corfee-Morlota, J. and Gagnon-Lebrunc, F. (2007) CDM: Taking stock and looking forward. *Energy Policy* 35: 15–28

Elsamawal, M. and Mohamed, A. (2006) The Role of Women Farmers in Traditional Rain Fed Farming System in North Kordufan. Ahfad University for Women. Available at www.highbeam.com/doc/1G1-147746140.html.

Elverland, S. (2009) 20 million climate displaced in 2008. Norwegian Refugee Council, 8 June. Available at www.nrc.no/?did=9407544.

Enarson, E. (2002) *Gender and Natural Disasters*. IPCRR Working Paper No. 1. Geneva: International Labour Organization.

Environmental Defense Fund (2008) *Environmental Defense Fund Launches First-of-its-Kind Independent Guide to High-Quality Carbon Offsets for Businesses and Consumers to Combat Climate Change*. Available at www.edf.org/news/environmental-defense-fund-launches-br-first-its-kind-independent-guide-br-high-quality-carbon.

Epstein, P. (2005) Climate change and human health. *New England Journal of Medicine* October: 1433–6.

EU Parliament (2011) *Climate Refugees' Legal and Policy Responses to Environmentally Induced Migration*. Directorate General for Internal Policies Policy Department C: Citizens' Rights and Constitutional Affairs, Civil Liberties, Justice and Home Affairs. Brussels. Available at www.europarl.europa.eu/RegData/etudes/etudes/join/2011/462422/IPOL-LIBE_ET(2011)462422_EN.pdf.

EURODAD (2012) *Cashing in on Climate Change?* Brussels: EURODAD.

European Commission (2008) *Climate Change and International Security: Paper from the High Representative and the European Commission to the European Council*. March. Available at www.consilium.europa.eu/ueDocs/cms_Data/docs/pressData/en/reports/99387.pdf (accessed 4 September 2009).

European Commission (2009) *Opinion on the Gender Perspective on the Responses to the Economic and Financial Crisis*. Advisory Committee on Equal Opportunities for Women and Men. 10 June. Available at www.equineteurope.org/opinuon.pdf.

European Commission (2010) More women in senior positions Key to economic stability and growth. Available at http://ec.europa.eu/danmark/documents/alle_emner/beskaeftigelse/more_women_in_senior_positions.pdf.

European Commission (2010a) *Water Scarcity and Droughts – 2012 Policy Review – Building Blocks*. Non-Paper Directorate-General Environment Directorate Water, Chemicals and Biotechnology ENV.D.1 – Water. Available at http://ec.europa.eu/environment/water/quantity/pdf/non-paper.pdf.

European Institute for Gender Equality (2012) *Review of the Implementation in the EU of area K of the Beijing Platform for Action: Women and the Environment Gender Equality and Climate Change*. EIGE, Luxembourg.

Everland, S. (2009) 20 Millions climate displaced in 2008. Norweigian Refugee Council 8 June 2009. Available at www.nrc.no??did=9407544.

Bibliography

Fankhauser, S. (2009a) *The Costs of Adaptation Centre for Climate Change Economics and Policy*. London: LSE.

Fankhauser, S. (2009b) The range of global estimates. In M. Parry et al. (eds), *Assessing the Costs of Adaptation to Climate Change: A Review of the UNFCCC and Other Recent Estimates*. London: International Institute for Environment and Development and Grantham Institute for Climate Change.

Food and Agriculture Organization (FAO) (1993). *Agricultural Extension and Farm Women in the 1980s*. Rome: FAO.

FAO (1995) *Women, Agriculture and Rural Development: A Synthesis Report of the Africa Region*. Rome: FAO.

FAO (1998) *Rural Women and Food Security: Current Situation and Perspectives*. Rome: FAO.

FAO (2003) *Women and Water Resources: Women in Development Service*. Rome: FAO.

FAO (2012) *The State of Food and Agriculture 2010–2011: Women In Agriculture Closing The Gap For Development*. Rome: FAO.

FAO (2009) 1.02 billion people hungry. Available at www.fao.org/news/story/en/item/20568/icode.

FAO (2009) *Rural Women and the Right to Food*. Rome: FAO.

FAO (2010) *What Woodfuels Can Do to Mitigate Climate Change*. Rome: FAO.

FAO (2011) *Highlights on Wood Charcoal 2004–2009*. Rome: FAO.

FAO (2011) *FAO at Work 2010–11. Women – Key to Food Security*. Rome: FAO.

FAO (2011) Policy roundtable: gender, food security and nutrition. Committee on World Food Security, 37th session, item V. 17–22, October. Rome: FAO.

FAO (2011) *The State of Food and Agriculture (SOFA 2010–11): Women in Agriculture: Closing the Gender Gap for Development*. Rome: FAO.

FAO, IFAD and ILO (2010) *Gender Dimensions of Agricultural and Rural Employment: Differentiated Pathways Out of Poverty – Status, Trends and Gaps*. Rome: FAO.

Felkerson, J. (2011) *$29,000,000,000,000: A Detailed Look at the Fed's Bailout by Funding Facility and Recipient (University of Missouri–Kansas City)*. Working Paper collection no. 698. New York: Levy Economics Institute.

Femke Vos et al. (2010) *Annual Disasters Statistical Review 2009: The Numbers and Trends*. Brussels: Centre for Research on the Epidemiology of Disasters CRED. Available at http://cred.be/sites/default/files/ADSR_2009.pdf.

Fernando, J. (2006) *Microfinance: Perils and Prospects*. London: Routledge.

Fichtner, W., Graehl, S. and Rentz, O. (2002) International cooperation to support climate change mitigation and sustainable development. *International Journal of Environment and Pollution* 18(1): 33–55.

Financial Express (2007) www.thefinancialexpress-bd.com/2007/12/20/20337.html.

Financial Times (2007) Europe to suffer as the world warms up. Available at www.ft.com/intl/cms/s/0/358a1bd0-9ce9-11db-8ec6-0000779e2340.html#axzz3bTfbFQO8.

First Assessment Report (FAR) (1990) *Climate Change: The IPCC Scientific Assessment*. Geneva: IPCC.

Fitoussi, J.P. and Stiglitz, J. (2009) *The Shadow GN: The Ways of the Crisis and the Building of a More Cohesive World*. Available at www.luiss.edu/system/files/ShadowGN_Final Document.pdf.

Floro, M. and Dymski, G. (2000). Financial crisis, gender, and power: An analytical framework. *World Development* 28(7): 1269–83.

Forbes (2008) *The New Green Business Model_For Investment*. Available at www.forbescustom.com/EnvironmentPgs/NewGreenBusinessModelP1.html.

Forbes (2012) *The New Green Business Model_For Investment (Peter C. Fusaro) International Research Center for Energy and Economic Development*. Available at www.forbescustom.com/EnvironmentPgs/NewGreenBusinessModelP1.html.

Fordham, M., 2003: Gender, disaster and development: the necessity of integration. In M. Pelling (ed.) *Natural Disasters and Development in a Globalising World*, pp. 57–74, London: Routledge.

Fordham, M., S. Gupta, S. Akerkar, and M. Scharf (2011) *Leading Resilient Development: Grassroots Women's Priorities, Practices and Innovations*. Northumbria University, UK/New York: UNDP and GROOTS international.

Fouillet, A., G. Rey, F. Laurent, G. Pavillon, S. Bellec, C. Guihenneuc-Jouyaux, J. Clavel, E. Jougla, and D. Hemon (2006) Excess mortality related to the August 2003 heat wave in France. *International Archives of Occupational & Environmental Health* 80(1): 16–24.

Friends of the Earth (2009) Subprime Carbon: Rethinking the world's newest derivative market. Friends of the earth/Chan, M. Available at www.foe.org/system/storage/877/77/4/452/SubprimeCarbonReport.pdf.

Friends of the Earth (2011) U.S. Recommendations for the Transitional Committee July 29, 2011 Role of Private Sector Finance and the Green Climate Fund. Available at www.foe.org/system/storage/877/6b/d/841/7-29-11_Friends_of_the_Earth_US_submission_Green_Climate_Fund_Transitional_Committee_private_sector_finance.pdf.

Fulton, M. (2014) *Investing in the Clean Trillion: Closing the Clean Energy Investment Gap*. Boston, MA: Ceres.

G8 Muskoka Declaration Recovery and New Beginnings Muskoka, Canada, 25–6 June 2010. Available at www.bundesregierung.de/Content/DE/StatischeSeiten/Breg/G8G20/Anlagen/G8-erklaerung-muskoka-en.pdf?__blob=publicationFile&v=2.

Gajigo, O. and M. Hallward-Driemeier (2011) *Constraints and Opportunities for New Entrepreneurs in Africa*. Washington, DC: World Bank.

Ganter, S. (2008) *Sink or Adapt*. Briefing paper. Berlin: Freidrich Ebert Foundation.

García-Pina, R., A. Tobías Garcés, J. Sanz Navarro, C. Navarro Sánchez and A. García-Fulgueiras (2008) Efecto del calor sobre el número de urgencias hospitalarias en la Región de Murcia durante los veranos del período 2000–2005 y su uso en la vigilancia epidemiológica. *Revista Española de Salud Pública* 82(2): 153–66.

Garnaud, B. (2009) *An Analysis of Adaptation Negotiations in Poznan* (IDDRI) Policy Brief No 01/2009. Paris: Institut For Sustainable Development and International Relations.

Garrity, D. (2009) Trees on farms key to climate and food-secure future. UNEP press release. Available at http://unep.org/Documents.Multilingual/Default.asp?DocumentID=593&ArticleID=6256&l=en.

GCCA (2008) *Gender and Climate Change Workshop Report*. 19–20 November. New York: GCCA.

GEA (2012) *Global Energy Assessment – Toward a Sustainable Future*. Cambridge/New York/Laxenburg, Austia: Cambridge University Press and the International Institute for Applied Systems Analysis.

GEF (2005a) *Achieving the Millennium Development Goals: A GEF Progress Report*. Washington, DC: GEF.

GEF (2005b) *GEF Data Base*. Washington, DC: GEF. Available at www.gefonline.org/projectList.cfm (accessed 10 July 2005).

GEF (2007) *Signposts: Joint Evaluation of the GEF Activity Cycle and Modalities*. Evaluation report no. 33. Washington, DC: GEF.

GEF (2008) *Report on the Completion of the Strategic Priority on Adaptation*. GEF/C.34/8. 9 October. Washington, DC: GEF.

GEF (2009) *Progress Report on the Least Developed Countries Fund (LDCF) and the Special Climate Change Fund (SCCF)*. Washington, DC: GEF.

GEF (2010) *Report of the Global Environment Facility to the Conference of the Parties of the 19th Session of the UNFCCC* November 2013. Washington, DC: GEF.

GEF (2010) *Report of the Global Environment Facility: A Note by the Secretariat*. November 2010. Washington, DC: GEF.
GEF (2011) *Gender Mainstreaming*. Washington, DC: GEF.
GEF 2012 *Report of the Global Environment Facility to the Conference of the Parties of the 18th Session of the UNFCCC*. FCCC/CP/2012/6. November 2012. Washington, DC: GEF.
GEF (2013) *Report of the Global Environment Facility to the Conference of the Parties of the 19th Session of the UNFCCC*. FCCC/CP/2013/3. November 2013. Washington, DC: GEF.
GEF (2014) *Report of the Global Environment Facility to the Conference of the Parties Conference of the Parties, Twentieth session*. Lima, 1–12 December 2014. Item X of the provisional agenda 2 September 2014 FCCC/CP/2014/2. Washington, DC, GEF.
GEF Evaluation Office (2010) Evaluation of the operation of the Least Developed Countries Fund for adaptation to climate change. Available at www.thegef.org/gef/sites/thegef.org/files/documents/LDCF_evaluation_rep0909web_no_annex_0.pdf.
Gender Action (2008) *Boom-time Blues: Big Oil's Gender Impacts in Azerbaijan, Georgia, and Sakhalin*. Washington, DC: Gender Action.
Gender Action (2009) *Doubling the Damage: The World Bank Climate Investment Funds Undermine Climate and Gender Justice*. Washington, DC: Gender Action/Heinrich Böll Foundation North America.
Gender CC Network – Women for Climate Justice (2007) *Gender: Missing Links in Financing Climate Change Adaptation and Mitigation*. Berlin: Gender CC Network – Women for Climate Justice. Available at www.gendercc.net/fileadmin/inhalte/Dokumente/UNFCCC_conferences/gender_cc_financing_positionpaper_bali_final.pdf.
Gender CC Network – Women for Climate Justice (2008) *Challenges and Recommendations for Clean Development Mechanism Aiming to Improve Women's Livelihood in the Pacific Region*. Berlin: Gender CC Network – Women for Climate Justice. Available at www.gendercc.net/fileadmin/inhalte/Dokumente/Topics/Women_CDM-Pacific.pdf.
Gender CC Network – Women for Climate Justice (2010) *In Retrospect: Gender in COP 15*. Berlin: Gender CC Network – Women for Climate Justice. Available at www.gendercc.net/fileadmin/inhalte/Dokumente/UNFCCC_conferences/COP15/Gender_in_the_Copenhagen_outcomes_final.pdf.
GFC (2007) The impacts of market-based biodiversity conservation on indigenous peoples, local communities and women. Available at http://globalforestcoalition.org/resources/market-based-conservation.
GFC (2009) *The Hottest REDD Issues: Rights, Equity, Development, Deforestation and Governance by Indigenous Peoples and Local Communities*. Commission on Environmental, Economic and Social Policies and Global Forest Coalition.
GGCA UNDP (2010) *Adaptation Fund: Exploring the Gender Dimensions of Climate Finance Mechanisms*. New York: UNDP.
GHF (2009) *Climate Change – The Anatomy of a Silent Crisis*. Climate Change Human Impact Report. Geneva: Global Humanitarian Forum.
Global Coolness (2007) Carbon-neutral is hip, but is it green? Available at www.ecoearth.info/shared/reader/welcome.aspx?linkid=73875.
Global Entrepreneurship Monitor (2005) *2005 Report on Women and Entrepreneurship*. London: Global Entrepreneurship Monitor.
Godquin, M. (2004) Repayment performance in Bangladesh: How to improve the allocation of loans by MFIs. *World Development* 32(11): 1909–26.
Godquin, M., and Quisumbing, A.R. 2008. Separate but equal? The gendered nature of social capital in rural Philippine communities. *Journal of International Development* 20(1): 13–33.

Goetz, A.M. (2003) Women's political effectiveness: A conceptual framework. In A.M. Goetz and S. Hassim (eds), *No Shortcuts to Power: African Women in Politics and Policy Making*, p. 246. Cape Town: Zed Books.

Goetz, A.M. (2007) *Gender Justice, Citizenship and Entitlements: Core Concepts, Central Debates and New Directions for Research*. Ottawa: IDRC.

Goheer, Nabeel A. (2003) *Women Entrepreneurs in Pakistan: How to Improve Their Bargaining Power*. International Labor Organization.

Goldstein, M. and Udry, C. (2005) *The Profits of Power: Land Rights and Agricultural Investment in Ghana*. Economic Growth Center Discussion Paper no. 929. New Haven, CT: Yale University.

Gomez, S. (2007) Offsets, the indulgences of today? Available at www.policyinnovations.org/ideas/briefings/data/offsets.

Goulden, M., D. Conway, and A. Persechino (2010) Adaptation to climate change in international river basins in Africa: A review. *Hydrological Sciences Journal* 54(5): 805–28.

GPFI – IFC (2011) *Strengthening Access to Finance for Women-owned SMEs in Developing Countries*. Washington, DC: GPFI.

GPFI-IFC 2011 *Strengthening Access to Finance for Women-Owned SMEs in Developing Countries*. Available at www.ifc.org/wps/wcm/connect/a4774a004a3f66539f0f9f8969adcc27/G20_Women_Report.pdf?MOD=AJPERES.

Grant, J. (2013) IPCC sets carbon budget PWC Blog 27 September 2013. Available at http://pwc.blogs.com/sustainability/2013/09/ipcc-report-dont-be-fooled-by-the-higher-carbon-budget-.html.

Green Climate Fund (2014) *Options for a Fund-wide Gender-sensitive Approach*. Document. B.06/13. Incheon, Republic of Korea: Green Climate Fund.

GreenBiz (2008) EcoSecurities: carbon offsetting trends survey 2008. Available at www.greenbiz.com/research/report/2008/09/24/ecosecurities-and-climatebiz-carbon-offsetting-trends-survey-2008.

GreenStream (2010) *Gender and the Clean Development Mechanism: Opportunities for the CDM to Promote Local Positive Gender Impacts*. Helsinki: Ministry of Foreign Affairs of Finland. Available at http://formin.finland.fi/public/default.aspx?contentid=220759&nodeid=40817&contentlan=2&culture=en-US.

GROOTS International and UNDP (2011) *Leading Resilient Development: Grassroots Women's Priorities, Practices and Innovations*. New York: UNDP.

Grown, C., Bahadur, C., Handbury, J. and Elson, E. (2006) *The Financial Requirements of Achieving Gender Equality and Women's Empowerment*. Working Paper no. 467. New York: Levy Economics Institute.

Grubb, M., Vrolijk, C. and Brack, D. (1999) *The Kyoto Protocol: A Guide and Assessment*. London: Royal Institute for International Affairs.

Grubb, M., Koch, M., Munson, A., Sullivan, F. and Thomson, K. (1993) *The Earth Summit agreements: A guide and assessment*. London: Earthscan and Royal Institute of International Affairs.

Gruebler, A. and Fujii, Y. (1991) Inter-generational and spatial equity issues of carbon accounts. *Energy* 16: 1397–416.

GTZ (2010) *Climate Change and Gender: Economic Empowerment of Women through Climate Mitigation and Adaptation?* Working Paper, October. Berlin: GTZ.

Guardian (2009) Women's touch helps hedge funds retain their values. *The Guardian*, 19 October. Available at www.guardian.co/uk/business/2009/oct/19/women-hedgefunds.

Guardian (2011) World carbon dioxide emissions data by country: China speeds ahead of the rest. *The Guardian*, 31 January. Available at www.guardian.co.uk/news/datablog/2011/jan/31/world-carbon-dioxide-emissions-country-data-co2#data.

Gupta, J. (2010) A history of international climate change policy. *WIREs Climate Change* 1(September/October): 636–53.

Gupta, S. and P.M. Bhandari (2003) Allocation of GHG emissions: An example of short term and long-term criteria in M.A. Toman, U. Chakravorty and S. Gupta (eds) *India and Global Climate Change, Perspectives on Economics and Policy from a Developing Country, Resources for the Future*.

Guttal, S. and Monsalves, S. (2011) Climate Crisis and Land. *Focus On Trade* 155(February/March). Bangkok: FOCUS.

GWA/UNDP (2006) *Mainstreaming Gender in Water Management*. Gender and Water Alliance.

Haites, E. (2011) Climate change finance. *Climate Policy* 11(3): 963–9.

Hamilton, K.S., Thomas, M. and Marcello, G. (2008) *Forging a Frontier: State of the Voluntary Carbon Markets 2008*. A report by Ecosystem Marketplace and New Carbon Finance. New York: Bloomberg.

Hansen, J. (2008) Tipping point. In Fearn, E. and Redford, K.H. (eds), *State of the Wild 2008*, pp. 7–8. Washington, DC: Island Press.

Hansen, J. (2012) Climate change is here – and worse than we thought. *Washington Post* August 3.

Hansen, J., Sato, M., Kharecha, P., Beerling, D., Masson-Delmotte, V., Pagani, M., Raymo, M., Royer, D.L. and Zachos, J.C. (2008) Target atmospheric CO_2: Where should humanity aim? *The Open Atmospheric Science Journal* 2: 217–31.

Harmeling, S., Esch, A., Griesshaber, L., Eckstein, D., Junghans, L., Nakhooda, S. and Fransen, T. (2013) *The German Fast-Start Finance Contribution*. Working Paper. Germanwatch, Bonn, World Resources Institute, Washington DC, and Overseas Development Institute, London. Available at www.wri.org/publication/ocn-ger-fast-start-finance.

Harris, J.M. (2008) *Ecological Macroeconomics: Consumption, Investment and Climate Change*. Working Paper no. 08–02. July. Medford: Tufts University.

Harris, R., Schalatek, S., Eggerts, E., Strohmeier, H., Wanjiru, L., Gore, T., Raczek, T., Eddy, N. (2012) *Gender and the Green Climate Fund: From Principles to Operationalization*. Available at www.gender-climate.org/Content/Docs/Publications/BM1_Gender_GCF_2-pager_FINAL_21Aug2012.pdf.

Hart, C. (2007) *The Private Sector's Capacity to Manage Climate Risks and Finance Carbon Neutral Energy Infrastructure*. Boston, MA: Massachusetts Institute of Technology.

Hartman, H. (2009) *The Impact of the Current Economic Downturn on Women*. Testimony presented to the US Congress, Joint Economic Committee, 6 June 2008. Washington, DC: Institute for Women's Policy Research.

Hazeleger, T. (2013) Gender and disaster recovery: Strategic issues and action in Australia. *Australian Journal of Emergency Management* 28(2): 40–6.

Heinrich Böll Foundation (2010) *Climate Governance in Africa: Adaptation Strategies and Institutions*. Berlin: Heinrich Böll Foundation.

Heinrich Böll Foundation (2011) *More than an Add-on: The Centrality of Gender Equality for Development and Climate Solutions*. Berlin: Heinrich Böll Foundation.

Hellmuth, M.E., Osgood D.E., Hess U., Moorhead A. and Bhojwani H. (eds) (2009) *Index Insurance and Climate Risk: Prospects for Development and Disaster Management*. New York: Columbia University.

Hemmati, M. (2005) *Gender and Climate Change in the North: Issues, Entry Points and Strategies for the Post-2012 Process and Beyond*. Berlin: Genanet.

Hendriks, C. (2007) *Carbon Capture and Storage*. Bonn: UNFCCC Secretariat Financial and Technical Support Programme.

Hirsch, P. and Wyatt, A. (2004) Negotiating local livelihoods: Scales of conflict in the Se San River Basin. *Asia Pacific Viewpoint* 45(1): 51–68.

Hoffmaister, J.P., Stabinsky, D. and Thanki, N. (2012) *Loss and Damage: Some Key Issues and Considerations for the Bangkok Regional Expert Meeting*. Briefing paper 2. Penang: TWN.

Hohne, N. and Kornelis, B. (2005) Calculating historical contributions to climate change – discussing the 'Brazilian proposal'. *Climatic Change* 71(1–2): 141–73.

Holmes, J. (2008) Opening remarks by Sir John Holmes, USG for Humanitarian Affairs and ERC at the DIHAD 2008 Conference. Available at www.reliefweb.int/rw/rwb.nsf/db900sid/YSAR-7DHL88?OpenDocument.

Holst, E. and Schimeta, J. (2012) Top-level management in large companies: Persistent male-dominated structures leave little room for women. *DIW Economic Bulletin* 4: 3–13.

Holt, S.L. and Ribe, H. (1991) *Developing Financial Institutions for the Poor and Reducing Barriers to Access for Woman*. Discussion Paper. Washington, DC: World Bank.

Hosier, R. (2009) *EF Support to Climate Change*. Climate Finance Workshop. July. Washington, DC: GEF.

Hossain, M. (1988) *Credit for Alleviation of Rural Poverty: The Grameen Bank in Bangladesh*. Research report no. 4. Washington, DC: International Food Policy Research Institute.

HPICA (2009) *Options for Reforming the Clean Development Mechanism*. Issue brief 2009–2010. Cambridge, MA: Harvard Project on International Climate Agreements.

Hulme, D. (1991) The Malawi Mudzi fund: Daughter of Grameen. *Journal of International Development* 3(3): 427–31.

Humphry, J. (2004) The clean development mechanisms: How to increase benefits for developing countries. *IDS Bulletin* 35(3): 84

Hunter M.L. and David, E. (2011) Displacement, climate change and gender. In E. Piguet, A. Pécoud and P. de Guchteneire (eds), *Migration and Climate Change*. Rome: UNESCO.

Hutton, G., Haller, L. and Bartram, J. (2007) Global cost-benefit analysis of water supply and sanitation interventions. *Journal of Water and Health* 5(4): 481–502.

IAASTD (2008) *Agriculture at a Crossroads*. Washington, DC: IAASTD.

ICICI Bank (2005) Grameen of USA set up JV for micro-finance. Available at www.nextbillion.net/news/icici-bank-grameen-of-usa-set-up-jv-for-micro-finance.

ICIMOD (2009) *The Changing Himalayas*. International Center for Integrated Mountain Development (ICIMOD), Kathmandu, Nepal: ICIMOD.

IDB (2007) *Promoting Gender Equality through Gender Mainstreaming and Investing in Women's Empowerment: A Report to the Board of Executive Directors on the Implementation of the Bank's Women in Development Policy 2002–5*. Washington, DC: Gender Equality in Development Unit, InterAmerican Development Bank.

IDB (2009) *Beyond Banking on Global Sustainability*. InterAmerican Development Bank November. Washington, DC: InterAmerican Development Bank.

IDB (2010) IDB Governors agree on financial terms for historic capital increase. NEWS RELEASE JUL 22 2010. Available at www.iadb.org/en/news/news-releases/2010-07-22/idb-governors-agree-on-a-capital-increase,7526.html.

IDB (2011) *IDB Integrated Strategy for Climate Change Adaptation and Mitigation, and Sustainable and Renewable Energy,* Vice-Presidency for Sectors and Knowledge, Infrastructure and Environment Sector, March 2011. Available at www.iadb.org/en/civil-society/public-consultations/climate-change-strategy/climate-change-strategy,6974.html.

IDB (2012) *Integrated Strategy for Climate Change Adaptation and Mitigation, and Sustainable and Renewable Energy*. Washington, DC: InterAmerican Development Bank.

Idowu Yetunde, O. (2009) Gender Dimensions of Agriculture, Poverty, Nutrition and Food Security in Nigeria Department of Agricultural Economics University of Ibadan, Nigeria. Available at www.ifpri.org/sites/default/files/publications/nsspbp05.pdf.

IEA (2006) (International Energy Agency) 2006. *Energy Balances and Statistics of OECD and Non-OECD Countries*. Paris: OECD/IEA.
IEA (2006) *Energy Technology Perspectives: Scenarios and Strategies to 2050*. Paris: OECD/IEA.
IEA (2008) *Energy Technology Perspectives 2008: Scenarios and Strategies to 2050*. Paris: OECD/IEA.
IEA (2010). Energy Technology Perspectives 2010: Scenarios and Strategies to 2050. International Energy Agency, Paris, France.
IEA (2012) *Energy Technology Perspectives 2012: Pathways to a Clean Energy System*. Paris: OECD/IEA.
IEA (2013) Redrawing the Energy-Climate Map. Paris: IEA.
IFAD (no date) *Adaptation for Smallholder Agriculture Programme*. Rome: IFAD.
IFAD-ASAP (2012) *The Adaptation for Smallholder Agriculture Programme (ASAP)*. Available at www.ifad.org/climate/asap/asap.pdf.
IFAD/UNEP (2013) *Smallholders, Food Security and the Environment*. Rome: IEA.
IFC (2006) *Diagnostic Study on Access to finance for Women Entrepreneurs in South Africa*. Washington, DC: IFC.
IFC (2009) *Women Entrepreneurs and Access to Finance*. Washington, DC: IFC.
IFC and Mckinsey (2011) *Global SME Finance Mapping*.
IFPRI (2008) *Are There Opportunities for Sub-Saharan Africa?* Discussion Paper 00832, December. Washington, DC: IFPRI.
IIED (2010) Baseline for trust: defining'new and additional' climate funding June 2010 The International Institute for Environment and Development (IIED). Available at http://pubs.iied.org/pdfs/17080IIED.pdf.
ILO (2008) *Zambia. Social Protection Expenditure and Performance Review and Social Budget. Executive Summary*. International Labour Office, Social Security Department, Geneva: ILO.
ILO (2012) Global Employment Trends 2012: Preventing a Deeper Jobs Crisis. January. Available at www.ilo.org/wcmsp5/groups/public/--dgreports/--dcomm/- publ/documents/publication/wcms_171571.pdf.
ILO/AFDB (2004) *Women and Labour Markets in Asia: Rebalancing for Gender Equality*. African Development Bank/International Labor Organization.
IMF (2009a) *Global Financial Stability Report*. Washington, DC: IMF.
IMF (2009b) *The Implications of the Global Financial Crisis for Low-Income Countries*. Washington, DC: IMF.
IMF (2010) *Financing the Response to Climate Change*. Washington, DC: IMF.
IMF (2011) World Economic Outlook (WEO) *Slowing Growth, Rising Risks*. September. Washington, DC: International Monetary Fund.
IMF (2012) *IMF Standing Borrowing Arrangements* (International Monetary Fund Fact Sheet). Available at www.imf.org/external/np/exr/facts/pdf/gabnab.pdf.
International Energy Agency, *World Energy Outlook 2012*. Paris OECD/IEA
International Energy Statistics (2011). Available at http://tonto.eia.doe.gov/cfapps/ipdbproject/www.guardian.co.uk/news/datablog/2011/jan/31/world-carbon-dioxide-emissions-country-data-co2#data.
International Research Institute for Climate Prediction (2005) *Sustainable Development in Africa: Is the Climate Right?* New York: IRI.
IPCC Second Assessment Climate Change 1995. *A Report of the Intergovernmental Panel on Climate Change*. UNEP WMO. Available at www.ipcc.ch/pdf/climate-changes-1995/ipcc-2nd-assessment/2nd-assessment-en.pdf.
IPCC (2007a) *Climate Change 2007: The Physical Science Basis*. Contribution of Working Group I to the Fourth Assessment Report of the Intergovernmental Panel on Climate Change. S. Solomon, D. Qin, M. Manning, Z. Chen, M. Marquis, K.B. Averyt, M.Tignor and H.L. Miller (eds). Cambridge: Cambridge University Press.

IPCC (2007b) *Climate Change 2007: Impacts, Adaptation and Vulnerability.* Contribution of Working Group II to the Fourth Assessment Report of the Intergovernmental Panel on Climate Change. M.L. Parry, O.F. Canziani, J.P. Palutikof, P.J. van der Linden and C.E. Hanson (eds). Cambridge: Cambridge University Press.

IPCC 2011 PCC (2011) *IPCC Special Report on Renewable Energy Sources and Climate Change Mitigation.* Prepared by Working Group III of the Intergovernmental Panel on Climate Change. O. Edenhofer, R. Pichs-Madruga, Y. Sokona, K. Seyboth, P. Matschoss, S. Kadner, T. Zwickel, P. Eickemeier, G. Hansen, S. Schlömer and C. von Stechow (eds). Cambridge/New York: Cambridge University Press.

IPCC (2012) *Managing the Risks of Extreme Events and Disasters to Advance Climate Change Adaptation.* A Special Report of Working Groups I and II of the Intergovernmental Panel on Climate Change. C.B. Field, V. Barros, T.F. Stocker, D. Qin, D.J. Dokken, K.L. Ebi, M.D. Mastrandrea, K.J. Mach, G.-K. Plattner, S.K. Allen, M. Tignor, and P.M. Midgley (eds). Cambridge: Cambridge University Press.

IPCC (2013) Summary for Policymakers. In T.F. Stocker, D. Qin, G.-K. Plattner, M. Tignor, S.K. Allen, J. Boschung, A. Nauels, Y. Xia, V. Bex and P.M. Midgley (eds), *Climate Change 2013: The Physical Science Basis.* Contribution of Working Group I to the Fifth Assessment Report of the Intergovernmental Panel on Climate Change. Cambridge: Cambridge University Press.

IPCC (2014) *(Citation for Part B: Regional Aspects (Ch 21–30)): Climate Change 2014: Impacts, Adaptation, and Vulnerability. Part B: Regional Aspects. Contribution of Working Group II to the Fifth Assessment Report of the Intergovernmental Panel on Climate Change.* Barros, V.R., C.B. Field, D.J. Dokken, M.D. Mastrandrea, K.J. Mach, T.E. Bilir, M. Chatterjee, K.L. Ebi, Y.O. Estrada, R.C. Genova, B. Girma, E.S. Kissel, A.N. Levy, S. MacCracken, P.R. Mastrandrea and L.L. White (eds). Cambridge/New York: Cambridge University Press.

IPCC (2014b) *Climate Change 2014: Mitigation of Climate Change. Contribution of Working Group III to the Fifth Assessment Report of the Intergovernmental Panel on Climate Change.* Edenhofer, O., R. Pichs-Madruga, Y. Sokona, E. Farahani, S. Kadner, K. Seyboth, A. Adler, I. Baum, S. Brunner, P. Eickemeier, B. Kriemann, J. Savolainen, S. Schlömer, C. von Stechow, T. Zwickel and J.C. Minx (eds). Cambridge/New York: Cambridge University Press.

IPCC (2014) *Climate Change 2014: Mitigation of Climate Change.* Contribution of Working Group III to the Fifth Assessment Report of the Intergovernmental Panel on Climate Change. O. Edenhofer, R. Pichs-Madruga, Y. Sokona, E. Farahani, S. Kadner, K. Seyboth, A. Adler, I. Baum, S. Brunner, P. Eickemeier, B. Kriemann, J. Savolainen, S. Schlömer, C. von Stechow, T. Zwickel and J.C. Minx (eds). Cambridge: Cambridge University Press.

IPCC (2014) *(Part A: Global and Sectoral Aspects, Ch 1–20): Climate Change 2014: Impacts, Adaptation, and Vulnerability. Part A: Global and Sectoral Aspects. Contribution of Working Group II to the Fifth Assessment Report of the Intergovernmental Panel on Climate Change.* Field, C.B., V.R. Barros, D.J. Dokken, K.J. Mach, M.D. Mastrandrea, T.E. Bilir, M. Chatterjee, K.L. Ebi, Y.O. Estrada, R.C. Genova, B. Girma, E.S. Kissel, A.N. Levy, S. MacCracken, P.R. Mastrandrea, and L.L. White (eds). Cambridge/New York: Cambridge University Press.

IPCC (2014) *Summary for Policymakers in Climate Change 2014: Impacts, Adaptation, and Vulnerability. Part A: Global and Sectoral Aspects. Contribution of Working Group II to the Fifth Assessment Report of the Intergovernmental Panel on Climate Change.* Field, C.B., V.R. Barros, D.J. Dokken, K.J. Mach, M.D. Mastrandrea, T.E. Bilir, M. Chatterjee, K.L. Ebi, Y.O. Estrada, R.C. Genova, B. Girma, E.S. Kissel, A.N. Levy, S. MacCracken, P.R. Mastrandrea and L.L. White (eds). Cambridge/New York: Cambridge University Press.

IPS (2009) Sunday 2 August. www.ipsnews.net.
IRENA (2013) *Renewable Energy and Jobs*. Abu Dhabi: IRENA.
ISDR (2009) *Global Assessment Report on Disaster Risk Reduction*. Geneva: ISDR.
Islam, R. (2009) Climate Change induced disasters and gender dimensions: perspective, Bangladesh. *Peace & Conflict Monitor* May: 4. Available at www.monitor.upeace.org/archive.cfm?id_article=616.
ITUC (2009) *Gender (In)equality in the Labour Market: An Overview of Global Trends and Developments*. Brussels: ITUC.
IUCN, UNDP and the Global Gender and Climate Alliance (2009) *Training Manual on Gender and Climate Change* (Aguilar Revelo, L. ed.). San Jose, Costa Rica. Available at https://portals.iucn.org/library/efiles/documents/2009-012.pdf.
Jackson, C. (2003) Gender analysis of land: beyond land rights for women? *Journal of Agrarian Change* 3: 453–80.
Jacobson, J. (1988) *Environmental Refugees: A Yardstick of Habitability*. Washington, DC: World Watch Institute.
Jacoby, H.D., Babiker, M.H., Paltsev, S. and Reilly, J.M. (2008) *Sharing the Burden of GHG Reductions*. MIT Joint Program on the Science and Policy of Global Change Report no. 16, November. Available at http://globalchange.mit.edu/fi les/document/MITJPSPGC_Rpt167.pdf.
Jacoby, H., Rabassa, M. and Skoufias, E. (2011) *On the Distributional Implications of Climate Change: The Case of India*. Washington, DC: World Bank.
Jenkins, P. and B. Phillips (2008) Battered women, catastrophe, and the context of safety after Hurricane Katrina. *NWSA Journal* 20(3): 49–68.
Johnsson-Latham, G. (2006) *Do Women Leave a Smaller Ecological Footprint than Men?* Study from the Swedish Ministry for Sustainable Development.
Johnsson-Latham, G. (2007) *A Study on Gender Equality as a Prerequisite for Sustainable Development*. Report to the Environment Advisory Council, Sweden.
Jones, A., Wolosin, M., Fransen, T. and Nakhooda, S. (2013) *The US Contribution to Fast-Start Finance: FY12*. Washington, DC: WRI.
Jonkman, S.N. and I. Kelman (2005) An analysis of the causes and circumstances of flood disaster deaths. *Disasters* 29(1): 75–97.
Journal of Blacks in Higher Education (2005) Hurricane Katrina's devastating effect on African-American higher education. Available at www.jbhe.com/features/49_hurrican_katrina.html (accessed 30 December 2011).
Julia and B. White (2012) Gendered experiences of dispossession: Oil palm expansion in a Dayak Hibun community in West Kalimantan. *Journal of Peasant Studies* 39(3–4): 995–1016.
Jumbe, C.B.L., and A. Angelsen (2007) Has forest co-management in Malawi benefited the poor? In. Dinello and V. Popov (eds) *Political institutions and development: failed expectations and renewed hopes*, pp. 171–99. Edward Elgar, Cheltenham, UK.
Kabeer, N. (1999) Resources, agency, achievements: Measurement of women's empowerment. *Development and Change* 30: 435–464.
Kabula, D. (2014) Presentation on Zambia, session, Mainstreaming Climate Resilience into Development Plans, Second Forum, UNFCCC Standing Committee on Finance, June 21, Montego Bay, Jamaica.
Kakota, T., D. Nyariki, D. Mkwambisi, and W. Kogi-Makau (2011) Gender vulnerability to climate variability and household food insecurity. *Climate and Development* 3(4): 298–309.
Kalimunjaye, S., Olobo, M. and Kyakulumbye, S. (2012) Carbon trade financing strategies and opportunities for competitiveness of private sector SMEs in Uganda. *Technology and Investment* 3(4): 244–51.

Kälin, W. (2008) The climate change–displacement nexus. The Secretary-General on the Human Rights of Internally Displaced Persons, Panel on disaster risk reduction and preparedness: addressing the humanitarian consequences of natural disasters, ECOSOC Humanitarian Affairs Segment, 16 July. Available at www.brookings.edu/speeches/2008/0716_climate_change_kalin.aspx.

Kaminker, Ch., Stewart, F. (2012) *The Role of Institutional Investors in Financing Clean Energy*. OECD Working Papers on Finance, Insurance and Private Pensions, No. 23, OECD. Available at http://dx.doi.org/10.1787/5k9312v21l6f-en.

Kanitkar, T., Jayaraman, T., D'Souza, M., Sanwal, M., Purkayastha, P., Talwar, T. (2010) *Meeting Equity in a Finite Carbon World Global Carbon Budgets and Burden Sharing in Mitigation Actions*. Background Paper for the Conference on 'Global Carbon Budgets and Equity in Climate Change', June 28–9. Tata Institute of Social Sciences.

Kartha, S. and Erickson, P. (2011) *Comparison of Annex 1 and Non-Annex 1 Pledges under the Cancun Agreements*. Working Paper WP-US-1107. Sommerville: Stockholm Environment Institute.

Kartha, S., Athanaisou, T. and Baer, T. (2012) The North–South Divide, Equity and Development – The Need for Trust-Building for Emergency Mobilization. In *Climate, Development and Equity: What Next?* Volume III. Development Dialogue no. 16, September. Uppsala: Dag Hammarskjöld Foundation.

Kauffman Foundation (2006) *An Untapped Pool of Equity for Entrepreneurs: Insight and Recommendations from Leading Women Angels*. April. Kansas City, MO: Kauffman Foundation.

Kaupp, H., Liptow, A. and Michaelaowa, A. (2002) CDM is not about subsidies – it is about additionality. *Energise* 1(3): 8–9.

Kelkar, U. and Bhadwal, S. (2007) *South Asian Regional Study on Climate Change Impacts and Adaptation: Implications for Human Development*. HDRO Occasional Paper 2007/27. New York: UNDP.

Kes, A. and Swaminathan, H. (2006) Gender and time poverty in sub-Saharan Africa. In M.C. Blackden and Q. Wodon (eds), *Gender, Time Use, and Poverty in Sub-Saharan Africa*. Working Paper no. 73. Washington, DC: World Bank.

Kevane, M. and Wydick, B. (2001) Microenterprise lending to female entrepreneurs: Sacrificing economic growth for poverty alleviation? *World Development* 29: 1225–36.

Kharta, S. and Erickson, P. (2011) *Comparison of Annex 1 and non-Annex 1 pledges under the Cancun Agreements*. Stockholm Environment Institute Working Paper WP-US-1107. Available at www.sei-international.org/mediamanager/documents/Publications/Climate/sei-workingpaperus-1107.pdf.

Khondker, H.H. (1996) Women and floods in Bangladesh. *International Journal of Mass Emergencies and Disasters* 14(3): 281–92.

Khor, M. (2007) Bali climate talks to decide fate of Kyoto Protocol. Climate Briefings for Bali 2 United Nations Climate Change Conference, Bali, 3–14, December 2007. Third World Network.

Khor, M. (2010) *The Equitable Sharing of Atmospheric and Development Space: Some Critical Aspects*. Research paper 33. Geneva: South Centre.

Khor, M. (2011) *Risks and Uses of the Green Economy Concept in the Context of Sustainable Development, Poverty and Equity*. Research paper 40, July. Geneva: South Centre.

Khor, M. (2012) A clash of paradigms – UN climate negotiations at a crossroads. In *Climate, Development and Equity: What Next?* Volume III. Development Dialogue no. 16, September. Uppsala: Dag Hammarskjöld Foundation.

Kim, K.A. (2003) *Sustainable Development and the CDM: A South African Case Study*. Tyndall Centre for Climate Change Research Working Paper 42.

Kirshen, P. (2007). *Adaptation Options and Costs in Water Supply*. A report to the UNFCCC Financial and Technical Support Division. Available at http://unfccc.int/cooperation_ and_support/financial_mechanism/financial_mechanism_gef/items/4054.php.

Koenig, D. (1995) Women and resettlement. In R.S. Gallin, A. Ferguson and J. Harper (eds), *The Women and International Development Annual*, vol. 4, pp. 21–49. Boulder, CO: Westview Press.

Kopecki, D. and Dodge, C. (2009) US rescue may reach $23.7 trillion, Barofsky says. Available at www.bloomberg.com/apps/news?pid=newsarchive&sid=aY0tX8UysIaM.

Kosatsky, T. (2005) The 2003 European health waves. *Euro Surveill* 10: 148–9.

Kovats, R.S. and Hajat, S. (2008) Heat stress and public health: a critical review. *Annual Review of Public Health* 29: 41–55.

Kovats, S. (2009) Adaptation costs for human health. In M. Parry et al. (eds), *Assessing the Costs of Adaptation to Climate Change: A Review of the UNFCCC and Other Recent Estimates*. London: International Institute for Environment and Development and Grantham Institute for Climate Change.

Krzysztof Hagemejer, K. and. Hagemejer, B.K. (2009) *Promoting Pro-poor Growth: Social Protection Can Low-income Countries Afford Basic Social Security? Affordability of Social Protection Measures in Poor Developing Countries*. Paris: OECD.

Lallement, D. (2014) *Gender, Renewable Energy, and Climate Change*. International Development Consultant Partnership Forum, Montego Bay, 23 June. Washington, DC: World Bank.

Lambrou, Y. and Piana, G. (2006) *Gender: The Missing Component of the Response to Climate Change*. Available at www.fao.org/sd/dim_pe1/docs/pe1_051001d1_en.pdf.

Lambrou, Y. and S. Nelson (2013) Gender issues in climate change adaptation: Farmers' food security in Andhra Pradesh. In Alston, M. and K. Whittenbury (eds.) *Research, Action and Policy: Addressing the Gendered Impacts of Climate Change*, pp. 189–206. Dordrecht, Netherlands: Springer Science.

LDC Watch (2014) Adaptation in the Mountains: Issues and Gaps beyond Boundaries. Asia Pacific Youth Forum and Training Workshop 2014, ICIMOD Headquarters, Kathmandu, Nepal, 22 September.

Le Queré, C. et al. (2008) Saturation of the Southern Ocean CO 2 Sink Due to Recent Climate Change. *Science* 319, 570c.

Lethbridge, J. (2012) *Impact of the Global Economic Crisis and Austerity Measures on Women*. London: Public Services International Research Unit, Business School, University of Greenwich.

Levina, E. (2009) *Financing Developing Country Mitigation and Adaptation: International Governance*. Washington, DC: Center for Clear Air Policy.

Life e.V. and Gender CC (2009) *Gender Mainstreaming and Beyond – 5 Steps Towards Gender-Sensitive Long Term Cooperation*. Berlin: Life e.V.

Lighting Africa (2011) Expanding women's role in Africa's modern off-grid lighting market. Available at www.lightingafrica.org/new-report-african-women-stand-to-gain-from-modern-off-grid-lighting.html.

Lim Li Lin (2010) In_session workshop on the numbers. AWG_KP 13. Third World Network. August. Bonn: UNFCCC.

Lindblade, K.A., Walker, E.D., Onapa, A.W., Katungu, J. and Wilson, M.L. (1999) Highland malaria in Uganda: prospective analyses of an epidemic associate with El Nino. *Transactions of the Royal Society of Tropical Medicine and Hygiene* 93: 480–7.

Litvak, V. (2007) *Priorities and Principles of Carbon Financing Within UNDP MDG Carbon Facility*. New York: UNDP.

Liverman, D. and Boyd, E. (2008) The CDM, ethics and development. In K. Olsen and J. Fenhann (eds), *A Reformed CDM – Including New Mechanisms for Sustainable Development*. Nairobi: UNEP-Risø Centre.

Locke, C. (1999) Constructing a gender policy for joint forest management in India. *Development and Change* 30(2): 265–85.

Loevinsohn, M.E. (1994) Climatic warming and increased malaria incidence in Rwanda. *The Lancet* 343: 714–18.

Logan, J.R. (no date) *The Impact of Katrina: Race and Class in Storm-Damaged Neighborhoods*. Available at http://asp.uibk.ac.at/nosi/report.pdf (accessed 30 December 2011).

López Torrejón, E. *et al.* (2012) The experience of El Almanario in ten indigenous communites in Guatemala. *Iberoamerican Journal of Development Studies* 1(1).

Lütken, S.E. (2008) CDM: developing country financing for developed country commitments? In K. Olsen and J. Fenhann (eds), *A Reformed CDM – including New Mechanisms for Sustainable Development*. Nairobi: UNEP-Risø Centre.

McArthur, R.H. (1972) *Geographic Ecology: Patterns in the Distribution of the Species*. New York: Harper and Row.

McCaffery, E.J. (1997) *Taxing Women*. Chicago, IL: University of Chicago Press.

McCarl, B. (2007) *Adaptation Options for Agriculture, Forestry and Fisheries*. A Report to the UNFCCC Financial and Technical Support Division. Available at http://unfccc.int/cooperation_and_support/financial_mechanism/financial_mechanism_gef/items/4054.php.

McGray, H., Hamill, A., Bradley, R., Schipper, E.L. and Parry, J.-O. (2007) *Weathering the Storm: Options for Framing Adaptation and Development*. Washington, DC: World Resources Institute.

MacGregor, S. (2010) 'Gender and climate change': From impacts to discourses. *Journal of the Indian Ocean Region* 6(2): 223–38.

McKibben, B. (2012) Global Warming's Terrifying New Math. *Rolling Stone* 19 July: 55–60.

Mckinsey (2009) *Pathways to a Low-Carbon Economy. Version 2 of the Global Greenhouse Gas Abatement Cost Curve*, McKinsey & Company. Available at www.mckinsey.com/.../mckinsey/.../pathways_lowcarbon_economy_version2.3/pdf.

McMichael, A.J., Campbell-Lendrum, D., Kovats, R.S., Edwards, S., Wilkinson, P., Edmonds, N., Nicholls, N., Hales, S., Tanser, F.C., Le Sueur, D., Schlesinger, M. and Andronova, N. (2004) Climate change. In M. Ezzati *et al.* (eds), *Comparative Quantification of Health Risks: Global and Regional Burden of Disease due to Selected Major Risk Factors*, vol. 2, pp. 1543–1649. Geneva: WHO.

Maitland, A. (2009) FT top 50 women in world business. *Financial Times* 26/27 September.

Malmberge-Calvo (1994) *Case Study on the Role of Women in Rural Transport: Access of Women to Domestic Facilities – Sub-Saharan Africa Transport Policy Program*. The World Bank and Economic Commission for Africa SSATP Working Paper 11.

Manzo, K. (2010) Imaging vulnerability: The iconography of climate change. *Area* 42(1): 96–107.

Maosheng, D. (2008) The Clean Development Mechanism: assessment of experience and expectations for the future. In K. Olsen and J. Fenhann (eds), *A Reformed CDM – including New Mechanisms for Sustainable Development*. Nairobi: UNEP-Risø Centre.

Marcucci, P.N. (2001) *Jobs, Gender and Small Enterprises in Africa and Asia: Lessons Drawn from Bangladesh, the Philippines, Tunisia and Zimbabwe*. SEED Working Paper 2001/18, WEDGE series. Geneva: International Labour Office.

Mary Robinson Foundation (2011) *Analysis of Gender References in UNFCCC COP 17 and CMP 7 Texts*. Available at http://mrfcj.org/pdf/Overview_on_the_status_of_gender_references_post-COP17.pdf.

Masika, R. (ed.) (2002) *Gender, Development and Climate Change*. Oxford: Oxfam Publishing. Available at www.oxfam.org.uk/resources/downloads/FOG_Climate_15.pdf.

Matsuo, N. (2003) CDM in the Kyoto negotiations. *Mitigation and Adaptation Strategies for Global Change* 8 (3): 191–200.

Mbow, C., Skole, D., Dieng, M., Justice, C., Kwesha, D., Mane, L., E. Gamri, M.,V. Vordzogbe, V., Virji and H. (2012) *Challenges and Prospects for REDD+ in Africa: Desk Review Of REDD+ Implementation in Africa*. Copenhagen, Denmark: GLP-IPO.

MDG Carbon facility. Available at www.undp.org/content/dam/aplaws/publication/en/publications/environment-energy/www-ee-library/climate-change/mdg-carbon-facility-brochure/MDGCF_Brochure_English_07.pdf.

Meinshausen, M. *et al.* (2009) Greenhouse-gas emission targets for limiting global warming to 2°C. *Nature* 458(30 April): 1158–62.

Mendelsohn, R. (2008) Warming to global warming. *Edmonton Journal* 24 November. Available at www.canada.com/topics/news/world/story.html?id=cff56e4b-5273-456c-9f31-5d3081e9aa3a.

Mendelsohn, R., Nordhaus, W.D. and Shaw, D. (1994) The impact of global warming on agriculture: A Ricardian analysis. *American Economic Review* 84(4): 753–71.

Mensah-Kutin, R. (2007) Gender and energy in Africa: regional initiatives and challenges promoting gender and energy. In G. Karlson (ed.), *Where Energy is Women's Business*. Leusden: ENERGIA.

Metz, B., Davidson, O.R., Bosch, P.R., Dave, R. and Meyer, L.A. (eds) (2007) *Climate Change 2007: Mitigation of Climate Change*. Contribution of Working Group III to the Fourth Assessment Report of the Intergovernmental Panel on Climate Change. Cambridge: Cambridge University Press.

Michaelowa, A. and Michaelowa, K. (2005) *Climate or Development: Is ODA Diverted from its Original Purpose?* Research paper 2. Hamburg: HWWI.

Minniti, M. and Naudé, W. (2010) Female entrepreneurship in developing countries. Available at www.wider.unu.edu/publications/newsletter/articles-2010/en_GB/08-2010-Female-Entrepreneurship.

Miralles-Wilhelm, F. (2012) *Recursos Hídricos y Adaptación al Cambio Climático en América Latina y el Caribe*. Banco Interamericano de Desarollo, Technical Note 478.

Mirza, M.M.Q. (2003) Climate change and extreme weather events: can developing countries adapt? *Climate Policies* 3: 233–48.

Mitchell, A. and Huq, S. (2008) *Principles for Delivering Adaptation Finance*. Available at https://cms.ids.ac.uk/UserFiles/file/poverty_team/climate_change/Adaptation%20Finance%20Briefing_final(1).pdf.

Mitchell, T., Tanner, T. and Lussier, K. (2007) *'We Know What We Need!' South Asian Women Speak Out on Climate Change Adaptation*. London: Action Aid International/Brighton: Institute of Development Studies, University of Sussex.

Mitchell, T., Haynes, K., Hall, N., Choong, W. and Oven, K. (2008) The role of children and youth in communicating disaster risk. *Children, Youth and Environments* 18(1): 254–79.

Möhner, A. and Klein, R.J.T. (2007) *The Global Environment Facility: Funding for Adaptation or Adapting to Funds?* Stockholm: Stockholm Environment Institute.

Mogues,T., Cohen, M. J., Birner, B., Lemma, M., Randriamamonjy, J., Tadesse, F. and Paulos, Z. (2009) *Agricultural Extension in Ethiopia through a Gender and Governance Lens*. Development Strategy and Governance Division, International Food Policy Research Institute – Ethiopia Strategy Support Program 2, Ethiopia. Available at www.ifpri.org/sites/default/files/publications/esspdp07.pdf.

Molitor, M.R. (ed.) (1991) *International Environmental Law – Primary Materials*. Boson, MA: Kluwer Law & Taxation.

Molony, T. (2011) Bioenergy policies in Africa: mainstreaming gender amid an increasing focus on biofuels. *Biofuels, Bioproducts and Biorefining* 5(3): 330–41.

Montes, M. (2012) *Understanding Climate Change Financing Requirements of Developing Countries*. Geneva: South Centre.

Montes, M. (2012) *Understanding the Long-Term Finance Needs of Developing Countries*. Bonn: UNFCCC.

Montgomery, J. and Young, B. (2009) *Home is Where the Hardship Is: Gender and Wealth (Dis)Accumulation in the Subprime Boom*. CRESC Working Paper 79. Milton Keynes: Open University/CRESC. Available at www.cresc.ac.uk/publications/home-is-where-the-hardship-is-gender-and-wealth-disaccumulation-in-the-subprime-boom.

Moore, T.G. (1996) *Health and Amenity Effects of Global Warming*. Washington, DC: Hoover Institution.

Moore, T.G. (2008) Quoted in Global warming – it's not all bad. *The Edmonton Journal*, November 23. Available at www.canada.com/edmontonjournal/news/sundayreader/story.html?id=dadb2fd1-be45-4493-999c-bcc69b02fbce#__federated=1.

Müller, B. (2008) *International Adaptation Finance: The Need for an Innovative and Strategic Approach*. Oxford: OIES.

The Munden Project (2011) *REDD and Forest Carbon: Market-Based Critique and Recommendations*. Available at www.mundenproject.com/forestcarbonreport2.pdf[.

Munich Re (2011) *2010 Natural Catastrophe Year in Review*. 10 January. Available at www.munichre.com/us/property-casualty/events/webinar/2011-01-natcatreview/index.html and Munich Re NatCatSERVICE www.preventionweb.net/files/24476_20120104munichrenaturalcatastrophes[1].pdf.

Murphy, D., Crosbey, A. and Drexhage, J. (2008) Market mechanisms for sustainable development in a post-2012 climate regime: implications for the development dividend. In K. Olsen and J. Fenhann (eds), *A Reformed CDM – including New Mechanisms for Sustainable Development*. Nairobi: UNEP-Risø Centre.

Muthoni, J.W. and E.E. Wangui (2013) Women and climate change: strategies for adaptive capacity in Mwanga District, Tanzania. *African Geographical Review* 32(1): 59–71.

Muylaert, M.S., Cohen, C., Pinguelli Rosa, L. and Santos Pereira, A. (2004) Equity, responsibility and climate change. *Climate Research* 28: 89–92.

Myers, N. (1993) Environmental refugees in a globally warmed world. *Bioscience* 43: 752–61.

Myers, N. (1995) *Environmental Exodus: An Emergent Crisis in the Global Arena*. Washington, DC: CI.

Nafo, S. (2012) *Defining 'Mobilized' Climate Finance: Solving a Fractal Conundrum*. Prepared for the Climate Change Expert Group (CCXG) Global Forum on the New UNFCCC Market Mechanism and Tracking Climate Finance, 19–20 March. Paris: OECD.

Nakhooda, S. (2012) *The Effectiveness of International Climate Finance*. London: ODI.

Narain, S. (2007) *Access to Finance for Women SME Entrepreneurs in Bangladesh*. Gender Entrepreneurship Markets, Mimeo, IFC. Bangladesh: South Asia Enterprise Development Facility (SEDF).

Narrod, C., Roy, D., Okello, J., Avendano, B., Rich, K. and Thorat, A. (2009) Public–private partnerships and collective action in high value fruit and vegetable supply chains. *Food Policy* 34: 8–15.

Nath, O. (2009) *CDM Potentials in SME*. Available at http://smallb.sidbi.in/sites/default/files/knowledge_base/presentation_cdm.pdf.

National Academy of Sciences (2007) Adapting to abrupt climate change. Available at http://dels.nas.edu/abr_clim/adapting.shtml.

National Council for Research on Women (2009) *Women in Fund Management: A Road Map for Achieving Critical Mass – and Why it Matters*. Available at www.ncrw.org/hedgefund.
Nature (2009) A safe operating space for humanity. *Nature* 461: 472–5.
Ndiaye, G. (2008) *Impact du Changement Climatique sur les Ressources en Eau du Sénégal*. Dakar: ENDA.
Neelormi, S., N. Adri, and A. Ahmed (2008) *Gender Perspectives of Increased Socio-Economic Risks of Waterlogging in Bangladesh due to Climate Change*. St. Petersburg, FL: International Ocean Institute.
Neelormi, S., N. Adri, and A. Ahmed (2009) Gender dimensions of differential health effects of climate change induced water-logging: A case study from coastal Bangladesh. *Proceedings of IOP Conference Series: Earth and Environmental Science* 6 (142026).
Nellemann, C., Verma, R. and Hislop, L. (eds) (2011) *Women at the Frontline of Climate Change: Gender Risks and Hopes*. Nairobi: UNEP.
Nelson, G.C. (ed.) (2009) *Agriculture and Climate Change: An Agenda for Negotiation in Copenhagen*. Washington, DC: IFPRI.
Nelson, G.C., Rosegrant, M.W., Koo, J., Robertson, R., Sulser, T., Zhu, T., Ringler, C., Msangi, S., Palazzo, A., Batka, M., Magalhaes, M., Valmonte-Santos, R., Ewing, M. and Lee, D. (2009) *Climate Change Impact on Agriculture and Costs of Adaptation*. Washington, DC: International Food Policy Research.
Nelson, K.C. and de Jong, B.H. (2002) Making global initiatives local realities: Carbon mitigation projects in Chiapas. *Global Environmental Change* 13: 19–30.
Neumayer, E. (2000) In defence of historical accountability for greenhouse gas emissions. *Ecological Economics* 33:185–92.
Neumayer, E. and Plümper, T. (2007) *The Gendered Nature of Natural Disasters: The Impact of Catastrophic Events on the Gender Gap in Life Expectancy, 1981–2002*. London: London School of Economics and Political Science with University of Essex and Max-Planck Institute of Economics.
New Carbon Finance (2009) *Fortifying the Foundation: State of the Voluntary Carbon Markets 2009*. New York: Bloomberg.
New Economics Foundation (2012) *Counting on Uncertainty: The Economic Case for Community-based Adaptation in North-East Kenya*. Available at www.careclimatechange.org/files/adaptation/Counting_on_Uncertainty_July12.pdf.
New York Times (2010) (C. Podkul) Private equity is bullish on clean energy. January 29. Available at http://green.blogs.nytimes.com/2010/01/29/private-equity-is-bullish-on-clean-energy/.
Nomura (2012) *Adaptation Needs in Developing Countries and Adaptation Sectors with High Potential for Contributions by Japanese Enterprises*. March. Tokyo: Nomura Research Institute.
Norad (2010) *Progress Report – Gender Mainstreaming in Norad's Energy Programme*. November. Leusden: ENERGIA.
Noy, I. (2009) The macro-economic consequences of disaster. *Journal of Development Economics* 88: 221–31.
Oakland Institute (2011) *Understanding Land Investment Deals in Africa Country Report: Ethiopia*. Oakland, CA. Available at www.oaklandinstitute.org/sites/oaklandinstitute.org/files/OI_Ethiopa_Land_Investment_report.pdf.
Obrador, P. (2008) *Implementing Program of Activities under CDM from the Point of View of the Managing Entities: Microfinance Institutions as an Opportunity for Developing Energy Efficiency PoAs in Latin America?* Latin American Carbon Forum, Chile, 28–30 October. KFW ForderBank. Available at www.latincarbon.com/2008/docs/presentations/Day3/Pablo Obrador.pdf.

O'Brien, K., R. Leichenko, U. Kelkar, H. Venema, G. Aandahl, H.Tompkins, A. Javed, S. Bhadwal, S. Barg, L. Nygaard and J. West (2004) Mapping vulnerability to multiple stressors: Climate change and globalization in India. *Global Environmental Change* 14: 303–13.

Obstfeld, M. (2011) *The SDR as an International Reserve Asset: What Future?* London: International Growth Centre, London School of Economics.

Odum, E.C. (2004) A prosperous way down. In E. Ortega and S. Ulgiati (eds), *Proceedings of IV Biennial International Workshop Advances in Energy Studies*, pp.1–10. Campinas: Unicamp.

Odum, H.T. (1973) Energy, ecology and economics. *Ambio* 2(6): 222.

Odum, H.T. and Odum, E.C. (2001) *The Prosperous Way Down*. Boulder, CO: University Press of Colorado.

Oduro, A. D., Baah-Boateng, W. and Boakye-Yiadom, L. (2011) *Measuring the Gender Asset Gap in Ghana*. Accra, Ghana: Woeli Publishing Services and University of Ghana.

OECD (2008) *Gender and Sustainable Development: Maximising The Economic, Social and Environmental Role Of Women*. Paris: OECD.

OECD (2011) *Development Perspectives for a Post-Copenhagen Climate Financing Architecture*. Paris: OECD.

OECD (2011) *Financing Climate Action Climate and Development Knowledge Network*. Paris: OECD.

OECD (2011) *First-ever Comprehensive Data on Aid for Climate Change Adaptation*. Paris: OECD.

OECD (2011) *OECD DAC Data Collection on Funding for the UN System Julia Benn Development Co-Operation Directorate*. Geneva: OECD.

OECD (2012) *OECD Environmental Outlook to 2050: The Consequences of Inaction*. Paris: OECD.

OECD-DAC (2002) *ODA and the Clean Development Mechanism*. Paris: OECD.

OECD-DAC (2011) *The Development Co-operataion Report 2011*. Paris: OECD

OECD and IEA (2009) *Financing Mitigation Support: Towards a Framework for Measurement, Reporting and Verification*. Paris: OECD.

Oldrup, H. and Breengaard, M.H. (2009) *Gender and Climate Changes Report. Nordic Summit Declaration, Abstract – Desk Study on Gender Equality and Climate Changes*. Available at www.norden.org/gender/doks/sk/Gender_and_climate_changes_Rapport.pdf (accessed 12 April 2009).

Olsen, K. (2006) *The Clean Development Mechanism's Contribution to Sustainable Development: A Review of the Literature*. Nairobi: UNEP-Risø Centre.

Olsen, K. and Fenhann, J. (eds) (2008) *A Reformed CDM – Including New Mechanisms for Sustainable Development*. Nairobi: UNEP-Risø Centre.

O'Neill, B. et al. (2010) Global demographic trends and future carbon emissions. *Proceedings of the National Academy of Sciences* 107(41): 17521–6.

Onkar, N. (2009) *CDM Potential in SMEs*. Available at http://smallb.in/sites/default/files/knowledge_base/presentation_cdm.pdf.

Oppenheimer, M. and Alley, R.B. (2005) Ice sheets, global warming, and Article 2 of the UNFCCC. *Climatic Change* 68: 257–67.

Oppong-Boadi, K. (2008) *Climate Change Impacts in Ghana*. Accra, Ghana: Environmental Protection Agency.

Orenstein, K., Redman, J. and Tangri, N. (2014) *The Green Climate Fund's 'No-Objection' Procedure and Private Finance: Lessons Learned from Existing Institutions*. Washington, DC: Friends of the Earth, Institute for Policy Studies and Global Alliance for Incinerator Alternatives.

Osei-Akoto I. DarkoOsei R. and Aryeetey E. (2009) *Gender and Indirect Tax Incidence in Ghana*. Ghana: Institute of Statistical, Social and Economic Research (ISSER) University of Ghana.

Oxfam (2007) *Adapting to Climate Change: What is Needed in Poor Countries and Who Should Pay?* Oxfam briefing paper 104. Oxford: Oxfam.

Oxfam (2008) Analysis of the Poznan Conference outcomes 2008. Available at www.oxfam.org/pressroom/pressrelease/2008-12-13/oxfam-analysis-poznan-conference-outcomes.

Oxfam (2010) *Righting Two Wrongs: Making a New Global Climate Fund Work for Poor People.* Oxfam briefing note, October. Oxford: Oxfam.

Oxfam (2011) *Owning Adaptation Country-level Governance of Climate Adaptation Finance.* Oxfam briefing paper 146, 13 June. Oxford: Oxfam.

Oxfam International (2013) *Promises, Power and Poverty.* Available at www.oxfam.org/sites/www.oxfam.org/files/bp170-promises-power-poverty-land-women-090413-en.pdf.

Pachauri R.K., Reisinger A. (2007) *Climate change 2007: Synthesis Report. Contribution of Working Groups I, II and III to the Fourth Assessment Report of the Intergovernmental Panel on Climate Change.* Geneva: Intergovernmental Panel on Climate Change.

Panitchpakdi, S. (2009) *Women Workers Will Be Hit Hardest.* Geneva: UNCTAD.

Panjwani, A. (2005) *Energy as a Key Variable in Promoting Gender Equality and Empowering Women: A Gender and Energy Perspective on MDG #3.* ENERGIA/EASE Discussion Paper. Leusden: ENERGIA.

Parikh, J. (2007) *Gender and Climate Change: Framework for Analysis, Policy and Action.* India: IRADe and UNDP.

Parkinson, D., C. Lancaster and A. Stewart (2011) A numbers game: Lack of gendered data impedes prevention of disaster-related family violence. *Health Promotion Journal of Australia* 22: 42–5.

Parry, M.L., Canziani, O.F., Palutikof, J.P., van der Linden, P.J. and Hanson, C.E. (eds) (2007) *Climate Change 2007: Impacts, Adaptation and Vulnerability.* Contribution of Working Group II to the Fourth Assessment Report of the Intergovernmental Panel on Climate Change. Cambridge: Cambridge University Press.

Parry, M., Arnell, N., Berry, P., Dodman, D., Fankhauser, S., Hope, C., Kovats, S., Nicholls, R., Satterthwaite, D., Tiffin, T. and Wheeler, T. (2009) *Assessing the Costs of Adaptation to Climate Change: A Review of the UNFCCC and Other Recent Estimates.* London: International Institute for Environment and Development and Grantham Institute for Climate Change.

Patz, J.A. *et al.* (2005) Impact of regional climate change on human health. *Nature* 438: 310–17.

PCF (2000) *Pro-type Carbon Finance.* Available at https://wbcarbonfinance.org/Router.cfm?Page=PCF.

PCFS (2012) *Not So Smart Climate Smart Agriculture.* Quezon City: IBON International.

Pearce, T., J. Ford, F. Duerden, B. Smit, M. Andrachuk, L. Berrang-Ford and T. Smith (2011) Advancing adaptation planning for climate change in the Inuvialuit Settlement Region (ISR): a review and critique. *Regional Environmental Change* 11(1): 1–17.

Pearl, R. (2003) *Commonground.Women'saccesstoNaturalresourcesandtheUnitedNations Millennium Development Goals.* WEDO (Women's Environmental and Development Organization). Available at www.wedo.org/files/common_ground.pdf.

Peiser 2008 Quoted in Global warming – it's not all bad. *The Edmonton Journal.* November 23, 2008.

Peraza, S., C. Wesseling, A. Aragon, R. Leiva, R.A. García-Trabanino, C. Torres, K. Jakobsson, C.G. Elinder and C. Hogstedt (2012). Decreased kidney function among agricultural workers in El Salvador. *American Journal of Kidney Diseases* 59(4): 531–40.

Perch, L., C. Watson, and B. Barry (2012) *Resource Inequality: Moving Inequalities from the Periphery to the Centre of the Post-2015 Agenda.* Background Paper for 'Addressing Inequalities' Global Thematic Consultation. New York: Addressing Inequalities Networked Alliance (AINA), co- led by the United Nations International Emergency

Children's Fund (UNICEF) and the United Nations Entity for Gender Equality and the Empowerment of Women (UN WOMEN) with support from the Governments of Denmark and Ghana, UNICEF.

Perlata, A. (2008) *Gender and Climate Change Finance – A Case Study from the Philippines*. New York: WEDO.

Perlata, A. (2009) *Gender Financing for Climate Change Mitigation and Adaptation in the Philippines: A Pro-poor and Gender Sensitive Perspective*. New York: WEDO.

Peterman, A., Quisumbing, A., Behrman, J., and Nkonya, E. (2010) *Understanding Gender Differences in Agricultural Productivity in Uganda and Nigeria*. IFPRI Discussion Paper 01003 July 2010. IFPRI Poverty, Health, and Nutrition Division

Peters, D. (2002) *Gender and Transport in Less Developed Countries: A Background Paper in Preparation for CSD-9 Co-Coordinator*. UN CSD Caucus on Sustainable Transport Background Paper for the Expert Workshop 'Gender Perspectives for Earth Summit 2002: Energy, Transport, Information for Decision-Making', Berlin, Germany, 10–12 January. London UNED Forum.

Peters, P.E. (2013) Conflicts over land and threats to customary tenure in Africa. *African Affairs* 112(449): 543–62.

Pew (2009) *Copenhagen 101: Mitigation*. Washington, DC: PEW.

Pew (2009) *The Timing of Climate Change Policy*. Available at www.pewclimate.org/policy_center/policy_reports_and_analysis/brief_timing_of_climate_chang/timing_options.cfm.

Porter, G. et al. (2008) *New Finance for Climate Change and the Environment*. Available at www.odi.org.uk/resources/download/2980.pdf (accessed 21 October 2009).

Posner, E.A. and Sunstein, C.R. (2008) *Justice and Climate Change*. Discussion Paper 08–04. Cambridge, MA: Harvard Project on International Climate Agreements.

Pouliotte, J., B. Smit, and L. Westerhoff (2009) Adaptation and development: Livelihoods and climate change in Subarnabad, Bangladesh. *Climate and Development* 1(1): 31–46.

Prikh, J. (2007) *Gender and Climate Change – Framework for Analysis, Policy and Action*. Available at www.gdonline.org/resources/UNDP_Gender_and_Climate_Change.pdf.

Project Catalyst (2010) Making fast start finance work. Briefing Paper, 7 June version. Available at www.project-catalyst.info/images/publications/2010-06-07_project_catalyst.

PWC (PricewaterhouseCoopers) (2011) *Counting the Cost of Carbon: Low Carbon Economy Index 2011*. London: PricewaterhouseCoopers.

PWC (2013) Busting the Carbon Budget Low Carbon Economy Index 2013. London: PricewaterhouseCoopers.

Quisumbing, A.R. and McClafferty, B. (2006) *Using Gender Research in Development*. Washington, DC: International Food Policy Research Institute. Available at www.ifpri.org/pubs/fspractice/sp2/sp2.pdf.

Quisumbing, A.R., N. Kumar, and J. Behrman (2011) *Do Shocks Affect Men's and Women's Assets Differently? A Review of Literature and New Evidence from Bangladesh and Uganda*. Washington, DC: International Food Policy Research Institute (IFPRI).

Rahman, A. (2001) *Women and Microcredit in Rural Bangladesh: An Anthropological Study of Grameen Bank Lending*. Boulder, CO: Westview Press.

Randriamaro, Z. (2008) *Strengthening the Role of Women in the Fight against Climate Change*. New York: WEDO.

Rashid, S.F. and Michaud, S. (2000) Female adolescents and their sexuality: Notions of honor, shame, purity and pollution during the floods. *Disasters* 24(1): 54–70.

Renton, A. (2009) *Suffering the Science: Climate Change, People, and Poverty*. Oxfam Briefing Paper No. 130. Boston, MA: Oxfam International.

Resnier, M., Wang, C., Du, P. and Chen, J. (2007) The promotion of sustainable development in China through the optimization of a tax/subsidy plan among HFC and power generation in CDM projects. *Energy Policy* 35(9): 4529–44.

Resurreccion, B.P. (2011) *The Gender and Climate Debate: More of the Same or New Pathways of Thinking and Doing?* Asia Security Initiative Policy Series, Working Paper No. 10. Sinagpore: RSIS Centre for Non-Traditional Security (NTS) Studies.

Reuters (2012) Global carbon market value rises to record $176 billion (Coelho, J.), May 30. Available at www.reuters.com/article/2012/05/30/us-world-bank-carbon-idUSBRE 84T08720120530.

Richards, P. (2005) Plant biotechnology and the rights of the poor: A technographic approach', in M. Leach, I. Scoones and B. Wynne (eds) *Science and Citizens*, pp. 99–214. London: Zed Books.

Richardson, K., Steffen, W. and Liberman, D. (2011) *Climate Change: Global Risks, Challenges, and Decisions.* Cambridge: Cambridge University Press.

Richardson, K., Steffen, W., Schellnhuber, H.J., Alcamo, J., Barker, T., Kammen, D.M., Leemans, R., Liverman, D., Munasinghe, M., Osman-Elasha, B., Stern, N. and Wæver, O. (2009) *Climate Change – Synthesis Report: Global Risks, Challenges and Decisions, Copenhagen 2009.* Copenhagen: University of Copenhagen. Available at www.climate congress.ku.dk.

Richardson, P., Howarth, R. and Finnegan, G. (2004) *The Challenges of Growing Small Businesses: Insights from Women Entrepreneurs in Africa.* Geneva: ILO.

Ringius, L., Torvanger, A. and Underdal, A. (2002) Burden sharing and fairness principles in international climate policy. *International Environmental Agreements: Politics, Law and Economics* 2: 1–22.

Rivera Reyes, R. (2002) Gendering responses to El Niño in rural Peru. In R. Masika (ed.), *Gender, Development and Climate Change.* London: Oxfam Publishing.

Riverson, K., Roberts, L. and Walker (2005) An overview of women's transport issues in developing countries the challenges in addressing gender dimensions of transport in developing countries: Lessons from World Bank's projects. TRB 2006 Annual Meeting CD-ROM. World Bank. Available at http://siteresources.worldbank.org/INTTSR/ Resources/462613-1152683444211/06-0592.pdf.

Robe, M. and Pallage, S. (2000) Foreign aid and the business cycle. *Review of International Economics* 9 (4): 637–8.

Roberts, B.H., Lindfield, M. and Bai, X. (2009) *Bridging the Gap Between Supply-side and Demand-side CDM Projects in Asian Cities in UNEP 2008.* Nairobi: UNEP.

Röhr, U. (2006) Gender and climate change. *Tiempo* 59: 3–7.

Röhr, U.G. (2009) *The Missing Link in Financing Climate Change Mitigation and Adaptation.* Berlin: Life e.V. and Gender CC.

Rose, K. (1992) *Where Women are Leaders: The SEWA Movement in India.* London: Zed Books.

Rosenthal, E. (2009) Third-world soot is target in climate fight. 16 April. Available at www.nytimes.com/2009/04/16/science/earth/16degrees.html (accessed 4 January 2012).

Sabarwal, S. and K. Terrell (2008) *Does Gender Matter for Firm Performance? Evidence from Eastern Europe and Central Asia.* Policy Research Working Paper 4705. Washington, DC: World Bank, Policy Research Department.

Saines, R.M. (2006) *Carbon Market Overview Legal Issues and Opportunities.* Chicago, IL: Baker and McKenzie LLP. Available at http://naem.org/Rick per cent20Saines.pdf (accessed 5 January 2012).

Sanchez, V. (2008) *Microscope on the Micro-finance Business Environment in Latin America and the Caribbean.* London: The Economist.

Sathaye, J.A. (2007) *Policies and Programmes in CDM: Observations Based on US Experience.* Available at http://ies.lbl.gov/ppt/policy0307bonn.pdf.

Schalatek, L. (2009) *Gender and Climate Finance: Double Mainstreaming for Sustainable Development.* Berlin: Heinrich Böll Foundation.

Schalatek, L. (2011) *A matter of Principle(s): A Normative Framework for a Global Compact on Public Climate Finance*. Berlin: Heinrich Böll Foundation.

Schalatek, L. (2012a) *Climate Financing for Gender Equality and Women's Empowerment: Challenges and Opportunities*. UN Commission on the Status of Women, 56th Session Interactive Expert Panel. 27 February–9 March. New York: UN.

Schalatek, L. (2014) *Of Promise, Progress, Perils & Prioritization Gender in the Green Climate Fund*. Berlin: Heinrich Böll Foundation.

Schelling, T. (1992) Some economics of global warming. American Economic Review 82 (1): 1–14.

Schneider, S.H., Semenov, S., Patwardhan, A., Burton, I., Magadza, C.H.D., Oppenheimer, M., Pittock, A.B., Rahman, A., Smith, J.B., Suarez, A. and Yamin, F. (2007) Assessing key vulnerabilities and the risk from climate change. In M.L. Parry, O.F. Canziani, J.P. Palutikof, P.J. van der Linden and C.E. Hanson (eds), *Climate Change 2007: Impacts, Adaptation and Vulnerability. Contribution of Working Group II to the Fourth Assessment Report of the Intergovernmental Panel on Climate Change*, pp. 779–810. Cambridge: Cambridge University Press.

Scholte, J. (2002) *Governing Global Finance*. CSGR Working Paper No. 88/02. Coventry: University of Warwick.

Schuberth, H. and Young, B. (2010) *The Role of Gender in Financial Market Regulation*. Available at www.garnet-eu.org/fileadmin/documents/policy_briefs/Garnet_Policy_Brief_No_10.pdf.

Schultz, I. and Stieß, I. (2007) *Emissionshandel und Gender*. Frankfurt am Main: Institut für sozial-ökologische Forschung.

Seck, M., N.A. Mamouda and S. Wade (2005) Senegal adaptation and mitigation through produced environments: The case for agricultural intensification in Senegal. In F. Yamin, A. Rahman and S. Huq (eds) *Vulnerability, Adaptation and Climate Disasters: A Conceptual Overview*, IDS Bulletin 36: 71–86.

SEI (2011) *Private Sector Finance and Climate Change Adaptation*. Policy brief. Stockholm: Stockholm Environment Institute.

Sequino, S. (2009) *The Global Economic Crisis, Its Gender Implications, and Policy Responses*. Paper prepared for presentation to the Commission on the Status of Women, 53rd Session, 2–13 March. New York: UN.

SERI, Global (2000) *Over Consumption? Our use of the World's Natural Resources*. Friends of the Earth Europe. Available at www.foe.co.uk/sites/default/files/downloads/overconsumption.pdf.

SESA (2011) *Forest Carbon Partnership Facility (FCPF) Readiness Fund. Common Approach to Environmental and Social Safeguards for Multiple Delivery Partners*. Available at www.forestcarbonpartnership.org/sites/forestcarbonpartnership.org/files/Documents/PDF/Nov2011/FCPF%20Readiness%20Fund%20Common%20Approach%20_Final_%2010-Aug-2011_Revised.pdf.

Sethi, N. (2012) India fights off cuts on agricultural emissions. *TNN* 3 December.

Shackleton, C.M., S.E. Shackleton, E. Buiten and N. Bird (2007) The importance of dry woodlands and forests in rural livelihoods and poverty alleviation in South Africa. *Forest Policy and Economics* 9(5): 558–77.

Sharan, D. (2008). *Financing Climate Change Mitigation and Adaptation Role of Regional Financing Arrangements*. Asian Development Bank, Manila, Philippines. Available at www.adb.org/Documents/Papers/ADB-Working-Paper-Series/ADB-WP04-Financing-Climate-Change-Mitigation.pdf.

Sharma, M. and Zeller, M. (1997) Repayment performance in group-based credit programs in Bangladesh: An empirical analysis. *World Development* 25(10): 1731–42.

Sikoska, T. and Solomon, J. (1999) *Introducing Gender in Conflict and Conflict Prevention: Conceptual and Policy Implication.* Available at www.un-instraw.org/en/docs/gacp/gender_and_conflict.pdf.

Singer, M. (2014) *Climate Change isn't Gender Neutral.* Available at www.anthropology-news.org/index.php/2014/04/07/climate-change-isnt-gender-neutral.

Skoufias, E., Rabassa, M., Olivieri, S. and Brahmbhatt, M. (2011) *The Poverty Impacts of Climate Change.* Washington, DC: World Bank.

Skutsch, M. (2002) Protocols, treaties and action: the 'climate change process' viewed through gender spectacles. In Masika, R. (ed.), *Gender, Development and Climate Change.* Oxford: Oxfam Publishing.

Skutsch, M. (2004) *CDM and LULUCF: What's in it for Women? A Note for the Gender and Climate Change Network.* Available at www.gencc.interconnection.org/skutsch2004.pdf.

Smith, K. (1991) Allocating responsibility for global warming: the natural debt index. *Ambio* 20: 95–6.

Smith, K. (1995) The basics of greenhouse gas indices. In Hayes, P., Smith, K. (eds) *The Global Greenhouse Regime: Who Pays?* pp. 20–50. London: Earthscan.

Smith, M.E., Phillips, J.V. and Spahr, N.E. (2002) *Hurricane Mitch: Peak Discharge for Selected River Reaches in Honduras.* U.S. Geological Survey. Available at http://pdf.usaid.gov/pdf_docs/Pnacp984.pdf.

Solomon, S. *et al.* (2009) Irreversible climate change due to carbon dioxide emissions. *Proceedings of the National Academy of Sciences* 106 (6): 1704–9.

Soren A. and Muchhala, B. (2010) *Fruits of the Crisis: Leveraging the Financial and Economic Crisis of 2008–2009 to Secure New Resources for Development and Reform the Global Reserve System.* January. Penang: TWN.

South Africa (2004) *A National Climate Change Response Strategy for South Africa Department of Environmental Affairs and Tourism.* Available at unfccc.int/files/meetings/seminar/application/pdf/sem_sup3_south_africa.pdf.

South Centre (2008) *Financing the Global Climate Change Response: Suggestions for a Climate Change Fund.* Geneva: South Centre.

South Centre/Khor, M. (2010) *The Equitable Sharing of Atmospheric and Development Space: Some Critical Aspects.* Research Paper 33, November. Geneva: South Centre.

South Centre (2011) *Emissions Budgets Under a 50 per cent below 1990 by 2050.* Informal note 71. Geneva: South Centre.

Srabani, R. (2008) Women's expertise key to rolling back deserts. Inter Press Service, 27 September. Available at http://ipsnews.net/news.asp?idnews=34899.

SREP (2009) Design document, June. Available at www.climateinvestmentfunds.org/cif/sites/climateinvestmentfunds.org/files/SREP_design_Document.pdf.

SREX/IPCC (2012) *Special Report, Managing the Risks of Extreme Events and Disasters to Advance Climate Change Adaptations.*

Stabinsky, D. and Hoffmaister, J.P. (2012) *Loss and Damage: Some Key Issues and Considerations Third World Network.* Briefing Paper 1. Penang: TWN.

Stadelmann M., A. Michaelowa, and J._T. Roberts (2013) Difficulties in accounting for private finance in international climate policy. *Climate Policy* 13: 718–37.

Stehr, H.J. (2007) The Clean Development Mechanism – evolving to meet climate and development challenges. In *Climate Action*, pp. 108–11. London: Sustainable Development International.

Stehr, H.J. (2008) Does the CDM need an institutional reform? In K. Olsen and J. Fenhann (eds), *A Reformed CDM – including New Mechanisms for Sustainable Development.* Nairobi: UNEP-Risø Centre.

Stern, N. (2006) *The Economics of Climate Change: The Stern Review.* Cambridge: Cambridge University Press.

Stilwell, M. (2012) Climate debt: A primer. In *Climate, Development and Equity: What Next?* Volume III. Development Dialogue no. 16, September. Uppsala: Dag Hammarskjöld Foundation.

Stilwell, M. (2012b) Climate finance: How much is needed? In *Climate, Development and Equity: What Next?* Volume III. Development Dialogue no. 16, September. Uppsala: Dag Hammarskjöld Foundation.

Stotsky, J.G. (1996) *Gender Bias in Tax Systems*. Working Paper no. 96/99. Washington, DC: International Monetary Fund.

Streck C. and Lin, J. (2008) Making markets work: A review of CDM performance and need for a reform. *EJIL* 19: 400–2.

Sulaiman, S. (2007) How is climate change shifting Africa's malaria map? SciDevnet, 1 August. Available at www.scidev.net/global/malaria/opinion/how-is-climate-change-shifting-africas-malaria-ma.html (accessed 14 April 2015).

Swain, R.B. and Floro, M. (2007) *Effect of Microfinance on Vulnerability, Poverty and Risk in Low Income Households*. Working Paper 31. Uppsala, Sweden: Department of Economics, Uppsala University. Available at www.nek.uu.se/Pdf/wp2007_31.pdf.

Swaminathan, M.S., 2005: Environmental education for a sustainable future. *Glimpses of the Work on Environment and Development in India*, J.S. Singh and V.P. Sharma, Eds., Angkor Publishers, New Delhi, 51–71.

Tacoli, C. (2009) *Crisis or Adaptation? Migration and Climate Change in a Context of High Mobility*. Available at www.unfpa.org/webdav/site/global/users/schensul/public/CCPD/papers/Tacoli%20Paper.pdf (accessed 27 July 2011).

Tanaka, S. (2014) *Gender-Inclusive Designs in Climate Finance Projects: ADB's Approach*. CIF 2014 Partnership Forum Gender Session, 23 June 2014. Bangkok: ADB.

TAR (Third Assessment Report, IPCC) (2001) *IPCC, 2001: Climate Change 2001: Synthesis Report. A Contribution of Working Groups I, II, and III to the Third Assessment Report of the Intergovernmental Panel on Climate Change*. Watson, R.T. and the Core Writing Team (eds). Cambridge/New York: Cambridge University Press.

TERI (2009) *Adaptation Financing*. TERI Viewpoint Paper 6. Available at www.realclimate economics.org/equity_global_distribution.html.

Tiejun, W. (2007) Deconstructing modernization. *Chinese Sociology and Anthropology* 49(4): 10–25.

Tiejun, W., Lau Kinchi, C.C., Huili, H. and Jiansheng, Q. (2012) Ecological civilization, indigenous culture, and rural reconstruction in China. *Monthly Review* 63(9): 29–35.

Tinker, I. (1994) Women and community forestry in Nepal: expectations and realities. *Society and Natural Resources* 7(4): 367–81.

Tirpak, D. (2008) The scientific basis for national and international policies, instruments and co-operative arrangements. Available at www.ipcc.ch/pdf/presentations/poznan-COP-14/dennis-tirpak.pdf.

Tirpak, D., Stasio, K. and Tawney, L. (2012) *Monitoring the Receipt of International Climate Finance by Developing Countries*. Washington, DC: World Resources Institute.

Tirpak, D., Gupta, S., Perczyk, D. and Thioye, M. (2008) *National Policies and their Linkages to Negotiations Over a Future International Climate Change Agreement*. New York: UNDP.

Todd, H. (1996) *Women at the Center: Grameen Bank Borrowers after One Decade*. Dhaka: Dhaka University Press.

Truitt G.A. (1999) *Female Agricultural Extension Agent in El Salvador and Honduras: Do they have an Impact in Training for Agricultural Development 1997–1998*. Rome: FAO.

TWN (2008) *No Additionality, New Conditionality: A Critique of the World Bank's Climate Investment Funds* (Celine Tan) Third World Network 30 May 2008 Briefing paper. Available at www.twn.my/title2/climate/.../TWN.BP.bonn.2.doc.

TWN (2009) *Historical Responsibility and Equity: The Key to a Fair and Effective Outcome in Copenhagen*. Briefing Paper #1. Penang: Third World Network.

TWN (2009) *Multilateral Financial Structure for Climate Change: Key Elements*. Penang: Third World Network.

TWN (2010) *Using SDRs to Finance Development*. Available at www.twnside.org.sg/title2/resurgence/2010/234/cover05.htm.

UC Davis (2012) *Study of California Women Business Leaders 2012–2013*. Available at http://gsm.ucdavis.edu/digital-publication/2012-2013-uc-davis-study-california-women-business-leaders and Top California Company Leaders Dominated by Men. Available at www.news.ucdavis.edu/search/news_detail.lasso?id=10427.

Udry, C., Hoddinott, J., Alderman, H. and Haddad, L. (1995) Gender differentials in farm productivity: Implications for household efficiency and agricultural policy. *Food Policy* 20(5).

UK Financial Services Authority Commodities Group (2008) *The Emissions Trading Market: Risks and Challenges*. March. Available: at www.fsa.gov.uk/pubs/other/emissions_trading.pdf.

UN (2006) *Empowerment of Women: Access to Assets*. Write up of Session 4, International Forum on the Eradication of Poverty, 15–16 November. New York: UN. Available at www.un.org/esa/socdev/poverty/PovertyForum/Documents/bg_4.html.

UN (2007) *51st Session of the United Nations Commission on the Status of Women*. 26 February to 9 March. Informal expert panel: Financing for Gender Equality and the Empowerment of Women. Moderator's Summary. New York: UN.

UN (2010) *Report of the Secretary-General's High-level Advisory Group on Climate Change Financing*. New York: UN. Available at www.un.org/wcm/content/site/climatechange/pages/financeadvisorygroup/pid/13300.

UN (2010) *The Millennium Development Goals Report 2010*. New York: UN.

UNCTAD (2009) *Citing Who About People Rely on Traditional Form of Fuels*. Geneva: UNCTAD.

UNDESA (2010) *World Economic and Social Survey 2009*. New York: UN.

UNDESA (2011) *World Economic and Social Survey 2010*. New York: UN.

UNDP (2006) *Human Development Report 2006 Beyond Scarcity: Power, Poverty and the Global Water Crisis*. New York: United Nations Development Programme.

UNDP (2007) *Human Development Report 2007/08*. New York: Palgrave Macmillan.

UNDP (2008a) Negotiations on Additional Investment and Financial Flows to Address Climate Change in Developing Countries. Erik Haites Margaree Consultants, Inc. Toronto. July. New York: UNDP.

UNDP (2008b) *Innovative Approaches to Promoting Women's Economic Empowerment*. New York: UNDP.

UNDP (2009a) *Resource Guide on Gender and Climate Change*. New York: UNDP.

UNDP (2009b) *Human Development Report 2009/10*. New York: Palgrave Macmillan.

UNDP (2010a) *Gender, Climate Change and Community-based Adaptation: A Guidebook for Designing and Implementing Gender-sensitive Community-based Adaptation Programmes and Projects*. New York: UNDP.

UNDP (2010b) *Price of Peace: Financing Gender Equality in Post-conflict Reconstruction*. Synthesis Report. New York: UNDP.

UNDP (2010c) *Human Development Report 2010/11*. New York: Palgrave Macmillan.

UNDP (2011) *Africa Adaptation Programme Experiences, Gender and Climate Change: Advancing Development through an Integrated Gender Perspective*. Available at www.undp.org/content/dam/aplaws/publication/en/publications/environment-energy/www-ee-library/climate-change/africa-adaptation-programme-experiences-gender-and-climate-change/AAP_Discussion_Paper1_English.pdf.

UNDP (2011) *Catalysing Climate Finance: A Guidebook on Policy and Financing Options for Support Green Low emission and Climate Resilient Development.* New York: UNDP.
UNDP (2012) *Gender and Adaptation.* Available at www.gender-climate.org/Content/Docs/Publications/UNDP_Policy-Brief-Gender-and-Adaptation.pdf.
UNDP (2012) The Climate Public Expenditure and Institutional Reviews (CPEIRs) in Asia-Pacific region: What Have We Learned?
UNDP/GGCA (2011) Ensuring Gender Equity in Climate Change Financing. New York: UNDP.
UNDP (2013) *The Rise of the South: Human Progress in a Diverse World.* New York: United Nations Development Programme.
UNDP/GEF (2012) *Gender in Action 2012.* Gender Report of UNDP/supported GEF financed projects. Available at http://web.undp.org/gef/document/UNDP-GEF%20Gender%20Report%202012.pdf.
UNECA (2009*) Financial Resources and Investment for Climate Change.* Special Session of the Africa Partnership Forum on Climate Change, in Addis Ababa on 3 September. Addis Ababa: United Nations Economic Commission for Africa (UNECA).
UNECA (2011) *Climate Financing: Global Imperatives and Implications for Sustainable Climate Resilient Development in Africa.* Working Paper 16. Addis Abba: UNECA.
UNECA (2011) *Development First: Addressing Climate Change in Africa.* The First Climate Change and Development in Africa (CCDA-1) Conference, Addis Ababa, Ethiopia Concept Note, 17–19 October.
UNECA (2011) *Filling the Gap: Expanding the financing for Adaptation under the UNFCCC through a Levy on International Transport Services.* Working Paper 21, Addis Abba: UNECA.
UNECE (2008) Europe Executive Committee on the implementation of the priorities of the UNECE reform for strengthening some activities of the committee. The Inland Transport Committee and Gender Issues in Transport. Note by the secretariat. Available at www.unece.org/fileadmin/DAM/trans/doc/2009/itc/ECE-TRANS-2009-08e.pdf.
UN ECLAC (2005) *Grenada: A Gender Impact Assessment of Hurricane Ivan – Making the Invisible Visible.* Santiago, Chile: Economic Commission for Latin America and the Caribbean (UN ECLAC), United Nations Development Fund for Women (UNIFEM) and United Nations Development Programme (UNDP), UN ECLAC.
UNEP (2008a) Increasing Access to the Carbon Market: New Countries, New Sectors. Geneva: UNEP.
UNEP (2008b) *Public Financing Mechanisms to Mobilize Investment in Climate Change Mitigation.* Geneva: UNEP.
UNEP (2008c) A reformed CDM: Including new mechanisms for sustainable development. In K. Olsen and J. Fenhann (eds), *A Reformed CDM: Including New Mechanisms for Sustainable Development.* Nairobi: UNEP-Risø Centre.
UNEP (2009) *Global Green New Deal.* Policy Brief. Geneva: United Nations Environment Programme.
UNEP (2010) *The Emissions Gap Report: Are the Copenhagen Accord Pledges Sufficient to Limit Global Warming to 2°C or 1.5°C?* Geneva: United Nations Environment Programme.
UNEP/UNEP RISO Centre (2008) *A Reformed CD: Including new Mechanisms for Sustainable Development.* Rotskilde: UNEP RISO Centre.
UNFCCC (1992) *United Nations Framework on Climate Change.* Signed 9 May, New York. Effective from 21 March 1994. Available at http://unfccc.int/files/essential_background/background_publications_htmlpdf/application/pdf/conveng.pdf.
UNFCCC (1997) *Implementation of the Berlin Mandate: Additional Proposals from Parties – Addendum – Note by the Secretariat.* 30 May. FCCC/AGBM/1997/MIS.1/Add.3. Bonn: UNFCCC Secretariat.

520 Bibliography

UNFCCC (1998) *Report of the Conference of the Parties on its Third Session*. Kyoto, 1–11 December 1997. FCCC/CP?1997/add.1 25 Marc. Available at http://unfccc.int/resource/docs/cop3/07a01.pdf.

UNFCCC (2004) *Oral Report of the Chair of the SBSTA on the in-session Workshops on Impacts of, and Vulnerability and Adaptation to, Climate Change: Vulnerability and risks, sustainable development, opportunities and solutions and Climate change mitigation: Vulnerability and risks, sustainable development, opportunities and solutions*. Delivered to the SBSTA Plenary on 21 June. Bonn: UNFCCC Secretariat.

UNFCCC (2007) *Investment and Financial Flows to Address Climate Change*. Bonn: UNFCCC Secretariat.

UNFCCC (2007a) *An Assessment of the Funding Necessary to Assist Developing Countries in Meeting Their Commitments Relating to the Global Environment Facility Replenishment Cycle*. FCCC/SBI/2007/21, 14 November. Bonn: UNFCCC Secretariat.

UNFCCC (2007b). *Investment and Financial Flows to Address Climate Change*. Bonn: UNFCCC Secretariat.

UNFCCC (2008) *Investment and Financial Flows to Address Climate Change: An Update*. FCCC/TP/2008/7 26, November. Bonn: UNFCCC Secretariat.

UNFCCC (2009) *Fact Sheet: Financing Climate Change Action*. Bonn: UNFCCC.

UNFCCC (2010) *Copenhagen Accord Decision 2/CP.15*. Bonn: UNFCCC Secretariat. Available at http://unfccc.int/resource/docs/2009/cop15/eng/11a01.pdf.

UNFCCC (2011) *Identification and Implementation of Medium- and Long-Term Adaptation Activities in Least Developed Countries*. Technical paper FCCCTP/2011/7. Bonn: UNFCCC Secretariat.

UNFCCC (2011) *Outcome of the Work of the Ad Hoc Working Group on Long-Term Cooperative Action Under the Convention*, Draft decision –/CP.16. Bonn: UNFCCC Secretariat. Available at http://unfccc.int/files/meetings/cop_16/application/pdf/c.

UNFCCC (2012) *CDM Methodologies Booklet*. Bonn: UNFCCC Secretariat. Available at http://cdm.unfccc.int/methodologies/index.html.

UNFCCC (2012) *The CDM and Women*. Bonn: UNFCCC Secretariat.

UNFCCC (2012) *The Rio Conventions: Action on Gender*. Bonn: UNFCCC Secretariat. Available at http://unfccc.int/resource/docs/publications/roi_20_gender_brochure.pdf.

UNFCCC (2013) *Executive Board Annual Report 2013: Clean Development Mechanism*. Bonn: UNFCCC Secretariat.

UNFCCC (2014) *Biennial Assessment and Overview of Climate Finance Flows Report*. Standing Committee on Finance. Bonn: UNFCCC

UNFCCC (no date) *Climate Change: Impacts, Vulnerabilities and Adaptation in Developing Countries*. Bonn: UNFCCC Secretariat.

UNFPA (2009) *Facing a Changing World: Women, Population and Climate*. State of the World Population 2009. Rome: United Nations Population Fund.

UNFPA (2010) UNFPA: Maternal health supplies being rushed to Haiti. Available at www.who.int/pmnch/media/news/2010/20100114_unfpa_for_haiti2/en/.

UNFPA/WEDO (2009*) Climate Change Connections A Resource Kit on Climate, Population and Gender*. Rome/New York: United Nations Population Fund and the Women's Environment and Development Organization.

UN-Habitat (2010) *Land, Environment and Climate Change. Challenges, Responses and Tools*. Nairobi: UN-Habitat.

UNHCR (2009) *Climate Change, Natural Disasters and Human Displacement: A UNHCR Perspective*. United Nations High Commissioner for Refugees. Available at www.unhcr.org/4901e81a4.html.

Union of Concerned Scientists (2007) *How to Avoid Dangerous Climate Change: A Target for US Emissions Reductions*. Available at www.ucsusa.org/assets/documents/global_warming/emissions-target-report.pdf.
UN Millennium Project (2005) *Taking Action: Achieving Gender Equality and Empowering Women*. Report prepared by the Taskforce on Education and Gender Equality, UNDP. London: Earthscan.
UN Millennium Project (2006) *Energy Services for the Millennium Development Goals*. New York and Washington, DC: UNDP, UN Millennium Project, World Bank, United Nations.
Unnayan Onneshan Innovators (2010) *Climate Change and South Asia: A Briefing Note*. Dhaka: Unnayan Onneshan Innovators Centre for Research and Action on Development.
UN-REDD (2009) Available at www.un-redd.org (accessed 28 December 2009).
UN-REDD (2011) *The Business Case for Mainstreaming Gender in REDD+. The United Nations Collaborative Programme on Reducing Emissions from Deforestation and Forest Degradation in Developing Countries* (UN-REDD). Geneva, Switzerland.
UNRISO (2011) Pipeline analysis and database CDM projects by type. Available at www.cdmpipeline.org/cdm-projects-type.htm.
USAID (2005) *Enhancing Women's Access to Markets: An Overview of Donor Programmes and Best Practices*. GATE Analysis Document. Washington, DC: USAID.
USAID-Adapt Asia (2014) *Sourcebook on Gender and Climate Change*. Washington, DC: USAID.
Usui, K. and Martinez-Fernandez, C. (2011) *Low-Carbon Green Growth Opportunities for SMEs*. November–December. Paris: OECD.
Van Den Hombergh, H. (1993) *Gender, Environment and Development: A Guide to the Literature*. Amsterdam: Jan van Arkel (International Books), for the Institute of Development Research.
Van der Werf, G.R, Morton, D.C., DeFries, R. S., Olivier, J. G. J., Kasibhatla, P. S., Jackson, R. B., Collatz, G. J. and Randerson, J. T. (2009) CO_2 emissions from forest loss. *Nature Geoscience* 2: 737–8.
Van Staveren, I. (2002) *Global Finance and Gender*. Brussels: Network Women in Development Europe (WIDE).
Villgrasa, D. (2002) Kyoto negotiations: reflections on the role of women. In R. Masika (ed.), *Gender, Development and Climate Change*. Oxford: Oxfam Publishing.
Vincent, K., T. Cull, and E. Archer (2010) Gendered vulnerability to climate change in Limpopo province, South Africa. In Dankelman, I. (ed.) *Gender and Climate Change: An Introduction*, pp. 160–7. London/Washington, DC: Earthscan.
Voluntary Services Overseas (2006) *Reducing the Burden of HIV and AIDS Care on Women and Girls*. Available at www.vso.org.uk/Images/RBHACWG_tcm8-8415.pdf.
Walby, S. (2009) *Gender and the Financial Crisis*. Paper for UNESCO Project on Gender and the Financial Crisis. Available at www.lance.ac.uk/fass/doc_libarary/sociology/Gender_and_financial_crisis_sylvia_walby.pdf.
Walby, S. (2013) Finance versus democracy: theorising finance in society. *Work, Employment and Society* 27(3): 489–507.
Walz, R. and Schleich, J. (2009) *The Economics of Climate Change Policies: Macroeconomic Effects, Structural Adjustments and Technological Change*. Heidelberg: Physica-Verlag.
Wamukonya, N and Skutsch (2008) *Is there a Gender Angle to the Climate Change Negotiations?* UNEP. Available at www.unep.org/roa/amcen/Projects_Programme/climate_change/PreCop15/Proceedings/Gender-and-climate-change/IsthereaGenderAngletotheClimateChangeNegiotiations.pdf.

Wara, M.W. and Victor, D.G. (2008) *A Realistic Policy on International Carbon Offsets*. Program on Energy and Sustainable Development Working Paper 74. April. Available at http://iis-b.stanford.edu/pubs/22157/WP74_final_final.pdf.

Ward, M., Streck, C., Winkler, H., Jung, M., Hagemann, M., Höhne, N. and O'Sullivan, R. (2008) *The Role of Sector No-Lose Targets in Scaling up Finance for Climate Change Mitigation Activities in Developing Countries*. London: International Climate Division, DEFRA.

Warrick, R. (2000) *Strategies for Vulnerability and Adaptation Assessment in the Context of National Communications*. Available at www.sprep.org/att/IRC/eCOPIES/global/172.pdf (accessed 4 January 2012).

WBGU (2009) *Solving the Climate Dilemma: the Budget Approach*. Berlin: German Advisory Council on Global Change.

WBGU (2011) *World in Transition – A Social Contract for Sustainability*. Berlin: German Advisory Council on Global Change.

WEDO (2003) *Common Ground, Women's Access to Natural Resources and the United Nations Millennium Development Goals*. New York. Available at www.wedo.org/files/common_ground.pdf.

WEDO (2008) *Gender, Climate Change and Human Security – Lessons from Bangladesh, Ghana and Senegal*. New York: WEDO.

WEDO (2012) *Womens Participation in UN Climate Negotiations, 2008–2012*. New York: Women Environment and Development Organization.

WEIGO (2014) About the informal economy. Available at http://wiego.org/informal-economy/about-informal-economy.

Wen, D.J. (2012) China and climate change: Spin, facts and realpolitik. In *Climate, Development and Equity: What Next?* Volume III. Development Dialogue no. 16, September. Uppsala: Dag Hammarskjöld Foundation.

Wewerinke, M. and Yu, Y.P. III (2010) *Addressing Climate Change Through Sustainable Development and the Promotion of Human Rights*. Research paper 34. Geneva: South Centre.

Wheeler T. and Tiffin R. (2009) Costs of adaptation in agriculture, forestry and fisheries. In Parry, M., Arnell, N., Berry, P., Dodman, D., Fankhauser, S., Hope, C., Kovats, S., Nicholls, R., Satterthwaite, D., Tiffin, R. and Wheeler, T. *Assessing the Costs of Adaptation to Climate Change: A Review of the UNFCC and Other Recent Estimates*, pp. 29–39. London: International Institute for Environment and Development and the Grantham Institute for Climate Change.

Whittenbury, K. (2013) Climate change, women's health, wellbeing and experiences of gender-based violence in Australia. In Alston, M. and Whittenbury, K. (eds) *Research, Action and Policy: Addressing the Gendered Impacts of Climate Change*, pp. 207–22. Dordrecht, Netherlands: Spring Science.

WHO (2003) Lives at risk: Malaria in pregnancy. Available at www.who.int/features/2003/04b/en/2009 (accessed 1 December 2009).

WHO (2005) Climate and health fact sheet. July. Geneva: World Health Organization. Available at www.who.int/globalchange/news/fsclimandhealth/en/index.html (accessed 24 July 2009).

WHO (2008) *The Global Burden of Disease. 2004 Update*. Geneva, Switzerland: WHO.

WHO (2011) *Gender, Climate Change and Health*. Geneva: WHO.

WHO (2014) *Climate Change and Health: A Tool to Estimate Health and Adaptation Costs*. Copenhagen, Denmark: WHO Regional Office for Europe.

WHO/UNICEF (2012) *Joint Monitoring Programme for Water Supply and Sanitation Progress on Drinking Water and Sanitation Update 2012*. Geneva: WHO.

Wieczorek-Zeul, H. (2009) IDA16 and gender equality. *GAP Newsletter*, October. Washington, DC: World Bank.

Wikipedia (2012) Available at http://en.wikipedia.org/wiki/Montreal_Protocol (accessed 31 May 2015).
Wikipedia (2013) Available at http://en.wikipedia.org/wiki/Environmental_policy_in_China.
Wilkinson P., K._R. Smith, M. Davies, H. Adair, B._G. Armstrong, M. Barrett, N. Bruce, A. Haines, I. Hamilton and T. Oreszczyn (2009) Public health benefits of strategies to reduce greenhouse-gas emissions: Household energy. *The Lancet* 374(9705): 1917–29.
Williams, M. (2009) *Women's Economic Empowerment in a Time of Recession*. New York: Division for the Advancement of Women, Department of Economic and Social Affairs, United Nations. Available at www.un.org/womenwatch/daw.
Williams, M. (2010) *Economic Development and the Triple Crises – Gender Equality betwixt and Between: The Impact of the Economic, Climate and Food Crises on Women's Empowerment and Well-being*. Geneva: South Centre.
Williams, M. (2014) *A Green Economy? Measuring the Right Things*. Uppsala: Dag Hammerskjold Foundation.
Winkler, H. (2004) National policies and the CDM: Avoiding perverse incentives. *Journal of Energy in Southern Africa* 15(4) (November).
Woestman (2010) *The Global Economic Crisis and Gender Relations: The Greek Case*. Association for Women's Rights in Development (AWID). Available at www.awid.org/sites/default/files/atoms/files/icw_2010_greekcase.pdf.
Women's Issues in Transport (2014) Bridging the Gap Proceedings, 5th International Conference. Paris 14–16 April. Available at http://wiit-paris2014.sciencesconf.org/conference/wiit-paris2014/pages/Proceedings_The_5th_International_Conference_on_WIiT_1.pdf.
WomenWatch Forum (2000) Summary of the WomenWatch online working groups on the 12 critical areas of concern of the Beijing Platform for Action E/CN.6/2000/PC/CRP.10. Available at www.un.org/womenwatch/forums/beijing5/.
Women's Working Group on Financing for Development (2008) Doha 2008: Women's Rights and Gender Equality in Financing for Development. Unpublished.
Women's Working Group on Financing for Development (2009) Submission to the NGLS Online Consultation for Inputs to the Stiglitz Commission. Unpublished.
Women's World Banking (1996) Available at www.soc.titech.ac.jp/icm/wind/wwb-report.html.
Wong, S. (2009) Climate change and sustainable technology: Re-linking poverty, gender, and governance. *Gender and Development* 17(1): 95–108.
World Bank (1995) *World Development Report*. Washington, DC: World Bank.
World Bank (2001) *Engendering Development: Through Gender Equality in Rights, Resources and Voice*. Oxford: Oxford University Press.
World Bank (2003) *World Development Report 2003: Sustainable Development in a Dynamic World – Transforming Institutions, Growth, and Quality of Life*. Washington, DC: World Bank.
World Bank (2005) *The Challenges in Addressing Gender Dimensions of Transport in Developing Countries: Lessons from World Bank's Projects*. 21 November. Available at http://siteresources.worldbank.org/INTTSR/Resources/462613-1152683444211/06-0592.pdf.
World Bank (2006) *Investment Framework for Clean Energy and Development*. Washington, DC: World Bank.
World Bank (2007) *Finance for All? Policies and Pitfalls in Expanding Access*. Washington, DC: World Bank.
World Bank (2009) *The Economics of Adaptation to Climate Change*. Washington, DC: World Bank.

World Bank (2009) *The Global Financial Crisis: Assessing Vulnerability for Women and Children*. Washington, DC: World Bank.

World Bank (2009) Women in 33 countries highly vulnerable to financial crisis effects. Press Release no. 2009/245/PREM, 6 March. Washington, DC: World Bank.

World Bank (2010) *Monitoring Climate Finance and ODA*. Washington, DC: World Bank.

World Bank (2010) *World Development Report 2010: Development and Climate Change*. Washington, DC: The International Bank for Reconstruction and Development/The World Bank

World Bank (2010a) *World Development 2010*. Washington, DC: World Bank.

World Bank (2010a) *Economics of Adaptation to Climate Change: Synthesis Report*, Washington, DC: The International Bank for Reconstruction and Development/The World bank.

World Bank (2010b) *Unfinished Business: Mobilizing New Efforts to Achieve the 2015 Millennium Development Goals*. Washington, DC: World Bank.

World Bank (2010c) *The Cost to Developing Countries of Adapting to Climate Change: New Methods and Estimates*. Washington, DC: World Bank.

World Bank (2011) *Social Protection and Climate Resilience Report from an International Workshop*. Addis Ababa, 14–17 March. Washington, DC: World Bank.

World Bank (2011) *World Development Report 2012: Gender Equality and Development*. Washington, DC: World Bank.

World Bank (2011b) *Mobilizing Climate Finance*. Paper prepared at the request of G20 Finance Ministers. Washington, DC: World Bank, Washington DC.

World Bank (2012) *Turn Down the Heat: Why a 4°C Warmer World Must Be Avoided*. November. Washington, DC: World Bank.

World Bank (2012) *World Development Report 2012: Gender Equality and Development*. Washington, DC: The International Bank for Reconstruction and Development/The World Bank.

World Bank (2013) *Expanding Women's Access to Financial Services*. Available at www.worldbank.org/en/results/2013/04/01/banking-on-women-extending-womens-access-to-financial-services.

World Bank (2014) *Getting a Grip on Climate Change in the Philippines*. Executive Report. Washington, DC: World Bank. Available at www.wds.worldbank.org/external/default/WDSContentServer/WDSP/IB/2013/06/25/000333037_20130625110039/Rendered/PDF/787940BRI0P1300chure0Reference0ONLY.pdf.

World Bank (2013) *Getting a Grip on Climate Change in the Philippines*. Washington, DC: World Bank. Available at www.worldbank.org/content/dam/Worldbank/document/EAP/Philippines/Final%20ExReport.pdf.

World Future Council (2012) *Breaking the Climate Finance Funding Deadlock*. Hamburg: World Future Council.

World Vision (2011) Drought relief update from Somalia, Kenya, and Ethiopia. Available at www.worldvision.org/news/drought-relief-update-somalia-kenya-ethiopia#sthash.GOup7Utk.dpuf and www.worldvision.org/news/drought-relief-update-somalia-kenya-ethiopia.

WorldWatch (2013) *Environment is a Growing Driver in Displacement of People*. Available at www.worldwatch.org/node/5888.

WRI (World Resources Institute) (2011) *Summary of Developed Country Fast-Start Climate Finance Pledges*. Available at http://pdf.wri.org/climate_finance_pledges_2011-11-18.pdf (accessed 19 December 2012).

WRI (2012) *The German Fast-Start Finance Contribution*. Available at www.wri.org/publication/german-fast-start-finance-contribution.

WWF-UK (2011) *Green Game Changers: Insights for Mainstreaming Business Innovation.* London: WWF and Verdantix.

York, R. (2012) Asymmetric effects of economic decline on CO_2 emissions. *Nature Climate Change* 2: 762–4.

Yotopoulos, P. and Floro, M. (1992) Income distribution, transactions cost and market fragmentation in informal credit markets. *Cambridge Journal of Economics* 16(3): 303–26.

Young, B. (2002) *The Gender Dimensions of the Global Financial Architecture Conference: Gender Budgets, Financial Markets, Financing for Development.* Berlin: Heinrich Böll Foundation.

Young, B. and Schuberth, H. (2010) *The Global Financial Meltdown and the Impact of Financial Governance.* Garnet policy brief no. 10. Available at www2.warwick.ac.uk/fac/soc/garnet/policybriefs/policybrief10.pdf.

Young, B., Bakker, I. and Elson, D. (eds) (2011) *Questioning Financial Governance from a Feminist Perspective.* London: Routledge.

Zhang J.J. and K.R. Smith (2007) Household air pollution from coal and biomass fuels in China: Measurements, health impacts, and interventions. *Environmental Health Perspectives* 115: 848.

Zhang, Z.X. and Maruyama, A. (2001) Towards a private–public synergy in financing climate change mitigation projects. *Energy Policy* 29(15): 1363–78.

Zvinavashe E., H. Elbersen, M. Slingerland, S. Kolijn, and J. Sanders (2011) Cassava for food and energy: Exploring potential benefits of processing of cassava into cassava flour and bioenergy at farmstead and community levels in rural Mozambique. *Biofuels, Bioproducts and Biorefining* 5: 151–64.

Zuckerman, E. and Garrett, A. (2003) *Do Poverty Reduction Strategy Papers Address Gender? A Gender Audit of 2002 PRSPs.* Washington, DC: Gender Action.

INDEX

AAUs (Assigned Amount Units) 46
ACC *see* anthropogenic climate change
accountability 54, 88, 483
acquisitions 376–7
adaptation 71, 72–7, 111n, 131–6, 139–40, 224, 381, 455–6, 463; costing 52, 267, 270–1, 284, 466–8; definition 131, 262; key sectors 124; mitigation linkages 151, 268–9, 417, 447, 449
adaptation deficit 76, 266–73, 351
adaptation finance 192, 261–88, 378–82, 399n, 409–10, 418
adaptation framework 31, 273–5, 462–5
Adaptation Fund 207, 212–18, 282–3, 352, 366, 369n
adaptation-mitigation gap 319–20
adaptation strategies 48, 77, 119–20, 122, 374
adaptive capacity 125–7, 131–2, 442
ADB *see* Asian Development Bank
additionality principle 180, 248, 416, 460–1n
adequacy principle 180, 416
Ad hoc Working-Group on Long-term Cooperative Action (AWG-LCA) 28–9, 38
Advisory Group on Climate Finance (AGF) 398–9n
AfDB *see* African Development Bank
Africa 41, 44, 100, 114n, 381, *see also individual countries*
African Development Bank (AfDB) 241–3, 353–5, 381
African Water Facility (AWF) 242

AGF (The UN Secretary General's Advisory Group on Climate Finance) 398–9n
aggregate climate financing 198–9, 266
aggregate emissions cut 59
agriculture 44, 50–1, 120, 133–5, 146, 162n, 265, 338n, 389–90, 400n, 447, 449–50, 467
'aid paradigm' 172, 174–5, 238
Alboher, S. 324–5
Alliance of Small Island States (AOSIS) 54–5, 179, 434
allowance-based transactions market 257
angel investors 189, 376, 392–3, 401n
Annex I countries 26–7, 46, 85, 179, 230n
Annex II countries *see* developed countries
anthropogenic climate change (ACC) 19, *see also* human change causation
AOSIS *see* Alliance of Small Island States
appropriateness principle 180, 416
ARs *see* assessment reports
Asian climate finance 182, 195
Asian Development Bank (ADB) 243–4, 245, 313, 356–7, 395, 473–4
assessment reports (ARs), IPCC 440–9
Assigned Amount Units (AAUs) 46
asymmetries 129–30, 339–69
atmospheric space 102, 104
austerity measures 365–6
AWF (African Water Facility) 242
AWG-LCA *see* Ad hoc Working-Group on Long-term Cooperative Action

Bali Action Plan (BAP) 28–9, 169, 185, 187, 274

Index

Bali bargain 61
Bangladesh 102, 112n, 135
banking/financial crisis 170, 363–4, 398n
banks, micro-finance 333, *see also* development banks; World Bank
BAP *see* Bali Action Plan
BASIC group 95–6
Beijing Platform for Action (BfA) 109–10
Berlin Act 97
Berlin Conference 113–14n
BfA (Beijing Platform for Action) 109–10
biases 339–69
biennial update reports (BURs) 182
bilateral finance 237–60, 290, 335n
biogas recovery 397
black carbon 143–4, 163n
black populations 81
bonds 189, 190–1, 377–8, 399–400n
bottom-up financial assessments 196
Brazil 112–13n, 230n, 327–8
Brundtland Report 63n
budgets 171, 409–10, *see also* carbon budgets
Buenos Aires Plan of Action 185, 274
burden of climate change 405–10
burden of disease 122
BURs (biennial update reports) 182
Busan agreement 238
business-as-usual aid paradigm 174
business model, GCF 220, 236n

CAF *see* Cancún Adaptation Framework
Canada 66n
Cancún Adaptation Framework (CAF) 136, 138, 273–5, 276, 287n, 464
Cancún Agreement 30–1, 46, 55, 169, 186
Cancún Decision 229n
Cancún emissions reduction pledges 45
capabilities 127–31
capacity building 123, 125–7, 131–2, 152, 154–5, 346, 442
capital infusion 387
capital market 421–2
cap and trade 193
carbon budgets 45–6, 103
Carbon Buyers 326
carbon credits 103, 193, 253, 254, 383, 426n
carbon dioxide (CO_2) 22–3, 39, 43–4, 52, 82, 102, 193, 404
carbon facility 393–6
carbon financing 192–3, 315–34, 388, 396–7
carbon market 192–4, 252–7, 269, 353, 383, 391–7, 401–2n, 420, 422–3

carbon offset 130, 193, 254
carbon space 90, 96–106
carbon tax 193, 420
carbon trading 193
Caribbean 45
Caribbean Development Bank (CDB) 245–6, 360
catastrophe bonds 377
CBA engendering 273–5
CBDR and gender 405–10
CDB *see* Caribbean Development Bank
CDM *see* Clean Development Mechanism
Certified Emission Reductions (CERs) 193, 212, 249, 251, 327, 333, 401n
CF *see* climate finance
change financing 363–7
Chavez, Hugo 228n
China 98, 101, 134, 172, 230n
CIFs *see* Climate Investment Funds
Clean Development Mechanism (CDM) 46, 144, 193, 249–52, 259n, 291, 315–34, 382, 401n, 420
Clean Technology Fund (CTF) 240, 301
climate advocacy 38–9
climate change: burden of 405–10; definitions 26, 63n; impacts/projection 42–3
climate, definition 62n
climate finance (CF): architecture 166–238; contemporary challenges 167–79; definition 167–79; distinctive features of 191–2, 194; engendering 415–21; evolution 185–7; flows of 232n, 239–46; historical background 167–79; 'mantras' 173; nature/scope of 375–84; paradigm features 226; post-2015 regime 403–30; scale/scope/needs 194–7; unravelling 454–6; useful terms 189–90; way forward 223–8
Climate Investment Funds (CIFs) 236n, 238, 240, 258n, 299–313, 350, 352, 369n
climate justice 96–106, 109, 115–16n, 403, 416
climate negotiations 28–33, 47–62
climate policy 187–8, 194, *see also* policies
climate proofing 132–3
climate protection 20–7, 28–33, 431–2, *see also* global climate protection
climate refugees 77–8
climate-related events 73
'climate-relevant finance' 167–8
climate risks, definition 156, *see also* risk
climate science 184, *see also* science
climate smart agriculture 390

528 Index

Climate Technology Fund (CTF) 302–3
CO₂ see carbon dioxide
co-benefits gap 321
co-financing 204, 234–5n
coherence of UNFCC mechanism 221–3
commodities 189
commodities markets 391
community groups 276–7
community vulnerability 119–20
competitive dynamics 177
compliance market 254
Conference of Parties (COP) 28, 33–4, 65n, 185–6, 205, 223, 229–30n, 235n
conflict 450
Congo Basin Forest Fund 242
conservation 145–53
COP see Conference of Parties
Copenhagen Accord 30, 54, 186
coping strategies 262
corrective justice 110, 413, 416–17
cost effectiveness, mitigation 146
costs: adaptation 52, 267, 270–1, 284, 466–8; of climate change 177, 407; health adaptation 284; mitigation 52, 292, 454–5, see also transaction costs
country groupings, UNFCCC 434–7
credit markets 344, 347
critical gender issues 262–6
CTF see Clean Technology Fund; Climate Technology Fund
currency risk 363

death rates 118
decision-making, UNFCCC 35
delivery mechanisms, finance 197–200
demand side finance 312
democracy 105–6
derivatives 189, 376–7
Designated National Authorities (DNAs) 317–18, 322, 324, 327
developed countries, main issues 50, 58, 61, 84, 97–8, 102, 180–1, 231n, 339–40
developing countries 61, 70–1, 73, 211, 271; atmospheric space 104; challenges 31, 49, 74; CO₂ per person 52; economic development 405; flow of finance to 57, 239–46; growth 76, 84–5; mitigation update 30, 101–2, 152; NAMAs 55; transfer of resources to 83
development/adaptation distinction 75, 267
development banks 240–1, 243–6, 313, 353–61, 473–4
development dimension 70–116, 153–4, 181, 411

development finance 168, 192, 373
development gaps 99–110
Development Outcome Tracking system (DOTs) 310, 311
development space sharing 96–106
differentiation needs 85
direct access, GCF 221
disasters 450
discriminatory norms 347–8
disease burden 122
distributive justice 110, 413, 416–17
diversity fund, IDB 358
DNAs see Designated National Authorities
Doha Climate Gateway 186
domestic risk analysis 159–60
DOTs see Development Outcome Tracking system
droughts 42
Durban Decision 31, 64n, 186
Durban Gender Decision 35–6
Durban meeting 32
Durban Outcomes 139–40, 425, 463
Durban Platform 38

early warning systems 442
earth summit see United Nations Conference on Environment and Development
economic development 74–5, 405
economic position, women 344–7
economics 47–53
economies in transition (EITs) 27
education investment 442
effluents ponds 397
'effort/burden' sharing approach 96
EIG (Environmental Integrity Group) 435
EITs (economies in transition) 96
elderly women 350
electricity generation 397
electrification 142
emissions gap 72, 96–110
emissions reduction purchase agreements (ERPAs) 394, 395
emissions reductions scenarios 45, 438–9
emissions trading 193, 250, 252
emotional distress 444–5
employment 144–5, 345–6, 364, 388, 390, 450–1
empowerment issues 117–65, 283–6, 295–9, 308–9, 421–6, 427
energy efficiency 122–3, 447–8
energy services 121, 332, 370, see also renewable energy
energy sources 451
energy use 141–4

entrepreneurship 144–5, 388, 390
environmental activism 20
environmental degradation 62n
Environmental Integrity Group (EIG) 435
environmentally sustainable technology 334
environmental protection 431–2
environment finance tools 472
equality, gender *see* gender equality/equity
equitable principle 87, 181, 416
equity gap 99–110, 321–3
equity issues 58, 70–116, 172, 175, 403–30, 438–9, 446, *see also* gender equality/equity
ERPAs *see* emissions reduction purchase agreements
ethics 70–116, 226
European Union (EU) 32–3, 368n, 434–5
extreme weather events 41–3, 76–7, 118, 125, 262–3

fairness issues 102–3, 105–6, 438–9
fallowing land 287n
Fast-Start Finance (FSF) 169, 223–4, 456–60
feminization of responsibility 445
Fiji 284–5
finance flows: developing countries 57, 239–46; engendering 285; mitigation 289–338; redirecting 353–61, *see also* flows
finance gap 96–106
financial/banking crisis 170, 363–4, 398n
financial barriers 475–8
financial markets 341–4, 348, 363–7, 375–91
Financial Mechanism, COP 223
financing regime structure 268
FIP *see* Forest Investment Program
fiscal policy, IMF 409–10
fishery sector 265–6
flexible market-based mechanisms 248–52, 315–34
floods 42–3
flows: adaptation finance 285; climate finance 167–8, 176, 183, 197–200, 232n, 239–46; mitigation finance 289–338; redirecting to women 353–61, *see also* finance flows
food production 264–6
food security 78, 264–6, 281
Forest Investment Program (FIP) 240, 303, 305, 336n
forestry 121, 145–53, 242, 276, 322–3, 338n
forwards 189, 376–7
FSF *see* Fast-Start Finance
fuelwood collection 163n
futures 189

GAP *see* Gender Action Plan
GCF *see* Green Climate Fund
GEF *see* Global Environment Facility
GEMCRA *see* gender empowerment and climate risk assessment
Gender Action Plan (GAP) 297, 311–12, 481–3
gender advocacy 467–8
gender asymmetries/biases 339–69
gender-blind policy 33–9
gender differences, mortality 448–9
gender empowerment 156–62, 298–9
gender empowerment and climate risk assessment (GEMCRA) 283–6, 421–6
gender equality/equity 115n, 117–65, 308–9, 323–30, 356, 360, 370–402, 425, 463
gender gaps 106–10, 344–7
gender justice 109, 403, 410–13, 416
gender mainstreaming 276, 296–7, 470–1
gender-sensitivity, finance regime 313, 403–30
geographical imbalances 320–1, 386
German Advisory Council on Climate Change (WBGU) 91–3
GGCA (Global Gender and Climate Alliance) 64n
Ghana 101, 125
GHGs *see* greenhouse gases
Global Adaptation Policy 274–5
global burden of disease 122
global climate change 18–69, 70–116, 166–238
global climate protection 28–47, 431–2
global environmental and climate protection 431–2
Global Environment Facility (GEF) 201–12, 233–5n, 241, 278–9, 294–9, 470–1, *see also* Small Grants Program
global equity gap 321–3
global finance 188, 197–200, 344–67, 390
Global Gender and Climate Alliance (GGCA) 64n
global governance framework 462–5
global mitigation policy 151–2, 454–5
global warming 41, 50–1, 62n, *see also* temperature rise
Gold Standard 326, 337–8n
governance 184–91, 310–11, 343, 431–2, 462–5

government role 418
'grandfathering' 94, 113n
Green Belt Movement 121
green bonds 190–1, 378
Green Climate Fund (GCF) 173, 176, 218–21, 236n, 264, 367n, 372–3, 404, 479–83
greenfield investments 376–7
greenhouse gases (GHGs) 22, 43, 46, 136, 229n, *see also* carbon dioxide

HDI *see* Human Development Index
health 51, 284, 444, 451–2, 467–8
heat generation 397
heatwaves 42, 77
hedge funds 189, 376, 399n
historical accountability 88
historical responsibility (HR) 67n, 87–9, 178
Honduras 397
host countries 326
household sector 144, 158, 291, 349
HR *see* historical responsibility
human change causation 23, 62n, *see also* anthropogenic climate change
Human Development Index (HDI) 81, 407
human displacement 79
hurricanes 42, 81

IAR (international assessment and review) 105
IDB *see* Inter-American Development Bank
IMF *see* International Monetary Fund
India 98, 101, 229–30n
indigenous peoples 106, 108, 349
Indonesia 101
inequality 77–85
infestation 43
information asymmetries 129–30
information services, Africa 381
information systems 442
infrastructure costs 468
insurance 361–3, 378, 380, 381, 400–1n, 426n
Inter-American Development Bank (IDB) 244–5, 357, 358–9
Inter-governmental Panel on Climate Change (IPCC) 24–6, 155, 440–9
international assessment and review (IAR) 105
international environment evolution 20–7
International Monetary Fund (IMF) 228n, 409–10

investment opportunities 192
investment programmes 313
investor countries 326
IPCC *see* Inter-governmental Panel on Climate Change

Jamaica 50
Japan 230n
joint implementation (JI) 250, 252
justice 96–106, 109–10, 115–16n, 403, 410–13, 416–17

Katrina hurricane 81
Kyoto Protocol 27, 32–3, 37, 38, 63–4n, 185, 249–50

LAD *see* loss and damage
land grabbing 377, 399n
land reform 150
land use availability 51, 153
land use and land use change and forestry (LULUCF) 46, 141
language use 425
Latin America 135, 230n
LDCF *see* Least Developed Countries Fund
LDCs *see* least developed countries
Least Developed Countries Fund (LDCF) 207, 208–10, 279–81
least developed countries (LDCs) 111n, 114n, 137, 178–9, 286n, 434
legitimization issues 97–9, 179–83
lending programmes 313
Like-Minded Group of Developing Countries (LMDC) 435
loan guarantees 189
long-term adaptation process 277
long-term finance 221–3
long-term global goals 59
loss and damage (LAD) 86, 228–9n
low-income countries 81, 240, 305–7
LULUCF *see* land use and land use change and forestry

Major Economies Forum on Energy and Climate (MEF) 229n
malaria 162n
male-biased policy 33–9
market-based mechanisms 46, 148, 237–60, 269, 315–34, 419
market makers 392
market risk 158
Marrakesh Decision 35
MATCH (Modelling and Assessment of Contributions to Climate Change) 426n
MDGs *see* Millennium Development Goals

measureable, verifiable and reportable (MRV) actions 30, 105, 182, 223
medium-term adaptation process 277
MEF (Major Economies Forum on Energy and Climate) 229n
men's access, financing 363–7
men's adaptation 133
men's employment/entrepreneurship 144–5
men's use, energy 141–4
mergers and acquisitions 376–7
MFIs (microfinance institutions), definition 368n
microfinance 330–4, 345, 348, 368–9n
microfinance institutions (MFIs), definition 368n
military spending 426n
Millennium Declaration 60
Millennium Development Goals (MDGs) 60, 69n, 332, 333, 393–6
mitigation 55, 72–7, 136–45, 181, 191–2, 454–5; adaptation linkages 151, 268–9, 319–20, 417, 447, 449; cost effectiveness 52, 146; global policy 71; private sector and 382–4; traditional knowledge/practices 145; update 30, 101–2, 152
mitigation finance 199, 204, 289–338, 409–10, 418–19
mitigation policy structure 151–2
mitigation projects 446
mitigation strategies 48, 120–2, 374
Modelling and Assessment of Contributions to Climate Change (MATCH) 426n
money market funds 189
Montreal Protocol 21–2, 62–3n
mortality 443–4, 448–9
MRV actions *see* measureable, verifiable and reportable actions
multilateral agreements 433
multilateral finance 237–60, 290, 335n

Nairobi Work Program 274, 463
NAMAs *see* Nationally Appropriate Mitigation Actions
NAP *see* National Adaptation Programme
NAPAs *see* National Adaptation Programs of Action
National Adaptation Programme (NAP) 136, 139–40, 273–5, 463, 465
National Adaptation Programs of Action (NAPAs) 136–7, 209–10, 273–5, 280
national communications 204, 314–15, 337n

national initiatives, insurance 362
Nationally Appropriate Mitigation Actions (NAMAs) 55, 99, 101–2, 151, 171, 182
national policies, Annex I countries 26–7
natural disaster numbers 79
needs, climate finance 194–7
Neumayer, Eric 94
NGOs (non-governmental organisations) 434–7
non-Annex I countries 179
non-financial barriers 475–8
non-governmental organisations (NGOs) 434–7
non-market-based mechanisms 419
non-targeted equality interventions 130–1
'no objection' process 340, 367–8n
'no regrets' options 151, 164n, 346
norms/normative issues 179–83, 184–91, 347–8
north-south imbalance 86

occupational hazards 444
ODA *see* overseas development assistance
OECD Development Assistance Committee (OECD-DAC) 183, 231n
offset test 255
operating risk analysis 158
opportunities: capabilities framework 127–9; mitigation finance 308–9, *see also* investment opportunities
options 189
Organisation for Economic Cooperation and Development *see* OECD Development Assistance Committee
overseas development assistance (ODA) 270–2, 278–9, 401n

parametric insurance 400n
Paris agreement 238, 257–9n, 410–13
participant risk analysis 160, 162
participatory research agenda 429–30
PDDs (project design documents) 324
peaking year, climate change 59
pension funds 190, 398n
performance mechanisms 418
personal security risk 158–9
Peru 101
pestilence 43
Philippines 172
Pilot Program for Climate Resilience (PPCR) 240
policies: climate protection 431–2; ethical dimensions 85–95; frameworks 123, 273–5, 355, 414–15; GCF 479–82; global climate change 18–69, 70–116;

mitigation/adaptation costs 454–6; structure 151–2, *see also* climate policy
politics 53–62, 179–83, 391–7
polluter pays principle (PPP) 90, 231n
portfolios, development banks 357, 473–4
post-2015 climate finance regime 403–30
poverty 70–1, 77–8, 81–2, 127, 316–30
poverty reduction 143, 272, 331
power dynamics 159
PPCR (Pilot Program for Climate Resilience) 240
PPP *see* polluter pays principle
PPPs *see* public-private partnerships
precipitation, heavy 42–3
predictability principle 181, 416
private equity funds 376
private sector 173, 220, 224–6, 339–40, 370–402, *see also* public-private partnerships
programmatic CDMs 249, 329
project-based transactions market 257
project cycle, GEF 206
project design documents (PDDs) 324
psychological distress 444–5
public finance 173, 224, 423–6
public-private partnerships (PPPs) 379–80, 397–8n, 476–8

qualitative risk analysis 156–62

rationalization, UNFCC 221–3
recovery risk analysis 160
REDD + *see* REDD Plus
REDD *see* Reducing Emissions from Deforestation and Forest Degradation
REDD Plus (REDD +) 147–51, 291
Reducing Emissions from Deforestation and Forest Degradation (REDD) 146–51, 291
refugees 112n
regional development banks 240–1, 353–61
regional initiatives, insurance 362
regional variation, mortality 448–9
regulations, REDD 150
renewable energy 144–5, 242–3, 305–7, 336n
rent seeking behaviour 255
repayment rates, micro-finance 348, 368–9n
resource allocation inefficiencies 347–63
resource sharing approach 95
resources and opportunities 127–9
resource transfer to developing countries 83

responsibility 54, 85, 445, *see also* historical responsibility
'responsibility and equity paradigm' 172, 175
'right to development' 74
rights: gender gaps 106–10; REDD 150
Rio Outcomes 433
risk: analysis 156–62; private sector 225, 391; types 164n, 165n, *see also* currency risk
risk assessments 283–6, 362, 421–6
risk insurance mechanisms 361
risk management 381, 387–8
Robinson, Mary 64–5n

scale, finance 194–7
scaling up long-term finance 221–3
Scaling-up Renewable Energy in Low Income Countries (SREP) 240, 305–7
SCCF *see* Special Climate Change Fund
SCF *see* Strategic Climate Fund
science: access to 154–5; of climate change 40–1, 184, 413–14; research 19
scientific imperatives, climate protection regime 39–47
scope of climate finance 194–7, 375–84
SD *see* sustainable development
SDRs *see* Special Drawing Rights
sectoral areas, vulnerability 153, 276, 449–53
sectoral imbalances 320
security 129–30, 158–9, 264–6
SED (Structure Expert Dialogue) 232n
SFCCD (Strategic Framework for Climate Change and Development) 300
SFDCC (Strategic Framework on Development and Climate Change) 239–40
SGP *see* Small Grants Program
SIDs *see* Small Island Developing States
Singapore 101, 231n
sinks 136, 163n
slow onset events 78–9
Small Grants Program (SGP) 202–8, 278, 295–9
small holders 446
Small Island Developing States (SIDs) 54, 114n, 178–9, 286n
small- and medium-sized enterprises (SMEs) 383–4, 386, 389, 399n, 401n
small-scale agricultural activities 146
SMEs *see* small- and medium-sized enterprises
social development 70–116
social equity 323, 355

Index 533

social function, carbon market 255
social position, women 344–7
social potentials, CIFs 304
social protection 196–7, 232n
social risk analysis 158–9
socio-economic activities 131–2
socio-economic development 111n
South Africa 101
South Asia heat waves 77
South Centre research 438–9
SPA (Strategic Priority for Adaptation) 202–8
Special Climate Change Fund (SCCF) 207, 210–12, 235n, 280–2
Special Drawing Rights (SDRs) 170, 224, 228n
Special Report on Emissions Scenarios (SRES) 115n
SREP *see* Scaling-up Renewable Energy in Low Income Countries
SRES (Special Report on Emissions Scenarios) 115n
Standing Committee on Finance 222–3
STAR (System for Transparent Allocation of Resources) 205
Stockholm Declaration 20–1
storms 18–19, 42
Strategic Climate Fund (SCF) 240, 301
Strategic Framework for Climate Change and Development (SFCCD) 300
Strategic Framework on Development and Climate Change (SFDCC) 239–40
Strategic Priority for Adaptation (SPA) 202–8
Structure Expert Dialogue (SED) 232n
sunset clause, CIFs 236n, 369n
supply risk analysis 157
survival 108–9
sustainable agriculture 133, *see also* agriculture
sustainable development (SD) 22, 75, 87, 316–30
sustainable energy 245
swaps 190
System for Transparent Allocation of Resources (STAR) 205

targeted gender equality interventions 130–1
TC (Transitional Committee) 367n
technological gap 320
technology access 122–3, 152, 452–3
technology funding 419–21
technology information systems 442
Technology Needs Assessments (TNAs) 211–12

technology perspectives 448
technology risk 160, 165n
technology transfer/development 153–4, 164n, 181, 334, 411
temperature goal 58, 71–2
temperature rise 23, 39, *see also* global warming
thriving imperative 108–9
time burden risk analysis 159–60
TNAs (Technology Needs Assessments) 211–12
top-down estimation, finance 195
tourism 51
traditional knowledge/practices 145
transaction costs 344, 346, 368n
transfer: burden of climate change 405–10; of resources 83; technology 153–4, 164n, 181, 334, 411
transformative climate finance 173, 175
Transitional Committee (TC) 367n
transportation 141–2, 452
trust fund, GEF 202–8

Umbrella Group 435
UNCED *see* United Nations Conference on Environment and Development
UNDP carbon facility 393–6
UNEP (United Nations Environment Programme) 21
UNFCCC *see* United Nations Framework Convention on Climate Change
United Nations Conference on Environment and Development (UNCED) 21, 433
United Nations Environment Programme (UNEP) 21
United Nations Framework Convention on Climate Change (UNFCCC) 19, 26, 56–7, 168, 179–83, 185–7, 434–7; adoption of 67n; funding outside of 237, 239–46; gender-blind 33–7; gender gap 107–8; GHG concentrations 46; historical responsibility and 89; mechanisms 221–3; operation of funds under 200–21; private sector role 372–5; way forward on climate finance 223–8
United States (US) 68n, 85, 178
urgent actions 173
US *see* United States

venture capital 190, 376, 392–3
violence 130
vision 60–1
voluntary carbon market 254

vulnerability 77–85, 118–28, 129, 153, 276, 415, 443, 445, 448–53, 463
'vulnerable employment' 364

Warsaw Dialogue 186–7
waste management 448
water 264–6, 272, 355, 420, 452, 468
WBGU (German Advisory Council on Climate Change) 91–3
weather derivatives 377
weeds 43
women-owned SMEs 384, 386, 389, 401n
women's access, financing 363–7
women's adaptation 133, 263, 265
women's business growth 475–8
Women's Caucus 64n
women's employment/entrepreneurship 144–5, 388, 390
women's empowerment 117–65, 295–9, 308–9, 427
women's groups 276–7
women's participation, UNFCCC 34, 36
women-specific vulnerabilities 153, 276, 415
women's position, economic/social 344–7
women's rights 106–10, 150
women's under-representation, financial markets 341–4
women's use, energy 141–4
women's vulnerability 153, 276, 415, 449–53
World Bank 217, 238, 239–40, 299–313, 333, 352, *see also* Climate Investment Funds
World Climate Conferences 23
World Climate Programme 24

Zambia 49